Benjamin Franklin
and the
Ends of Empire

Benjamin Franklin and the Ends of Empire

CARLA J. MULFORD

UNIVERSITY PRESS

OXFORD
UNIVERSITY PRESS

Oxford University Press is a department of the University of Oxford. It furthers
the University's objective of excellence in research, scholarship, and education
by publishing worldwide. Oxford is a registered trade mark of Oxford University
Press in the UK and certain other countries.

Published in the United States of America by Oxford University Press
198 Madison Avenue, New York, NY 10016, United States of America.

© Oxford University Press 2015

First issued as an Oxford University Press paperback, 2020

Library of Congress Cataloging-in-Publication Data
Mulford, Carla, 1955–
Benjamin Franklin and the ends of empire / Carla J. Mulford.
pages cm
Includes bibliographical references and index.
ISBN 978–0–19–938419–8 (cloth) | ISBN 978–0–19–009007–4 (paper) |
ISBN 978–0–19–938420–4 (updf)
1. Franklin, Benjamin, 1706–1790—Political and social views. 2. Franklin, Benjamin, 1706–
1790—Knowledge and learning. 3. Statesmen—United States—Biography. 4. United States—
Intellectual life—18th century. 5. Great Britain—Colonies—America. I. Title.
E302.6.F8M93 2015
973.3092—dc23
2014041810

For Ted

Contents

EIGHT

Rebellion to Tyrants, Obedience to God   274

NINE

"I intended well, and I hope all will end well"
Franklin's Last Years   316

CONCLUSION   344

Preface

Benjamin Franklin and the Ends of Empire is both a literary biography and an analysis of the evolution of Franklin's theories of empire. As an intellectual biography, my study focuses on Franklin's written and oral expression (including private and published letters, pamphlets, newspaper articles, notes to himself, and speeches in meetings), paying great attention to Franklin's public and private views on the British Empire and its fiscal, social, legal, and military problems. As a study of Franklin's views about empire in North America, I show how Franklin's social and political theories evolved across his lifetime in response to the changing fiscal, legal, and political conditions placed on the lives of the American colonists, Native Americans, and Africans and African Americans. Franklin's changing viewpoints indicate an early embracing of and then a developing critique of British leaders, especially those who sought to hinder the freedoms of others while gaining for themselves both political power and property.

Biographical in orientation, my book addresses Franklin's intellectual life specifically related to early modern liberalism and imperial theory. But it also speaks to the very literariness of Franklin's expression, focusing again and again on the methods Franklin used to express his ideas to the different audiences he was writing for. For Franklin, the life of the mind was an ideal made palpable in the act of writing. For this reason, my study is attentive to the content of Franklin's writings but also to their literary expressiveness. Scholars frequently remark about the very literariness of Franklin's autobiography. I attempt to show similar literary qualities are evident in Franklin's writings about fiscal, social, and political policy. My book offers consolidated analyses of Franklin's writings on monetary policies, on social and political problems, and on the ideology of freedom that came to define American liberal thought during the political transformation that took place as the colonies were becoming states. It offers, in essence, a literary study of Franklin's lifetime of writing about society, economics, and politics. I reveal Franklin's evolving intellectual life as he was figuring out that the best government was one that could secure the best possible lived experience for the greatest number of peoples around the globe.

Literary biography is something of a hybrid form, blending the qualities of historical documentary biography with aesthetic concerns about the life of the mind. It is this special concern for both documented story and imagined mental world that gives literary biography its special place among biographies of well-known and lesser-known people, whether writers, political leaders, orators, or philanthropists. The biographer writing in this mode engages in an imaginative investment in the subject, attempting to articulate the intellectual world her subject circulated in and wrote for. The biographical imagination is grounded in contemporary evidence—from historical documents to the cultural and social conditions of the period to the subject's own writings and speeches—and then articulated as narrative story. Where my book offers extended quotations from Franklin's writings, the goal is to enable readers to gain access not just to the content of Franklin's thinking but to its method of expression. Michael Benton has remarked that "literary biography often deals with subjects who stand apart from society's norms and whose intertwined lives and writings offer a critique of the world" inhabited by others. In Benton's view, the literary biographer's subject often "tends to adopt an individualistic, critical view of the principles and practices of society which, on particular issues, may develop into outright opposition."[1]

Benton's point about literary biography is especially true in Franklin's case, because Franklin entered political life seeking to become a part of the British social and political scene but concluded that he would always be apart from the values and goals of people and politicians in Britain. Such a renunciation came at great personal cost, making a literary biography of Benjamin Franklin and his theory of empire a fruitful task. Understanding early modern liberalism as the backdrop to Franklin's life story and his writings helps us grasp an important aspect of Franklin's beliefs in and expressions about how personal liberty and the common good are intertwined. Understanding the backdrop also helps us see that Franklin's ultimate turn against the British Empire did not arise from pique at Alexander Wedderburn's denunciation of him in the Cockpit, as many historians have suggested, but instead developed across an extended period of time as a result of serious deliberations about the nature of empire and its impact on colonial peoples.

This literary biography of Benjamin Franklin is also a study of political life in the eighteenth century, especially as it relates to the British Empire and its colonial holdings. As an intellectual history of British colonial relations articulated by and through Benjamin Franklin, it is a first of its kind, because of its thoroughgoing analysis of Franklin's writings about economy, society, the environment, and imperial politics. In conversing with older works like Alan Houston's *Benjamin Franklin and the Politics of Improvement* (Yale, 2008) and Douglas Anderson's *The Radical Enlightenments of Benjamin Franklin* (Johns Hopkins, 2000), it adds to a stream of scholarship out there already, but it departs from others in its emphasis on Franklin's evolving theories of empire formulated as political goals for North America. Especially in its effort to ground Franklin's thinking by attending to his early modern liberal values adopted in his youth, the book will, I hope, shed a different light on one of British North America's greatest economic, social, and political theorists.

In some ways, my work extends into the present century different conversations about Franklin that began over a century ago, in studies written by economic and political historians. In 1895, W. A. Wetzel produced a monograph on Franklin's economic views as they were evident in several of Franklin's most important writings.[2] Lewis J. Carey entered his own opinions on Franklin's economic thinking with a longer study, *Franklin's Economic Views*, published in 1928.[3] Carey's study is noteworthy not only because it was produced well before the Franklin papers project began but because, though it is quite rudimentary, it remains the most complete account of Franklin's economic thinking. While taking up Franklin's views on economy and society, my work also engages some of the questions embraced in the work of Verner S. Crane, Gerald Stourzh, and Paul W. Connor, whose interests in Franklin are those more typical of the political historian.[4] Like these scholars, I focus on Franklin's writings on trade, economics, and political theory, but unlike them, I treat Franklin's studies of populations, for instance, in the context of his concern about the people's pragmatic and ethical impact on the land. I am also preoccupied by Franklin's early acceptance of imperialist notions about superior and subjected peoples and his eventual critique of such notions as he recognized that nation-formation in Britain contradicted the very foundations of liberal subjectivity.

Benjamin Franklin and the Ends of Empire is organized in roughly but not rigidly chronological fashion, with chapters as much thematic as chronological. After an introduction describing the intellectual roots of Franklin early modern liberalism, the book moves (chapters 1 and 2) into Franklin's

family history, especially the family's background in England, and iden-
tifies Franklin's intellectual and humanistic roots in early modern times.
These chapters speak to the many writers whose works emerged during the
seventeenth and early eighteenth centuries, with an attention to Franklin's
youthful understanding of imperial economic theory and his fascination
with late seventeenth-century writings about personal liberties, including
freedom of conscience and freedom of the press. I'm interested in the ways in
which Franklin's early reading and analysis of British culture and imperialism found voice in his writings about free trade and free peoples. Then the
book takes up (chapters 3, 4, and 5) Franklin's young adult and middle years,
when he was involved with Pennsylvania politics and learning strategies
for political negotiation. During these years Franklin carefully developed
a socioeconomic view supporting both free trade and a politics of imperialism. His goal was to negotiate with Crown and Parliament an administrative
policy that would establish among all the colonies an equable laboring and
trading situation with Britain, in effect creating a commonwealth (and commonly held ideas about liberties and benefits) among all trading partners.

As his intellectual, social, and political world widened, Franklin began
to conceive that the ideology of British freedoms had extended to the colonies with the first settlers. Thus he believed that freedom as a natural right
ought to be available to all British Americans, who were, after all, merely
Britons geographically dispersed. The extension of political freedoms to
British North Americans would work ideologically, he thought, to solidify
people in North America who were otherwise politically and culturally
diverse. Franklin's mature years as the colonies' chief representative and
cultural ambassador in Britain and Europe form the content of chapters 6
and 7, which elucidate Franklin's disgruntlement with the British ministry
and with British colonial administrations that worked to undermine the
well-being of Britons in North America. These two chapters address the
pivotal years of Franklin's rejection of Great Britain and attend to Franklin's
significant concerns about Britain's expansive imperialism, especially with
regard to Ireland and India. Chapter 8 treats the years of the Revolution
against Great Britain, especially Franklin's diplomacy in France and his
mature views of sovereignty and human justice. Chapter 9 discusses the
last period of Franklin's life, from his triumphant return to Philadelphia to
his last days. The chapter discusses Franklin's last years, including his work
in American abolition and his concerns about the subjection of peoples
throughout the globe. I hope readers will find that my book helps them
understand just how very important to Franklin's philosophy and his values were his formative years spent around the table, hearing his family's
stories, and his youthful reading in early modern liberal writings.

Acknowledgments

This book began over two decades ago as a study of Benjamin Franklin's experiences with and writings about Native peoples of North America. It went through different iterations in the intervening years. Some material originally intended for this volume has reached print already, because it no longer suited the scope of the project. I was fortunate to receive several fellowships in the work's earliest stages. The National Endowment for the Humanities provided a summer research stipend in 1992. The Andrew W. Mellon Foundation provided residential fellowships administered by two major archives in Franklin studies, the Library Company of Philadelphia and the American Philosophical Society, where I performed significant research in 2000–2001 and continued to cull collections in intervening years. The American Council of Learned Societies granted me a fellowship to continue drafting the book in 2006–7. And Penn State's College of Liberal Arts granted me two research leaves, one in 2000 and one in 2006. Penn State's Institute for the Arts and Humanities provided a small grant for much-needed released time in 2010, so I could move the writing forward. Without the research opportunities these fellowships afforded, the book would not have reached fruition.

So many scholars and friends formed audiences for papers delivered, read portions of the manuscript, and provided moral support as the work proceeded that it is difficult to imagine my completing the work without their support. Some of my closest friends—J. A. Leo Lemay, William Pencak, Jeffrey Richards, and Frank Shuffelton—did not live to see the result of their gentle nudging toward my completion of the project. But many remain who deserve my sincere thanks for their goodwill and interest in the work. Some wrote letters in my behalf. Others cheered me on across many years. Still others invited me to their institutions to deliver lectures related to Franklin. For their inspirational interest in the work, I thank Douglas Anderson, Robert Arner, Nina Baym, Richard Bell, Richard Bernstein, George Boudreau, Louis Cellucci, Deborah Clarke, David Curtis, Paul Erickson, Armin Paul Frank, John Frantz, Ed Gallagher, Dustin Gish, Roy Goodman, James Green, Sandra Gustafson, Sharon M. Harris, Tamara Harvey, Matthew S. Holland, Nian-Sheng Huang, Paul Kerry, Daniel Klinghard, Annette Kolodny, Ned Landsman, Paul Lauter, James Lilley, David Lincove, Janet Lindman, Rodney Mader, James May, Donald Mell, Marietta Messmer, Randall Miller, Dennis Moore, Wilson Moses, Charles Nicol, Marcy North, Hugh Ormsby-Lennon, Frank Parks, John Pollack, Daniel Richter, Marion Rust, Doreen Alvarez Saar, Eleanor Shevlin, David Shields, Sheila Skemp, Scott Slawinski, Herb Sloan, Laura Stevens, Larry E. Tise, John Van Horne, W. M. Verhoeven, Marianne Wokeck, and Michael Zuckerman.

Many students, faculty, and friends formed audiences that raised useful questions of the work when it was delivered in a variety of invited lectures at Cliveden, the Franklin Institute, the Library Company of Philadelphia, the Joseph Priestley House, the McNeil Center for Early American Studies, the Columbia Seminar on the History of the Atlantic World, the Washington DC Area History Seminar, and at a number of academic institutions, including Cambridge University (England), Georg-August University at Göttingen (Germany), the University of Groningen (the Netherlands), and several American institutions, including Belmont University, California State University at Channel Islands, the College of the Holy Cross, Columbia University, Drexel University, Indiana State University, Lehigh University, the Ohio State University Libraries, Princeton University, the University of Kentucky, the University of Maryland, the University of Tulsa, Florida State University, and Western Michigan University.

I would like to thank the staffs of the various libraries where I worked on my book, including the American Antiquarian Society, the American Philosophical Society, the Beinecke Rare Book and Manuscript Library, the British Library, the Library Company of Philadelphia, and the Special Collections Library of the Van Pelt Library at the University of Pennsylvania. For their assistance with the illustrations for this volume, I would particularly thank Mary Ellen Budney (Beinecke Rare Book and Manuscript Library), Anna Clutterbuck-Cook and Elaine Heavey (Massachusetts Historical Society), Nicole Joniec (Library Company of Philadelphia), Valerie-Ann Lutz (American Philosophical Society), and Jaclyn Penny (American Antiquarian Society). I also am very grateful for the assistance of the student researchers who helped me during the last phases of writing, especially the Penn State undergraduate interns Marvee Shah, Adison Godfrey, and Aleksander Smolij. Penn State Ph.D. Katie Owens-Murphy helped me manage the editing of the manuscript when it became too unwieldy in its final stages. I am grateful for her efforts to assist my work.

Brendan O'Neill of the Oxford University Press has been the writer's ideal editor, providing critical suggestions and important guidance all along while remaining enthusiastic and confident about the importance of the work. The series of anonymous readers of the manuscript asked probing questions, suggested revisions, and spotted errors. I thank them for their generosity in helping make this a better book. I'd also like to thank press coordinators Stephen Bradley and Eswari Marudhu and the manuscript's copyeditor, Richard Isomaki, for the care taken with the manuscript.

My family has waited too long for the work to conclude. Irene and Ted Lehmann, Ellen Clendenning and Jerry Fallas, and Marjorie and John Gardner have never quite known whether to ask how the writing was going, but they probably always knew it would conclude when they least expected it. I appreciate their kind interest in the project from its infancy. To Robert L. Giuntoli II, Frank Guillard, Tim Foust, Kimberly Albright, Patricia Gaughan, Elaine Sterrett, and Rosemary Shaner I owe very, very special thanks for helping me get by in the ways that only they know best.

Work on the manuscript took place in several different locations in State College and Boalsburg until Franklin and I found our home at the Wren's Nest, a living historic home originally built before 1783 in the town now called Bellefonte, where Ted Conklin suggested we might share a life together. The Wren's Nest was the perfect place to conclude the writing. I am grateful to Ted for making this writer's life possible amid the changing circumstances of our lives, including my major surgery, the challenges of my university work life (including an office move for building renovations), the arrival and departure of several rescued cocker spaniels, and the arrival and continued stay of my inspiring mother. The completion of the book is owing to his loving-kindness, grit, generosity, and steadying presence.

Benjamin Franklin
and the
Ends of Empire

Introduction

Late in the year 1768, Benjamin Franklin penned a strong statement about war and civil liberty. Employing an uncharacteristically emotional tone, Franklin revealed his anxiety about the prospect of the continued warfare of two governments working to deny the personal and civic liberties of their subjects. "A horrid Spectacle to Men and Angels is now about to be exhibited on the Stage of this Globe," he exclaimed. The Atlantic world was in disarray. Referring to the British Parliament's imposition of the Townshend Acts on the American colonies and France's similarly imperial move to control uprisings in Corsica (which had succumbed to French forces), Franklin articulated a view of freedom as a "common right" belonging to all people. He wrote that "Two great and Powerful Nations are employing their Forces in the Destruction of Civil LIBERTY, that heavenly Blessing without which Mankind lose half their Dignity and Value!" He complained that one of these "great and Powerful Nations" was destroying civil liberty by "oppressing and enslaving a handful of Men the last brave Assertors of it within the Bounds of the old Roman Commonwealth," and "the other" was "crushing in its Infancy, the first Appearance of it in the Western World." Franklin was writing about the French, who were suppressing the Corsicans, led by Pasquale Paoli (1725–1827), champion of representative democracy, and about the British, who were making every effort to suppress the Britons in North America simply for seeking the same civil and political rights afforded to Britons in England. To Franklin, France had "lost Sight of its antient Name and State, *Franks* from the *Freedom* it once enjoy'd," whereas Britain, even "while it boasts of enjoying Freedom itself, would ruin others for vindicating their common Right to it." Continuing the diatribe, Franklin said that France was "acting a cruel, a mean and unmanly Part, thus to use its vastly superior Force against People so unable to resist it." But France's behavior was, he said, "*more excusable*" than Britain's, because at least in France's case, "the People to be oppress'd and enslav'd, are NOT"—adopting the parent/child metaphor typical in propaganda of the day—"her *own Children!*"[1] Franklin's diatribe gave voice to his frustration with governments that sought to reduce the "Dignity and Value" of "Mankind" by destroying "Civil Liberty."

My preoccupation with Franklin's statement lies in his strategic linking of civil liberty with the personal ideals of dignity and value (meaning the feeling of self-worth, in this context) and with political freedom as a "common Right" for all people. Franklin pointed out that Britain's vaunted liberal notions of freedom conflicted with its view of its role as an imperial power. The statement makes clear Franklin's recognition of problems inherent in imperial nation-states: imperial authoritarianism, when set in a context of global warfare, would fall into conflict with notions of ancient civil liberties that, in his ideal conception, belonged to all people. Imperial goals were superseding individual rights and freedoms. Franklin was concerned about a plan beginning to emerge in Britain to consolidate fiscal and military policy so as to streamline the administration of the American colonies and make them more like the structure emerging for the administration of British India. Despite British "boasts of enjoying Freedom itself," such plans would occur at the expense of Britons around the globe, in Franklin's view.

This was not a new line of argument for Franklin. In the early 1750s, he had expressed his views that the formation of nation-states ought not to occur at the expense (both fiscal and personal) of colonial peoples. This view was most notably expressed in a series of mid-1750s letters he wrote to William Shirley (1694–1771), a lawyer and colonial official serving as governor of Massachusetts, explaining his conception of colonial self-governance. In the letters to Shirley, Franklin articulated a clear plan for administering colonies without denying them legal representation and access to trade. He suggested an intercolonial system to increase intercolonial trade and mutual assistance, all under the umbrella of British Parliament and the king. Britons in North America would have the same rights, privileges, and representation as those in England.

Franklin believed that those living outside England ought to have the same political standing as those in England. It was a view he expressed often, especially from the 1750s onward. For instance, in a letter to his friend, Peter Collinson (1694–1768), a botanist and member of the Royal Society of London, Franklin wrote in 1754 that "Britain and her Colonies should be considered as one Whole, and not as different States with separate Interests," adding that "Instructions from the CROWN to the Colonies, should have in View the Common Weal of that Whole, to which partial Interests ought to give way." In Franklin's view, on behalf of the "Common Weal," the Crown should never "Aim at extending the Prerogative beyond its due Bounds, nor abridging the just Liberties of the people." Instead, all instructions, like all laws, "should be plainly just and reasonable."[2] In a just and liberal commonwealth, Franklin thought, the interests of the people would be considered paramount, with government held in "due Bounds" and the people's liberties guiding decision-making. The "Common Weal" of the whole ought to determine policy.

Franklin was articulating his concerns about governments that were "abridging the just Liberties of the people" at the time when France, Spain, the Netherlands, and Britain were flexing their military muscles in a global movement for control of the seas and the transport trade. Franklin was speaking at the moment when Britain was shifting to a policy of full support for a strategic fiscal-military state—to gain full control over land-bases in India while retaining complete trade and legislative oversight of North America—that would undoubtedly work to undermine the local rights of Britons used to mouthing and participating in liberal citizenship.[3] John Brewer has shown that the late seventeenth and eighteenth centuries "saw an astonishing transformation in British government," a transformation that required Britain to work hard "to shoulder an ever-more ponderous burden of military commitments" by increasing taxation, organizing a public deficit (a national debt), and developing "a sizable public administration devoted to organizing the fiscal and military activities of the state."[4] Franklin's remarks provide apt evidence for what Brewer has identified as the perpetual conflict that emerges as the buildup of a nation-state undermines the rights of the individuals within that state. Franklin's remarks are also a perfect example of what historian Sophus A. Reinert has described as the nationalist propensities of competing European powers to mimic (and challenge) Britain's aggressive global expansion.[5] The conflict between individual rights and state power indicates the challenges pressuring several of the most important ideals undergirding early modern liberalism.

Early Modern Liberalism

In using the phrase *early modern liberalism* to describe the intellectual, civil, and political values of Franklin's world, I am making an effort to recuperate a rich array of ideals articulated in writings that circulated in England, on the Continent, and in North America. Intellectual and political historians have employed a cluster of terms to describe the tenor of the era. The word *republicanism* was in vogue in the eighteenth century and among historians of the late twentieth century, but there were many disagreements about what the word meant (in Franklin's day) and how scholars in recent times should define it, whether loosely or precisely.[6] As with the term *republicanism*, the term *Whig* has the burden of archaism and political confusion, because of the shifting values of the eighteenth century and the "party" ideology attached to it as a political label. Because both terms were used during the eighteenth century, but used differently by different people, it is difficult to disentangle their meanings for use now. Like intellectual and literary historian Annabel Patterson, I prefer the phrase *early modern liberalism* to describe the values Franklin admired precisely because it did not exist as a label in Franklin's day. The phrase etymologically affiliates with *liberty*, and its subsequent emergence (unlike the word *republicanism*, which was used to describe political theory or systems of governance) included religious, legal, and economic issues, from the past and present day. To those who might suggest that using the term is anachronistic given the term's particular impact in nineteenth-century thought, I think it useful to consider the antecedents to nineteenth-century liberal thought, because in those antecedents arose the range of concepts in constant interplay *prior to* when the idea of liberalism became more fixed as a platform in the nineteenth century.[7]

This approach speaks to work by key historians of early modern Britain, particularly Annabel Patterson and Stephen Pincus, and work by only a few historians who study colonial and revolutionary America, particularly Joyce Appleby. It used to be common to use the term *liberal* in the context of early America. Indeed, Appleby long argued that it should never have been abandoned, at least for the Early Republic. In the historiography, other descriptions of what constituted liberal thinking prevailed, including *Whig, radical Whig,* and *Commonwealth* thought. The matter was further confused by the literature on *republicanism* and *classical republicanism* by historians of early America, such as Bernard Bailyn, J. G. A. Pocock, and Gordon Wood, who downplayed the impact of figures like John Locke (1632–1704). Pincus's is, to my thinking, a most convincing analysis of a series of writers who shared many of the tropes common to classical republicanism, especially those reflecting an interest in "the common good" and a "hatred of tyranny." But rather than denouncing increasing commercialism as corruption, these writers instead celebrated the new commerce-driven "vocabulary of interests and rights in defense of the common good." Pincus has pointed out that in examining histories of liberalism, scholars must be attentive to the complete range of writings resulting from the commonwealth tradition, because many of these writings, rather than articulating distress about the emerging commercial society of England, expressed "a new ideology applicable to a commercial society, an ideology that valued wealth but also the common good, an ideology, in short, that celebrated neither possessive individualism nor the anti-commercialism of republican Sparta."[8] As used by both Patterson and Appleby, the phrase *early modern liberalism* helps to cut a clear path through the staggeringly confusing historiography. The phrase comprehensively embraces values that occurred in a wide array of writers during the seventeenth and eighteenth centuries. Using the term to discuss Franklin's life and writings places Franklin in line with Algernon Sidney (1623–1683), John Locke, John Milton (1608–1674), John Trenchard (1662–1723), Thomas Gordon (c. 1691–1750), and many others—all writers studied by Patterson, Appleby, and Pincus.

By employing the phrase *early modern liberalism*, I am referring to formulations about two key freedoms based, as historically conceived by Protestant writers of the sixteenth and seventeenth centuries, in the ancient liberties of the Magna Carta: liberty of person (freedom from oppression by a tyrannical monarch and freedom to enjoy the fruits of one's own labor) and liberty of conscience (freedom to worship in the ways that one chose to worship the Christian God). Central writers in this tradition (e.g., Algernon Sidney and John Milton, among many lesser-known writers), after facing hostility for the expression of their views, came to embrace freedom of speech as another central freedom individuals ought to hold as dear as their lives. Writers (such as Trenchard and Gordon, among others) in the liberal tradition of the seventeenth and early eighteenth centuries took up the challenge to articulate their own sense of urgency about individual freedoms. Eventually, such arguments would address issues such as trade guilds, emigration (and its prevention, for certain trades), and slavery—all issues that Franklin wrote about during his lifetime.

Some of the writers who adapted for late seventeenth century and early eighteenth century use the writings of Sidney, Locke, Trenchard, Gordon, and others spoke of their values as "country" values. These values also informed Franklin's notions about early modern liberalism. "Country" ideology circulated among a coalition of Tories and Whigs from roughly the 1680s to the 1740s. Those who supported the country ideology (which was more a platform of values than a "party" in the modern sense) tended to articulate a view that *the whole country* should benefit from policymaking, not just members of the court, whose interests could often dominate political life. Their writings favored policies supporting personal liberties, an efficient and representative government developed through frequent elections, moral and ethical accountability, and the duty of those in power to work toward the nation's interests. They also argued for an orderly government that would act solely according to the consent of those governed. In general, country ideology tended to emphasize rights and privileges (whether individual, local, or parliamentary) above the power of the monarch and ministry, and it fostered the notion that the government should operate to assist the whole population.[9] Country ideology had a long history, and like the foundational texts of liberal values, it was attractive to Franklin from his youth. Indeed, "country" views formed a touchstone in his writing throughout his life.

By studying early modern liberalism as a stream of writing on matters of conscience, economy, and statehood, we are able to see Franklin's ideas more clearly, as he, early on, wrote to the problems inherent in the economic literature and then sought to embrace the developing marketplace economy and the literature of commercialism complementing that economy. Franklin's original goals for the colonies were that they remain within the British imperial system. He held on to these goals for a long time, attempting to find workable solutions to the political and social impasses that he continually faced while attempting to negotiate reasonable taxing and defense policies, first for Pennsylvania alone and then for all of the colonies, when he was living in England. While in England, he began to realize, slowly but steadily, that he was being treated as a subaltern. He also realized the extent to which the discourse of nationhood that was the foundation for England's imperial imaginings was, first, alienating of the disparate peoples living within the British commonwealth system and, second and more importantly, masking a political inequality Franklin perceived more and more to be acutely the condition of British American, Irish, and many Scottish people, not to mention the peoples in Asia and Africa that Britain was attempting to colonize. In these London years, Franklin's tone became more trenchant than conciliatory, more accusatory than accommodating.

Franklin was rankled that Britons in England did not consider British people equal under the social compact that bound them all. He became deeply troubled that Britain's vaunted liberalism, a liberalism he had been raised to admire and cultivated as his own, was a sham. In some ways, Franklin's turn against England seems finally to be a turn into a political consciousness—indeed, political self-consciousness—that he had avoided recognizing for many years because he seems truly to have believed in the traditional conception of love of country, a key aspect of the rhetoric of old Whig liberalism and country ideology, that he often articulated in his writings when critiquing the imperialist policies and culture fostered under George III. In effect, by using the term *early modern liberalism*, I am attempting to evoke a constellation of values important to Franklin across his long life.

Franklin's Views

Part of the problem Franklin faced as the most important negotiator for the colonies in England was the fact that he was regarded as a lowborn American and a tradesman. His background among laboring people enabled him to understand, from the colonial perspective, problems inherent in Britain's imperial system. But precisely because of his background among laboring people, he had difficulty (despite his international renown as a scientist) securing the support of the powerful men in London who were designing imperial policies. Status, educational credentials, and birthplace mattered more to Britons in power than Franklin wished to acknowledge. By looking at some of the British cultural meanings associated with the word *liberal*, we can come closer to the complexity of values that Franklin faced as a colonial American.

An interesting and telling example of the attitudes that cultured Britons held toward laborers, tradespeople, and all those in the marketing ends of commerce (as opposed to leaders in administration who were bankrolling certain transport trades) appears in Samuel Johnson's 1755 *Dictionary of the English Language*, where Johnson (1709–1784) reported: "Of the laborious and mercantile part of the people, the diction is in a great measure casual and mutable," and thus not worthy of his dictionary.[10] For Johnson, it was not lamentable that the words of laborers, tradespeople, and merchants would not appear in his dictionary. His clarifying remark indicates Johnson's condescension toward the work of most such people: Their "fugitive cant, which is always in a state of increase or decay, cannot be regarded as any part of the durable materials of a language, and therefore must be suffered to perish with other things unworthy of preservation." Claiming that, for the purposes of his dictionary, he "could not visit caverns to learn the miner's language, nor take a voyage to perfect my skill in the dialect of navigation, nor visit the warehouses of merchants, and shops of artificers, to gain the names of wares, tools and operations," Johnson concluded, "it had been a hopeless labour to glean up words, by courting living information, and contesting with the sullenness of one, and the roughness of another." Laboring people were dull-witted and certainly unskilled in language, Johnson assumed. Worse, they were sullen and rough. Johnson's assumptions presumably described but also instructed the "cultured" gentleman what he should think about the English language and laborers. Johnson thus taught the same values to all those who would read his dictionary in an effort better to know the English language. Surely Johnson was well aware that his presumed record of the language was both emancipating (through education) and disciplining (through his elucidation of "proper" attitudes) of the middle classes who were increasingly becoming literate during the century.

Whereas Benjamin Franklin, who often visited wharves, ships, mills, and manufacturing plants, always had abundant curiosity about how things worked, how calculations were derived, by what methods the laborers did certain things, and where they did them, Samuel Johnson would not stoop to do so, as the language of the laborer was, he sniffed, mere "fugitive cant." The uses of language—its diction, its speech method, its rhetorical power among initiates—differentiated people in Samuel Johnson's world. Franklin, well understanding this fact of life in his era, proposed that the primary skills students should learn in his English school and his Academy (college) be tied to the linguistic arts of reading, writing, and oratory. And for Franklin, himself once a laborer and merchant, Johnson's classed explanation about which diction was "worth" recording and which was not, would surely have been noted. Yet Franklin knew the audience he was seeking to persuade in England, and for that audience, Dr. Johnson served as a crucial instructor in taste and a self-cultivated sense of refinement. Franklin seems genuinely to have admired Johnson's learning. He quoted Johnson in his Poor Richard almanacs, and he was happy to have opportunities to meet with him amid his round of clubbing in London during the 1760s.[11]

Franklin's and Johnson's views on the word *liberal* (as it was defined in Johnson's dictionary) are evident in the way each talked about his culture. The two primary meanings Johnson offered for the word in his dictionary, when he employed *liberal* as an adjective, imply class differentiation signaling elite group assumptions about culture, precisely the elite group assumptions that Franklin came to understand and quarrel with when attempting to negotiate for the colonies in England. Johnson's etymology for the word, used as an adjective, is based in Latin and French usages, and his definitions are these: "1. Not mean; not low in birth; not low in mind. 2. Becoming a gentleman." A liberal person, to Johnson, was one born relatively high and one who had high-minded qualities, as became a gentleman. The third meaning that Johnson attached to the word indicates qualities of generosity: "3. Munificent; generous; bountiful; not parcimonious." Johnson taught that liberal gentlemen should be bountiful, even though they should consider themselves above those who labored with their hands for a living.

Examining Franklin's writings, one finds that Franklin used the term primarily to suggest two meanings, the first (and less frequent) usage indicating "generosity," and the second as a descriptor for education, as in "liberal education." Franklin never used the term to suggest class, as Johnson did. Franklin conceived that the use of the term *liberal* ought to convey generosity, as, for instance, when he revised and quoted the poem, "For Liberality," from *The Genuine Works* (1736) of George Granville, Baron Lansdowne (1667–1735) in *Poor Richard Improved*, 1750:

> Tho' safe thou think'st thy Treasure lies,
> Hidden in Chests from Human Eyes,
> Thieves, Fire, may come, and it may be
> Convey'd, my Friend, as far from thee.
> Thy Vessel that yon Ocean sails,
> Tho' favour'd now with prosp'rous Gales,
> Her Cargo which has Thousands cost,
> All in a Tempest may be lost.
> Cheats, Whores and Quacks, a thankless Crew,
> Priests, Pickpockets, and Lawyers too,
> All help by several Ways to drain,
> Thanking themselves for what they gain;
> The *Liberal* are secure alone,
> For what they frankly give, for ever is their own.[12]

In his quotation, Franklin emphasized the word "Liberal" by taking the printer's liberty of italicizing it for his almanac readers. Franklin agreed with Johnson's third definition of *liberal* but clearly disagreed with the notion that the word had any particular association with those of the upper class. Illiberal people were alike subjected by "Whores, Quacks, . . . Priests, Pickpockets, and Lawyers"—that is, a full range of people from all classes. The poem provides a good idea about Franklin's use of the term, for it emphasizes generosity and the feeling of personal freedom and security that such generosity made possible. The example illustrates how Franklin used "country" ideology to support a liberal agenda.

Franklin's educational models emphasized what he called a liberal education, but his educational plans were a far cry from what was typical for gentlemen in England. The differences in his educational plans for Philadelphians, when compared to English models and to the existing American colleges, are many: He wanted a school not for the well-to-do alone but for ordinary people, including "handicrafts" (his word for tradesmen or artisans). He framed educational plans that included the classical trivium and quadrivium, but rather than focusing exclusively on this traditional body of learning, he aimed to train young men in practical arts and sciences to assist their everyday work and their self-tutelage during the hours when they were not working. Franklin also considered essential a significant amount of training in English and other contemporary, continental languages and literatures.[13] For reading, Franklin suggested contemporary authors and those whose work influenced the great liberal philosophical traditions he appreciated in his youth. Such authors as Algernon Sidney, John Milton, John Locke, and John Trenchard and Thomas Gordon formed just a small part of Franklin's pantheon of liberal thinkers and writers.[14] He admired these writers for their expressions about just government, the rights and liberties of subjects, and the duties of the monarch. He also admired them for their clear statements about the separation of church and state. His educational plan modeled liberalism for the students.

As he did with his educational plan, Franklin used his almanacs to inform his readers about their cultural roots in liberal traditions and the potential for liberty in British North America. These were roots Franklin was fond of speaking about, roots that arose from the seventeenth century in the English civil wars, roots evocative of what was popularly conceived as the original charter of personal liberties embodied in the Magna Carta. For instance, he called up the memory of Algernon Sidney for his readers in 1750's *Poor Richard Improved*. Under the entry for December, Franklin remarked:

On the 7th of this Month, 1683, was the honourable Algernon Sidney, Esq; beheaded, charg'd with a pretended Plot, but whose chief Crime was the Writing an excellent Book, intituled, *Discourses on Government*. A Man of admirable Parts and great Integrity. Thompson calls him the British Cassius. The good Lord Russel and he were intimate Friends; and as they were Fellow Sufferers in their Death, the Poet joins them in his Verses,

> Bring every sweetest Flower, and let me strow
> The Grave where Russel lies; whose temper'd Blood
> With calmest Chearfulness for thee resign'd,
> Stain'd the sad Annals of a giddy Reign,
> Aiming at lawless Power, tho' meanly sunk,
> In loose inglorious Luxury. With him
> His Friend, the British Cassius, fearless bled;
> Of high, determin'd Spirit, roughly brave,
> By ancient Learning to th' enlighten'd Love
> Of ancient Freedom warm'd.[15]

Franklin quoted the Scottish poet James Thomson (1700–1748) sentimentally to offer the view—so that it is not his almanac's Richard Saunders's view alone—that Algernon Sidney and Lord William Russell (1639–1683) died unjustly at the hands of a monarch who loved luxury, for a "plot" with which, it was said at the time, neither had anything to do. Sidney had been accused, with Russell, of being involved in the Rye House Plot, aimed at taking the lives of Charles II and his brother, James (heir to the throne), shortly after the Crown was restored to the Stuart line. A Parliamentarian, Sidney believed in representative government. His *Discourses concerning Government*, which circulated widely in manuscript during his lifetime, was published under several different titles beginning around 1698. By combining Thomson's poetry and his own argument, Franklin reminded his readers that liberty of speech, liberty of person, and legislative freedoms are all contested values, not to be taken for granted. By memorializing and thus celebrating Sidney's and Russell's martyrdoms for their presumed part in the Rye House Plot, Franklin informed and reminded his readers about the bravery involved in honoring "th' enlighten'd Love / Of ancient Freedom." This was an essential part of liberalism, to Franklin: honoring ancient freedoms by challenging government when it attempted to usurp individual liberties.

Associated with ideas of liberalism in Franklin's writings are ideas about liberty. He admired the work of writers from the 1680s through the 1720s who spoke about civil freedom. During his youth, John Milton, Thomas Gordon, and William Trenchard were particularly influential on his developing beliefs about civil society. While his brother James was incarcerated for challenging local government officials by printing criticisms of them in his newspaper, Franklin ran the paper. He printed Thomas Gordon's "Cato's Letter" of February 4, 1721, where Gordon identified free speech as a "publick Liberty." Franklin reprinted some of the most important passages of Gordon's message, indicating his own belief (with which James Franklin concurred) that freedom of speech, like freedom of conscience, comprised a "sacred privilege" most "essential to free government." Franklin quoted Gordon at length in Silence Dogood No. 8, published in the *New-England Courant*, July 9, 1722. He opened with Gordon's opening, "Without Freedom of Thought, there can be no such Thing as Wisdom; and no such Thing as publick Liberty, without Freedom of Speech." Calling freedom of speech the "Right of every Man, as far as by it, he does not hurt and controul the Right of another," Gordon linked free speech with enlightened and free government and the security of property: "This sacred Privilege is so essential to free Government, that the Security of Property, and the Freedom of Speech always go together; and in those wretched Countries where a Man cannot call his Tongue his own, he can scarce call any Thing else his own. Whoever would overthrow the Liberty of the Nation, must begin by subduing the Freeness of Speech; a *Thing* terrible to Publick Traytors." Gordon used an exemplary story about the absence of freedom of religion under King Charles I to illustrate the problems that occurred for the people when freedom of speech was not protected by the monarch. Under Charles I's "wicked ministry," he wrote, "People were forbid to talk of Religion in their Families: For the Priests had combined with the Ministers to cook up Tyranny, and suppress Truth and the Law." In Gordon's view, as in Franklin's, "The Administration of Government, is nothing else, but the Attendance of the *Trustees of the People* upon the Interest and Affairs of the People." That is, good governors serve the people, not themselves. If they are doing their jobs well, governors ought not to fear public scrutiny of their activities. For "as it is the Part and Business of the People, for whose Sake alone all publick Matters are, or ought to be, transacted, to see whether they be well or ill transacted," then "it is the Interest, and ought to be the Ambition, of all honest Magistrates, to have their Deeds openly examined, and publickly scan'd: Only the *wicked Governours* of Men dread what is said of them," Gordon concluded.[16] By printing Gordon at this moment, Franklin was using the newspaper to support both the freedom of the Franklin press and the freedom of speech. Franklin admired and promulgated such ideals as freedom of speech, freedom of conscience, and the freedoms of person and property as he matured in political knowledge.

Franklin long supported the ideals of freedom of speech and freedom of conscience. As he grew into increasing political prominence, he came to value especially the ideal of the freedom of person, in which inhered the right to own the fruits of one's own labor. As will become clear, while Franklin worked to find an equable solution to the trade and navigation laws imposed on the colonies, Franklin realized, finally, that by supporting Britain and the empire in North America, he was supporting a corrupt system. The sources of the values Franklin believed in might seem conflicting, in the historical scholarship, but in general, the values Franklin admired had their root in the social contract theories of the seventeenth century, theories that articulate the differences between what philosophers called the state of nature and the state of civil society. In these theories reside the political concept that all human beings are equal in the state of nature and thus have equal rights by nature's laws, rights that become constrained when they enter into civil society, which they enter, by choice, in order to protect their natural rights.

Franklin tended to admire John Locke and to distance himself from Niccolò Machiavelli (1469–1527) and Thomas Hobbes (1588–1679), all of whom wrote—differently—about state power, civil society, and natural rights of common men. As his writings attest, Franklin was a voracious and eclectic reader and a superb rhetorician. He could at times reference Machiavelli in denigrating terms, for instance, but at other times, he commended him. In short, Franklin was a master rhetorician, and he was willing to use whatever theoretical position would be most useful at any particular time. Franklin's writings reflect a remarkable flexibility of thinking, an inquirer's capacity to embrace a position at one point but to reflect upon issues continually in an effort to reach a better or more appropriate conclusion. As illustrated by the famous instance of his publishing and then retracting his "little metaphysical piece," *A Dissertation on Liberty and Necessity, Pleasure and Pain* (London, 1725), Franklin would work to get to know a position, test it out as he wished, use it if it proved important to do so, and change his mind about it at some later point. He was unafraid of pointing out such self-contradiction in his autobiography. He privileged process in his intellectual life, and he constantly sought out new ways of thinking about things, as his scientific bent indicates. Franklin's theories on imperialism, liberalism, natural rights and obligations, the social compact—all were open to continual interrogation, revision, reformulation. His view of the dignity and value of labor never changed.

Franklin's mature position on liberalism began to take shape during the 1750s. In that decade, he created and started publicly to circulate his goals and strategies for retaining the British Empire intact. He was developing self-conscious intellectual, social, and structural policies that he explained to leaders such as Cadwallader Colden (1688–1776), Thomas Pownall (1722–1805), and William Shirley. He understood that the liberalism he was advocating was in stark contrast to the special-privilege liberalist assumptions—the "interest politics" typically associated with "court" ideology—operating in England. In addition to the lobbying of the ministry by the well-to-do, there was, across the middle part of the eighteenth century, an increasing pressure on government deriving from the mercantile and trade sectors, who were lobbying Parliamentarians and the ministry in order to gain advantages for themselves at the expense of Americans. Fearing North Americans' economic independence and the political consolidation of the disparate peoples living within the boundaries of British-identified territories, propagandists in England argued for punishing controls over colonial production and trade. Most Americans conceived that their interests did not matter to those in power in England. This bothered Franklin, who was himself lobbying to relax the trade and navigation laws hindering, among other things, American manufacturing. He argued that the constraints on trade, meant to undermine the economic stability and power of the American colonies, was shortsighted. By critiquing the special-privilege assumptions of those in power, Franklin was attempting to put reins on the growing fiscal-military state that, he saw, relied on the jostling of trade organizations, lobbyists, and groups of merchants and financiers.

Franklin's Ends of Empire

One of the fairly consistent strands in Franklin's thinking across his lifetime is his conception of what ought to be the ends of empire. Those ends ought to be the creation, material support, and protection of the best possible living circumstances for the greatest number of people living within the borders of territories held as one national community. To make such ends of empire possible, he thought, governments should foster ideals like those associated with the ancient British liberties often talked about during the sixteenth and seventeenth centuries by a range of writers Franklin read as a youth and came to admire. Freedom of conscience (often called freedom of religion), freedom of speech (to protect those who might question social and political decision-making), freedom of movement, freedom to work and keep the fruits of one's labor, and several other related freedoms became ideals Franklin spoke about again and again. He considered that good government ought to foster the lives of the people. Franklin's views are evidenced repeatedly, in what he wrote privately and what he printed in his newspapers and pamphlets—whether speaking about the peopling of North America, Native Americans and imperial relations, immigrant non-Britons within British boundaries, colonial administration and changing colonial policies, or slavery and the conditions of living without owning one's own labor. Especially in the 1750s and early 1760s, when Franklin conceived that Britain's colonial problems might still be resolved by an improved relationship between the British administration and British colonial peoples, he took every possible opportunity to make known his position about the mutual dependence and common bonds—the "interest of humanity," as he often called it—of Britons on both sides of the Atlantic. For Franklin, the ends of empire were the interests of humanity and the interests of the people.

Unlike his friends in Great Britain and Europe, Franklin had witnessed great changes in North America and understood the environmental and political promise of a consolidation of the colonies as productive parts of the British Empire. Even though he could conceive of Britons in North America living in their own independent fiscal and legal confederation—as evidenced in his 1750s Albany Plan of Union and his letters to William Shirley—Franklin nonetheless attempted to offer workable solutions to Britain's growing fiscal and military problems, solutions that would, he hoped, preserve the individual rights and freedoms he had grown to admire as particularly British. As his efforts at negotiation wore on in the 1760s and early 1770s, though, Franklin increasingly realized that his suggestions for building a stronger Atlantic empire would not be countenanced in England. He grew restive and began explicitly addressing the problems with the existing—and constantly changing—navigation and trade policies of Great Britain. Franklin gradually came to terms with his concerns about imperial goals and individual values, and the evolution of his thinking on these matters brought him to the place where he would call into question any empire that worked against the welfare of its people. My argument is based in my view that Franklin for the most part adhered to early modern liberal values as they came down to him in the eighteenth century, though at different periods in his life, for different reasons, he emphasized different aspects of liberalism. He adapted the liberal writings to frame up his arguments across time, and he relied on the tradition for major support when he started to pull away from thinking of himself as an imperial nationalist.

While historians have typically considered Franklin's turn from the British Empire as having occurred when he was publicly castigated in the Cockpit by Alexander Wedderburn (1733–1805) and deprived of his position as postmaster-general (in 1774), I am arguing that Franklin's evolving turn away from the British Empire advanced in three major stages. It began in the 1750s, with his letters to Governor William Shirley (which he strategically republished in 1766). It reached a new point when Franklin was taken by Alexander Wedderburn on a tour through the countryside in Ireland and shown the agricultural laborers there in 1771. Franklin's letters about this experience, written in embittered tones, register his disbelief that Britain could allow its laborers to live in squalor and destitution, without sufficient clothes on their backs and food on their tables. He sought a legal challenge to Britain's supremacy. By 1773, British intrusions in Ireland and India prompted Franklin to begin formulating positions about the complicated question of political sovereignty. He argued at first tentatively but then more forcefully that sovereignty fell not to the imperial governments that chartered territories but to the individuals who made the original treaties with indigenous peoples and paid for the land thus acquired by treaty with them. By thinking through the problems in North America, Ireland, and India, Franklin had developed a firm resolution toward American independence, a resolution founded in a series of legal arguments about American sovereignty. Franklin's turn from the British Empire had already reached its logical endpoint in necessary independence well before his denunciation in the Cockpit by Wedderburn in 1774 and his removal from the postmaster-generalship. After the event at the Cockpit, Franklin's was a sad but not a sudden or reluctant turn away from Britain, as many have argued, but a turn that had been deliberated for over twenty years, beginning with the letters he formulated and wrote to William Shirley.

Some of the core values of Franklin's mature liberalism lie in the insistence on individual dignity; the essential equality of all persons as social and political agents; the necessity for freedom of inquiry and freedom of expression; and the centrality of the freedom of labor (that one could own one's own labor) to the function of both local and global communities. Franklin formulated a theory of empire that was based in the primacy of labor and the importance of a living wage for all persons who ought to be considered equal politically in terms of their status and who could be interconnected with one another across land and water. If we wish to trace a shift in Franklin's views about empire, that shift can best be associated with Franklin's critique of the discourse of nationalism and the racializing characteristics of the British nation, a view of nationalism that Franklin at one time embraced and then discarded when he realized the illiberal tendencies of such views. Franklin finally argued, fully and consistently, in behalf of a necessary transparency of power that liberalism itself could often leave mystified or inarticulate. Franklin's greatest challenge and his greatest accomplishment was to identify and speak to the glaring inconsistencies in a system that yoked imperialism to the language of liberalism while denying that any inherent rights and liberties belonged to those most valuable to the commonwealth, the laboring people.

His writings on economy and society during this era are clear statements based on data he collected, readings he had done, and inquiries he had personally made among leading economic, social, and political theorists. Recognizing the significant discrepancies between Britain's oppressive trade policies and its public, liberal face given to those policies, whether in Scotland, Ireland, North America, or India, Franklin engaged in a campaign to reveal the fractures in the facade. His many public letters to the British press, his letters both public (that is, circulated to third parties) and private to friends, his newspapers essays, and his pamphlets from the 1750s through the early 1770s—all reveal his effort to speak about the troubled intersections of fiscal-military state-building and the challenge to individual freedoms that resulted. Franklin finally left England in 1775, sailing for North America in full recognition that he had failed to persuade others about his views of Britain's potential commonwealth. His profoundly difficult leave-taking marked Franklin's final and complete understanding of the extent to which liberalism as practiced in Britain was an empty promise of prosperity only for the few, not the many whom Franklin embraced as the most worthy—the laborers, the farmers, the manufacturers who simply, as he had done, wanted to live peaceful lives with hope for a better future for their children.

One

"THIS OBSCURE FAMILY OF OURS WAS EARLY IN THE REFORMATION"

On Family Memory

The civil wars of the early modern era had a significant impact on Benjamin Franklin's English ancestors. To fully understand Franklin's attitudes about war and liberty requires attention to the role that the political and religious controversies of the seventeenth century played in the family's stories about itself. We know from Franklin's autobiography, numerous family letters, and his uncle Benjamin's personal writings that the family's experiences during the Reformation and the battles that took place in the English Midlands during England's Civil War influenced their views of English history and presumed ancient British liberties. Franklin learned his family's history early on, mostly from his father Josiah (1657–1745) and beloved uncle Benjamin (1650–1727), for whom he was named. He read the books they brought over with them, listened to their conversations around the dinner table, and absorbed as a youth their storied lives. We cannot know exactly what happened to the family in England, but it is worth pausing to consider just how difficult their lives must have been that they would risk an ocean crossing toward an unknown future.

Historians have said that Franklin's father's family emigrated to New England so that the men could seek a livelihood. Such a reading follows a mid-twentieth-century explanation that featured economic concerns above religious ones. Arthur Bernon Tourtellot, for instance, concluded that "all evidence suggests that it was a spirit of independence . . . rather than controlling doctrinal persuasions, that led the two Franklins, Benjamin the Elder and Josiah, who became Puritans, to follow that course" of moving to New England.[1] Tourtellot's reasoning is sound. The cost of living was somewhat lower in New England, and wages were two to three times higher for laboring people. But other factors, including doctrinal concerns, informed the family's decision to emigrate.[2]

Josiah Franklin decided to leave England for two reasons—to be able to practice his religion without interference from authorities and to earn a living sufficient to support a growing family. According to Franklin family lore, the men were seeking suitable employment, where a greater variety of trades were available for workers, where wages would be higher, and where land was less expensive; but they were also and perhaps even more importantly seeking the opportunity to worship as they felt their consciences directed. The evidence supplied by family records suggests that the family was significantly concerned about matters of religious conscience. Several of the major battles of the civil wars, which had taken place just decades before, happened in the vicinity of Ecton, Banbury, and Oxford, where the extended family lived. As the years ensued, the family expressed deep sympathy with those on the Parliamentarian side who were lost during the wars. This chapter will touch on the family's experiences during the English Civil War, their 1683 leave-taking from their homeland, and their family stories' impact on Benjamin Franklin.

"This obscure Family of ours was early in the Reformation"

The Franklin family came from an area of England's Midlands that was under serious contest during the Reformation and through the era of the English Civil War. Key battles of the mid-seventeenth-century Civil War took place on the very farms and roadways of the communities where the extended Franklin family lived. Josiah Franklin's and his brother Benjamin's stories about their ancestors suggest that the family feared for their lives in the era of Queen Mary, when efforts were made to re-introduce Catholicism and suppress Protestantism in England in the 1550s. Stories about Queen Mary, or "the bloody Queen," appear with some frequency, especially in Uncle Benjamin's writings, suggesting that anxiety over religious toleration (and its absence) was a constant concern for the family. But they likewise feared the monarchy of their own lifetime, especially when, under a series of acts designed to enforce conformity, they grew concerned about freedom to worship in a dissenting way, according to their conscience.

As dissenters leaning toward Puritanism, the Franklin family supported the Parliamentarians during the war, yet they often found themselves among Royalist supporters traveling toward Parliamentarian-held areas. Townspeople were challenged from all sides during the war in their midst. Some joined the ranks of both sides of the army for pay and plunder; others joined because they believed in the cause. But when battles concluded with clear winners and losers, many decided to shift sides in order to continue receiving pay. In the words of historian Brian Manning, "Soldiers who served only for pay were indifferent as to which party they served, providing they were paid."[3] They plundered local people and even their own battlefield compatriots. Desertion was frequent, especially after major campaigns, and most of those who were fighting would (if not injured) straggle along, unmotivated as they were by lack of pay, arms, food, clothing, and incentive to fight.[4] Historian Ian Gentles has remarked that the "armies of both sides were like mushrooms, shooting up almost overnight, and then disappearing even more quickly." One historian of the era has noted that the people living in the Midlands were, when the Royalists were around, pestered by "incessant demands" and endured "continuous abuse" from the king's soldiers. Royalists often demolished private residences to secure their fortifications, and they thought nothing of confiscating valuable objects made of silver and gold in order to have them melted down in order to pay the king's troops.[5] Surely the family's location in the Midlands subjected them to intermittent foraging from soldiers of both sides. [See Figure 1.1.]

Such a family history associated with civil unrest gives us good insight into why Benjamin Franklin a century later might have chosen to work as hard as possible to avoid war against people in England and the British Crown. The Franklin family's context sheds light on the political and theological difficulties that all Britons faced as questions of civil and religious authority emerged in uneasy tension with cultural struggles over individual rights, civil liberties, and religious freedom. The complex and indeed conflicted relationship in early modern England between the person and body of the king (or queen), on the one hand, and the established church, Privy Council and ministry, Parliament, and the people, on the other, were long-standing problems remaining unresolved in Franklin's day, problems that Franklin had hoped would have been resolved well before a revolution would take place between the colonies and Great Britain.

Figure 1.1 The Civil Wars in the English Midlands. Significant battles between the king and parliamentarians took place in the English Midlands, especially between the town centers of Oxford and Ecton, where the extended Franklin family lived. Ecton is located near the major battles at Edgehill and Cropredy Bridge. Map, engraved and published by Bormay and Co., New York, 1901. Private collection.

"This obscure Family of ours was early in the Reformation," Franklin wrote into the opening pages of his memoir in late July or early August 1771.[6] He was reflecting upon the notes he had made from family contacts at the time when he and his son, William (c. 1731–1813), toured the countryside of Northamptonshire and Oxfordshire, in central England, just north and northwest of London, back in the summer of 1758.[7] During that trip, Franklin was working partly from his own childhood memory of stories told by family members and partly from some notes and letters given him by his father Josiah and his uncle Benjamin. Surely the opening lines of Uncle Benjamin's nostalgic verse about Ecton, written while he was living in London in 1702, were among Franklin's recollections: "This is the Church Whose preacher I did fear," Uncle Benjamin had written. "These are the Bells I did Delight to Hear."[8] [See Figure 1.2.] He visited the country and town parishes where the Franklin ancestors had lived, and he made contact with the remaining relatives who were known to the New England Franklins, most notably a first cousin, Mary Franklin Fisher (1673–1758).[9] Thinking on the many hours he had spent listening to stories about the family, Franklin was interested in collecting what further information he could glean from parish records and burial grounds.

The tour in 1758 had personal and ideological importance for Franklin. He had been under duress to explain to the ministry and Board of Trade why the Quaker-dominated Pennsylvania Assembly continued to seek redress against the Penns, the Proprietors of Pennsylvania. The year 1757 had been particularly difficult. The Assembly defended itself against its maligner, William Smith (1727–1803), who (as a key informant to the Penn family) was agitating against the Assembly in behalf of the Penns and petitioning that the Assembly be dissolved. Tired of Smith's attacks, the Assembly incarcerated Smith for contempt. Franklin was the one who had to explain the Assembly's actions to the Penn family and the Board of Trade. He was also expected to explain the repeated appeals (which he personally supported) that lands held by the proprietors be taxed by the local Assembly. Both positions worked from the Pennsylvania colonists' assumption that the Assembly, an elected body, had every right to assume to itself local juridical action.

The argument goes to the foundation of the early modern liberal principle of the right of representation by a body of one's elected peers. During the spring of 1758, Franklin had been summoned to appear before the Board of Trade to defend the Assembly's appeals. He assisted legal counsel in drawing up arguments to support his contention that the Assembly, as an elected representative and legislative body for the colony's affairs,

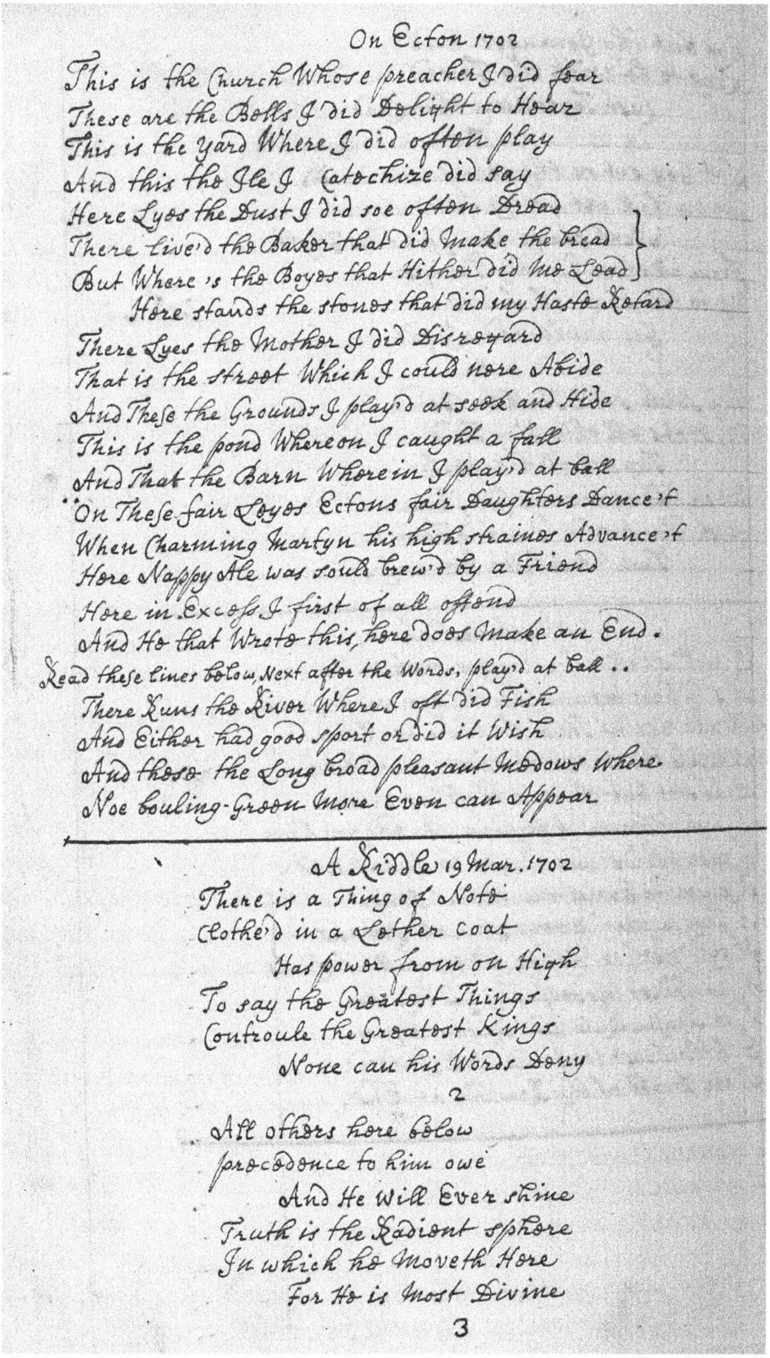

On Ecton 1702

This is the Church Whose preacher I did fear
These are the Bells I did Delight to Hear
This is the yard Where I did often play
And this the Ile I Catochize did say
Here Lyes the Dust I did soe often Dread
There live'd the Baker that did make the bread ⎫
But Where 's the Boyes that Hither did me Lead ⎭
    Here stands the stones that did my Haste Retard
There Lyes the Mother I did Disregard
That is the street Which I could nere Abide
And These the Grounds I play'd at seek and Hide
This is the pond Whereon I caught a fall
And That the Barn Wherein I play'd at ball
On These fair Leyes Ectons fair Daughters Dance't
When Charming Martyn his high straines Advance't
Here Nappy Ale was soule brew'd by a Friend
Here in Excess I first of all offend
And He that Wrote this, here does make an End.
Read these lines below, Next after the Words, play'd at ball ..
There Runs the River Where I oft did Fish
And Either had good sport or did it Wish
And these the Long broad pleasant Medows Where
Noe bouling-Green More Even can Appear

A Riddle 19 Mar. 1702
There is a Thing of Note
Clothe'd in a Lether coat
        Has power from on High
To say the Greatest Things
Controule the Greatest Kings
        None can his Words Deny
                2
All others here below
proceedence to him owe
        And He will Ever shine
Truth is the Radient sphere
In which he Moveth Here
        For He is most Divine
                3

Figure 1.2 Uncle Benjamin's Verse about Ecton, 1702. Benjamin Franklin (the Elder, Franklin's uncle Benjamin), composed a nostalgic verse about Ecton in 1702, while he was living in London. The verse shows the strength of family memory in the Franklin household. Benjamin Franklin (the Elder), MS Commonplace Book, American Antiquarian Society. Courtesy, American Antiquarian Society.

had every right to defend itself against libelous speeches and writings like those by William Smith and to seek tax monies from the Penns. Smith, having written and published complaints against the Assembly in the German press in Pennsylvania, penned an appeal to the king in counsel and to Parliament complaining of mistreatment at the hands of the Assembly. Smith's argument was based in the legal assumption that the king in counsel and Parliament had rights of jurisdiction that superseded the Pennsylvania Assembly's rights. To Franklin, a dangerous precedent might occur if Smith's argument found support in England, because the Pennsylvania Assembly held that it had a right, as a representative and elected body, to secure its own territory against malefactors (real or imagined). Franklin argued that the Assembly was the colony's primary representative and governing body, according to the original charters granted from the king and according to timeworn custom. "The Petitioner's Committment, is merely for a Contempt," Franklin argued, "and he might have been discharged" had he simply submitted to the superior authority of the Assembly to jail him for libel. "Is this Mans Case then such as calls for an Enquiry into the privileges of the Representatives of the people in Pennsilvania? nay in all the several Colonies in America," he queried. He was basing his legal argument on the logic that all the colonies' representative bodies would be implicated should the Crown and Parliament take over the rights and obligations typically (and by charter) granted to local jurisdictions. Further, he explained, the people in the colonies, "these large and distant provinces," all had rights to representative bodies that acted in their behalf, much as people in England had, from those in "the House of Lords down to the lowest Court of Justice" and indeed justices of the peace.[10]

Franklin and the lawyers won their point eventually: the Smith case was dismissed, and the Penns agreed to a small degree of taxation. But the legal case argued against the Penns was still pending at the time Franklin took his country sojourn with his son into their ancestral homeland in 1758. The pressure of thinking through the legal precedent he was arguing, the implications regarding rights for local representation, the necessary justice (to his thinking) behind the request for taxing the Proprietary—all these had to be weighing on him while Franklin traveled through the Midlands to discover for himself what was left of his family's past.

As he began his memoir for his son thirteen years later, Franklin created a narrative focusing on the family's tradition of dissent. He explained that their family members were "Protestants thro' the Reign of Queen Mary, when they were sometimes in Danger of Trouble on Account of their Zeal against Popery." Franklin was recalling that the family, despite injunctions against nonconforming worship, remained true to the Protestant Anglican Church under Catholic Queen Mary,[11] until they eventually turned into dissenters against Anglicanism under Charles I. From our perspective today, Franklin's mention of his family's activities in the sixteenth century and through the era of Queen Mary has little resonance. But in his own day, especially for Protestants, mentioning Queen Mary evoked a shared memory of a fearful time. References to Queen Mary spoke to a continuing sense of horror and fear about questions of conscience for people of Franklin's generation. Franklin's specific mention of Queen Mary's reign and his family's having been "sometimes in Danger of Trouble on Account of their Zeal against Popery" signals his awareness of the family's dissenting past even as it reveals the importance of his memorial recollection of their stalwart belief in the justice of their cause of conscience.

Memorials to martyrs under Mary appeared regularly in the *New England Primer*, a widely used schoolbook, from its earliest (1690) printings, thus keeping alive the British colonists' sense of mission to practice their religion as they chose. Protestant history was featured in the *Primer*, which originated in London in 1679 as *The Protestant Tutor* and became *The New English Tutor*.[12] The *Primer* that Franklin knew featured the execution of Protestant John Rogers (1500?–1555), a very popular preacher who had worked on translating the Bible for Protestant worship. [See Figure 1.3.] When Queen Mary came to the throne, Rogers was forced into a form of house arrest and stripped of his position. He received no pay during this interim, and his wife and children—featured in the *Primer*'s version of his story—suffered. Rogers's house arrest lasted for five years, during which time he was labeled a seditious preacher and then condemned to death. At the time of his execution, he was taken on a cart to Smithfield amid a throng of people who celebrated his constancy in his faith and gave public testimony to the importance of Protestantism, thus ritualizing his execution. His wife, with their eleven children, one a newborn, reportedly accompanied him during this trip to his execution. Even Catholics, it is said, remarked about his heroic fortitude amid the flames that took his life.

John Rogers's verses and their association with Queen Mary were commonplace for Franklin's elders. Rogers's memorialization in the *New England Primer* and John Foxe's *Book of Martyrs* (1563), a popular book in the colonies, presented him as an exemplary martyr for the cause of Protestant religious freedom. The popularity of the *Primer* is itself a testament to the propaganda effect of the evocation of Rogers's memory. This at her Breaft, following him to the Stake ; with which forrowful Sight he was not in the leaft daunted, but with wonderful Patience died couragioufly for the Gofpel of Jefus Chrift.

Some few Days before his Death he writ the following Exhortation to his Children.

G I V E Ear my Children to my Word,
  Whom God hath dearly bought,
Lay up his Laws within your Heart,
  and print them in your Thoughts.
I leave you here a little Book,
  for you to look upon,
That you may fee your Father's Face,
  when he is dead and gone,
Who for the Hope of Heavenly Things,
  while he did here remain,
Gave over all his golden Years
  to Prifon, and to Pain.

M R. *John Rogers*, Minifter of the Gofpel in *London*, was the firft Martyr in Queen *Mary*'s Reign, and was burnt at *Smithfield*, *February* the Fourteenth, 1554. His Wife, with Nine fmall Children, and one

C   Where

Figure 1.3   John Rogers Woodcut in Franklin and Hall, *New England Primer* (1764). For their popular *New England Primer*, Franklin and Hall published this woodcut of the death of John Rogers. They took the 1727 *Primer* published by Kneeland and Green in Boston as their source text. John Rogers Woodcut, The New-England Primer Enlarged. For the more easy attaining the true reading of English. To which is added, the Assembly's catechism. Philadelphia: Printed and sold by B. Franklin, and D. Hall, in Market-street, 1[7]64. Courtesy, Beinecke Library, Yale University.

primer was in use in Boston during Franklin's boyhood, and before he framed a partnership with David Hall (and thus before complete records were made), Franklin printed numerous copies of a *New England Primer* that featured Rogers's story. After the partnership, the two printed and sold between the years 1749 and 1756 at least 35,100 copies of the *Primer*, according to their records. Franklin selected as his text one that offered a beautiful woodcut and the pages of the John Rogers verses. According to C. William Miller, Franklin "apparently settled early in his career on the text of the primer he would print; it is identical with that printed in Boston in 1727 by Kneeland and Green," exhibiting none of the changes later introduced by other printers.[13] Indeed, Franklin was fond of marketing the Rogers story to evoke public memory of a more valiant past, thus suggesting his awareness that the story not only had resonance for his readers but that such resonance repaid his print shop.[14] Whether printed and circulated in Boston or Philadelphia or Charleston, John Rogers's verses brought home to colonial readers, especially those whose families had risked an Atlantic crossing as a result of the English Civil War, the idea that self-sacrifice, in cases of conscience, was central to the practice of spiritual and civil freedom.

Franklin used the opportunity of writing his memoir in 1771 to place his lineage firmly in a line of descent from the initial early modern liberalizing moments in British and European history. English heresy laws meant that dissenters could be put to death for disobeying the Crown's established religion. Despite this, Franklin's family nonetheless practiced its dissenting faith privately. In speaking about the Reformation activity of his family, Franklin linked himself with the liberalizing tendencies of the era, both the era in which his ancestors lived and the one in which he was himself situated. The link reveals a recognition that he was participating in a long line of struggle against political and religious tyranny.

Lest that point be missed by contemporary readers of his memoir, Franklin followed his general assertion about his family's Reformation activities with a specific instance that his father had mentioned in a 1739 letter.[15] Franklin's story in the autobiography follows his father's explanation of the events. "They had got an English Bible," Franklin wrote,

> and to conceal and secure it, it was fastened open with Tapes under and within the Frame of a Joint Stool. When my Great Great Grandfather read in it to his Family, he turn'd up the Joint Stool upon his Knees, turning over the Leaves then under the Tapes. One of the Children stood at the Door to give Notice if he saw the Apparitor coming, who was an Officer of the Spiritual Court. In that Case the Stool was turn'd down again upon its feet, where the Bible remain'd conceal'd under it as before.[16]

The story about the jointed stool indicates the strictness of the heresy laws.[17] In the process of disobeying the laws proscribing dissenting practice, even the Franklin children were put to use. The labor of practicing one's faith and the fear about so doing had to have been strenuous, as evidenced by the fact that the story had been passed down for several generations.

There is no mistaking Franklin's interest in associating himself, in his memoir, with a family whose history intersected with dissent during an era rhetorically constructed by colonists as tyrannical in matters both spiritual and political. To be sure, the Puritans residing in Boston were as intolerant of religious difference as the Anglicans had been of Puritans in old England. As the family told its story, however, pious dissent was idealized, indeed memorialized. Franklin's record of the family history here also attests to an understanding of the shifting religious and political climate that his family faced. From the mid-sixteenth-century reference to Queen Mary and the English Bible, Franklin turned, mid-paragraph, to the mid-seventeenth-century religious and political traumas that led to his father's decision to emigrate to New England. The paragraph synthesizes around the theme of dissent among sincere and pious people laboring over questions of conscience, even as it touches two centuries in its diachronic relation of family events.

Northamptonshire and Oxfordshire during the English Civil War

According to the Franklin family accounts, the family remained, in public, with the Anglican Church, though they clearly, by the time of Thomas Franklin's generation, had nonconformist leanings. Uncle Benjamin wrote about Thomas Franklin II (1598–1682), his father, that he was "a lover of good men of all denominations," yet "he was most Inclin'd to the presbiterian Government and discipline, but when charles 2ᵈ return'd he went to church alsoe for peace and order sake."[18] Uncle Benjamin's explanation suggests that although his father was inclined toward Puritanism, he kept up church attendance in the Anglican Church "for peace and order sake." Many people of Thomas Franklin's generation found it most expedient to behave in this fashion.

Uncle Benjamin's and his father's stories about their ancestors fascinated Benjamin Franklin. In his memoir, Franklin credited Uncle Benjamin for passing on to him the family records: "The Notes one of my Uncles (who had the same kind of Curiosity in collecting Family Anecdotes) once put into my Hands, furnish'd me with several Particulars, relating to our Ancestors."[19] According to Uncle Benjamin and to the parish records Franklin himself discovered in 1758, the Franklins came from a line of people who had lived in different small towns in the eastern and central Midlands of England, roughly thirty to fifty miles northward from London, for over three hundred years before Benjamin Franklin was born.[20] Family lore indicated that they were at one time landowners and members of the professional classes.[21] Indeed, the word *franklin* in the fourteenth and fifteenth centuries referred to a freeholder of free but not noble lineage. Various spellings—Franklin, or Francklyne, or Franklyn—of the family name survived.[22] The oldest ancestor known to Uncle Benjamin from the stories he recalled hearing as a youth involved his great-grandfather, Henry Francklyne, who probably flourished in the early to middle years of the sixteenth century. Uncle Benjamin reported that he was an attorney who had had a significant amount of "free Land."[23] The land was, in other words, unenclosed land held in tenure as a family freehold on which day laborers would have worked for the family but also on which people were permitted to set up their families and engage in subsistence agriculture. According to Uncle Benjamin, this ancestor lived in Houghton, a town in Northamptonshire near Northampton and a local farming area called Ecton, a predominantly agricultural area of sheep-grazing and subsistence farming.

Uncle Benjamin's story about Henry Francklyne is as interesting as it is ironic. The irony is in the method Uncle Benjamin used to relate it, because the story revealed how Henry Francklyne's interest in "Right" undermined the family's inheritance of the land and his businesses: "In his dayes the Gent^s of that town were for having their Land Inclosed," he wrote. But Henry Francklyne, "being of honest principles, knowing the Laws in force against it, and that it would be a great wrong to the poor, opposed their designe & stood in deffence of the poor Inhabitants and soe spent his Estate and did himselfe nor them any good therby for Might overcame Right." Uncle Benjamin's wry concluding comment about Henry was a remark that, "[h]aving thus spent his Estate[,] his son was put to a blacksmith" and lived in Ecton, four miles east of Northampton. The perceived justice of Henry Francklyne's cause was lost on Uncle Benjamin, who seemed to lament the loss of the estate because of Francklyne's concern about poor people and his disregard for the enclosure laws. He refused to enclose his commons.

The story emphasizes the absence of patrimony and the laboring roots in the Franklin family. Henry Francklyne could offer his son no patrimony, because he had not enclosed his land for personal use and profit. He chose instead to let the land remain in common use, thus diminishing his estate's value, and he ended up seeing that his son Thomas Francklyne was apprenticed to a blacksmith, so that when he came of age, he would have a trade.[24] The son did have his own freehold, evidently, but he was forced to become a tradesman, and he evidently worked his own land. The son's estate, less than a quarter the size of his father's, seems to have been used for cattle and farming, and he served his farm and his neighbors as a blacksmith.

During the sixteenth century, Henry was living through the first phase of an enclosure process that would extend through the nineteenth century. The issue of enclosure is itself a mark of the changes taking place in rural areas across all of England but especially England's Midlands during the sixteenth century. Those living at subsistence were at risk, and they were arriving in the Midlands, where Henry Francklyne lived, in increasing numbers. In the Midlands, vagrancy laws were enacted, and town watchmen were enforcing the laws. Sanitation problems prompted towns to pass laws requiring the cleaning of the streets on appointed days. Anxiety about employment emerged among the laboring classes. Artisans and tradesmen signed themselves into guilds (a medieval practice carried on into this era) in order to secure their places in a crowded labor market. Above the laboring class of apprentices, only freemen of boroughs could trade at fairs and market days. And those who ran inns or taverns would be given stiff fines or imprisonment for lodging beggars or vagrant persons.[25] Those favoring enclosure could improve their fields through crop rotation, employ new farming methods, and improve the land's productivity, all of which would lead to a higher yield and better income. Hindsight enables us to see this as environmental improvement. Hindsight enables us to see the irony, too, that Benjamin Franklin, who believed in the benefits of owning and using private property, came from an ancestor who embraced the medieval system rather than the modern one, rejecting the move to economic self-sufficiency and the privileges of private property ownership made possible by modern laws and agricultural innovation. In any case, Uncle Benjamin's remarks about Henry Franklyne's land, remarks written down in 1717, suggest that these matters came under discussion in the family during Benjamin Franklin's youth.

Thomas Franklin (Benjamin Franklin's grandfather) remained in Northamptonshire for all of his working life. Born, by Uncle Benjamin's account, "at Ecton in Northamptonshire on the 8 day of Oct: in the year 1598," Thomas Franklin was "naturally of a chearfull temper, pleasant conversation, Just in his dealings." Uncle Benjamin reported of his father that he was "as to his trade an Exelent workman, a man of understanding, in the best things, a constant Attender on ordinances, and family dutys, a great observer of the works of providence." He was locally admired for the range of his skills. He was "a Turner, a Gun-Smith, a surgeion, a scrivener, and wrote as pretty a hand as ever I saw," reported Uncle Benjamin. In addition, he had knowledge of "Astronomy and chymistry which made him acceptable company to m^r John Palmer the Arch-Deacon of Northampton," according to Uncle Benjamin. He kept a farm on his freehold, and he was a blacksmith as well. Thomas Franklin evidently was a polymath by inclination and ability, like his famous grandson.[26]

Thomas Franklin had nine children born between the years 1637 and 1657 with his wife, Jane White Franklin (1617–1662).[27] Josiah Franklin, Benjamin Franklin's father, was the last child, born December 25, 1657. Josiah's brother Benjamin, the Uncle Benjamin of this account, was seven years older, born March 20, 1650. The problems of this era are manifold, and a young and growing family would have needed security against civil unrest. Thomas and Jane White Franklin married during difficult times, when people of all stations were facing problems over taxation and civil and ecclesiastical authority under King Charles I, ending in an era of unrest and a series of battles and skirmishes across the English Midlands.

Considering the years of their childrens' births, Thomas and Jane White Franklin did well merely to survive the ongoing difficulties prompted by political and religious dissension: most of the births of their children took place at the height of the Civil War, with several significant battles taking place nearby. Their sons Thomas, Samuel, John, and Joseph—all born between the years 1637 and 1646—entered the world during wars and rebellions in Scotland, Ireland, and England. In fact, during the height of Jane White Franklin's childbearing, several conflicts of the Civil War took place in England's Midlands between Banbury (in Oxfordshire), where Jane White had been born and raised, and Ecton (in Northamptonshire), where she had moved to live with her husband. In the vicinity of these towns and Oxford, where members of the extended family had moved (all within about thirty-five miles of each other), the Parliamentarians battled Royalists led by King Charles and, later, Prince Rupert. The first battle of the war took place at Edgehill, not far from Banbury, in October 1642. It ended inconclusively as to whether the Parliamentarians or royal troops won, but for each side, about five hundred men died and 1,500 were wounded. In March 1643, the king was determined to take over the region and sent several troops of horse, a demi-cannon known as Roaring Meg, and several footsoldiers from Banbury to bombard the Parliamentarian center at Hopton Heath. Between the Royalists' cannon blows and several cavalry charges, the Parliamentarians withdrew. For the April 1643 sieges of Birmingham and Lichfield, Prince Rupert's troops ran right through Banbury from Oxford. The area was a prime target for both the Parliamentarian forces and the Royalists. Key battlefields and eventually Banbury Castle became sites of siege and devastation. Banbury town and Castle were repeatedly taken by the different sides. Between the years 1643 and 1644, according to parish and combat registers in Banbury, close to five hundred people died in the town and Castle.[28] Reports of the smell of carnage, the absence of food and clean water, and generally unsanitary conditions clarify that the residents' quality of life was poor. Vagrants and deserters walked the farmlands and roadways. The area was unsecured and subject to repeated intrusions by strangers.

A husbandman and blacksmith, Thomas Franklin would have seen his lands in Ecton crossed and recrossed by soldiers, deserters, and camp followers. These were bloody battles, with troops on foot wielding hand-held weaponry and soldiers of horse wielding axes and pikes, reaping bloody carnage. As in most wars, townspeople's farms and animals would have been ransacked by both sides. Thomas Franklin's wide range of skills, along with his landholdings, probably brought both sides to call on him for various needs, from allowing use of his land for the quartering of retinue (including militia, camp followers, and animals) to assisting with repairs of equipment. Jane Franklin surely struggled with her repeated pregnancies under wartime stress. Indeed, at some point among the births of her children, Jane Franklin watched two sons, twins, die as newborns. Perhaps they were stillbirths. In any case, the family records indicate twins, boys, died.[29] The records are silent as to the causes of their deaths, but the wartime situation might account for the loss of the boys. Uncle Benjamin, Hannah, and Josiah Franklin were born just after Charles I was beheaded, during the years of Cromwell's Commonwealth and "Protectorate" (1649–60).[30] It is hard to imagine a more troubled moment to raise a family. How much the children knew about the events going on around them can only be surmised. But surely, in their adult years, they understood the religious, civil, and political implications of the battles won and lost on or near the family's homestead.

The children were raised in a very pious household, given Uncle Benjamin's account of his parents. According to his recollection, the childhood home had been decorated with biblical verses appealing to believers in Christian grace. "On the Wall of My Fathers parlour," he wrote, "Was Writen in Church-Text, Round about the Room, near the floor above it, the 16 and 17 verses of 3 John. God so loved the World that He gave his only begotten son that Whosoever beleeveth in Him Should not perish but have Everlasting life. For God sent not his son into the world to condemn the world but that the world through him might be saved."[31] The parents taught their children a belief that their present condition, however trying, was merely temporary, and that the condemnations of the world from whatever quarter, fruitless. Hope resided in Christ's dispensation. Such an attitude of total faith in Christian grace is Calvinist at heart. Uncle Benjamin recalled that his mother was "Exact in her morals," and he reported that "she was Religiously Educated & alsoe Religiously Inclin'd and kept up a Thursday meeting of her godly woman Neighbours[,] . . . which they spent in prayer, conference, and repetition of the foregoing Lords day serm[on,], [and] singing."[32] Josiah Franklin's dissenting parents were well matched in piety, and they raised their children to become pious as well.

The pastors in the family's midst were also dissenters, whether at Ecton or at Banbury. William Whately (1583–1639) was vicar of Banbury (and son of the mayor) and a celebrated moderate Calvinist when Jane White was a child there. His place was eventually taken over in 1648 by a native of Oxford, Samuel Wells (1614–1678), reputed for his intelligence and his religious devotion and a favorite of the Franklin family, which his daughter Hannah joined in 1683. Wells was a chaplain to Parliamentarian forces under Robert Devereux (1591–1646), third Earl of Essex, during the Civil War. Both Whately and Wells were Calvinist in their leanings, but both tended to be moderate in their practice. It was Wells under whose vicarage the town of Banbury became noted for its Puritanism, but Wells, in fact, was moderate when compared with some of his peers. He put himself on the line at the time Charles I was imprisoned and about to be tried in special tribunal in Westminster in January 1649. Parliament had resolved to try the king for high treason, which could only end in Charles's execution. Gathering to himself a group of clergy from Oxfordshire and Northamptonshire, Wells formally petitioned Parliament to reconsider its resolution. The petition was denied, and the king was executed.[33]

With the 1660 restoration of the Stuarts, the Puritans entered a new phase in their dissenting ways, and life became more complicated. The Clarendon Code—named for Edward Hyde (1609–1674), first Earl of Clarendon, Charles II's Lord Chancellor—effectually re-established the Anglican Church, and toleration for dissenters, even those who had gone against the regicides, disappeared. The Clarendon Code was a series of four legal statutes aimed at making ecclesiastical dissent difficult. The Corporation Act (1661) required all municipal officials to take Anglican communion and formally reject the Solemn League and Covenant of 1643. This effectively excluded nonconformists from public office. The Act of Uniformity (1662) made the use of the Book of Common Prayer compulsory in religious services, wherever they were held in England. The Conventicle Act of 1664 forbade conventicles (worship in private—and, hence, unauthorized worship—among people who were not members of the same household) and in effect prevented dissenting religious groups from meeting. The Five Mile Act (1665), aimed at nonconformist ministers, forbade ministers from coming within five miles of incorporated towns or the places of their former livings. The Clarendon Code brought about a good deal of religious controversy.

When he refused to conform under the Act of Uniformity, Samuel Wells, along with about two thousand other leading ministers, was ejected from his church in 1662. Like them, he gathered up those who left his parish church and met with them for private worship, until the Conventicle Act made this impossible. Thereafter, he continued to work in the area, until the Five Mile Act proscribed his very presence in the area, and he was forced to move to Deddington in Oxfordshire, where he took up his pen and wrote weekly letters to members of his former congregation, giving spiritual advice and encouragement. He returned to Banbury in 1672, after Charles II issued an indulgence of religion, and he died there six years later.

Wells's history reveals the extent to which Puritan faithful would go in an effort to practice their religion. Samuel Wells was well known to the Franklins. Uncle Benjamin would eventually marry Samuel Wells's daughter, Hannah. The marriage took place just months after Josiah Franklin set sail with his family for Boston. Uncle Benjamin retained significant bitterness over the ousting of Samuel Wells for nonconformity. When speaking of Hannah's father, he wrote into his "Short Account," "This Mr W. was one of those 2000 that were turn'd out soon after King Charles 2^d restoration, on 24 Aug 1662, comonly called, Black Bartholomew Day."[34] In bringing up Bartholomew's Day, Uncle Benjamin linked Samuel Wells's ousting with the wave of Catholic violence against Huguenots (French Protestants) that began on August 24, 1572, with the murder of several Huguenot leaders in Paris. For Protestants, August 24, St. Bartholomew's Day, would ever be linked with the assault on Protestants that began on that day and lasted for over two months, resulting in the deaths numbering as high as 100,000 persons. In Uncle Benjamin's view, Catholics' anti-Protestantism was, in effect, little different from Anglicans' anti-Puritanism.

The family's emigration to New England thus occurred in the context of significant civil and religious unrest in England, a context memorialized by Uncle Benjamin. Protestant sympathy and anti-Catholic sentiment are likewise evident in Uncle Benjamin's account when he described Josiah's decision to leave for New England. Of Josiah, Uncle Benjamin wrote that, after having been apprenticed to his brother John to learn the dying trade, he "married Ann Child of Ecton the Daughter of Robert Childe there. but things not succeeding there according to his mind, wth. the leave of his frinds and father he went to New England in the year 1683. in order to which voyage he was come up to London at the time when the Noble Lord Russel was murder'd."[35] The double entendre evokes Russell's being of noble lineage and a noble soul, in Uncle Benjamin's view. Lord William Russell (1639–1683), sometimes called by dissenters "The Patriot" and "The Martyr," rose to have a significant career in the House of Commons. He shared with many in the House fears that the restoration of the Stuarts would plunge England, and perhaps all of Britain, into Catholicism again, because Charles II and his brother James, Duke of York, would favor France, Catholicism, and absolute power. He became especially outspoken during the Exclusion Bill crisis (1678–1681), and he rose often to support the bill, introduced into Commons with the intention of excluding James Stuart from succeeding to the throne after Charles II. When Charles dissolved Parliament in 1681, after the bill's third presentation, public anxiety diminished, but Lord Russell continued with private meetings of like-minded Protestants. When a plot was discovered in 1683 to assassinate King Charles II and James, Duke of York, several people pointed their fingers at Russell, identifying him, unjustifiably it seems, as a conspirator. He was sent to the Tower, tried at the King's bench, and found guilty of high treason. He was executed at Lincoln's Inn Fields, London, on July 21, 1683—the same month Josiah Franklin and his family sailed from London, venturing toward an unknown future in New England.

In Uncle Benjamin's stories, the Franklin family was linked to Protestantism and to civil laws that would allow for the exercise of freedom of conscience. Taken in the context of his comments about Samuel Wells and then Lord William Russell, Uncle Benjamin's support of the civil right to dissent in both civic and religious duties clarifies that for the Franklins, dissent in the civil arena and nonconformity in the ecclesiastical one were central to the exercise of personal freedom. Personal freedom associated with the conventicles also seems to have dominated the thinking of Josiah Franklin during these years. In Benjamin Franklin's autobiography, Josiah's decision to leave England is related this way: "The Family continu'd all of the Church of England till about the End of Charles the Second's Reign, when some of the Ministers that had been outed for Nonconformity, holding Conventicles in Northamptonshire, Benjamin and Josiah adher'd to them, and so continu'd all their Lives. The rest of the Family remain'd with the Episcopal Church."[36] Franklin's relation is, in essence, the story of Samuel Wells.

Josiah Franklin talked over his concerns about his own and his family's situation with his father, Thomas, just before Thomas died. Josiah evidently traveled with Uncle Benjamin to take part in services (the "Conventicles") held by nonconforming ministers, most surely Samuel Wells, at the time when the Clarendon Code prevented ministers from remaining in their hometowns. Perhaps the death of his father (which released Josiah of caregiving for him) in 1682, the upcoming marriage of his brother Benjamin to Hannah Wells in 1683, and his own questions of conscience weighed heavily on him. The crisis over the Exclusion Bill and the house arrest of Lord William Russell must also have been worrisome. He set sail with his wife,

Anne Child Franklin, and their three children in the summer of 1683. This was just about the time when Russell was executed. Surely that execution had some impact for a man of conscience who wished to practice without imposition from civil or ecclesiastical authorities.

Dissent's Descent

Benjamin Franklin's recollections in his autobiography underscored the problems of religious liberty that lived on into Franklin's own day. As Franklin framed the story, "The Conventicles having been forbidden by Law, and frequently disturbed, induced some considerable Men of his Acquaintance to remove to that Country, and he was prevail'd with to accompany them thither, where they expected to enjoy their Mode of Religion with Freedom."[37] By mentioning the conventicles in the context of his family lineage as he opened his long family story purportedly written for his son, Franklin was seeking a context in family experience for understanding the present crisis with Britain. He was writing his life story around the lives lived by his grandfather, father, and uncle. Like his grandfather, he publicly kept a seat in the Anglican church in Philadelphia while he privately kept his spiritual notions to himself. Like his more distant ancestor, Henry Francklyne, he was always ready to lend funds or a helping hand to assist those who were willing to labor in their own behalf, even though he was unwilling to give mere welfare to the poor. Like his Uncle Benjamin, he created an autobiographical record that could be passed down across the generations, so that the family stories about questions of conscience and about attempting to do the right thing would be known to future generations. Indeed, Franklin seems to have found in his ancestors approximations of himself as he thought about his family history.

Thus, Franklin's opening of the memoir with a long reflection upon his family ties and his trip to his family's ancestral lands in England ought not to be taken so lightly as his biographers have taken them. Most who have studied Franklin have persisted in interpreting Josiah Franklin's move to the New England colony as having occurred primarily for economic reasons. Perhaps this results from hindsight gained from Benjamin Franklin's business acumen. But in light of Benjamin Franklin's (and Uncle Benjamin's) quite clear, alternate story about the move, we begin to see the ways in which the family story underscores Franklin's own concerns about liberty of person and property.

The appearance of his family's story in the opening pages of the autobiography facilitates Franklin's emphasis on inheritance and cultural heritage, to be sure. But those opening pages also remind us that, to someone who in essence gave up his homeland, what that homeland represented to him was centrally important. To my thinking, when he sat down to begin his memoir, Benjamin Franklin was not, on the heels of a pleasant excursion, merely being nostalgic about his family's ancestral home. Especially considering that he was writing this part of his memoir at a turbulent era in his own representation of the colonies, after the events now called the Boston Massacre and during a lull in his services as representative of Massachusetts (because he was not getting recognition as representative of Massachusetts), the issues raised regarding the family's ancestral positioning of dissent are quite noteworthy. When he sat down and started writing the memoir in the summer of 1771, he was doing so knowing that he would not be accepted by Hillsborough as the colonial agent for Massachusetts (their stormy interview about Franklin's appointment by the Massachusetts House of Representatives had taken place in January). He knew as well that the House of Commons was taking action against printers (in February) who published their debates. Indeed, he felt he was witnessing a shutting down of the whole liberal project of the transparency of government proffered by the printing revolution. Information from Crown and Parliament was tightening. Printing freedom was being challenged in England. He also was aware, on the heels of fighting off complaints sent to England by the Pennsylvania Anglican, William Smith, that Britain might eventually impose Anglican bishops throughout the colonies. Franklin was facing distrust both from Massachusetts and from Crown and ministry in his efforts to find a peaceful resolution to the conflicts over representation and taxation.

In recreating, in the memoir, his own record and interpretation of the family's stalwart resistance to tyranny both political and religious and its adherence to the idea of independence of thinking, Franklin established the connection between his own turbulent times—indeed, how history sometimes repeated itself—and those suffered by his ancestors. The family's stories featured the failed relationships among the people, the Crown, and Parliament, and they bespoke questions associated with ancient liberties. Perhaps Benjamin Franklin might have aimed for so long to avoid war with England in part because of his family's collective memory of the ways in which wars had so wracked the lands of his forebears. Perhaps, too, he was hoping for a return of the presumably liberal opportunities that his forebears had themselves hoped for, centuries earlier. A rich understanding of his family's stories about their removal to New England, coupled with a close reading of the opening of Franklin's memoir, helps to explain why questions of liberty of conscience and the associated liberties of person worked deeply into the fabric of Franklin's life.

Two

"I HAD SUCH A THIRST FOR KNOWLEDGE"

Franklin's Boston Youth

Franklin's interest in learning about his family and their dissenting English past yielded him an ample store of materials that resonate in his writings. He began to develop from these early years a conception of what ought to constitute political freedom, and though his conception deepened and its emphases shifted across time, it was a view of liberalism that lay at the heart of Franklin's constant questioning of any imperial project that did not put first those—the artisans, laborers, farmers, and merchants—who were assisting the empire. One way of looking at Franklin's writings on imperialism and early modern economic theory, which undergirded Britain's early imperial imaginings, in fact, is to envision them as an outcome of his inquiry into early modern liberalism. From the time he was a youth, his reading and writing regularly addressed the several freedoms associated with early modern liberalism—educational liberalism and its concomitant freedoms, including the freedom of speech and the press, freedom of conscience, and freedom to question the authority of those in government.

To examine the shifting courses of Franklin's attitudes about liberalism and social and political economies, it will be fruitful to consider Franklin's early readings and writings, so as to track his intellectual and ideological frames of reference. Such an investigation helps us gauge the intellectual life of the community in which Franklin was raised as well. This chapter explores Franklin's earliest ideas about politics, society, and the role of government in individuals' lives by examining the materials he worked with during in his youth. By taking into account what went to press during Franklin's apprenticeship years in his brother's print shop and by looking into Franklin's own earliest published writings in Boston, we observe an early preoccupation with personal and civic freedoms.

Franklin's Reading

When he was a youth, Franklin was obsessed with learning about England and British history. A voracious reader, he sought out both historical materials and contemporary ones. Franklin's 1771 recollection about his childhood reading suggests an eclectic array of volumes directed to a general, English-speaking readership. But he was also reading in social and political philosophy, with an emphasis on British and classical history and culture, on personal and social ethics (especially doing good), and on the philosophical problem of the nature of the virtue. Franklin reported in the autobiography that he admired several books, including Daniel Defoe's *An Essay upon Projects* (1697) and Cotton Mather's *Bonifacius. An Essay Upon the Good* (1710). Both books offered suggestions for mutual aid societies directed to personal, civic, and economic improvement. Franklin also reported having read Plutarch's *Parallel Lives*. These were comparative biographies that paired Greek and Roman leaders. About this reading, he commented, "I still think that time spent to great Advantage."[1] He read John Bunyan's *The Pilgrim's Progress* (1678), followed by a collection of Bunyan's "Works, in separate little Volumes," which he "afterwards sold" so as to purchase R. Burton's *Historical Collections*, a series of small chapbooks ("and cheap, 40 or 50 in all") about English history, written by Nathaniel Crouch and attributed to Richard and then Robert Burton.[2]

Franklin lamented as an adult "that at a time when I had such a Thirst for Knowledge, more proper Books had not fallen in my Way." Literary historian Kevin J. Hayes has made an interesting analysis of Franklin's strategy in creating the early reading section of the autobiography. Centering on Franklin's "story of the Bunyan-for-Burton exchange," Hayes argues that Franklin was thus showing that he had "outgrown the simplistic religious sentiments" of Bunyan and was signaling his more mature view of what books might offer.[3] He was also showing his desire to inculcate useful knowledge rather than metaphysical speculation. The mature Franklin, the greatest natural philosopher of his era, knew at the time he made this remark that Enlightenment ideology had taken hold in Britain and Europe. He was also aware of the Enlightenment's abhorrence for religious disputation and acrimony over spiritual matters and religious doctrine. Although the seventeenth-century writings that formed part of his own upbringing were still part of the common intellectual heritage and living memory of people of his generation, he was interested in fostering more modern ideas.

Franklin expressed disdain for his father's library of books in what he called "polemic Divinity." While it would be easy to dismiss any inquiry into what these books might have been, given Franklin's later-in-life dismissal of them, it is nonetheless fruitful to glance at what polemical divinity Franklin might have encountered, because we are attempting to gather an understanding of his intellectual life in his formative years. Franklin reported that the books in his father's library were not numerous, but they formed his first reading matter. It is likely that Josiah Franklin brought a few books over with him in 1683, when he came over with his little family. Perhaps the books were timely, in his day, and came from the era right after the civil wars, during Cromwell's interregnum, or the restoration of the monarchy to the Stuarts. "Father's little library consisted chiefly of Books in polemic Divinity," Franklin said, indicating that he had read most of these books. At the time he was writing his autobiography, what Franklin called "polemic Divinity" had become the province of complicated historical memory of religious schism and sectarian violence. For those of Franklin's generation seeking to rationalize government and to establish more representative political processes that would supplant the tradition of inherited monarchy, the acrimony about religion and divine right formed part of the aged system they were hoping to eradicate.

What were these books owned by Josiah Franklin on polemic divinity, and why did Franklin refuse, when an aging statesman, to credit them any impact on his intellectual life? The phrase *polemic divinity* could refer to many kinds of writing commonly read by Josiah Franklin's generation, whether in New England or old. The books could have been about local matters in England—the Puritans in Banbury, the siege of the castle there during the civil wars, or the Levellers who had attempted to take over affairs there during Cromwell's rule. Perhaps the books were a mix of highbrow, Royalist writings that favored monarchy and criticized Puritans and republican government. Or perhaps they were Parliamentarian or Puritan writings favoring parliamentary maneuvers, Puritanism, and representative government. Well-known Parliamentarian polemicists of the era of the civil wars included two often read and reprinted writers, Joshua Sprigg (1618–1684) and Richard Vines (1600?–1656), whose renown and writings were surely known to the Franklin family, which was, as Uncle Benjamin's records show, reasonably well read. Joshua Sprigg was a well-known polemicist whose *Anglia Rediviva; England's Recovery*[4] formed its own rebuke against monarchy in favor of a republican form of government in its celebration of Sir Thomas Fairfax (1612–1671). Richard Vines was well known for casting the Puritan ascendance as a just reward from God. His *Happinesse of Israel* (1645), a sermon, assisted in inaugurating the new regime as if it were God's hand upon a chosen people, a rhetorical maneuver employed often in Puritan writings, especially in New England.[5]

On the other side of the religion and monarchy debate, writings favoring the Stuarts and monarchy in general came from several places. Obvious in this context is Thomas Hobbes (1588–1679), whose *Leviathan* (1651) argued that human beings in their natural state exist in a condition of perpetual struggle, thus requiring an absolute sovereign to keep their fears and obsessions in check so as to avoid continual civil warfare. All of these texts were likely known to people in the Franklin household. Yet perhaps the best-known and circulated text was *The history of the rebellion and Civil Wars in England* by Royalist Edward Hyde (1609–1674), Earl of Clarendon.[6] Clarendon's account was widely circulated in manuscript, and it reached print at a time when oppositional writings from the seventeenth century were being—as Annabel Patterson pointed out long ago—edited, circulated, and republished for a new generation of readers. A battle of competing histories was being waged, and publications from the middle seventeenth century were being compiled and published for the newest generation of readers. Clarendon's manifesto of conservative monarchic ideology (two key components of which included the conception of divine right and passive obedience to authority) was posthumously published by Crown supporters to counterbalance the publication or republishing (between 1697 and 1701, with coordinated reprintings in succeeding years) of the more liberal writings of the pantheon of liberal writers Franklin was getting to know, including John Milton (1608–1674), Algernon Sidney (1623–1683), James Harrington (1611–1677), Edmund Ludlow (c. 1617–1692), and Henry Neville (1620–1694).[7] Clarendon's *History* became a rallying point for High Church and Tory conservatism under Queen Anne. The public acclaim for the Stuarts received renewed support from Tory writers in London at the turn into the eighteenth century.[8] Indeed, even the Whig publicist John Oldmixon (1673–1742) remarked in 1727 of Clarendon's elegantly produced *History* that "Prepossession in Favour of his Lordship's Book, was so strong, for several Years, that no Body would have given a Hearing to any one, who should have said a Word against it."[9] Clarendon's admirers were so numerous and outspoken that Daniel Defoe (c. 1660–1731), a favorite of Benjamin Franklin at this time, roundly criticized Clarendon and his polemic in *Jure Divino* (1706), a satiric epic poem against the renewed Stuart interests. I surmise that Benjamin Franklin read these materials while still a youth. But even if he did not, he surely became aware of them in his young adulthood, as his insatiable curiosity and appetite for everything British brought him into literate company learned in British values and British history.

As he began the life of a writer, Franklin chose to favor nonsectarian debates like those prevalent in the London newspapers of the early eighteenth century. Indeed, Franklin's earliest writings (the Silence Dogood papers published in James Franklin's *New-England Courant*) make light of doctrinal disputatiousness and religious hypocrisy. Yet as a mature philosopher in 1771 (when he wrote about his father's library), Franklin knew the extent to which these printed materials on religious controversy represented an important efflorescence of diverse views about religion and religious practice. Several of the Parliamentarian leaders and Puritans and some of those who professed a belief in liberty of conscience whom Franklin cited in his mature years—Algernon Sidney, John Hampden (c. 1595–1643), John Pym (1584–1643), John Locke (1632–1704), John Milton, for instance—were being reprinted widely. Their writings took on significant importance for their expressions about religious toleration and freedom of speech during these times of polemic sectarian debates. Franklin surely understood the relationship that obtained between the ideals of personal liberty he would espouse much of his life and the protest literature of the English Civil War era.

Franklin rarely engaged in metaphysical arguments, because such arguments took one out of the realm of the community and had no practical basis for determining accomplishment. As he phrased it in the autobiography, he decided to put away "metaphysical Reasonings" at about the time he attempted to recover and destroy all copies he had printed of his deistic pamphlet, *Dissertation on Liberty and Necessity, Pleasure and Pain* (1725). He concluded that although he found some aspects of freethinking had some merit, freethinking, in practice, could not assist the search for happiness: "I began to suspect that this Doctrine tho' it might be true, was not very useful. . . . I grew convinced that *Truth, Sincerity and Integrity* in Dealings between Man and Man, were of the utmost Importance to the Felicity of Life," he concluded.[10] Franklin was, as his earliest readings and writings attest, highly interested in several related concepts that emerged from the era of the civil wars, including freedom of conscience, freedom of speech and print, freedom of inquiry, and freedom of person in the pursuit of economic prosperity.

Apprenticeship

In addition to reading his father's and uncle's books, Franklin probably read or skimmed everything that passed through or was published by the printing office of James Franklin when he served his apprenticeship there. These years—roughly 1718, when Franklin was apprenticed at age twelve to his brother in the new print shop, to 1723, when he absconded from Boston, hidden indentures uncontestable—were crucial years in Franklin's development as a tradesman, an intellectual, and a Briton. Any investigation of Franklin's social and political philosophies should account for his experiences in James Franklin's printing house.

Evidence from Franklin's earliest writings clarifies that Franklin enjoyed the writings popular in the metropolitan London world that his brother James had experienced when he went to London to buy press machinery and type for his newspaper, the *New-England Courant* in 1721.[11] James had an exciting time in London, and he was impressed by the club scene and the literary qualities of news there. A commentator in London's *Freeholder's Journal* about that time remarked that "a crowd of papers" in London "encumber the town, and make the tables of our coffee-houses look like the counter of a Pamphlet-shop." In the *Weekly Journal, or British Gazetteer*, another writer remarked that "there is not a place under the sun, that is so fruitful of scribblers of all denominations and qualifications, as this famous City of London."[12] The London Grubstreet style employed wit and ribaldry, melodrama and overwrought sentimentalism, and it appealed to both court and commoners alike. Ridicule, a chief means of expression, was sometimes aimed at improving readers' ethics, their social behavior, or their political views, but it more frequently devolved to unsophisticated sarcasm for mere entertainment and surprise. A range of materials were popular in London in the late seventeenth and early eighteenth centuries. These included writings about immediately contemporaneous events; writings of practical instruction and piety; official proclamations, laws, and court findings; writings that played on the contest between the sexes, with some materials of relatively explicit sexuality; polemic writings in the vein of the sectarian controversies of the civil wars; and writings testing or embracing relatively newly found freedoms related to speaking and printing in public critical opinions about religion, court, and government policy.

The first issues of the *Courant* sound much more like London papers than the Boston papers, which seem quite boring by comparison with their mere shipping news and news about the government and local leaders.

The two existing newspapers, the *Boston News-Letter* (an older paper) and the *Boston Gazette* (a newer one), tended to favor the governors above the Assembly (an elected body), and both directed their fare toward the political and economic leadership. Indeed, in the words of print historian Charles E. Clark, both papers "treated the lower orders of town and country with anonymity and occasional contempt."[13] By contrast, James Franklin's *New-England Courant* mimicked London newspapers in content and political slant. The *Courant* was a new genre of newspaper for New England, and the "club" of writers associated with it signaled that this was a new kind of publisher.

The books, pamphlets, and old newspapers available in the library of James Franklin's print shop appealed to the intellectual and verbal versatility of Benjamin Franklin, who enjoyed reading there in his leisure hours. Indeed, Benjamin Franklin was sufficiently proud of the press library and sufficiently interested in informing others of the cosmopolitan nature of that library that he printed a list of the books at the print shop during the period when he was publishing James's paper alone. [See Figure 2.1.] Printed July 2, 1722, the list names a wide selection of writings contemporaneously admired in Britain and on the Continent. James likely acquired in London many of the "large and valuable Collection of BOOKS," which would assist the writers' goals of "writing on Subjects Natural, Moral, and Divine" and "cultivating those which seem the most Barren."[14] These books included works in natural history, astronomy, cosmography, geography, and politics, along with early modern social and political theory by John Milton, Bishop Gilbert Burnet (1643–1715), John Oldmixon, the Port Royal logicians, and copies of the *Spectator* and the *Athenian Oracle*. Benjamin Franklin's literary career began under the influence of such materials as these, some of the most important writings well known by literate modern Britons.

Franklin's apprenticeship as a writer originated with two ephemeral broadside ballads he printed and sold in the streets, encouraged by his brother to make money for the print shop. James suggested Franklin write the broadside ballad, *The Light House Tragedy* (1718), about the loss (in rough waters) of the family of lighthouse-keeper, George Worthylake. Franklin's little tragedy "sold wonderfully," which "flatter'd my Vanity," Franklin wrote.[15] His other ballad, "a Sailor Song on the Taking of *Teach* or Blackbeard the Pirate," probably sold well enough that their father, Josiah Franklin, thought it best to put a stop to what he considered frivolous writing that required little intellect or verbal skill and had no pious outcome. "They were wretched Stuff, in the Grubstreet Ballad Stile," Franklin said,

SHOULD we inform the World of our Accomplifh-
ments, either Natural or Acquir'd, it would favour
too much of Vanity. We fhall therefore only add,
that we are furnifh'd with a large and valuable Collection of BOOKS ; which may be of vaft Advantage to us, not only in making *Indexes*, but alfo in
writing on Subjects Natural, Moral, and Divine, and
in cultivating thofe which feem the moft Barren.
We fhall at this Time favour you with a fmall part
of our Catalogue, *viz.*

        Pliny's Natural Hift.
        Jofephus Ant.
        Ariftotle's Politicks.
        Hiftory of France.
        Roman Hiftory.
        Her. Moll's Geography.
        Athenian Oracle, Four Volumes.
        Britifh Apollo.
        Heylin's Cofmography.
        ————— Sum of Chriftian Theology.
        Cot. Mather's Hiftory of New England.
        Oldmixon's Hiftory of the American Colonies.
        Sandy's Travels.
        Du Barras.
        Burnet's Hiftory of the Reformation.
        ————— Theory of the Earth.
        Virgil.
        Hudibras.
        Milton.
        The Spectator, Eight Volumes.
        The Guardian, Two Volumes.
        The Turkifh Spy.
        Art of Thinking.
        Art of Speaking.
        The Reader.
        The Lover.
        Cowly's Works,
        The Ladies Pacquet broke open.
        The Ladies Calling.
        Hiftory of the Affairs of Europe.
        Oldham's Works.
        Shakefpear's Works.
        The Tail of the Tub.
        St. Auguftine's Works.
A. B. Tillotfon's, Dr. Bates's, Dr. South's, Mr.
    Flavel's, & Mr Charnock's Works, *&c. &c.*
    &c. &c. we have alfo a great Number of Latin
    Authors, and a vaft Quantity of Pamphlets.

Figure 2.1 List of Books in James Franklin's Print Shop. While his brother was incarcerated for
insubordination, Benjamin Franklin published a list of several of the books in the print shop. The
list reveals the liberal concerns of the writers behind the *New-England Courant*. Published in the
New-England Courant, July 2, 1722, 2. Courtesy, Massachusetts Historical Society.

even while he acknowledged their immense popularity at the time. So the young Franklin found himself in an odd quandary as his career began: he discovered in himself a significant ability to write pleasing pieces that sold well and assisted in supporting his brother's press, but he was told by his father that "Verse-makers were generally Beggars," and thus he should give up such writing. Franklin evidently gave up the public pursuit of versification. But he nonetheless became extremely well read in contemporary literature. His earliest writings make reference to popular writers, such as Daniel Defoe and Isaac Watts (1674–1748), and popular essays from the *London Journal*, the *Spectator*, and the *Guardian*. He grew used to employing both classical Latin and modern English epigraphs. Franklin cited contemporary writers such as John Dryden (1631–1700), Jonathan Swift (1667–1745), and Alexander Pope (1688–1724), yet the allusive nature of his writing and the quality of his satirical pieces suggest a wide and deep awareness of important satire of the era. Franklin's turn into more studious prose writing seems to date from this period of his life, yet the popular writing apprenticeship he experienced would later become more fully realized in the immense success of his almanacs.

James Franklin required all kinds of support to get his press underway in Boston, so it is not surprising that he would set his younger, newly apprenticed brother to work in an effort to take advantage of local events of an ephemeral nature. James Franklin had probably trained as a pressman in New England and then, as biographer J. A. Leo Lemay has shown, with the funding from a loan his father obtained to assist him, traveled to England in 1717 or 1718 to procure type and press machinery.[16] He returned to Boston ready to set up a complete print shop, publish local titles, reprint important British titles, and engage in newspaper-writing and circulating materials in New England like those he had found and enjoyed in old England. To start up a press without patrons, as printers were forced to do in New England, was risky business. At the time he set himself up, there were five presses operating in Boston, so competition was steep. To supplement his income, James initially took advantage of the family's laboring heritage by using their special methods for dying cloth. Josiah and Uncle Benjamin had been dyers in England, so James used their formulas to print—as he advertised his wares—"Linens, Calicoes, Silks, &c in good Figures, very lively and durable Colours, and without the offensive Smell which commonly attends the Linens Printed here" in New England.[17]

James initially secured work for himself by printing sermons and other works of piety, including writings by pastors Thomas Prince (1687–1758), Solomon Stoddard (1643–1729), Cotton Mather (1663–1728), and Benjamin

Colman (1699–1747).[18] Indeed, of the over twenty broadsides, pamphlets, or books printed in James Franklin's printing house by 1720, well over half of the items were religious in nature. James Franklin also printed practical materials, some of them by local authors and some reprints from England. He took on a large project with *Hodder's Arithmetic*, a costly production printed for seven booksellers, that would be, according to Lemay, "the first separately published mathematical textbook printed in the colonies."[19] He also published some scientific writings, including Thomas Robie's *Letter to a Certain Gentleman* (1719) about the aurora borealis (mistaken for a meteor shower, by Robie's assessment). James Franklin's printing business began to flourish by 1719, increasing fivefold from its meager beginning in the summer of 1718.

James Franklin's Imprints on Social, Political, Economic, and Ecclesiastical Matters

Two clusters of publications by James Franklin's print shop have significance for the study of his younger brother's intellectual and ideological beginnings. The Franklins published a number of materials related to the Puritans, church matters, and religious practice. They also published a growing literature about the local economy, its relationship to the British Empire's economy, and the efforts of laboring colonists who sought decent wages and decent standards of living. These two groups of titles made a significant impression on Benjamin Franklin's development, and they had a lasting impact on his career as printer, diplomat, and social and political theorist.

In matters of religion and conscience, James Franklin supplemented the publication of the local ministers' tracts by reprinting materials that were well known in England. One of the most important titles in this line was Richard Bernard's *The Isle of Man* (originally published in 1627), which would have an appeal among local Puritans, but especially descendants from the *Mayflower*. Bernard (1568–1641), an English Puritan and associate of several *Mayflower* Puritans, wrote the *Isle of Man* as an allegory about approaching the heavenly city of Revelation and the means by which one should conduct oneself according to Christ's path of compassion and rectitude. The *Isle of Man* reached its sixteenth edition in 1683, the year Josiah Franklin sailed for New England. Was this one of the volumes in "polemic divinity" from Josiah's library that young Benjamin Franklin read? Very likely. It was the sixteenth edition that James Franklin acknowledged he was printing on the title page of his volume. James Franklin's bringing the *Isle of Man* into print in Boston ensured him an audience looking for more titles from renowned Puritans beyond their New England locale.

Reprinting Bernard also afforded the Franklins an opportunity to speak about the injustices of the witch trials carried on in New England by the area's earnest leaders. Such publication drew attention to appalling injustices sometimes done under the guise of law to those accused of sorcery, whereas compassion ought to have been offered, instead. That is, in the epistle to the reader, Bernard inveighed against the conduct of then-recent witch trials in England: "*The death of five brethren and sisters lately condemned and executed for* Witches," Bernard wrote, "*one more yet remaining, formerly brought before a Judge, and now in danger to be questioned again*"—these events, he said, "hath moved me to take this pains" to inquire after the spiritual well-being of all prisoners, not just those of conscience and those of unproven guilt. Bernard's point was that he was troubled by the actions against witches brought by "*vain Accusers,*" and while he did not wish to "prevent Justice, *nor to* hinder legal proceedings," he felt concern for "*the state of Poor* Prisoners . . . *and how their Souls safety is neglected.*"[20] Bernard called for toleration, asking his readers to make an effort to understand difference and show compassion for those who were unlike themselves. The parallel circumstances regarding witches in New England and old would have been lost on no reader of the era, especially the Franklins. In *A Guide to Grand-Jury Men* (1627), another work Bernard originally published in the same year as the *Isle of Man*, Bernard had allowed that witches were active in the world, but he pointed out that many people who simply acted with peculiar manners were being mistaken as witches and executed, whereas some of their behaviors might reasonably be explained according to simple and natural explanations. In his *Guide*, Bernard asserted that the hostility raging toward presumed witches was "vaine, dissolute, and irreligious," and he requested "patience" and forbearance toward those accused.[21] To the generation of leaders (such as the Mathers) who had taken part in the New England witch trials of the 1690s, Bernard's name surely carried a purifying and corrective weight. And to Samuel Sewall in particular, the sole witch trial judge who recanted his role in the events, Bernard's voice was a beacon of reason and righteous self-justification.[22] Bernard's books spoke less to the letter of the law than to the spirit of personal ethics grounded in respect for all persons, a theme that became common in Benjamin Franklin's writings throughout his life.

James Franklin's press also printed several pamphlets resulting from a controversy over the New North Church that was being established in

Boston. The controversy over the church brings to light some of Boston's disparities in social ranking, financial means, and educational opportunity at the time the Franklin brothers were coming of age. The existing churches were five: the Calvinist and theologically conservative First Church; the Second or North (later called the Old North) Church; the Franklins' church, the more liberal Third or South (later called the Old South) Church, which employed the Half-Way Covenant adopted in 1662; the King's Chapel (called Queen's Chapel during the reign of Queen Anne), the sole Anglican Church at the time; and the Brattle Street Church, an architecturally and theologically innovative and fashionably liberal church, where Benjamin Colman preached.[23] These existing churches were supported by leading citizens, some of whose families descended from original settlers, and by others whose families achieved some prominence after emigrating to New England. In 1714, a cluster of tradesmen and mechanics decided that a church was needed to give special encouragements to men in trades, and so they founded a New North Church.[24] Their goal was to retain independent status. That is, they did not wish to have consociational status with the other churches nor to be a part of any ecclesiastical system wherein the existing churches (especially the more conservative First Church, sponsored by the Mathers) would establish doctrine for all churches. When the New North Church called together a congregation in its new building in 1720, they installed as assistant pastor the Reverend Peter Thacher (1677–1739) of Weymouth, a nearby fishing and agricultural town. Some members within the group thought it troublesome that Thacher absconded from his position in Weymouth, arguing, "Ministers shall not be vagrants, nor intrude themselves of their own authority into any place which best pleaseth them."[25] Thacher was criticized from within his own church by those who questioned the potential loyalty of his leadership and from outside his church by the Mathers and others who sought ecclesiastical control over all of the Boston churches. Some of Thacher's critics were likely troubled by the social status of the members of this new church.

Thacher responded to his critics in a manuscript he gave to James Franklin to publish. Thacher's *A brief declaration of Mr. Peter Thacher, and Mr. John Webb, Pastors of the New-North-Church in Boston, in behalf of themselves* (1720) makes a strong case for freedom of conscience, freedom of movement for worship, and the right to speak against oppression in spiritual matters.[26] Against the insistence that all churches be tied to the same ecclesiastical authority, Thacher declared that the New North Church was following the Cambridge platform of church discipline of 1649 and the plan of the synod of 1662, insisting (particularly to the Mathers, who wished to oversee all Congregational church discipline) "that the great Foundation Principle of *Congregational* churches . . . is the *Equality* of particular Churches, and a *Fulness of Power and Authority* in every particular Organized Church regularly to manage all their own affairs . . . without being *subject* to any other Ecclesiastical Jurisdiction whatsoever." Making observations upon texts from the doctrine established in 1649 and 1662, Thacher concluded that "it is an Essential Right belonging to particular Churches to enjoy a free Liberty within themselves" to look into matters laid before them, and then, "as becometh Creatures endued with Reason and Conscience," to make their own judgments upon issues of spirituality and ecclesiastical policy. The pamphlet concluded by saying that the two new pastors agreed with "the Venerable Dr. Increase Mather" in abhorring any singular "Society of Men" who intentionally set themselves apart from and outside of church discipline, by "arrogat[ing] to themselves an exemption from giving an account of themselves," arguing instead that the New North Church and its pastors had acted clearly with high regard for the church discipline established in 1649 and 1662.[27] The defense is interesting for its insistence on the church's having followed the Cambridge discipline in the face of charges that the pastors had acted with disruption and malice in creating their own church. The language bespeaking equality of conscience and opportunity when the "Society of Men" creating a church was sincerely invested in the traditional church establishment evokes a central foundational principle of early modern liberalism and the concomitant measure, freedom of association, that such liberal professions enacted. Benjamin Franklin, likely the most speedy and accurate pressman in James's shop, was probably asked to set the type for this pamphlet. Both Franklins evidenced a growing interest in the way that liberal values and ancient British liberties were argued for in England. The language of Thacher's tract coalesced with the stories told in their family about their personal investment (in removing to New England). Thacher's tract coalesced with the brothers' deep and growing commitment to the liberal philosophies of the early eighteenth century.

Similarly important and more liberal titles were printed at James Franklin's press, most notably *English liberties, or The Free-Born Subject's Inheritance*, a rousing document created by Henry Care (1646–1688) during the era of English revolutions.[28] James Franklin reprinted Care's 1682 *English Liberties* in 1721 for several booksellers.[29] Care's name itself was tied to the several liberties at issue in the Franklins' Boston, especially religious toleration, press freedom, and representative court justice. Under the guise of "a Lover of true Protestants," Care achieved notoriety, according to his biographer Lois G. Schwoerer, "as the most persistent polemical voice against Catholicism, the Church of England, and the Stuart court," and he achieved fame among those who were like-minded as "the most passionate proponent of Dissent, religious toleration, law (as he saw it), and exclusion."[30] Henry Care was one among many writers of the civil wars whose works were reprinted posthumously for new generations in the face of increasing concerns about monarchical power and the rights of British citizens. Care's editor, Benjamin Harris, was the one who continued to bring out his works, updating the sets of British common laws included with each new edition.

James Franklin's publication of Care's *English Liberties* works as a bridge between the two lines of print jobs—religious and secular—that he took on. Care's volume speaks to matters of religion and conscience, but it also very clearly addresses the crucial concept of civil liberties through the rhetorics of ancient liberties, jurisprudence, and economics. There are several reasons why James Franklin might have chosen to publish Henry Care's *English Liberties* at this time: the Massachusetts Charter controversy; concerns about voting rights, court representation, and jurisprudence; concerns about press freedom (and particularly the Franklins' press freedom); and the document's evocative language supporting the liberties of all subjects, even if they dispraised government. The Massachusetts Charter controversy was quite actively being pursued at the time, with a very large group of Old Charter proponents who favored by-then mythic freedoms of the original charter granted to the Massachusetts Bay trading company. The New Charter proponents—including the Mathers, who had input into the New Charter and supported it—had been said to have given away some of the more fundamental rights enjoyed by original settlers. In mythic folk memory, the Old Charter was much like the Britons' Magna Carta, which Care had reprinted in *English Liberties*: it was a text known in collective memory to offer basic freedoms and rights, including freedom of conscience and speech, representative voting and representative justice, and local jurisdiction rather than regional encumbrance to a Crown-appointed authority. The New Charter regulated that Massachusetts had to accept governance appointed by the Crown. It made property rather than church membership the basis for franchise. Anyone opposed to governance by England tended to support the Old Charter, because the New Charter enabled London to dominate local governance. The divisions between the Old Charter and New Charter groups were clear, yet it should be acknowledged that few could realistically expect the British administration to restore the Old Charter, which meant restoring almost total self-government. The Old Charter supporters hoped for certain rights that the Old Charter had guaranteed, particularly that the elected assembly had the right to pass laws. Governors were aware that they needed the colonial legislatures to cooperate, because without cooperation, very few laws would get passed.[31]

The Franklins reprinted in 1721 the fifth edition, a large book (288 pages) just published in London, of Care's *English Liberties*.[32] This particular version of Care's text, essentially a reprinting of the 1719 edition, served as a crucial reminder to Britons in both old England and new that an understanding of *English* liberties needed to remain in place in the face of the changing policies, politics, and financial problems of the Hanoverian succession under George I in 1714. George I's decision to spend much of his time in Hanover meant the implementation of a policy of relying on a cabinet of ministers to rule England. The absence of the king made court-related appointments of utmost importance. The new king installed Robert Walpole (1676–1745) as prime minister. Walpole would become in essence the majority leader in the House of Commons. With the South Sea Company Act 1720, members of the court and ministry engaged in running England into furious (and unsupported) speculation in company shares. The South Sea Company was relying on presumed improved relations between Spain and Britain that would yield a monopoly of trading rights for England in Spanish South America. The company was designed to trade enslaved Africans to South America, but its financial basis was a flimsy scheme whereby individuals holding short-term government bonds were persuaded to exchange their roughly £10 million in bonds for new stock in the company. Members of the aristocracy, the Bank of England, and even unwitting independent speculators who knew nothing of the project sought shares. Company stock reached a period of fast inflation, rising a hundredfold per share from meager beginnings. The price of stock—£1,000 per share in April 1720—collapsed five months later to £150 per share. Banks, the aristocracy, goldsmiths, and ordinary people had wagered England's financial security on a scheme fostered by the administration. And though he did not support the scheme, Robert Walpole, who had just been named First Lord of the Treasury, was blamed for the significant depression felt throughout Britain, but especially in London.

There were problems in the New England economy that resonated from the panic about specie resulting from the South Sea Bubble. As historian Margaret Ellen Newell has shown, Massachusetts had early on worked to establish economic policies independent of England. In seeking to create an economic foundation on local goods (rather than imports), tax incentives (abatements and subsidies), low loan rates, and protective tariffs, New England secured economic stability interrupted only by European wars and disrupted trade routes. Yet by the first quarter of the eighteenth century, New England's early success stagnated in uneven shipping because of perpetual European wars and recurring years of specie scarcity, which caused severe internal depression and anxiety about prices of primary exports.[33]

It was into this context of political and economic instability that the Franklins thrust their new edition of Henry Care's *English Liberties*. The opening of Care's book—an encomium addressed to *"all the true Lovers of the Liberty and Welfare of their Native Countrey"* would have impressed New Englanders, as it eloquently referenced past oppressions and punishments suffered by people at the hands of government. Recalling *"our renowned Forefathers,"* who *"so dearly bought"* British *"Laws and Rights,"* *"at the Expence of so much Blood and Treasure,"* the preface concluded with a statement linking liberty and life: *"when Liberty is once gone, even Life it self grows insipid, and loses all its Relish."*[34] The fundamental precepts of every person's rights and liberties form the opening chapter of Care's volume. In "The Constitution of our *English* Government (the best in the world)," Care wrote, there is "a most excellently mixt, or qualified, Monarchy, where the King is vested with large Prerogatives, sufficient to support Majesty; and restrain'd only from the Power of doing himself and his People Harm; which would be contrary to the very End of all Government." Care took pains to speak to England's rule by mixed authority while also clarifying the nature of that rule, a rule by law rather than tyranny, because liberty was every person's birthright: "in *England*, the Law is both the Measure and the Bond of every Subject's Duty and Allegiance, each Man having a fixed fundamental Right born with him, as to Freedom of his Person, and Property in his Estate, which he cannot be deprived of, but either by his Consent, or some Crime, for which the Law has impos'd such a Penalty or Forfeiture." Such a means of governance assured every person that each had a right to enjoy freedom of person and of property without intervention from government: "This original Happy Frame of Government is truly and properly call'd an *English Man's Liberty*, a Privilege, not to exempt from the Law but to be freed in Person and Estate from Arbitrary Violence and Oppression." Care's volume printed a version of the Magna Carta and other important documents outlining inherited rights of free Englishmen, along with series of laws enacted over the centuries relating to the practices of free people.

Benjamin Franklin would embrace Henry Care's values and articulate them throughout his life. Care's expression of fundamental liberties marks a cornerstone in early modern liberalism, especially considering the number of editions of this text and the frequency of its use in England and British North America. Care's work served, with John Locke's *Two Treatises of Government* (1690), as the practical foundation for many of the theoretical expressions about freedom admired and espoused by colonial leaders.[35] Franklin knew the volume intimately, and he also no doubt became aware when he reached Philadelphia that William Penn had incorporated whole sections of Care's book into his own *Excellent Priviledge of Liberty and Property Being The Birth-Right Of the Free-born Subjects of England* (Philadelphia, 1687).[36] Franklin so appreciated Care's *English Liberties* that as a mature man he kept copies of the title in his private library, donated a copy to the Library Company of Philadelphia, and advertised the volume in other volumes he published.[37] Given Franklin's public stances on liberty during the course of his long career, I cannot overstate the importance of this book to Benjamin Franklin.

Henry Care spoke to the issues of every individual's having both freedom of person and property in his estate, unless the person engaged in criminal activity and thus forfeited his rights. Personal freedom and the right to earn and thus to own inheritable property both were concerns in the Franklins' Boston, and the Franklin print shop published several tracts more that followed a line of reasoning that all individuals were free—and had inalienable rights given them in the Magna Carta—to earn sustenance for themselves and their families without interference by government, which could not usurp the rights of individuals. Care's volume thus also fell into the line of writings James Franklin published on the local economy, its relationship to the British imperial measures to obtain specie and regulate taxes, and the efforts of colonists seeking to better themselves economically and socially. In this sense, Care's volume affiliates with other James Franklin imprints by some well-known local writers—Benjamin Colman (1673–1747), John Wise (1652–1725), and John Colman (1670–1753)—as they all, in one way or another, engaged in the developing discourse of civil and economic rights in Boston.

Matters of the local economy and its relationship to British imperial policies were of significant concern to James Franklin and (perhaps most especially) the merchants served by newspapers and other media Franklin printed. The Franklin print shop was a virtual clearinghouse for pamphlets on the local economy and civil policy. Because these matters would become crucial to Benjamin Franklin's experiences in Philadelphia, we ought to examine the range of materials James Franklin printed. Franklin took up some local concerns about marketing and fair access to goods when he printed a brief pamphlet, *Some Reasons and Arguments Offered to The Good People of Boston And adjacent Places, for The setting up Markets in Boston* (1719), by Benjamin Colman, pastor of the Brattle Street Church. Colman argued that the city should allow farmers to set up markets in a designated area of Boston and create a designated market day, when people could make their purchases of fresh vendibles without the intercessions of merchants. He argued that a market day by farmers would save townspeople time, increase their virtuous use of their time, and make more level (because of availability of goods to all) the purchasing power of rich, middling level, and poor people. "To lose our time is to throw away our money and our life (not to say our Souls) and to injure the Commonwealth, as well as our Families," Colman averred, because "[a] Market would promote Industry, and prevent abundance of Idleness."[38] His argument linked industriousness with the well-being of a country: "Industry is of great Account to the temporal weal of any Country."[39] And it lent notice to the discrepancies faced by poorer people in the face of wealthy people who could afford the time or servants to secure sustenance. To Colman, a market would bring both riches and virtue to the town. People, but especially poor people, were oppressed under the current system, because without means to get to the country to get goods, they were subject to town merchant-hucksters who bought cheaply and sold dearly, and they thus had to give proportionally more for their daily sustenance than others did. Colman concluded his remarks with an appeal to ancient custom, that prosperous cities of old always had markets.[40] Colman's argument, based in equity for all, contained in its position a central thesis that persons of higher status were afforded greater opportunities than persons of low status. He considered the situation unjust. His appeals to equity, justice, and virtue all relate to an early modern liberal conception supporting the greater good of the commonwealth based in the larger freedom of circulation of persons, their labor, and thus their wealth. This would be an argument Benjamin Franklin would take up fully in the years to come.

Other pamphlets addressed monetary problems more directly, and in their approaches to the problem of Boston's deficit of coinage (and its credit) are clear reminders of the extent to which local people were subjected to the schemes and difficulties of a Crown and ministry who had little understanding of local conditions, even though they insisted on taxation by and allegiance to Crown and Parliament. News of the South Sea Bubble debacle would arrive in British North America by the end of 1720, causing difficulty for already troubled merchants in towns whose shortage of hard specie (silver) might prove their downfall in light of the calling in of debts in England. The introduction of paper money and bills of exchange to supplement the declining level of specie assisted towns in the short run, but because hard coinage was required in England for purposes of taxation and for import payments, specie eventually disappeared, leaving New Englanders in a situation of having to pay too dearly with their paper notes and thus causing tremendous cycles of inflation.

Two camps developed to deal with the problem of money shortages, and James Franklin published the output from both sides of the debate. Writers attempted to consider the funding and goods crisis in macroeconomic terms but employed different means of analysis based on different assumptions about the social formation. One cluster of writers—Edward Wigglesworth, Thomas Paine, and a few others—argued for retrenchment on the part of a people indulged by trade advantages. This became a morals argument based in class assumptions that worked against poor or laboring people. The other cluster—notably, John Colman and John Wise (1652–1725)—argued that the local economy could expand if a system of credit could be put in place to sponsor local business and settlements further westward.

Those favoring retrenchment relied on traditional assumptions (later called "mercantilism," by Adam Smith) about what happens when luxury goods (goods that serve needs other than basic needs) get into the hands of the poorer sort. The argument assumes that the poor have no need for splendorous nor even high-quality goods, no need for free time (because they would use it in vain amusements), and no need for amusements of any kind (because in amusements they would increase their already profane behavior). That is, the argument went, the poorer sort deserved fewer spending options, because they did not choose wisely and bought superfluities, mimicking the rich. These writers argued in behalf of a general disengagement with trade in luxury items, saying that the excess materials used at home and in everyday business were essential to making the rich happy and keeping them spending their money, but such materials ought not to be available to poor people, because the poor would develop extravagant spending habits. By correcting spending habits of everyone but the elite, most from this camp contended, money woes would be alleviated.

James Franklin started printing pamphlets on Boston's funding crisis in Boston in 1720. That year, he printed the work of the usher at the Old South Church, Edward Wigglesworth (c. 1693–1765),[41] who argued that while paper bills seemed to work in the short run, bills should be used only under strict regulation and, even then, only until hard specie returned to the region. Wigglesworth's arguments, smacking distinctly of the conservative economic writings of their era, offered a linkage between the morals of the commonwealth and her ability to have a positive balance of trade with foreign powers: in other words, corrections in an uneven and infelicitous (for Britain) balance of trade were essential to the well-being of Britain and her colonies. Wigglesworth sought to reform local habits and external trade rather than attempting to develop internal markets that could commercially thrive and thus buoy the economy. Wigglesworth tended, too, to blame economic woes on the rising class of merchants who were bringing in diverse goods to market.

With the publication of Wigglesworth's pamphlet, James Franklin's press became a clearinghouse for pamphlets on economics and the funding crises of New England and old. For New Englanders, Thomas Paine (1694–1767) in 1721 summed up the funding crises acutely: they arose because of the poor morals and poor choices made by people, from the "gentry" to the "commonalty." Paine's pamphlet, a dialogue James Franklin printed in 1721, claimed to entertain the diverse opinions on the paper money crisis but ultimately argued, in effect, that conspicuous consumption was the problem driving Boston to its ruin. Paine's position is clear in the long title of his pamphlet, *A discourse, shewing, that the real first cause of the straits and difficulties of this province of Massachusetts Bay, is it's extravagancy, & not paper money.*[42] Writing as Philopatria, Paine contended that the debates about the colony's funding should not revolve around the contention (by consumers) that paper money brought on all of New England's problems or the contention (made by merchants) that all that was needed in the colony was a medium of trade. Instead, Paine asserted, "the foundation of our straits is our Extravagant Consumption of foreign Commoditys." He based his evaluation of the problem on a somewhat negative view of human nature: people desired goods for two reasons, from their personal greed and their love of status, as long as they could be on top. Paine articulated it thus: "Grandeur so naturally springs up among us, that every one is ready (I suppose by their management so) to fancy themselves the progenie of the *rich and honourable*. This seems to be the unquenchable desire of everyone. . . . Our Gentry, yea our Commonalty must be dress'd up like Nobles, nothing short of the finest of Broadcloths, Silks, &c. will serve for their Apparel, and outlandish slaves almost in endless order must wait upon all their Entertainments."[43]

Paine was echoing the analysis offered by Edward Wigglesworth, whose primary rhetorical tool was a morals charge wherein financial ruin indicated moral decay. In drawing his conclusion about the problem, Wigglesworth asserted in *A Letter from One in the Country to His Friend in Boston* that people imported luxury goods too often and "send off all our Silver and Gold to the perplexing and almost ruining the whole Country." They also have "catch'd eagerly at every thing fit to be exported, and by doing so have rais'd the price of such things." He denigrated the credit economy that resulted from luxury imports, saying that "we simple Country People being mightily pleas'd with fine things far fecht and dear bought (so long as we could have goods without paying ready mony for them) made no scruple, many of us, to take up much more upon trust than we earnt mony to pay for, hoping that a plentiful Crop of Corn or some other Smile of Providence would enable us to pay for all, one time or other."[44] In making his points about paper bills and the problems of a credit economy, Wigglesworth argued that "ready money" brought extravagance to a "simple" and profligate people who could otherwise manage to do without superfluous goods.[45] Like Paine, Wigglesworth suggested that country people were unable to understand their dilemma. He concluded that because the people themselves could not be expected to eschew luxuries, it was up to their governors to do away with legislation that made paper bills and land banks possible: "Upon the Whole, it is the Duty of Civil Rulers to consult the Welfare of the Publick," he said. "Our Legislators saw the Door, at which all of our Calamities have broken in upon us, standing wide open: They have pusht it partly to; and so have in some measure checkt the madness of the People, who without Fear or Wit were running into Debt, to their own Ruin, and the Ruin of them that trusted them, and of the Whole Country."[46] Wigglesworth's central economic argument was against a paper bill and credit economy and in favor of more stringent fiscal controls enacted through legislation. Anxious about taxation to repay the forfeitures resulting from too easy credit, he ended his commentary with a series of rhetorical questions: "Must men Spend more than they earn? Must publick & private Banks be establish'd, that so when People have spent all they have earnt, they may know where to go and borrow more, to lay out for things they have no need of? And must the Lands of the Country groan under Taxes and Mortgages to uphold these Fooleries?"[47] Wigglesworth's emotionally heightened appeals, designed to create economic fear, were common fare among writers who complained about the poorer sort or about those whose spendthrift profligacy might impoverish the community. Unable to consider potential benefits of a growing commercial economy, writers like Paine and Wigglesworth sought to contract spending rather than enhance it and to enforce the status quo rather than attempt innovative solutions to age-old economic shortfalls.

Wigglesworth's pamphlet was a response to *The Distressed State of the Town of Boston, &c. Considered. In a Letter from a Gentleman in the Town, to his Friend in the Countrey,* by John Colman.[48] Colman had argued in behalf of a private bank (as opposed to a government-sponsored bank) run as a stock company by philanthropic and compassionate individuals as a means to end the financial crisis. The use of private banks would enable consumers to bypass taxing policies and shore up the local financial situation outside of government interference. For this reason, the government sought to suppress any private banks and lending. "The Medium of Exchange, the only thing which gives life to Business, Employs the Poor, Feeds the Hungry, and Cloaths the Naked, is so Exhausted," Colman wrote, "that in a little time we shall not have wherewith to Buy our Daily Bread, much less to pay our Debts or Taxes."[49] Colman was already known for his land bank proposal when he published his pamphlet in 1720. Because he had been criticizing the government's policies regarding currency and debt, Colman was arrested and tried for disturbing the peace at a difficult time. Colman's argument in behalf of a private banking plan was merely one among a number of the lines of defense against specie scarcity. Colman was, like some others, attempting to come up with macroeconomic answers to the problems by suggesting something more akin to the now classic arguments in behalf of capital exchange, arguments commonly appreciated best by the commercial classes in cities—that all people ought to have more liberal expectations and take advantage of more fluid resources.

John Colman and John Wise (1652–1725)—both printed by James Franklin—argued for a greater leniency in exchange, supported by a reissuing of paper currency and a new banking system whereby land would secure credit. Both Wise and Colman favored reissuing paper money, with credit secured by land, and they sought to ease the local economy by creating banks whose basis or security lay in land. They refuted concerns reflecting the backward-looking economic arguments about balance of trade and hard specie and instead argued for more fluid monetary, social, and political policies based in commercial ties that would strengthen rather than sever relations across community boundaries. Colman and Wise and others of this more liberal economic camp favored paper money for its potential to fuel internal development, enable the creation of raw products for export, and assist in the expansion of farming, manufactures, and trade. In Margaret Newell's words, "Government's role, in this formulation, was to 'let trade in a manner go free' and to stimulate the economy by making loans to enterprising individuals or by chartering private banks."[50] Benjamin Franklin, who likely set type for these pamphlets on economics, was gaining early lessons in economic theory.

James Franklin was fortunate that John Wise brought him the manuscripts for *The Freeholder's Address to the Honourable House of Representatives* (1721), *A Friendly Check, from a Kind Relation* (1721), and *A Word of Comfort to a Melancholy Country. Or the Bank of Credit Erected in the Massachusetts-Bay* (1721). All three pamphlets urged, with brilliant rhetorical flourishes, the support of local commercial endeavors that would both secure the failing economy and assist—by creating employment opportunities—those already distressed. John Wise enjoyed local renown as a defender of the ancient charter of British civil liberties. His strong voice in behalf of the ancient rights of all subjects emerged during the controversy over taxation and religious oppression under the Dominion of New England (1686–89) and the appointed governor, Sir Edmund Andros (1637–1714). A pastor at Ipswich during the Dominion period, Wise encouraged his congregation to ignore the poll and property taxes that Andros had imposed on all Massachusetts residents. The town of Ipswich (leading several other towns) refused to appoint tax collectors for Andros's levies, unless they were directed to do so by the Massachusetts General Assembly. The resistance actions brought Wise fines and imprisonment for twenty-one days. He was also suspended from his ministry.[51] When the Dominion of New England was abolished in 1689, Wise was exonerated, but his reputation for arguing in behalf of ancient liberties was secured.

In the funding crisis of the 1720s, John Wise favored a greater independence of funding possibilities so as to encourage expenditures by individuals and businesses and create better living standards for those already among the categories of the poor. In the *Freeholder's Address*, Wise began by alluding to the South Sea debacle as contributing to the problems the government was facing in its currency. Wise proposed that the General Court emit £50,000 credit, at 5 percent, in the form of paper bills and secured by land.[52] He then suggested that the interest on loan money was to be repaid as produce or goods (flax, hemp, wheat, rye, corn, pork, beef, fish, oil, camblets, druggets, serges, and so forth) that would be sold for ready money or retained in their raw form and used to sponsor a number of public projects administered by "Gentlemen" for the relief of the poor. He favored spinning schools for the poor women and children of the province, who could, by spinning and producing threads and yarns, take part in their own upkeep and gain, by their own productivity, access to goods in New England. He also considered that goods could be placed into a storehouse to supply garrisons with provisions and clothes. The goods could also be used in trade to bring silver back into the country, as, for instance, in trade to Portugal. He argued that it would be useful to develop a paper mill, and he sought the construction of buildings and a hospital for the poor. He favored housing poor boys who would be trained in the use of languages and in mathematics, so that they would be prepared for business.[53] Of course, these social projects are ones that Benjamin Franklin himself would take up in Philadelphia.

Unlike John Colman, whose private banking plans revealed a distrust of government, Wise conceived that attaching a public banking endeavor to the Massachusetts government would assist in keeping activities free from scrutiny in England yet suggest an understanding of the importance of good governance affiliated with the Crown. He concluded by expressing hope that the Assembly would "grant us a further Supply of this Miracle working Paper Medium, that we as well as others may reap the Benefit of them, and raise to our selves noble Estates as they have done before us: This will remove our present unhappy prospects, and rejoyce the hearts of the People, and cause them with chearful hearts Honorably to support their Government, the Ministry, and Schools of Learning, and add to their now Wonderful Loyalty to King George, and submission to his Government."[54]

Wise's *Word of Comfort to a Melancholy Country* offered a different argument still, one based less on a need for any bill of exchange like paper money than on a system of bills of credit. He began his extended analysis of how bills of credit would solve the financial crisis in Massachusetts with a crucial assertion indicating that the means for resolution of the problem lay not in God's hands, nor in London's, but in Massachusetts alone: "The Means of our Relief are in our own Hands; and we can save our selves, as easily, as to say the Word."[55] "*We are Defective in Nothing, or in Nothing so much as in want of a Sufficient Medium of Trade,*" he insisted. Arguing that "*All Prudent Men and Civil Nations, upon long Experience, find that a Convenient Medium must be had, and made use of to Support Trade and Commerce with due Advantage,*" Wise asserted that "*A Medium of Trade need not be Costly, if it be but convenient and safe.*"[56] In Wise's view, the days of hard specie brought significant hardship and inequity among people, and it laid good people at the mercy of extortioners who charged dearly for basic commodities.

Wise offered a solution based in a medium directly suited to local circumstances and local labor. He argued that bills of credit would "bring things nearer to the Rule of Equity; and Adjust matters in Commerce so fairly, that all Men may live and thrive, upon their Labor and Profits." Such economic parity might breed a happier social formation, and it would "bring the Bills to such a Level, as the Money ought to be at in a Country of Trade, and Religion, where Men should love their Neighbours as themselves; and do as they would be done by."[57] Wise believed that people would be more willing to take part in such a system, because it promised greater equity, something important to a "Country of Trade, and Religion." This kind of system would, Wise believed, make everyone more "Willing, that others should live Prosperously, upon their Means, their Incomes, their Labour, and Profits, as well as themselves."[58] Wise emphasized generosity of spirit throughout his pamphlet, favoring a language of benefits that would arise from plenty. The opposite behavior of niggardliness—that constrained financial conditions augur constrained and indeed perfidiously usurious social conditions—was the negative circumstance Wise was, in effect, speaking to.

Where Edward Wigglesworth and Thomas Paine had questioned the effects of paper money or bills of credit on the industriousness and moral fiber of the people, Wise and Colman propagandized that New Englanders' habits of industry and neighborliness would be enhanced by the effects of a greater market participation that more ready money, whether as paper money or bills of credit, would afford people. In the hands of these writers, debt was emptied of its negative implication, replaced instead with a more positive interpretation, that if New Englanders were indebted, this situation simply arose because of the usury of those seeking to keep hard specie in place combined with the absence of opportunity for those most willing to seek to better their lives. As Margaret Newell has explained it, "Advocates of increasing the money supply expressed confidence that industrious New Englanders would use credit rationally to invest and improve, rather than merely to consume."[59]

Working in his brother's print shop, the young Benjamin Franklin must have been intrigued by the arguments offered by people he knew on such expansive problems as Britain's economic system and its local fiscal ramifications. It is clear from his writings, even at this stage, that while he understood and appreciated the traditional economic positions taken by those more conservative, he considered that opportunities for expansion of both the local economy and the empire far outweighed the local concern about temporary contractions that ready money could produce. Into his mature years, he carried with him some of the more conservative writers' attitudes about the poor, to be sure. Overall, however, as his later writings made abundantly clear, Franklin cast his lot with those favoring commercial stimulation, and he agreed with the quotation John Wise made of Sir Edward Coke in his *Word of Comfort*, that *"Trade & Traffick, is the Life of a Common Wealth."*[60]

Franklin's Turn

Franklin had read conservative British economic theorists during his earliest years. We gain a sense of Franklin's views from his earliest writings. In Silence Dogood No. 10, published in the *New-England Courant*, August 13, 1722, for instance, Franklin copied from Daniel Defoe's book *An Essay Upon Projects* (1697) a chapter on relieving widows that referenced Sir William Petty (1623–1687), scientist, mathematician, economic theorist, and fellow of the Royal Society who survived service under Oliver Cromwell, Charles II, and James II.[61] In Franklin's newspaper essay, Silence Dogood is discoursing on a project for relieving widows by quoting arguments set forth by Daniel Defoe (c. 1660).[62] Defoe, Silence pointed out, employed mathematical calculations to conclude that for a very small sum, regularly paid, members who voluntarily contributed to a *"Friendly Society"* could assist the widows, who might otherwise be bereft of support while still raising children and thus forced to rely upon community charity (by way of public taxation) rather than individually funded resources.

Few of Franklin's New England readers would have missed the striking similarities between Silence, voicing Defoe, and John Wise. Silence's comments resonate with (but do not exactly duplicate) the tone and context of Wise's *A Word of Comfort*. Indeed, perhaps Franklin counted on his reading audience's knowledge of John Wise when he echoed Wise's arguments that helping another person did no harm to one's own economic well-being. Franklin's Silence mimics Wise's stance on public support: Silence "would leave this to the Consideration of all who are concern'd for their own or their Neighbour's Temporal Happiness," believing as she does that "the Country is ripe for many such *Friendly Societies*, whereby every Man might help another, without any Disservice to himself." This sounds quite like Wise's comment "that Men should love their Neighbours as themselves; and do as they would be done by." While this remark of course reverberates with the proverbial golden rule, it nonetheless gives space to the conception that it should be expected that people love themselves first, a theme common to the writings of Thomas Hobbes and Bernard Mandeville (1670–1733), among others.

In Daniel Defoe's world, as in John Wise's and Benjamin Franklin's, Thomas Hobbes's, and Bernard Mandeville's, self-love functioned to assist one's love of community. That is, their understanding of human nature was such that individuals were self-interested and would assist others only if their own interests were sufficiently met in so doing. To phrase Silence's Defoe another way: "without any Disservice to himself," a person could take part in friendly societies that helped others, and this was a chief commendation for the establishment of friendly societies. In Defoe's and Franklin's views, giving credence to a person's self-interested nature might make that person more willing to assist others outside himself (and herself) and their family. Like Mandeville and Hobbes, then, Defoe and Franklin held that self-interest could benefit the community. Self-love, in this way, could provide social benefits.

This is an important aspect of Franklin's view, even as a young man, and it provides a small glimpse of his complicated understanding of human nature. It would be very easy to take some of Franklin's writings and construct a model of Franklin that suited the traditional classical republican view, which is that he argued a liberal agenda in behalf of social improvements from a disinterested and democratic perspective. But Franklin had a more interestingly complicated view of human nature than this, and he seems to have followed the modern natural law tradition as it was fostered by some of the more nuanced liberal writers, including John Trenchard (1662–1723) and Thomas Gordon (c. 1691–1750).[63] As he phrased it in the autobiography, Franklin always gave vanity a fair hearing, because it could be productive of social benefit: "Most People dislike Vanity in others whatever Share they have of it themselves," Franklin wrote in 1771, "but I give it fair Quarter wherever I meet with it, being persuaded that it is often productive of Good to the Possessor and to others that are within his Sphere of Action."[64] This duality of thought—that self-love fostered love of others—is Mandevillian, for it assumes at its basis that private vices (such as self-interest) can be put to use for public benefits.

Opposing Authority

Nearly from its beginning, James Franklin's press tended to adopt an oppositional stance regarding church and state policies, almost as if Franklin were taking his lead from the best-known presses in London at the time. As we have seen, many of the titles James Franklin printed relate to or extend early modern liberal thinking and monetary policies to New

England. The Franklin print shop also participated in the pamphlet wars about the religious conflict in the region, not just about the formation and purpose of churches but the sectarian differences surrounding the require-ments for church members. The position taken by the press was one that local authorities eventually managed to suppress, but not without signif-icant liberal protestation from the Franklin brothers. The line of books that James Franklin printed could not fall under punishable behaviors, but James Franklin's newspaper, the *New-England Courant*, did, from its inception.

The opening numbers of the *Courant* expostulated against the attempts by the Mathers to enforce smallpox inoculation. It is with deep irony that the Franklins, who themselves seem to have favored the *idea* of smallpox inoculations, ended up on the side opposing them, but the situation was complicated by the Mathers' notion that smallpox inoculations ought to be carried out in the community as a matter of law—everyone should receive the inoculation. James Franklin decided to use his paper as a public forum to test the community's willingness to have a conversation about the mat-ter. The writers he gathered around him criticized the pro-inoculation articles appearing in the *Boston Gazette*. Their concern was less about the inoculation itself than the method being employed to carry it out. The debates between the papers (and those between the Mathers and Franklins) became heated, so much so that the Mathers and their friends dubbed the collection of writers encircling James Franklin and his paper a "Hell-Fire club." Cotton Mather obsessed about the paper's open criticism of church-men's power. Mather wrote in his diary, December 1721: "Warnings are to be given unto the wicked Printer, and his Accomplices, who every week publish a vile Paper to lessen and blacken the Ministers of the Town, and render their Ministry ineffectual."[65]

Finding his press the subject of castigation, James Franklin fought back with an eloquent statement supporting toleration for differing points of view as long as they were fairly and publicly expressed. Following the rea-soning of John Milton and John Locke, James Franklin complained that "to anathematize a Printer for publishing the different Opinions of Men, is as injudicious as it is wicked." He argued that the "*Courant* was never design'd for a Party Paper." To the contrary, he insisted, "I have once and again given out, that both Inoculators and Anti-Inoculators are welcome to speak their Minds" in the paper, and he made yet another invitation: "I hereby invite all Men, who have Leisure, Inclination and Ability, to speak their Minds, with Freedom, Sense and Moderation, and their Pieces shall be welcome to a Place in my Paper."[66] The newspaper would be used, he argued, for open discussion of matters of society and government, not for offering ideas associated with one particular side or another.

Yet James Franklin did use his press to criticize social and political policies of those, including the Mathers, holding the reins of government. Other numbers of the *Courant* took up the Massachusetts Charter controversy and other local political and ecclesiastical issues. The newspaper did offer news, fictional pieces, gossip, satires, and memoranda from other papers.[67] Indeed, much of the material seems to have been intended as entertainment. But a good deal of Franklin's paper was critical of prominent local church authorities, their elitism, their support of inoculation for smallpox, their preaching regarding piety and conformity, and their anxiety about keeping public discourse in the hands of churchmen rather than those whom the Mathers characterized as "knaves" and "scribblers." To Increase Mather, James Franklin's *New-England Courant* was "a *Cursed Libel*," "a *Wicked Paper*" likely to bring down the heavens' wrath upon New England because of its lack of respect for the authorities of church or government.[68]

James Franklin was bringing a bit of old England to New England in his newspaper. The oppositional press in London (i.e., the press supporting the liberal notions the Franklins admired) was quite strong at the time James Franklin was over there buying his press type and learning the trade. The oppositional press in London, especially at the time of the Hanoverian succession, ridiculed place-seekers in government and spoke to matters of conscience in religion. Beyond the literary cultural matters imitated by James Franklin's cluster of writers, Franklin was, in effect, imitating the successful papers in London by offering fare critical of the government and of the state church. The *Courant* embraced the oppositional stance like the one taken by the best-known paper in London, the *London Journal*. The *London Journal* was one among about forty political weeklies published in London in 1720, when it started printing John Trenchard and Thomas Gordon's series of letters signed by "Cato" (and thus called Cato's Letters). Soon most of the weeklies were publishing reprints of the letters. The paid circulation of the *London Journal* reached between 10,000 and 15,000 subscriptions at the height of the publication of Cato. The *Journal*'s circulation was higher than any other paper, including the *London Gazette*, the official newspaper. The newspaper became available in the country towns far from London, and it was considered among the most reliable resources for news of government. The *New-England Courant* was the sole outlet in New England offering an array of oppositional materials much like those offered in the *London Journal*.

In effect, by printing in New England materials that were entertaining or controversial, or both, James Franklin was attempting to present the local readers with reading fare similar to papers in London. The trouble was, he was in New England, not in old England. And so while he found a useful way to sell his newspapers and pamphlets, he also found himself getting into serious squabbles—brought on by the kinds of materials he was printing in the paper—with the authorities. They considered his behaviors impudent and impious, and they feared social insurrection might occur as a result of the challenging of their authority. On January 15, 1723, a special committee devised explicitly to render a decision about James Franklin's newspaper and drawn from members of the Massachusetts Council and the Assembly made public its findings regarding James Franklin's *New-England Courant*. It averred "That the tendency of the said Paper is to Mock Religion, and bring it into contempt, That the Holy Scriptures are therein Prophanely abused. That the Reverend and Faithful Ministers of the Gospell are injuriously reflected on: His Majesty's Government Affronted: The Peace and good Order of His Majesty's Subjects of this Province disturbed by the said Courant."[69] The committee's recommendation, in effect, was to shut down the press unless James Franklin, who was both printer and publisher, submitted to authorities—prior to publication, for approval—all materials in advance of printing them. The committee conceived that Franklin should be punished for past printing offenses and proscribed from future ones. Its finding and recommendation "humbly propose[d]" that "for prevention of the like Offenses" in future,

> *James Franklin* the Printer and Publisher . . . be strictly forbidden by this Court to Print or Publish the *New-England* Courant, or any Pamphlet or Paper of the like Nature, except it be first Supervised by the Secretary of this Province. And the Justices of His Majesty's Sessions of the Peace . . . be directed to take Sufficient Bond of the Said *Franklin*, for his good Behaviour for Twelve Months time.[70]

Such a move would not only silence Franklin and his press but take away a mainstay of his livelihood. This seems to have been the goal of the committee and those in government whom it was designed to serve. Shutting down Franklin's press had been the aim of the Mathers from the start, especially Cotton Mather, who rankled from the attacks against the inoculation plan he had organized. Their actions resembled England's seventeenth-century licensing acts (the Printing Act of 1662, renewed in 1693), which were "based on the theory that the freedom to print was hazardous to the community and dangerous" to the leadership, to borrow Jeremy Black's words.[71] The Printing Act in England was designed to protect the Church of England and officers of government, and it required prepublication submission. The assumption of the leadership seems to be that their official finding would take care of the problem.

Despite the finding against him, James Franklin challenged the government by printing his newspaper, as if no action had been taken against him, on January 21, 1722, the week after the vote for supervising his press had passed the Council and Assembly. As local news, Franklin reproduced the motion made and agreed to on January 14 by the House and Council to suppress the open publication of his paper. By reproducing the statement made against him, Franklin provided an impudent rebuke of the authorities, enabling readers to participate in the rebuke by purchasing and reading his newspaper. The brothers behaved fearlessly as they challenged the authorities' actions.[72] James Franklin was selling his papers while legitimately challenging the rights of any colonial legislature to regulate printing. Local authorities called for James Franklin's arrest, causing him to go into hiding. Young Benjamin Franklin took over the publication of the newspaper.[73]

While his brother was in hiding, Benjamin Franklin printed (among other things such as mock "rules" for editing the newspaper) a reprint series of materials taken directly from the London press, including Cato's Letters from the *London Journal*. Silence Dogood No. 8, published July 9, 1722, reprinted Trenchard and Gordon's Cato's Letter No. 15 from the *London Journal*, number 80, February 4, 1721, on the freedom of the speech in a free country. Replete with references to Charles I's proclamations abolishing parliaments, this letter by "Cato" observed that "Without Freedom of Thought, there can be no such Thing as Wisdom; and no such Thing as publick Liberty, without Freedom of Speech; which is the Right of every Man, as far as by it, he does not hurt or controul the Right of another: And this is the only Check it ought to suffer, and the only Bounds it ought to know." The liberal manifesto, arising under the hand of the younger brother, taunted the authorities significantly more than they could have anticipated by calling them "Publick Traytors." Crucial to the strategy advancing free speech is that it find an audience among those whose speech was purportedly being suppressed. Crucial too is the link established between free speech and the security of property. Free speech, a "sacred Privilege . . . so essential to free Goverments," secured one's ability to protect one's property. Only free government could assure the people "that the Security of Property, and the Freedom of Speech always go together." Indeed, Franklin used Cato to say that "in those wretched Countries where a Man cannot call his Tongue his own, he can scarce call any Thing else his own," because "Whoever would overthrow the Liberty of a Nation, must begin by subduing the Freeness of Speech; a *Thing* terrible to Publick Traytors."[74]

The linking of freedom of speech with natural rights logic, a hinging typical of many of Trenchard and Gordon's Cato's Letters, aptly suited the situation of James Franklin's press. The language of liberty the newspaper article offered is a central premise of the liberal political theory common in Franklin's day. By calling freedom of speech a "sacred Privilege," the article assured *New-England Courant* readers, without speaking the statement explicitly, that the meddlesome government was usurping the rights of the printer and, in so doing, was encroaching on the rights of every person in the community. By implying that an ideological attachment obtained between the Massachusetts government and the court of King Charles I, Franklin's Silence Dogood (and her erstwhile publisher/author) could effectively evoke the living memory of England's civil wars without making charges directly against the local government.

Benjamin Franklin's Silence Dogood No. 9 reprinted another of Cato's Letters, this time No. 31 from the *London Journal* of May 27, 1721. Silence was reproducing the materials "from an ingenious Political Writer in the London Journal, the better to convince . . . Readers, that Publick Destruction may be easily carry'd on by *hypocritical Pretenders to Religion*."[75] This letter by Thomas Gordon, a pseudophilosophical diatribe against weaknesses and inconsistencies in human nature and aimed at the South Sea debacle, is used by Silence Dogood in answer to her rhetorical question opening her essay, "Whether a Commonwealth suffers more by hypocritical Pretenders to Religion, or by the openly Profane?" Silence concludes that those in state offices, "publick Hypocrite[s]," can deceive people into thinking them great public-spirited men, whereas they are knaves, in reality. Silence used her platform to argue that "we cannot better manifest our Love to Religion and the Country, than by setting the Deceivers in a true Light, and undeceiving the Deceived, however such Discoveries may be represented by the ignorant or designing Enemies of our Peace and Safety."[76]

Silence Dogood No. 9 has been understood (by the editors of Franklin's papers, among others) as a specific remark on the former Massachusetts governor, Joseph Dudley, who had studied for the ministry but entered political life. J. A. Leo Lemay argued that the letter is a diatribe against Samuel Sewall, who was serving as chief justice overseeing the court actions taken against James Franklin. While these hypotheses bear up under examination, I believe they miss the larger point: Silence Dogood's No. 9 essay criticizes all those who would argue that they serve the people when they are really serving themselves primarily. Its point is especially directed against those who hypocritically serve others under the guise of religion, but the essay speaks more fully to all "Political" hypocrites. Indeed, if we remove ourselves from the local concerns and consider Silence Dogood No. 9 in the broader context of liberalism and its foundations, we discover that Franklin is using Silence to make a significant philosophical comment on the human condition and on the nature of power—that power corrupts even the best of people and even those who claim to profess a higher calling, that of serving their God. Unlike self-love, to which Franklin gave some credence because it might lend itself to doing good for others, self-serving hypocrisy corrupted the individuals who embodied it and the people whom they, presumably, should be serving.

As indicated in the (commonly quoted) epigraph Franklin employed, "*Corruptio optimi est pessima*" ("The best, when corrupted, are the worst"), corruption in those who ought to be above reproach was an unconscionable misuse of divinity. Two source texts seem possible. The expression had been used against the Anabaptists in New England in a small volume by Samuel Parker (1640–1688) published anonymously in London in 1673, about the supposed slaying of the author's brother, Josiah, who had been called to serve the ministry first in Virginia and then in New England but was slain by Baptists.[77] Franklin's Latin quotation matches the one used by Parker exactly, just as his theme—the desperate nature of hypocrites in religion who are more interested in power than in spiritual truth—is similar to Parker's.[78] The use by Franklin is particularly interesting, if he got it from Parker, from the notoriety with which the authorship and facts of the book were challenged by the Privy Council. But a similar line was also used by Royalist Sir John Denham (1614?–1669) in his poem "The Progress of Learning," published in *Poems and Translations with the Sophy* (1668). Denham's lines are remarkably akin to Franklin's. Both spoke about the extent to which Protestant theology overwrote history and, while wresting learning from the hands of Catholicism, nonetheless also crushed free inquiry:

> No longer by Implicite faith we erre,
> Whilst every Man's his own Interpreter;
> No more conducted now by *Aarons* Rod,
> Lay-Elders, from their Ends, create their God.
> But seven wise men, the ancient world did know,
> We scarce know seven, who think themselves not so.
> . . .
>
> Then, from the clashes between Popes and Kings,
> Debate, like sparks from Flints collision, springs:
> As Ioves loud Thunderbolts were forg'd by heat,

The like, our Cyclops, on their Anvils, beat;
All the rich Mines of Learning, ransackt are
To furnish Ammunition for this War:
Uncharitable Zeal our Reason whets,
And double Edges on our Passion sets;
'Tis the most certain sign, the world's accurst,
That the best things corrupted, are the worst.[79]

If Franklin's readers knew Denham's poem, they might have delighted in the ironic turn against the local Puritan leadership. That Franklin might have been mimicking a Royalist line of argument against the likes of Luther and Calvin (the poem also called printing the pernicious instrument of Lucifer, who brought about printing so as to create "Wild controversie" among people) probably was delightful to read.[80]

Finally, this particular Silence Dogood number could apply as much to Oliver Cromwell—whom Franklin would later characterize as "conqueror and protector (some say the tyrant) of three great kingdoms" (*Poor Richard's Almanack*, 1748)—as it might to Governor Dudley or Samuel Sewall. Silence Dogood No. 9 is a critique of anyone whose self-loving hypocrisy interferes with societal betterment, and it finds that those especially heinous in this offense are those who hide behind the surplice. The letter clearly separates goodness and justice (qualities with which an uncorrupted natural man is born) from deception and fraud (qualities that occur when society has fallen to a corrupted state) masquerading under the countenance of religion. This line of argument is worth underscoring as belonging to Benjamin Franklin's canon from his earliest years. It is a sign that from his entrance into print, Franklin was willing to take significant risk and to oppose authority.

In his autobiography, Franklin explained his departure from Boston as having arisen from personal pique against his brother, an act of will in behalf of his own freedom against his brother's authority. Such might have been the case, and it *is* the story that has come down across the years. Yet it is also likely that, having rubbed up against the authority of Boston's leaders, Franklin considered it most expedient to aim for a new start in another community lest he himself eventually be thrust into jail for contempt. The authorities *were*, after all, still the authorities, and whatever political philosophy Franklin believed in would not stand to keep him out of jail unless it were the same philosophy held by those in his midst. He broke his secret apprenticeship with his brother's press and left—first sailing for New York but ending up in Philadelphia—in September 1723. Earlier that year, he had a chance to see his brother discountenance, once again, those in power. In a long essay supposedly authored by "Philo-Dicaios" in the May 6, 1723, *New-England Courant*, James Franklin, speaking of the Magna Carta, queried, "Is it not notorious that 'the Bulwark of our Liberties and Properties, the *Magna Carta*, or *Great Charter* of *England*, a Charter purchas'd with the *Treasures*, and seal'd with the *Blood* of our Ancestors,' has been sometimes but little minded by the Legislative Power?"[81]

We might attribute to politics and to the cause of testing the freedom of the press James Franklin's continued publication of materials critical of ecclesiastical and civil governance, but we ought also to be mindful of two things: first, James Franklin believed his newspaper was appropriately mimicking modern London fare, and second, he was fully aware that the materials he was offering were timely and would sell papers. His newspaper was remarkably successful from its inception, perhaps especially because of its oppositional stance. The amount of ink spent detracting and defending James Franklin's *New-England Courant* is an index to the anxiety about their authority felt by those in civil offices. In New England as in old, where the state and state religion had a merely tenuous hold over a diverse population, draconian measures, such as attempting to ensure the demise of dissident voices, were considered the sole means by which civil unrest could be averted.

By way of conclusion, it will be useful to speak to the issue of conflicting narratives regarding liberalism and classical republicanism that were as common in Franklin's day as they are in our own. My purpose is not to rehash the too frequently discussed contest by scholars about the oppositional rhetoric of Trenchard and Gordon, known as Independent Whigs, nor to attempt to identify Franklin's writings, early and late, as falling into some particularly paradigmatic line of reasoning indicating that he was always pro-American independence or pro-empire.[82] Instead, I would like to underscore my sense that, like his brother James, Benjamin Franklin in his youth took an oppositional stance (rather than a clearly adumbrated ideological position) on matters of religion and governance.

Franklin's youthful reading was haphazard, and his search for a speaking voice was varied, producing a rhetorical positioning that was both fluid and inconsistent. Franklin was nothing if not an expert rhetorician. And rhetorically, he could embrace a variety of viewpoints, not because he was intentionally inconsistent or Machiavellian, nor incoherent in his views, but because he would embrace whatever rhetorical position best suited the oppositional situation he was writing to, at any given time. Franklin's liberalism, then, gave great credence to some of those—such as Hobbes, Mandeville, and even Machiavelli—who believed that private interests might have public benefits. It is not entirely clear to me that Franklin ever believed in disinterested virtue, a quality of virtue that was entirely other-directed without being self-seeking for financial gain or for reputation. In his thinking, he allowed for, though he personally tried to avoid, the negative human feelings of jealousy and greed.

Should this force us to assume that he was not liberal in his overall social and political policies? Most of us adjust our opinions as we learn more or meet up with those who think differently. Franklin, especially early in his career, adopted a rhetorical position much like that adopted by Thomas Gordon in Cato's Letter No. 31, which Franklin quoted (though quoting a different part) in Silence Dogood No. 9. Gordon had written, "Of all the passions which belong to human nature, self-love is the strongest, and the root of all the rest; or, rather, all the different passions are only several names for the several operations of self-love." Granting that self-love operated in all human beings, Franklin sought to establish civic and political instruments and institutions whereby the greatest degree of good could accrue to the largest number of people. Franklin, quoting Gordon, wrote: "Upon the whole, we must not judge of one another by our fair pretensions and best actions; since the worst men do some good, and all men make fine professions: But we must judge of men by the whole of their conduct, and the effects of it." In Gordon's as in Franklin's world, self-love could prompt public benefits. Perhaps this helps explain why Franklin would go on to launch a significant number of public service projects beginning in the late 1720s.

Three

FRANKLIN'S IMPERIAL IMAGININGS
"Coined Land" and Global Goals

Franklin's initial decades in Pennsylvania give witness to his abiding concerns about the British colonial situation, both the American colonies' ideological position as part of the growing British state and their potential for expansion of the empire onto Indian lands that were, as yet, without British or European claim. Indeed, his earliest writings are testaments to Franklin's preoccupation with the imperial pretensions of Britain's structural and fiscal policies for the American colonies. Franklin's experiences as a printer and merchant in Philadelphia enabled him to understand better the different administrative operations for the colonies. In Boston, he had learned a good deal about the difficulties faced because of the funding crises and the Massachusetts Charter. In Philadelphia, he coped with the constrained political, fiscal, military, and social conditions underlying the Penn family's land grants. Generally speaking, Franklin sought internal social and fiscal improvements for Pennsylvania while also seeking to enhance the colony's status within the British Empire.

Pennsylvania's Proprietary leadership produced local complications, within Pennsylvania, and distant ones, with regard to policies emanating from London. This chapter will examine Franklin's developing views with regard to the British administration's goals for the colonies by looking into Franklin's key writings on the financial crisis in Pennsylvania, the premiere problem faced by Philadelphians at the time Franklin arrived there. These years reveal the extent to which Franklin was preoccupied with the administration's confusing attempt to decide upon and implement an imperial colonial policy. Franklin became a leading figure in Philadelphia while still a young man, and he happily embraced his new working life and his civic goals. But the Pennsylvania colony, its leadership, and its inhabitants were in difficult legal, social, and economic circumstances. Among the many problems that Franklin attempted to address during his Pennsylvania years, roughly from 1723 to 1758, four have relevance to this study: problems with money and systems of exchange; problems relating to taxation, which was integrally linked to the circulation of currency and goods; problems concerning the legal status of the Proprietary and the Pennsylvania Assembly, especially as these related to defense of the colony; and problems with the numerous and diverse immigrants coming across the Atlantic to live in Pennsylvania. This chapter and the next two take up these sets of concerns preoccupying Franklin.

Like Boston (and Massachusetts generally), Philadelphia (and the Pennsylvania colony) lacked available hard currency that would enable the city to promote production and commerce. During Franklin's Philadelphia years, he found the local inhabitants were unable to pay continually rising taxes for normal operations, yet higher taxes needed to be levied in part because of the nature of the Pennsylvania Charter and its Proprietary. He also discovered that Philadelphians were stressed morally, with quarrels erupting during wartime among Quakers who supported defense and those who did not. There were quarrels as well among Presbyterians, some of whom favored High Church practices. In addition, Philadelphians were concerned about serious economic stagnation. They were worried in the 1740s and 1750s about matters of defense in borderlands to the north and west against the French, Indian peoples, or both combined. They were inexperienced in dealing with an influx of foreign immigrants—most notably, the Palatinate Germans—and the problems that ensued from the mixing of different European cultures, especially in the absence of a common system of exchange in terms of money and language.

The situation in Pennsylvania was similar to but different from Franklin's experiences in Boston. Franklin understood that any colony having so diverse a population would experience difficulties requiring adjustments to the changing social and economic scene. Pennsylvania's issues were exacerbated by the fact that large tracts of land were held by those who were, in effect, nonresidential landlords (i.e., the Proprietors), and these lands were exempt from taxation by Pennsylvania's Assembly, the governing body for the colony. Problems in systems of linguistic and monetary exchange among diverse peoples, problems in culture arising from cultural diversity, problems in defense—all were made worse by the seeming stranglehold, whether by the Crown, British merchants, or the Pennsylvania Proprietors, on funding and decision-making regarding defense and civic improvements. As I will attempt to show in this and succeeding chapters, the ideologies and rhetoric of early modern liberalism that Franklin spent his youth learning assisted his formulation of new ideas in political theory about economics, trade, and the potential for self-governance, governance indeed independent of control by the Pennsylvania Proprietors, Parliament, and eventually, even the Crown. Franklin's conversance with economics and economic theory enabled him to begin to conceive how the ends of empire should directly relate to the lives of the people working the empire's lands and circulating their goods in its networks.

The "true Interest of Pennsylvania": Franklin, the Imperial Currency Crises, and "making Money plentiful"

Within the first ten years of his residence in Philadelphia, Franklin witnessed monetary constriction and its deleterious effects on merchants, laborers, trade, and land values. He recalled much later, when writing his memoir, that the year of his arrival was particularly difficult for Philadelphians: "I saw most of the Houses in Walnut street between Second and Front streets with Bills on their Doors, to be let; and many likewise in Chesnut Street, and other Streets; which made me think the Inhabitants of the City were one after another deserting it," he wrote.[1] His Boston experiences had taught him that the wealthier people might be uninterested in expanding paper currency circulation. But Franklin believed that with a greater amount of money available for exchange, land and property values along with food prices might balance out and stabilize, numbers of jobs would increase, and merchants' businesses could stabilize and perhaps increase.

Franklin arrived in Philadelphia in time to witness the region improve as a result of the city's currency acts of 1723, the effects of which were evident within his very first years there. These acts created bills of credit totaling £45,000, all but £7,500 of which was loaned to individuals at 5 percent interest and based in real estate mortgages (that is, the bills of credit were on land and property).[2] Whereas he had originally walked streets where houses were unoccupied, after the 1723 currency acts took effect, he became "persuaded that the first small Sum struck in 1723 had done much good, by increasing the Trade, Employment, and Number of Inhabitants in the Province, since I now saw all the old Houses inhabited, and many new ones building."[3] But the improvements of the early part of the 1720s could not be sustained, because the bills of credit began to stabilize the city's situation at about the time that they also started to "sink," or get paid off. Some people argued for another set of currency acts to improve the flow of money. Others, "Rich Men," Franklin said, disliked the idea of increasing monetary flow, because the wealthier people were making significant money on interest for monies lent, and usury would diminish if the wealth were more widely spread.

Benefiting from his Boston experiences and his reading of colonial writers such as John Wise and benefiting as well from his knowledge of then-current economic theories emerging in England, Franklin entered the debates on Philadelphia's crisis with his pamphlet *A Modest Enquiry into the Nature and Necessity of a Paper-Currency*, published in April 1729. His remarks on monetary exchange, fiscal independence, and the "true Interest of [his] Country" provide the foundational principles of Franklin's views on money, trade, land, and populations, all themes that reverberate throughout his writings on society and economy. A careful examination of his pamphlet shows the extent to which Franklin had taught himself by reading the leading economic theorists. The pamphlet also reveals Franklin's conversance with the central tenets of more recent economic theory that land and labor, working in productive collaboration, were essential for building a stable commercial community. Pennsylvania, with its abundance of land and diverse laboring population and with its relatively peaceable relations with the indigenous populations, had the possibility of becoming, in Franklin's assessment, the key North American imperial center for trade around the globe. In Pennsylvania Franklin sought to create a test case for his land and labor theories and his imperial trade designs. Franklin's pamphlet entered a stream of discourse—ranging from Thomas Mun (1751–1641) to Adam Smith (1723–1790) in Britain and to the Physiocrats in France—about specie, economic stability of states, and commercial activity.

The contents and tenets of Franklin's *Modest Enquiry* enable us to see how Franklin adapted and created innovations in existing economic discourse to the situation of Philadelphia.[4] The pamphlet has five major movements.[5] The first movement attempts to explain, in easy-to-grasp terms and by way of rudimentary analysis, the nature of money as a currency, the value of which (as specie and as interest, or what the money might purchase) will fluctuate according to supply and demand. *"There is a certain proportionate Quantity of Money requisite to carry on the Trade of a Country freely and currently,"* Franklin explained. Too much money would be *"of no Advantage in Trade,"* and too little, *"exceedingly detrimental to it."*[6] The task of all communities, then, was to determine the level of money necessary to keep the local and external economy fluid. Determining this quantity (and the value) of money is important, because the level of currency flow would affect land values and house rents, internal and external trade, agricultural and manufactory production, job stability (whether in agriculture, manufactures, or trade), population stability and diversity, and the rate of importation (and cost) of durable goods from other countries.

Franklin used plain language, avoiding the highly histrionic self-reflection found, for instance, in John Wise's pamphlets.[7] His goal was to explain principles then under discussion by the most current economic newspaper writers and pamphleteers. Franklin's attention to his audience's diverse linguistic and emotional needs reveals a conscious literary style he would use again and again. Employing a rhetorical method common to such economic literature aimed for the wider public, Franklin explained in this first part of his pamphlet the price-specie-flow mechanism sometimes still attributed to David Hume (1711–1776), whose formulation occurred much later. In fact, as economic historian Lars Magnusson has shown, Hume's views regarding the flow relationship (i.e., the flow or fluctuation according to availability) among prices, money, and supply, as explicated in his writings on trade, were earlier articulated by at least three economic theorists: Nicholas Barbon (1640–1698), in *A Discourse on Trade* (1690) and *A Discourse concerning the Coining the New Money Lighter* (1696); Jacob Vanderlint (d. 1740), in *Money Answers to All Things* (1734); and Isaac Gervaise (1680–1739), in *The System or Theory of the Trade of the World* (1720).[8] We know that Franklin was well read in the writings of William Petty (1623–1687) by the time he wrote this pamphlet, and close examination of Franklin's commentaries indicates his familiarity with many other writers on economic matters. He adapted their arguments to suit the current circumstances of Philadelphia.

Some economic writings were available in newspapers Franklin admired that were published in London. Sir Richard Steele's essay "Vincit Amor Patriæ," in No. 200 of the *Spectator* (1711), for instance, carried a useful commentary on "Political Arithmetick" (referencing Petty) to show the extent to which the sovereign ought to be interested in the riches of the people and the extent to which there was a direct correlation between the land's productivity and the available working population. Franklin recognized the importance of making sound economic decisions for Philadelphia. Franklin's explanations of economic concepts are valuable indicators of, first, his wide reading in economic literature, even at this relatively early stage of his public career, and, second, his pragmatic interest in applying his theoretical understanding toward a practical solution of the fiscal dilemma faced by Philadelphians specifically and Pennsylvanians generally.

Like Petty in his *Political Arithmetick* (written in the 1670s, published posthumously, 1690), Richard Steele emphasized that the love of one's country required one to wish for the best economic circumstances for all the people: he titled his remarks "Vincit Amor Patriæ" (i.e., "love of country conquers," or "love of country surpasses all things"). Just so, Franklin began his own pamphlet by referring to love of country, which became a common theme for him, but pushing further into the realm of self- and community "interest" rather than mere *amor patriæ*. Franklin opened by saying, "There is no Science, the Study of which is more useful and commendable than the Knowledge of the true Interest of one's Country." He emphasized in his conclusion, "I think it would be highly commendable in every one of us, more fully to bend our Minds to the Study of *What is the true Interest of* Pennsylvania."[9] The pamphlet falls into a group of economic writings that offer great leniency to the pursuit of self-interest. While some economists in his day suggested that the pursuit of self-interest was antithetical to the community's well-being, Franklin gave self-interest fair quarter by eliding any difference between self-interest and the interest of the community at large. The question that economic theorists faced was how the common good might be accomplished when self-interest was allowed fair play in the world. From Mandeville to Grotius to Pufendorf to Hume, the common connection between private vice and public benefits was standard fare among economists.[10]

Accepting the economic value of self-interest, Franklin's second movement in his pamphlet made observations about the potential opposition to such arguments as those he was making. Franklin's goal was to assure self-interested people that their situations would actually improve with an increased flow of currency. Franklin acknowledged that a cluster of well-to-do Philadelphians, those who enjoyed financial protections derived from their elite economic status, might make objections: (1) usurers, who loaned money out at a high rate, might object from a fear that increasing money flow, making money more plentiful, would decrease their ability to loan money out at high interest; (2) land speculators, who possessed large sums of money that they laid out in land, might object from fear that others would also be able to buy land, thus increasing land's prices; (3) lawyers and others who worked the courts might object because they could lose business from those who normally need legal assistance to create and to fight off writs and injunctions; and (4) those who depended on usurers, land speculators, and lawyers, "whether as holding Offices, as Tenants, or as Debtors," might object out of a sense of duty that they should "*appear* to be against a large Addition" of money due to their dependence on the elite.

Franklin continued by speaking to the local and metropolitan London interest politics. Those who loved trade and manufacturing would like his ideas, he argued, because trade and manufacturing would be significantly enhanced if the proposals were followed. Those who supported the Proprietor's interest ought to support the increase in money supply because an increase in money supply would raise land values, and "we all know the Proprietary has great Quantities to sell."[11] Franklin merged his economic lesson with interest politics in Britain. "A Plentiful Currency," he said, "will be so great a Cause of advancing this Province in Trade and Riches, and increasing the Number of its People; which, tho' it will not sensibly lessen the Inhabitants of Great Britain, will occasion a much greater Vent and Demand for their Commodities here." Britain needed British Americans as consumers. Increasing the money supply would increase demand for British goods, he argued. And as "the Crown is the more powerful for its Subjects increasing in Wealth and Number," Franklin said, "I cannot think it the Interest of England to oppose us in making as great a Sum of Paper Money here, as we, who are the best Judges of our own Necessities, find convenient."[12] Franklin deftly combined the imperial project (in favor of the Crown) with his own recommendations for local fiscal changes, all while indicating that local people knew best what they needed for a secure economy.

The availability of currency would bring people to Pennsylvania, Franklin argued. With more people in Pennsylvania, a greater number of products and services would be required. For merchants in England, Pennsylvania's enlarged population would mean English merchants could "Vent" their commodities to an increasingly greater demand. Franklin played on the point of self-interest, allowing that merchants ought to be self-interested. Instead of holding onto the older economic notion that a country benefits from an influx of bullion from foreign shores (called the "balance of trade" argument), Franklin was arguing for a newer theory usually called the "foreign-paid income" theory. Also called the "labor balance of trade" or the "export of work theory," this newer notion held that countries, to succeed, should export products with as much value added as possible and import as few of such products as possible. That way, specie would flow in as a result of labor and economic stimulation inside the country. Josiah Child (1630–1699), Charles Davenant (1656–1714), Nicholas Barbon, John Pollexfen (1636–1750), John Cary (d. 1720?)—all pointed out the significance of manufactures and the importance of employing all people, especially the poor, rather than worrying about where the income came from.[13] The foreign-paid incomes argument grew in importance, especially after the Treaty of Utrecht in 1713.[14] Those who propounded this theory supported the idea that selling commodities and manufactures to foreign countries was sound economic policy, because one's countrypeople would be employed. This theory of paying for labor is thus appropriately called the "foreign-paid income theory": production was possible as long as incomes were paid, and in these situations, foreigners paid the incomes when they purchased the value-added commodities produced by the laborers. Franklin was allowing for the self-interest of English merchants: why should merchants complain, he suggested, as long as their goods were "vented" to the colonies and paid for by those outside England. And he was participating in supporting the theory of foreign-paid incomes, suggesting that colonists were substituting as the "foreigners" in this instance.

The Crown would therein become more powerful, because subjects of the Crown would increase in wealth and number. Pointing out that while some in England might not like to see the colonies expand in population and self-sustenance, these people, whoever they were, might not have the purest motives. Franklin was hinting about the problems with the Proprietary and at court. "I should think the Government at Home [i.e., in England] had some Reasons for discouraging and impoverishing this Province, which we are not acquainted with," if the government did not approve such a plan as this one.[15]

With these remarks, we find Franklin's thinking was very clear about the extent to which economics and economic policies were political in the broadest sense. In some ways, Franklin's remarks presage the kind of definitional writing that Adam Smith would much later engage in, in the *Wealth of Nations* (1776). Franklin might not have called this pamphlet a foray into "political economy," yet it is clear that as early as 1729 Franklin understood quite well the relationship between the economic well-being of his colony and the sense of political well-being at "Home" in England. Over fifty years later, in the introduction to Book IV, "Of systems of political economy," Adam Smith defined the subject in *The Wealth of Nations* in this way: "Political economy, considered as a branch of the science of a statesman or legislator, proposes . . . first, to provide a plentiful revenue or subsistence for the people, or more properly to enable them to provide such a revenue of subsistence for themselves" and second, "to supply the state or commonwealth with a revenue sufficient for the public services. It proposes to enrich both the people and the sovereign," Smith wrote.[16] Franklin concurred with Smith's later expressed notion of "Political Economy"—that political economy should be a system of economic thinking wherein both the people and the sovereign would achieve positive outcomes. But he developed his own thinking much earlier, based on his own understanding of economic theory.[17]

Franklin's third movement in *A Modest Enquiry* directly related to his understanding of "political arithmetic" and his reading in Petty. In this central part of the pamphlet, Franklin defined money, explained how bills of credit worked, and argued for creating bills of credit with the security based in land—the argument that Petty perhaps most influentially expressed, although Franklin had found the argument in John Wise as well. To address Franklin's opening query to the section, "*Whether a large Addition to our Paper Currency will not made it sink in Value very much*," the pamphlet offered some remarks on "the Nature and Value of Money in general." "Providence," Franklin said, has created the world in such a way that, first, different countries and even different parts of the same country have peculiar productions (products that come solely from that locale), and second, different men have different abilities and skills ("genius's") in a variety of "Arts and Manufactures." So "Commerce," defined as "the Exchange of one Commodity or Manufacture for another," is "highly convenient and beneficial to Mankind." Money is needed to advance the possibilities of commerce, Franklin concluded, because the "immediate exchange of commodities" between willing parties is "tedious" and has "inconveniences." Thus, "Money, properly called a *Medium of Exchange*," has been found useful: "through or by its Means Labour is exchanged for Labour, or one Commodity for another."[18] Here Franklin clearly adumbrated the view of money that was the premise of many economists' tracts: money assists in the exchange of both goods and services, and, given that different countries produce different goods and services and that even within the same country, different goods and services are available, money is needed to make exchange convenient. Money assists commerce, in other words, and commerce is "beneficial to mankind." The pamphlet clarified central economic tenets of his era in a language and style attentive to the needs of a wide swath of readers. The pamphlet, in fact, functions as an educational tract on money, and it was an educational project just as important as the Junto and library company.

That commerce had a civilizing function was central to some of the newer writings, such as those by David Hume and Adam Smith, on trade and civilization that Franklin would come to know much later. Yet even Thomas Mun (1571–1641), among the early theorists, pointed out that commerce with strangers assisted in the creation of "humane policy."[19] With dismay, Mun acknowledged the accomplishments of the Dutch people who, though they had little land, had made a success of themselves in "purchas[ing] great wealth and strength by their industrious commerce with strangers." Jealous of the Dutch success, Mun remarked about "how wonderfully . . . they [i.e., the Dutch] improved in all humane policy."[20] And Josiah Child commented that trade, along with increased communication, would assist in cultivating "the unsociable Tempers of many barbarous People."[21] Earlier than Franklin—and thus earlier than either Hume or Smith—these writers had pointed out the extent to which commerce had a civilizing function. Franklin seems to have imbibed this thinking, as evidenced by his expression that "Commerce" was "beneficial to Mankind." Franklin's assertions in this area reveal his appreciation of the fundamental need to establish economic principles along the newer premises associated with commercial societies.

Franklin's interest in the diversity of the land's productivity and the diversity of labor (from agriculture to the "handicrafts" to merchant business) reflects common concerns of the earliest economic discourse, beginning as early as the 1640s. Lewes Roberts (1596–1641) and Henry Robinson (c. 1604–c. 1664) both argued, as Lars Magnusson has explained, that "the British economy must become more diversified in order to become less economically vulnerable" to the success of Britain's neighbors.[22] Between the 1650s and 1720s, writers continually pointed out that product diversity, in terms of both commodities and manufactures, would help the British economy remain stable. Samuel Fortrey (1622–1681) and John Houghton (fl. 1670–90) in the 1670s pointed out that if trade were free, there would be a more effective allocation of resources. Pointing to the diversity of productive capacity of the land, England could "furnish all our neighbours" with horses, sheep, and bullocks and instead import corn (rather than growing it).[23] This resource allocation thesis, as economic historian Marian Bowley called it,[24] is a formulation that Franklin perhaps more than most in his generation saw as a great potential for Britain, if it would seek to diversify its landholdings in Britain and all of its colonies and to deregulate all trade.

The diversity of kinds of money interested Franklin, too, as he continued in the third movement of his pamphlet to explain that men have identified as money whatever it is they have chosen to be their common commodity—"Gold, Silver, Copper, or Tobacco"—as the means of exchange. His insertion of "Tobacco" into the list is a wonderful example of the ways Franklin inserted American products into his otherwise British- and European-oriented discussions. Historically, he pointed out, "those Parts of the World which are engaged in Commerce, have fixed upon Gold and Silver as the chief and most proper Metals for this Medium," "they being in themselves valuable Metals for their Fineness, Beauty, and Scarcity." But these metals have no permanent value; their value works out to be whatever arises from the flow of supply and demand. It is better, Franklin concluded, "to fix upon Something else, more proper to be made a *Measure of Values*." He asserted, "This I take to be *Labour*."[25]

This is the famous labor theory of value. As Franklin explained this economic theory, Franklin (following Petty) compared the getting of silver in a mine to the raising of a corn crop and bringing it in.[26] He concluded, after employing the example from Petty, "Thus the Riches of a Country are to be valued by the Quantity of Labour its Inhabitants are able to purchase, and not by the Quantity of Silver and Gold they possess; which will purchase more or less Labour, and therefore is more or less valuable, as is said before, according to its Scarcity or Plenty." Franklin pointed out that, in European states, silver and gold will always operate to inflate and deflate markets according to their scarcity or plenty, at any given time. Franklin thus entered the specie flow debates while drawing attention to the obvious difference for Britain if Britain would take into account the potential value of Pennsylvanians' potential contributions to trade and thus to the Crown.

Franklin's illustration features his own central themes of intercolonial cooperation and imperial expansion rather than the mere imperial (and mercantilist) goal of regulating all manufactures so that all industry will be in England. There being more land in North America, making labor the standard of value might mean more people would come to Pennsylvania rather than to England. Franklin insisted that the economic stability and strength of the Pennsylvania colony would supplement Britain's strength, not compete with it. Thus, by making the comparative standard one of labor rather than metals, Britain would be in a better position than its European rivals, because of the strength and productivity of Britain's colonial holdings and the presence of the colonial trade.

Most striking about Franklin's pamphlet is its extended conversation with the economists he was reading. Again following some of the examples Petty and John Wise had offered, Franklin turned his discussion to bills of credit. In taking major trading cities (Hamburg, Amsterdam, London,

Venice) into his calculus, Franklin argued that the banks in these cities that issued bills of credit essentially stabilized their trading markets. Like Petty, Franklin argued that for reasons of their compactness, relative ease and safety of carriage (their light weight), and for other reasons, bills of credit are preferable, in trading cities, to the use of money. In the context of an argument simply about the use of paper currency, Franklin seems to spend an inordinate amount of time explaining how bills of credit would assist international markets. But he had to educate Philadelphians and Londoners about the growing importance of Philadelphia to Britain. Most remarkable is that Franklin could foresee Pennsylvania's potential to enter into the world markets so as to become as important as, say, London or Hamburg. He was attempting to show all Philadelphia and London—and especially the merchants and lenders there—that the colony could be a player on the world's economic stage.

Franklin explained the workings of international markets and the international banking system based in bills of credit by showing the important role of trade in both internal and external markets. Calling banks "the general Cashiers of all Gentlemen, Merchants and great Traders in and about" the major cities of London, Hamburg, Venice, and Amsterdam, Franklin illustrated how the system worked: "they deposite their Money, and may take out Bills to the Value, for which they can be certain to have Money again at the Bank at any Time: This gives the Bills a Credit." Bills of credit, so exchanged, "are never less valuable than Money, and in Venice and Amsterdam they are generally worth more." Further, Franklin said, "the Bankers always reserving Money in hand to answer more than the common Run of Demands (and some People constantly putting in while others are taking out)" are in a position to "lend large Sums, on good Security, to the Government or others, for a reasonable Interest, by which they are paid for their Care and Trouble." Without this secondary use for the money laid into the banking system via bills of credit, Franklin concluded, "the Money which otherwise would have lain dead in their Hands, is made to circulate again," making money plentiful. "Thus the Running Cash of the Nation is as it were doubled," which "is an exceeding great Advantage to a Trading Country, that is not over-stock'd with Gold and Silver."[27] Franklin was arguing that trading became easier in such trading cities: bills of credit brought both ease of use and a more secure medium for trade than gold or silver, which can fluctuate widely in value. Franklin was also pointing out that if the larger business of a trading country were taken up in bills of credit, then common money would be available for the day-to-day needs of the community.

Franklin here engaged some of the current theoretical debates about money. During most of the seventeenth century, British economists had argued about how much money, as bullion, was essential to the well-being of the country. Basing their concern on what they called the "balance of trade," most writers in this vein expressed distinct concern about a monetary imbalance in gold and silver, an imbalance occurring to England's detriment. By the end of the seventeenth century, the debates began to center on trade, and the argument shifted from an obsessive concern about an imbalance in the metals in Britain's coffers to one based in Britain's trade. If Britain could increase its exports, the argument went, then the money flow to Britain would increase. Thus, several writers argued in favor of a balance of trade (meaning that Britain ought to be seeking to have more trade than, say, France and Spain) rather than arguing obsessively about having money available to the Crown and commonwealth. In other words, trade fueled wealth, so exports and imports rather than amassed specie ought to be favored.

This was a "nation" argument that Franklin adapted to a commercial argument. Franklin was writing at the moment of transformation in economic thinking, when the defensive postures of the older mercantilists regarding trade were being challenged by newer commercial theories, or what came to be called "laissez-faire" economics. Franklin was inserting himself into the midst of this transformation and attempting to show how Philadelphia was central to the empire's economic well-being. He was addressing those who believed in the quantity theory of money; these people believed that money needed to remain in a country rather than be sent out of it in payments for imports. Franklin argued that if Philadelphia and the Pennsylvania colony could participate in an international monetary credit system like the great trading cities he mentioned, Philadelphia's economy would stabilize, Philadelphia's merchant trade would improve, and overall wealth would increase. He used this opportunity to teach his readers that bills of credit existed between countries. In an effort to make this sound like a real possibility for Philadelphians, he concluded that "so here, in some of the neighboring Provinces [namely, in New England], we engage our Land" by using land as the security for bills of credit.[28] Given the great extent of land available, given the potential for an increasing population in Pennsylvania, and given that "Trade" is "nothing else but the Exchange of Labour for Labour," then "the Value of all Things" is "most justly measured by Labour," assuming that there is a constant value in a day's labor, whereas the value of money fluctuates.

The labor theory of value was relatively common at the time. It can be found in Petty and John Wise, but it was also available in the writings of Josiah Child and a few others earlier than Petty.[29] Franklin could apply the theory to Pennsylvania because of the immense tracts of land claimed by the colony. In Franklin's view, availability of land was central. Land could be productive, he argued, so it would be best to base currency in land rather than in accumulated bullion. Franklin attempted to explain this in terms appropriate to the discourse taking place in England, but for his Philadelphia audience, he wrote: "It is certain that the Value of Money has been continually sinking in England for several Ages past," "because it has been continually increasing in Quantity. But if Bills could be taken out of a Bank in Europe on a Land Security, it is probable the Value of such Bills would be more certain and steady, because the Number of Inhabitants continue to be near the same in those Countries from Age to Age." This led him to his remarkable conclusion: "For as Bills issued upon Money Security are Money, so Bills issued upon Land, are in Effect *Coined Land*."[30] Franklin pushed this idea of basing bills on land because the population in Pennsylvania kept increasing "and will be further increased" by the help of an increase of currency (paper money), and "land in consequence is continually rising." He argued that "in case no Bills are emitted but what are upon Land Security," then, so long as any of the acts for bills of credit were duly executed and enforced, "it is absolutely impossible such Bills should ever sink below their first Value, or below the Value of the Land on which they are founded."[31]

Franklin's recognition of land's importance is worth underscoring. His point about land's productivity is one he would argue repeatedly, so much so that the French Physiocrats with whom he later came in contact would borrow and extend upon Franklin's views of land in North America. Franklin's contribution to the debate in the 1720s was his focus on the productive uses to which land could be put, placing land's productivity as the real source of national wealth, with paper money as currency being the key means by which land resources could be tapped. Paper money facilitated land's productivity. Thus, bills of credit based on land would always retain or increase their value, but never fall short of their original value. Also worth underscoring here is Franklin's effort to position Philadelphia as the central British North American trading metropolis having the potential of a Hamburg, London, or Amsterdam. With navigation acts that would support rather than hinder colonial productivity, Philadelphia could be the jewel in England's crown.

In a fourth part of his pamphlet, Franklin worked out further points about money, its intrinsic and extrinsic worth, and interest, or levels of "usury," as interest was frequently called in the economic literature. Crucial to the situation in Pennsylvania was determining the level of interest that would resolve the current crisis in currency without leading to inflation or deflation, the point made in the opening of the pamphlet. Franklin argued that money had both intrinsic value, as coinage or bullion, and extrinsic value, as it was a currency used in exchange. Its use in exchange caused its value to rise and fall. Franklin explained it this way: "in order to make a true Estimate of the Value of Money, we must distinguish between Money as it is Bullion, which is Merchandize, and as by being coin'd it is made a Currency: For its Value as a Merchandize, and its Value as a Currency, are two distinct Things; and each may possibly rise and fall in some Degree independent of the other." In both instances, whether speaking of quantity of money as bullion (intrinsic worth) or speaking of money used as currency, the value of money would rise and fall. "Thus," Franklin explained, "if the Quantity of Bullion increases in a Country, it will proportionably decrease in Value; but if at the same Time the Quantity of current Coin should decrease, (supposing Payments may not be made in Bullion) what Coin there is will rise in Value as a Currency, i.e. People will give more Labour in Manufactures for a certain Sum of ready Money."[32] Franklin here articulated a key point against the quantity theory of money: having money for money's (intrinsic) sake was less useful than having of money to serve a community. He made this point mostly to get back to his original argument, which essentially addressed the question of developing the optimum level of interest in relation to the amount of paper currency to be created. Paper currency would have the same sets of values: if paper currency were founded on land, it would have a value as land, but it would also have an additional value as currency. He added that currency has an additional value in terms of the time and effort it saves the person who employs it as a means of exchange: "*Money, as a Currency, has an Additional Value by so much Time and Labour as it saves in the Exchange of Commodities.*" That is, "If, as a Currency, it saves one Fourth Part of the Time and Labour of a Country; it has, on that Account, one Fourth added to its original Value."[33]

The twofold nature of the value of paper currency, Franklin argued, meant that it was very important to determine the level of interest, what he called the "natural standard of Usury" that could be expected from paper currency based upon land as security.[34] This important step—allowing that self-interested individuals would want to reap some kind of benefit from lending their money—clarified Franklin's understanding that the only way Pennsylvanians would accept an additional set of paper currency acts would be if some, especially those who were in a position to reject the acts, could make money from them. He also allowed for consideration of the level of risk on loans of money: "where the Security is undoubted, at least the Rent of so much Land as the Money lent will buy" is appropriate, but allowing for an additional "ensurance," just in case the fiscal situation should change, would be important. "On such Accounts," he allowed, "it is no wonder if People ask a greater Interest for their Money than the natural Interest; and what is above is to be look'd upon as a kind of *Praemium* for the Ensurance of those Uncertainties, as they are greater or less." Thus allowing for a level of self-interest in his argument, Franklin could conclude, "Now it is certainly the Advantage of a Country to make Interest as low as possible, . . . and this can be done no other way than by making Money plentiful."[35] He thought that, taking everything into consideration, a 4 percent interest would be sufficient to keep commerce moving.[36]

Franklin's arguments employ ideas from the leading economic theorists of his era. He especially admired William Petty's *A Treatise of Taxes and Contributions* (1662).[37] Petty's fifth chapter of his treatise, "Of Usury," clarified that the economic system should allow people to seek emolument for the risks or inconveniences they absorbed: "Wherefore when a man giveth out his money upon condition that he may not demand it back until a certain time to come, whatsoever his own necessities shall be in the mean time, he certainly may take a compensation for this inconvenience which he admits against himself: And this allowance is that we commonly call Usury." Like Petty, Franklin embraced the newer seventeenth-century ethic that removed the opprobrium from those who engaged in lending money at interest. From the Middle Ages through the sixteenth century, those who engaged in usury were considered morally suspect, because they were taking advantage of the poor and others for their own personal gain.[38] By the seventeenth century, the idea of personal gain as a result of the loaning of money at interest was less frequently chastised. Early economic theorists such as Thomas Mun and Edward Misselden (1608–1654) helped inaugurate the early modern sensibility regarding the lending of money to assist individuals while assisting the commonwealth.

As this is a view Franklin embraced wholeheartedly, it is likely that he gained his ideas not from Petty alone but from some of the other economic theorists he was reading, many of whose books he owned. For instance, Thomas Mun reflected on usury in *England's Treasure by Forraign Trade* (1664): "Let us then begin with Usury, which if it might be turned into Charity, and that they who are Rich would lend to the poor freely; it were a work pleasing to Almighty God, and profitable to the Commonwealth." By lending money, Mun had argued, "the rich giveth opportunity presently to the *younger & poorer* Merchants to rise in the world, and to enlarge their dealings; to the performance whereof, if they want means of their own, they may, and do, take it up as interest." Thus, Mun said, "Our money lies not dead, it is still traded." As we have seen, this idea appealed to Franklin. "How many Merchants, and Shop-Keepers have begun with little or nothing of their own," Mun wrote, "and yet are grown very rich by trading with other men's money?"[39] These are Franklin's views precisely. "One mans necessity becomes another mans opportunity," Mun said,[40] and Franklin agreed. This then-modern conception of the economy as functioning apart from the moral world of right and wrong naturalizes usury as simply a means by which forces might be balanced in a market economy.[41] Franklin was participating in the debates to improve conditions within the Pennsylvania colony, but he was also invested in the idea that Philadelphia could be a central trading city for the empire. The network he imperially imagined would place Philadelphia (of all places outside London in the British Empire) on the map of a global exchange network.

Franklin concluded this section by turning to potential objections to the rates of interest proposed. If rates were low and terms easy, then too many people might wish to take out bills of credit to an extent that could not be supported by the current trade in goods, labor, and land. No one would want to sell his land for less than what he bought it for, Franklin argued, so people would be careful about borrowing. His argument is based in the idea of economic flow: the proportion of borrowing, and the available land, would eventually—after initial fluctuation—work in flow with one another. Others might object to a large addition to the currency: with a large addition, the people of the province would increase. If the increased population all engaged in husbandry, then the value of products brought to market (his example is flour) would decrease from that increased productivity. The argument is based in the market flow of supply and demand. "We can never have too many People (nor too much Money)," he said, because "when one Branch of Trade or Business is overstocked with Hands, there are the more to spare to be employed in another. So if raising Wheat proves dull, more may (if there is Money to support and carry on new Manufactures) proceed to the raising and manufacturing of *Hemp, Silk, Iron*, and many other Things the Country is very capable of, for which we only want People to work, and Money to pay them with."[42]

These issues—the proportional relationship of the population to the land's productivity, the proportional relationship between the flow of money and trade's stability and increase, the desirability of keeping people laboring (attending to primary wants) rather than in luxury (attending to artificial needs)—all of these themes became Franklin's trademark concerns. His argument offers two strategies for social and economic improvement. First, currency (money) was needed, so that the population could increase. Second, a diverse population, once it was dispersed widely, would bring diversity of laborers and thus their crafts, which would foster a diversity of productions. These positions are not new with Franklin, but they are relatively new to the colonies, and they represent the growing recognition of the potential productivity of the American colonies compared to Britain's other imperial lands, particularly Ireland (which preoccupied Franklin) and Scotland.

Franklin repeatedly and explicitly insisted that Pennsylvania was part of Britain's "trading" network. He used the contraction of money in Pennsylvania to point out the extent to which older economic policies based in older economic theory and in agendas of colonization like those in the West Indies undermined any empire attempting to create a global reputation and nationalized wealth: "Upon the Whole it may be observed, That it is the highest Interest of a Trading Country in general to make Money plentiful; and that it can be a Disadvantage to none that have honest Designs."[43] Whereas the people in Ireland were suffering from want and neglect, the people in Pennsylvania (and the other mainland colonies) only needed an opportunity to show their ability to assist the British commonwealth and Crown, and that opportunity lay in another paper currency act. This example provides a fascinating instance of Franklin's insights not only about the existing economic (really, macroeconomic) problems faced by the British Empire's desire to expand at a time of fiscal contraction but also about the potential for future British global power if Crown and Parliament would relinquish the trade and navigation policies that restricted the colonists' productivity and their consumption. Trade and navigation acts placed colonies into secondary and tributary roles rather than equal, contributing roles. As equal partners, the colonies could stimulate collaborative, globalized growth for the empire.

At this stage of his argument, Franklin again expressed a recognition of the importance of self-interest. He addressed the needs of lenders, merchants, the Crown, and the Proprietor one last time. An increase in the money supply would not hurt usurers, he argued, because usurers would simply have more money to lend. And an addition to the money supply would not hurt merchants who might hold outstanding debts, because a greater availability of money would enable people to pay off their debts sooner rather than leave merchants without merchandise. Indeed, everyone would see the importance of introducing additional paper currency, because the paper currency addition would *serve* Great Britain *and* the Proprietor:

> It cannot hurt the Interest of Great Britain, as has been shewn; and it will greatly advance the Interest of the Proprietor. It will be an Advantage to every industrious Tradesman, &c. because his Business will be carried on more freely, and Trade be universally enlivened by it. And as more Business in all Manufactures will be done, by so much as the Labour and Time spent in Exchange is saved, the Country in general will grow so much the richer.[44]

Working to differentiate the situation in Pennsylvania from the situation in New England and South Carolina, Franklin concluded that objections based on the relative failures of New England and South Carolina were unjust, because neither place emitted its currency with such "Prudence" or "such good Security as ours is." Besides, Franklin chauvinistically implied, Pennsylvania was better situated as a prospective imperial trade center than either New England (hampered by a more limited range of products) or South Carolina (hampered in its production by a plantation and slave-driven economy that would prevent freeholds and thus the range of produce that might otherwise emerge).

Franklin called for conversation about his ideas. He was especially interested in hearing from those whose opinions might be contrary to his, because he hoped for debate in print, before any voting would occur: "I think it would be highly commendable in every one of us, more fully to bend our Minds to the Study of *What is the true Interest of* Pennsylvania," he wrote. He expressed a concern not simply that it would be important for Pennsylvanians "to reason pertinently with one another; but, if Occasion requires, to transmit Home [i.e., to England] such clear Representations, as must inevitably convince our Superiors of the Reasonableness and Integrity of our Designs."[45] The passage is remarkable for a number of reasons. The call for open debate reveals Franklin's view of the public uses to which print might be put. "I sincerely desire to be acquainted with the Truth," Franklin wrote, "and on that Account shall think my self obliged to any one, who will take the Pains to shew me, or the Publick, where I am mistaken in my Conclusions." An open exchange of ideas about economic matters would enable Pennsylvanians to recognize that they ought to have an investment in the fiscal decisions being made. Not only did Pennsylvanians have a "true Interest," but their interest needed to be explained to those back in England, so that the colonial administration, Crown, and Proprietary would understand Pennsylvanians' (arguably) transparent goal of having a paper currency based in "Reasonableness" to emphasize the "Integrity" of the people. His rhetorical emphasis upon integrity, reasonableness, and transparency would become his trademarks in economic and political propaganda in years to come.

In examining Franklin's *A Modest Enquiry into the Nature and Necessity of a Paper-Currency*, we can begin to trace Franklin's understanding and application of the ideas of his era's key economic theorists. We also witness his inventive, pragmatic applications of such theory. Franklin's paper currency pamphlet reveals that he was participating in the more modern discourse of economics and trade common for the generation of the 1690s rather than the older economic theory of the sixteenth century. Earlier economists—Josiah Child and William Petty perhaps most notably—had tended to blame the poor for their condition, an idea that carried over well into the eighteenth century. For instance, John Cary had argued—in *An Essay, towards Regulating the Trade, and Employing the Poor, of this Kingdom* (London, 1717)—that he was "endeavour[ing] to shew, how the Habit of Laziness and Beggary first crept in amongst us, how it may be prevented from spreading further, how Imployments may be provided for such as are willing to Work, and a Force put upon those who are able but Idle."[46] Franklin disagreed with such disparaging views of the poor.

Indeed, Franklin's pamphlet's opening salvo strove to separate its author from those economists who belittled the poor for their condition. Franklin pointed out how unfair it was to blame the poorest workers for buying luxuries when superfluous goods were all that was available for them to be paid with, in the absence of currency. "Working Men and their Families," he wrote, "are . . . induced to be more profuse and extravagant in fine Apparel and the like, than they would be if they were obliged to pay ready Money for such Things after they had earn'd and received it, or if such Goods were not imposed upon them, of which they can make no other Use." He admonished those who offered such goods to poor laborers: "how unreasonable would it be, if some of those very Men who *have been a Means* of thus forcing People into unnecessary Expence, should be the first and most earnest in accusing them of *Pride and Prodigality*." And he concluded, chiding the wealthy who lacked compassion for others, that "tho' this extraordinary Consumption of Foreign Commodities may be a Profit to particular Men, yet the Country in general grows poorer by it apace."[47] Rather than focusing on obligations to the poor or on blaming impoverished people for their own condition, Franklin focused on training and employing all people. It is a position that forms the core of his economic theory.

Franklin's discussion of the science of trade (that trade works like a machine or a natural entity) was entirely modern, in contrast to the older (sixteenth- and early seventeenth-century) idea regarding economic stature as representing his countrymen's moral stature (the rich were creditable, the poor, debased). For Franklin, bills of credit should be based in land, a view held by both Wise and Petty. He spoke of the intrinsic and extrinsic worth of money, as did John Locke (1632–1704). He considered the idea of foreign-paid incomes to be feasible. And he assumed the presence of economic elasticity, creating arguments that revealed his belief in a specie-flow, supply-demand mechanism. His aim was to show the impact of trade on local agriculture, construction, and merchant activities and to speak as well to the positive imperial consequences when a local situation (the Pennsylvania colony) could be improved and brought online within a global network (the empire's trade).

Franklin was also preoccupied with the more modern notion that a country's wealth resided in its lands, not simply the mineral wealth that could be wrested therefrom but the potential productive wealth that came from the laborer's hand, whether in agriculture, manufacturing, or commerce. That is, to Franklin (as to some others interested in securing fiscal stability), a country's real wealth resided in its land and its free (even if indentured) laborers. In *A Plan of the English Commerce* (1728), Daniel Defoe had remarked, for instance, that "the Funds of Trade in any Nation, and upon which the Commerce that is rais'd . . . [as] the Trade of the Nation," rely on two areas: "The Produce of the Soil, and The Labor of the People." A nation's successful trade depended upon the extent to which the land was productive and the people involved in labor.[48] Defoe was building on the previous generation's assessments, as Franklin would. In 1691, Dudley North (whom Franklin read) had pointed out in his *Discourses on Trade* that some of those who engage in labor "are more provident, others more profuse; some by their Industry and Judgment raise more Fruits from the Earth, than they consume in supplying their own occasions; and then the surplus remains with them, and is Property or Riches." Arguing against the tendency to hoard specie, North pointed out that in the land and in its laborers resided a country's wealth. North argued, as Defoe and Franklin later would, that surplus from the land resulted from provident labor, making the lands and the laborers the greatest source of wealth of the nation.[49]

While a cluster of writers around the turn into the eighteenth century agreed that land and labor ought to be the key factors in determining a nation's wealth and its potential for economic stability, there was considerably less agreement as to whether land or labor should be considered the more important, when factoring productive potential.[50] Several writers supported the importance of agriculture and manufacture, and they frequently addressed the means by which the natural riches of the kingdom should be improved. London merchant Lewes Roberts, in *Treasure of Traffike* (1641), for instance, had argued that land that lay wasted and unproductive caused money to be unavailable to the commonwealth. Franklin would have agreed. Mercantilist discussions generally tended to take a form similar to Roberts's arguments. The "riches of the earth" were, Roberts attested, "the fountaine and mother of all the riches and abundance of the world." Landlords and those who worked the earth had obligations that they were not meeting, in Roberts's view. "Some of them through Ignorance, some by negligence, and too many by bad husbandry," he wrote, "content themselves with the yearely rents thereof, or at most with the Revenues, that their predecessors drew therefrom before them." He complained that these landlords were "loath to take the paines, either by industry, improvement or care, to increase those their demesnes and estates, either by planting, cleansing, or manuring a waste or barren piece of ground, or by drayning a marshy bogge, or the like, and thus to inrich themselves by a faire advancement of their own."[51] Roberts was excoriating those, such as manor lords in Ireland, who simply collected rents on their lands, left laborers in poverty, depleted soils, and thus wasted precious land rather than assisted economic and agricultural progress. Such a critique could easily be extended to Pennsylvania's absent Proprietors, Franklin realized.

Pennsylvania, Ireland, and the Traffic of Empire

An examination of the literature of the era indicates economists' and politicians' preoccupation with what was happening in Ireland. Franklin was reading this literature, including William Petty's *Political Anatomy of Ireland* (written in 1672, published 1691). The attraction to the study of Irish issues related to the way nonresident landlords in Ireland handled the management of lands there but also to how significantly British policies regarding Ireland differed from those related to Scotland. Because economic theory often addressed Ireland and because concerns about land use predominate that literature, it behooves us to consider, before concluding discussion of Franklin's earliest economic theories, the literature on Ireland that Franklin knew even this early in his career. Excoriation over the misuse of land would become Franklin's theme with regard to the lands held by the Proprietors, who were neither using the good lands held in trust nor paying taxes on the lands. The lands were being wasted. Given Franklin's reading in the older economic tracts that frequently used Ireland as a negative but potentially positive example and given his understanding of the taxation and defense quandary into which Pennsylvania had fallen as a result of extensive lands held in the Proprietary interest, we should take a moment to examine the situation faced in Ireland and Franklin's concerns about potential problems in Pennsylvania arising from a burgeoning influx of Irish immigrants.

The development of plantations in Ireland during the sixteenth and seventeenth centuries had left Ireland's society and economy unstable. Combined with obvious religious turmoil (Protestant ascendants, native Catholics, recent immigrants) and cultural stratification (Britons and Anglo-Irish people over Gaelics and other native and immigrant populations), the social and economic disparity led to distinct poverty for a majority of the people in Ireland. Ireland's external trade was driven by a plantation system favoring absentee Anglo-Irish landlords who, along with their subletting agents, personally benefited from an extractive system that left significant portions of Ireland deforested, with mineral veins (for iron, chiefly) emptied and potential agricultural areas denuded. Agricultural harvests were created largely for export, with the factoring of beef and pork into vendible meats or related subsidiary industries (e.g., butter- and cheese-making, salting, tanning, wool production, spinning, and so forth), leaving large areas without reasonable dietary sustenance for the laboring poor. Several areas (though by no means all) of eastern Ireland were enclosed. Historian J. H. Plumb pointed out long ago that "three quarters of Irish land belonged to Englishmen or to Anglo-Irish Protestant families. By the middle of the century three quarters of a million pounds in rent was leaving Ireland each year for the pockets of the absentee landlords living in England." Wool, a staple in the Irish economy, could be exported only to England. Its manufacture inside Ireland was illegal. Further, Ireland could not trade directly with the American colonies, despite the fact that the Irish economy (based in the manufacture of linen) depended on the American colonies, which supplied the flax seed and potash for bleaching linen. "What little prosperity Ireland enjoyed," Plumb concluded, "hardly touched the vast majority of the peasantry, who lived in want and in fear of starvation. Thousands shipped themselves to the [American] plantations on terms little better than slavery, which were preferable to the slow starvation at home."[52] Plumb's account seems melodramatic, but it is confirmed by contemporaneous accounts.

Some had, for nearly a century, argued for the importance of keeping Ireland impoverished for fear of a general uprising among the indigenous, displaced Catholics. Such arguments led to continued scheming to get Protestant Scots to continue to settle Ireland. Concerned that a successful uprising on the part of the majority Catholics would return a Catholic Stuart to the English throne, the government employed economic repression to contain Irish rebellion. Fear-mongering over an Irish Catholic uprising lasted through the seventeenth century and made a convenient means by which Anglo-Irish landholders could continue to seek preferment from England, whether seeking enclosures for their land or accommodation in trade. William Petty, among others, was troubled by inequities in Ireland. In his *Political Anatomy of Ireland*, Petty wrote, "The British protestants and church have three fourths of all the lands; five sixths of all the housing; nine tenths of all the housing in walled towns and places of strength, two thirds of the foreign trade. That 6 of 8 of all the Irish live in a brutish, nasty condition, as in cabins, with neither chimney, door, stairs, nor window, feed chiefly upon milk and potatoes, whereby their spirits are not disposed for war."[53] The situation changed very little—indeed, perhaps it worsened—by the first quarter of the eighteenth century.

Similarly, Jonathan Swift, whose satire Franklin admired, famously lamented the condition of Ireland in a number of tracts. Swift's *A Short View of the State of Ireland* (1727) took a strong position about Ireland's poverty, illustrating the preposterousness of some of the older English economists' undemonstrated assertions that part of the problem in the balance of trade (i.e., the absence of specie) was that the settlements of Ireland, Scotland, and East India caused money to flow from England to these colonies rather than vice versa.[54] This argument, which had emerged in the economic debates in the 1620s, continued through the seventeenth century. Their prevalence in the early eighteenth century is unmistakable, given Swift's excoriation of English people who would assume Irish people had significant money. Swift's pamphlet works out its own economic theory explaining the means by which a kingdom would thrive. Swift's list could be Franklin's, in Franklin's writings about Philadelphia. The "cause(s)" of a "kingdom's thriving," Swift asserted, were the following: the "fruitfulness of the soil," so that inhabitants can "produce the necessaries and conveniences of life" for themselves and for export; "the industry of the people, in working up all their native commodities to the last degree of manufacture"; "safe ports and havens, to carry out their own [manufactured] goods . . . and bring in those of others as little manufactured, as the nature of mutual commerce will allow"; the ability to "export and import . . . goods in vessels of their own timber, made in their own country"; "the privilege of a free trade in all foreign countries which will permit them, except those who are in war with their own prince or state"; the right of people, as "a free people," to be "governed only by laws made with their own consent"; the "improvement of land, encouragement of agriculture, and thereby [the] increasing the number of their people[,] without which any country . . . must continue poor"; "the residence of the prince, or chief administrator of the civil power"; "the concourse of foreigners, for education, curiosity, or pleasure, or as to a general mart of trade"; the disposal of "all offices of honour, profit, or trust, only to the natives; or at least with very few exceptions, where strangers have long inhabited the country, and are supposed to understand and regard the interests of it as their own"; the spending of "the rents of land and profits of employment . . . in the country which produced them, and not in another"; "the public revenues being all spent and employed at home, except on the occasions of a foreign war"; "after the manner of all civilized nations," the freedom of people, "unless they find it for their own interest or conveniency, to receive . . . moneys," only "of their own coinage by a public mint"; the favoring of "a disposition of the people of a country to wear their own manufactures, and import as few incitements to luxury, either in clothes, furniture, food, or drink, as they possibly can live conveniently without."[55] Swift's points underscore the extent to which self-rule was lacking in Ireland, forcing depressed circumstances for the majority of the people. The kinds of arguments Swift was making about Ireland just as easily applied to Pennsylvania—point for point—and to the other American colonies. Franklin showed this in his own economic tract.

Swift complained about "the miserable dress, and diet, and dwelling of the people. The general desolation in most parts of the Kingdom. The old seats of the nobility and gentry all in ruins, and no new ones in their stead. The families of farmers who pay great rents, living in filth and nastiness upon butter-milk and potatoes, without a shoe or stocking to their feet, or a house so convenient as an English hog-sty to receive them."[56] Swift lamented that land rents by Irish or Anglo-Irish laborers were not even put back into service in Ireland but were spent in England. "One third part of the rents of Ireland is spent in England, which with the profit of employments, pensions, appeals, journeys of pleasure or health, education at the Inns of Court, and both Universities, remittances at pleasure, the pay of all superior officers in the army and other incidents, will amount to a full half of the income of the whole Kingdom, all clear profit to England."[57] Swift's complaints bear witness to the inequities existing in Ireland. The conditions of Ireland were poor, with an English or Anglo-Irish cluster of well-to-do landholders retaining the majority and best of eastern lands and with Irish people (including Irish Catholics, immigrants from Europe, and many laboring Protestants) landless, disfranchised, and living in significant poverty.

Ireland's situation was of intense interest to Franklin not simply because of his reading about the Irish people but because of his awareness that the situation with the Proprietary in Pennsylvania was beginning to look much like that of the landed interest of the English and Anglo-Irish in Ireland. Many of the complaints that Swift made about Ireland match several points Franklin ended up making about the Proprietors' treatment of Pennsylvania and Britain's of the American colonies. Like Swift, Franklin argued in his *Modest Enquiry* several similar points: that Pennsylvania's land was good and deserved to be tilled by people who could benefit from it by working it and selling their surplus; that an economic system sufficient to the needs of the colony's laborers and residents was needed; that suitable work and housing were required; that the carrying trade should be free to transport goods and foodstuffs from the Pennsylvania colony elsewhere; that ships ought to be built by the colonists themselves; that tradespeople would be happy to settle, would remain industrious, and would pay off any debts if only they could be free from having to rely on barter; and that the general standard of living would be improved were money more freely in circulation. Franklin's ideas at this time, like his pamphlet, mirror those Swift offered regarding Ireland's social and economic crises.

Franklin remained attentive to the situation in Ireland. He seems to have considered the American colonies, but Pennsylvania particularly, in parallel circumstances with Ireland. Or, perhaps more accurately, he sought to make sure that England did not treat the American colonies the way that it was handling affairs in Ireland. He was aware that Catholics had been ousted from their homelands. He was also aware that the political elite in Ireland was Anglican, not Presbyterian. The series of Penal Laws enacted in the medieval and early modern era would have been of interest to Franklin, especially Poynings' Law of 1495, devaluing the Irish Parliament's legal power and implementing its subservience to the English Parliament, and the various Declaratory Acts, which, in historian Martyn Powell's words, "legally enshrined the right of the British parliament to legislate for Ireland."[58] The legal situation for Catholics and Protestant dissenters was not quite the same, but dissenters were, in effect, legally dispossessed, and the series of Navigation Acts in 1663 and 1671, the Cattle Act of 1667, the Woollen Act of 1699, and the Act of 1733—all served to channel

Irish trade activity into the hands of the ruling Anglican elite. Essentially, Ireland's economy was forced into trading streams that would not compete with Britain (as England, Scotland, and Wales),[59] thus creating what historian Louis Cullen has called a "profoundly colonial" situation for Ireland.[60] As another historian, James Kelly, phrased it, "Ireland remained a separate kingdom in name, but . . . a colony in practice."[61] Franklin was concerned about the statutes that subjected both Catholics and dissenters to English Anglicans and subjected Anglo-Irish to British (as opposed to Irish) laws. The concern lasted his lifetime, as we will see. He was quite sure he did not wish a similar situation to occur in the American colonies.

When significant numbers of Irish people began to land on the shores of North America, Franklin took clear notice, and he evidently hoped to bring attention to their plight (and to the situation of American Britons, as well) by printing information about the newcomers. Franklin turned his attention to Ireland not long after presenting his *Modest Enquiry* to Pennsylvania readers. He was self-consciously beginning to establish himself as a colonial leader whose interests demonstrably were enmeshed with the interests of the British Empire. What happened in Ireland could easily happen in a province like Pennsylvania, where an absent landlord held a majority of the best land that could be tenanted by freeholders. To inform Philadelphians of the situation in Ireland, Franklin used his newspaper to print what he called "Affairs of Ireland" (*Pennsylvania Gazette*, November 20, 1729). He wrote of "the unhappy Circumstances of the Common People of Ireland," who no longer were needed to till the land (in the raising of corn), because the land had been taken over for the raising of cattle and sheep. He noted that "Poverty, Wretchedness, Misery and Want are become almost universal among them," while the "Trade and Manufactures of the Nation [were] being cramp'd and discourage'd." Without work and without land, "the labouring People have little to do," Franklin reported, so they could not purchase bread. What made the situation worse, Franklin said, was that "Taxes are nevertheless exceeding heavy, and Money very scarce; and add to all this, That their griping avaricious Landlords exercise over them the most merciless Racking Tyranny and Oppression." Franklin pointed out that the laboring poor were thus forced to emigrate to North America, "notwithstanding the general Disrespect and Aversion to their Nation that they every where meet with among the Inhabitants of the Plantations."[62] The unspoken message was all too clear: Irish immigration was occurring, because avaricious landlords who were enclosing their land were creating a situation where labor was not needed because land was unavailable, thus making livelihoods nonexistent.

Franklin was not alone among printers making this point about Ireland in 1729. Irish immigration had been reported in the *New-England Weekly Journal*, August 25, 1729. The *Journal* reported that about two thousand immigrants from Ireland had just arrived, with more expected. In the middle colonies, between April and November, about six thousand emigrants had arrived.[63] Having hypothesized a correlation between land and labor, Franklin was aware that too great a sudden influx of laborers would depreciate laborers' wages. This would create yet another crisis in the local economy.

For Franklin's economic schemes to work, a relative balance between laborers and available work was essential. He was preoccupied by the land and labor balance. Too rapid an expansion of labor could prove troublesome. By 1732, when Germans, too, had begun to reach Philadelphia in increasing numbers, Franklin developed a series of questions to be asked of the members of his Junto regarding laborers and the rights of individuals regarding their sovereign. Franklin wondered:

Does the Importation of Servants increase or advance the Wealth of our Country? Would not an Office of Insurance for Servants be of Service, and what Methods are proper for the erecting such an Office? . . .

If the Sovereign Power attempts to deprive a Subject of his Right, (or which is the same Thing, of what he thinks his Right) is it justifiable in him to resist if he is able?[64]

All of these questions suggest the range of Franklin's concerns about Pennsylvania, the American colonies, and the presumed common wealth of Great Britain.

The case of Ireland revealed what happened when land was held by a few who held taxing authority over the population, creating a situation where labor was not needed. This negative example of what could happen when land was unavailable to the majority of a population revealed Franklin's growing sense that an imperial crisis with regard to the American colonies might be at hand. He considered it time to develop a cooperative imperial network, with an equitable distribution of money and trading opportunities among all the colonies of Britain, whether Ireland, the North American colonies, or the island colonies. Franklin would later see firsthand Ireland's predicament. In that later time, he would attempt to ameliorate laborers' conditions by working with ministers there. But he eventually gave up trying to bring Irish peers over to his positions regarding free trade and economic self-sufficiency. At this time, in 1730, the influx of Irish immigrants was a threat to local economic and social stability.

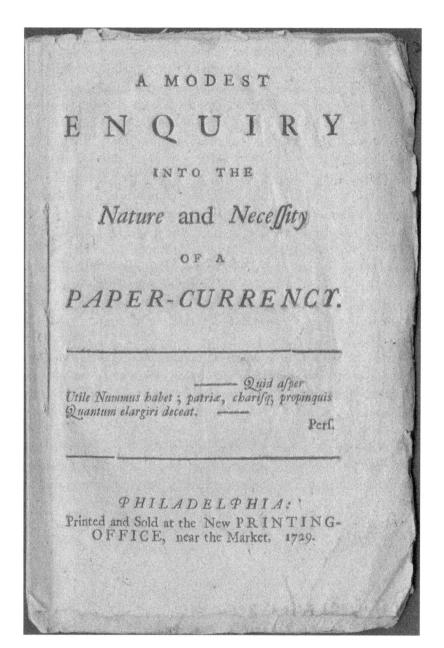

Figure 3.1   Title Page, A Modest Enquiry into the Nature and Necessity of a Paper Currency (1729). Franklin's *Modest Enquiry* is his first major statement about the usefulness of paper currency (called bills of credit) to stimulate local economies. Courtesy, Library Company of Philadelphia.

In Pennsylvania, for the time being, the Assembly's currency acts kept the colony solvent, easing local stresses for landholders and laborers. If the Assembly had *not* acted when it did to fund the sinking city of Philadelphia, the colony would have been in dire straits, and colony policy likely would have required that the Crown take over the debt and administration of the colony. Yet as it stood, Philadelphia and the Pennsylvania colony together benefited significantly from the issuing of paper money based on the series of currency acts passed by the Pennsylvania Assembly in 1723, 1729, and 1739.[65] [See Figure 3.1.] The acts for emitting bills of credit worked so well in Pennsylvania that the Assembly continued issuing paper bills of credit between 1726 and 1746. By passing acts for re-emitting the bills, the Assembly made it possible for the money to remain in circulation rather than being "sunk" or removed from circulation once the loan was repaid. This alleviated the chronic shortage of currency faced especially by laboring people, the poor, and the newcomers, who had the most to lose. The Assembly recognized the critical importance of issuing bills of credit, especially during periods of economic downturns.

But the Assembly's issuing of bills of credit, even as they assisted in stabilizing an otherwise depleted economy and improved the overall standard of living of working people, was looked upon with suspicion by the wealthier sort, by some colony leaders, and particularly by Pennsylvania's Proprietors and their representatives, the governors and others sent to the colony to secure the interest of the Proprietary. While the economic crisis was averted, the colony was far from avoiding a sort of political showdown that would eventually place Benjamin Franklin front and center in the theater of empire.

Four

PENNSYLVANIA POLITICS AND THE
PROBLEMS OF EMPIRE

By midcentury, the Pennsylvania economy was thriving. The Assembly's series of currency acts and other stimulus efforts made Pennsylvania's economy sufficiently stable that the Proprietors, first Thomas Penn (1702–1775), son of William Penn, and then his nephew, John Penn (1729–1795), launched an inquiry as to why monies were not being given them as quitrents and as duties on interest. What began as an inquiry into Pennsylvania's economic well-being led to a bitter dispute about power, a dispute dominated by behind-the-scenes negotiations between the Proprietary and the Board of Trade. By the 1740s, concerns were developing in London about the possibility of total self-rule in the colony of Pennsylvania, where, the Proprietors feared, the Assembly (an elected body) held significant sway.

Benjamin Franklin's ideas about the consolidation of the empire arose from these difficulties in the Pennsylvania economy and in the political life of Philadelphia. Examining Franklin's response to pressures from the tensions between the Proprietary and the Assembly will help underscore his influence in the city of Philadelphia, the colony of Pennsylvania, and the larger Atlantic imperial network. As a hard-working, intelligent tradesman who was competitive yet community-oriented, Franklin found the antagonism among the governor, Council, Assembly, and Proprietary baffling at first. He carefully cultivated friendships and social and business relations among all sorts of people in Philadelphia, from tradesmen to the colony's leaders. As the government's printer, he got business from both the Assembly and the Proprietors. He had established for himself a network of political and intellectual correspondents across the colonies and across the Atlantic. And his successes in a number of areas—from securing the government's printing jobs to establishing community-oriented projects to establishing himself as a scientist—all suggest Franklin's significant interpersonal talents in addition to his economic acumen.

Both Philadelphia as a city and Pennsylvania as a colony were being challenged by an increasingly diverse population and by stresses along border areas requiring significant defense. Especially during the middle decades of the eighteenth century, the arrival of great numbers of immigrants put pressure on communities. Piracy by competing empires along the waterways and at the western borders created difficulties for those involved in managing the colony. This chapter and the next work in tandem to discuss Franklin's maturing views, first regarding the conditions specific to Pennsylvania politics (the present concern) and then (in the next chapter) regarding his views of the empire and his growing sense of the potential that the colonies could be self-sustaining. In a sense, this chapter addresses Franklin's local concerns, the next, his imperial ones. Examining Franklin's responses to Pennsylvania politics creates a backdrop to our understanding of his ideas about what ought to be the purposes and goals of empire, especially regarding manufacturing and commercial freedom, self-rule, and self-determination. Franklin's work as a tradesman interested in social projects, his service to Philadelphia, and his concerns about the Assembly's relationship to the Proprietors, especially as these related to the essential need to defend the Pennsylvania colony—these form the basis of this chapter.

Franklin of Philadelphia

When Franklin arrived in Philadelphia in the early 1720s, the city was just about to experience a major expansion in population, which brought increased intercolonial traffic in goods. The increased population meant that more goods and services were needed, creating a relatively higher standard of living for most people when compared to other colonies, particularly Massachusetts. After several months in the city, Franklin returned to Boston, well dressed for a leather-apron man, with a watch and "nearly Five Pounds Sterling in Silver" that he displayed, as "a kind of Raree-Show," to the pressmen in his brother James's shop.[1] Once he became established in the city, he entered civic and political life, enjoying the free exchange of ideas made possible by the city's toleration, economic expansion, and increasing size.

Some of Franklin's success can be attributed to his ability to converse, even as a young man, with people from all walks of life. After some time in Philadelphia and largely as a result of the colony's problems with the Proprietary, Franklin would have to take sides in political debates, but early on, he sought to make friendships with people from all stations, regardless of their rank or political disposition. Franklin could converse with learned men, including the governor and leading Quakers, and with apprentices, dockworkers, shipmen, and men of all trades. His learning matched his skill and obvious physical strength as a workman. Seeking out men from all stations, Franklin could learn from both the landed and laboring classes how to thrive in his new surroundings. By using politeness or flattery (appealing to the elite group's sense of self-worth and honor) and earnest talk, mixed with occasional raillery (appealing to the intelligence and wit of those less wealthy), printer Franklin eventually won the support of the colony's leaders and its tradespeople.

As a printer, Franklin early practiced a good deal of toleration for differing points of view, and though he did not always print all sides to a debate, during his early business days, he found it useful to claim he tolerated all views. Franklin famously wrote in his memoir that he "carefully excluded all Libelling and Personal Abuse" in his newspaper, the *Pennsylvania Gazette*. He said that when he "was solicited to insert any thing of that kind, and the Writers pleaded as they generally did, the Liberty of the Press, and that a Newspaper was like a Stage Coach in which any one who would pay had a Right to a Place," he would answer that he "would print the Piece separately if desired, and the Author might have as many Copies as he pleased to distribute himself."[2] This is, of course, a good strategy to gain extra income, because the sale and distribution would be guaranteed, and the newspaper itself would not be involved in the particular fray at hand. In a humorous article in his *Gazette*, June 10, 1731, Franklin explained that his paper would present all sides: "Printers are educated in the Belief, that when Men differ in Opinion, both Sides ought equally to have the Advantage of being heard by the Publick," because "when Truth and Error have fair Play, the former is always an overmatch for the latter." Besides, Franklin joked, both sides will then "cheerfully serve all contending Writers that pay them well." Franklin pleaded the excuse of tolerating all points of view as a measure of the liberty of his press. In so doing, he was calling up recollections of a past when the press was not free and was under the disposition of the Crown and court and subject to official scrutiny according to various seventeenth-century licensing acts. But the key point for an up-and-coming printer was that toleration of different points of view paid the printer well.

Many of Franklin's earliest and closest friends were among the leading men in Philadelphia. He developed professional and personal friendships with the governor, many leading Quakers, and many tradesmen. In his memoir, Franklin himself made much of his youthful friendship with Pennsylvania's governor, Sir William Keith (1669–1749), who had encouraged him to go to London to identify and purchase type for his new press, promising letters of introduction and credit that never materialized when Franklin reached London. Of Keith, Franklin wrote, "He wish'd to please everybody; and having little to give, he gave Expectations."[3] Other connections he made did benefit him, however. With James Logan (1674–1751), an Irish Quaker who had come to Philadelphia as an agent for William Penn, Franklin forged a close friendship based on their mutual love of books and knowledge of the natural world.[4] Logan opened his extensive library to Franklin and became one of his more confidential advisors. William Allen (1704–1780), a wealthy merchant who became the Proprietors' chief justice for the colony, also supported Franklin in many endeavors from these earliest days. Allen initiated the negotiations that eventually brought Franklin the offer of deputy postmaster in 1751. Along with Richard Peters (1704–1776), rector at Christ Church, Allen assisted Franklin's plans for an academy, providing Franklin access to his wide connections and helping him fund his plans. Richard Peters was the Penn family's central correspondent during the years leading up to the fracture between the Assembly and the Proprietary, and he often offered good advice about working with the Proprietors. Peters helped foster Franklin's scientific inclinations. He worked with Peter Collinson (1694–1768), a merchant and botanist in England, to secure—as a gift from the Proprietor—the electrical apparatus with which Franklin made his initial great discoveries.[5] These well-to-do men seem to have liked Franklin, and they sought to increase his opportunities for assisting the community.

Among tradespeople, Franklin circulated easily and was lucky to have discovered several men equally talented as he and equally interested in self-improvement. With like-minded men such as Hugh Roberts (c. 1706–1786) and Philip Syng (1703–1789), Franklin remained lifelong friends. With others, he worked to establish a public library and a variety of projects for civic improvement. When he formed the Junto, which he described in his memoir as "a Club, for mutual Improvement," he included only his most "ingenious Acquaintance" as members.[6] The standing queries for Franklin's Junto, a group of tradesman interested in self-improvement, eventually published in 1779, indicate the concerns of these men. Several topics point to notions of personal service, reputation, and community assistance that were Franklin's hallmarks. The standing queries are fascinating for what they reveal about Franklin's thoughts on community spirit and personal investment in one's friends:

> Do you think of any thing at present, in which the Junto may be serviceable to mankind? to their country, to their friends, or to themselves? . . . Hath any deserving stranger arrived in town since last meeting, that you heard of? and what have you heard or observed of his character or merits? and whether think you, it lies in the power of the Junto to oblige him, or encourage him as he deserves? . . . Do you know of any deserving young beginner lately set up, whom it lies in the power of the Junto any way to encourage?

Additional standing queries addressed larger social and political concerns: "Have you lately observed any defect in the laws of your country, [of] which it would be proper to move the legislature for an amendment? Or do you know of any beneficial law that is wanting?" and "Have you lately observed any encroachment on the just liberties of the people?"[7] Taken together, the standing queries emphasize service to one's friends, community, and country, and they suggest an active course of obliging others while securing the success of one's own interests. Establishing a cluster of tradesmen in one group, the Junto also fostered a network of cooperative groups beyond the original Junto. In all cases, these community-spirited groups worked from a core set of personal and civic values: maintaining self-respect and respect for others; determining upon and then performing one's civic duty; aspiring to achieve moral self-governance, with the understanding that if one could govern oneself well, one would be contributing to the possibility of joining a positive, self-governing community. Self-regulation was thus a cornerstone supporting the foundational goals of personal and political growth.

Pennsylvania Politics

Largely due to its religious toleration and its agricultural potential, Pennsylvania attracted significant numbers of immigrants during the early decades of the eighteenth century. As we have seen, Irish immigrants came in large numbers. So did Scots-Irish, Germans from the Palatinate, and some Dutch, Swedish, Swiss, and Welsh immigrants.[8] Most who came were laborers and tradespeople, attracted by William Penn's promises of toleration. Penn's writings, some of which were being reprinted at the turn into the eighteenth century, argued a line of thinking common among dissenters in the late seventeenth century that, in the words of historian Mary Maples Dunn, "persecution had serious economic consequences"[9] and that dissenters, who were a large part of the laboring and merchant classes, were being ruined by harassment, fines, and fees, simply because of their dissent. Like the originator of the Society of Friends, George Fox (1624–1691), and a few other theorists about society at the time, Penn argued that Britain's unwillingness to address its policies of intolerance at home undermined its potential for imperial expansion and social and commercial stability.[10] By pointing to his colony as one that would tolerate the many different sects seeking asylum from religious constraints in Britain and Europe, Penn initiated the colony's success. Pennsylvania became a magnet for members of different Protestant sects, and it also served as the primary place where Quakers sought to reside.

The diversity of people and beliefs proved to be the colony's strength but also an area of its potential weakness. The Quakers' commitment to pacifism, a fundamental principle of Quaker practice, had a long history dating to a peace testimony made to King Charles II in 1660. The civil wars over power and religious practice struck the Quakers as abhorrent, the harassment for their religious ideals intolerable. The commitment to pacifism and their belief in toleration of others brought many Quakers to Pennsylvania in the 1680s, seeking a place where they could reside without being chastised, kept outside government, and murdered. Moreover, they thought, they would never be forced to take part in European wars. Many of the original Quaker settlers were Welsh, and they sought to establish their own community west of Philadelphia (on a grant of land offered by Willian Penn) apart from other groups of Quakers who resided in the city or other areas just outside it. Quakers came to Pennsylvania in great numbers, but so did non-Quakers interested in taking advantage of Pennsylvania's official policy of toleration.

The very diversity of the population, even within the Quaker population, brought tension to Philadelphia and its surrounding region. The Council had been set up by William Penn to represent him in the colony, and it became in effect the high court of the colony in the absence of the Proprietor. The much larger General Assembly, which proclaimed as its model England's House of Commons, in effect had little power, as it was devised by Penn, but it cultivated its power across the initial decades of the colony's settlement as the Council members and different governors continually changed. Tensions within the Council and tensions between the Council and Assembly made governance difficult. In effect, Penn had devised what historian Gary Nash has described as a "tightly knit economic and political partnership" in Philadelphia, leaving Quakers from the Lower Counties (Sussex, Kent, and New Castle) with less power than those acting on upper-class presumption and largely with approbation by the Proprietary in Philadelphia. Following Gary Nash's analysis, Joseph E. Illick summarized the situation well: "A non-Quaker population antedating the establishment of Pennsylvania, the visibility of Penn's friends on the powerful Council[,] and a proprietary land policy which always appeared to be opportunistic gave rise to Quaker pro- and antiproprietary factions, in Council and Assembly respectively, and to a party from the Lower Counties."[11] An "Act of Union" had been designed to blend the two together, but decision-making did not occur peaceably among the different groups of Quakers.[12]

The problems had a long history, and they continued into the first half of the eighteenth century. The Council presumed (in 1686) all rights to create bills without consulting with the Assembly and then denied the Assembly's power to amend any bills. The Assembly protested. The protest, as historian Mary Dunn said long ago, "implie[d] power of debate," whereas "the council insisted that the lower house had rights to assent or dissent only" (meaning that the Assembly had no right to debate with the Council).[13] The constant bickering about power annoyed Penn, who, in Dunn's words, "thought the Pennsylvania government a new model, not at all comparable to that of England."[14] He considered that the Assembly was intentionally obstructing government in Pennsylvania. The result was legal chaos in Pennsylvania, almost from the moment of its inception, and frequent appeals to Whitehall for redress of perceived infractions.

William Penn had come of age in a world in which status and power were tied together: one's status conferred upon one the right and duty of making decisions for others, especially those less well-to-do. In Penn's world, one's "interest" lay with the number of friends one had at court or in the ministry. While Penn seems thoroughly to have believed in the concepts of liberty of conscience and while he also attempted to create a state structure that might provide a space for the practice of individual liberties, he also—at the very same time—considered that his role as Proprietor was one of supreme ruler. But what good was a supreme ruler, one who conceived that he owed allegiance only to the Crown, who was physically distant (across the ocean, like an absentee landlord) and politically self-absorbed? Penn's alliances with the Court and with the Board of Trade in effect contradicted the liberal project that informed his "holy experiment." Religious toleration did not necessarily mean that individuals would remain free of concern about holding powerful leadership positions.

Several in the British administration, particularly Edward Randolph (1632–1703), surveyor general of the colonies, sought to consolidate colonial holdings and policies by pulling back colonial charters and Proprietary governments, but the Pennsylvania Charter was restored to Penn in 1694. Still, the Crown and Parliament sought ways to organize the colonies for better administration. The result was Parliament's 1696 passage of a new Navigation Act that was, in Nash's words, "designed to extend and coordinate the authority of the Crown in the colonies."[15] By establishing colonial vice-admiralty courts empowered by the Crown and by requiring that Whitehall approve all governor appointments, the Crown, ministry, and Board of Trade attempted to constrain the colonies into one system. Smuggling came to the attention of Whitehall in the 1690s. Even Penn's court friends were unable to prevent the Board of Trade from delving into the illegal trading practices taking place in Pennsylvania. By 1700, the House of Lords aimed to annul Proprietary and charter governments.[16] Penn believed the Pennsylvania Charter would be annulled in 1701.

Adding to the difficulties the Penn family faced was its high station and relative poverty. Leading Quakers in the colony, concerned about their land rights and investments, started to wonder whether the colony could continue as a proprietary colony. They were concerned about their investments in the colony. When he went to England, James Logan, as the Penns' agent, offered to sell Penn's government to the Crown in 1710–11. When William Penn had a stroke in 1712, most of the leaders in the colony considered permanent royal government imminent.[17] After Penn's death, to borrow the words of historian William Hanna, "Confusion, distraction, and poverty were the hallmarks of the proprietary family."[18] Yet the Proprietary family managed to keep the colony as Penn lay incapacitated, and it found an able and admired new governor in Sir William Keith, who had been serving as surveyor general of customs for the southern colonies.

Philadelphia was growing fast during this time, with population growth and economic development outpacing any other city in the British Empire.[19] The huge growth brought increased pressure on the Proprietors to accept the Assembly's move that the Proprietors' lands be taxed for defense of the British Empire and to accept that the Assembly, as a representative body, should have a say in legislation over the colony's diverse population. The history of the squabbles between the Assembly and the Proprietors has long been of interest to historians of Pennsylvania, its Quakers, and the Proprietary. It is of general interest here primarily as the background to some of the particular moments when Franklin was forced, finally, to express his personal opinions or to take a side or develop a strategy for dealing with obstructions from the different squabbling groups. Our purpose will be to examine Franklin's proposals for the British Empire in North America, attempting to elucidate Franklin's systemic analysis yielding possible imperial strategies in the face of the internal squabbling within colonies and among different colonies and, more expansively, in the face of the wars among European powers for empire in North America.

The Assembly spent several decades battling over questions of legal prerogative, taxation of Penn lands, trade with the Indians inside and outside the colony's borders, and funding for imperial defense. The Penn family had long believed that the Assembly was attempting to usurp the Proprietary prerogatives in legal matters and dispose of tax dollars according to its own decision-making rather than observing its obligations to the Proprietary (with due deference to the Proprietor's governors). Thomas Penn, who became the family's principal Proprietor in the mid–1740s, retained an extremely ungenerous view of the Assembly. Yet the Assembly had had to take over the fiscal operations of the colony (including taxation) within decades of the colony's founding, because the Penn family lacked the funds necessary to administer the colony. As historian James Hutson has pointed out, the Assembly was forced to take over taxation because "during the early decades of the eighteenth century[,] someone had to pay for the administration of government, for gifts to Indians, and for other expenses and, the proprietary family being impoverished, the Assembly was obliged to step into the breach, raise the money, and do the job."[20] The Assembly blamed the Proprietor for neglecting his duties to the people of the commonwealth. The Proprietor, suspicious of popular leadership and of the intransigence of antidefense and anti-Proprietary Quakers (whether elected as members of or outside the Assembly), blamed the Assembly for usurping the role, duties, and obligations of the Proprietary. By 1750, the governance of the colony was costing the Proprietary more than the funds that were gained from quitrents and other fees the Proprietors attempted to exact from settlers in the colony. The issue was that people frequently settled on Penn's lands without paying rents, and travelers avoided paying the fees for traveling across the lands and using ferries to cross the rivers. This was a problem that gradually increased as the decades wore on. By 1752, Richard Peters, agent for Proprietor Thomas Penn, wrote in a letter to him that "Your Quit Rents are shamefully in Arrears—Your Ferrys wrested out of your hands—Your Manor Lands and appropriated Tracts are settled . . . promiscuously [i.e., by squatters]." He added that the "Assembly [is] provoked by Paper Money being demanded and not likely to be granted—The Sheriffs are the Creatures of and subservient to the People—The Juries without virtue in Proprietary Disputes and no Court of Equity."[21] Peters bemoaned his situation as intermediary for the Penns and underscored that administration of the colony was difficult, with competing groups forcing the government to be in disarray.

The Proprietors had considered that the wealth of the settlers was dependent on Proprietary lands and efforts without due recognition (financial and deferential) given to Proprietary agents. Egged on by his advisors and agents, Thomas Penn resented the Pennsylvania Assembly's control of public monies, and he was determined to seek redress against the Assembly's presumed usurpation of administration of laws. The creation and administration of laws was supposed to be in the hands of the governors of Pennsylvania, and their agents.[22] The Penns refused to allow the Assembly to tax Proprietary lands for the public defense. The Assembly continued to threaten to petition the Crown for redress against such behavior. After years of such threats, the Assembly started making petitions to the Crown. Yet the Penn family had friends in court. Despite these friendships, however, the ministry became so concerned about Thomas and then John Penn's inability to lead the colony that it offered the Penn family an opportunity to sell Pennsylvania's government back to the Crown.[23] In general, the situation in Pennsylvania was an annoyance to Whitehall. As it turned out, the ministry in 1755 was not disposed toward Penn, but the Board of Trade nonetheless supported him against the Assembly's repeated petitions to the Board for redress of the stalemate caused by the Penn family's unwillingness to see their tracts taxed.

"Tribune of the People": Franklin's Projects for Philadelphia and Pennsylvania

Franklin claimed he wanted to avoid the fray in these political battles, but in effect his public projects suited the goals of the Assembly, Council, and Proprietary. That is, Franklin's projects for intellectual and social amelioration—the Junto (1727), the academy and English school (1749), the hospital (1751–52), the fire companies merging as an insurance cooperative (1751), for instance—all were civic projects with social and political ends. William Hanna once observed that Franklin practiced no politics before

1751,[24] but the paper money proposal was a political project. Franklin was always participating in programs that effectively served the political ends of both the Assembly and the Proprietary, and in several instances, he was forced to take controversial stances as a result. Hanna also remarked that Franklin lacked a theory of government, that his writings from the 1730s and 1740s "reveal no serious speculations about political matters or problems of government and no analysis of or suggestions for improving local conditions."[25] Franklin's remarks about paper currency, his many contributions to his *Pennsylvania Gazette* and *General Magazine*, and his plans for social institutions, including institutions assisting the defense of the colony (such as the Association) all indicate Franklin's concerns about social and political life. In many of Franklin's writings and in some of his letters—particularly those to Cadwallader Colden (1688–1776) and James Logan—Franklin expressed clear civic and political goals for Pennsylvania.

Franklin's goals resonate with his views of the potential liberal operations of empire. Britain was involved in the early 1740s with the War of the Austrian Succession, a prolonged series of confrontations among most European powers about the succession of the Hapsburgs to the throne. In British North America, the imperial warfare occurring among the French, Spanish, and British was called King George's War, which was carried out on both land and sea from Nova Scotia to Maryland. Piracy was a key strategy of control of the seas, and Pennsylvanians were suffering from repeated raids by French and then Spanish cruisers. If Pennsylvania were freed from fears of attack by French and Spanish privateers on the seaboard and from the French and their Indian allies on its western border, and if Pennsylvania became free of constraints on its trade, Pennsylvania could thrive on its own. If Pennsylvanians could be unencumbered from paying for taxes supporting the defense (including defense of Proprietary lands) and instead focus on their own lands, labor, and needs, then the labor on the land would seem much lighter, and taxation would seem a necessary function of self-governance and colonial self-improvement. Philadelphia could become a booming metropolitan center of trade and culture—all working to the greater glory and the global network of the British Empire.

Franklin was aware of the rich potential of the Pennsylvania colony. It was agriculturally fecund and located in a sufficiently mild climate; its population of laborers was used to working the land, and they brought diverse sets of skills for the different trades; and its laws, regularly under contest by the Assembly, were open to flexible interpretation. In his newspapers, pamphlets, and magazines, Franklin informed the colonists of their particular good fortune, just as he also illustrated to the Crown and ministry Britain's good fortune in having the Pennsylvania colony at its disposal. As we have seen, his pamphlet supporting paper currency had suggested that Philadelphia could become a leading metropolitan center for the empire, equal in trading capacity to London, Hamburg, Amsterdam, and Venice. Franklin wanted to see that his arguments were understood both locally and across the Atlantic. Take, for instance, his interesting article in the opening issue of his magazine, the *General Magazine, and Historical Chronicle, for all the British Plantations in America* (vol. 1, January 1741). In his "Account of the Export of Provisions from Philadelphia," Franklin listed the numerous and diverse goods entered for export between December 25, 1739, and December 25, 1740. These exports ranged from wheat, flour, barley, and Indian corn to pork, beef, and pickled sturgeon, to beer, peas, and beans. After presenting his twenty-five-item listing, Franklin concluded,

> The above Account is a Proof of the Fertility of this Province, and of the great Plenty wherewith God has bless'd the Industry of the Inhabitants; who in a few Years have made a Garden of a Wilderness, and, besides living well themselves, have so much Food to spare to other Countries. By means of this and the neighbouring *Provision Colonies*, the British Fleet and Forces in the West-Indies are at this Time supplied with Provisions at a moderate Price, while the Enemy is starving in Want; which shows that these Colonies give Great Britain a considerable Advantage over its Enemies in an American War, and will no doubt be an additional Inducement to our Mother Country to continue us its Protection.[26]

Franklin emphasized that Pennsylvania was the basis for British prosperity and defense. This commentary and those like it in many of Franklin's incidental publications and private writings reveals Franklin's growing mission to show how freedom of labor (the absence of sumptuary laws and workers' guilds and strict limitations on numbers of apprentices in any given trade) led to individual happiness and increased productivity and how these (happiness and productivity) could combine to assist other areas of the Empire. By fostering its productive colonies, the empire could be secured from want, would have a market for the circulation of goods, and would be able to overcome an enemy. Franklin used this little piece to point out the "considerable Advantage" afforded the empire because of its important colony, Pennsylvania, and its key city, Philadelphia. Such pronouncements as this are not coincidental; instead, they illustrate a design on Franklin's part to inform both colonists and officials of the importance of colonies like Pennsylvania to the greater British Empire. [See Figure 4.1.]

An ACCOUNT *of the Export of Provisions from the Port of* Philadelphia, *in* Pennſilvania, *betwixt the* 25*th of* December 1739, *and the* 25*th of* December 1740.

Wheat 314,570 and half, Buſhels.
Bread, 49 and half, Tons ; 7,980 Tierces, 9,573 Barrels, 885 half Barrels, 881 quarter Barrels, and 9 Cags.
Flour, 100 Tierces, 53,970 Barrels, 147 half Barrels.
Barley, 40 Buſhels.
Indian Corn, 418 Tierces, 298 Barrels, 126,418 Buſhels.
Rye, 17 Barrels, and 1574 Buſhels.
ɔ ork, 7 Tierces, 2978 Barrels, 137 half Barrels, 16 Cags.
Bacon, 10 Hogſheads, 218 Tierces, 258 Barrels, 1 Hamper, 5 Boxes, and 700 *lb.*
Beef, 313 Barrels, 75 half Barrels, 6 quarter Barrels.
Beer, 497 Barrels, 26 half Barrels, 1 Hogſhead.
Butter, 1 Tub, 1 Barrel, 371 Firkins, 207 Cags, 1 Box, 4 Pots, and 400 *lb.*
Fiſh, 1 Hogſhead, 594 Barrels.
Cyder, 2 Hogſheads, 26 Barrels.
Apples, 1 Hogſhead, 17 Barrels, 4 Half-Barrels, 2 Cags.
Dry'd Tongues, 1 Barrel, 2 Boxes, 1 Cag.
Potatoes, 2 Barrels.
Hickery Nutts, 3 Barrels.
Pickled Sturgeon, 15 Cags.
Peaſe, 27 Barrels.
Beans, 4 Barrels.
Cheeſe, 1 Tierce, 102 ſingle Cheeſes, and 3,300 *lb.*
Hogs Lard, 28 Barrels, 42 half Barrels, 13 quarter Barrels, 46 Cags.
Sage, 1 Cheſt.
Oats, 4 Hogſheads, 3 Tierces, 370 Buſhels.
Onions, 50 Barrels, 730 Bundles, 221 Strings.

> *The above Account is a Proof of the Fertility of this Province, and of the great Plenty wherewith* G O D *has bleſi'd the Induſtry of the Inhabitants ; who in a few Years have made a Garden of a Wilderneſs, and, beſides living well themſelves, have ſo much Food to ſpare to other Countries. By means of this and the neighbouring* Provifior Colonies, *the* Britiſh *Fleet and Forces in the* Weſt-Indies *are at this Time ſupplied with Proviſions at a moderate Price, while the Enemy is ſtarving in Want ; which ſhows that theſe Colonies give* Great Britain *a conſiderable Advantage over its Enemies in an* American *War, and will no doubt be an additional Inducement to our Mother Country to continue us its Protection.*

Errata, *Page* 5. *line* 16 *from the Bottom, for* 1665 *read* 1655.
Page 72. *line* 8 *from the Bottom, for* 50,000 l. *read* 250,000

Figure 4.1 "An Account of the Export of Provisions from Philadelphia". Franklin published his account of the provisions exported from Philadelphia in his new (but not long-lived) journal, the *General Magazine, and Historical Chronicle, for all the British Plantations in America* (vol. 1, January 1741), 75. He seems to have made separate print runs of the journal, with this account of provisions appearing on p. 77 of some issues. Courtesy, Beinecke Rare Book and Manuscript Library and Historical Society of Pennsylvania.

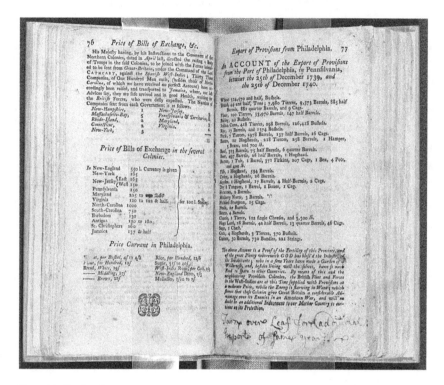

Figure 4.1 Continued.

In short, Franklin seems always to have had his eyes on improving his own and his adopted colony's prospects. He understood the usefulness of publicity about things like Philadelphia's place in the trade networks of North America. He also understood that Philadelphia's exports needed protection from tariffs by the home country or the Proprietor and from theft by privateers sailing for other countries in the coastal waterways of North America and the trading islands in the Caribbean. By instructing the other North American colonies, the so-called West Indian colonies, and England about the importance of Philadelphia in the global trade theater, Franklin was also instructing Great Britain about the need to protect the potential wealth of such a colony as Pennsylvania.

With regard to defense against marauding enemies to the British Empire, Franklin understood but did not agree with conservative Quakers and men of conscience who did not wish to take part in or fund efforts for self-protection in the war for empire in North America. This is not to say Franklin was a warmonger—indeed, I believe he wanted to avoid war, which wasted talent, money, and life. He did, however, believe it important to defend one's empire, because such defense preserved one's way of life. Franklin also understood but did not agree with the Proprietor's position regarding taxation and the other fees sought to exact from the hard-working colonists. He ultimately seems to have believed that reasoned argument might win some of these men over to an understanding of the rich promise of the colony of Pennsylvania and to Pennsylvania's central importance to the prospect of a British North America.

So, once he started to "retire" from the printing business by handing over more of his business to David Hall (1714–1772), Franklin started working more openly toward a political career and a greater leadership role. The key issues prompting Franklin's decision to enter into the public political arena were the dual issues of the conduct of the Indian trade and matters of defense of the empire. Of the two issues, defense seemed the more pressing to Philadelphians. There were two matters of defense that the colony had to consider. The first was a problem local to Philadelphia: Spanish and French privateers had always sailed along the eastern seaboard, but during the spring and summer of 1747, piracies and depredations were taking place with much greater frequency off the Delaware capes. The second issue of defense related to the defense of not only the colony but the greater British Empire: skirmishes were increasing in Pennsylvania's westernmost borders with Ohio Indians and the French, so the issue of funding defense became a central issue faced by Pennsylvanians.

Franklin's *Plain Truth* (1747), his plan for defense (which he called the Association), and his calling for a lottery (to fund defense)—all indicate the extent to which he had thought long and hard about the necessity for colonists' defending themselves, whether or not their government (either the local government in Pennsylvania or the Crown) saw fit to assist the effort. His plans were so well conceived that when he circulated his ideas he found warm support among members of the elite, like James Logan, and among his tradespeople associates. Franklin developed plans whereby the British people across the Atlantic and Britons in North America might systematically work together to build a stronger British Empire. What was lacking was a system, a system free of the prejudice of religious conscience, status, and ethnicity, that could serve to bring people together rather than tear them asunder.

Franklin's strategy of playing the middle ground between the Proprietor and the colonists, between the conservative and more liberal Quakers, and between British colonists and most others comes to the fore in *Plain Truth*, published November 17 on his own press. Prompting the timing of the pamphlet was piracy along the eastern seaboard that had continued unchecked and in recent months had escalated and entered a path up the Delaware River. During much of the year, settlements that lay along the Delaware had been attacked, some fully ransacked. Settlers were being harassed, and some were wounded during the raids for goods and slaves. When the Philadelphia Council attempted acting to protect the area by closing the Delaware to foreign vessels, privateers got around the act by sailing up on the New Jersey side. Even though they would be the first protected by defensive action, settlers from the Lower Counties were offended that Council was abrogating their power by making defense decisions.

The Assembly essentially stalemated any action the Council sought to make. The result was that privateering continued, and without redress, it increased. Council president Anthony Palmer (d. 1749) complained to the Assembly on October 16, 1747, that "From the Success which attends our Enemies by Cruizing in our Bay without risque or opposition, it may reasonably be expected that they will continue their Depredations in the Spring, and in all likelyhood block up the Trade of this flourishing Colony—a Loss which we apprehend will be sensibly felt by all sorts of People."[27] Palmer's argument suggested that the Council sought action not just to protect the wealthy but to protect the commonwealth. The Assembly responded to Palmer's plea by asserting that the pilots for the ships (the guiding boats) were at fault, if they brought enemy ships upriver. With regard to the Council's concern about an attack on Philadelphia, the Assembly replied, "We hope there is no Danger."[28]

Most residents—all but the most conservative Quakers, who were pacifist, and some of the wealthier sort, who wanted to avoid additional taxes—thought something ought to be done regarding defense, but concerted action seemed impossible. James Logan, in an open letter six years earlier to Friends at the Yearly Meeting on September 22, 1741, had attempted to persuade pacifist Quakers to supply funds for defense, but the Meeting refused to read his message to those gathered. He then paid Franklin to print the letter as *To Robert Jordan, and others of the Friends of the Yearly Meeting for Business, now conven'd in Philadelphia* (1741). In December 1747, recollecting that moment six years earlier, Logan wrote to Franklin about his chagrin at the pacifists among his Quaker friends: "Our Friends spare no pains to get and accumulate estates, and are yet against defending them, though these very estates are in a great measure the sole cause of their being invaded, as I showed to our Yearly Meeting, last September was six years, in a paper thou then printed."[29] All during the fall, Franklin worked with Logan, Tench Francis (d. 1758), William Coleman

(1704–1769), and Thomas Hopkinson (1709–1751) to strategize how to approach the problem. His friends agreed with him that the ideas he would offer in *Plain Truth*, spoken as if "By a Tradesman of Philadelphia," might work to help people realize how their inaction jeopardized their lives and livelihoods. Franklin's pamphlet, *Plain Truth: Or, Serious Considerations on the Present State of the City of Philadelphia and Province of Pennsylvania*, offered a vehicle that residents could rally behind.

Plain Truth brought up several key themes common in writings about defense at this time, but it also had a particularly Franklinian ring to it, especially in its opening and in its interesting calculations about the population. In advancing a point about the nonaggressive nature of the inhabitants, the pamphlet opened by implicating qualities of the British character (as opposed to the French and Spanish characters) as issues that undermined self-protection. It spoke as well to the wealth (and thus the desirability) of Pennsylvania and its defenseless state when compared with all other seaboard colonies. This defenselessness was a result of the stalemate among members of the Council and the Assembly, Franklin made clear: Quakers were "against all Defence, from a principle of Conscience," and though "Our late Governor did for Years sollicit, request, and even threaten them in vain" and though "The Council have since twice remonstrated to them in vain," it seemed that "Their religious Prepossessions are unchangeable, their Obstinacy invincible."[30] Calling attention to this impasse was risky, for it publicized the predicament to residents in a way that might have increased the rancor.

But Franklin's strategy was effective because he used the factionalism to stress the need for solidarity in "this now flourishing City, and greatly improving Colony."[31] Some of the factionalism was based on differences in ethnicity and wealth, so Franklin worked to differentiate middling-level people from those of higher station. Using a series of rhetorical questions, he directed attention to the lives of tradespeople and those like them. He pointed out that the piracy would continue, because "to refuse Defending one's self or one's Country, is so unusual a Thing among Mankind, that possibly they [i.e., the pirates] may not believe it, till by Experience they find, they can come higher and higher up our River, seize our Vessels, land and plunder our Plantations and Villages, and retire with their Booty unmolested." If such gradual encroachments proved successful, he indicated, then the pirates would be given "the greatest Encouragement to strike one bold Stroke for the City, and for the whole Plunder of the River."[32] In fact, this is the situation that existed from mid-July 1747, forward. Franklin used the situation to draw attention to the fact that the Quakers were significantly outnumbered, given the recent levels of immigration and the prosperity of non-Quakers in the colony. He pointed out that if such a place as this were "destroy'd and ruin'd, it will not be for want of Numbers of Inhabitants able to bear Arms in its Defence."[33] As Franklin framed it, both the deleterious effects on trade that piracy created and the faction- alism that was dividing the commonwealth worked together, creating a situation such that "we . . . my dear Countrymen and Fellow-Citizens; we, I mean, the middling People, the Farmers, Shopkeepers and Tradesmen of this City and Country . . . tho' we are numerous . . . are quite defence- less."[34] Franklin separated out "the Rich," who, he pointed out, "may shift for themselves," given that the "Means of speedy Flight are ready in their Hands,"[35] from the community of others who might, if they could muster "the Prudence and the Spirit to apply it,"[36] take the lead in creating change.

Many leading Quakers were wealthy merchants, but Franklin was speaking less to them than to the large numbers of middling-level people in his midst.[37] Franklin employed several appeals to this new community of diverse people he was calling into being as one group. He appealed to social constructions of hardy masculinity, to the experience of people who earned their living and lived from the animals of the land: "'Tis computed that we have at least (exclusive of the Quakers) 60,000 Fighting Men, acquainted with Fire-Arms, many of them Hunters and Marksmen, hardy and bold." He also appealed to the several different ethnic peoples who were settled in Pennsylvania. He promoted a positive construction of "the BRITISH RACE" by pointing to the model of "Our Neighbours of New-England," who "afford the World a convincing Proof, that BRITONS, tho' a Hundred Years transplanted, and to the remotest Part of the Earth, may yet retain, even to the third and fourth Descent, that *Zeal* for the *Publick Good*, that *military Prowess*, and that *undaunted Spirit*, which has in every Age distinguished their Nation." He appealed likewise to "the *brave* and *steady* Germans," who came from "*that warlike Nation*" who once "fought well" even for their "Tyrants and Oppressors." He also spoke favorably about the Scots-Irish, using the siege of Londonderry, Ireland, to evoke a memory of bravery:

What Numbers have we likewise of *those brave People*, whose Fathers in the last Age made so glorious a Stand for our Religion and Liberties, when invaded by a powerful French Army, join'd by Irish Catholicks, under a bigotted Popish King! Let the Memorable Siege of Londonderry, and the signal Actions of the Iniskillingers, by which the Heart of that Prince's Schemes was broken, be perpetual Testimonies of the *Courage* and *Conduct* of those *noble Warriors!*[38]

Here, Franklin called up the memory of the civil wars and the problems faced by peoples who had repeatedly been settled and resettled. Franklin was calling into being support for a greater Britain based on support from diverse ethnic populations. The propagandistic rhetorical gesture was a socially consolidating one, based in ethnic and cultural diversity, suggestive of the provocatively new idea that embracing diversity in one's community was a powerful, solidarity-building imperial stance.

In speaking to a particular memory about the Scots-Irish, Franklin might have benefited from advice from his friend, James Logan. Logan developed his lands west of Philadelphia (Donegal township) by settling Scots-Irish people there. Logan had once written to James Steel (fl. 1714–45), receiver-general for quitrents, and then, later, to Thomas Penn that he had decided to settle a group of Scots-Irish in Donegal because of their brave defense, back in Ireland. As Logan explained it, around 1720, "considerable Numbers of good Sober People came in from Irel'd who wanted to be Settled, at ye Same time Also it happen'd that we were under some apprehensions from ye Northern Indians. . . . I therefore thought it might be prudent to plant a Settlem[en]t of Such Men as those who formerly had so bravely defended Derry and Inniskillin as a frontier in case of any Disturbance."[39] In effect, Logan was using the newcomers as buffers against a presumed enemy, but his expressed purpose underscored the idea of the bravery of the Irish, his countrymen—those who had once fought might be willing to do so again, since their new land had come at a great personal sacrifice. By calling upon the different ethnic populations that were being threatened, Franklin was suggesting that a new union, one that avoided the ethnic biases of former times, could effectively stand and deliver against those who were attempting to stand in the way of their "most precious *Liberty* and *Property.*"[40]

The literary qualities of *Plain Truth* are rarely discussed, but they are worthy of notice. Like the tradesman he represented as author and like the Poor Richard of his almanac fame, Franklin created a peroration that began with a homespun metaphor based in huswifery and concluded with military-oriented, pithy sententiae. The passage accrued its power as it progressed:

At present we are like the separate Filaments of Flax before the Thread is form'd, without Strength because without Connection; but Union would make us strong and even formidable: Tho' the *Great* should neither help nor join us; tho' they should even oppose our Uniting from some mean Views of their own, yet, if we resolve upon it, and it please God to inspire us with the necessary Prudence and Vigour, it *may* be effected. . . . Were this Union form'd, were we once united, thoroughly arm'd and disciplin'd, was every Thing in our Power done for our Security, as far as human Means and Foresight could provide, we might then, *with more Propriety*, humbly ask the Assistance of Heaven, and a Blessing on our lawful Endeavours. The very Fame of our Strength and Readiness would be a Means of Discouraging our Enemies; for 'tis a wise and true Saying, that *One Sword often keeps another in the Scabbard.* The Way to secure Peace is to be prepared for War.

The concept of strands of fiber in a thread was an interesting and compelling metaphor to describe the disparate community that formed Pennsylvania. Working together, the different people could spin a mighty militia. Informing them that the plan being offered was both lawful and blessed, Franklin hoped to gain support from reluctant readers. What was lacking, in Franklin's view, was the resolve of the community to defend itself. Franklin's use of religious rhetoric to fashion part of his argument resembled many a pamphlet from the era of the English civil wars. His generalized appeal to an overseeing deity ("God") enabled him to call attention to religious principle or conscience. Much of the tone and content of this part of *Plain Truth* hearkens back to the pamphleteering of Cromwell's era. This is especially true of the last phrases of the pamphlet, where Franklin invoked God again and wrote what was, in effect, a benediction to his readers:

> *May the* God *of* Wisdom, Strength *and* Power, *the Lord of the Armies of Israel, inspire us with Prudence in this Time of* Danger; *take away from us all the Seeds of Contention and Division, and unite the Hearts and Counsels of all of us, of whatever* Sect *or* Nation, *in one Bond of Peace, Brotherly Love, and generous Publick spirit; May he give us Strength and Resolution to amend our Lives, and remove from among us every Thing that is displeasing to him; afford us his most Gracious Protection, confound the Designs of our Enemies, and give* Peace *in all our Borders.*

The pamphlet's signal irony, of course, is that by highlighting social divisions, Franklin promoted unity.

Plain Truth experienced resounding success. Franklin had promised in the pamphlet that the author would create a paper that would, in effect, serve as a document for an Association for defense that he was calling into being. This he did a few days later, after first having a meeting that was very well attended. Franklin's editors report that more than five hundred people signed the Association documents on November 24 and that "within a few days the number of signatures exceeded 1,000."[41] Even with all of this support, the Quaker-dominated Assembly did not come out in support of defense. By contrast, the Council resolved "to give all due Protection and Encouragement to the Members of the Association."[42] When the Associators met in early December in front of the Court House, Richard Peters, Council secretary, announced to the men that their "Proceedings are not disapprov'd by the Government."[43] Franklin was energized. He proposed a lottery that would assist in funding the Associators so that they could purchase what was needed for defense. The group solicited cannon and materiel from the Proprietors and from neighboring New York. A fast day—the first in Philadelphia, with the statement authored by Franklin—was proclaimed. The lottery succeeded well beyond expectation.

Indeed, all of Franklin's plans met with resounding success. On November 27, Franklin wrote to Cadwallader Colden of New York, who was intensely interested in the situation in Philadelphia: "Tho' *Plain Truth* bore somewhat hard on both Parties here, it has had the Happiness not to give much Offence to either. It has wonderfully spirited us up to defend our selves and Country, to which End great Numbers are entring into an Association."[44] About this time, Richard Peters shot off to the Proprietors a lengthy description of the events leading up to the formation of the Association. Peters observed that "the Scheme took its rise from the just fears and apprehensions all sorts of People were under for their Lives and Properties." And in an effort to present the best case, he clarified that, in his view, the Association really sought the approval of the Proprietor, who would benefit from any successful defense the colony could muster. In Peters's words, "Tho' there may be at the bottom of it a personal antipathy to Quakers who brought the Country into this dilemma, yet they really desire to recommend themselves to the Proprietaries."[45] As Franklin suggested, the Associators would elect officers from among themselves, and they gathered in common places and marched in the streets. Peters reflected that their "Conduct hitherto has been remarkably regular and moderate, without any angry Expressions or blustering behaviour."[46]

As it turned out, by the time the Associators were ready to defend Philadelphia and Pennsylvania, peace between Great Britain and Spain and France was close to being established. The Treaty of Aix-la-Chapelle, signed on October 18, 1748, ended the War of the Austrian Succession.

Territorial hostilities lingered in the background, but the treaty officially ended attempts by French and Spanish privateers to enter into the Port of Philadelphia and disrupt the inhabitants of Pennsylvania. Relative peace ensued, perhaps because people understood that they could indeed muster up a force, if they needed to so do.

Plain Truth, the Association, the lottery—all were personal successes for Franklin, who gained a significant sense of his importance to the community as an organizer. He had given leadership roles in most of the organizing to others, but the community knew quite well whose initiative drove the plans for the Association and the lottery. Thomas Penn was threatened by the organizations, especially the idea that members would elect their leaders, which might set a precedent for general elections and eventually self-rule. Penn sniffed in a letter to Richard Peters (whom Penn eventually persuaded to his point of view) that Franklin was "a dangerous Man and I should be very Glad he inhabited any other Country." Penn grudgingly concluded that Franklin was, in effect, "a sort of Tribune of the People," and so had to be "treated with regard."[47] In fact, Franklin *was* a tribune of the people in these important decades of the 1740s and 1750s. Many of his activities, conducted alongside his newspaper and almanac businesses, his electrical experiments, and his various other scientific and social efforts, involved his playing a central role in formulating, developing, and organizing a series of endeavors for the public welfare. It was Franklin who arranged for and proposed funding of the specimen-collecting trip of botanist John Bartram (1699–1777) in 1742 and the development of the society for "useful knowledge," which became the American Philosophical Society; Franklin who proposed the Academy and English School in 1749; Franklin who planned for and helped establish the Pennsylvania Hospital in 1751–52, based on a joint venture between public finances and private; Franklin who proposed to merge the different Philadelphia city fire companies into one insurance company, the Philadelphia Contributorship, in 1751; and Franklin who worked out plans for communication via print (newspapers) and rider post. Franklin's friends and associates in Philadelphia and his scientific, business, and other correspondents in the other colonies and in London well understood his contributions to the local community and to the empire. Franklin attained roles of increasing importance to Philadelphia and the Pennsylvania colony.

Franklin was named justice of the peace for Philadelphia in 1749. On August 13, 1751, he took his seat in the Pennsylvania Assembly (a post to which he was annually re-elected until his famous defeat in 1764). He became alderman of Philadelphia in 1751. And on August 10, 1753,

Franklin was named a joint deputy postmaster for the American colonies (jointly with William Hunter [d. 1761], printer for Williamsburg), an appointment he had solicited.

Franklin's activities during the local defense crisis resulting from the War for the Austrian Succession laid the groundwork for his taking on several different roles both locally and on behalf of the empire and formed the basis as well for his delving into British imperial strategies. He saw that his ideas were admired by many people from diverse backgrounds, and he considered he could be useful to the empire, because he understood well the colonial situation in North America. He was corresponding with key leaders in all of the northern colonies, and he had some admirers in London—indeed, in Europe—as a result of his agricultural correspondence and his electrical experiments.

Franklin's Ideas for Securing the Empire

During the 1740s and 1750s, Franklin was in the process of studying population growth and dispersal in the American colonies, along with trade practices, imperial laws, and the American Indian question. He was able to put his knowledge to use once again when the war between Britain, Spain, and France continued, despite the declaration of peace and the treaty at Aix-la-Chapelle. This time, the warfare would directly hit North America, have significant impact on Indian relations, and cause the colonies considerable anxiety about defense. Franklin would yet again devise a plan of union—not of the disparate people of Pennsylvania but of the North American colonies. Franklin's *Albany Plan of Union* (1754) reveals his systemic analysis of the problems faced by the colonies in North America and his impressive imperial plan to address colonial defense, the colonies' relationships with one another, and the colonies' relationship to the imperial center. With the *Albany Plan*, we begin to see glimpses of Franklin's mature sense of what the British Empire might become.

The related problems of Indian affairs and colonial defense dominated Franklin's thinking at this time. The French were making their way down the Mississippi and Ohio Rivers, creating alliances with the Native peoples to the West against the Iroquois and their neighbors in the East. The Indian trade, carried on as it was by individuals and in anything but a systematic fashion, caused hardship and animosity among Indian peoples and, by extension, their recently settled neighbors. Traders often used alcohol to confound the Natives' judgment about the deals being made.[48] Franklin was concerned about the ethnic populations in western Pennsylvania. Some of those (German Catholics and Lutherans) who came to Pennsylvania and settled in the western parts could, the (probably unfounded) argument went, become French sympathizers who might not support British defense measures established by Protestants to the eastward. Franklin was likewise concerned that if the colonies were attacked—all at once—by French forces, they could not ably defend themselves, because they were divided in their interests and loyalties, and they lacked a coordinated system of communications, defense strategy, and munitions. He was deeply engrossed in his scientific experiments and his correspondence about electricity, but Franklin nonetheless worked hard in the early 1750s to conceive a plan whereby these many different issues could be addressed.[49]

The French were making plans to settle the territories west of the established borders of Pennsylvania and Virginia.[50] Preparing to occupy the Ohio Valley in 1753, the French were reputed (incorrectly) to be attempting to settle Germans into the Ohio area to secure them to the French side. Like many others in leadership positions, Franklin watched the French with concern about the future of the British Empire. In May that year, Governor Hamilton (based on a report from New York's Governor Clinton) told the Pennsylvania Assembly that a large party of French and Indians had been reported passing the town of Oswego, heading for the Ohio country. Likewise, Hamilton mentioned that the Iroquois (who were putatively in alliance with the British) at Onondaga were alarmed by the French movements through their territory.[51] The Iroquoian alliance with the British was strong, but it was always subject to competition with the French. In fact, separate private agreements about defense occurred between both French and English representatives, making the alliance with Britain as much a cipher as that with the French. The Iroquois, interested in protecting themselves, were playing the French and British Empires against each other in an effort to secure unity and power to the Iroquoian peoples, not the European peoples.[52]

The French were seeking to infiltrate British-claimed territories and create military fortifications behind British settlements. Their plan was to advance further into the Ohio country in 1754. In the interim, they built forts, one on the shore of Lake Erie at Presque Isle (now Erie, Pennsylvania) and one at an area they called Rivière aux Boeufs, which entered a tributary of the Allegheny River about fifteen miles south (an area now called French Creek), near present-day Waterford.[53] In response, the British government, represented by Robert D'Arcy (1718–1778), fourth

Earl of Holderness, who was serving as secretary of state, sent a circular letter of August 28, 1753, to all colonial governors. Holderness ordered the governors to "repel Force by Force," but only "within the undoubted limits of his Majesty's Dominions."[54] Based on the directive from Holderness, Robert Dinwiddie (1693–1770), lieutenant governor of Virginia, sent George Washington (1732–1799) out to Fort Le Boeuf with a directive that the French withdraw from Virginia territory. Washington returned in January 1754, with a message that the French had refused to comply with the directive. Dinwiddie was concerned that the French were going to take over the Ohio territory and use it as a means to attack the western reaches of Virginia.[55] Encouraged by Britain to do so, Dinwiddie called for a joint session of the governors of all the other colonies.

In Pennsylvania, Governor Andrew Hamilton (c. 1676–1741) in February met with the Assembly to seek its grant of immediate assistance for defense, so that Pennsylvania could support Virginia during this territorial crisis. The Assembly balked, expressing a concern about Pennsylvania's boundaries, and instead named a group of seven men, Benjamin Franklin among them, to report on the far boundaries of Pennsylvania, so that boundaries for defense would be on record. This was clearly a delay tactic by an Assembly committed to pacifism. After receiving the report, the Assembly took a recess. In fact, the Assembly was divided: some were willing to grant a sum of money in defense "for the King's Use" (a euphemism to avoid mentioning armaments), and some were not.

The British colonies' differences—both within the colonies and among them—as they considered how to respond to challenges by the French only served to heighten French interest in the lands west of the British settlements. Franklin was aware that the impasse in Pennsylvania was compromising the defense of its borders. He understood the importance of securing the Iroquois interest to the side of the British and developing a system whereby the colonial governments could work in concert with one another and defend the borders of the British Empire in North America. Franklin was actively engaged in working out a solution for managing both the Indians and the different colonial governments. From William Clarke (1709–1760), a Boston surgeon who joined the Louisbourg expedition in 1745, Franklin received information about the activities of the French and the English in two letters in 1754. On May 6, Clarke observed to Franklin that the jealousies among the colonies would always prevent an association for mutual protection. "I cannot help thinking," wrote Clarke, "that unless there be a united and vigorous opposition of the English Colonies to them, the French are laying a solid Foundation for being, some time or other, sole Masters of this Continent; notwithstanding our present Superiority to them, in point of Numbers."[56] The British colonists numbered, against the French, a proportion roughly of fifteen to one, so Clarke's view was accurate.[57] Clarke continued, "this Union is hardly to be expected to be brought about by any confederacy, or voluntary Agreement, among our selves. The Jealousies the Colonies have of each other, with regard to their real or imaginary different Interests, &c. will effectually hinder any thing of this kind from taking place." Even if a union were possible, Clarke said, the separate colonies would likely "never agree about the Form of the Union, or who should have the execution of the Articles of it." He concluded that the difficulties would continue, despite the necessity for "mutual Safety and preservation of these Colonies" until "we are forced to it, by the Supreme Authority of the Nation. And how little Attentive those that have the management of this authority are, and have been, to the Affairs of the Plantations, we know but too well."[58] Clarke and Franklin agreed that a directive from Britain was necessary. Franklin, in fact, was busy attempting to sort out what a united front could effect in Britain's behalf and how a union of the colonies might be arranged. He concluded that with an act of Parliament or else authorization by the Crown, a union of the colonies might be possible.

In the meantime, Franklin was busy trying to incite interest in the problem. He devised his famous "Join or Die" newspaper cartoon, the first of its kind in any American papers, and he accompanied it with a long paragraph of news that spoke to defense problems. [See Figure 4.2.] On May 9, 1754, the *Pennsylvania Gazette* carried a detailed description of the different French and Indian activities, including the British surrender of an indefensible fort on the Monongahela River in the face of over one thousand French forces and eighteen pieces of artillery. Indian trader William Trent (1715–c. 1787) had been commissioned to raise a company of volunteers to protect the small fort on the Ohio until reinforcements arrived, but he managed to muster fewer than fifty men. The French compelled the surrender. After providing significant details about the movements and armament of the French and French-allied Indians, the losses of traders and their goods, and the general alarm caused by these activities, Franklin observed, "The Confidence of the French in this Undertaking seems well-grounded on the present disunited State of the British Colonies, and the extreme Difficulty of bringing so many different Governments and Assemblies to agree in any speedy and effectual Measures for our common Defence and Security." He pointed out that "our Enemies have the very great Advantage of being under one Direction, with one Council, and one Purse." The British colonies, known to have no organization, in effect enabled the success of the French, who "presume that they

Figure 4.2 "Join or Die." Franklin published his snake cartoon, "Join or Die," in the *Pennsylvania Gazette*, May 9, 1754, during the height of concerns about defense of the colonies against the French and their Indian allies. Courtesy, Library Company of Philadelphia.

may with Impunity violate the most solemn Treaties subsisting between the two Crowns, kill, seize and imprison our Traders, and confiscate their Effects at Pleasure (as they have done for several Years past)," in addition to "murder[ing] and scalp[ing] our Farmers, with their Wives and Children, and take an easy Possession of such Parts of the British Territory as they find most convenient for them." He concluded with a warning: "if [the French] are permitted to do" this, the result will be "the Destruction of the British Interest, Trade and Plantations in America."[59]

Franklin's method was to inscribe fear into an article asking for nationalist pride. In Franklin's view, the British colonies' destruction was the consequence of inaction, lack of defense, and absence of coordination of the British colonies. His goal was to make people believe that their whole way of life was in jeopardy, so that they might begin to unite. The border settlers, here characterized largely as farmers, depended upon peaceable relations between traders and the surrounding Indians and settlers. Trade with the Indians constituted a feature of a fruitful trade system that benefited people locally and across the Atlantic. When the lives of settlers and traders in their midst were disrupted, the British Empire was in jeopardy.[60]

PLAN of the Town and Harbour of *LOUISBURGH*.

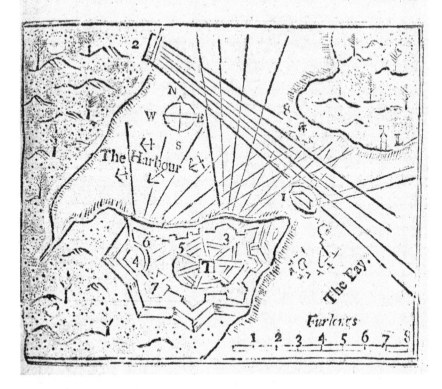

Figure 4.3 The Fortress at Louisbourg. Franklin created and published a woodcut of the supposedly impregnable fortress at Louisbourg, Cape Breton island, in the *Pennsylvania Gazette*, June 6, 1745. The woodcut map, considered the first map illustrating a news event in American journalism, shows the defenses at Louisbourg that the New England militia successfully captured. Franklin considered the militia's victory over the French, June 16–17, 1745, as an exemplary sign of British Americans' courage and military ability in the face of an imposing enemy. He apologized for the rudimentary nature of his woodcut, which he himself probably made, but let James Parker use it for a similar story in Parker's *New-York Weekly Post Boy* on June 10. Courtesy, Library Company of Philadelphia.

Franklin had invested much time and effort in defending the empire against France and supporting the Indian trade. In 1745, to remind colonists about the importance of defending the empire and supporting settlers living far from town and city centers, Franklin devised and then printed a woodcut of the supposedly impregnable fortress at Louisbourg on Cape Breton, shortly after New Englanders had captured it from the French.[61] [See Figure 4.3.] He sent his woodcut on to James Parker, so that Parker could use it just days later in his own paper, the *New York Weekly Post Boy*. From the 1740s, then, Franklin had been looking into how colonists might defend themselves against attacks by the French. He wondered whether the colonists should have to risk themselves, since they were fighting the French to assist the British Empire. French incursions into the Ohio country brought these questions to the fore for Franklin in the 1750s.

One result of Franklin's concerns about both the treatment given Native peoples and the best defenses against the French was his being commissioned by Governor James Hamilton (c. 1710–1783) to meet with the Ohio Indians who were returning home after a meeting with Virginia representatives in September 1753. With fellow commissioners Isaac Norris (1701–1766), speaker of the Assembly, and Richard Peters, Franklin made a hasty trip across the Susquehanna to meet with the party in Carlisle. The French had been pushing into the Ohio area. In addition to their forts at Presque Isle and Le Boeuf, they created one at Venango. The Indians allied with the British had attempted to rebuff the French, but they suffered losses and sought recompense and additional support from Virginia and Pennsylvania. One of the members of the treaty party, Tanacharison (Tanaghrisson, or Scruniyatha; 1700–1754), a civil chief among the Senecas known as "Half King," expressed particular concern about trade in the Ohio, indicating that if the British did not build and secure their own forts, they should expect that the French would take over the territory completely, because the Indians would no longer defend themselves and their purported British allies against the French.

Scaroyady (also Scarouady or Scarouyady; n.d.), an Oneida chief sent to represent the Iroquois at this meeting, complained about the trading methods of the British. Speaking on the Natives' behalf, Scaroyady complained that the traders brought the Indians too much "Rum and Flour" and ought instead to bring "Powder and Lead," because "The Rum ruins us."[62] Scaroyady also remarked that "English goods are sold at too dear a rate to us," and he followed up with this: "If only honest and sober Men were to deal with us, we think they might afford the Goods cheaper." Franklin was aware of unfair practices in trade with Native peoples, but this was perhaps the first time he conceived the British Empire might be at stake. Scaroyady explained that the locations of trading forts and the methods traders used were unfair. Scaroyady suggested that the British set up trading fortresses that would be secured with the assistance of Indians. He said that the French "look on the great Number of your Traders at Ohio with Envy; they fear they shall lose their Trade." To the Natives, the British had too many different traders in Indian country. Scaroyady complained, "You have more Traders than are necessary; and they spread themselves over our wide Country, at such great Distances, that we cannot see them, or protect them. We desire you will call back the great Number of your

Traders, and let only three Setts of Traders remain," asking for trade posts at "Logs-Town, the Mouth of Canawa, and the Mouth of Mohongely." He promised that "the Indians will then come to them, and buy their Goods in these Places, and no where else. We shall likewise look on them under our Care, and shall be accountable for them." Scaroyady made several important points that Franklin took note of: the too numerous traders created too much attention from the French; the traders were widely dispersed, causing undue hardship for the Indians, especially those designated to protect them; and the traders dealt scurrilously with the Indians by giving them alcohol prior to negotiating the trades and offering unsuitable goods when the exchanges took place.

Franklin learned much from these negotiations. He considered them so important that he printed a written version (probably much edited) of the negotiations as *A Treaty Held with the Ohio Indians, at Carlisle, In October, 1753* (1753). His British friends William Strahan (1715–1785) and Peter Collinson asked for copies of the treaty, and Franklin saw that copies were circulated widely in Britain and North America. Franklin used the documents in an effort to inform local settlers and those in Britain and Europe about the difficulties faced by colonists, including the processes of negotiation with Native peoples. Such negotiations were central to the British Empire in North America. They required patience, time, funding for gifts, and reliable communication networks, including trustworthy translators. In addition, it was difficult to find Indians who were, in fact, accepted spokespersons for their groups and difficult to distinguish friendly from duplicitous advice. Franklin understood the importance of these negotiations to the Empire. He printed the proceedings so that people in Britain, especially, would begin to understand that the colonists were not dealing with just one or two potential allies or potential enemies but with multitudes of potential allies and enemies from different tribal cultures, with different and competing goals, and unpredictable outcomes. Franklin understood and hoped others would understand that diplomacy was a complicated relation among British, Indian, and other European parties rather than a contest for empire simply among Europeans.

As it turned out, Franklin wanted to figure out a way to reduce the tensions between British settlers (and thus the British Empire) and the Indians. Indeed, he would publish in 1768 in London a satirical captivity narrative, "The Captivity of William Henry," to draw attention to the ways Native peoples were treated.[63] In the 1750s, Franklin became especially interested in the Indians' unhappiness caused by traders. For instance, in 1751, Franklin drafted the Assembly's statement to the Proprietor remonstrating against the Proprietor's lack of interest in developing good relations with the Indians. The Proprietor, through Governor Hamilton, had offered to assist funding a defensive fort based on the Indians' request at a meeting at Logstown in May of that year.[64] The Assembly expressed concern that the settlers were alone bearing the costs of treating with the Indians to keep relations in good stead. The settlers, in other words, were paying the costs of supporting the Proprietor's lands. The Assembly wanted the governor to recognize that if people unsuitable to be traders were creating problems for the Indians, the Pennsylvanians' costs were moot: the Indians would turn against British settlements. The Assembly's remonstrance thus makes two key points: first, a defensive fort might be useful, but more useful would be contributions to the gifts being made at treaty councils, and second, the selection of traders needed to be more careful, to ensure that only those of probity and concern for the British colonies' well-being would be invited to trade with Indians.

At the 1753 treaty council at Carlisle, Franklin was also concerned about Pennsylvania's defense, and he liked the Indians' suggestion about having designated trading posts. Immediately after the meeting at Carlisle, on October 18, 1753, Franklin wrote to Boston merchant James Bowdoin specifically to ask that Bowdoin send him the trading house laws established for Indians in the Boston area.[65] He liked the idea of regulating the Indian trade. In a letter to James Parker (c. 1714–1770) in March 1751, for instance, Franklin had remarked that the Indian trade would be enhanced with a system of public trading houses: "Publick Trading Houses would certainly have a good Effect towards regulating the private Trade; and preventing the Impositions of the private Traders; and therefore such should be established in suitable Places all along the Frontiers." He also thought that the Indians would benefit from having metalsmiths set up nearby. "Every one must approve the Proposal," he wrote at that time, "of encouraging a Number of sober discreet Smiths to reside among the Indians. They would doubtless be of great Service. The whole Subsistance of Indians, depends on keeping their Guns in order; and if they are obliged to make a Journey of two or three hundred Miles to an English Settlement to get a Lock mended; it may, besides the Trouble, occasion the Loss of their Hunting Season."[66] Franklin clearly was thinking of the Indians as affiliated with the British and working in the British interests, but he was also concerned that their needs were met, so as to retain their alliance.

In his letter to Bowdoin, he had asked how to go about creating the regulations and what had been the outcome. In his return letter about the trading posts, called "truckhouses," Bowdoin replied, "The best method we can go into, is to supply them with what they want at the cheapest rate possible, which will not only undermine the French Trade with them, but in proportion thereto bring them into our Interest and Friendship against the French." Bowdoin's conclusion was Franklin's, as well: this approach worked best, because "Trade and Commerce between Nation and Nation, especially when carried on to mutual advantage, have a natural Tendency to beget and confirm a mutual and lasting Friendship."[67] The intersection between equitable trade relations and the cementing of imperial alliances was indisputable. Trade and defense were mutually significant: the Indians' interest was the British interest, and the British interest was the Indians' interest. To neglect this point would be costly in terms of money and lives. Franklin, across his long life, had a variety of different views about indigenous peoples, but at this crucial moment in building a British Empire in North America, he argued that Indian interests, like colonial ones, were integral to the whole.

Franklin was again chosen by Governor Hamilton to attend an intercolonial conference, called the Albany Congress, in 1754. The Albany conference arose from the erosion of relations with the Six Nations Iroquois, centered in New York. The Iroquois had for decades attempted to engage in neutrality in the war between France and Britain on Iroquoian lands, and they justifiably were troubled by the problems caused them by irregular and inequitable trading practices and by the proximity of the British and the French and French-allied Indians on their western borders. In the fall of 1753, the Board of Trade asked that the colonies of New York, Virginia, Pennsylvania, Maryland, New Hampshire, Massachusetts Bay, and New Jersey send commissioners to a conference with representatives of the Iroquois, so that they all might engage together in "burying the Hatchet and renewing the Covenant Chain," a reference to the agreements made between the Iroquois and the British representatives suggestive of their mutual respect and alliance.[68] As it turned out, Virginia and New Jersey declined to take part, and Rhode Island and Connecticut were invited to participate by Governor James DeLancey (1703–1760) of New York. The commissioners were to engage in creating "one general Treaty to be made in his Majesty's Name."[69]

Franklin was in the midst of working through the details related to the Pennsylvania Hospital, but he attended the conference with John Penn and Richard Peters of the Council and Isaac Norris, speaker of the House. When meeting with his cohort prior to the actual conferences, the representatives generally agreed that it would be difficult to find a way to get the different colonies to unite in their plans and policies. Franklin drafted a brief that he shared, in advance of the official meeting, with several of his colleagues. The plan Franklin devised is strikingly similar to the one he had mentioned in his March 20, 1751, letter to James Parker, and it aligns with the plans suggested by Archibald Kennedy for winning the Indian interest to the British interest. Three key issues mark Franklin's plans. First, the plans acknowledged that the Indians had been treated unfairly and with inconsistency (especially by unscrupulous traders and by settlers who, in effect, gave only a pittance for extensive lands), so a unified strategy would be essential to keep the Iroquois allied with the British. Second, the plans argued for a centralized administration with supporting staff from among the different colonies as the best way to administer Indian affairs and defense against the French and French-allied Indians. And finally, the plans suggested ways in which a commonly funded treasury could aid in defense of British and Indian lands. In Franklin's view, defense concerned not just forts and land locations but also coastal or riverine locations.

The public plans under discussion at the Albany meeting required a kind of public subterfuge on the parts of both the Iroquois and the group representing Pennsylvania. Franklin was aware that private negotiations for land acquisitions were taking place between the Proprietary agents and the Indians. He was also aware that the Iroquois were selling large amounts of land settled by other Indians, principally Delawares, along with a range of non-Indian settlers who were not paying quitrents for the lands they were inhabiting. Private dealings (by their very nature) were less easily controlled than public ones. But the very publicity of Franklin's plans, along with the debates that would take place over them once the negotiations concluded and decisions were made in councils, helped defeat the impact of private negotiations for the larger community.

The version of Franklin's plan that made it through the debates differed from what he had originally suggested to his associates at the time they arrived in Albany. Still, the Albany Plan of Union, largely Franklin's creation, offered a significantly centralized imperial blueprint for administration that suggests the range of Franklin's thinking on imperial matters. The Albany Plan allowed for representation of the individual member colonies by way of a Grand Council, the members to be selected by election, and it allowed for a chief administrator, selected by the Crown. Franklin was suggesting a mixed form of government, one that allowed for an optimal possibility of representation, based on a colony's population, while also having the imperial "check" on this representation with a leader selected by the Crown. Funds for the Union would be based on contributions made by the individual colonies: "That the said General Government be administered by a President General, To be appointed and supported by the Crown, and a Grand Council to be Chosen by the Representatives of the People of the Several Colonies, met in their Respective Assemblies." Under the president general's direction, "with the Advice of the Grand Council," would be all Indian treaties and the right to "make Peace or Declare War with the Indian Nations." The president general would also "make such Laws as they Judge Necessary for regulating all Indian Trade." And finally, the president general would handle all land transactions, "mak[ing] all Purchases from Indians for the Crown, of Lands not within the Bounds of Particular Colonies," and "Grant[ing] Lands in the Kings Name," to new settlements, "till the Crown shall think fit to form them into Particular Governments."[70] This plan allowed for a consistent centralized administration, regular communication with the Crown, and equal opportunities for all settlers. The last point was an important one for Franklin: it would prevent individuals or groups from creating competing, private agreements over the same territories, and it might mitigate the competition among the colonies resulting from the different charters and founding documents.

The significance of Franklin's suggestions was not lost on his colonial peers. Franklin's friend William Clarke drew up his own observations about the importance of keeping the Iroquoian interests on the side of the British and the usefulness of the colonies to British maritime trade and imperial power.[71] Clarke published his *Observations on the late and present Conduct of the French, with Regard to their Encroachments upon the British Colonies in North America* in 1755 with an addendum of Franklin's *Observations concerning the Increase of Mankind*, originally written in 1751 and circulated in manuscript from the point when it was first written. Clarke's position on defense and on the importance of the colonies to the imperial power of Great Britain dovetailed with Franklin's. Both men understood the importance of keeping active, positive connections with the Iroquois, even as they also knew that the Iroquois were selling out other Pennsylvania Indians, chiefly the Delawares. Both also recognized the precariousness of the colonies' military defense in the face of French support by western Indians and French fortifications bordering British areas. And both knew how important the riverine system was to keeping strong trade networks within and between British colonies.

Franklin and Clarke believed that Parliament, ministers, and Crown were unable to comprehend two key aspects of Britain's problem in North America. First, there was a problem of the North American terrain, which was difficult to traverse, making the calculations of miles only part of the equation when dealing with arming soldiers or militia, because the central problems of movement—trees, waterways, and mountains—were incomprehensible to armchair wartime theorists.[72] Second, Clarke and Franklin worked to show the extent to which the colonies' products were central to Great Britain's current wealth.[73] Like Franklin, Clarke pointed out the advantage the French had over the British in a most crucial aspect of military strategy: French settlements were under the centralized control of a single commander. As Clarke phrased it, "This may appear very extraordinary at first View, considering the superior Number of Inhabitants within the *English*, to those of the *French* Colonies, especially as the English are Masters of such a large Sea-Coast," but "the Form of Government in the French Colonies" worked to give the French great "Advantages": "All the French Settlements in *North-America*, how many small Governments soever they may be divided into, are under the absolute Command of the Governor of *Canada*."[74] The British colonies, by contrast, were, "exclusive of *Georgia* and *Nova-Scotia*, "divided into eleven distinct Governments," with different assemblies that ordered their separate governments. As Franklin often noted in his 1750s correspondence, the different governments and remoteness of their capitals produced great difficulties in getting the colonists to agree upon the importance of defense funding to thwart French incursions.

Taken in the context of his friendships with men of high station who were interested in influencing imperial decision-making, Franklin's Albany Plan of Union was quite sweeping in its recommendations. Like William Clarke and Massachusetts governor William Shirley (1694–1771), Franklin understood that trade, defense, and empire were intricately intertwined, and concerted action was essential to the future stature of the colonies and Great Britain. Getting those who had no experience in the colonies to understand the predicament of Great Britain's interests became the crucial challenge Franklin faced in the later 1750s and the 1760s.

Franklin's Idealism

In the 1754 Albany Plan of Union Franklin offered a strategy for controlling Indian relations and the Indian trade across the British settlements in North America. He also spoke to the importance of building a defensive posture that would work to establish British fortifications against French and French-allied Indians in British North America. Franklin's imperial theory was systems-based. That is, he worked out a strategy that allowed for a systematic and controlled series of relationships that would work internally, within each colony and by way of elected representatives, and externally, from colony to colony and all equally with the Crown, on behalf of the British nation. Far from being naive about colonial problems, Franklin understood that the British interest in North America would best be represented if the colonists could find a way to work with one another and with common friends among the Indians and work collaboratively against their common enemies, the French, Spanish, and their Indian allies. The plan failed to get adopted by the individual assemblies and was rejected by Crown officials. Franklin's views were idealistic, but not uninformed. Franklin had not given sufficient credence to the interest politics being pursued both in the colonies and in Britain.[75]

Although his Albany Plan met with little approval, Franklin continued to work aggressively in behalf of the British Empire in North America. When the Crown sent Major General Edward Braddock (1695–1755) as commander-in-chief of British forces in North America, Franklin was there to assist him in finding men and materiel. He set up postal communications for Braddock, and he became part of the team Braddock consulted—though Braddock did not listen to the advice Franklin and others gave him—as he attempted to prosecute military operations in North America. The result of Braddock's unwillingness to attend to the colonial advisers' suggestions about conciliatory gestures to friendly Indians and about defending British interests was a disastrous defeat at what has come to be called the Battle of the Monongahela in 1755.

With Franklin's help in the Assembly, the colony of Pennsylvania continued to develop its own strategies for defense in the absence of an imperial program. Franklin convinced the Assembly to pass a Militia Act in the fall of 1755. The act allowed for the creation of an all-volunteer force, much like the one the Association had created in the 1740s. The Militia Act, along with an act to supply the troops, passed the Assembly and enabled a system of defense for Pennsylvania as the French and French-allied Indians continued to harass Pennsylvania's settlers and friendly Indians. But the border defenses would always be plagued by a need for funds, and Franklin increasingly became convinced that Pennsylvanians' lives and estates should receive the protection of the Proprietor or else of the Crown. In the year 1757, Franklin accepted the nomination by the Pennsylvania Assembly to be its representative and chief negotiator in England, after the Assembly recognized a need for its own representation directly with the Crown in its disputes with the Proprietor. Franklin set sail for England in 1757, hopeful that if he could simply get the Penn family to meet with him, he could lay out the problems of Pennsylvanians in a reasonable way and help the family come to understand better Pennsylvania's imperial potential. He seems to have continued believing, as he had written to James Parker back in 1751, that by sending out "Men of good Understanding and Address" and by "furnish[ing] them with a reasonable Scheme and proper Instructions," a better understanding might occur. In 1751, he was talking about creating a union of the colonies. Franklin seems always to have held that "reasonable sensible Men, can always make a reasonable Scheme appear such to other reasonable Men, if they take Pains."[76]

External imperial matters of trade and defense and internal (i.e., intra- and intercolonial) matters of social stability and cohesion—these were Franklin's political and social concerns during the years when Pennsylvania was challenged by significant immigration, piracy by the French in its seaports, and war by the French and their Indian allies on the northern and western borders. As government printer and postmaster and as an assemblyman and civic leader, Franklin was at the hub of activity during the 1740s and 1750s. As we have seen, Franklin had a range of social connections among both wealthy and laboring peoples, and he was frequently called upon by members of the Assembly and by the Proprietary and its representatives to assist in working to balance out the needs of the community and the empire. To phrase his position succinctly: Franklin was at the center of the colony's political and social decision-making.

Five

"PEOPLE IN THE COLONIES . . . BETTER JUDGES"

Observing Empire at Midcentury

Benjamin Franklin became one of Europe's most influential imperial theorists, though he went largely unacknowledged in England during the 1750s, when he began to establish himself as a statesman. In public letters to the press, private correspondence among a variety of acquaintances, and pamphlets and other publications, Franklin represented the American colonists' side in debates about British colonial administration. His writings show that Franklin the tradesman had turned into an imperial mathematician. It is almost as if Franklin pondered the question, What would it take to make Great Britain the strongest European power in North America and around the globe? His answer rested in multiple sets of criteria: availability of a superior land mass of fertile and productive soil; a proportionate population of healthy, independent laborers tilling their own freeholds; a culturally diverse population that would be able to create diverse products and consume others' products via fair trade networks; a body of laws supporting self-governance; and security of property and person from the depredations of foreigners. Because he knew well the different areas of North America about which he was concerned, Franklin was among the best-informed imperial theorists of his day.

In many of Franklin's projects we can observe an intersection of interests. The colonies were, he conceived, nearly self-sufficient. They could produce their own goods, if left unhampered by trade regulations. Considering the colonies as part of an empire, he believed they were a ready market for Britain. He talked about internal trade with the Indians and establishing fair trade policies with neighboring nations. He wrote about land use and, by association, labor, in the colonies and in Great Britain. He studied populations in different locales and examined the likelihood of increase. Franklin's theorizing about empire was intricately tied to his thoughts about the proportional relationship between the number of laboring people and available land for tillage and manufacturing.[1]

Most striking is Franklin's sense that different parts of the empire might benefit from other parts of it in a cooperative and collaborative network. Franklin's views of land and its productivity reveal sensitivity to geographical locale, soil quality, and methods of husbandry, indicating a concern about the impact of both humans and animals on the environment. Close examination of Franklin's writings reveals his concomitant interests—like many a European geographic demographer—in concepts associated with ethnicity and the contributions that people of different backgrounds might make to a commonwealth. Franklin's demographic analysis related to his theories of imperial relations; the two are entwined in most of his political tracts from this era. Complementing the previous chapter's discussion of Franklin's involvement in Pennsylvania politics, this chapter pauses to explore Franklin's early 1750s views about agriculture, the environment, population, and imperial idealism. As Franklin's "Observations concerning the Increase of Mankind" and his letters to William Shirley clarify, he was even in the 1750s considering that the colonies' potential for self-rule was strong. Indeed, his writings from this era reveal many of Franklin's mature views of the potential for an American empire free of British intrusion.

Agriculture and Imperial Policy

In the early 1750s, Franklin was involved with his electrical experiments and with drawing up plans for and setting up the Academy, the English School, and the Pennsylvania Hospital in Philadelphia. He exchanged correspondence with people in North America and Britain about the cultivation of lands, the best ways to help both land and people prosper, and the latest advice about ways to improve husbandry. Beginning in the late 1740s, agriculture had begun to fascinate him, just as it did his many learned correspondents. Agriculture and studies in husbandry increasingly formed part of Franklin's reading, and they entered his experimental investigations and thus written exchanges with people on both sides of the Atlantic.

Franklin's concerns about improving agriculture found their way into his plans for education, both in the plan for the Academy (a college) as for the English School (a day school). Indeed, the study of agricultural matters was such a matter of course for him that he used it as an opening metaphor in his "Proposals for the Education of Youth" in 1749: "If Men may, and frequently do, catch . . . a Taste for cultivating Flowers, for Planting, Grafting, Inoculating, and the like, as to despise all other Amusements for their Sake, why may we not expect they should acquire a Relish for that *more useful* Culture of young Minds," Franklin asked.[2] Study in these areas was explicitly called for in his proposal, to complement readings in natural history. And the students were to "now and then" make "Excursions" to visit "the neighboring Plantations of the best Farmers," to observe "their Methods" so that these might be "reason'd upon for the Information of Youth." Besides, he concluded, "The Improvement of Agriculture . . . [was] useful to all, and Skill in it no Disparagement to any."[3] Franklin's ideas were innovative, compared to existing educational models, which emphasized classical learning above practical learning. His ideas represent some of the newest thinking available in North America on the importance of understanding husbandry and land management.

Franklin was one among a circle of correspondents whose members were inquiring into different agricultural models. Franklin shared his thoughts on agriculture, among other topics, with several friends, mostly notably Cadwallader Colden (1688–1776) and Jared Eliot (1685–1763). Colden, the lieutenant governor of New York and a leading botanist, agricultural philanthropist, and physician and a friend of Swedish botanist and zoologist Carl Linneaus (1707–1778), was at the time North America's best-known student of botany and zoology. Colden's tract on yellow fever had caught Franklin's eye, but their letters ranged on topics from theories of perspiration and "animal oeconomy" to the speed of travel east and west across the Atlantic Ocean and the value of tar water in treating human diseases. Colden encouraged Franklin to offer classes on agriculture in his academy, and he helped Franklin circulate his ideas, from those on land use and population to those on electricity. Jared Eliot learned of Franklin's interest in his work and opened up a correspondence with him in the late 1740s by sending Franklin his manuscripts and then his published *Essays upon Field-Husbandry in New-England*, published between 1748 and 1759. Eliot encouraged silk culture in Connecticut, designed a process for creating iron from black sea sand, and ran repeated agricultural experiments on his farms, which he shared in his *Essays*. Eliot's friendship and shared values helped Franklin develop his own ideas about agricultural improvements. He often launched his agricultural ideas first with Eliot, trying them out against Eliot's knowledge and experience, and improving his ideas from the suggestions he received. The two talked about various agricultural processes, from draining swamps and meadows in order to cultivate hemp, to the causes of mildew in corn and hay, to the foundations of springs on high grounds, to the reasons for the striations in the rocks of New England. The 1740s and 1750s found Franklin acutely interested in all aspects of the natural world, including the study of what today might be called environmentalism and sustainability, in addition to the better-known work in electrical theory.

Franklin was in the thick of activity as a member of Pennsylvania's Assembly as he pondered the predicament of the colonies with regard to British colonial policy.[4] An immediate cause for alarm arose from the significant amount of crime arising from convict servants in Virginia, Maryland, and Pennsylvania. Franklin's *Pennsylvania Gazette* for April 11, 1751, carried a long article about the mayhem—arsons, murders, robberies, and so forth—caused mostly by convicts brought to the colonies under new laws established in Britain. In earlier times, the colonies enacted laws against the importation of convicts or regulated high duties on their importation. But beginning in 1717, when Parliament passed a new Piracy Act providing for the transportation of felons to the colonies, colonial governments were prevented from passing their own laws limiting the importation of convicts. Pennsylvania's attempt in August 1749 to pass its own law placing a high duty on the importation of convicts was never presented to the Board of Trade. Pennsylvanians learned in January 1751 that their act had been scuttled by Pennsylvania's agents and the Proprietors for fear—given newer efforts to bring the colonies into one standard policy—that the constitutionality of all of Pennsylvania's acts and the colony's proprietary status would be questioned.[5]

Franklin was incensed. His response to the scuttling of Pennsylvania's efforts to control the influx of convicts was an acerbic satire on "rattlesnakes for felons" in the *Pennsylvania Gazette* for May 9, 1751.[6] Addressed "To the Printers of the Gazette," the article began by referring to the April 11 issue reporting on the problems with convicts. Under the pen name *Americanus*, Franklin ironically observed, "I understand that the Government at home will not suffer our mistaken Assemblies to make any Law for preventing or discouraging the Importation of Convicts from Great Britain, for this kind Reason, '*That such Laws are against the Publick*

Utility, as they tend to prevent the IMPROVEMENT *and* WELL PEOPLING *of the Colonies.'*" In return for such thoughtfulness, which "call[ed] aloud for the highest *Returns* of Gratitude and Duty," Franklin proposed that rattlesnakes be sent to Britain, to be "carefully distributed in St. James's Park, in the Spring-Gardens and other Places of Pleasure about London; in the Gardens of all the Nobility and Gentry throughout the Nation; but particularly in the Gardens of the *Prime Ministers*, the *Lords of Trade* and *Members of Parliament*; for to them we are *most particularly* obliged."[7] The exchange of rattlesnakes for felons would work well, of course, for venomous satirical implication, but the idea of *exchange* between the colonies and Great Britain also served to illustrate that, in Franklin's view, the colonists ought to send out exports in return for imports.

Britain's plan for populating the colonies by sending its poor and its convicted felons to America struck a sore nerve in Franklin. Franklin was in the process of developing his own theories about how to manage poverty (frequently the cause of crime) and sickness, but exporting criminals to the colonies would never suit a progressive imperial agenda like the one he was developing. He worked hard as an assemblyman and provincial leader to show Great Britain the potential for imperial power that might accrue to the empire with the right management and defense of the colonies. It was difficult for him to believe that Parliament and ministry could support the peopling of the colonies with the social outcasts of Great Britain. Britain was in the process of developing a series of new colonial policies. Franklin wanted to be sure that colonists' ideas received a hearing.

British colonial policy during the first decades of the eighteenth century had been largely an unofficial policy of "salutary neglect."[8] The ministry was tending to matters of concern internal to Great Britain, including repeated fiscal crises and problems with land distribution and use, labor, and the politics of administration. So the different colonial American assemblies tended to the internal matters of each colony. The need for comprehensive imperial measures began to emerge as the goals of different colonial administrations changed and as the French continued their encroachments on the interior of North America. As James Henretta has explained it, members of the new Board of Trade in the 1760s found themselves "at the center of a struggle between two distinct types of colonial administration, each justified . . . by its own theory of empire."[9] One system of governance relied upon colonial assemblies for legislation and governance. This system—which was not a system at all but instead a series of haphazard circumstances based on the differing original charters of the different colonies—came into particular turmoil during the late 1740s and the 1750s, as the colonists grew increasingly restive in the face of French maneuvers on colony borders and the tightening of trade and navigation policies set into place in Great Britain. The second system sought constraints on production and commerce. Again in the words of Henretta, "The proponents of a system of strong central supervision of the American possessions now occupied key posts in the colonial bureaucracy and were seeking parliamentary sanction for administrative measures which would embody their own theory of empire."[10] In later years, Franklin would understand Britain's attempt to streamline colonial policy as one seeking to dovetail American affairs with those in British India. But in these middle decades, Franklin conceived the situation as a misunderstanding on the part of Britons in Great Britain about how to manage lands, people, and resources in North America and a misapprehension of the colonies' value to the so-called mother country.

The plan to send convicts to the colonies was one among a cluster of policies developed or reauthorized by Parliament to improve circumstances for Britons in England. Other acts in place or being developed around this time displayed Britain's ignorance of the social and economic situation in the British colonies of North America, whether speaking of the mainland colonies or the Caribbean islands. In addition rankling at Parliament's reauthorization of the Piracy Act, Franklin grew alarmed by the Iron Act of 1750 and the Currency Act of 1751. The Iron Act, called the Importation, etc., Act of 1750, changed the situation regarding production of iron in the North American colonies. The act was designed to encourage the colonial exportation of raw iron products, including pig iron and bar iron, and to prevent the further development of iron furnaces for iron production in British North America. In effect, the act was to restrict colonial production of iron and steel, forcing exportation of raw materials rather than allowing for manufacturing in America. Such a move might straiten the circumstances of Pennsylvanians, who had a significant stake in iron manufacture and export. The Currency Act of 1751 likewise created havoc for Pennsylvanians, who had, across the previous decades, used the emission of paper money as a stimulus to the local economy and an aid to the distribution of goods and services. As we have seen, Franklin was particularly fond of the role that paper money could play in assisting the economic well-being of Pennsylvania and New England. But beginning in the 1740s, the London merchants whose complaints were receiving a greater hearing from the Board of Trade and Parliament, complained that they did not wish to have to accept colonial currency, particularly the currency of New England, for goods they exported to the colonies. In effect, the act assisted British merchants at the expense of Britons in North America who had grown used to emitting and recalling currency as a matter of boosting local economies yet controlling for internal inflation. The key problem seems to have been that, in Great Britain, the idea that the colonies were a significant part of the British Empire and indeed central to the future prospering of the empire was inconceivable.[11] In most instances, the acts worked to diminish colonial prospects for manufacture and trade while enhancing the quality of life for Britons back home.

Colonial administration had long been a topic of serious debate among political and social theorists in Great Britain and in North America. The threat of French encroachments and of shifting Indian alliances made the situation precarious for Britons in North America. The competition over territories and peoples in North America formed part of a larger imperial challenge faced by Britain and France: how might land be used to foster the greatest amount of production for the greatest number of people. As environmental historian Richard H. Grove has pointed out, in the middle of the eighteenth century, Britain was attempting to develop a land-use strategy to address its soil depletion and deforestation at home. The goal in Britain was to shift the burden of resource depletion onto British colonials and British colonial holdings.[12] If Britain could also thrust upon the colonies its convicts and the poor, who did not enhance production and social stability but instead used up significant resources, Britain might have a greater chance to improve the quality of life of those living inside Britain.

The effect, environmentally speaking, was to displace the social and economic problems resulting from environmental degradation and depletion onto the colonies, distancing resource depletion onto regions outside the mainland. Consider the case of timber extraction. In England, from the late seventeenth century through the late eighteenth century, anxiety about shipbuilding for the British navy prompted a move to conserve and enlarge existing woodlands. But landowners in England fought—indeed, riots occurred—against the increasingly restrictive forest acts designed to protect timber. Landholders argued in behalf of their rights to use their private property as they pleased. Anxiety about timber remained, however, so Britain determined on a policy of extraction of American forests. In Grove's words, "Between 1690 and 1776 increasingly interventionist attempts were made to utilise and secure timber supplies from the American colonies." The goal behind successive acts was "to secure exclusive forest rights for the Crown over larger and larger areas of New England."[13] Despite England's diverse timber tracts, in other words, landholders in England were protected from extraction; instead, timber extraction would occur in North America.

By contrast, the French had begun, under the original leadership of Jean-Baptiste Colbert (1619–1683), minister of finance and secretary of the navy, to study, systematize, and regulate agricultural holdings. Of particular interest were the studies of forest science and soil management. The result of Colbert's oversight of the forests, the Forest Ordinance of 1669, revealed, in France, what Richard Grove has described as "a political commitment to control" agricultural production that stands "in stark contrast to government attitudes in England at the same period, where common rights to land use were far more politically potent." The French worked to create systems of conservation of resources, evidenced by various land management acts to protect forests. Following Colbert, groups of horticulturalists and botanists associated with the Jardin du Roi developed for over a century a system of intervention in France to ensure timber cultivation and protection. The goal was to conserve agricultural products in France. Grove has concluded, "In England many resource demands were displaced to the colonies, while in France an attempt was made instead to devise a more systematic form of land management" at home.[14] The difference in practice occurred throughout the eighteenth century.

As Franklin's writings attest, Britons felt superior to the colonists. The British debates about colonial policy at this time centered on metropolitan concerns and featured three key goals: to gather into a colonial network a system of dispersed colonies that would augment the wealth and diversity of manufactures of England; to ensure that the costs of administration and defense of the colonies would be displaced onto those who lived on or held money-making property in the colonies; and to control the trade of the colonies so that England's surplus goods would be manufactured and sold to those living in British holdings. In essence, this was a revival and reuse of some older economic theories. Writers tended to express fear that there was a drain upon English purses due to wars in North America. Such a drain on England did not benefit the British people at home, so, the argument went, Britons in North America should make up the difference by exporting raw materials to England for manufacture. If Americans were permitted to manufacture, their products would interfere with British manufacturing and sea trade. The imperial goal was to obtain raw materials, process the products, and then make of the colonies an additional market for British goods manufactured in England.

There was less concern in England (when compared with France) with long-term effects on the environment, whether on the mainland or in the colonies. In the French model, resources were controlled by the state rather than by individuals. The French imperial model meant that laws enacted in France impacted French colonies, because the colonies were under the control of the French Crown. Perhaps because it was more populous than England, France began conservation measures during the seventeenth century. It carried such conservation into the eighteenth century not just in policy but by intellectuals frustrated with the classed system in France. Arguments about the need for social and political reform found expression, Richard Grove points out, "in terms of natural history, agronomy and attitudes towards climatic theories and fears of climatic change."[15] In the context of Grove's analysis, the rise of the cluster of intellectuals who called themselves Physiocrats is unsurprising, given French issues of overpopulation and the tightening of land. Grove has concluded that British and French differences in approach "affected the whole pattern of development of the conservation policies of the two countries in their colonial possessions." Their fundamental differences were being registered in their political conduct during the eighteenth century.

It is no wonder that Franklin's views about the relationship of flow between land use and population would eventually receive much more attention in France, particularly from the Physiocrats, than they would in England. Franklin's writings about the British colonial system, even at this stage in his life, suggest concerns about economic impact on the American colonies of Britain's constraining system. But Franklin was concerned as well about environmental problems in North America if Britain were to ride roughshod over American lands. Deforestation and its concomitant impact on wildlife in New England was something Franklin himself had seen as a youth. Living in Pennsylvania, Franklin conceived that the British colonies would not survive the onslaught of colonists (and colonial processes) without careful management of resources and immigrant peoples and without military protection in areas bordering with French peoples and Indians hostile to British settlements. Nowhere is this more clear than in his work for the Assembly,[16] the Albany Plan, and his "Observations concerning the Increase of Mankind," an essay he began writing in the late 1740s, concluded in 1751, and circulated widely thereafter.

Having served at Indian treaty negotiations, Franklin understood from the Indians' perspective the success of France's state model of military power and its centralized policies on Indian relations. France streamlined its policies regulating interactions with Native peoples, and its methods had, in effect, befriended them.[17] Franklin believed that the single military head model used by France in North America made it possible for France to dominate in North America. Britain's colonies were too divided and competitive. It was for this reason that Franklin had devised the Albany Plan so as to create a single military leader for British North America. Whether considering the environmental or the military impact of the British, Franklin considered that Great Britain ought to alter its model of imperial expansion if it wished to retain the North American colonies as part of the greater British Empire. As we have seen, Franklin's involvement in matters of colonial administration prompted his inquiry into Indian trading policies and practices in all the colonies. He also sought—as demonstrated in his Albany Plan—a more stable and secure standing for the colonies internally (i.e., among themselves) and externally (i.e., with regard to the British Empire and global expansion).

He was fascinated by debates about the empire. From an unidentified copyist, Franklin received some notes, probably about this time, drawn from *Discourses on the Public Revenues, and on the Trade of England* (London, 1698) by Charles Davenant (1656–1714), an economist and politician. The notes are from Part 2, Discourse 3, "On the Plantation Trade." Their presence among Franklin's papers indicates Franklin's awareness of Davenant's long and influential tract on trade and navigation and the effect of Britain's navigation policies on its social, political, and economic conditions.[18] Davenant's views, on some matters, are quite similar to Franklin's. Davenant wrote, for instance, that the colonies "are a Spring of Wealth to this Nation," because "they work for us, . . . their Treasure centers all here . . . and . . . the Laws have ty'd 'em fast enough to us; so that, it must be through our own Fault, and Misgovernment, if they become independent of *England*."[19] Davenant had been interested in implementing the series of Navigation Acts that began in the seventeenth century. He took some of his material from a plan laid before the Board of Trade by William Penn in February 1697.[20] Davenant liked Penn's plan for a centralized government in America, with representatives from each active colony attending meetings hosted in New York (considered geographically central). He wrote fully about such a plan in his *Discourses*. Davenant also supported the rights of colonial assemblies to enact their own laws, as long as the laws agreed with those enacted by Parliament. Davenant attempted to discuss the situation of labor in the colonies, but without good information about them, he could not understand the extent to which the Navigation Acts' constraints on manufacturing and trade hindered labor opportunities in the colonies. This is where Franklin could advocate for a more comprehensive policy.

Franklin's Observations on the Increase of Mankind

Few in Great Britain recognized that by diminishing the environmental and economic circumstances of the colonies, Britain was diminishing its own potential for growing the empire both at home and in North America. Franklin aimed to explain his views regarding Britain's need to protect the natural resources in the colonies, support manufacturing there, and provide for an English-speaking, skilled (rather than convict) labor force to emigrate there. He wanted to show how important it was to implement an administrative policy that would benefit the colonies, because by assisting the colonies, he conceived, colonial policy could assist the empire. To this end, he accumulated information and started drafting his long essay on trade, the "increase of mankind," and the "peopling of countries."

When he began drafting "Observations concerning the Increase of Mankind" in 1750, Franklin (as a member of a special committee of the Assembly) had been studying the productions of Pennsylvania. He used his ability with numbers to work out a proportional relationship between population and land availability, quality, and use. Employing the concept of flow he developed when writing about paper money, Franklin argued that the large amount of land and the diversity of potential agricultural produce would bring about a natural increase in the inhabitants of North America. The people would have a high standard of living, and they would live longer than people inhabiting a territory with natural delimitations and depleted soils. The venting of England's criminals did not fit into his plan, nor did the idea of making the North American colonies merely extractive resource colonies rather than manufacturing and productive contributors to the commonwealth. Franklin's theories about empire required freedom from trade constraints. It also depended on a free and diverse labor force. Built on an assumption that indentured laborers would eventually wish to hold their own freeholds, Franklin's theories were based in an expansionist commercial model affording a wide market for the flow of a variety of agricultural products and manufactured goods.

In his "Observations," Franklin addressed specific anti-free trade and pro-dependent colony arguments that imperial theorists commonly took regarding the American colonies. One of the common arguments was based on the old economic debates about constraining trade. The concern in Great Britain was that the best artisans in the most productive and important trades would leave England for British North America, thus depriving England of its best laborers. If the people in the American colonies were permitted to engage in manufacturing of their own goods, they would be competing with British manufacturers and merchants.[21] This was the argument used by the manufacturing interest in Great Britain, which claimed that labor there would become more costly, because fewer highly skilled laborers would remain in England if they were permitted to emigrate to improve their quality of life. With fewer workers, both agricultural products and manufactures would become more costly, the argument went. To counter this, Franklin said that with so much land available in North America, it would take "many Ages to settle . . . fully" the colonies. "The Danger . . . of these Colonies interfering with their Mother Country in Trades that depend on Labour, Manufactures, &c. is too remote to require the Attention of Great-Britain," he wrote.[22] Hindsight, of course, enables us to see the weakness in such arguments. Franklin was attempting to employ his rhetorical skills to persuade a reading audience fearful about an economic power shift toward the colonies, a power shift that Franklin himself surmised might eventually occur.

Franklin also addressed a challenge faced in North America: labor could never be cheap there, because most tradespeople eventually sought to own their own land and become independent. Thus, laborers were difficult to find, which drove up the wages of laboring people. This view, based in a freehold (and nonplantation) agricultural model rather than a manufacturing model, assumed the dominance of the independent farmer who owned his own plot, took care of his own land, and either manufactured his own goods or traded for those goods he could not manufacture. It ran counter to a theory more frequently propounded at the time Franklin was writing, that a manufacturing population would prompt the best use of land and support the largest population.[23] Whereas earlier economic theorists had expressed what economic historian Klaus Knorr long ago called a "predilection for industry and trade as against agriculture,"[24] Franklin was arguing for a mixed economy of independent agriculturalists whose backgrounds as tradesmen would enable them to achieve a mixed use of land. This reasoning suggests a concern to establish a balanced set of agricultural methods that would work in flow with manufacturing and benefit from economic policies associated with free trade.

Working to counter the British arguments supporting the restrictions on trade and the flow of laborers to the colonies, Franklin also took up the issue of slavery. In the case of chattel slavery, one of the arguments in Britain was that labor in the colonies, being performed by slaves, would undercut the cost of free or indentured labor in Britain and thus always undercut the cost of any goods manufactured in England. To this argument Franklin responded, "'Tis an ill-grounded Opinion that by the Labour of Slaves, America may possibly vie in Cheapness of Manufactures with Britain.

The Labour of Slaves can never be so cheap here as the Labour of working Men is in Britain."[25] Franklin, perhaps because he tried owning slaves, was attempting to address an economic problem that slavery entailed on the colonies, particularly the plantation colonies. It was a problem that would enter the original draft of the Declaration of Independence, and it was based on an understanding that forced dehumanization of Africans came at a cost not just to the slave but to the owner of the slave, a position Thomas Jefferson would later embrace.

In an effort to "Compute" the cost of owning slaves and keeping them at their labors, Franklin added up not just the cost of paying for the slave, the slave's clothing, the driver of the slave, the maintenance of the slave, and so forth, but the cost in money of interest on the money one lost while paying for all of the extra costs associated with slave-keeping. That is, economic theorist that he was, Franklin computed the raw costs (the actual costs borne by the slaveowner), along with the costs of the use of money (if that money had been put to use as an investment, instead). If one were to "compare the whole Amount with the Wages of a Manufacturer of Iron or Wool in England," Franklin argued, "you will see that Labour is much cheaper there [i.e., in England] than it ever can be by Negroes here." "Why then will Americans purchase Slaves?" he asked. "Because Slaves may be kept as long as a Man pleases, or has Occasion for their Labour; while hired Men are continually leaving their Master (often in the midst of his Business,) and setting up for themselves." The answer itself underscored the earlier point about the costs of labor always remaining high in North America, because free laborers want to own their own land and the product of their labor.

Franklin's argument against slavery, at this time in his life, was an economic one based on appropriate land use in balance with productivity rather than one formed from moral or humanistic concerns. The extractive quality of plantation culture, which took over acres of lands and required the use of unfree labor for agriculture, depleted the soils and undermined the economic livelihood of independent laborers. This was costly to the British commonwealth, because slave plantation culture deprived poor people of a potential livelihood, and it created, in the rich, a dependence on foreign luxuries and an enfeebling of both the Africans and the slave-owners who held Africans in perpetual bondage. His examples related to plantation slavery in the Caribbean:

> The Negroes brought into the English Sugar Islands, have greatly diminish'd the Whites there; the Poor are by this Means depriv'd of Employment, while a few Families acquire vast Estates; which

they spend on Foreign Luxuries, and educating their Children in the Habit of those Luxuries; the same Income is needed for the Support of one that might have maintain'd 100. The Whites who have Slaves, not labouring, are enfeebled, and therefore not so generally prolific; the Slaves being work'd too hard, and ill fed, their Constitutions are broken, and the Deaths among them are more than the Births; so that a continual Supply is needed from Africa. The Northern Colonies having few Slaves increase in Whites. Slaves also pejorate the Families that use them; the white Children become proud, disgusted with Labour, and being educated in Idleness, are rendered unfit to get a Living by Industry.

In Franklin's view, slavery was a harmful practice leading to laziness among the wealthy rather than laziness among the poor. What an inverse of the older notion that poverty arose from laziness! What an inversion, too, of the common economic argument in Britain that the plantations were an asset to Great Britain and the empire and that the African slave trade proved a "nursery to seamen" and thus would assist in increasing Britain's naval power.[26] To be sure, Franklin owned three domestic slaves during these years. He finally assessed that attempting to hold people in bondage was difficult and costly to the individual slaveholder, because of the time spent in keeping the slave enslaved and because the slave took up the laboring potential of an independent laborer who would eventually become a producer himself.[27] Franklin would, once he circulated in London, begin to think about antislavery not just along economic imperial lines but along humanitarian ones as well. In the 1750s, however, he was working on developing a strategic system of building an empire of English-speakers in North America. Franklin's imperialist orientation made him think about conceiving an environmental logic for colony-building. Plantation agriculture was inherently wasteful of the environment and economically unsound for the empire. Franklin's goal centered on formulating an imperial philosophy built upon environmental circumstances and enabling the greatest number of well-meaning and healthy people to enjoy the greatest possible standard of living. Plantation slavery, like the venting to the colonies of the poor, unhealthy, or criminal peoples, worked to undermine such a goal.

By subjecting colonies to constraints in trade and labor, the British administration was seeking to enhance the quality of life in the home country at the expense of developing a rich potential in the American colonies. Franklin seems to have believed that with sufficient data and with a tone of reasonableness, he might be able to convince Parliament and the ministry that a policy of constraints, oppressive at its base, actually worked to undermine the British commonwealth by creating a weaker economy and, in effect, poorer and less healthy people. He was uninterested in an imperialism based in absentee landholding and extractive measures built upon forced labor. Instead, he proposed land-use policies adapted to the different environmental and social conditions obtaining in different parts of the British Empire. Based on his correspondence with people from many different locations, Franklin was calling for an environmental logic for British colonization in the face of clear English economic and cultural anxiety about losing a grip on the status quo in England. In effect, Franklin was inventing a strategy that could change the existing marketplace of goods and labor.[28] He would later, in his so-called Canada pamphlet, propound his ideas more fully.

Franklin's *Observations concerning the Increase of Mankind, Peopling of Countries, etc.* is most frequently spoken of as a pamphlet about population rather than about environment, the economy, labor, and society. In his manuscript essay, which he circulated for several years in advance of letting the essay get published, Franklin estimated that the population in the English colonies in North America doubled about every twenty-five years.[29] Demographic historians have shown the relative accuracy of this estimate. In the mainland English-speaking colonies, between 1700 and 1770, the population rose eight times, from roughly 275,000 to 2,210,000.[30] In addition to the convicts brought over, large numbers of Germans, Scots, Irish (both Scots-Irish Protestants and Irish Catholics), Africans and African-descended peoples inhabited North America, taking over the lands of Native peoples. The ancestral British population (that is, those Britons born to the generations of initial immigrants) was a minority beginning in the year 1700, drastically so from about 1725, because of the arrivals and increase of non-English immigrants.

At the time he began writing the "Observations," Franklin was working out what he conceived to be a useful proportional relationship between land and people, on the one hand, and the land's productivity, on the other. He knew his Hobbes and Locke. He was also aware of the ethnizing tendency of population study being conducted in Europe. Carl Linnaeus, for instance, the famous Swedish naturalist, botanist, and zoologist whose work had become known to Franklin through James Logan, had established in his *Systema Naturae* (1735) an arrangement of all species into a system identifiable by class, genus, and species where mankind was no longer considered to be apart from other animals. To Linnaeus, mankind was arranged according to classifications identifying racial characteristics: *Homo ferus, Europaeus albus, Americanus rubis, Asiaticus luridus, Afer niger*. Of Europeans, Linnaeus reported such character traits as "ingenious, white, sanguine, governed by law." Of Africans, his descriptive characteristics included "lazy, careless, black, governed by the arbitrary will of the master." The idea of a taxonomy of humankind was employed famously by Georges-Louis Leclerc, comte de Buffon (1707–1788), who developed further distinctions among mankind. Such ideas were embraced by leading social theorists, who were seeking to establish a relationship between people's skin pigmentation, geographical locale, and personality. This kind of anthropology was called environmentalism in Franklin's day, and in ours, it smacks of dangerous racial stereotyping.[31] Fear of strangers, as British political theorist Bernard Crick once reminded us, is an ancient prejudice.[32]

As part of his analysis of population, Franklin repeated some of the different stereotypes employed in the standard literature about the different peoples of the globe. It is worthwhile for us to consider what Franklin said regarding the different populations, because his comments were employed against him in a smear campaign during the Assembly elections in 1764 and in some of our own contemporary debates about racism's undergirding of founding ideologies. What commentators have lost sight of is the rhetorical situation into which Franklin was attempting to insert his ideas. Franklin was attempting to speak to population theorists about ethnic population categories and the kinds of labor they performed. For this audience of North American and British theorists on social and political economies, he couched his discussion in terms his well-read audience would expect.

Earlier in his life, like his friend James Logan, Franklin learned to admire the Scots people, especially the Highlanders. In his pamphlet on defense, *Plain Truth* (1747), Franklin presented the story of the Scots-Irish, "*those brave people*," who had gathered together to fight off James II as he attempted return to power during the siege of Londonderry, Ireland. In *Plain Truth*, Franklin cast the Scots, Irish, and Scots-Irish as noble and courageous, as we have seen. Franklin also spoke of the Germans in that pamphlet. Of the Germans, Franklin remarked that they were "*brave* and *steady*" as they fought well and heartily, even for leaders who were their "Tyrants and Oppressors."[33] Such an approach to the disparate peoples of Pennsylvania served his effort to gather members of disparate groups into a consolidated effort of defense. Writing in *Plain Truth* for the local audience about local defense matters, it made good sense, as we have seen, to employ this approach while discussing the people who made up Pennsylvania's population.

Yet Pennsylvania's German population was more complicated than Franklin let on in *Plain Truth*.[34] During the late 1740s, poorer and less healthy Germans had been arriving in Pennsylvania, and the Assembly and colony leaders faced difficulties in deciding how to house the new-comers, care for their numerous sick, and educate them. The manuscript draft of Franklin's "Observations concerning the Increase of Mankind" was composed for high-status colonial and British leaders. It was destined to enter the stream of British and continental economic thought. For that audience, Franklin adopted the position and even the diction frequently taken among elites and often by those whose interests lay in defining what the British nation was, politically, and defining precisely who it was who made up the so-called British nation. Indeed, as we watch Franklin shift his perspective about nationhood while speaking on the Germans living among the English-speakers, we come to understand better how language of nation formation can end up relying on ethnic stereotypes.

In the middle of the eighteenth century, German-speaking immigrants were second only to the Africans brought forcibly to the colonies. Germans far outnumbered all other European emigrants. Germans outnumbered immigrants from England by more than two to one in the 1740s and more than three to one in the 1750s. Moreover, English-speakers emigrated to many different colonies when they arrived; German-speakers, on the contrary, usually landed in Philadelphia, clustered in Pennsylvania first, and moved on to other areas if greater opportunities arose elsewhere. As historian A. G. Roeber has indicated, "Germans in almost all parts of North America by the 1750s affirmed Philadelphia's role as *Oberamt*"—in effect, Philadelphia was the Germans' clearinghouse.[35] The concern among English-speakers was expressed in three key areas. First, German-speakers who were farmers tended to cluster homesteads together rather than to intersperse their farms among farms held by other groups. Franklin was concerned that the absence of agricultural diversity might exhaust soil quality and fecundity. Second, Germans preferred to keep to themselves culturally, and they refused to learn the English language and use English domestic methods inside their households. For Franklin the imperial-ist, such behavior would reduce markets for English-speakers and British goods. And third, until the great migrations of the 1750s, Germans were highly employable, because they "undersold" their labor, compared to other workers, thus driving down wages. Franklin argued that they were taking potential jobs away from English laborers.

Germans were perceived by some to be industrious, so, it was argued, they were useful to the empire. For this reason, Henry Pelham (1694–1754), First Lord of the Treasury and Chancellor of the Exchequer, the prime minister from 1743 to 1754 (when he died), and George Montagu-Dunk (1760–1771), second Earl of Halifax, president of the Board of Trade from 1748 to 1761, schemed together and with the Board of Trade to settle German and Swiss Protestants in Nova Scotia. Virginia's plan for the Ohio territory included settling Protestant Germans there as a buffer (beyond the British settlements) against the French. There were plans to settle Germans in Massachusetts, as well, as Franklin knew. Joseph Crell (d. 1765), a German who originally had settled in South Carolina, moved north and developed a plan for a glass factory in Braintree, Massachusetts, in the late 1740s and early 1750s. Crell (also Crellius) worked with three men—Franklin's brother John (1690–1756), stocking weaver Peter Etter (1715–c. 1786) of Braintree, and Norton Quincy (n.d.)—to establish a glass factory. The factory landed in other directors' hands in 1752, but in the meantime, Crell and the others worked hard to attract German artisans and establish a community in the town. They purchased parcels where factory directors had laid out the lots, streets, and squares with names like Hague, Hanover, Zurich, Manheim, and so forth. Benjamin Franklin himself took part in this plan to create a German community of glassmakers. He bought some parcels of land as part of the scheme sponsored by his brother John. Crell also brought over a group of German immigrants to settle western Massachusetts, but the plan fell through. These Germans were assisted by those already in Braintree, and some found employment in the glass factory owned by John Franklin.[36]

Because of a change in the population of Germans emigrating in the late 1740s and early 1750s, anxiety developed in Philadelphia about whether the community could handle the ensuing problems. The German-speakers arrived in need of immediate medical assistance. They were perceived by townspeople as economic burdens upon the existing systems, because they brought with them a variety of contagions (including smallpox and typhus).[37] The position taken among Britons in North America was complicated. The older argument about labor remained active: German-speakers who were healthy stole jobs from English laborers, because they sold their labor more cheaply than did English people. But other arguments against Germans also emerged. German-speakers who arrived in tremendous numbers from the poorest classes in their homeland brought illness and created, in addition to a health hazard, a financial (tax) burden because they required charity. The situation worsened when more and more German-speakers arrived in Philadelphia. In the year 1758, German printer Christoph Sauer (1695–1758) estimated that two thousand passengers on fifteen ships, due to arrive in that year, perished en route.[38]

Given this context, it is no wonder that in Philadelphia between the years 1751 and 1755, Benjamin Franklin was involved with petitioning for and then managing the erection of the Pennsylvania Hospital. Franklin also wished to see an English School and a Charity School erected in Philadelphia. He had sincere concerns about the situation of the Germans, but his writings also reveal a particular British characterization of the situation. To James Parker (c. 1714–1770), he remarked in a letter dated March 20, 1751, that he was concerned about the potential Germanization of Pennsylvania: "This will in a few Years," he wrote, "become a German Colony." "Instead of their Learning our Language," he continued, "we must learn their's, or live as in a foreign Country." He said that English-speakers disliked living among Germans: "Already the English begin to quit particular Neighbourhoods surrounded by Dutch, being made uneasy by the Disagreeableness of disonant Manners." He expressed anxiety that "in Time, Numbers will probably quit the Province for the same Reason." Most troubling, however, was that (Franklin claimed), "the Dutch under-live, and are thereby enabled to under-work and under-sell the English; who are thereby extreamly incommoded and consequently disgusted, so that there can be no cordial Affection or Unity between the two Nations." He turned the economic argument into a nation-formation one: "How good Subjects they may make, and how faithful to the British Interest, is a Question worth considering."[39]

Franklin's concerns reflected common thinking about Germans among English-speakers in Pennsylvania but especially Philadelphia, and his attitudes are not particularly attributable, as Francis Jennings once charged, to a peculiar ill-will toward German-speakers.[40] Indeed, as historian Simon Finger has shown in his recent book on public health in Philadelphia, Philadelphians "recognized that disease and debility were shared problems, and in recognizing that the problem was collective, they embraced a public responsibility to preserve and promote the common welfare, which they tried to fulfill to the best of their abilities."[41]

Like others in Philadelphia, Franklin worried that the Germans might join forces with the French, who were moving down into the territory of the indigenous peoples they called the Illinois. Even so, Franklin tended to favor a proposal circulating among some Philadelphia leaders that Germans be forced to settle in border areas, as buffer peoples between the English-speakers to the east and the Indians surrounding western settlements. Although this might make a German alliance with the French easier to establish, it seemed to be a risk worth taking, because of what was conceived as the Germanization of Pennsylvania. Taken together, Franklin's writings about Germans from this time, both published writings and letters and pamphlets that were widely circulated, reveal the cultural tensions having to do with Germans' clustering together, with their retaining their own domestic and language practices, and with their taking potential jobs away from English laborers. All three of these issues crop up in his imperialist-oriented, British-inflected "Observations concerning the Increase of Mankind."

Like many theorists in Britain and Europe, Franklin made remarks about Germans based on an understanding of ethnic identity then conceived as the newest kind of social science. Franklin's ethnizing remarks would come back to haunt him in the Philadelphia elections in the mid-1760s, when he was courting the German vote. Yet voters in Philadelphia had significantly different views than the audience of colonial and British leaders whom Franklin was seeking to impress when circulating his manuscript. For this audience, whether the one in North America, where he initially circulated the essay, or the one in London, which the printed essay would ultimately reach, Franklin drew up remarks based in the developing science of environmental ethnology. "A Nation," he wrote in 1751, "well regulated is like a Polypus; take away a Limb, its Place it soon supply'd; cut it in two, and each deficient Part shall speedily grow out of the Part remaining." To Franklin, it was in Britain's interest to regulate the colonies' immigration more firmly, because, in the absence of English-speaking laborers, Germans would arrive, supply the place of English laborers, and take over the Pennsylvania colony.

The "Observations" expounds more fully on the ideas Franklin mentioned in his March 1751 letter to James Parker. In the "Observations," Franklin wrote, "Since Detachments of English from Britain sent to America, will have their Places at Home so soon supply'd and increase so largely here; why should the Palatine Boors be suffered to swarm into our Settlements, and by herding together establish their Language and Manners to the Exclusion of ours? Why should Pennsylvania, founded by the English, become a Colony of *Aliens*, who will shortly be so numerous as to Germanize us instead of our Anglifying them, and will never adopt our Language or Customs, any more than they can acquire our Complexion." Franklin was explicitly addressing his concern to the larger audience of British readers who were establishing colonial policy. He concluded that

the Number of purely white People in the World is proportionably very small. All Africa is black or tawny. Asia chiefly tawny. America (exclusive of the new Comers) wholly so. And in Europe, the Spaniards, Italians, French, Russians and Swedes, are generally of what we call a swarthy Complexion; as are the Germans also, the Saxons only excepted, who with the English, make the principal Body of White People on the Face of the Earth. . . . [W]hy increase the Sons of Africa, by planting them in America, where we have so fair an Opportunity, by excluding all Blacks and Tawneys, of increasing the lovely White and Red? But perhaps I am partial to the Complexion of my Country, for such Kind of Partiality is natural to Mankind.[42]

The language here of swarming and herding, the insistence upon the alien qualities of the Germans, the reference to the color of the skin (what Franklin calls "complexion"), the linguistic construction of same-group partiality as "natural"—all reflect the ethnizing tendencies of nation-formation discourse, where cultural anxiety born of population density, land and labor problems, health concerns, and language fears are made to seem like insurmountable obstacles caused by racial and ethnic aliens who will never attempt to blend into what the group considers normative.

The language is racist, and it privileges fairer complexion. In the context of his own day, however, Franklin's arguments were based in theories that were circulating in Europe about ethnic identity and geographical location. As he was addressing a British and European audience involved in colonial administration, he played up positions suitable to their cultural assumptions of their own superiority. Franklin was attempting to call into being a British nationalist identity among those of British descent, whether on the English mainland or in the colonies of British North America. More importantly, however, Franklin was working hard to inform people in England that they should care about what was happening to colonists who represented British enterprises both material and cultural.

Britain's failure to establish firm immigration and defense strategies put British Americans at risk, he thought. Britons in North America were concerned about being boxed in by the French in the West and eventually forced off their lands. If non-English speakers came to the British colonies in greater numbers, the English speakers would eventually move out. Franklin addressed the concern by suggesting that if Britain failed to defend the colonies, then the British Empire would ultimately lose its colonial holdings. If Great Britain wished to retain the colonies and foster a greater British Empire, then its policies should protect the colonists against foreign immigrants as well as foreign invaders. Franklin pointed out that an empire would always diminish in its power and population if it permitted "foreigners" to people its lands. Among the things that would "diminish a Nation," Franklin wrote, was "The Importation of Foreigners into a Country that has as many Inhabitants as the present Employments and Provisions for Subsistence will bear." In effect, he reasoned, this importation "will be in the End no Increase of People; unless the New Comers have more Industry and Frugality than the Natives, and then they will provide more Subsistence, and increase in the Country; but they will gradually eat the Natives out. Nor is it necessary to bring in Foreigners to fill up any occasional Vacancy in a Country; for such Vacancy (if the Laws are good, . . .) will soon be filled by natural Generation."[43]

Because his ultimate audience was centered in England primarily, Franklin attempted literally to bring home the point about available land and the potential curtailing of the population base by developing an argument about France invading the English mainland. Listed among the things that "must diminish a Nation," Franklin wrote that loss of territory would affect population (the number of marriages likely being diminished in a circumscribed space). He used the example of Wales within England. Pointing to England's history, Franklin argued that "the Britons being driven into Wales, and crowded together in a barren Country insufficient to support such great Numbers, diminished 'till the People bore a Proportion to the Produce, while the Saxons increas'd on their abandoned Lands." He concluded that thus "the Island became full of English. And were the English now driven into Wales by some foreign Nation, there would in a few Years be no more Englishmen in Britain, than there are now People in Wales."[44] In other words, population displacement by foreigners, whether in England and Wales or in the British colonies of North America, ought to be unacceptable to Britain. Couched this way, the argument might have a greater influence with the British audience than any other argument.

As a social theorist, economist, scientist, and demographer, Franklin was attempting to prove that those in the Old World who thought they understood the colonies, their environment, their population, and their productivity did not in the least understand the potential loss to the empire that might eventually occur from poor management, simply because they had miscalculated what was possible in North America. Calculations based on Old World notions had nothing to do with the potential of a new country. By basing their calculations on assumptions having to do with the environmental conditions of the Old World, members of Parliament and ministry were misapprehending the circumstances faced by colonists in North America. False information and incorrect assumptions effaced the colonists' rights to a fair hearing of their complaints.

Franklin attempted to offer a proper understanding of the colonial problems, with accurate data and with an eye to keeping the empire intact and growing. This is clear if we consider the very opening of Franklin's "Observations." It opened by pointing out that any calculations "made upon the Bills of Mortality, Christnings, &c. of populous Cities, will not suit Countries; nor will Tables form'd on Observations made on full settled old Countries, as Europe, suit new Countries, as America."[45] The colonies were growing, Franklin attested, adding that with a growing population, there would be an increase in productivity: "In Proportion to the Increase of the Colonies, a vast Demand is growing for British Manufactures, a glorious Market wholly in the Power of Britain, in which Foreigners cannot interfere, which will increase in a short Time even beyond her Power of supplying, tho' her whole Trade should be to her Colonies: Therefore Britain should not too much restrain Manufactures in her Colonies."[46] Grow the population, allow for a free labor market of free laborers, and you will grow the empire, Franklin reasoned.

Franklin's Imperial Theories in Circulation

Like many men in the republic of letters, Franklin had grown used to circulating his thoughts among friends and acquaintances, so he could test them, gain further information, and develop arguments that would counter whatever objections his candid readers had with his work. Franklin's "Observations" was completed in 1751, and he circulated it for some time thereafter. We can catch a glimpse of his thinking on the idea circulating manuscripts in letters to leading Americans engaged in science and agriculture, including James Bowdoin (1726–1790), Jared Eliot, and Cadwallader Colden. Franklin had been corresponding with Bowdoin about Colden's theories about air and solidity. He wrote to Bowdoin on May 14, 1752, "I always tho't it wrong to print private Letters without the Consent of the Writer; but to communicate now and then a philosophical Epistle, to a discrete philosophical Friend, as it tends to mutual Improvement, I do not think it amiss."[47] That is, sending along someone's manuscript was not, to his thinking, inadmissible, as this was a sort of publication (though in manuscript) only among friends whose interests might coincide with the author's. Circulating handwritten materials to friends offered an opportunity for information-sharing, critique, and mutual improvement. Scholars today call this form of communication scribal publication. Print publication prevented the generous correction of friends as well as the congenial circulation among those whose thoughts one might like to solicit before sending something into print. To Eliot he wrote, December 19 of that year, that he was sending along his meteorological observations, written "in order to digest and methodize a few of my own thoughts."[48] Circulating his thoughts by way of manuscript was a method—indeed, a form of coterie publication—that Franklin used when he was still thinking about his data and his positions on various topics.

Franklin wanted to continue refining his thinking about populations, labor, and settlements of the colonies, so he circulated his "Observations concerning the Increase of Mankind" widely. He sent the essay to several correspondents, but he also allowed others to send it around for him or to mention it to their correspondents. In effect, he used his scribal publication network to get feedback on his tract. Richard Jackson (c. 1721–1787), Dr. John Perkins (1698–1781), and Peter Collinson (1694–1768) all helped get Franklin's manuscript read by numerous people who were not directly in Franklin's network of correspondents. In the colonies, the essay was so admired that correspondents heard of it from friends and then asked Franklin for a copy, so that they might read it.[49] John Perkins remarked from Boston in October 1752 that the "Observations . . . is a very informing Piece and I think it should be read and well considerd by every Englishman who wishes well to his Country But more especially by those in power and Ability to promote the Nation's Intrest."[50] Peter Collinson, then Franklin's most helpful correspondent about electrical matters, wrote to Franklin in September 1752 about both the electrical experiments and his "Observations." Of Franklin's experiments, Collinson insisted, "All Europe is in Agitation on Verifying Electrical Experiments on points. All commends the Thought of the Inventor," to which he added (having been the publisher of Franklin's experiments): "I wish my Dear Friend you'l oblige the Ingenious part of Mankind with a publick View of your Observations &c. on the Increase of Mankind. I don't find anyone has hit it off so well."[51] Franklin's reputation as a scientist helped secure him a reputation as a social and imperial theorist. His reputation ensured that his views might be taken more seriously.

When Cadwallader Colden learned of the tract from their mutual friend Peter Collinson, he asked Franklin to send it to him.[52] In response, Colden wrote that he was "exceedingly pleased with your observations on the increase of mankind." Yet Colden offered a suggestion. "I think with our friend Bartram," he wrote, "that the last Paragraph is the only one liable to exception."[53] The material Colden questioned is the material frequently remarked upon today, the part where Franklin had originally concluded that he wished there were more white people on the globe. His friends urged Franklin to publish the piece. He finally consented to its release in print in 1754, without the offending concluding section. He permitted it to be published as an appendix to William Clarke's *Observations on the late and present Conduct of the French, with Regard to their Encroachments upon the British Colonies in North America* (Boston: Samuel Kneeland, 1755). Both Clarke's and Franklin's pamphlets were reprinted immediately in London; Franklin's essay, alone, in the *Gentleman's Magazine* in November, 1755, and the *Scots Magazine*, April 1756. It was appended to later editions of Franklin's scientific experiments, and when Franklin became the primary representative for the colonies in the 1760s, he again sent the essay into print. In some of the reprintings, Franklin's authorship was identified, and in most, the comments that had troubled Colden were removed.

"The People in the Colonies . . . better Judges"

Franklin was, in essence, the leading colonial theorist on imperial matters. Along with *A Modest Enquiry into the Nature and Necessity for a Paper Currency* (1729), the *Observations concerning the Increase of Mankind* (1754) clarifies the correlation Franklin would consistently argue between imperialist expansion and land and labor. If the colonists were to succeed as mainland British subjects were permitted to succeed, then they would need land for both the increase of population and the increase of internal productivity and trade. They would need the freedom to develop their own laws relevant to their colonial situation. They would have to be able to calculate and collect their own taxes as necessary to their own government officers and requirements for defense. In Franklin's view, if the administration wanted to grow the empire, then it needed to allow the empire to grow. It needed to reduce or do away with constraints such as the Navigation Acts, and it needed to permit the free flow of people and goods, in behalf of the empire, around the globe.

By 1755, Franklin was aware that rather than opening up markets for labor and trade, the administration seemed interested in devising additional constraints upon the colonies. This suggested to Franklin that however he might try to persuade Parliament and the ministry about the situation on the ground in the colonies, his views—despite his growing fame and the respect accruing to his renown as a scientist and state theorist—would be held in suspicion, if only because he was a colonial

American "subject" rather than a Briton who came of age in England. He was upset that talented American Britons received insufficient recognition in Britain. In his Poor Richard's almanac for April 1753, Franklin quipped, "The Good-Will of the Govern'd will be starved, if not fed by the good Deeds of the Governors." By December 1755, he was making more pointed remarks about the extent to which colonial Britons were being given unequal treatment at the hands of those in administration. In "A Dialogue between X, Y, and Z," published in the *Pennsylvania Gazette*, December 18, 1755, Franklin reminded readers of their putatively common heritage with Britons in England: "British Subjects, by removing to America, cultivating a Wilderness, extending the Dominion, and increasing the Wealth, Commerce and Power of their Mother Country, at the Hazard of their Lives and Fortunes, ought not, and in Fact do not thereby lose their native Rights."[54] His insistence that Britons in North America "do not," simply by the location, "lose their native rights" signals the kind of reading Franklin was then engaged in regarding the legal status of the colonies. Franklin's frustration with British colonial administration grew steadily during the 1750s, along with his certainty that great potential lay in the lands and free peoples of British North America.

Franklin's sense of the injustice of the difficulties faced by Britons in North America becomes clearer when we examine his letters to Governor William Shirley (1694–1771), a barrister in London who had emigrated to Boston in 1731 and served as governor in 1741–49 and then again in 1753–56. Like Shirley, Franklin had conceived a plan for colonial union prior to the Albany conference in 1754. Although neither his plan nor Shirley's was approved in Britain, Franklin considered Shirley an able leader, one who was willing to try to cope with the colonial difficulties based on his long residence in Massachusetts. Franklin appreciated Shirley's legal knowledge. The two men struck up a friendship in the mid-1750s, a friendship so strong that Franklin opened up to Shirley his views about the colonial administration's current plans. Shirley had specifically solicited Franklin's views regarding the Albany Plan and other plans for defense and administration. Franklin knew Shirley would help him formulate his plans more deeply, and he also knew that Shirley would circulate his letters among leaders in government. Indeed, the letters would become famous when Franklin's friend, William Strahan (1715–1785), printed them in his *London Chronicle*, February 8, 1766, while Franklin was attempting to represent colonial Britons during the Stamp Act crisis.

In opening his correspondence with Shirley, Franklin spelled out his dislike for any plan that would tax the colonists while also leaving them subject to governors appointed by the Crown and to laws enacted by Parliament. Franklin created for Shirley a full statement of his views, indeed his first major articulation of the rights of citizens-subjects and the obligations of government. These letters are evidence of a very important turn in his thinking about the British Empire: if the empire would not assist its subjects and give them equal rights with all Britons, then the empire was not fulfilling its obligations to its colonies. Franklin argued that it was unfair to oblige the colonists to accept control and decision-making by members of Parliament who knew very little about life in the colonies. On December 3, 1754, he argued that "excluding the *People* of the Colonies from all share in the choice of the Grand Council, will give extreme dissatisfaction, as well as the taxing them by Act of Parliament, where they have no Representative." Here was Franklin's clear statement about the rights of the colonists to participate in their own government. He continued with a statement that reads much like a Poor Richard maxim, that people "bear better when they have, or think they have some share in the direction," so if heavy burdens were to be laid on them, it would be "useful to make it, as much as possible, their own act." The next day, he spelled out his thinking more fully: Parliament ought to have no jurisdiction over the colonies, because Parliament, being distant, could not understand the colonists' needs and goals. Further, governors, often assisted by placemen, frequently used their offices for profit and were just as often selected to be governors not from their qualities as leaders but as reward or benefit from service rendered in some other sector. Franklin attempted to assure Shirley that the colonists were "loyal, and as firmly attach'd to the present Constitution and reigning Family, as any Subjects in the King's Dominions." He continued: "The People in the Colonies, who are to feel the immediate Mischiefs of Invasion and Conquest by an Enemy, in the Loss of their Estates, Lives and Liberties, are likely to be better Judges of the Quantity of Forces necessary to be raised and maintain'd, Forts to be built and supported, and of their own Abilities to bear the Expence, than the Parliament of England at so great a Distance."[55]

The letters to William Shirley from the 1750s are of a piece with Franklin's representations to Parliament, administration, and British people (in letters to the press) in the 1760s: the colonists had every right, as loyal subjects of the king, to develop their own plans for securing their borders, electing officials, extracting resources, manufacturing products, and managing taxation to support good government. These letters form a major step in Franklin's firming up of his views on the legal rights of British subjects. When Shirley pursued the topic of rights with him,

Franklin wrote again on December 22, 1754, to clarify his views about representation, legislation, and taxation of the colonies. After professing to having enjoyed "the conversation your Excellency was pleased to honour me with, on the subject of uniting the Colonies more intimately with Great Britain, by allowing them Representatives in Parliament," Franklin considered more fully what colonial representation in Parliament might look like and how representation might affect policy. He wrote that he believed "such an Union would be very acceptable to the Colonies, provided they had a reasonable number of Representatives allowed them." But his conditions were clear: if representation were to occur, then "all the old Acts of Parliament restraining the trade or cramping the manufactures of the Colonies, [should] be at the same time repealed, and the British Subjects on this side the water put, in those respects, on the same footing with those in Great Britain." Once a new, consolidated Parliament were elected and called to order, a Parliament "representing the whole," *then* it would be time for reconsideration of those old laws. If the new Parliament considered it in "the interest of the whole to re-enact some or all of them," then they could do so. It was not that he thought the colonies would have an abundance of representatives in Parliament so as to "have any great weight by their numbers." Instead, he wrote, "I think there might be sufficient to occasion those laws to be better and more impartially considered, and perhaps to overcome the private interest of a petty corporation, or of any particular set of artificers or traders in England, who heretofore seem, in some instances, to have been more regarded than all the Colonies, or than was consistent with the general interest, or best national good."[56]

In the group of letters to William Shirley, Franklin spoke directly to the Navigation Acts and the additional acts restraining manufacture and trade and to the interest politics that allowed the manufacturing and merchant sectors in England to sway legislation. By repealing all acts that worked against the colonies until a new Parliament were elected that included American representatives, Parliament could forestall the operation of the different interest groups in Britain—and particularly of the London merchants—from having undue power over legislation. The idea of representation in Parliament was tantalizing to Franklin, whose ideas about the empire were becoming more realistic and better grounded in an understanding of how politics operated in Great Britain.

Knowing that his letters to Shirley would be circulated widely among those in the British administration, Franklin offered a persuasive note of relativity to the potential power that might accrue to the colonial representatives in Parliament. Couching his ideas with the persuasive language of reasonableness and of "the interest of the whole," Franklin employed his most celebrated method of arguing a case "in terms of modest diffidence" rather than "dogmatical method." He used in his letters with Shirley words of indirection, words indicating possibility, words like "imagine," "perhaps," "might," and "seem."[57] Clearly, in Franklin's view, the constraints placed on colonial trade and manufacturing were unjust, but by phrasing the situation as a form of interest politics, he avoided, for the moment, a dogmatic assertion and instead revealed an understanding of the political landscape in London that was negatively impacting the colonists in North America.

Of Indians, Their Lands, and the British Empire

The discussion thus far might suggest that Franklin was not accounting for the situation of Indians, their sovereignty over their own lands, their understanding of the negative cultural and environmental impact on their tribes of the Europeans in their midst, and their consistently self-interested method of playing the European powers against each other by creating only tentative alliances with them. Franklin's writings about the British Empire sometimes seem to imply that the land was free of people, as if he were adopting the Europeans' arguments based in *terra nullius* theory. Yet Franklin was well aware that the lands were inhabited by indigenous peoples. As a Pennsylvania assemblyman, he had personally been involved in working through problems with the various Native populations living along Pennsylvania's borderlands. He was interested in Native polities, and he was interested as well in working out the best and fairest means by which Indians could be treated with regard to their goods in trade and their homelands.

Franklin's writings such as his *Observations concerning the Increase of Mankind*, directed to a wider, imperial audience, took on the dispassionate tones and assumptions of discourses on population and on the foundations of civil government. Franklin's *Observations* thus echoed and conversed with tracts on land and society rather than on Native polity. His tract addressed concerns similar to those found in John Graunt's *Natural and Political Observations . . . upon the Bills of Mortality* (London, 1662), William Petty's tracts again made available in Thomas Short's *New Observations, Natural, Moral, Civil, Political, and Medical . . . on Bills of Mortality* (London, 1750), and Scottish philosopher Robert Wallace's *A Dissertation on the Numbers of Mankind in Antient and Modern Times*

(Edinburgh, 1753).[58] Like Graunt (1620–1674), Franklin used mortality numbers to work up estimates of the probability of longevity. Like Short (fl. 1750–70) and Wallace (n.d.), Franklin disparaged the state of luxury in European urban centers, because luxury had a deleterious effect on people. Instead, Franklin praised (as they did) the benefits of simplicity, frugality, and hard work.

To Franklin, at least in theory, a country location would be better than an urban one. Native lands would be required if the colonies were going to continue to receive European immigrant populations and achieve the best suitable living conditions, with an appropriately mixed use, on the greatest amount of available land. In contemporary European legal opinion, land might be obtained by different means: (1) land might be claimed by right of conquest, whether as a holy war (the "just war, holy war" concept) or a war (as to the death) with a political opponent; (2) land might be overtaken and claimed as territory, if the land were uninhabited (the *terra nullius* theory); (3) land might be taken if it were not being "improved" and used productively (according to European views of land tenure requiring husbandry). There was little precedent for William Penn's experiment in treating with the Indians for their lands as one sovereign entity with another, thereby gaining a presumably legal and just title for the settlers to use in perpetuity. The singular feature of Pennsylvania's politics was the Proprietor's effort to prove (on paper, according the British and European imperial policy) a clear title, one created by treaty and appropriate, agreed-upon payment, to Native lands.

If we consider Franklin's friendships and business networks along with some of the printing jobs he took upon himself, we begin to see that Franklin's long-standing interest in population figures matched his long-standing interest in the Indian treaty situation in Pennsylvania. In 1731, Franklin began printing in the *Pennsylvania Gazette* several extracts from *The Political State of Great Britain* (vol. 40, 1731) providing physical, moral, and political observations on London's bills of mortality.[59] By printing as well a table of the burials in Boston between 1700 and 1731, Franklin illustrated that "not above a 40th Part of the People of that Place [Boston] die yearly, at a medium." Like John Graunt and Thomas Short before him, Franklin placed high value on rural districts. There, he argued, work would be plenty, and where work was plenty, couples bore more children and lived longer. If Britain sought to prosper, then large land masses would be required. And if large land masses were required, it was necessary to secure the legal title to the lands that would be inhabited in behalf of Great Britain.

Franklin began examining the treaties of Pennsylvania probably beginning in the late 1720s under the tutelage of his friend James Logan, the
Proprietor's representative after 1701. Eventually, Franklin conceived the
plan to print the treaties and began doing so in 1736. Franklin's selection
of treaties represents a self-conscious effort to identify Pennsylvania's treaties as legitimate in the face of challenges to Pennsylvania's borders (by
Virginia and New York, on the one hand, and by France, on the other). The
treaty record would also assist in handling the conflicts between settlers and
Indians. Treaties made permanent by print had a more reliable basis than
treaties lying inaccessible in the offices of governors. The original treaties
drafted by William Penn had been made with Delawares (Lenapes) close
to Philadelphia.[60] By the 1720s and 1730s, the Iroquois (Haudenosaunee)
argued for presumptive and sovereign rights to the entire territory that
had been the Lenapes'. If the Delawares could be perceived by the Iroquois
as not having jurisdiction over their own ancestral lands, the original and
subsequent treaties made by the Proprietor with the Delawares might not
remain valid in Indian country. Franklin became aware of the contested
sovereignty during his treaty negotiations in Albany and in his different
conversations about the Indians with various colonial representatives.
Surely he conceived that by printing the treaty documents, he might add a
form of permanence to documents that were really, in effect, quite tenuous,
regardless of what the paper on which they were written was supposed to
signify to the British and European empires.

Just as surely, Franklin was concerned that the Indians be treated fairly.
He himself had been involved in skirmishes against Delawares in the
Wyoming territory of Pennsylvania. But by the time of the Easton conferences beginning in 1756, Franklin understood the complexities of dealing
with the Iroquois while also attempting to engage in continuing peaceful
land acquisition with the Delawares, who had first been displaced from
New Jersey, and then from the forks of the Delaware River, and then from
the area called Wyoming in northeastern Pennsylvania, along the upper
eastern branch of the Susquehanna River. The Delawares were moving into
the Ohio area, an area Franklin himself had set his sights on as possible
settlement territory for Great Britain.

At issue in the 1750s were the representations made by some Delawares
but particularly by Teedyscung (1700–1763), the self-named "King of the
Delawares," that the Penns (especially Thomas and Richard Penn) had lied
about original agreements, particularly the infamous "Walking Purchase"
of 1737 and other land deals the Delawares considered fraudulent, leaving the Delawares stranded in territory that was not their homeland.[61]

Because of their displacement from their ancestral lands, the Delawares had great difficulty practicing cultural and political autonomy. Especially because the Iroquois had, on and off, been courted to form a league with Pennsylvania, the Delawares' sense of autonomy in negotiations was challenged. The Iroquois claimed primary negotiating privileges with the British and French, which thwarted the Delawares' efforts to seek reparations for the misdealing of the past decades. According to the stories told privately at the 1756 Easton treaty conference, Teedyscung did not stick with the scripted points originally given him. Instead, he used the conference to point to the injustices the Delawares faced at the hands of the Proprietary interests, a point that surely interested Franklin and the Assembly.

Given Franklin's goal to discredit the Proprietary, it has been easy for historians to point to Teedyscung's representations in the Easton conferences as playing into the hands of the Pennsylvania settlers' anti-Proprietary factions. It has also been easy to suggest that Teedyscung was a tool in the hands of the anti-Proprietary Quakers, led by Israel Pemberton (1715–1779), a prominent businessman who assisted Franklin in founding the Pennsylvania Hospital, among other things. The speech did, in fact, point to the Penns' and their representatives' questionable dealings with the Delawares. The Proprietors' interest in developing a strong relationship with the Iroquois, in an effort to replace Albany with Philadelphia as the center of Iroquois interest and obligations, played out in disappointing ways for the Delawares.[62] Teedyscung's speech was evidently much longer than what came to be reported in the various translations and records secured for the Pennsylvania colony, and it was likely more plaintive than most who had not been there would recognize. As James Merrell has remarked, the "colonists who heard Teedyuscung at Easton in 1756 and then read the official account thought that his 'Warmth and Earnestness' regarding 'the Wrongs that had been done them' was, on the page, 'much too faintly expressed.' "[63]

Franklin's interest in the treaties related to his goal of securing more land for Pennsylvania and the British Empire. But when Franklin took the records of Teedyscung's speeches to London with him in 1757, it is also possible that Franklin was concerned about the readiness of the settlers to find ways to damage Indian claims and to displace Indians onto lands that were not their original territories. In terms of mere legal title to Indian lands, several legal questions arise, questions that Franklin surely would have considered important. If Indians were displaced from their original territory, how might they create treaties based upon their presumed sovereign title to the territory sought by British and Europeans? If Indians felt demeaned from mistreatment by the settlers and by neighboring Indians, how could their representations of authority over land, representations given at any treaty council, be used authoritatively and credited in perpetuity so that the settlers would have a just and irrevocable title to lands that had been the Indians'? Clarifying the original title to the lands, in other words, would clear the way for a legally binding land agreement—a treaty—to take place. Clearing the original title was the only legal method, Franklin conceived, to assume sovereignty over the lands in question.

When Teedyscung complained in 1756 about the treatment the Delawares were receiving, the grievances needed to be taken seriously, or the land on which Pennsylvanians had settled would be questioned. It is likely for this reason that Franklin went along with the Quakers when they—to appease Teedyscung, who had asked for his own recorder—suggested that Charles Thomson (1729–1824), a master at the Friends' school in Philadelphia, become the amanuensis to Teedyscung. Must we assume (as various historians have done) that there were only nefarious reasons (i.e., the desire to discredit the Penns and the Proprietary) behind their willingness to provide Teedyscung the presumed legitimacy—a recorder of his speeches—that he was seeking? Perhaps there was something in Teedyscung's representation that struck a chord with Franklin, who was interested in seeing the Indian lands in settlers' hands so that productive use might be made of the soil. Franklin's interest was one of fostering the empire by peopling the land with English-speakers. But he understood that peaceful relations needed to follow treaty meetings, because settlers' lives were at stake. Speaking to the imperial audience, Franklin had somewhat blithely pointed out in his "Observations" that

> America is chiefly occupied by Indians, who subsist mostly by Hunting. But as the Hunter, of all Men, requires the greatest Quantity of Land from whence to draw his Subsistence, (the Husbandman subsisting on much less, the Gardner on still less, and the Manufacturer requiring least of all), The Europeans found America as fully settled as it well could be by Hunters; yet these having large Tracks, were easily prevail'd on to part with Portions of Territory to the new Comers, who did not much interfere with the Natives in Hunting, and furnish'd them with many Things they wanted.[64]

In order to assert that the Indians "were easily prevail'd on to part with Portions of Territory to the new Comers," Franklin had to feel assured that the Indians were treated properly. If they were not, then there would be uprisings in the midst of settled colonists. He seems to have understood full well the necessity for peaceful dealings with Indians. It almost seems as if in the 1750s he had prescience of what would occur in the 1760s—a series of uprisings by Indians against colonists that would threaten the very heart of the settlements in Pennsylvania. Franklin's growing concerns about regulating the Indian trade, behaving with fairness and equity with Indians of all groups, and securing forts and forest rangers in border areas—all attest to his legal and ethical concerns about appropriate diplomacy.

Another aspect of Franklin's interest in the Indians was his awareness that Europeans were fascinated with ideas of the "primitive" or "natural man" and thus in Indian speeches. His printing thirteen sets of these treaty council minutes attests to his own fascination with Indian oratory and, perhaps more importantly, his belief that the Indians' representations about their land dealings were essential matter upon which future settlement would depend. As Daniel Richter has argued, it is likely "that much of what the Indian speakers intended found its way to paper."[65] Franklin was among those who conceived that Indian speeches, like Indian people, were worth caring for and preserving. Indeed, traditional stories among the Haudenosaunee (the Iroquois) indicate a centuries-long affection for Franklin as a friend to Indians.[66]

To most British and Europeans, American Indians would be disposed of, eventually, whether by conquest or by attrition because of their proximity to whites.[67] Franklin's *Observations* acknowledged his awareness of the stadial theory of civilization (evidenced in the quotation above)—that mankind moved along a progress model of civilization from hunting to pasturage (husbanding) to farming (gardening) to manufacturing and commerce. But his remarks also clarify a richer comparatist angle than typically associated with the stadial model. That is, he seems to have understood that the Indians' cultural lives, like their livelihoods, were deeply embedded in the natural world they inhabited. Note that when he spoke about Indians as hunters, he did not seem to assume that they would eventually become manufacturers. Instead, his assumption—naive as it seems today—seems to have been that Indians uninterested in British lifeways would move off to tracts further westward.

Considering that Franklin's audience was largely one of imperial theorists and those in the colonial administration, it should be expected that Franklin's imperial writings from midcentury employed the assumptions and terminology of the imperial theorists with whom he was conversing. Yet, unlike many of those theorists, Franklin had personal experience with Indian peoples. As printer for the colony of Pennsylvania, he was interested in the extent of territory that trappers and traders covered. We have already accounted for his interest in economic growth in the region. He knew well the chief merchants of Philadelphia as well as the field agents who transacted their business in the interior. He printed thirteen of the treaties with Indians between 1736 and 1762. He had himself taken part in treaty negotiations or conferences with Indians, including the Logstown Indian conference in 1748, a trip to the area of the Susquehanna Valley in 1751, and the conference at Carlisle in 1753, prior to the Albany conference in 1754. His activities prompted an interest to settle a territory in the Ohio valley, written up in pamphlet form as "A Plan for Settling Two Western Colonies in North America" in 1754. This was eventually published again by Benjamin Vaughan (1751–1835) in his edition of Franklin's *Political, Miscellaneous, and Philosophical Pieces* (1779). At the time he died, Franklin had significant landholdings in the area, "Depreciation Lands" that lay west of the Allegheny River but called "Ohio" lands.[68] His plan for a colony in the Ohio territory never materialized, but it supplies evidence of his sense that only those most experienced in North America should lead colonies there. In the context of his own interest to settle the western territory, his warnings about the possibilities that the French might yet draw the Iroquois to their side in the Europeans' contest for empire in North America and gain additional western territories reveal a persistent line arguing for expanding the British territories.

Liberty, Property, and Defense in Pennsylvania

For the Pennsylvania Assembly, Franklin formulated several positions about liberty, property, and government. His views invoked key aspects of the early modern liberalism he had admired from his youth. He believed that people ought to be able to elect representatives who would formulate and pass the laws of the commonwealth, revealing a core belief in the right of citizens to elect representatives who would legislate for them. Franklin believed it the duty of governors to defend liberty by finding ways to assist those governed, whether in matters of health, education, or personal and public safety. He argued for transparency in government, so that the people knew the beliefs, values, and operations of their leaders. All of these beliefs are evidenced in Franklin's activities during the 1750s, a difficult time for Pennsylvanians because of legal tangles with the Proprietary government and taxation disputes to support the defense of border areas with France. Evidence of these beliefs appears in the letters on government written to William Shirley, as we have seen.

Franklin wrote many of the communications between the Assembly and the Pennsylvania governor. While writing for the Assembly, Franklin frequently employed the rhetoric of liberty as a natural right and the defense of the people by their governors as one of the supreme rules of the social contract among people in a commonwealth. Take, for example, the Assembly message to then governor Robert Hunter Morris (c. 1700–1764) that Franklin composed and sent in November 1755. The ground warfare against France had continued for several years, leaving western settlers prey to attacks by the French and their Native allies. When British-led troops failed to secure the area, Pennsylvanians were left, again, with the problem of defending British territory and their own homesteads. The attacks by Indians in border areas put Pennsylvania's western settlers on edge. Easterners held the seat of power, and to eastern Pennsylvanians fell the decision-making about the defense of western Pennsylvania. Taxes would need to be levied to fund local militias and secure the borders of Pennsylvania. Yet again, however, the Pennsylvania Assembly reached an impasse over the issue of taxation of the Proprietary lands. Expressing the Assembly's sincerity "as dutiful Subjects," Franklin clarified to Morris that the House had continued drafting bills for defense, despite their constant rejection. Fusing a rhetoric of sentiment with a rhetoric of equity and rights, Franklin wrote that because the members of Pennsylvania's House were "deeply affected with the present distressful Circumstances of the Frontier Counties," they had "determined to do, for the publick Safety and Welfare, every Thing that could reasonably be expected from them, either as dutiful Subjects to the Crown, or Lovers of their Country."[69]

The governor, whose written instructions from the Proprietors were secret, continued refusing the Assembly's right to tax Proprietary estates to assist in the common defense of Pennsylvania. The House had, under Franklin's leading arguments, decided to seek recourse with the Crown and thus bypass both governor and Proprietary. Franklin announced the decision to Morris, couching it in a way that sounded threatening: "We being as desirous as the Governor to avoid any Dispute on that Head [with regard to the taxation of the Proprietary], have so framed the Bill as to submit it entirely to his Majesty's Royal Determination, whether that Estate has or has not a Right to such Exemption." The goal in this exchange was to remind the governor about the importance of retaining the goodwill of Pennsylvania's Indians and keeping the people of Pennsylvania secure from internal disputes and external harm. But Franklin went farther: he articulated a position about political equity among members of a political community geographically dispersed but under one imperial leader. Surely the governor could see that "the Proprietaries Conduct, whether as Fathers of their Country, or Subjects to their King, must appear extraordinary, when it is considered that they have not only formally refused to bear any Part of our yearly heavy Expences in cultivating and maintaining Friendship with the Indians, . . . but they now, by their Lieutenant, refuse to contribute any Part towards resisting an Invasion of the King's Colony." Franklin's message went on to say that the inhabitants in the borderlands with Indian country did not wish their defense to be at the expense of fellow Pennsylvanians, who had long supported them, but at the expense of the Proprietors, whose interests they were assisting by living in and thus establishing the colony's western border. Thus, the message concluded, "We have taken every Step in our Power, consistent with the just Rights of the Freemen of Pennsylvania, for their Relief, and we have Reason to believe, that in the Midst of their Distresses they themselves do not wish us to go farther." That is, those living in the western areas being attacked did not wish to rely on easterners for defense. Further assistance, in effect, would imply an opportunity, among the wealthier eastern Pennsylvanians, to govern those more vulnerable members of the commonwealth to the west. Franklin added to the statement the now famous dicta: "Those who would give up essential Liberty, to purchase a little temporary Safety, deserve neither Liberty nor Safety."[70] The border peoples had an obligation and a right to protect themselves rather than continuing to rely on their neighbors, even though their governors were not providing for their common defense. This was a position he had employed in his letters to William Shirley. He now adapted it for use in behalf of the Assembly of Pennsylvania.

Franklin's trenchant expression about not giving up "essential Liberty" in order to feel secure from harm has consonance with some of the most important articulations about liberty and governance in early modern liberal expression. Remarks making similar points about how good governors ought to be protecting their people can be found in Cato's Letters. Thomas Gordon (1692–1750) had pointed out in Cato's Letter No. 11 a "primary law of nature and nations," related to the benefit and safety of the people: "The sole end of men's entering into political societies, was mutual protection and defence; and whatever power does not contribute to those purposes, is not government, but usurpation."[71] Franklin agreed, as evidenced in his messages to the Pennsylvania governor. To Franklin and the Assembly, the people's liberty was being usurped, in hidden governance, by a governor who represented a Proprietary that felt no stake in the preservation and happiness of the settlers of Pennsylvania. If they should, in their time of need, have to turn to their neighbors for additional assistance, they would lose, in effect, all the freedom that inheres in their rights as equally free subjects. For Franklin, liberty and security were intertwined. His own defense activities indicate this crucial belief in the concept that one had a right to self-defense in order to preserve his freedom of action. This was not a mere rhetoric of liberty for Franklin but a belief he acted on.

Franklin had tried for several years to keep the conversation going between the Assembly and the different governors of Pennsylvania, but compromise had become untenable in the mid-1750s, as defense problems increased. The notorious defeat in 1755 of the regiments under General Edward Braddock (1695–1755) and the general's own death in July at a battle at Great Meadows (now Farmington), Pennsylvania, left Franklin fielding questions about the supplies he had vouched and paid for by himself, a debt that amounted to nearly £20,000. He was frustrated by the pacifists in the Assembly and frustrated as well that the Proprietors refused to understand the extent to which absence of funding for defense might prompt Pennsylvania's capitulation of its western region to the French and a retreat eastward of the settlers. When he learned that the Proprietors had, in a secret clause, required that the governor never agree to taxation of their estate, Franklin was enraged. He wrote in the Assembly's behalf yet another message to Morris on August 8, 1755, addressing the governor's stated reasons for refusing to allow the Proprietors' lands to be taxed. Asking the governor why he would allow himself to be "the hateful Instrument of reducing a free People to the abject State of Vassalage," Franklin wrote that the members of the Assembly were "entreat[ing] him to reflect with what Reluctance a People born and bred in Freedom, and accustomed to equitable Laws, must undergo the Weight of this uncommon Tax." By allowing the colonists to bear a disproportionate burden of taxation while the Proprietors' lands lay untaxed yet protected by the colonists was, in essence, a method "of depriving us of those Liberties, which have given Reputation to our Country throughout the World, and drawn Inhabitants from the remotest Parts of Europe to enjoy them." Franklin argued that the liberties enjoyed by Pennsylvanians were "Liberties not only granted us of Favour, but of Right; Liberties which in Effect we have bought and paid for."[72]

He joined forces with the Quakers in the Assembly who were aiming to tax Proprietary estates for defense. In October 1755, he was chosen to be a colonel in a regiment of foot raised in Philadelphia. When the Assembly passed Franklin's Militia Bill in late November, approving £60,000 for defense, Franklin and his son William traveled in the middle of wintertime to key border areas, going as far as Gnadenhutten, Ohio, to build forts and organize defense. In October 1756, he went on a tour of military inspection to Carlisle, Harris's Ferry, and New York, and he conferred with a group of disgruntled Indians at Easton in November that year. Franklin knew the issues firsthand, because he was actually working on fortifications and overseeing operations. He was quite willing to work, for himself and others, to support the common good—in this case, to gain safety and shore up the people's essential liberty. Liberty and security were enmeshed.

When Governor Morris was removed from office, Franklin was hopeful that the new governor, William Denny (1709–1765), a British army officer, would be more effective, as he would understand defense matters. At a public celebratory dinner, Denny took Franklin aside and tried to flatter him. As Franklin later reported in his autobiography, Denny offered him recompense if he would reduce his opposition to the Proprietary government. Over "a Decanter of Madeira, which the Governor made liberal Use of," Franklin wrote, Denny's "Solicitations and Promises" increased. "My Answers were to this purpose, that my Circumstances, Thanks to God, were such as to make Proprietary Favours unnecessary to me." Franklin also said to Denny that his only dispute with the Proprietary was that its measures were not always "for the Good of the People," but that if the Proprietors would embrace the people's good, then "no one should espouse and forward [the Proprietors' measures] more zealously than myself, my past Opposition having been founded on this, that the Measures which had been urg'd were evidently intended to serve the Proprietary Interest with great Prejudice to that of the People."[73] The impasse between the governor and the Assembly worsened through 1756, as Denny rejected every bill seeking to tax the Proprietary. In January 1757, the Assembly voted to send Franklin to London as its agent to represent its concerns directly to the Proprietors. Franklin's primary goal was to persuade the Proprietors to agree to taxation of their lands. If he failed in that mission, the Assembly asked that he approach British administration to seek a ruling on what the Crown conceived to be the duty of the Proprietors toward Pennsylvania. Franklin prepared himself during the spring that year, and he set sail in June 1757 on his mission for Pennsylvania.

Surely Franklin and the Assembly were convinced that his reputation as a natural philosopher and imperial demographer would assist his negotiations. He had been awarded honorary degrees by Harvard (1753), Yale (1753), and William and Mary (1756). The Royal Society of London awarded Franklin its Copley Medal in November 1753. In fact, William Denny presented this medal to Franklin in 1756 at the celebratory dinner where he tried to persuade Franklin to join forces with the Proprietors rather than to quarrel with them. While Franklin was busy that year, planning appeals for defense monies from the Proprietary and then erecting forts on the western borders of British settlements, the Royal Society unanimously elected him to membership, admitting him with the enticement to join by giving him a waiver of the customary fees. His election to the Royal Society of Arts, largely an innovative agricultural society, followed this in a matter of months. His electrical experiments were the talk of London and, especially, of Europe—so much so that the Abbé Nollet had published his own *Lettres sur l'Electricité* in 1753, which prompted the publication of Franklin's own "supplemental" experiments. Indeed, Franklin's reputation in Europe exceeded his reputation in London.

As an agent, Franklin would have to be mindful of the fact that his postmaster-generalship, a coveted position he shared with William Hunter (d. 1761), was an appointment from Parliament and the British ministry. But he was in a position, everyone thought, to use this appointment to his advantage, for it added to his prestige as a British colonial representative. Along with his other accolades and achievements, Franklin was the ideal representative for the Assembly in the legal tangle with the Proprietors. His esteem was so high that Richard Peters (c. 1704–1776), the provincial secretary who supported the Proprietary party but who also was a member of Franklin's Library Company and board of the Academy, feared Franklin would succeed in his mission, based on his reputation alone. To Thomas Penn (1702–1775), Peters wrote on January 31, 1757, after Franklin had been selected by the Assembly for the mission, fretting about Franklin's appointment: "Certain it is that B.F.'s view is to effect a change of Government, and considering the popularity of his character and the reputation gained by his Electrical Discoveries which will introduce him into all sorts of Company he may prove a Dangerous Enemy." Peters was concerned about Franklin's Royal Society friends who might assist him in gaining access to court circles: "Dr. Fothergill and Mr. Collinson can introduce him to the Men of most influence at Court and he may underhand give impressions to your prejudice. In short Heaven and Earth will be moved against the

Proprietors."[74] Thomas Penn was unconcerned. He reassured Peters that the definite classed structure of Britain, especially London, would prevent Franklin from being effective. "I think I wrote you before," Penn said, "that Mr. Franklin's popularity is nothing here, and that he will be looked very coldly upon by great People, there are very few of any consequence that have heard of his Electrical Experiments, those matters being attended to by a particular Sett of People, many of whom of the greatest consequence I know well, but it is quite another sort of People, who are to determine the Dispute between us."[75] Franklin prepared himself for his mission during the spring of 1757, and he set sail for London in June.

Six

FRANKLIN IN LONDON'S THEATER OF EMPIRE

Franklin spent most of the years between 1757 and 1775 in London and other parts of Britain and Europe. He first traveled to London in 1757, on a mission for the Pennsylvania colony. When that mission faltered in the mid-1760s, he returned to Philadelphia. Franklin traveled again to London for Pennsylvania, and he remained there until 1775, when he returned home to America, having failed to create a peaceful solution to the impasse between the British administration and the British colonies in North America. These were intense years for Franklin. He was lionized across Europe for the accomplishments of his electrical experiments and his theories on topics as diverse as the course and causes of the Gulf Stream, the origin of musical sound using glass tubes, the causes and effects of temperature change in maritime climates, the usefulness of crop rotation to agricultural productivity, and the chemical properties of matter. He received accolades from many different countries, including France, Germany, Italy, and the Netherlands. He was a favorite companion of leading scientists and philosophers, from Sir John Pringle (1707–1782) to David Hume (1711–1776) and Henry Home (1696–1782), Lord Kames.

Franklin was chastised in Britain for the seeming intransigence of the American colonies. In the colonies, some doubted the sincerity of his messages to those in the British administration about the colonies' defense and taxation predicament, while others were jealous of his ability to negotiate so well with members of the aristocracy, given his workingman's background. Franklin spent nearly two decades in negotiation with Great Britain, first representing Pennsylvania in its quarrels with the Proprietary and then representing several of the colonies, when the different colonial assemblies asked him to become their representative in England in the face of the series of acts related to trade and navigation, then the Stamp Act, and then the so-called Coercive Acts. Franklin's activities during these years reveal several theoretical and practical political strategies. Whether considering some of his most important and influential writings or lesser-known letters to the British press and to individuals, we can see a tension between his liberal values and what he was experiencing and reporting on. That tension between values he idealized and the events he was taking part in forced a gradual evolution of his ideas about the British Empire. His first turn in thinking about the possibility of eventual colonial self-sufficiency had arisen in his letters to William Shirley, where he outlined his ideas about a colonial union with representative governance. Those letters, which resulted from the colonies' need for defense against the French, hinted at Franklin's understanding of the colonies' potential power and self-sufficiency. His experiences in London during the period under discussion brought him to embrace the necessity of the independence of the colonies.

Franklin's decades in negotiation with Great Britain preoccupy this chapter and the next. This chapter takes up Franklin's activities during the years 1757 to 1769. It examines Franklin's life in London and the social and political complexities of his mission for Pennsylvania, the outcome of his negotiations, his brief return to Pennsylvania, and then his return to London amid the controversy caused by several oppressive measures designed to tax colonial Britons. Franklin continued to argue for political representation and for economic and trade policies that would assist the colonies and bind them in a collaborative and not subordinated relationship with Great Britain. In the 1760s, when Franklin made public his thoughts on the advantages of retaining Canada in the peace treaty with France and then when he published in London his 1750s letters to William Shirley, he was already turning away from the idea of keeping together an empire that seemed to privilege some Britons (those on an island near Europe) above others (those in British colonies). Chapter 7 takes up Franklin's life and writings, roughly speaking, from 1769 to 1775, key years in the evolution of Franklin's ideas about agriculture, constitutional reform, and commerce, years leading to a recognition of the possibilities for the colonies as independent states.

The Theater of Empire

It will be useful to pause and reflect on Franklin's life in London and take into account the complexity of his mission during the decades he spent away from Philadelphia. These years—1757 to 1769—were filled with activities going well beyond Franklin's negotiations for Pennsylvania and then the colonies. Franklin worked tirelessly in the theater of empire. By employing the phrase *theater of empire*, I am calling attention to the various roles Franklin embraced on the different stages in Britain and Europe where he was, perforce, acting. In London, that theater included the taverns and coffeehouses where his newspaper articles were read, the clubs where he tried to persuade his learned associates about the various points he was making, the estate rooms and hallways where important negotiations were stalled or furthered, and the different locations at court and in Parliament where Franklin sought a fair hearing for colonial problems and offered his suggestions for compromise. Franklin was on stage—as an entrepreneur, a natural philosopher, a colonial statesman, a man of letters, and an imperial theorist. But extending the metaphor, the theater of empire Franklin played in was also a theater of war, as Franklin struggled to address, as if in strategic warfare, the various attacks on his character and on the colonists' demands and expectations. He was sometimes ill, emotionally and physically out of sorts, and weary of his mission, but still he pressed forward toward what he hoped would result in a fair hearing of Americans' grievances.

As respite from his tense times in London, Franklin also enjoyed the life of an esteemed intellectual, and he took part in many trips that enabled him to see his influence outside London. Franklin enjoyed a diverse social network. He established friendships and associations with some of the most important intellectuals, natural historians, and political philosophers in Britain and Europe. He enjoyed London's club culture, and he established a social routine shortly after his arrival in London. On Mondays, he frequently met and dined with scientists, philanthropists, and explorers at the George and Vulture, where he enjoyed the company of John Ellicott (1706–1772), famed clockmaker, fellow of the Royal Society, and astronomer who would become clockmaker to King George III, and, occasionally, James Cook (1728–1779), who was in the midst of launching his military career with the navy. Alternate Thursdays found Franklin dining with his favorite group, the Club of Honest Whigs, at St. Paul's Coffeehouse. Here Franklin met key scientists, philosophers, and political theorists whose friendships lasted his lifetime. Regulars included (when they were in town) John Canton (1718–1772), the physicist (son of a weaver) and fellow of the Royal Society who was the first in England to confirm Franklin's theories about the properties of electricity; Richard Price (1723–1791), a dissenting minister whose writings on politics and economics formed the basis of his reputation in London at the time; Joseph Priestley (1733–1804), whose innovations in education and natural philosophy interested Franklin; James Burgh (1714–1775), whose *The Dignity of Human Nature* (1754) resembled Franklin's *Poor Richard* almanacs; Andrew Kippis (1725–1795), theologian, masterful writer, and eventually author of a narrative about James Cook's voyages. Here Franklin also met William Rose (1719–1786), Scottish schoolmaster, classical scholar, and friend of Samuel Johnson, and, occasionally, James Boswell (1740–1795), lawyer and Johnson's famous biographer. On Sunday, Franklin dined often with Sir John Pringle, a Scottish physician who gradually replaced Franklin's old friend, printer William Strahan (1715–1785), as Franklin's closest friend. Philosopher David Hume was a dining companion when he was in town.

In addition to his club rounds and evenings with particular friends, Franklin also was consulted for his opinion on various scientific matters. In May 1758, he spent a week at Cambridge engaged in experiments related to latent heat and cooling processes from evaporation with physician and chemist John Hadley (1731–1764). That summer, he traveled with his son William on the now famous tour of the ancestral family's towns in England's Midlands, contemplating the family's past, the English civil wars, and the Americans' current predicament. By December, he had invented a damper for stoves and chimneys. His opinions were sought on many things, and he enjoyed the company of his friends. With these associates, some of them close friends and others part of a larger community of military, civic, and scientific leaders, Franklin shared his thoughts on matters ranging from natural history to pure science and political theory. Through them, he would meet some of the most important politicians and philosophers of his time and shore up his understanding of imperial politics, on the one hand, and the importance of essential liberty, on the other.

Political life in London was complicated by the dizzying rate at which leaders were in or out of favor with king and Parliament during Franklin's many years of negotiations with Britain. Between 1754 and 1782, when Franklin was negotiating the Treaty of Paris, there were nine different ministries, some of them led by friends to America and some by those seeking repressive measures. It is no wonder that Franklin was uncertain about how to approach negotiations, and with whom, to be most effective. After the long ministry—from 1743 to 1754—of Henry Pelham (1694–1754), a Whig, the ministry fell for two years to his brother, Thomas Pelham-Holles (1693–1768), first Duke of Newcastle, who was also a Whig. Newcastle eventually fell from power as a result of perceptions that he had mishandled England's situation in the ongoing European wars. An interim, "caretaker" government emerged upon Newcastle's ouster, under William Pitt (1708–1778), first Earl of Chatham, known as the "Great Commoner" and famed for his oratory. Pitt was the wartime leader during the war for empire in North America. A friend to British North America, he did his best to advocate for British imperial superiority and against government corruption.

But the Whigs were factionalized, and Pitt did not get along with Newcastle, so in May 1757, King George II—upon the advice of William Cavendish (1720–1764), fourth Duke of Devonshire, and Newcastle—authorized Philip Yorke (1690–1764), first Earl of Hardwicke, to negotiate a coalition between Newcastle and Pitt. The result was another change in the ministry, with a combined effort of Newcastle and Pitt (1757–62) to prosecute the war against France in North America. Working together, with Pitt attending to defense and foreign policy and Newcastle directing financial matters and working behind the scenes to control the personal interests of different factions, the two were successful until Newcastle was forced to resign upon the accession of George III, who favored the Scot John Stuart (1713–1792), third Earl of Bute, as prime minister. Bute served from 1762 to 1763 only, however, because he was forced out by those who did not approve of the purportedly lenient terms he had accepted in the Peace at Paris of 1763, which concluded the war between Britain and France in North America. The Grenville Ministry (1763–65) followed, led by imperialist George Grenville (1712–1770), best known for the Stamp Act he sought to impose on the American colonies. King George III grew to dislike Grenville and installed Charles Watson-Wentworth (1730–1782), first Marquess of Rockingham, as prime minister. But the Rockingham Whigs lasted only a brief time (1765–66) in Rockingham's first ministry. William Pitt replaced him in 1766 and effectively served two years as prime minister until, under pressure for not managing to negotiate an alliance with Prussia, he left the government (1768). Imagine being Benjamin Franklin, trying to keep up with what was going on behind the scenes at court and in Parliament during these decades crucial to the eventual split between Britain and America.

"I am too old to think of changing countries"

Franklin arrived in England in July 1757. He stayed with his scientific friend, Peter Collinson (1694–1768), while finding living quarters. Hopeful that his appeal to the Penns would succeed, Franklin worked on the two primary legal concerns that had brought him to London. First, Franklin and his friends in the Assembly conceived that the Penns had denied the Assembly its right to legislate tax policy including the taxation of proprietary lands. The Assembly's reasoning was that just as the king's lands were taxed according to laws made in Parliament, so should the Proprietors' lands be taxed according to laws made by the Pennsylvania Assembly. Second, Franklin's Assembly friends—especially Joseph Galloway (1731–1803)—conceived that the Assembly had the right to appoint and remove judges, according to a precedent set by the British Act of Settlement of 1701. Instead, in Pennsylvania, the Proprietors were appointing judges who served at the pleasure of the Proprietary, preventing the Assembly from removing those judges who seemed to be overstepping their offices or otherwise not fulfilling their duties. The Assembly was again seeking the same legal parity with Parliament. As historian Benjamin Newcomb has argued, these positions taken by Franklin, Galloway, and their friends dominating the Assembly indicate the extent of their belief that by curtailing executive prerogative and enlarging the legislative power of the Assembly the Assembly would preserve the "fundamental . . . liberties of Englishmen on both sides of the Atlantic."[1]

Franklin began by attempting to cultivate relationships with members of the ministry in an effort to win them to his side in the debates about Pennsylvania Proprietary government and the legal tangle with the Assembly. He soon discovered, however, that the Assembly's position about its authority was as disagreeable among members of the ministry as it was to the Proprietors. His friend and advisor, Richard Jackson (c. 1721–1787), a British lawyer who would later serve as agent of the Pennsylvania Assembly and who became a friend of America in Parliament, explained at the outset of his stay that the ministry would not support the Assembly's attack on the Penns. Instead of pressing for a settlement of the dispute, Jackson advised Franklin to "keep up the Ball of Contention, 'till a proper Opportunity offers" from a more favorable administration.[2] The ministry was, in fact, hostile to colonial ambitions. Franklin learned this in his first meeting with John Carteret (1690–1763), first Earl of Granville and president of the Privy Council. Granville warned Franklin that, in England, the king was considered the supreme legislator of the colonies. Franklin knew that, at least according to the charters, this view was incorrect, but he nonetheless understood from this interview that his undertaking was much more difficult than he or the Assembly had anticipated.[3] Granville, related to the Penns by marriage, would protect the family. His warning boded ill for Pennsylvania's Assembly and the series of laws it had enacted, but Franklin continued hopeful that a resolution could be reached with the Proprietors, believing that by a reasonable representation of grievances he might persuade the Penns to take up the interests of the Pennsylvanians as their own.

He met with Proprietors Richard Penn (1706–1771) and Thomas Penn in August, when he gave them, on behalf of the Assembly, a list of grievances regarding governance and taxation. Although Franklin fell ill during this period, he continued exchanging messages with the Proprietors and again met with Thomas Penn in November, when he was well enough to get out again. Franklin conferred with the Penns from January through May 1758, and he defended the Pennsylvania Assembly in hearings before the Board of Trade. Finally, on November 27, 1758, the Penns agreed, at least in theory, that limited taxation of the Proprietary might be conceivable, but they were uncertain about the goals of both the Assembly and its representative.[4] Franklin continued to try to meet with the Penns during 1759 and early 1760, but when their exchanges became heated, they refused to give him an audience and instead said he needed to work with their solicitor. In fact, the Penns had been intercepting Franklin's mail to America. From reading a letter Franklin wrote to Isaac Norris, January 14, 1758, they learned that Franklin had characterized Thomas Penn's treatment of his legal arguments with "a Kind of triumphing laughing Insolence, such as a low Jockey might do when a Purchaser complained that He had cheated him in a Horse." Franklin had been arguing with Penn about the rights of the Assembly according to William Penn's original charter, which, Franklin said, had advertised that "the Assembly of Pennsylvania shall have all the Power and Privileges of an Assembly according to the Rights of the Freeborn Subjects of England, and as is usual in any of the British Plantations in America." Penn retorted that his father had granted rights to the Assembly that he had had no right to grant, essentially insinuating that his father had cheated people in order to get them to settle the colony. Franklin remarked to Norris that he was "astonished to see him thus meanly give up his Father's Character." From that moment, Franklin said, he conceived "a more cordial and thorough Contempt for him than I ever before felt for any Man living."[5]

The Penns felt above having to deal with Franklin, forcing him to begin making appeals to the Board of Trade and Privy Council. Hearings on the various acts of the Assembly began before the Board of Trade in May 1760. In the view of the Penns, the Assembly aimed "to establish a Democracy, if not an Oligarchy," under a charter that "betrayed the rights of the Crown."[6] The Penns feared that if the charter were upheld in the way the Assembly represented it, then the Penns would be required to pay most of the colony's expenses by way of taxation of their extensive landholdings. When he was called to appear before the Board of Trade, Franklin based his defense of the different acts of the Assembly on the rights presumably granted the Assembly by charter. He argued that although the Proprietors had executive privilege, they nonetheless were required to meet the legal expectations placed on all landholders and pay their taxes. He also said that it was the will of the people and their right to pass acts via their legislatures. Despite Franklin's arguments based in a reasonable view of the law according to the charter, the Board of Trade rejected, June 24, seven of nineteen acts passed by the Pennsylvania Assembly, including the taxes on the Penns' estates.[7] Franklin appealed to the Privy Council, which in a ruling on August 27 and through the intercession of William Murray (1705–1793), first Earl of Mansfield and chief justice, approved the taxation of the proprietary lands at the lowest possible tax rate, as long as their unimproved lands were not taxed and they would retain the right to appeal future taxes. In overturning the ruling on taxation made by the Board of Trade, the Privy Council granted the position that the Penns were now, at least in principle, no longer above the law and had the same responsibilities of other landholders in the colony.[8]

During these years of negotiations with the Penns, Franklin continued to meet with important and influential members of the British government. He felt convinced that he might still be able to sway leaders to assent to the Assembly's views on administration of the colonies. He impressed some people, but his status as a Briton from North America would always hamper his political aspirations. Nonetheless, his friend Richard Jackson proposed to him the flattering idea of seeking election to Parliament. When writing of this to his young Philadelphia ally, Joseph Galloway, Franklin sighed, "I am too old to think of changing Countries," adding, indeed, "[I] am almost weary of Business, and languish after Repose and my America."[9] Franklin might have been able to set sail for Philadelphia at this point, except that he was obligated to remain in Britain in order to organize and manage the parliamentary reimbursement owed for Pennsylvania's military expenses in the war against France.[10]

The Interest of Great Britain

While in the middle of Pennsylvania's legal fray against the Proprietors, Franklin entered the pamphlet war taking place over the disposition of Canada and Guadeloupe in the aftermath of the imperial wars in North America. This was his first lengthy attempt to explain directly to English Britons the idea of a British Commonwealth geographically dispersed. *The Interest of Great Britain Considered, with Regard to Her Colonies and the Acquisitions of Canada or Guadeloupe* (1760), frequently called the "Canada pamphlet," was written during the protracted discussions by leaders of state about the various proposed wartime reparations that ought to be sought from France at the conclusion of the Seven Years War (the peace finally settled in 1763). Franklin was attempting to persuade British ministry and Parliament of the usefulness of keeping colonies together that were both geographically conjoined and similar in terms of their commodity extraction and production.

Several ministers—those holding interests in sugar plantations—liked the idea of additional island acquisitions and thus sought to retain Guadeloupe in the peace settlement. These colonizers argued according to a long-standing theory of empire that imperial self-sufficiency would best obtain when the colonial empire retained differentiated landholdings, dispersed widely in terms of climate, geography, and topography. Others—and here most notably Benjamin Franklin—argued that such a widely dispersed empire of different extractive and productive qualities did not assist the mixed commercial empire that Britain had become. Like Franklin, theorists of the newer commercial empires pointed out that British manufactures would have better assistance from a system that enabled an increase in domestic English manufacture.

The complicated sets of arguments regarding colonies and differential production that emerged in Britain and France during the 1750s and 1760s reveal growing tensions over how to resolve local, monarchical, land-limited, and land- or sea-locked differences while also retaining, maintaining, and manipulating their colonial possessions in the Americas. Hindsight enables us to see that Britain's policy of using its colonies to support manufacturing on the mainland was depleting resources in its colonial landholdings. Franklin would have seen this in the fur and fishing trades during his youth in New England, when the historically large numbers of beaver pelts and offshore fish (cod, particularly) were significantly diminished. He would have witnessed as well the deforestation around New England resulting from the increase of shipping and shipbuilding in North American and British ports. Surely these factors weighed on him as he considered what might be the best way to address trading problems between the colonies and Great Britain and the defense at sea against France and Spain.

We can best examine Franklin's imperial philosophy if we take into account the conversation into which Franklin's "Canada pamphlet" was entering. Franklin's *Interest of Great Britain Considered, with Regard to Her Colonies* was his second contribution to the pamphlet war over whether Britain should seek the French Caribbean island Guadeloupe or French Canada at the conclusion of the Seven Years War. His first effort was "Humorous Reasons for Restoring Canada," printed in the *London Chronicle* December 25–27, 1759.[11] Franklin's Canada pamphlet responded to two pamphlets, one supporting the acquisition of Canada and one articulating a contrary position and favoring Guadeloupe. The first pamphlet, *A Letter Addressed to Two Great Men, on the Prospect of Peace; and on the Terms necessary to be insisted upon in the Negociation*, supported the annexation of Canada. (The two great men were Newcastle and Pitt.) It was written by a Scot, John Douglas (1721–1807), and published anonymously.[12] The other pamphlet Franklin was responding to was published anonymously by William Burke (1729–1798), who had been named secretary and register of Guadeloupe and who thus used his *Remarks on the Letter Address'd to Two Great Men. In a Letter to the Author of that Piece*[13] to support the position that Guadeloupe was by far the superior acquisition.

Burke's *Remarks on the Letter Address'd to Two Great Men* is preoccupied with ministerial concerns and support of colony men living in London. His examples are few. Burke—whom Franklin called "the Remarker"—employed numerous rhetorical flourishes to incite fear into the aristocracy. He expressed concern about the depopulation of England, the potential losses to manufacturing if the northern American colonies stabilized as manufacturers, and the necessity of controlling the seas around the Caribbean. Burke's arguments were designed to retain the status quo of the older model of the mercantilists, whereby large landholders, who controlled the wealth coming from the colonies, were primary recipients of the distribution of goods in London, and employed poor, landless, working people (in the case of Guadeloupe, enslaved Africans). Burke warned that protracted negotiations with France over Canada would bring about "extravagant expectations" and "render the negotiation for peace a work of infinite difficulty." He argued that English mainland "blood and treasure" were being "expended . . . in the cause of the colonies" and that English people were "making conquests for them."[14] He commented that if the colonists would only employ their own "strength and watchfulness," they could secure their land with a series of forts at key points, so as to prevent French and Spanish access to British territory.[15] The strategy Burke employed was one of blame: if the colonists felt they were at risk, then it was their fault for being colonists in the first place.

The British debates about the processes of colonization at this time centered metropolitan concerns and featured three key goals: to gather into a colonial network a system of dispersed colonies that could assist the wealth and diversity of Britain; to ensure that the costs of administration and defense of the colonies would be displaced onto those who lived on or held money-making property in colonies; and to control trade so that surplus colonial goods would benefit Britain rather than the colonies producing the surplus. Writers tended to express fear that protracted colonial wars drained English purses, that supporting the colonists did not benefit the British people at home, and that Britons in North America would develop their own manufactures, thus interfering with English manufacturing and sea trade. We have seen Franklin address such concerns before.

Franklin published his Canada pamphlet in mid-April 1760.[16] He targeted a wide reading audience, including political leaders, the "great men" of the elite administration, but also the larger audience of merchants, agricultural laborers, tradespeople, and shippers whose livelihoods integrated across the commercial economy that would be influenced by the decision about acquisition. Speaking as an imperial statesman, Franklin pointed out that "great abilities have not always the best information,"[17] thus speaking to the ministers' and others' reliance upon an older, Elizabethan-era scare about depopulation of England and Europe and their ignorance of the actual situation in North America and Canada. As Franklin phrased it, "The objection I have often heard, that if we had Canada, we could not people it, without draining Britain of its inhabitants, is founded on ignorance of the nature of the population in new countries." He politely asked the Remarker to take a "farther reflection"[18] on matters before attempting to create an analogy between the land situation in North America and that of Europe.

To the Remarker's comment that the war in North America was noteworthy for "the blood and treasure expended"[19] on Britain's part, Franklin pointedly observed, "I believe this is too common an error" before going on to explain that the war was of national interest and imperial conse- quence, its cost borne by Americans. He repudiated arguments about the self-interest of the American Britons with an observation upon human behavior—in this case, the behavior of the "Remarker": "Those who would be thought deeply skilled in human nature, affect to discover self-inter- ested views every where at the bottom of the fairest."[20] And he indicated that any interested reader could read about the expenses on record: "The accounts at the treasury will tell you . . . [about the] amazing sums . . . necessarily spen[t] in the expeditions against two very trifling [French- held] forts, Duquesne and Crown Point."[21] Franklin spoke of real-world situations, using examples drawn from shipping charts; population cal- culations; his own experiences as a laborer, Indian diplomat, and wartime leader; and his knowledge of the social and natural environments of North America and the Caribbean. Indeed, Franklin's pamphlet is striking for its critical specificities, its arguments based on environmental considerations, on experience, and on a comparative analysis relating the situation in the Americas to that in Europe.

Arguments for retaining Guadeloupe held that Canada was too large an expanse to defend easily, was less valuable a land mass to protect, and was likely to be inhabited by the laborers, especially mechanics and arti- sans, who could best benefit the British empire by remaining in England. To address such arguments, Franklin developed his own position featur- ing details on population, land availability and use, and manufacturing. Franklin had already published on population in his pamphlet *Observations concerning the Increase of Mankind*. His study of birth records indicated to him the remarkably accurate assessment that the free population in British America doubled every twenty to twenty-five years (about half the time it took for population to double in England).[22] He could thus point out in his Canada pamphlet that agricultural practices and the possibility of free landholding meant that people married at younger ages and thus produced more children. If Canada were acquired as a result of the war, there would be more land in England's dominion. More land in the hands of Britons in North America would bring about a natural increase in inhabitants there, not by a venting or depopulation of the sovereign island but by natural increase.

Bringing home his points about land and the laboring classes, Franklin noted that mechanics who arrived in North America found it easier and more lucrative to enter into agriculture than continue with their trades. The greater dispersal of independent wealth caused by agricultural (rather than manufacturing) subsistence meant less crime. And he concluded with an economic and environmental analysis that rewrote some of the assumptions of mercantilists he had read in his youth, assumptions that continued to emerge during this pamphlet war. "A people spread thro' the whole tract of country on this side the Mississipi, and secured by Canada in our hands," he said, "would probably for some centuries find employment in agriculture, and thereby free us at home effectually from our fears of American manufactures." He insisted that "manufactures are founded in poverty. It is the multitude of poor without land in a country, and who must work for others at low wages or starve, that enables undertakers to carry on a manufacture." To the contrary, he insisted, "No man who can have a piece of land of his own, sufficient by his labour to subsist his family in plenty, is poor enough to be a manufacturer and work for a master." His conclusion was that "while there is land enough in America for our people, there can never be manufactures to any amount or value." Franklin's views, favoring the agricultural sector over manufacturing, were designed to address the merchant groups favoring the suppression of American manufacturing. In the presumed absence of their own manufacturing—because Americans would prefer agriculture, he said—the Americans would become Britain's consumers of goods, a ready market for British manufactures, because the colonists were too busy working their lands. His implications regarding the potential expansion of trade would not have been lost on the manufacturers and merchants who were lobbying Parliament regarding the necessity of constraining rather than freeing up colonial trade and manufacture.[23]

The Remarker had expressed concerns about the hatmakers in England who complained that Britons in North America were engaged in the hat-making trade. The hat trade was used to exemplify the loss of manufacturing in England to colonial American manufacturers. To this Franklin commented that "the exports thither are not diminished by . . . manufacture but rather increased." Franklin used the Remarker's dated example to draw attention to two things—Burke's absence of detailed and up-to-date information and his inability to conceive that ecological and environmental conditions never remained constant and were always in flux. Franklin pointed to the Remarker's ignorance of the American environment and the natural limits of productivity caused by depletion and extraction as primary engines of colonial economy. Of Burke's example of the hat trade, Franklin said, "It is true there have been ever since the first settlement of that country, a few hatters there, drawn thither probably at first by the facility of getting beaver, while the woods were but little clear'd, and there was plenty of those animals." But—drawing attention to the deforestation

and animal losses—he wrote that "the case is greatly alter'd now. The beaver skins are not now to be had in New England, but from very remote
places and at great prices." The impact on human ecology from the losses
of the forest and animals was palpable. "The trade is accordingly declining there," he concluded, "so that, far from being able to make hats in any
quantity for exportation, they cannot supply their home demand; and it
is well known that some thousand dozens are sent thither yearly from
London, and sold there cheaper than the inhabitants can make them of
equal goodness."[24] The colonies were thus, Franklin said, "losing the few
branches [of manufacturing that] they [had] accidentally gain[ed]."[25] This
was, of course, only a partial truth, but its relevance to the specific case of
hatmakers was clear, and the argument was based in the environmental
concerns that had formed a central part of his argument in this pamphlet
as in the *Observations*. The two tracts were, in fact, so much of a piece
that he appended his *Observations* to the Canada pamphlet when it was
printed in London and then in Dublin, Boston, and Philadelphia, in 1760.
Franklin's facts and figures and his comparative data (comparing Europe
or Africa with North America or the Caribbean) provided a compelling argument for acquiring Canada. Franklin's pamphlet is replete with
information about North America, its environment and productions. His
commentaries featured an informed evaluation of the human and animal
ecological changes that had taken place and the necessity for continual
adjustment of expectations to the changing circumstance in the environment. His sensitivity to ecological changes and his continued use of data
proved a distinctive contribution to the pamphlet debates, and his pamphlet worked to correct the misinformation being tossed about.

What seems to have bothered Franklin more than the absence of information about North America was the prejudice against British Americans
that such ignorance fostered. Franklin was troubled about the ways that a
language of politeness obscured the needs and lived experiences of the colonists. Indeed, in reading Franklin's pamphlet, we gain a keen perspective
on Franklin as a rhetorician aware of the linguistic implications of effete
abstractions. He expressed a growing sense of annoyance at those who
used vague language to mystify the difficulties of and the losses incurred
during colonization. For example, Franklin castigated the Remarker
for his comment that the French were "an enemy to be apprehended" as
"an expression . . . too vague to be applicable to the present, or indeed
to any other case."[26] The comment that most inflamed Franklin, however,
related to the administration's presumed desire to "check the growth" of
the British North American colonies. The Remarker had commented that

the French should be allowed to remain in North America to "check the growth of our colonies," because otherwise "they will extend themselves almost without bounds into the in-land parts, and increase infinitely from all causes."[27] The Remarker "reserved" himself from further discussion of the issue, for it was, he said, a subject "not fit for discussion."

Franklin scoffed at the language of humanism that mystified what the Remarker really meant, and he excoriated the Remarker for being "reserved" in saying this was "not a fit subject for discussion."[28] For Franklin, failing to discuss the reasons behind curbing the growth of the colonial population worked against British nationalism and against humanity. He remonstrated, drawing attention to the Remarker's rhetorical maneuvering and giving witness to the colonists' personal difficulties. Britons in England needed to be informed about the devastation caused by the war in North America. Playing on Burke's notion of "checking" North America's growth and drawing attention to Burke's obscuring language, Franklin wrote:

> We have . . . seen in what manner the French and their Indians check the growth of our colonies. 'Tis a modest word, this, check, for massacring men, women and children. The writer would, if he could, hide from himself as well as from the public, the horror arising from such a proposal, by couching it in general terms: 'tis no wonder he thought it a "subject not fit for discussion" in his letter, tho' he recommends it as "a point that should be the constant object of the minister's attention!" But if Canada is restored on this principle, will not Britain be guilty of all the blood to be shed, all the murders to be committed in order to check this dreaded growth of our own people? . . . I would not be thought to insinuate that the remarker wants humanity. I know how little many good-natured persons are affected by the distresses of people at a distance and whom they do not know. There are even those, who, being present, can sympathize sincerely with the grief of a lady on the sudden death of her favourite bird, and yet can read of the sinking of a city in Syria with very little concern.[29]

Franklin was insinuating that the supposed humanity of the Remarker was a flimsy cover for the scurrilous idea that Americans, if they died at the hands of the French, would be no loss to Britain. The Remarker lacked basic human decency but couched his expressions as humane. Franklin's insight—that people often show greater sorrow over the losses of those near them, including little caged birds, rather than those afar (who are assisting the Empire)—provides us a striking lens into the problems he faced while negotiating with administrative leaders in Britain.

Franklin was also talking about problems related to the global imperial projects of both Britain and France in his pamphlet, making every effort to account for the positions taken by those in administration who had a larger agenda than figuring out how to address problems related merely with the Atlantic colonies. In this regard, the reference to Syria (above) is interesting, especially in light of some comparative comments Franklin had earlier made in the pamphlet regarding threats to empire in Algiers, Tunis, and Tripoli. Franklin's comment about "the sinking of a city in Syria" is a reference to two major earthquakes along the Levant fault zone.[30] Franklin was studying earthquakes at the time, attempting to discover patterns in their duration and effects.[31] The entire Levant region was under observation and investigation by both Britain and France as an imperial zone where a contest for empire would likely occur. Franklin's mention of Syria, Algiers, Tunis, and Tripoli indicates his awareness that although he was arguing about colonies in North America, he was attentive to British and French imperial projects underway on the other side of the globe.[32] In his pamphlet, he signaled his awareness of the power of the different peoples in Asia and associated the power of tribal peoples there to the power of the indigenous population—especially if that population were to be assisted by France—in North America. Imperial projects would require resources for containment, he concluded, making a striking comparative analysis among several different populations and regions, including Asia, Scotland, Ireland, and North America:

> Algiers, Tunis and Tripoli, unequal as they are to this nation in power and numbers of people, are enemies to be still apprehended; and the Highlanders of Scotland have been so for many ages by the greatest princes of Scotland and Britain. The wild Irish were able to give a great deal of disturbance even to Queen Elizabeth, and cost her more blood and treasure than her war with Spain. Canada in the hands of France has always stinted the growth of our colonies: In the course of this war, and indeed before it, has disturb'd and vex'd even the best and strongest of them, has found means to murder thousands of their people and unsettle a great part of their country. . . . Canada has also found means to make this nation spend two or three millions a year in America.[33]

In all instances, whether speaking of indigenous peoples of Asia, Scotland, Ireland, or North America, Franklin warned, it was best not to underestimate their desire to hold onto their land. It would take a significant military presence in lands—as in India, for instance—where the European empire was a hostile alien.

While the Remarker's rhetoric of empire seemed to occlude the losses of indigenous and imperial peoples, Franklin's idea was to lay bare the realities of defensive war. Imperial projects, his pamphlet insists, are not humane ones, whether one is talking about the American colonies or events in Syria. Franklin's point about the mystifying discourse of empire that constrained humane action in its effort to enhance one power's geographical and trade expansion was clear: self-love always supersedes love for others; self-love enabled one to ignore others' lives and losses. To defer, to avoid speaking about inhuman slaughter of one's brethren, merely obfuscated the detail that might have shown the injustice and inhumanity of such thinking.

By critiquing the language associated with sensibility and humanism, Franklin showed how a discourse of humanism could enable one sentimentally to detach oneself from others' hardships. This method was common in Franklin's writings. Still playing on the Remarker's comments about the need to check the growth of the colonies, Franklin offered a Swiftian modest proposal: "If it be, after all, thought necessary to check the growth of our colonies, give me leave to propose a method less cruel." His proposal was simply to murder the colonists, "a method of which we have an example in scripture." The "murder of husbands, of wives, of brothers, sisters, and children whose pleasing society has been for some time enjoyed, affects deeply the respective surviving relations: but grief for the death of a child just born is short and easily supported," he insisted. Franklin's satiric comment was studded with reasonableness and humanity:

> The method I mean is that which was dictated by the Egyptian policy, when the "infinite increase" of the children of Israel was apprehended as dangerous to the state. Let an act of parliament, be made, enjoining the colony midwives to stifle in the birth every third or fourth child. By this means you may keep the colonies to their present size. And if they were under the hard alternative of submitting to one or the other of these schemes for checking their growth, I dare answer for them, they would prefer the latter.

The central point was that Britons' lives in America were in the hands of Britons in England. It would be more merciful, quicker, and less expensive to kill colonial people as babes than to leave them unprotected from French attacks against them on the borderlands of North America. Franklin's modest proposal mocked the effect of a civic humanism that worked to obscure the real, lived experiences of colonial people whose lives would be changed by the decisions under discussion. By employing specifics in his arguments, he would not have anyone, especially pamphleteers and ministers, hide from themselves or the public what was really being discussed when arguments were put forward to let Canada remain in French hands.

Franklin had developed an imperial theory that featured farming smaller freeholds so as to enjoy commercial success with excess produce. Franklin allowed for commerce in his theory, but he added environmental conditions into the commercial equation. Showing an awareness of the problems of soil depletion and atmospheric change—especially showing a sense that neither were constants, especially in North America, where he was charting reports about wind and theorizing about the Gulf Stream—Franklin allowed for a system of flexible trade and laboring practices. He considered the widest possible impact, whether one were a laborer or a colonial administrator. To be sure, Franklin clearly had North American laborers in mind, but he also accounted for the interest of those involved in capital development and distribution. In revealing his superior knowledge of colonial environments, colonial affairs, and the lived experiences of laborers, Franklin's analysis worked to disabuse readers of the misinformation they had been given.

Franklin's pamphlet expressed concern about the social and natural worlds in the Americas as these were increasingly negatively impacted by commodity extraction and regulation without concern for the laborers and the land. Of course, Franklin had an imperialist orientation at this time, but it is also important to recognize that, unlike other pamphleteers, Franklin was developing an environmental logic for colony-building. He was uninterested in an imperialism based in extractive measures built upon forced labor (such as slavery in the Caribbean) and instead proposed land-use policies adapted to the different environmental and social conditions obtaining in different parts of the British Empire. By attending to environmental conditions, Franklin underscored the importance of the American colonies to the British imperial system while also clarifying that resources *do* decline dramatically when the colonial policy is merely for extraction rather than careful cultivation of resources.

Franklin sent his pamphlet to David Hume, among others, to learn what Hume thought of his views. Having read Hume's essays "On Commerce" and "On the Jealousy of Trade" (and evidently commingling them in his memory), Franklin used the opportunity of his letter to extend a long and urbane compliment to Hume for his presumed understanding of the economic situation of laboring peoples in colonial lands. Hume's letter to Franklin has not been found, but some of his meaning can be garnered from Franklin's response to it. "I am not a little pleas'd to hear of your Change of Sentiments in some particulars relating to America," he wrote, "because I think it of Importance to our general Welfare that the People of this Nation should have right Notions of us, and I know no one that has it more in his Power to rectify their Notions, than Mr. Hume."[34] Franklin's message both complimented and instructed Hume. Franklin made sure Hume understood the compliment by identifying, with great subtlety, what Hume's message *should* be. As the newly eminent historian of Britain whose examination of the British Empire and its history was then being published, Hume should inform Britons in Great Britain about the circumstances of Britons in colonial areas such as North America.

Franklin played on the language of interest politics germane to the colonial system to make a point to Hume regarding the common interests, interests of humanity, of Britons in North America and those in Great Britain. Franklin spoke warmly about Hume's work. "I have lately read with great Pleasure, as I do every thing of yours, the excellent Essay on the *Jealousy of Commerce*." He hoped it would "have a good Effect in promoting a certain Interest too little thought of by selfish Man, and scarce ever mention'd, so that we hardly have a Name for it; I mean the *Interest of Humanity*, or common Good of Mankind." He continued that he "hope[d] particularly from that Essay, an Abatement of the Jealousy that reigns here of the Commerce of the Colonies, at least so far as such Abatement may be reasonable."[35] The rhetorical maneuver, typical of Franklin when addressing a learned audience, could draw polite and witty attention to the negative condition being discussed (jealousy of commerce) by emphasizing the construction of a conceived opposite (the interest of humanity). In other words, jealousy of commerce prevented the operations that might benefit "*Humanity*, or the common Good of Mankind."

In making such an analysis, Franklin framed an elaborate and extended compliment to Hume's own views. Hume had pointed out in his essay "Of Commerce" that war, by drawing people away from wealth-producing livelihoods, detracted from the ability of a nation to create wealth. He argued that nations should not fight with one another in an effort to gain exclusivity over the seas or in commerce. Instead, nations should aim to support freedom of commerce and trade by remaining in peace with one another. In so doing, they could generate more products and thus greater profits to agricultural, manufacturing, and merchant groups. Hume's critique of mercantilism was one that Franklin himself had been fond of making during these years, so Franklin seized the opportunity to affirm Hume's assertions, despite the fact that such assertions were, to Franklin, neither new nor particularly clearly phrased. Hume had written in his essay "Of the Jealousy of Trade" that it was "obvious, that the domestic industry of a people cannot be hurt by the great prosperity of their neighbours; and as this branch of commerce is undoubtedly the most important in any extended kingdom, we are so far removed from all reason of jealousy." Hume went farther, however, and "observe[d], that where an open communication is preserved among nations, it is impossible but the domestic industry of every one must receive an increase from the improvements of others."[36] That is, rather than being a threat, a neighbor's wealth was a bonus, as it could be used to increase one's nation's wealth: a neighbor's wealth created a great opportunity for exporting, at potential profit, one's own surplus manufactured goods. Such a system could promote better livelihoods within both nations, and it would sponsor an increase in and greater variety of commercial goods. Hume's particular case in point was the woolen manufacture, but his point leans toward the laissez-faire model already publicly favored by Franklin and adumbrated later on by Adam Smith.

In addition to confirming his agreement with Hume, Franklin's letter clarified the extent to which Britons in England did not seem to care about the situation of Britons in North America, whether in peace or in war. Defense in North America, Franklin argued, was falling increasingly to the colonial people alone, and they were prevented from appointing official military leaders from among themselves, as appointments occurred at the prerogative of the Crown and ministry. Franklin reminded Hume that colonial troops were left defenseless in Canada in 1746, after the colonial administration in London had offered to support troops and regimental leaders willing to make an expedition to Canada. "Tho' I am satisfy'd by what you say, that the Duke of Bedford was hearty in the Scheme of the Expedition, I am not so clear that others in the Administration were equally in earnest in that matter," Franklin wrote. He politely quibbled with what evidently had been Hume's supportive construction of the British administration's concern about what happened to the North American colonies abutting Canada in the war there between Britain and France. Franklin acknowledged that it was "certain that after the Duke of Newcastle's first Orders to raise Troops in the Colonies, and Promise to send over Commissions to the Officers, with Arms, Clothing, &c. for the Men, we never had another Syllable from him for 18 Months." During this time, Franklin said, "the Army lay idle at Albany for want of Orders and Necessaries; and it had begun to be thought at least that if an Expedition had ever been intended, the first Design and the Orders given, must, thro' the Multiplicity of Business here at home, have been quite forgotten."[37] Franklin's reply indicates that Hume had defended the administration, evidently, indicating that it had shown concern about the colonists. Essentially, Franklin's message to Hume was this: experience in North America and Canada belied Hume's armchair representation of the administration. The letter amplifies the point of the pamphlet itself: experience must always be taken into account when policy is devised, so that people are not left risking their lives and livelihoods attempting to save a British Empire that does not seem interested in saving them.

From a rhetorical standpoint, however, the most telling moment in Franklin's long letter to Hume is his defense of his word *colonize* in the Canada pamphlet. Franklin, fond of expressive neologisms, had used the word *colonize* as a reminder of an original intent regarding the lands of North America that present-day Britons, in their fears of drawing talent away from the mainland, had forgotten. He drew upon arguments he had been making, beginning in the 1720s, against the old mercantilist theories and in behalf of commercial and manufacturing freedoms. He attempted to remind Hume that the original intent of the colonies had been to vent England of its less desirable laborers. Franklin's arguments about economies and the commonwealth reveal a sophisticated theoretical understanding of the positive proportional ratio of land to population in areas not densely settled. In the older economic system, colonies were chartered typically to assist joint stock companies, some of whose lead investors were either in or close to the administration. The original goal was to bring mineral (and, later, fur) wealth back to England—and that, quickly—so as to assist individuals' net worth, which, it was argued, would enhance the nation's wealth. The private vice (i.e., greed), in Bernard Mandeville's terms, was a public benefit.[38] Individuals benefiting from trade advantages created the nation's benefits. Franklin pointed out in the Canada pamphlet that at one time, it was administrative policy to send people overseas. Such venting occurred originally to secure better working conditions for a greater number of people in England. Venting also helped Britain gain a toehold for colony-building and natural resource extraction, whether of minerals, fur, timber, animals, or other common or exotic products. In the Canada pamphlet, Franklin invoked that past initiative in an effort to remind readers that benefits would accrue to Great Britain with a greater number of people in North America, because they could take advantage of the productive *richesse* of the lands there. It is an environmental argument based in population dispersal, productive labor, and artisanal accomplishment.

In case Hume had missed these points in the Canada pamphlet itself, Franklin worked to differentiate the earlier goals from the current situation in North America. He was attempting to disabuse Hume of misunderstanding about the colonial situation. He wrote: "The objection I have often heard, that if we had Canada, we could not people it, without draining Britain of its inhabitants, is founded on ignorance of the nature of population in new countries. When we first began to colonize in America, it was necessary to send people, and to send seed-corn; but it is not now necessary that we should furnish, for a new colony, either one or the other."[39] Colonizing, Franklin insisted, required assistance from Britain. The colonies, now no longer dependent, no longer required Britain.

In this portion of the Canada pamphlet when Franklin spoke to the original colonization efforts, his point was similar to the arguments Hume was making in his essays "On Commerce" and "On the Jealousy of Trade." Yet Franklin's point was that having available land for cultivation was an actual support for the manufacturing interests in England. He suggested that with policies of free trade possibilities and the free movement of laboring people, Britain would flourish. "The annual increment alone of our present colonies, without diminishing their numbers, or requiring a man from hence, is sufficient in ten years to fill Canada with double the number of English that it now has of French inhabitants," Franklin wrote.[40] British North America could people itself, he indicated, without taking population or livelihood from people in Britain. To clarify for Hume the detailed background of his 1760 Canada pamphlet, Franklin appended his much-circulated treatise, originally written in 1751, *Observations concerning the Increase of Mankind.*[41]

Franklin's economic analyses always led him back to concerns about establishing the greatest good for the greatest number of people. Herein he knew his view conflicted with the interest politics of the current administration and with the views held by the Pennsylvania Proprietors, who worked from the assumption that the people of Pennsylvania owed them allegiance and freedom from taxes out of gratitude for the opportunity that being in Pennsylvania afforded. Franklin believed that a free laborer ought to be able to earn a living wage sufficient to his and his family's needs and sufficient, too, that he would be able to sell his surplus goods from his own labor and free as well to begin setting aside an additional sum (whether in currency or in land) from his earnings for the proverbial rainy day. To Franklin, such an approach devoid of any jealousy over another's good fortune in commerce was, in effect, "the *Interest of Humanity,* or common Good of Mankind." Franklin understood that this was not the view of the good of mankind that most political theorists of his time supported. He had become painfully aware of the extent to which the discourse of "the nation" was trumping the opportunities of the nation's people, especially those living in colonial situations in North America, East Asia, Ireland, and even in parts of Scotland not typically discussed by the legal, social, and political philosophers born there.

So in the end Franklin used the word *colonize* to portray his view of the situation: Britons in North America were colonizing the lands and peoples in order better to serve the empire. Yet David Hume, a Scot whose own country had its own burden of a peaceable but nonetheless colonized history, found trouble with the word and the very notion of colonizing lands for England. The word sounded harsh, brutish, too unusual to be useful. Responding to Hume's remarks about the word, Franklin wrote, "I thank you for your friendly Admonition relating to some unusual Words in the Pamphlet. It will be of Service to me. The pejorate, and the *colonize*, since they are not in common use here, I give up as bad; for certainly in Writings intended for Persuasion and for general Information, one cannot be too clear, and every Expression in the least obscure is a Fault."[42] Franklin attempted to gloss over, as a difference of opinion regarding word usage merely, a difference of opinion regarding how to use facts as one sees them. Yet his polite wording to Hume clarified his view that the word might be unpersuasive. If he gave up anything, it was the word, but not the position, which he considered accurate.

The editors of Franklin's papers have said that his Canada pamphlet should be regarded as one of Franklin's most important pamphlets.[43] It cemented Franklin's reputation as an important imperial strategist whose analyses bore up under examination, even if his message was lost on those in administration. Unlike his friends in Great Britain and Europe, Franklin had witnessed great changes taking place in North America and understood the environmental and political promise of a consolidation of the colonies as productive parts of the British Empire. As he increasingly realized that his views would not be credited nor countenanced in England, he grew restive and began explicitly addressing the problems with the existing (and constantly changing) trade policies of Great Britain. His writings on economy and society are clear statements based on data he collected, readings he had done, and inquiries he had personally made among leading theorists. Recognizing the significant discrepancies between Britain's oppressive trade policies and its public, liberal face given to those policies, whether in Scotland, Ireland, North America, or India, Franklin continued in his campaign to reveal the fractures in the imperial facade.

Philadelphia Interlude

Franklin's mission to London in behalf of the Pennsylvania Assembly had concluded with a small victory for the Assembly but no clear resolution to the ongoing issue of taxation of the Proprietary estates. Franklin remained in London to make sure that Pennsylvanians would be reimbursed for their expenses to support the British military in the war against France in North America. By the time he set sail for Philadelphia by way of Portsmouth in August 1762, Franklin was ready for a change of scene. He had long hoped that his son William would marry his young friend Polly Stevenson, but William had his sights on upper-class society and held Tory leanings. He married a planter's daughter, Elizabeth Downes (1728–1777), in September, shortly after gaining the royal appointment as governor of New Jersey. Franklin missed the wedding by setting sail in advance of the nuptials. He arrived in Philadelphia on November 1. Early in 1763, Franklin had the honor of welcoming his son home with his new bride, as the royal governor of New Jersey.

By summer, Franklin was again working on colonial matters. He wanted to make sure the American communications networks were strong, so he toured the colonies, traveling first to Virginia (from April to May) and then northward again, through New Jersey, New York, and New England (from June to November) to inspect post offices. He made his extensive tour with John Foxcroft (d. 1790), secretary to Virginia governor Francis Farquier (1704?–1768), and his daughter Sarah.

The trip was a lull before a storm of controversy that would emerge again over settlers and Indians in western parts. On November 8, Franklin met with other commissioners to sign orders for defense, a situation necessitated by warfare between Indians and British settlers from the Ohio territory through Detroit. Organized by Pontiac, who began by attacking settlements at Detroit, a collection from different Native tribes made repeated attacks against settlements up and down the interior. The skirmishes resulted in warfare in border areas in Pennsylvania. A cluster of settlers in Lancaster County attacked peaceable Indians and created a firestorm of protest and anxiety from Lancaster to Philadelphia. Franklin was angered by the massacre of peaceable Indians who were living amid the settlers. He drafted a bill, January 4, 1764, to set into law that whites could be tried for capital offenses against peaceful Indians. The bill was unpopular, and the Assembly dropped it.

But Franklin would not be silenced. He published his tract *A Narrative of the Late Massacres* on January 30, written to excoriate the so-called

Paxton Boys.[44] Writing to evoke moral outrage, Franklin tried to wake up Pennsylvanians. "Let us rouze ourselves," Franklin wrote, because of the shameful actions of a few men who engaged in a heinous crime.[45] He argued that the "Hands of Government" needed strengthening, so "that JUSTICE may be done, the Wicked punished, and the Innocent protected." Franklin's angry and emotional response to the murder of peaceful Native peoples revealed a humanitarian concern for justice but also his anxiety that such murders could set off an Indian war the settlers were unprepared for. The pamphlet reveals Franklin's deft handling of information so as to produce emotional responses in his readers. The details are vivid: the Conestoga Indians who had been away from home had returned to find the "butchered half-burnt Bodies of their murdered Parents and other relatives" left strewn about. He implored his audience to remember the peacemaking of former times. "These poor People have been always our Friends. Their Fathers received ours, when Strangers here, with Kindness and Hospitality. Behold the Return we have made them!" Franklin reminded readers of their obligations to Natives who were willing to assimilate: "When we grew more numerous and powerful, they put themselves under our *Protection*. See, in the mangled Corpses of the last Remains of the Tribe, how effectually we have afforded it to them!" Franklin contrasted the disgusting behavior of the Pennsylvania settlers with the hospitality of ancient heathens and Christians. "Heathens, Turks, Saracens, Moors, Negroes, and Indians"—all had been hospitable, he said. He concluded that the Conestogas "would have been safer among the ancient Heathens, with whom the Rites of Hospitality were *sacred*." Franklin grew even more incensed when the men involved marched eastward to Philadelphia in February, claiming that they would slaughter all the Indians seeking refuge there. Franklin believed that Native peoples everywhere would take the massacre as a sign of the treachery of all settler peoples. The massacre would make treaty agreements far more difficult, and it would be the touchstone behind all future attempts to purchase and use Indian lands in Pennsylvania. Franklin was called upon by the governor and members of the Assembly to quell the potential violence, and he succeeded in doing so.

Problems with defense and the disruptions by border settlers continued to plague Franklin and the Assembly's legislative situation. The continued intransigence of the Penns prompted members of the Assembly ultimately to conclude that Pennsylvania ought to be a royal colony. In April 1764, Franklin drafted and then published *Cool Thoughts on the Present Situation of Our Public Affairs* about the

Assembly's plan to seek a royal charter. Factions arose in favor of the Proprietors, but the anti-Proprietary party was able nonetheless to get Franklin elected speaker of the Assembly. In May, Franklin drafted a petition to the king requesting a formal change of government, which he signed as speaker in May 1764. Additional controversy reached his speaker's desk from Massachusetts, when Franklin was asked by the Massachusetts House of Representatives to support its protest of Grenville's proposed Stamp Act, a parliamentary measure intended to raise revenue on all printed matter in the colonies. This tax would disrupt the free flow of information and cause extra hardship for those involved in activities from papermaking to printing and distribution of printed materials. Franklin was so involved with Assembly matters that while he was concerned about the Stamp Act, he let Assembly concerns dominate his activity. Still, in September, he presented the Assembly with his proposal to instruct its London agent, Richard Jackson, to oppose the passage of the proposed Stamp Act; seek modifications of the Sugar Act (which had been enacted April 5); and argue that only the Pennsylvania legislature had the right to pass legislation imposing taxes in Pennsylvania. As speaker, Franklin signed the instructions to Jackson.

Despite his efforts to support the colony of Pennsylvania, Franklin faced significant difficulties during the fall election campaign for the Assembly. Perhaps he had been away too long. He had developed enemies. Some of his assailants wrote that the reason he favored royal government was that he coveted a governorship. Others said he had drawn a large income from public monies while serving as Assembly agent. Still others criticized his use of public funds while in London. Worse, they tried to impugn his character by saying that his son William's mother had been a black maidservant named Barbara, whom it was said he had buried in an unmarked grave. Franklin's detractors used the opportunity of the election to malign Franklin for having called German immigrants "Palatine boors" when he first drafted the "Observations concerning the Increase of Mankind." By reviving Franklin's slur, the anti-Franklin group managed to get Germans to vote against him. He was defeated in the voting in October 1764, but his party retained its majority and appointed Franklin to join Richard Jackson as Assembly agent in London. He set sail for London on October 26, sailing from Chester, where three hundred friends and admirers accompanied him to his ship. His passage was difficult, but he arrived in London in December.

"To wear their old clothes over again, till they can make new ones"

Franklin's interlude in Pennsylvania had been a turbulent one, but he was ready to work again for the colonies when he reached London in late 1764. Arguing for the repeal of the Stamp and Sugar Acts would require all the rhetorical skill and political acumen he could muster. In addition to defending the colonies against stringent measures that placed colonial free enterprise in jeopardy, Franklin had specific duties regarding Pennsylvania's status with the Crown. Franklin was being called upon to represent the rights and grievances of Pennsylvania again, but this time he was tasked with requesting the Crown to take on Pennsylvania as a royal government. Franklin would spend much of his time in London attempting to influence imperial policies on trade, taxation, and political representation. Parliament was increasing its attempts to find a method for taxing the colonies. The argument for taxation was based on the increasing debt caused, according to British views, because of the expenses of the imperial wars on the interior. To the thinking of those in power, the defensive wars were being fought to protect the American colonists, not the British Empire in North America.

The first step in arguing against oppressive tax measures was an interview on February 2, 1765, with First Minister George Grenville (1712–1770) to protest the imposition of stamp duties in America. Working with other colonial agents, Franklin attempted to explain the situation in North America. Grenville nonetheless introduced his annual budget in Parliament, one that included his proposal for the Stamp Act. Working with Thomas Pownall (1722–1805), who favored fostering better ties between Great Britain and British North America, Franklin met with Grenville again on February 12 to offer an alternative proposal for raising revenue in America by issuing paper money at interest. The suggestion was dismissed. The Stamp Act passed the House of Commons on February 27 and received the king's assent on March 22. It was scheduled to take effect November 2, 1765.

Franklin considered the matter concluded when the vote took place, so when Grenville asked Franklin to nominate someone to serve as Pennsylvania's stamp distributor, Franklin nominated his friend, John Hughes (c. 1712–1777). Being in London, Franklin did not realize the radical strength of the anti–Stamp Act protests taking place in North America. He was alarmed by reports of mob action against Britain. In Pennsylvania, Franklin's nomination of Hughes caused quite a stir. Franklin's detractors used the opportunity to say that Franklin supported the stamping measure, because he was seeking office in Britain—an argument that Franklin detractors have employed against him to this day. Although he believed self-rule could work in the colonies, he was still trying to keep the empire together at all costs. Franklin and Pownall were more successful in April 1765, when they worked together to get the Quartering Bill amended. The change brought about the elimination of the forcible quartering of British troops in private dwellings in America; the amended act passed May 3. Yet this was a very minor victory in light of the ongoing Stamp Act protests in North America.

Through the summer and fall of 1765, Stamp Act protests spread through all the colonies. In Philadelphia, growing unrest brought about several attacks on the stamp distributors. Franklin's home was threatened in September—so much so that Sally Franklin went to New Jersey to live with her brother as the fury raged on the streets. In mid-September, Deborah armed herself against the mob gathered outside her home, refusing to flee. Her bravery was rewarded by the assistance of more than eight hundred people who showed up to quell the angry protestors and dissolve their effort to storm the Franklin home. On November 1, 1765, the Stamp Act failed to go into effect as local courts refused to convene and administer it. The administration of government in the colonies was at a standstill. Late in the year, Franklin presented the Privy Council with Pennsylvania's petition to become a royal government, given the stalemate that had taken place over Assembly laws. The proposal was tabled. Franklin turned to writing for the press during the winter months. He wrote a number of newspaper articles defending the colonies and agitating for repeal of the Stamp Act. Early in 1766, he designed an anti–Stamp Act cartoon, had it printed on cards, and used the cards as calling cards when sending out his messages.

Given the double-headed issue of taxation and representation, a cause he had eloquently discussed formerly in his letters to William Shirley, Franklin decided it was time to lay out his arguments to the public, so that the people of Britain might better understand the Americans' grievances. With a preface signed "Lover of Britain," Franklin's friend William Strahan strategically timed his republication of Franklin's letters to Shirley (originally written December 3, 4, and 22, 1754) in the *London Chronicle,* February 8, 1766. Strahan's method was to cast, with Franklin, a friendly gauntlet into the public arena in an effort to get Britons more invested in the equal rights of American Britons. By bringing his 1750s letters to light again, Franklin was attempting to assure contemporary readers that the Americans' aversion to taxation without just and equitable representation had antedated by more than ten years the current crises. Franklin's decision to republish the Shirley letters signals his re-evaluation of his opinions about Great Britain. He would continue to argue for a greater Britain, one with a global reach and imperial maritime significance. But in his dealings with the Board of Trade and Privy Council, Franklin had begun seriously to question the ability of Britons to understand or at least have compassion for the situation of Britons in North America. For this reason, it is reasonable to conclude that Franklin's letters to William Shirley, published in 1754 and then republished in 1766, mark his first clear public statement that the colonies could, if they cooperated with one another, form a more cohesive state, of themselves, than as colonies bound to Great Britain. These letters were Franklin's first major statement that the liberties associated with early modern liberalism were more important to him than any attachment to an empire that did not care about its peoples. The Franklin-Shirley letters were reprinted widely. They would have a significant impact on the liberty language employed during the American Revolution by supporters of the colonies in Britain and by those seeking redress in the colonies. In fact, these letters were perhaps the most widely reprinted of Franklin's writings in Franklin's day.[46] After Strahan's printing, they were copied in the London *Gazetteer* (February 10) and then in the *London Magazine* and *Gentleman's Magazine*.[47] In the colonies, the letters were printed May 15, 1766, in the *Pennsylvania Gazette*; the *Providence Gazette*, February 7, 1767; the *Boston Gazette*, December 5, 1768; and the *Pennsylvania Chronicle*, January 16, 1769.[48]

The republication came at a strategic time in 1766, during his negotiations regarding Pennsylvania's status as a colony and the conflict over the Stamp and Sugar Acts. Franklin's strategy at this time was to challenge the lobbying efforts in Parliament, particularly from the mercantile sector, which was pushing for constraining measures against colonial trade. The letters had a clear message about Britons in North America, who were ready for self-rule if Britain failed to provide for representation and freedom from trade restrictions. This became clear eight years later, when Thomas Pownall revived them as he published in London the fifth edition of his *Administration of the British Colonies* (1774). James Burgh (1714–1775) also printed them in his *Political Disquisitions* in London in 1774, and they were reprinted in Burgh's Philadelphia imprint in 1775. They appeared again in 1776 and in 1778 in both an English and French edition. Even more telling with regard to the impact of these letters on the colonies is that they were reproduced in an article, "The History of the War in America," in the *Vermont Gazette or Freeman's Repository*, March 13, 1784.

The Shirley letters would have a long, active life during these years of negotiations as well as during the war and treaty years.

Days after sending the Shirley letters to press, Franklin had to attend
the House of Commons to face questions about the American colonies
and their allegiance to the Crown. He appeared for a long interview there
on February 13, 1766. When questioned before Commons about taxation,
the war debt, and the colonists' riotous intransigence against Britain, especially regarding the implementation of the Stamp Act, Franklin repeated
his frequent argument that the war between Britain and France over territory in North America was fought not for the colonists' sake but because of
Britain's territorial battle with France about the limits of Canada and Nova
Scotia and about the right of British trade in the Ohio country.[49] When
questioned about Pennsylvania's taxation and trade and the American
contention that the colonies lacked the specie required by tax, Franklin
pointed out the circuitous trade routes Pennsylvania merchants followed
in order to gain enough specie for taxes. He described the bartering system
that formed the complicated trade-route system.[50] With a later question, he
took the opportunity to point out that British North Americans' annoyance with Parliament increased as a result of the trade restraints on the
colonies, because merchants could no longer bring foreign gold and silver
into the colonies, could not manufacture their own money, and were held
subject for stamp taxes.[51] Aware of the stable markets in North America
and the ability of Britons there to produce their own goods, Franklin
believed that American boycotts of British manufactures would succeed
if Britain continued its policy of repressive measures. Indeed, Franklin's
writings both private and public continually argued that boycotts would
secure Americans rights that the ministry was unwilling to grant.

Franklin bemoaned his inability to persuade to his side the politicians
and populace in Britain, but the records of his remarks before the House
of Commons on February 13 give evidence that his views on American
affairs were being considered with care. When questioned in Commons,
"What was the temper of America towards Great Britain before the year
1763," Franklin replied, "The best in the world." This provided him an
opening to evoke a mythic story of common heritage of the Britons in
North America and those in England. "They submitted willingly to the
government of the crown, and paid, in all their courts, obedience to acts
of parliament," he offered. Indeed, "They had not only a respect, but an
affection for Great-Britain, for its laws, its customs and manners, and even
a fondness for its fashions." For the constituency supporting restrictions
against American manufacturing, he added that this "greatly increased

the commerce." The honor granted to those from Britain also found its way into Franklin's representation: "Natives of Britain were always treated with particular regard; to be an Old England-man was, of itself, a character of some respect, and gave a kind of rank among us," he said.[52] Franklin's rhetorical method was to construct a sense of common lineage, common goals, and common values, matching the themes of his many articles in the public press.

The period of questioning was long, and it must have been tiring when we remember that Franklin stood through the process and was expected to be ready to handle well any question that might arise. After expressing himself on the national pride of colonial Britons, Franklin stood through several more series of questions—hours' worth, in fact—before he was permitted to withdraw. The last questions he was asked concerned the Americans' feeling of attachment to Britain.

Q. What used to be the pride of the Americans?
A. To indulge in the fashions and manufactures of Great Britain.
Q. What is now their pride?
A. To wear their old cloaths over again, till they can make new ones.[53]

Franklin attempted throughout the proceeding to emphasize how British colonial policies had driven a wedge between the Great Britain and the American colonists. He worked hard to explain his complicated view that the empire was assisted and not undermined by the colonies. The repeated questions on matters of policy, taxation, population, importation, and exportation were numbing in their insistence on detail, and their very phrasing bespoke an obvious sense of superiority that members of Parliament felt toward British Americans. Franklin affected a transparency of political thinking that is representative of the contents of his voluminous writings for the press, to friends, and to those in power. Franklin's long defense of the colonies before the House of Commons contributed to the repeal of the Stamp Act on February 22, 1766.

But Franklin's work had only just begun. He spent the year 1767 campaigning against parliamentary taxation of the colonies in series of letters to the London newspapers. In letters to North America, he attempted to explain the situation in London. Franklin was caught in a difficult position. He was attempting to create arguments supporting the colonies and their affection for Great Britain at precisely the time when colonists were agitating against several measures intended to fortify Britain's hold over them. The colonists had reached a point where they considered it might be better to have complete legislative freedom. Franklin's themes in his numerous essays for the press during this period spoke to what the editors of his papers identify as "the necessity of mutual understanding and, for Britain, the price of misunderstanding in terms of taxes and commerce lost."[54] Franklin recommended that the ministry begin to understand this discrepancy before the empire was further imperiled.[55] By freeing up American trade and especially by reducing the restrictions upon imports and exports, he asserted, the ministry could increase revenues going to England and still retain British North Americans' allegiance. His argument that a distinction existed between the right to regulate trade, conceived as an external tax, and the right to create internal laws for internal taxes fell on deaf ears.

Franklin worked long hours writing for the public press and writing private letters to friends of the colonies in an effort to win their support for the Britons in North America. For instance, Franklin offered to his friend, Lord Kames, a series of comments on the American disputes. To Kames, Franklin wrote on February 25, 1767, expressing a wish for imperial unity. Using the tone and language of an impartial imperial theorist, he wrote, "It becomes a Matter of great Importance that clear Ideas should be formed on solid Principles, both in Britain and America, of the true political Relation between them, and the mutual Duties belonging to that Relation." Kames evidently agreed with Franklin on most points, because Franklin made an effort to shore up Kames's support by saying, "I am fully persuaded with you, that a consolidating Union, by a fair and equal Representation of all the Parts of this Empire in Parliament, is the only firm Basis on which its political Grandeur and Stability can be founded." He confessed to Kames that what was troubling was the sense out there, among the general population, that "Every Man in England seems to consider himself as a Piece of a Sovereign over America; seems to jostle himself into the Throne with the King, and talks of OUR *Subjects in the Colonies*."[56]

For the public press, he tried again and again to offer arguments about the legal and moral problems of assuming that colonial Britons were mere subjects of subjects. In a summary article "On the Propriety of Taxing America" written under the name "Benevolus" and published April 11, 1767, in the *London Chronicle*, Franklin included many of his primary arguments regarding American affairs. When Charles Townshend (1725–1767), Chancellor of the Exchequer, proposed additional duties in the House of Commons in May, Franklin worked even harder (and with growing anger) to attempt to persuade people of the wrongheadedness of these and other oppressive measures. The Townshend proposals passed in

July, causing more unrest in the colonies, unrest Franklin did not witness but heard about.

In the meantime, Franklin decided take a break and go to visit with some of the French philosophers and scientists who made up his growing number of European correspondents. With his friend Sir John Pringle, Franklin took a tour of France from August through October. Franklin had numerous friends at court under the reign of King Louis XV. He had a significant following as well among the leading natural philosophers and economists of France. The king himself expressed sincere admiration for Franklin's experiments. He had, back in the 1750s, asked that Franklin's electrical experiments be performed, so that the French could verify Franklin's findings. When the experiments were successfully performed at Marly, the French Royal Academy was informed that Franklin's experimental vision was a reality. Learning of Franklin's visit in 1767, the king asked to meet Franklin, so his friends arranged to have both Franklin and Pringle presented to the king at Versailles. The visit to France allowed Franklin to see the extent of his renown in Europe and to test the possibility of political amity between the Americans and the French government.

In his writings for the press from 1766 through 1769, Franklin often emphasized his sense of the common natural rights of all Britons, wherever they were situated globally. These were ancient rights, in the commonwealth tradition, extending back to the charter rights in the Magna Carta. In a statement published in the *London Chronicle* January 5–7, 1768, Franklin insisted that Americans, as British citizens, had a "natural right" to develop, manufacture, and use their own goods, form their own assemblies, and make their own laws. "There cannot be a stronger natural right than that of a man's making the best profit he can of the natural produce of his lands," Franklin wrote. "It is of no importance to the common welfare of the empire, whether a subject of the King's gets his living by making hats on this or that side of the water."[57] According to a formulation Franklin was fond of at this time, the colonists were British subjects, and they should be held accountable to the king for their actions. But only the king held dominion over them ultimately. Any other laws regulating colonial activities should emanate from the colonists' own elected assemblies, not from those (members of Parliament) whom Franklin called the king's subjects.

Franklin's article published in the *Gentleman's Magazine*, January 1768, articulated this position most clearly. "The British state or empire consists of several islands and other distant countries, asunder in different parts of the globe, *but all united in allegiance to one Prince, and to the common law* (Scotland excepted) as it existed in the old provinces or mother country, before the colonies or new provinces, were formed," he said. He argued that although they had "separate assemblies, the allegiance of the distant provinces to the crown will remain for ever unshaken, while they enjoy the rights of Englishmen." The most important of these rights was, "with the consent of their sovereign, the right of legislation each for themselves," because self-rule "puts them on an exact level, in this respect, with their fellow subjects in the old provinces . . . . But if the old provinces should often exercize the right of making laws for the new," Franklin warned, the colonists "would probably grow as restless as the Corsicans, when they perceived they were no longer fellow subjects, but the subjects of subjects."[58]

Franklin's characterization of the British Empire is worth examining closely. His imperial project was essentially a global overseas empire with separate legislative assemblies (like separate parliaments). All entities would ally with the king and operate under the same rules of common law with Britain, but each would create its own laws for its internal operations. Franklin featured the ancient rights of English people in the formulation, even as he emphasized the equality of each citizen before the sovereign (the Crown). Finally, note the warning Franklin offered: if such an imperial situation does not emerge, then rebellion would be likely. The formulation allows for a potential schism, if Britons in England do not soon grasp that the colonists have the right to make their own laws and determine their own internal operations and, in effect, develop their own trade and labor laws and practices. Colonists were not "subjects of subjects" (that is, not subject to England's Parliament); colonists were subjects of the king of England.

Such were the arguments that Franklin boldly offered British readers in an effort to insist upon the equal rights because of common heritage of the Britons in North America with Britons closer to the seat of power in London. His remarks in this *Gentleman's Magazine* provided an explicit statement of an argument he had been making for years: that the colonies ought to be considered subject only to the Crown and the legislatures that the Crown had, in effect, chartered (i.e., the colonial legislatures). The colonies were not possessions but equal partners in the commonwealth; the colonists' rights were equal to—indeed, the same as—the rights of all Britons, according to the ancient rights guaranteed by the Magna Carta. Franklin's arguments here, much like the letters to William Shirley, indicate that despite his polite appeals to reason, he was, in effect, writing explicitly about the alternative of an independent America.

In Franklin's analysis, some of the misunderstanding between Britain and America resulted from the different stages of development of the two land masses. He sought a theoretical solution to the practical problem

of political impasse. He took the theorist's logic a bit further by applying the stadial theory of civilization to the economic issues of commerce
and taxation. Because the land in England had been settled for centuries,
he argued, English trade and taxation were based upon the manufacturing and commercial stages of production. In British North America, he
argued—notwithstanding the supposedly minor problem of the indigenous peoples—land was plentiful. As he had urged in the Canada pamphlet, in America, agriculture, not manufacture, formed the basis of the
economy. As the two were unequal in commodity and production (i.e.,
agriculture preceding manufacture), the two should not be obligated to the
same trade policies and thus should not be equally taxed.

Franklin's ideas featured the colonial agricultural situation as opposed
to the manufacturing enterprise in England, and they were based on the
assumption he retained from the late 1720s that agriculture was productive of new wealth. As he wrote in a letter dated February 20, 1768, to
Philadelphia physician Dr. Cadwalader Evans (c. 1716–1773), with whom
he shared many similar political as well as scientific and philanthropic
views, "Agriculture is truly *productive of new wealth*; Manufacturers only
change Forms; and whatever value they give to the Material they work
upon, they in the mean time consume an equal value in Provisions."[59] The
British people and Parliament, he suggested, narrowly wanted all of the
immediate trade advantages, and they wanted American taxes as well,
even though Britons in North America had a different internal economic
model based in agriculture. Franklin's negotiating difficulties become
apparent in the letter to Evans. His role to mediate between the colonists
and people in Britain was complicated by growing unrest in the colonies.
Britain was not acting fast enough, and the colonies had become relatively
self-sufficient. Manufacturers on both side of the Atlantic clamored for
attention. The manufacturing interests in Boston were seeking to defy
manufacturing and trade regulations from Great Britain at the same time
that Franklin was attempting to negotiate differential regulations for the
American colonies. Franklin alluded to his difficulty: "The Boston People
pretending to interfere with the Manufactures of this Country, makes a
great clamour here against America in general. I have endeavoured therefore to palliate matters a little in several public Papers."[60] The publications Franklin referred to included his famous letter on the causes of the
Americans' discontents before 1768, published in the *London Chronicle*,
January 5–7, 1768; his famous comment on the cabinet post (as secretary
of state for the American colonies) designed for Wills Hill (1718–1793),
Lord Hillsborough (who had served as president of the Board of Trade

and Plantations, 1763–63), published in the *Gazetteer and New Daily Advertiser*, January 21; and his comments on the "subjects of subjects," published in the *Gentleman's Magazine* at the end of January. These three publications show very clearly Franklin's legal analysis that, given the natural rights of all Britons, wherever they lived, the American colonists had equal rights, constitutionally created when charters were granted, with the king's subjects in England. Massachusetts Britons were not seeking special dispensation; they were seeking to have their rights upheld in England.

Franklin's mature view of empire was that the colonies ought to be able to engage in legislation and fiscal policy creation to address matters internal to their mutual economic well-being and their defense. Again and again he attempted to explain his thinking to different key members of the Privy Council and Commons. His efforts reached an impasse during the late 1760s. He became weary of the project. In a letter to his son William in March 1768, Franklin poignantly observed, "As to my own sentiments [on matters of taxation and colonial representation], I am weary of suggesting them to so many different inattentive heads, though I must continue to do it while I stay among them." His role as representative required Franklin to seek out some common ground for Britons in Great Britain and those in North America. He devised a plan for internal and external revenue generation, but no one wished to consider his theory of such a regulated empire. In truth, the complications that would ensue from an effort to tax both externally and internally were insurmountable, but Franklin nonetheless kept trying to develop a system that would work. In the letter to William, Franklin remarked about the schemes John Dickinson (1732–1808) had suggested in his "Letters from a Farmer," which had begun appearing in the colonies and then in Britain.[61] Dickinson, a lawyer, had argued in his series of twelve letters published between 1767 and 1768 that Parliament might be able to create laws regulating the trade in North America, but it could not create laws for raising revenue, for this would be unconstitutional. Dickinson urged the colonists to avoid violence, but he conceived that the current situation would lead to future conflict.

In his letter to William, Franklin commented, "The more I have thought and read on the subject the more I find myself confirmed in opinion, that no middle doctrine can be well maintained." He probed the matter of parliamentary power, concluding that "Something might be made of either of the extremes; that Parliament has a power to make *all laws* for us, or that it has a power to make *no laws* for us; and I think the arguments for the latter more numerous and weighty than those for the former." He compared the situation of the colonies with that of Scotland. "Supposing," he wrote, "that doctrine established"—that Parliament was not empowered to make laws for Britons in North America—then "the colonies would then be so many separate states, only subject to the same King, as England and Scotland were before the Union." In that situation, Franklin said, "the question would be, whether a union like that with Scotland would or would not be advantageous to *the whole*." He conceived that he "should have no doubt of the affirmative," that the relationship would be advantageous, "being fully persuaded that it would be best for *the whole*, and that though particular parts might find particular disadvantages in it, they would find greater advantages in the security arising to every part from the increased strength of the whole." He concluded with a sigh, however, that "such union is not likely to take place while the nature of our present relation is so little understood on both sides the water, and sentiments concerning it remain so widely different."[62] In effect, Franklin was proposing a system whereby the colonies would be united for mutual assistance in terms of economic well-being and defense, and their relationship to greater Britain would be something like Scotland's. The colonies would have allegiance to one another internally, with internal legislative and taxing authority, and with each citizen having the rights to the common law as a function of the obeisance due the king as the ultimate ruler. Parliament might rule over matters relating to the whole empire, but not to matters internal to the independent colonies. In many ways, this mature formulation dovetails in its essential features with the arguments Franklin had made in the letters to William Shirley back in the 1750s. His views had not changed so much as they matured and hardened. He had examined legislation, read an immense amount of commentary on imperial matters, and found a solution to the problems created by the current situation in Britain.[63] Franklin the scientist was bringing to bear his ideas about land, labor, and productivity into a system of mutual cooperation and mutual defense.

The "unerring oracles" of Britain: Franklin and the Physiocrats of France

When clear argument failed, Franklin often turned to satire. In June 1768, he published a captivity hoax that drew upon his analyses of the land, natural productions, and peoples of North America even as it illustrated the self-importance and self-absorption of Britons in England. The storyline about trading practices among the Indians hearkened back to Franklin's days at the treaty negotiations with Indians in the 1750s. Indeed, the story draws upon remarks made by the Indians about inequities they experienced at the hands of traders. But the storyline also featured Franklin's interest in agricultural productivity and the potential of using agricultural produce for trade in an interconnected imperial system, an idea Franklin had been discussing with his French friends connected to a growing republic of letters across Europe. His French friends had helped arrange for his introduction to Louis XV in 1767. Franklin used satire to let off steam and make fun of cultural ignorance and pretension. His captivity hoax is thus of a piece with some of his early satirical writing that burlesqued British ignorance of North America and English Britons' smugness. Like his series of newspaper hoaxes—most notably his "Grand Leap of the Whale" supposedly up the falls at Niagara—published the previous year, Franklin's captivity narrative burlesqued British fascination with what British North Americans would recognize as an outlandish fiction.[64] Each of Franklin's newspaper satires offered pointed critiques of British readers amid reasonably reliable material about North America. The smugness of British cultural pretension and Britons' assumptions about having better knowledge of North America are the focus of most of Franklin's satires from this time.

Likely written around the middle of the 1760s, Franklin's literary hoax "Extract from an Account of the Captivity of William Henry in 1755, and of his Residence among the Senneka Indians six Years and seven Months till he made his Escape from them. Printed at Boston, 1766. 4to, Pages 160" was printed by his friend Strahan in the *London Chronicle*, June 23–25 and 25–28, 1768.[65] Franklin's narrative parodied captivity narratives popular at the time by including purported Indian stories and speeches, thereby mocking ignorant British readers who sought exoticized, purportedly "authentic" stories about Indians. His "Captivity of William Henry" in effect offered a pointed commentary upon British ethnocentric bias, obstinacy, arrogance, selfishness, and pride, in dealings with the supposedly "subject" Indians and American colonists. Whereas in the usual captivity narrative the speaker gains personal insight, the speaker in this narrative proudly remains blindly ignorant. This was Franklin's point about the British.

William Henry, the speaker of the narrative, was writing about supposed abuses he suffered from British "Handlers" (traders), who were charging him too high a price for the Bible he wished to procure so that he could proselytize among the Indians. William Henry complained about how difficult it was (in both time lost and expense) for Alaguippy, a fictional Seneca, to get him a Bible. Henry was essentially subject to the Indians who were themselves subject to the Albany Indian traders, or handlers: "This [the problem in getting the Bible] and other Impositions I suffer'd from the Handlers while I liv'd as an Indian among the Indians, serv'd to make me see in a stronger Light the Enormity of my own Conduct." Presumably, William Henry was about to explain his remorse over the enormity of his own conduct, in trade, with the Indians.[66] What he reveals, however, is his own bias. The situation described in the procuring of the Bible—a situation of trade abuse common among New York traders—is something like the trade and tax abuses that, in Franklin's view, subjected the colonies to the whims of English ministers.

William Henry used his narrative to relate several Indian tales. The last Indian tale, ostensibly about the arrival of evil in the land, spoke to the trade impasse between the Albany handler and the Indians, but really between Britain and the colonies. The story Henry reported in his narrative was purportedly told to him by Canassatego. At the time of creation, Canassatego related, the good Manitta said, "Ye are Five Nations, for ye sprang each from a different handful of the seed I sowed; but ye are all brethren, and I am your father, for I made ye all."[67] According to the story, Manitta outlined the fact that each tribe received a different agricultural commodity and then announced, "As I have loved and taken care of you all, so do you love and take care of one another. Communicate freely to each other the good things I have given you, and learn to imitate each others virtues." The nations lived well and communicated "freely to each other as their wants required" until the "evil Manitta came among them, and put evil thoughts into their hearts." Following this, Franklin offered a parable about commerce: the "Mohocks" decided they would not trade their corn except for "a *good deal* of fruits, beans, roots, squashes, and tobacco, for a *very little* corn," so they could "live in idleness and plenty, while [the others] labour[ed] and live[d] hardly." When, like the "Mohocks," the other nations sought trade advantages for themselves at the expense of their fellows, "discord, animosity, and hatred" ensued. As a result, the good Manitta punished them all:

> Wretches, said he, did I not freely give to each of you different kinds
> of good things, and those in plenty, that each might have something
> in his power to contribute to his brother's happiness, and so increase
> the happiness and strengthen the union of the whole; and do you
> now abuse those gifts and oppress each other; and would one brother,
> to make himself *in imagination* more happy, make four brethren *in
> reality* more miserable!

The good Manitta took away the sun and rain for nine years. The distress made the five nations begin to help one another. Because they were helping one another, other nations took notice and began to seek an affiliation with them: "The nations among whom they were scattered now began to esteem them, and offered to incorporate them among themselves: But they said, No we are still a people, we chuse to continue a people; perhaps our great Manitta will restore us to our country, and we will then remember this your offered kindness." Franklin reported that the great Manitta returned them to their former agricultural glory, from whence arose the "inviolable rule and custom among the nations, that *every Brother is welcome to what a Brother can spare of the good things which the great spirit has caused to spring for him out of the earth.*" Another version of the "do unto others" lesson, this lesson arose from an agricultural lifestyle, free trade, and mutual assistance. A parable about the potential for the British Empire in North America, the hoax offers the positions Franklin had been arguing, in private and public, across the many years of his negotiations in London. By creating a parable on the English and American trade imbalance Franklin could reflect on undeserving ("lazy") Britain's acquisitiveness at the expense of American activity. By hinting about the "other nations" taking notice of the friendly trade alliances, Franklin hinted about the French as potential allies with the colonies. This provides us a tangible sign of Franklin's willingness to consider other options for British North Americans, should Britain continue oppressing the colonists with taxes while denying them free trade and representation.

After telling this tale, Franklin had Canassatego draw out the analogy for William Henry, in a different way, by saying that the English and French traders "had long practiced the same wickedness towards them [the Indians], making every thing dear that they exchanged with them," and even when trading among themselves the English and French used such practices and were left to "lift the hatchet, brother against brother." The point made about trade—that cooperative trade practices would bring the greatest mutual benefit—is quickly rejected by William Henry. Henry responded with a verbalized sniff. He said that the tale was dubious, because it had been "trusted to memory only" and passed "from woman to woman, through . . . many generations." Henry snubbed Canassatego as if he were stupid to think Indians could have anything of substance to offer. The snubbing illustrates that William Henry (the Englishman) learned nothing from his captivity, either from his own experience as one subjected to British trading practices or from the Indian tales themselves. Indeed, in the narrative's conclusion, William Henry arrogantly asserted that Canassatego's stories are foolish Oneida tales and that he is not like other captives "who have before me been among these Indians" and "reported highly of their stories, as if there were something super-excellent in them." Instead, Henry reported, "these poor creatures labour under" a "miserable darkness," with their "best instructions" being "far inferior" to "the unerring oracles that we [the English] possess."[68] This formulaic denigrating response is typical in captivity narratives of a religious nature; its repetition here, however, underscores the hypocritical ignorance of the speaker who has, ethnocentrically, been unable to hear a tale about mutual assistance.

Franklin's point was not lost on his Physiocratic friends, to whom he sent his article. Although the hoax had been published anonymously in London, Franklin's French friends guessed he was the author. Franklin's reputation in France is worth considering in light of this hoax captivity narrative and his growing reputation outside Britain. Franklin sent the essay, along with several of his other articles, to his French friend Jacques Barbeu-Dubourg (1709–1779), a polymath whose many interests (science, medicine, botany, mathematics, electricity, history, economics, political theory, rhetoric) neatly aligned with Franklin's.[69] The friendship solidified during the 1760s, as Franklin worked in London and began publicizing his political, social, and economic writings. Their surviving correspondence indicates that Franklin and Barbeu-Dubourg had a long-standing friendship that probably dated to the original publications of Franklin's electrical experiments. Barbeu-Dubourg was mentioned to Franklin in one of the first letters he had received from the French admirers of his electrical experiments. When Thomas-François Dalibard (1709–1799), a French naturalist, published in 1752 a literal translation of Franklin's electrical experiments with "the Approbation & Privilège du Roy," Franklin's reputation was established among French intellectuals. Indeed, Franklin was so popular among the intelligentsia that Dalibard brought out a second, enlarged French edition of Franklin's experiments in 1756. In 1773, Barbeu-Dubourg would bring out an even more complete edition of Franklin's writings, also with the "Approbation & Permission du Roi," titled simply *Œuvres de M. Franklin*. Dalibard and Barbeu-Dubourg were among a cluster of theorists who called themselves Physiocrats. The group included, among others, notable natural philosophers and economists such as François Quesnay (1694–1774), Anne-Robert-Jacques Turgot (1727–1781), Pierre Samuel du Pont de Nemours (1739–1817), and Victor de Riquetti (1715–1789), marquis de Mirabeau. They believed that economic systems should be tied to agricultural production, a line of argument that Franklin had been fond of making through much of his life. Like Franklin, they believed that labor on the land ought to be the sole determinant of a country's national wealth, and they sought to convince others of this position through a series of contacts with correspondents extending across Europe and, originally through Franklin, across the Atlantic.

Franklin's ideas dovetail so well with the Physiocrats that it is difficult to discern whether they were reading his writings before he read theirs, or whether simply the co-emergence of such ideas was bound to happen, given the situation of agricultural productivity in North America and the preoccupation with limited land masses in Europe. The group wrote and published their own journal, *Ephémérides du citoyen, ou bibliothèque raisonnée des sciences morales et politiques* (1765–72), which featured their ideas and offered extracts of articles from other periodicals on topics related to areas of their common interest. Beginning in 1766, they published several of Franklin's articles, including (probably with Barbeu-Dubourg's translations) "On the Price of Corn, and Management of the Poor," Franklin's published statement about his examination before the House of Commons, and his "Positions to be Examined," about issues in free trade, all originally published in the *London Chronicle*, and several other works of later dates.[70] In early 1769, his friends published Franklin's captivity hoax in the *Ephémérides du citoyen* as "Mithologie et Morale Iroquoises."[71] While the title featured the "mythology" of Indian peoples, the group nonetheless must have been agreeably impressed by Franklin's deft and devastating satirical handling of British trade policies, even as they would have enjoyed his analysis of land economies, which makes agricultural products the basis of wealth, of a balance of trade, and of "common" benefit to all.

Defending the "Imperium in Imperio"

In essay after essay for the London press, Franklin wrote about the wrongheadedness of Parliament to assume it could tax the colonists, about the unfounded fears of the mercantile sector that worried that the colonies would take jobs from and sap the population of Great Britain, and about the equal rights of all Britons, wherever geographically located, to the classic liberties of speech, conscience, labor, and equality before the law. Yet Franklin was tilting at windmills, imagining a community of equals, despite what he knew—that British interests would always trump concern about Britons in North America.

He was frustrated by the internal political gaming taking place as each new administration jockeyed itself into power. Privately, he had written of his frustration about the behind-the-scenes dealmaking to William, "This whole venal nation is now at market, will be sold for about Two Millions; and might be bought out of the hands of the present bidders (if he would offer half a million more) by the very devil himself."[72] He finally spoke publicly about the internal politicking in Britain in a plaintive letter to the *Gazetteer*, September 18, 1768. Writing as "Expositor," Franklin defended Britons in North America by acerbically attacking the ignorance of English Britons, especially their lack of interest in learning about and attending to the issues that Americans were complaining about. He mocked the complacence of Britons in England and their willingness to be led by self-interested politicians: "Whoever . . . will give themselves the trouble to look at these acts, which the Americans refuse to comply with, will at once see the whole is a piece of ministerial policy," he wrote, a policy "designed not for the good of Great Britain or her colonies, but for an American establishment, whereby they may be able to provide for friends and favourites." Franklin's goal was twofold: to inform the general population about things they knew little about, and to goad the ministers by exposing the level of the private negotiations that interfered with a transparent and equitable British imperial strategy. The remark about the "American establishment" spoke to his concern about the number of men associated with the West Indian sugar lobby who held sway in administration. To the end of exposing the proverbial foxes guarding the hencoop, Franklin concluded the piece with a comparative analysis about the situation of North America as opposed to that in Ireland: "The Irish establishment has been much talked of as a sinecure for friends and favourites, and cast-off mistresses," Franklin scoffed, "but this American establishment promises a more ample provision for such-like purposes." He concluded, "That this is the truth of the case, every one that will give himself the trouble must see, unless troubled with the present very polite disorder of being short-sighted.[73] Franklin had always been interested in Ireland's political status, as we know. He considered Ireland a negative example of what could happen in America. He thus used Ireland here to criticize how individuals were gaining financial and personal goods (money and mistresses, in this mocking instance) from their "sinecures" in Ireland. Franklin was already aware of the political situation in Ireland. He would keep his eye on it until he witnessed firsthand the debased conditions of Irish laborers, an experience that confirmed his belief that separating from Britain might be the best way to gain legislative and economic freedom.

By October, Franklin made another effort to couch his analyses of the problems in a narrative conveying historical and ideological significance, a storyline related to the commonwealth tradition he so admired. He again offered his theory of an imperial system, this time explicitly speaking to cultural memory of the English civil wars. In an essay in the *London Chronicle*, October 20, 1768, he worked hard to attach his political system to history, and in a deft move, he called up into common memory the civil wars that had encompassed England, Wales, Ireland, and Scotland in the seventeenth century. He was addressing various remarks made in the press against Britons in North America. Some complained that the Americans' "claims are founded on an impossibility, an *imperium in imperio*," Franklin acknowledged. He again employed the precedent offered by the political situation of Scotland and directed attention to the history of the British civil wars. His comparative analysis indicated that the Americans—but really Franklin—conceived that "a King may be constitutionally King of two different states, as was formerly the case" in England, "when the Parliaments of England and Scotland were absolutely independent of each other." He argued that "the Americans do not claim all the immunities which Scotland formerly enjoyed, yet they may constitutionally enjoy a legislation, as to their internal government, consistently with sound policy." Here followed his argument based in his view of constitutional law: "to shew that [the Americans] have enjoyed such legislation," he said,

> they set forth, that when the colonies were first established, our Kings believed, they had a right to send forth some of their people into another world, if I may so say; and as an encouragement, gave them an internal legislative power, which no Parliament at that time found fault with, and which they have enjoyed ever since, except during the abolition of government in Britain, when even Scotland, an independent kingdom, was brought under subjection by Cromwell, to the English Parliament. So much was King Charles II of this opinion, that, at the restoration he revived the American forms of their governments: yea, if my memory fails not, rebuked the English House of Commons for intermeddling in matters relating to the constitution of the colonies, as being what they had no concern in.[74]

Based on his understanding of legal and constitutional precedent, Franklin had concluded that Americans were subject to the king, not to members of Parliament. If Britons in England would merely grant parity to their compatriots in North America, Franklin insisted, legislation could pave the way for a true commonwealth, one that protected the liberties of all Britons while keeping them secure, wherever they were globally situated. Despite his accumulated evidence—raised in statistics he offered again and again to numerous people and in his letters to the press—Franklin was unable to convince many people of the viability of his system.

Franklin was committed to the viability and potential durability of an extended British Empire, and so, as we have seen, he developed several possible strategies for assisting free Britons in North America and elsewhere while attempting to preserve the British Empire for England. What Franklin insufficiently accounted for, and what finally led, in my view, to Franklin's ultimate despair about Whitehall's unwillingness to attend to the petitions of British colonials in North America, were the different assimilationist policies exercised between England and its other colonized areas, Scotland, Ireland, and India. Whitehall's model of colonization, ideally based on its Plan of Union for Scotland, was neither Franklin's nor that of several of the Irish leaders Franklin admired. Likewise, Franklin was experiencing growing concern over what he was reading in the newspapers about events in India and the ministry's support of the flailing East India Company. Franklin the rational economist, laissez-faire theorist (well before Adam Smith's publicity of that term), and natural philosopher hoped peacefully to persuade Whitehall to consider establishing a constitutional empire with British North America. Without having legislative change, however, he understood the impossibility of reaching his goal. And he had, in fact, already concluded that the British North American colonies would be better off if free from the political constraints laid on them by Britain.

Seven

LOVE OF COUNTRY

Franklin's belief that the American colonies would do better without being part of the British Empire was confirmed during the late 1760s and deepened until he left England in 1775, the years under discussion in this chapter. Franklin's writings and activities during these years reveal three central preoccupations. First, Franklin's views about agriculture's being the real source of a nation's wealth deepened into a principled view of agrarian economic theory. Second, Franklin's belief that constitutional reform was essential to secure Americans' rights hardened into a policy of seeking for Pennsylvania a royal government and pressuring for a constitutional monarchy for all the American colonies. Third, Franklin's ideas about governance reached a new recognition about the dangers of imperial intervention in matters of defense and the marketplace. Franklin came to believe and then articulate more fully a view that the freedom of trade among colonies and from colonies to all other ports was essential to the American colonies' economic stability and political right. These matters form several of this chapter's central concerns.

In examining these concerns, we will be able to consider more fully Franklin's shift away from the British Empire. As we have seen, Franklin's thinking began to shift in the 1750s, with the letters to Massachusetts governor William Shirley that Franklin wrote, circulated, and published. As this chapter clarifies, his ideas about the potential self-sufficiency of the colonies developed into clear political theory in the 1760s, a theory embracing constitutional monarchy. Franklin's turn against the empire reached clear articulation in 1771, after Franklin toured Ireland and Scotland. Further, in groping toward a legal opinion regarding British Americans' original sovereignty over their colonies—thus denying the British nation's jurisdiction over American lands—Franklin conceived that lands in North America acquired peacefully from the Native peoples there belonged to the new possessors alone.

Franklin's views on American sovereignty derived from his consideration of the East India Company's invasion, supported by the British government, into India. Such invasions, unparalleled in North American experience, confirmed Franklin's disgust with Britain. He may have liked his royal office as postmaster general, but he had no affection for British colonialism. Franklin was not a pro-empire man until the middle 1770s, as many historians have argued. In fact, Franklin was a pro-American man in the 1750s and 1760s. His reservations about the British Empire had been expressed decades earlier in Pennsylvania. By 1775, Franklin knew it was time to break off any effort to keep ties with Britain and to sail homeward, for love of country and his countrypeople, the British North Americans.

"Agriculture the only honest Way" to Create Wealth

Franklin had always been interested in the relationship between agriculture, trade, and the development of a nation's economy, as we have seen. While he considered manufacturing and trade valuable for nations seeking wealth, Franklin began to assert with greater frequency in the 1760s a view supporting agriculture as the foundation of a nation's wealth. The problem with manufacturing and trade was that markets could be manipulated by unscrupulous individuals and parliaments. Finding a fair market for goods when navigation laws could be passed without input and representation from those creating the produce proved unacceptable to the colonies. Working with his French Physiocratic friends and friends in England, Scotland, and Ireland interested in agriculture, Franklin developed a rhetoric of agricultural nationalism that featured agriculture and agricultural laborers as the true center of a nation's wealth. His thinking dovetailed with the Physiocrats, who had long admired his writings on land and agricultural economies and coalesced as well with many friends among the new agricultural societies cropping up in England and Scotland.

Although he was now saying that agriculture was the chief element in a nation's wealth, Franklin still valued manufacturing but gave it secondary importance. This position about agriculture was slightly different from the labor theory of value, which had assumed that marketable productions from the land were what mattered. Instead, Franklin now focused on the individual farmer who owned his own property and farmed his land and thus created the nation's wealth while remaining free of the potential corruption of markets. This position, later articulated by his friend Lord Kames, was a form of agricultural patriotism. Franklin had grown distrustful of markets that were trammeled by the engineering of governments uninterested in letting the markets determine the value of goods. In an economy employing middlemen, as the British system did, price-fixing (e.g., import and export duties, which artificially raise or reduce prices) designed to supply wealth to England would always interfere with free trade. During the years under current discussion, Franklin argued this position in several letters to the press, in conferences with those in the ministry, in the marginalia of pamphlets he was reading, and in private letters to British, French, and North American friends that circulated among an extended network of readers.[1]

An especially interesting example of Franklin's evolution in thinking about agriculture appeared in his "Positions to be Examined," which originally had served as Franklin's notes for discussions with those in the ministry about agriculture, trade, and a country's wealth. Franklin decided to converse with his friend Henry Home, Lord Kames, about his thoughts. In January 1769, he sent Kames the statement of his "Positions": "To commence a Conversation with you on your new Subject," he wrote on January 1, "I have thrown some of my present Sentiments into the concise Form of Aphorisms, to be examin'd between us, if you please, and rejected or corrected and confirm'd as we shall find them most proper."[2] Kames returned some remarks on the use of oxen in farming. Franklin wrote again on February 21, after Kames had been elected president of the Edinburgh Agricultural Society. He developed for Kames a comparative analysis of the use of oxen versus horses to till soil, pointing out that horses take more space and fodder for upkeep. He then remarked on the centrality of agriculture to a nation's fiscal well-being: "Food is *always* necessary to *all*, and much the greatest Part of the Labour of Mankind is employ'd in raising Provisions for the Mouth. Is not this kind of Labour therefore the fittest to be the Standard by which to measure the Values of all other Labour?" Franklin asked Kames.[3] Their correspondence helped both Franklin and Kames solidify their attitudes about agriculture as the foundation of a nation's economy and morals. Franklin ended up publishing his "Positions" in a compendium of British and European agricultural and manufacturing writings. Signed "B.F." when published April 4, 1769, Franklin's "Positions" appeared originally in *De re Rustica; or, The Repository for Select Papers on Agriculture, Arts, and Manufactures* (London, 1769). Sandwiched between an article on laburnum wood in Scotland and the Alps and a letter and related article from the Physiocrats' *Ephémérides du Citoyen* on corn and the food supplies to poor people, Franklin's "Positions" articulated a view linking husbandry with moral purity and commerce with cheating. The article was circulated in Britain and France via Strahan's *London Chronicle*, July 1, 1769, and the *Ephémérides du Citoyen* 10 (October 1769), 6–16, in French translation.[4] Benjamin Vaughan (1751–1835) would later publish it among Franklin's works in his 1779 edition.

The argument of Franklin's "Positions" showed Franklin's movement away from predominantly market arguments based solely in trading wealth toward arguments based in the agrarian patriotism that was becoming common in England and Scotland. Franklin opened with two premises, that "All Food or Subsistence for Mankind arise from the Earth or Waters" and that the "Necessaries of Life that are not Foods, and all other Conveniencies, have their Values estimated by the Proportion of Food consumed while we are employed in procuring them." Saying that manufactured goods are merely "Subsistence metamorphosed," Franklin concluded next that "*Manufactures* are only *another Shape* into which so much Provisions and Subsistence are turned as were *equal in Value* to the Manufactures produced." Thus, any labor that goes into creating productions from the land is paid for by the produce of the land itself, and such productions are merely subsistence that has been changed into goods. In a fair trading circumstance, equally valued goods will be traded with one another, taking into account the cost of the transportation of the goods for exchange. As Franklin phrased it, "*Fair* Commerce is where equal Values are exchanged for equal the Expence of Transport included." In an equitable situation, "Where the Labour and Expence of producing both Commodities are known to both Parties[,] Bargains will generally be fair and equal," Franklin argued. "Where they are known to one Party only," however, "Bargains will often be unequal, Knowledge taking its Advantage of Ignorance."

The argument emphasized the practice of local and free trade carried on without the interference in the marketplace either of middlemen or the long arm of the government, with its taxing hand in producers' pockets. Franklin then went on to dispute his own point about the labor theory

of value argued decades earlier. Formerly, he might have said that manufacturing added value to the goods produced, thus creating the nation's
wealth; now, he insisted that the only benefit attained from manufacturing
was its transforming subsistence or raw new products into more trans-
portable goods for foreign markets. Franklin made an acerbic comment
on the current trading assumptions of British mercantile and manufacturing sectors by arguing against his own labor theory of value. He said that
"the Advantage of having Manufactures in a Country, does not consist
as is commonly supposed, in their highly advancing the Value of rough
Materials, of which they are formed"—a central point behind his former
labor theory of value, that labor enhanced the value of a raw production like
flax. In fact, "Sixpenny worth of Flax may be worth twenty shillings when
worked into Lace," but the higher value resulted from the fact that "it has
cost nineteen shillings and sixpence in Subsistence to the Manufacturer"
of that lace. The greater cost was passed on to foreign markets, he said,
making the "Advantage of Manufactures" simply this: "under their [manu-
factured] shape Provisions may be more easily carried to a foreign Market;
and by their means our Traders may more easily cheat Strangers." The
argument reflects Franklin's bitterness over the manufacturing and trade
lobby in Parliament in the middle eighteenth century. He concluded that
British North Americans would be better off without having to operate
under trading legislation established in Britain. Franklin concluded his
"Positions" with similar acerbity. "Finally," he wrote, there are "but three
Ways for a Nation to acquire Wealth"—"by *War* as the Romans did in
plundering their conquered Neighbours. This is *Robbery*"; "by *Commerce*
which is generally *Cheating*"; and "by *Agriculture* the only *honest Way*
wherein Man receives a real Increase of the Seed thrown into the Ground,
in a kind of continual Miracle wrought by the Hand of God in his Favour,
as a Reward for his innocent Life, and virtuous Industry."[5]

Franklin's insistence on the importance of agriculture here matched his
interest in agricultural experimentation and production. Given his understanding of the comparative environmental circumstances of the colonies
and Great Britain, it is not surprising to find that Franklin was beginning to argue that, contrary to England's situation, North America was
more conducive to a growing, economically viable, productive agricultural enterprise. In England, where the supply of raw materials along with
the control of production and marketing was, in historian Joanna Innes's
words, "concentrated in the hands of a few large manufacturers, effectively
employing large sectors of the work force,"[6] the general population came
to consider itself as a consumer society.[7] Agriculture in England accounted

for only about 30 percent of national income. Wealth lay instead in private hands or in the trading wealth and industrial capital of middling-level people.[8]

Franklin harbored great hope in the independent farmers of North America, arguing that they wished to remain free laborers on their own lands without having extensive tax structures foisted on their property (i.e., their property in land and labor). Franklin's writings indicate his increasing annoyance about Britons' lack of knowledge about American life. "How little this Politician knows of Agriculture!" he gasped in the margins when he was reading an anonymously published pamphlet, *The True Constitutional Means for Putting an End to the Disputes between Great-Britain and the American Colonies* (London, 1769). "Is there any Country where 10 Bushels of Grain are generally got in for one sown? . . . No Farmer of America, in fact, makes 5 percent of his Money. His Profit is only being paid for his own Labour and that of his Children."[9] For all of England's attention to agricultural improvement, few involved in decision-making for the colonies showed any concern about learning about North America and its peoples.

Franklin continued to think and talk about agricultural innovations and the importance of the land in the 1770s. In the year 1770, with James Burgh (1714–1775) and some other friends from the Club of Honest Whigs, Franklin and his friends launched a series of Whiggish essays for the British newspapers, imitating the tone of British statesmen, taking up the constitutional question of taxation without representation, and hearkening back to the rhetoric of the English civil wars.[10] In eleven "Colonist's Advocate" essays published between January and March, the authors combined agriculture-centered arguments about the North American economy with political arguments about the injustice of taxation without representation. Their arguments were similar to those Franklin had employed back in the 1750s. In this instance, the effort was to win the repeal of all the parliamentary measures pernicious to the colonists.

In the essay series, Franklin and his friends used the argument that North American lands were best for those who were independent farmers. They pointed out that the colonies actually formed the basis of Britain's wealth during the seventeenth and early eighteenth centuries. In "The Colonist's Advocate," No. 4, printed in the *Public Advertiser*, January 15, they asserted that the "Colonists have made our Merchants Princes, while themselves are, for the most Part, Farmers and Planters." Because of their productive labor, the colonists "have employed our Hands, increased our People, consumed our Manufactures, improved our Navy, maintained our Poor, and doubled, or trebled our Riches."[11] For the Advocate's essay published February 1, they used Franklin's statements made during his examination before the House of Lords: "The Colonists are almost all Farmers, depending on the Produce of their Lands, contented till lately, and happy, but in no Condition to pay us Taxes, otherwise than by their enabling us to pay our Taxes out of the great Advantage we gain by them."[12] Franklin and his friends employed a view that land, agricultural production, and taxation—especially the constitutional question about the right of Parliament to levy taxes on the colonies—needed to be considered in tandem with national policies beneficial to both producers of raw and finished goods and their consumers, wherever they lived.

Constitutional Questions: Crown, Parliament, and Colonies

The "Colonist's Advocate" essays spoke about many matters beyond the importance of agriculture. Franklin and his friends used the essays to discuss key constitutional questions under discussion in Parliament, the Privy Council, the American colonies, and Ireland. It will be fruitful to consider Franklin's ideas on these issues in light of arguments being made regarding Ireland and its colonial relationship to England. To Franklin, the constitutional question regarding the American colonies had been clear for a long time: only if Parliament allowed the colonies to have representation *in* Parliament should the right of Parliament extend to colonial legislation. And if representation did occur, all existing laws regarding the colonies would need to be rescinded and new laws created by the newly elected Parliament. If he failed in his efforts to adjust parliamentary control, Franklin believed a constitutional monarchy the best method to achieve equity for the king's subjects in North America.

Franklin created his ideas of justice and the rights of Britons in North America from his reading, his understanding of the English civil wars, and his inquiry about Ireland's status as, in effect, a colony of England. His view of early modern liberalism was an amalgamation of beliefs adapted from several writers prominent from the time of the English civil wars, including Locke, Hampden, Sidney, and Milton. Using these writers, the "Colonist's Advocate" essays argued for basic freedoms for the colonists as subjects of the king equal in status with subjects in England, including members of Parliament. In Franklin's view, the colonists' constitutional rights inhered in their basic freedoms as British subjects, rights that they had carried over with them when they left England and settled in British colonies. British subjects' rights were clarified by the constitution deriving from the era of the civil wars, a constitution founded on ancient British liberties. "This Constitution," argued the Colonists' Advocate, "is founded on the prime Maxim of all free Government, viz. That no Subject is to be deprived of any Part of his Property, but by his own Consent, given either personally, or by his Representative."[13]

Franklin and his friends were specifically addressing problems resulting from the initial imposition of the Townshend duties in 1767 and the resultant unrest in Boston. The Townshend Acts, passed by the British Parliament, had provided for import duties on items in daily use, including tea, glass, lead, paint, and paper, and they established a Board of Customs Commissioners for America, stationed in Boston. In early 1768, because the people in Boston protested the duties and were becoming more radical in their resistance, the customs commissioners asked for army assistance to fortify Boston against the protests and to protect the commissioners as they attempted to carry out their duties. When troops arrived late that year, the people of Boston were outraged. Clashes started to occur as businesses were boycotted or vandalized. The situation worsened during 1769 as the people of Boston hardened in their rebellion against the army in their midst. In the "Advocate" essay printed February 1, 1770, with unusual prescience in advance of the "Boston Massacre" of March 5, Franklin wrote in irony: "We have been taught by our Forefathers to look upon the British Government as free. What our Sons may call it is not yet certain." Although the anecdotes related to other events, Franklin used those events to comment on contemporary circumstances: "Free Government depends on Opinion, not on the brutal Force of a Standing Army," he said, concluding that members of Parliament, who were (like all other subjects) fallible, did not act properly regarding the colonies. Taking the tone of an elder British statesman, Franklin wrote: "our Laws for regulating our Colonies, and their Commerce, have not always been framed according to the purest Principles of Wisdom, Justice, and Humanity. These Errors ought to convince us, that our Parliaments (what are P——s but Assemblies of fallible Men?) are but incompetent Judges of the State and Abilities of our remote Fellow-Subjects."[14] In these essays and with the help of Burgh and his other Club of Honest Whig friends, Franklin consistently set forth a brief regarding the freedom of all subjects, wherever they lived, opposing constraints placed on one group of subjects by others among the Crown's subjects.

Franklin became entrenched in the 1760s in his decision to seek royal government for Pennsylvania. He wanted the Pennsylvania colony to be a Crown colony rather than a Proprietary one. The decision to appeal for royal government grew from the frustration Pennsylvanians felt over the unwillingness of the Proprietors to have their estates taxed. Franklin had done a significant amount of reading on the rights of subjects and obligations of the Crown, constitutional monarchy, and colonial Ireland. Franklin's frustration with parliamentary legislation and Parliament's insistence that it should be the ultimate legislative power over colonial America grew steadily as he faced continued wrangling in England over the laws enacted by Parliament, whose members knew very little—and seemed to care even less—about life in the colonies. Franklin dug in his heels.

Historians have long characterized Franklin as an "Empire man," a "loyal Englishman," an "unabashed" and "committed" royalist until his denunciation by Alexander Wedderburn (1733–1805) in the Cockpit, linking his turn of heart away from Britain to that moment in 1774 when he lost his postmaster generalship and was humiliated before his British friends and enemies in administration.[15] The support for such arguments arises in Franklin's attempts to secure for Pennsylvania a royal government, his interest in acquiring western lands in the Ohio territory and, later and for William Franklin, the Illinois territory, and his willingness to consider the possibility of his joining administration in England, whether in Parliament or in colonial administration.[16] There is some basis for this position, but as I have been arguing, if we focus more fully on Franklin's early modern liberalism and more specifically on his views of the potential for a constitutional monarchy articulated as early as the 1750s in his letters to William Shirley and in his public and private writings on the rights of British subjects on both sides of the Atlantic, we reach a different conclusion: Franklin was seeking a systemic solution to problems in legislation for the colonies. His solution was a constitutional monarchy whereby the independent colonies combined together as states, with legislatures of their own, underneath the Crown as titular head but with legislation arising from assemblies—independent parliaments—created by popular election. He was attempting to find a legal means by which to end the impasse with the British Parliament. He worked tirelessly to bring his plan to the attention of people in government offices and the general population.

Franklin's arguments about the American colonies' relationship to the Crown mirrored those of Irish writer William Molyneux (1656–1698), whose controversial book *The Case of Ireland's being Bound by the Acts of Parliament in England, Stated* (1698) argued that Ireland deserved independent legislative status from the British Parliament. Franklin owned a copy of Molyneux's book and used his historical analysis as early as the 1750s.

We know he was consulting it during the period under discussion, because in April 1770 he sent the newest edition to his Boston associate, Samuel Cooper (1725–1783), a pastor active in the Massachusetts resistance. In sending an edition hot off John Almon's press, an edition with an incendiary preface ("shrewdly written," in his view), Franklin signaled his belief that the American colonies needed to be forewarned about what might be in store for them, if they were unsuccessful in their efforts to challenge the legislative privilege of the British Parliament. Indeed, Franklin conceived that it might be useful to align with Ireland. "Our Part is warmly taken by the Irish in general, there being in many Points a Similarity in our Cases," Franklin wrote to Cooper.[17]

Molyneux's work had helped Franklin think through American issues. Ireland's colonial history and its present state were of immense relevance to Franklin's views about constitutional monarchy, so it is worthwhile to examine Ireland's colonial situation and Molyneux's book. Literary historian Oliver Ferguson once observed that "Though in title a kingdom, eighteenth-century Ireland was in fact virtually an English colony."[18] All important government and ecclesiastical positions were held by English appointees, thus producing a constant drain on Ireland's economy. Ireland had its own Parliament, but under Poynings' Law, an old law passed under Henry VII, only the king's consent made possible the convening of the Irish Parliament, and it could pass no laws without the king's approval. Once in session, the Irish Parliament could create and send "Heads of Bills" to England for approval, but the Privy Council could delete, add to, or reject these bills. After the Revolution of 1689, Parliament was customarily convened every other year, not to create legislation for Ireland but to vote on funding bills to cover the costs of administration.

In commerce, Ireland was constrained by a series of acts passed by the English Parliament after its restoration that crippled the livestock, meat, and wool industries. For instance, the Navigation Act of 1663 prohibited exportation of goods from Ireland to any English colony unless those goods were loaded in English ships at English ports. Members of Parliament in England held that these laws were their right to pass. They conceived that England had every right to advance its interest at the expense of its colonies, so that England maintained a so-called balance of trade favorable to itself.[19] For the Anglo-Irish who had been settled in Ireland for half a century, the Wool Act of 1699 was the last straw. This act prohibited Ireland's exporting woolen goods to any country and permitted the exportation of unworked wool only to a few specific English ports, thus giving England a monopoly in Irish raw wool. The Irish woolen industry was crippled to support English weavers. Economically speaking, however, absentee landholders produced perhaps a worse problem than the oppressive trading legislation. Many landowners were English families who had been given Irish land confiscated during the civil wars or the Revolution of 1689; other landholders were men who had bought estates during the high speculation resulting from these wars. During the first half of the eighteenth century, many descendants from older Anglo-Irish families left their estates for London. In addition to draining off the money to England, then, the system led to high land prices destructive to the peasantry, as landholders hired middlemen who sublet at a profit.[20]

The Parliament in England took advantage of its powerful appointments in Ireland. Socially, Ireland was divided into three major groups: the native interest, the ancestral Gaelic Catholic population; the English interest, sometimes called the New English, who were recent English appointees and Anglo-Irish supporters of English policies, clearly the most powerful group because they controlled the Irish Parliament; and the Irish interest, sometimes called the Old English, largely Anglo-Irish Protestants whose families had been settled in Ireland the previous century. This group acknowledged England's sovereignty over Ireland but refused to submit without protest to the economic and legislative restrictions placed on Ireland by the English Parliament. Franklin was interested in the situation of the Anglo-Irish, the Old English whom he sometimes called the Patriots, who were descended from those who had settled in Ireland decades earlier. The status of Anglo-Irish residents was based in a political theory that Ireland was dependent on the Crown of England, but not on the Parliament. The Anglo-Irish conceived that as descendants of the original English settlers of Ireland, they had equal rights with their fellow subjects in England. Thus, they argued, the English Parliament was interfering in Irish affairs, and it was, in effect, encroaching on both the king's prerogative and the rights of Englishmen in Ireland.

Franklin appreciated Molyneux's book, which traced five hundred years of history in Ireland. Molyneux argued that England did not take Ireland by conquest in the era of Henry II, because the Irish had willingly submitted to Henry. When Henry gave Ireland to John, when John was crowned king, he became the king of England and Ireland. Thus, Ireland was a separate, distinct kingdom, Molyneux argued, one having its own constitution, acts of the English Parliament, and title in the monarch's name. Ireland was not a subject of the British Parliament but of the Crown, Molyneux said, arguing as well that as the first English settlers had been regarded as English subjects, so their descendants had the same rights, as had English people of later migrations. Molyneux was asserting the rights of the subject under a constitutional monarchy. Molyneux's view thus critiqued Parliament's claim of legislative supremacy over Ireland by establishing the point that the rights of Anglo-Irish subjects were being usurped by a Parliament that had no legitimate authority over Ireland.

Molyneux's arguments were attractive to Franklin, who was searching out possible lines of argument to use regarding American affairs. He was tired of the privilege given by Parliament to the arguments of lobbyists for the manufacturing and merchant sector while his own arguments about legal parity between Britons in North America and those in England fell on deaf ears. His writings evidence his exasperation with those in and surrounding Parliament—place-seekers, lobbyists, and men of privilege, he thought, rather than accomplishment—who could presume their rights more important than the rights of the American colonists. Likewise, he was troubled that key cabinet posts were going to people who had come home from India with records of poor management and disastrous military campaigns that endlessly pitted tribal groups against each other. He observed that trade advantages accrued to the East India Company and other trading companies associated with the Asian trades. Those in Parliament whose wealth or family ties lay in India favored policies relevant for India (to protect investments by the British Treasury) more than for North America. American concerns were taking a back seat to East Indian politics. Franklin waited, and he continued to refine his ideas about calling the American colonies a constitutional monarchy.

Franklin never understood, despite his affection for the presumed rights accorded as ancient British liberties, rights for which the civil wars had occurred, that his desire to have royal government would never be acceptable to members of the British Parliament. Franklin's ideas about a constitutional monarchy would have required a divided government, with the Crown having sovereignty over each colonial legislature in addition to sovereignty in England. The editors of Franklin's papers have remarked that both the Lords and Commons "and for that matter the King" would have conceived this method of division unconstitutional.[21] Further, England's civil wars occurred largely because King Charles I assumed he had greater authority than Parliament, an assumption that in effect cost him his life. The British Parliament, anxious to curb royal prerogative, would never submit again to Crown privilege. Even Franklin's friends in Parliament considered preposterous Franklin's idea that the king rather than Parliament should have sovereign rule over the American colonies. As Franklin's editors have acknowledged, "Any sphere of royal influence outside the purview of Parliament was suspect, as appeared soon afterward in the controversies over reforming the government of India."[22] Hindsight enables us to recognize how fruitless Franklin's efforts were. Yet Franklin pressed on, attempting to gain acknowledgment for his mission and to reveal the colonists' views of both allegiance to the Crown and rights to self-rule.

"You are not appointed": Hillsborough's Response to Franklin's Challenge

As the first trial growing out of the Boston Massacre was taking place in October 1770, Franklin was about to be chosen the agent of the Massachusetts House of Representatives. The appointment was made October 24. The appointment by the Massachusetts House made Franklin the elected agent for four colonies, Pennsylvania, Georgia, New Jersey, and Massachusetts. Franklin prepared to present his credentials to Wills Hill (1718–1793), second Viscount Hillsborough (known as Lord Hillsborough in the colonies), secretary of state for the colonies. Franklin's relationship with Hillsborough had begun when Hillsborough became, under George Grenville (1712–1770), president of the Board of Trade and Plantations in 1763. Under William Pitt (1708–1778), first Earl of Chatham, Hillsborough became joint postmaster general in 1766. Hillsborough took up the new position of secretary of state for the colonies in 1768, a post in which he served (along with the Board of Trade position) until 1772. Franklin had initially considered having a new position for a secretary of state for the colonies a good thing for North America. Having a secretary for the colonies would provide him with a specific sounding board for his ideas about handling North American concerns. But Franklin quickly grew to distrust Hillsborough, who followed a platform of refusing all concessions to the colonies.

Having been appointed by the Massachusetts Assembly without the oversight of the Massachusetts governor, Franklin understood that Hillsborough would not be willing to recognize him as a representative, because he had not received the appointment according to the rules established by Crown officers. Hillsborough would not concede that Franklin was the colonies' legitimate representative, because all authority derived from Crown appointments, not from elections carried on by colonial assemblies. Even so, Franklin presented his credentials to Hillsborough as Massachusetts agent, January 16, 1771. Hillsborough had been attempting to regularize colonial operations. Prior to 1765, the policy had been that agents sent to act in their colony's behalf were appointed by both houses in the colonial legislatures *and* the colonial governor. That is, all three groups (commons, house, and governor) were expected to concur on the agent's appointment. After the furor about the Stamp Act, the situation changed, and agents were appointed without this process of multiple concurrences, because of the animosity that colonists showed their governors. Hillsborough intended to use Massachusetts as the test case for restoring the older system. He wanted to force upon Massachusetts particularly a model of the authority of his office.[23]

Franklin wanted to see what happened when he attempted to press Hillsborough to accept his role as the Massachusetts representative. Franklin showed up at Hillsborough's interior public office (the "Levee Room") on the morning of January 16, 1771, with his paper showing his selection as agent. The porter at first sent him away without an audience, but as Franklin's coach was driving away, the porter ran out, interrupted Franklin's departure, and said that Hillsborough would see him. Hillsborough, "whose Countenance chang'd" at Franklin's statement that he wanted to show him his appointment by the Massachusetts House, insisted, "You are not appointed." Hillsborough then proceeded to say he had a letter from the Massachusetts governor, Thomas Hutchinson (1711–1780), indicating he would not give his assent to the bill appointing Franklin. But when Franklin pursued this with him, Hillsborough called in John Pownall (1720–1795), secretary to the Board of Trade and undersecretary of the American Department, who was waiting in an interior chamber for consultation. In front of Franklin, in answer to Hillsborough's question about the supposed letter, Pownall denied there was any such letter in the packet Hillsborough received. It is difficult to determine whether it was Franklin's appearance there as agent or Pownall's public denial of Hillsborough's claim that angered Hillsborough more. Working from his own political agenda, Franklin politely remonstrated, "I cannot conceive . . . why the Consent of the *Governor* should be thought necessary to the Appointment of an Agent for the *People*." Hillsborough grew contemptuous: "I shall not enter into a Dispute with you, Sir, upon this Subject." Hillsborough told Franklin that he should have gone directly to the Board of Trade, not the American secretary's office, with his paper, announcing that he (Hillsborough) would continue to "persevere in the same FIRMNESS" toward Massachusetts that he had been using all along. "No such Appointment shall be entred" in the records, he said. Franklin withdrew.[24]

This singular interview reveals the extent to which constitutional questions and questions of authority over colonial decision-making rankled Hillsborough, from an imperial standpoint, almost as much as they troubled Franklin. It also shows the length to which Franklin was willing to press for an audience on colonial matters. Franklin's appointment would normally have been presented to the secretary of the Board of Trade and recorded in the records of that office.[25] But Franklin wanted an opportunity to bring the issue of representation to a head with the colonial secretary. Hillsborough was known to have a high temper. To Hillsborough's rancor, which Franklin characterized as *"a mix'd look of Anger and Contempt"* at one place and as *"Warmth"* in another, Franklin returned politic politeness combined with a clear sign that he would, regardless of Hillsborough's views on the matter, consider himself the colonies' agent. Franklin's politic conclusion of the interview underscored Hillsborough's rancor, confirmed his message that he would remain agent, and articulated a politeness unexpected under the circumstances: "I beg your Lordship's Pardon for taking up so much of your time," he said, concluding, "It is I believe of no great Importance whether the Appointment is acknowledged or not, for I have not the least Conception that an Agent can *at present* be of any Use, to any of the Colonies."[26] In his effort to revive an older method of creating agents, the one requiring the affirmation of both houses and the governor, Hillsborough alienated the colonies' representative and the colonies at precisely the time when the colonies recognized their potential for intercolonial cooperation on several fronts, including the import-export trade.

At the time of his difficult interview with Hillsborough, Franklin had already worked out a constitutional argument that—given their original relationship with the king in Council (via their charters)—the colonies were, from the moment of their political formation, distinct states. He had written as much to Samuel Cooper in June 1770. Franklin's arguments were similar to Molyneux's. Knowing that Cooper would share the letter with the other activists, Franklin created a statement of carefully reasoned argument:

That the Colonies originally were constituted distinct States, and intended to be continued such, is clear to me from a thorough Consideration of their original Charters, and the whole Conduct of the Crown and Nation towards them until the Restoration. Since that Period, the Parliament here has usurp'd an Authority of making Laws for them, which before it had not. We have for some time submitted to that Usurpation, partly thro' Ignorance and Inattention, and partly from our Weakness and Inability to contend. I hope when our Rights are better understood here, we shall, by a prudent and proper Conduct be able to obtain from the Equity of this Nation a Restoration of them.[27]

Franklin's view had evolved to a position that the separate parliaments of Ireland and the American colonies were, in effect, legally on a par with the Parliament of England. He argued this position based on original charters for the American colonies and on the idealized conception of ancient British liberties. Shortly after his confrontation with Hillsborough, Franklin renewed his correspondence with his Massachusetts correspondents, this time writing to Thomas Cushing (1725–1788), merchant and politician elected to the Massachusetts House. To Cushing on February 5, 1771, Franklin expressed his wish that Britons in England better understood the political relationship between the colonies and their sovereign and between their agent (himself) and those in administration in England. His anger about the treatment received from Hillsborough spilled into this letter: "When they [i.e., the colonies] come to be considered in the light of *distinct states*, as I conceive they really are, possibly their agents may be treated with more respect, and considered more as public ministers."[28] In addition to revealing this stance regarding the colonies' legal status as independent states, Franklin's private letters to friends and his official letters to the Massachusetts House of Representatives illustrate Franklin's view that the colonies might at any moment decide to break with England. He seems almost poised to make a run for a ship, for his own personal safety.

Perhaps this was mere strategy for the private audience in the British ministry who were intercepting his outgoing mail in order to scrutinize what he was saying to colonial representatives. Perhaps for that audience, too, Franklin wrote to his American friends that the colonies have come to the attention of "foreign courts" (the French court) and that each colony, given the growing population in North America, would do well to develop and support its own local economies by developing its own manufactures for internal use, especially in the cloth trade. In a long letter to Cushing, Franklin wrote on June 10, 1771, that "considering our Increase in America," Britain would not "be able much longer to supply us with Cloathing." Franklin had formerly argued that American manufactures would never supersede British manufactures but now suggested that British North Americans ought, in fact, to increase their manufacturing of durable goods. He understood the rich potential for productivity in North America if the colonists would avoid importation from Britain. "Necessity," he wrote, "as well as Prudence, will soon induce us to seek Resources in our own Industry." Pressing for nonimportation, he offered a rationale based in thrift, hard work, and keeping American money in North America. "Family Manufactures will alone amount to a vast Saving in the Year," he said. In addition, "a steady Determination and Custom of buying only of your own Artificers wherever they can supply you, will soon make them more expert in Working, so as to dispatch more Business." Risk of loss would be significantly reduced in this way: "The lowness of Provisions with us, compar'd with their daily rising Price here, added to the Freight, Risque and Commissions on the Manufactures of this Country, must give great Advantage to our Workmen, and enable them in time to retain a great deal of Money in the Country." The policy of nonimportation might work, he concluded, although Massachusetts should still retain enough trade "to render our Friendship of the greatest Importance to this Nation."[29] The argument for nonimportation had been around since the days of the Stamp Act protests. By conveying his positive views relating nonimportation to an improvement in the capacities of workers, Franklin was clearly suggesting to his North American friends as well as to those who were "secretly" reading his mail that, like the colonies he was representing, he was ready to consider an alternative political model for the "distinct states" of British North America.

Franklin's Tour of Ireland and Scotland, 1771

The pressures of his political activities surely caused Franklin to seek some solace for reflection and mental rejuvenation. During the summer of 1771, Franklin decided to tour the countryside and meet with some of his various philosophical friends in England, Ireland, and Scotland. He was developing an acquaintance with a liberal prelate, Jonathan Shipley (1714–1788), and he decided to visit Shipley at Twyford in June (17–24) and again July 30 through August 13, 1771. During the latter visit, he began his memoir. The opening movement in the memoir reveals that he was reflecting upon the departure of his ancestors from England at a time when they were facing serious religious and social problems caused by an overbearing monarch. As his ancestors had faced issues related to their rights, so he was mulling over the best course of action, not just for himself, but for all the people in the American colonies. He was, in effect, reliving the family's history. His interlude in Twyford was one among a number of visits made during the summer and fall of 1771.

Having accumulated information from his friends and his readings about the constitutional situation of Scotland and Ireland, he wanted to learn more about agriculture there, and he made a tour to both places in 1771. He traveled with Richard Jackson (c. 1721–1878) to Ireland and stayed some of the time at Hillsborough's estate. In Scotland, he stayed with David Hume (1711–1776), Lord Kames, and other friends. Franklin's travels were partly for pleasure and partly to witness agricultural practices in Ireland and Scotland. He saw firsthand the treatment of Irish agricultural laborers at the hands of middlemen on English manorial estates, and he saw the systems of agriculture in place in Scotland. When Franklin saw for himself in 1771 the oppression particularly of Irish laborers, the population of his special concern because of his idea of creating American legislative parity with Ireland, he was forced to recognize (and he wrote about) the ingrained assumptions of superiority that kept British people from recognizing their common heritage of rights and obligations to secure liberty, property, and personal freedom for all Britons, wherever they lived.

Franklin's letters about what he witnessed in Ireland reveal his disgust with Britain, and they mark the extent of Franklin's desire to leave the British Empire. Ireland's conditions prompted Franklin's second major turn away from Britain and toward a different political future for North America. Franklin's writings on the Irish and the question of the status of Ireland within the British Empire enable us to focus on his critique of any imperial policy that would support absentee landlords and resource extraction, leaving no wealth in the hands of the very peoples whose labor created the land's value to the commonwealth in the first place. It will be useful at this juncture to examine Franklin's conclusions about the colonized situation of Ireland and the relationship he felt might exist between Ireland and North America (and especially the New England and middle Atlantic colonies).

As we have seen, Franklin had been mulling over constitutional questions about Ireland and America for some time. The trip he took in the fall of 1771 was a culmination of a decade-long inquiry into Scottish and Irish affairs and decades-long correspondence with many Scottish and Irish political and natural philosophers. During the 1760s, in the midst of the imperial debates, Franklin had begun to make references to both Scotland and Ireland in some of his writings on the British Empire. His Pennsylvania experience had taught him to be deeply suspicious of absentee landlords, and he grew increasingly concerned about absentee landlords in the American colonies and in Scotland and Ireland. Hillsborough, a member of the Irish peerage, was one such landlord. Hillsborough owned Hillsborough Castle in northern Ireland and the Blessington Estate in county Wicklow. Franklin had also come to know well (and indeed entertained in Craven Street and later at Passy) several Irish members of Parliament, including Sir Edward Newenham (1732–1814), who sympathized with British America, and Gervase Parker Bushe (1745–1793), author of *The Case of Great Britain and America* (1769).[30] Newenham was enthusiastic in his friendship with Franklin and his praise of Franklin's views. The young Bushe and Franklin shared interests in the economics of colony-holding, in methods of taxation, and in population analysis. Franklin admired and likely collaborated with Gervase Parker Bushe during the 1760s. He developed a friendship with the younger man in part to discuss some of his questions regarding Ireland.

We have seen that Franklin appreciated Molyneux's stance on Ireland. Franklin judged that Parliament should have no control over the colonies and that the American colonies should have separate parliaments, as Ireland did. Franklin had written for the *London Gazetteer* a series of brief essays in 1766 linking the situation of the American colonies with Ireland. Most pointedly, he questioned why people in England should despise British settlers elsewhere: "Why despise your own English, who conquered and settled Ireland for you; who conquered and settled America for you," he inquired."[31] He had conceived there might be potential parity in the situations of Ireland and North America.

For his five-week tour in 1771, Franklin had several questions about Ireland. He was interested in understanding better Ireland's administration within the imperial system. He also wanted to learn about the quality of life of the agricultural laborers, to see if any parity existed between their lives and those of agricultural workers in North America. What Franklin witnessed in Ireland, especially with regard to the situation of the laborers on the land, saddened and disgusted him. By placing Franklin's 1771 trip to Ireland in the context of his ongoing discussions about Ireland, America, and the British Empire, we can more clearly see the rationale behind Franklin's disaffection for Britain. Perhaps more than any other event he faced at this crucial time, Franklin's trip to Ireland confirmed his belief, for good and all, that the British administration had no interest whatsoever in the colonists as people who were extending the British nation and that, to the contrary, the ministry's sole concern was with finding the most expedient ways to extract wealth from its dominions. Franklin's tour made him admit that there could be no good empire, and no national pride, where the people who lived on and worked the land were not the primary concern of those in administration. Far from being a pro-empire man, Franklin was conceiving a legitimate cause necessitating a break with Britain: Britain was starving its laborers to feed its wealthiest classes.

Franklin was taken aback by conditions in Ireland. He had thought he had understood well the situation there, given his knowledge of the political system and his conversations with his friends Newenham and Bushe. Ireland was controlled by the English interest, its political life in the hands of peers and members of Parliament whose appointments, of relatively recent date, enabled them to control land prices, manufactures, small farmers, and tenant farmers. These relatively new appointees—sometimes called in Ireland the New English and called by Franklin the courtiers—had displaced older English Protestant settlers, the Anglo-Irish settlers sometimes called in Ireland the Old English (to Franklin, the Patriots). This displacement enabled the even older English Catholic settlers to amalgamate some of their interests among city-dwellers in the eastern portions of Ireland and among some of the native Irish people. These were difficult, potentially turbulent times in Ireland.

But what seems most to have impressed Franklin was the obvious destitution and depression of the laborers. He developed detailed and emotional accounts of what he witnessed. To his old friend, Joshua Babcock (1707–1783) a physician of Rhode Island, Franklin wrote on January 13, 1772, that in Scotland and Ireland, "a small Part of the Society are Landlords, great Noblemen and Gentlemen, extreamly opulent, living in the highest Affluence and Magnificence: The Bulk of the People Tenants, extreamly poor, living in the most sordid Wretchedness in dirty Hovels of Mud and Straw, and cloathed only in Rags." Later in the same letter, he made sad mockery of the discussion taking place in London about the economy of the empire, discussions built on ignorance of the lived experiences of laboring people. He wrote that if Americans should "ever envy the *Trade* of these Countries, I can put them in a Way to obtain a Share of it." In an uncharacteristically emotional outpouring, Franklin offered a bitter denunciation of the existing oppressive system of colonial measures used toward Ireland. Should Americans ever envy Ireland's trade success, he said, "Let them with three fourths of the People of Ireland, live the Year round on Potatoes and Butter milk, without Shirts." By doing so, their merchants could "export Beef, Butter and Linnen." He continued, "Let them with the Generality of the Common People of Scotland go Barefoot, then may they make large Exports in Shoes and Stockings." And, speaking of laborers in England, he wrote, "if they will be content to wear Rags like the Spinners and Weavers of England, they may make Cloths and Stuffs for all Parts of the World." Franklin bitterly concluded:

> If my Countrymen should ever wish for the Honour of having among them a Gentry enormously wealthy, let them sell their Farms and pay rack'd Rents; the Scale of the Landlords will rise as that of the Tenants is depress'd who will soon become poor, tattered, dirty, and abject in Spirit.[32]

Franklin was dismayed by the poverty and destitution of the laboring people in Ireland, Scotland, and England, dismayed as well that those with whom he was associating as a diplomat had no concern for the populations that served them and, in fact, perpetuated the old, worn-out economic argument that the laboring poor deserved to live the way they did.

The situation in Ireland was much worse than that in Scotland because of Ireland's historically different path in the area of economic integration. To protect England's farmers, beginning in 1688, Ireland was prevented from marketing in England its dairy products. Scotland, by contrast, was permitted to market its pastoral goods after 1701. The situation forced Ireland to rely on its export trade to the French and English Caribbean colonies and to North America, trade that was constantly interrupted by imperial wars on land and seas. Ireland was also unable to participate in the lucrative East India trade, except via shipping and market channels in England. Finally, Ireland's lands, after 1750, were enclosed at a time when the population in the countryside had increased. Commercial landlords and absentee landlords, old Anglo-Irish populations, held the majority of lands, putting older joint and communal tenures, especially for grazing rights, under duress. Without land, a man would be a "boy," a farmer's day-laborer, and would likely have to remain single because he could not own enough in his labor, let alone any land, in order to make marriage viable. Excluded from landownership and a say in the economic system, groups of men, mostly Catholics, formed a "Whiteboy" movement in the mid-1760s aimed at restoring ancient commons and personal liberties.[33]

During the 1760s, Franklin had been seeking points of similarity between Ireland and the American colonies, with a goal of establishing procedural precedents for administration of the American colonies. But after this 1771 trip to Ireland, Franklin would comment again and again on the extent to which manufactures could bring about the ruin of a nation if they ran unchecked, if they were controlled by a ruling elite or court power, and if they were operating in such a way as to make the laboring people destitute. In the letter to Babcock, he concluded that "the Effect of this kind of Civil Society seems only to be, the depressing Multitudes below the Savage State that a few may be rais'd above it."

Franklin's letter to Joshua Babcock had begun with an assessment of the importance of agriculture as the key stage (using the traditional stadial theory) for the best subsistence. Franklin believed that improvements on the land could create prosperity and advantages in a free trade market while creating opportunities for equality of status among agricultural laborers. He offered his ideas to his Scottish friend Lord Kames in their frequent exchanges about agriculture. Eventually, Kames embraced Franklin's suggestions and created his own set of writings on agriculture, published just a few years after Franklin's visit in Scotland as *Sketches of the History of Man, In Two Volumes* (Edinburgh, W. Creech, and London: W. Strahan, 1774) and *The Gentleman Farmer. Being an Attempt to Improve Agriculture, by Subjecting It to the Test of Rational Principles* (Edinburgh, W. Creech; London, W. Cadell, 1776). At the time of Franklin's visit to Scotland, it was undergoing a process of agrarian change that brought greater attention to ideas of improving the land. Crop rotation, the raising and use of different kinds of animals, attention to soil quality and arability—all attested to a new concern with agrarian utility and fostered a renewed sense that in Scotland, farming and agricultural improvement were the "natural" interests of gentleman, who could use farming to practice their ideas of benevolence because, closer to the land, they could avoid the temptations of corruption that came with commerce.[34] As Franklin had been doing, Kames would go on to argue that the best state in society was that of an independent farmer positioned to compete with his goods and labor for the best land available for agriculture. He wrote that commerce brought corruption, like the entailing of properties. Absentee landlords took up land that virtuous farmers could be harvesting. Just as Franklin had argued against the Proprietors, Kames argued about absentee landlords and the process of entail: "To the possessor, an entail is a constant source of discontent, by subverting that liberty and independence, which all men covet, with respect to their goods as well as their persons."[35] A few pages later, Kames again used an idea gained from Franklin, "It is now an established maxim, That a state is powerful in proportion to the product of its land: a nation that feeds its neighbors, can starve them."[36] Kames would go on in 1776 to make the kind of claim Franklin was fond of making in the early 1770s. In Kames's words, agricultural patriotism was phrased thus: "Agriculture justly claims to be the chief of arts: it enjoys beside the signal pre-eminence, of combining deep philosophy with useful practice."

To Kames, Britain was "fundamentally . . . indebted" to agriculture "for the figure it makes all the world over."[37] To be sure, Kames was speaking more to gentlemen farmers than independent freeholders in his writings, but the ideas about agriculture that he was offering and the speculations he was making about the link between agrarianism and nationalism were links that Franklin himself had been making at the time the two had first entered into discussions on agricultural matters in 1769.

Franklin formulated these views for Babcock, when he was writing about Ireland. In this letter, Franklin referred to farming as "the most honourable of all Employments, . . . as being the most useful in itself, and rendring the Man most independent."[38] In laboring on the land, people could experience a good quality of life and retain their independence. Here we begin to see what were his differences of opinion with his Irish friends, friends like Sir Edward Newenham, whose anxiety about Protestant control overrode his concern about equity and fair dealings with Catholic laborers and townspeople. Franklin was walking a fine line here: surely he understood that an ideal agrarian existence might be possible for manor lords in Scotland but was not possible in Ireland precisely because of religious as well as economic disparity.

Joshua Babcock was just one of the correspondents to whom Franklin wrote about his trip to Ireland. He wrote in a similar vein to Thomas Cushing on the same day he wrote to Babcock. Franklin's remarks spoke in a comparative context, but Franklin's point was to show the great contrast between Ireland and North America. "Ireland is itself a fine Country, and Dublin a magnificent City," he wrote. But there were significant differences between Ireland and North America: "the Appearances of general extreme Poverty among the lower People, are amazing: They live in wretched Hovels of Mud and Straw, are clothed in Rags, and subsist chiefly on Potatoes. Our New England Farmers of the poorest Sort, in regard to the Enjoyment of all the Comforts of Life, are Princes when compar'd to them." He complained that absentee landlords and their middlemen discouraged the laborers. "Such is the Effect of the Discouragements of Industry," he insisted, because of "the Non-Residence not only of Pensioners but of many original Landlords who lease their Lands in Gross to Undertakers that rack the Tenants, and fleece them Skin and all, to make Estates to themselves, while the first Rents, as well as most of the Pensions are spent out of the Country." Franklin was deeply troubled about so much poverty, the likes of which he had never seen. Manor culture and absentee landlords promoted a poor quality of life of the laboring people, with few opportunities for social and political improvement among the majority of people. Franklin had had ample time to examine the country situation closely, for he had been invited by Hillsborough to visit Hillsborough Castle. Hillsborough took him on a forty-mile carriage excursion (a very uncomfortable one at that, because Franklin was unwell), attempting to impress on Franklin the success of the Irish system as a result of Britain's control. Franklin reported that "an English Gentleman there [in Ireland]" had implied that something was wrong with the British North Americans, because they did not produce certain kinds of goods for commodity trade with other British colonies (which trade supported the English treasury, because it was taxed). Hillsborough "could not understand," Franklin reported, "why we did not rival Ireland in the Beef and Butter Trade to the West Indies, and share with it in its Linen Trade. But he was satisfy'd when I told him, that I suppos'd the Reason might be, *Our People eat Beef and Butter every Day, and wear Shirts themselves*."[39]

Franklin had gone to Ireland with a list of queries revealing the imperial economist at work, with queries such as "Can the Farmers find a Ready Money Market and a good Living Price for the Produce of their Lands?"[40] He came away from Ireland shocked by the disparity of wealth but, it seems to me, especially shocked that the laborers, having no share of their own productions, had the least share of the commonwealth. To be sure, Franklin was not the first and only person to notice the infinite misery of laboring people and the unremitting opulence of landholders in Ireland. After a pages-long discussion of the means by which Ireland was rich in exports—that "the chief Exports of Ireland seem to be pinch'd off the Backs and out of the Bellies of the miserable Inhabitants"—Franklin did report to Thomas Cushing that "Schemes are now under Consideration among the humane Gentry, to provide some Means of mending if possible their present wretched Condition."[41]

Indeed, the issue of the *Hibernian Magazine, or Compendium of Entertaining Knowledge* for October 1771, which Franklin probably read and certainly contributed information to,[42] included several patriotic items belittling the nobility, including an unsigned piece called "The Immorality and Depravity of our present Nobility bid fair for the realization of the underneath portrait of posterity . . . in the Year 1971," which satirized the hedonism deriving from luxury and the extent to which Ireland was under the so-called leadership of pensioners and ne'er-do-wells, all under the pretense of being a nobleman's journal for 1971. The date is interesting: Was this a typographical error, for 1771, or 1791? Was it a sly, fantasy projection into the future about the indolence and decay of Ireland as a result of poor leadership there? Another item from the *Magazine* titled "A

Picture of Europe for 1771" provided literary portraits of the several states of Europe. The portrait for Great Britain is that she is "On her knees. The Cabinet Council playing at backgammon. A Secretary of State fingering the red Rose at a candle. Neptune supporting the throne, with his head off." And Ireland, placed just after the account for Great Britain, is pictured with succinctness: "IRELAND. Barefooted. Singing the Irish howl."[43] The comments are so striking as to make me wonder whether Franklin wrote these bits. In any case, Franklin's comments about Ireland reflect what was, in some circles, growing concern about the instability of any economy that would rob the poor of their wealth—that is, the wealth they held in their own labor on the land—in order to pay off rich, absentee landholders who had little concern for common people. To Franklin, the situation in Ireland was a perfect illustration why Pennsylvanians needed to be rid of its Proprietary relationship with the Penns and with Britain. Indeed, Franklin's views probably gained some force from his visits to a number of different houses of Patriots, to several printers, and to the Irish Parliament.

Franklin's letters about his tour of Ireland serve as significant telltales regarding the changing winds of empire.[44] The utter poverty of the laboring people, the conditions of their households, their bare tables, their bare feet—all seem to have registered in Franklin a profound distrust of the ministers with whom he was dealing and the motives behind their sometimes smiling faces. Hillsborough—who just that year had remarked to Strahan that Franklin was "a factious, turbulent Fellow, always in Mischief, a Republican, Enemy to the King's Service, and what not"[45]—had, during Franklin's tour of Ireland, insisted upon hosting Franklin and Richard Jackson, and did so with magnanimous courtesy and compliments. To Cushing, Franklin commented wryly that this was only so much subterfuge, as "by patting and stroaking the Horse to make him more patient while the Reins are drawn tighter and the Spurs set deeper into his Sides."[46]

As a colonial agent, Franklin would have to deal with the absentee landlords like Hillsborough, that "small Part of the Society . . . living in the highest Affluence and Magnificence," but as a British American, descended from laboring people in New England, he was made to recognize that, from the viewpoint of those involved in determining colonial policy for Britain, he was merely a dressed-up and intelligent version of the shirtless peasants of the countryside, the horse that pulls the chaise around the circles of court. It was precisely his odd position, neither of the British gentry nor of the local laboring people, that enabled Franklin to create a formulation of empire that allowed for self-governance and connection among colonies (an internal system) all under an external, cooperative set of laws governing mutual benefits. Franklin's Ireland trip convinced him that the British administration should not be permitted to regulate internal trade, develop and administer legislation, and name and require that the colonists pay for governors in America. He was hoping to interest the Irish Patriots, "dispos'd to be Friends to America," to join his cause, but he was unsuccessful.[47]

Made at a crucial moment in his thinking about imperial policies, Franklin's trip to Ireland clarified his doubts about an imperial system that based its power over its colonial holdings in resource extraction and depletion, population control through taxation and poverty, and a trading imbalance such that specie was never available in the colonies. The assumption seemed to be that colonial people could best serve the commonwealth by not serving themselves properly. Notions of self-love and self-respect were not part of the equation here. Where people could not demonstrate love of themselves and their comrades because they were left destitute and in misery, how could they possibly enjoy love of country? In such a case as this, manufacturing in the sovereign country was more a cost than a benefit, in terms of taxation, particularly if manufacture took as raw materials the very stuff of life of the laborer. What Franklin saw of Irish peasant life and what he heard around the manors he visited of the gentry convinced him that to assume that the wealth of a country resided in its extraction and export of raw materials and its potential output for manufacture and distribution elsewhere undermined what he considered to be the real wealth of any nation: its people and the independent labor of those people.

In the effort to examine Franklin's attitudes during these years crucial to decision-making about rebellion of the American colonies, historians have tended to overlook Franklin's views about Ireland and particularly this 1771 visit to Ireland. Perhaps because he called it variously a "tour," a "journey," and an "expedition," scholars have tended to focus upon his writings explicitly about American policy and British administration. What is clear about the effects of Franklin's journey to Ireland and his witnessing of the lives of Irish people is that the rhetoric of similarity he had been using to suggest possible affiliation between Britain's administration of Ireland and that of the American colonies changed to a rhetoric of difference. Franklin was still quite interested in Ireland, but he would not again suggest that the situation of Ireland was like that of the British colonies in North America. The native Irish were too oppressed, the settled Anglo-Irish too smug for Franklin's taste. He admired the Patriots, and he hoped that, should rebellion become necessary, they would support the

American colonies. But he could not determine upon any plan that could reconcile Ireland's administration with anything he wanted to happen in the British American colonies.

Indeed, when a new act was talked about (in 1773) to prevent emigration from Scotland and Ireland to America, Franklin developed a commentary, never published (because the plan aborted), that reveals his thinking about what he considered to be the imprisonment of laborers on islands that robbed them of their independence. As he wrote in 1773, his solution to the problem of emigration was this: "Let them [absentee landlords] return to their Family Seats, live among their People, and instead of fleecing and skinning, patronize and cherish them; promote their Interest, encourage their Industry, and make their Situation comfortable. If the poor Folks are happier at home than they can be abroad, they will not lightly be prevailed with to cross the Ocean."[48] Franklin's was still a view of empire, but empire with a difference from any he witnessed in Europe. Franklin's would be an empire that viewed as its greatest potential the property it might have in its free people.

Entangled Empires: North America and India

Franklin's agency for the American colonies took place during critical years in Britain's imperial expansion in the East, as it made major inroads in India by supporting the East India Company. This context—Britain's expansion into India—is important, because those in Parliament and the ministry faced larger questions than those associated with American affairs. It will be useful to pause here and consider the background to Franklin's efforts to work with the ministry while the ministry was attempting, mid-century, to achieve a global empire. Competing with news on American affairs in the London newspapers during the late 1760s and early 1770s was increasing coverage of events in India and the various business straits of the East India Company. Franklin conceived by 1764 that a duty on East India tea would actually assist the colonies, because East India goods fell into the category of luxuries rather than necessities.[49] Nonimportation of India goods would be relatively easy for Britons in North America, because India goods were based on manufactured needs rather than basic needs. Britain was assisting the East India Company in its military wars in India while seeking to tax the colonies with oppressive measures presumably to support war efforts, trade, and administration in North America.

Franklin grew more uneasy with the extended political and economic reach of Parliament in North America while it was willing to bankroll invasions by a private company into India. While he was in London, Franklin read the newspaper accounts of the invasions and speculated on the relationship between the administration of the American colonies and of India. In an interview with Gottfried Achenwall (1719–1772) in 1766, Franklin had identified inequities in the American colonial and East Indian trade policies. He was troubled by the Navigation Acts imposed on the colonies while the East India Company enjoyed exclusive trade rights in certain enumerated goods.[50] Writing as "Benevolus" to the *London Chronicle*, April 11, 1767, Franklin explained his views regarding colonial taxation without representation in the context of what he knew to be the need, in the British Treasury, to fund expeditions in India rather than North America. At their own expense, Franklin argued, the American colonies engaged in war against France in North America. "Advantages were obtained by that war," he reminded his readers: "to wit, greater security of trade and settlement free from the interruptions of the French, and a great extent of territory and dominion." The free trade assisted the colonists, he argued, while "the territory and dominion acquired appertain to the crown." The colonists "never pretended to lay claim to the least part of either of these latter advantages," yet their adversaries in the current administration, "who think *another trading Company* (in exactly *similar* circumstances) have a right to both, must at least allow, on the same principle, that the colonies in this particular [i.e., the desire for free trade] are modest, however silly it may have been in them to waive their pretentions in favour of government."[51]

The East India Company was in the middle of protracted negotiations with the ministry regarding taxation of Company shares. Company shareholders considered that any funding the Company received from tribes in India was Company money, not government money. The issue came to the fore in the mid-1760s, when after a series of crises, the Company finally won the support of local leaders in India. In 1765, the nawab of Bengal and other local rulers transferred the financial administration of Bengal, Behar, and Orissa to the Company, thus making available more than £2 million sterling in the Company's coffers. As a result, extensive speculation occurred on shares of Company stock. Company stockholders wanted the money distributed in dividends to them, as a result of their investment. Yet some officers of government thought a large share of the income should ease the British Treasury's financial difficulties, based on the notion that the funds arose from political sources and were not profits from trade.[52] Franklin's sly reference to this situation in his Benevolus essay indicates that India had become a target of his concerns.[53]

Similar evaluations of the American and East Indian situations flew from Franklin's pen in these years. To Thomas Crowley (d. 1787), an English Quaker who made public proposals about creating a united federation of all colonies including colonies in India, Franklin replied in London's *Public Advertiser*, October 21, 1768, that the Americans "have never engag'd Britain in any War on our Account, but have constantly manag'd our Indian Wars ourselves, without asking Help from hence either of Men or Money." He reminded his readers that "by our Connection with Britain we are unavoidably drawn into all her Wars, and always have, as it was our Duty, borne our Part of them without murmuring." But now, the administration was finding it convenient to pass over its costly problems with "Hanover, Portugal, and the East India Company, whose Protection was expressly intended by Britain, and indeed, highly expensive to her," leaving them "entirely out of your Account," "that the Odium of the whole may be laid on us.[54] Franklin was angered by a ministry and population obdurate regarding their own people, Britons in North America, but avaricious for more wealth in another part of the world. He considered that North Americans would eventually be asked to pay for wars in East India, and he concluded that the Britons in North America might be better off on their own, with no ties to such a rapacious government.

During the years 1772 and 1773, Franklin repeatedly saw American affairs tabled so that Parliament and the ministry could consider affairs in India. But he was thrilled to point out again and again to his American friends his belief that the Americans' nonimportation of East India goods brought the Company's trade to a deficit. He avidly followed American newspaper reports on the strategy of nonimportation. He happily reported to Joseph Galloway (c. 1731–1803) on December 2, 1772, for instance, that he had enjoyed reading in the *Pennsylvania Gazette* for October 21 that "the present Difficulties of the India Company and of Government" were caused by Americans' nonimportation: "The Company have accepted Bills which they find themselves unable to pay, tho' they have the Value of Two Millions in Tea and other India Goods in their Stores, perishing under a Want of Demand." He pointed out that "it is known that the American Market is lost by continuing the Duty on Tea, and that we are supply'd by the Dutch." Over the course of the previous five years, if the duty on tea had been removed, the Americans "might probably have otherwise taken off the greatest Part of what the Company have on hand, and so have prevented their present Embarrasment, yet the Honour of Government is suppos'd to forbid the Repeal of the American Tea Duty."[55]

The sheer irony that the administration would insist on having its way with North America while funding wars in India was too great for Franklin to avoid. Knowing that his letters were being intercepted did not hinder Franklin's disparaging remarks on administrative policies. He could make no sense of a government that would table American affairs for what were perceived the more pressing matters associated with military problems in India and the extent to which the British government was funding shareholders' wars there. Yet it was already too late to repair the damage caused by what he considered to be illegal administrative policies in North America. Still Franklin tried to convince the administration and the British populace about their wrongheaded notions of Britons in North America. Using an ideology based in presumably ancient and common heritage, he wrote again and again to the newspapers and to friends of the colonies about the colonists' common goals and ancestry.

One final issue regarding Franklin's views of affairs in India is worth noting, especially as it provides an intriguing glimpse of the legal theoretician at work while also indicating Franklin's growing notion that because of their personal sacrifices in hardship and monies, the settlers of North America—rather than the king—held sovereignty over their land, a sovereignty granted when they made agreements with or took over by conquest Native lands. In several pieces from the year 1773—an essay titled "On Claims to the Soil of America," his "An Edict by the King of Prussia," and a letter to William Franklin dated July 14, 1773—Franklin began to articulate his thinking about land acquisition, land tenure, and sovereignty.

Franklin's letter to his son William formulated a clearly new position about sovereignty. In the letter, Franklin outlined his views on land obtained in areas occupied by Britain. He concluded, "I think that any Englishman or Number of Englishmen may if they please purchase Lands of an Indian Nation[,] unite with it and become Subject to its Government; or if they do not chuse that, and their Numbers be sufficient, they may, purchasing with the Lands a Freedom from Indian Authority, erect a new State of their own." Franklin reached this conclusion through a series of postulates that, because they have never been fully discussed, are worthy our examination. He opened by remarking that "my Opinion, as being somewhat of a Civilian," differs a bit from opinions of lawyers. His postulates followed:

1. That it is the natural Right of Men to quit when they please the Society or State, and the Country in which they were born, and either join with another or form a new one as they may think proper.

   The Saxons thought they had this Right when they quitted Germany and established themselves in England . . . .

2. Those who thus quit a State, quit [Submission] to its Protection, but do not therefore become its Enemies.

3. If they purchase Territory in another Country, it may [be only] on Terms of submitting to the Sovereignty and Laws before established therein or, Freedom from that Sovereignty may be purchas'd with the Land. This latter I take to be the Case with respect to Lands purchas'd of the Indian Nations in America.

4. If a Freedom from the Sovereignty is purchased with the Land, the Purchasers may either introduce there the Sovereignty of their former Prince, if they chuse it as needing his Protection; or they may erect a new one of their own, if they are sufficient to their own Defence.

This quasi-legal opinion—that land belonged to the actual people engaged in taking over lands, not to the monarch ruling the land they came from—resulted from Franklin's observations on a decision rendered in Britain regarding land the East India Company conquered in Bengal. Considering the situation in North America in the context of the growing situation in India, Franklin now believed that even the Crown had no legal rights to the lands in North America.

Franklin's opinion arose from his reading of the legal opinions raised to support the Crown's takeover of territories in India. When he wrote to his son William, Franklin had just finished reading the Pratt-Yorke opinion regarding the petition of the East India Company to gain lands in India. He was reading William Bolts's *Considerations on India Affairs; Particularly Respecting the Present State of Bengal and Its Dependencies* (London: J. Almon, 1772). Because he was not a lawyer and his view about these matters differed from Pratt and Yorke, Franklin called his opinion that of a "Civilian," even as he acknowledged that his own view "goes a little farther than that of those great Common Lawyers." The backstory of Franklin's opinion was a situation in India. Robert Clive (1725–1774), first Baron Clive, had been engaging in several military expeditions against different tribal groups in India in the late 1750s. The Company considered that the lands and peoples Clive had thus "secured" ought to be granted to the Company. The legal decision rendered by Attorney General Charles Pratt (1714–1794), later first Earl Camden, and Solicitor General Charles Yorke (1722–1770) distinguished between two kinds of territory. Where land was acquired by conquest, they argued, the Crown held both sovereignty and title to the land. Where land was acquired by peaceful cession between two groups, the original holders of the land and those making the acquisition, then the Crown was sovereign, but proprietary rights inhered to the new holders of the land, not the Crown. According the Pratt and Yorke, the land acquired by Clive and his forces was held under the sovereign, because held by British people, though the land did not belong to the Crown but to the Company.

Franklin took up the Pratt-Yorke opinion and began to make a sharper distinction about land tenure in America that essentially left the Crown out of the equation. His position showed up originally in an essay for the *Public Advertiser*, March 16, 1773, where he spoke about the questionable assumption that the colonists who went to North America did so for Britain, not for themselves. Franklin created an analogy he would later use in his letter to William and in his satirical "Edict by the King of Prussia." In the *Advertiser* article, he was attempting to point out the parallels between British subjects in North America and those in England. "To me . . . it seems, that the Subjects in the two Countries are . . . upon a Level." The analogy was plain, and it is worth quoting at length:

> Britain was formerly the America of the Germans. They came hither in their Ships; found the *Cream* of the Land possessed by a Parcel of Welsh Caribbs, whom they judged unworthy of it, and therefore drove them into the Mountains, and sat down in their Places. These Anglo-Saxons, our Ancestors, came *at their own Expence*, and therefore supposed that when they had secured the new Country, they held it of themselves, and of no other People under Heaven. Accordingly we do not find that their Mother Country, Germany, ever pretended to tax them; nor is it likely, if she had, that they would have paid it. So far then the Level is clear; for unless Great Britain had a Property in the Lands of America before the Colonists went thither, it does not appear how they could take Lands of her to hold on any Terms.

The same analogy would be used in his "Edict": If America belonged to Britain, then England belonged to Germany. The colonists in America were, in fact, the owners of their property in America.

While Franklin's expression of these views had reached a new place in 1773, they had been on his mind for some time. In marginalia to pamphlets arising during the crisis in American affairs in 1769 and 1770, Franklin began to work out a different notion about sovereignty and the acquisition and settlement of foreign lands. In one pamphlet, Franklin wrote into the margins, "The Lands [in North America] did not belong to the Crown but to the Indians, of whom the Colonists either purchased them at their own Expence, or conquer'd them without Assistance from Britain."[56] In another, Franklin articulated a theory about distinct states of the empire, even as he spoke about the colonists as the original agents over the land they secured in North America: "*British Empire*, a vague Expression," he sputtered. "All these Writers (almost all) confound themselves and Readers with the Idea that the British Empire is but ONE State; not considering or knowing that it consists of many States under one Sovereign." He went further, however, regarding North America: "The British Nation had no original Property in the Country of America. It was purchas'd by the first Colonists of the Natives, the only Owners. The Colonies [were] not *created* by Britain, but by the Colonists themselves." These sentiments, still nascent in 1770s, reached a fuller articulation by 1773, precisely resulting from Franklin's understanding of Britain's growing preoccupations with India. Seeing what was happening in India helped Franklin draw more fully a sense that his business in England would shortly be at an end, given the impasse in his negotiations. He was not sanguine about such an outcome.

Power on Display: A Bull-Baiting in Britain's Cockpit

Franklin had been working to bring about a peaceful means for meeting the competing trade, manufacturing, and social goals of both the Crown and the colonists in British North America. He had repeatedly been called upon by different representatives working on behalf of the Crown and the individual colonies to come up with a plan that would consolidate British imperial power while addressing the seemingly ever-increasing demands of the residents in the colonies of North America. The winter of 1773 to 1774 was difficult for Franklin, not just because negotiations for Massachusetts and the other British colonies in North America had hit a standstill in London, but because it seemed he was also being mis-understood by some of the New Englanders whose interests he was repre-senting. He understood that his friends in the colonies were living under duress, but he seriously miscalculated their anger about the intrusions in their everyday lives. He still conceived of his role as one of mediation. The various measures that he was arguing against—the quartering of troops among them, the closure of harbors, severe customs watches—all brought to Boston a police state both intrusive and unfamiliar. Franklin drafted plan after plan for potential conciliation. He wrote satires about the blindness of imperial ministers. He tried to meet with (and was often rebuffed by) ministers who offered him little courtesy and less respect. The evidence among his papers indicates that Franklin wanted both sides to be informed about what was happening, so that the British Americans would understand the negative impact of their restiveness, on the one hand, and so that the British ministry and especially the manufacturing interests and general population would understand the legitimate grievances of British North Americans, on the other.

Franklin was sandwiched between significantly radicalized colonial assemblies with high expectations and imperial leaders with no patience for hearing complaints. Under these circumstances, Franklin was called in January 1774 before the Privy Council Committee for Plantation Affairs to explain the petition that it was his duty, as the Massachusetts agent and representative, to lay before Council. The Massachusetts House was petitioning for the removal of the Crown-appointed governor, Thomas Hutchinson (1711–1780), and Lieutenant Governor Andrew Oliver (1706–1774), because the House considered they might better serve in some other capacities, given what the House understood to be their negative attitudes about the people of Massachusetts as indicated by their repeated requests for British military assistance and additional coercive means to control the population. Their views had become public, because their letters had been stolen and sent to resistors in Massachusetts.

The House inquiry was the result of an exchange of letters between the governor and lieutenant governor with the late Thomas Whately (c. 1728–1772). By undisclosed means, Franklin had secured the letters from the possession of the Whately family and had sent them to his contacts in Boston, where they were printed. The Massachusetts representatives were outraged—as Franklin had known they would be—by the negative characterizations given the colonists' behaviors. Britons were outraged that private correspondence of political leaders had surreptitiously been acquired and sent and had been published. William Whately (n.d.), presumably to defend his honor against charges that he had stolen and transmitted the letters from his brother Thomas, engaged in a duel with John Temple (1732–1798), who likewise believed his honor was being called into question as the author of the mischief. After a politely inconclusive duel took place between the two men, Franklin made a public avowal that he was the one who had obtained the letters and sent them to Boston. He was called to explain his actions before the Privy Council in an area called the Cockpit.

The hearing in the Cockpit occurred at a pivotal moment in Franklin's negotiations with the administration. The hearing would offer a public spectacle of British Empire at the expense of the colonies' most renowned agent, a person of high standing as a natural philosopher and man of letters on the Continent. Franklin was experiencing what might be described as a subaltern status. His presumed role as a native informant—that is, his role as putative negotiator between the colonies and Great Britain, as represented by Whitehall—was overshadowed by considerations of empire (and an ideology of empire) over which he had no control and about which he was, at least as a public platform of political self-consciousness, attempting to remain neutral. The imperial structure called upon Franklin to perform the role of "American," even as it negated his part in the unfolding drama. The administration intended to discipline the North American colonies by humiliating—in a kind of civic pillory—their most active agent.

Intellectual and political historians and biographers of Franklin have commented that the public humiliation was, in effect, the primary motivation behind Franklin's turn against the British Empire. For example, one historian has remarked that "the Cockpit incident altered Franklin's vision," adding, "The Cockpit changed Benjamin Franklin, pushing him toward a decision that he had been trying with increasing difficulty to avoid."[57] The stripping of his postmaster generalship did acutely hurt Franklin's pride, but as we have been seeing, long before the event in the Cockpit, Franklin had grown weary of Britain's stranglehold on the colonies. Franklin's course of action and his views of the British Empire had already been established back in the 1750s, evidenced in his letters to William Shirley. He believed the Americans had a legitimate right to colonial assemblies that determined and executed their own laws. As he developed his views into a full-fledged conception of a constitutional monarchy, with the Crown as the sole sovereign over the colonies, he examined closely the situation in Ireland. His experiences on tour in Ireland and Scotland in 1771 made such a goal unthinkable, as we have seen. Franklin's vision had long been altered, and in 1773, as he began to reason about the legal position that might be made regarding American sovereignty over their lands, he was aware that such a position would negate Britain's stranglehold. His opinion against Britain had been shored up as he examined the legal decisions being rendered about India. Franklin ultimately concluded that the Americans were the sovereigns over the lands they had peacefully negotiated for and acquired from the Native peoples in North America. He had already turned away from hoping for imperial unity by the time Wedderburn denounced him publicly.

The Cockpit was, historically speaking, a scene of entertainment. It was a large chamber within the block of buildings on or near the site of the Cockpit erected by Henry VIII opposite Whitehall in London. Here the king's Privy Council collectively met to examine legal matters. It was a long room with a central floor, in amphitheater style, surrounded by raised balcony-like platforms for observers and outside participants. It has been said that the Stuart kings once fought their specially bred fighting roosters in this location within the palace.[58] The Cockpit entertainment in January 1774 involved Solicitor General for the Crown Alexander Wedderburn (1733–1805), a Scot by birth and training who had found a place in the British ministry, and Benjamin Franklin, postmaster general for the colonies, elected representative for several colonies but in this case representing Massachusetts, and a second-generation British colonist in North America.

Franklin's goal was twofold: to attempt to keep alive the Massachusetts petition before the Privy Council and to refuse to name the party with whom he was complicit in obtaining and transmitting the letters that had revealed what the Massachusetts people considered the perfidy of their court-appointed governors. Of course, at this stage in his career, Franklin was enjoying significant international celebrity for his scientific achievements. He was a friend of the French court and nobility, a chief representative of everything that Europeans wished "America" to be. And he was proud of these achievements and his public renown. Being called into the Cockpit to defend his agency for Massachusetts, Franklin knew that his part in the letters affair would be mentioned. For Franklin, the day would not be a good one. He was not given sufficient advance notice of the Cockpit hearing to find a legal representative to assist him. So he called upon the services of John Dunning (1731–1783), the appointed legal representative of the Massachusetts House. Dunning, a former solicitor general, was well aware of the law and gave Franklin appropriate legal advice, all things considered. But Dunning was unwell, and his infirmities would, in essence, enable the Lords and others present to shout him down quite easily. Oratorical skill and superior volume when speaking—these would be necessary, because a large gathering was expected, given the events that had recently come to light. Nine days before the Cockpit hearing took place (January 29, 1774), London received news that the East India Company's 342 chests of tea were thrown overboard by "Indians" to prevent their being landed and thus perforce made available for market in New England.

Alexander Wedderburn was well chosen to represent imperial concerns. With a loud voice and a penchant for rhetorical flourish, Wedderburn was already at that time a powerful lawyer-orator in Britain.[59] Having begun his legal practice in Edinburgh, where he was on familiar footing with leading Scottish philosophers and political theorists, he joined the London bar in 1757. He had come of age in Edinburgh as the city was reaching its cultural apex as the center of arts, letters, and philosophy in the British Empire. He was on the fast track in London. Aware that his noticeable accent might hinder his ability to get ahead as a barrister in London, Wedderburn took lessons in elocution. Within four years of joining the London bar, he entered Parliament as the protégé of the former prime minister, John Stuart (1713–1792), third Earl of Bute. Under the administration of Frederick North (1732–1792), known as Lord North, Wedderburn became so insistent with his legal probing in opposition to the government that he was, in essence, persuaded by an appointment as solicitor general to develop an allegiance to the Crown.

Franklin knew that an imperial entertainment was about to unfold at his expense. As he understood it, he was ostensibly to be questioned about a matter in which, from the imperial standpoint, he knew he had no legal standing: colonial governors did not—nor did colonial agents—serve by the choice and consent of the governed but by the pleasure of the Crown. He understood the Crown's legal position, which was central to its controlling the populations of the British North American colonies. Yet the legal question was ultimately moot: Franklin was really to be the butt of questions relating to the letters he had admitted to having received surreptitiously and sent to New England.

Franklin's attire befitted his station and legal brief: he wore a full-dress wig (though he was not given to wearing wigs), and he appeared in Council wearing a suit of Manchester velvet. But it didn't matter how Franklin dressed. The Council was packed full of Crown representatives—thirty-four lords and ministers were in attendance for a hearing that typically drew no more than a dozen persons for short briefings. The Council and public landings in the Cockpit included only a few of Franklin's close friends. In Council were Francis Dashwood (1708–1781), fifteenth Baron le Despencer, and William Legge, (1731–1802), second Earl of Dartmouth, who had seemed interested in conciliation prior to this event. Both shared Franklin's concerns about the imperial stranglehold on American trade in the absence of parliamentary representation and the imposition of coercive measures presumably to control activities among Britons in Boston. Also in the chamber were the American Edward Bancroft (1741–1821); noted spokesman in behalf of the American colonies, Anglo-Irishman Edmund Burke (1729–1797), whose ideas on this particular issue were unclear; and

Franklin's scientific friend Joseph Priestley (1733–1804). Franklin understood the importance of his performance that day, but nothing could have
prepared him for the spectacle that happened.

Several records of the Cockpit drama survive. Although some records
are more complete than others, all reveal that Franklin was attacked, scurrilously so, and in personal terms.[60] No one among his friends called for
the floor in his behalf. In effect, the attack Franklin received had nothing
to do with the legal or imperial issues at hand. Wedderburn opened the
session remarking upon the size of the crowd there to listen to the hearing,
using his opening to underscore, as he phrased it, "the presence of so great
a number of Lords, and of so large an audience" that the hearing "appears
to have excited." He continued, "It is a question of no less magnitude, than
whether the Crown shall ever have it in its power to employ a faithful
and steady servant in the administration of a Colony." But Wedderburn
did not stay long with the supposedly pressing legal and imperial questions. As witness William Bollan (c. 1710–c. 1776) later reported, "I had
the grievous mortification to hear Mr. Wedderburn . . . wandring from
the proper question before their Lordships, pour forth such a torrent of
virulent abuse on Dr. Franklin as never before took place within the com-
pass of my knowledge of judicial proceedings, his reproaches appearing to
me incompatible with the principles of law, truth, justice, propriety, and
humanity."[61] Wedderburn abused Franklin in personal terms unbecoming
anyone who walked in polite circles. Examining the records of the long
hearing—which Franklin, age sixty-eight, endured while standing—one
has a sense that Wedderburn focused his negative rhetorical constructions
around three key areas: Franklin's reputation as a scientist and natural
philosopher; Franklin's reputation as a man of letters; and Franklin's reliability and trustworthiness as a colonial agent, friend to Britain, and friend
to anyone. The attack created the impression that Franklin was the master-
mind behind a plot of radical incendiaries harboring the most treacherous
thoughts about the Crown and administration.

With regard to Franklin's reputation in science and natural philosophy, Franklin was mockingly called "Dr." Franklin, especially frequently
at the opening but throughout Wedderburn's performance. Wedderburn
described Franklin as moving "in a different orbit from that of other
Colony Agents," such that he "gravitates also to a very different center."[62]
In a salvo near the opening of the diatribe, Wedderburn invoked the audience's presumed desire for order and stability, characterized as a righteous
zeal for truth and humanity. He enjoined his auditors to understand that
the honor of Britain was at stake: "I hope, my lords," he said, "you will

mark [and brand] the man, for the honour of this country, of Europe, and of mankind."[63] In Wedderburn's characterization, Franklin had "forfeited all the respect of societies and of men. Into what companies will he hereafter go with an unembarrassed face, or the honest intrepidity of virtue. Men will watch him with a jealous eye; they will hide their papers from him, and lock up their escritoires." Wedderburn then made a most striking rhetorical blow, given Franklin's high reputation as a philosopher and litterateur: "He will henceforth esteem it a libel to be called *a man of letters; homo* trium *literarum!*"[64] Rhetorically speaking, Franklin was constructed as beyond the pale of human and humane society.

In contrast with this insulting characterization of Franklin as the embodiment of sheer malevolence and incivility, Wedderburn treated the Crown-appointed governor and lieutenant governor and those who supported the imperial cause with a rhetoric of sentimental humanism and universal, self-sacrificing benevolence. He characterized Thomas Hutchinson as "a faithful and steady servant," the choice of the king, who followed the wishes of "his people," "A native of the country, whose ancestors were among its first settlers. A Gentleman, who had for many years presided in their Law Courts; of tried integrity; of confessed abilities; and who had long employed those abilities, in the study of their history and original constitution."[65] In Wedderburn's portrayal, Hutchinson was a man who acted a "very laudable and friendly part . . . on every occasion for the good of the colony."[66] Hutchinson had long spent his time—until the letters Franklin sent arrived in Massachusetts—"enjoying the people's confidence."[67] He displayed, in the letters then before the Council, "good sense, . . . great moderation, and . . . [a] sincere regard to the welfare of that his native province."[68] By speaking of Hutchinson in this way, Wedderburn developed for his willing audience—expressions of assent were vocal, and frequent—a character of Hutchinson based in the sentimental and polite qualities of honesty, sincerity, and goodness. In Wedderburn's hands, Hutchinson became the person who acted with humility and self-sacrifice in service to his country, thus creating a position of unaccountable surprise that the people of Massachusetts should be unhappy.

Wedderburn's rhetoric articulates Franklin as a kind of Miltonic Lucifer or Marlovian Faustus, incendiary in his machinations, secretive, lying, disputatious. Wedderburn said, for instance, "Your Lordships will not wonder that I consider Dr. Franklin not so much in the light of an agent for the Assembly's purpose, as in that of a first mover and prime conductor of it for his own; not as the Assembly's agent for avenging this dreadful conspiracy of Mr. Hutchinson against his native country; but as the actor and secret spring, by which all the Assembly's motions were directed: the inventor and first planner of the whole contrivance."⁶⁹ Franklin had behaved with "suspicion" and "treachery," and he had created a situation such that "a whole province [has been] set in a flame."⁷⁰ In Wedderburn's construction, Franklin was "the true incendiary, . . . the great abettor of that faction at Boston, which, in form of a Committee of Correspondence, have been inflaming the whole province against his Majesty's government."⁷¹ He continued, "But Dr. Franklin, whatever he may teach the people at Boston, while he is *here* at least is a subject; and if a subject injure a subject, he is answerable to the law." The significant irony in this remark is that Franklin had for years been arguing that the subjects of the Crown in England were injuring the subjects of the Crown in America, of course. Wedderburn continued by taunting Franklin: "The rank in which Dr. Franklin appears, is not even that of a Province Agent: he moves in a very inferior orbit."⁷² Wedderburn cast Franklin as a lawless ruffian, a rank upstart, a petty criminal, one who deserved to be shunned from civil society.

By mocking Franklin as a man of letters—with all the oratorical flourish possible to enjoin the double entendre—Wedderburn scored a significant degree of opprobrium for the colonies' representative, to be sure. But Wedderburn added another obviously negative, personalized barb to his dramatic rendering: he cast Franklin as an African. Franklin had performed, Wedderburn insisted, the part of Zanga, the enslaved and debased Moor in the popular 1721 play *Revenge*, by Edward Young (1681–1765). "Amidst these tragical events," Wedderburn importuned, referring to the duel that had taken place, "Amidst these tragical events, of one person nearly murdered, of another answerable for the issue, of a worthy governor hurt in his dearest interests, the fate of America in suspense." Then, probably with all the histrionics of great theater, Wedderburn pointed to Franklin, we can assume, and said, "Here is a man, who with the utmost insensibility of remorse, stands up and avows himself the author of all. I can compare it only to Zanga in Dr. Young's *Revenge*." Wedderburn quoted a few lines from the well-known play, lines that culminate with Zanga's saying, "I hated, I despised, and I destroy." And he concluded, "I ask, my Lords, whether the revengeful temper attributed, by poetic fiction only, to the bloody African; is not surpassed by the coolness and apathy of the wily American?"

Franklin was thus likened to the central dramatic villain of a revenge tragedy, an African, and then castigated as the wily American. Wedderburn was relying on his audience's knowledge of Young's tragedy and, more importantly, on his audience's willingness to associate those in colonies with untrustworthy, darker peoples. The rhetorical association Wedderburn made is a reliable index of most self-respecting, "polite," upper-class Britons' assumptions: Africans and American colonists are both subhuman peoples to be subjected. It is unlikely that Wedderburn would have used that rhetorical ploy were this not the case.

Hindsight enables us to understand how Wedderburn's characterization of Franklin as Edward Young's Zanga came at an important moment in Franklin's shifting personal beliefs about Africans and the slave trade. Consider the interesting conjunction between Wedderburn's use of Zanga in this speech and a letter Franklin sent to Anthony Benezet (1713–1784) in 1773, a conjunction so fascinating that it invites speculation as to whether Franklin's letter to Benezet had been intercepted in London. After 1770, authorities had more frequently been seizing Franklin's letters, copying them, and sending them on. Franklin's letter to Benezet of February 10, 1773, written in London, opened with the notice that he was enclosing Edward Young's *Night Thoughts*. The brief letter also included the information that Franklin "commenc'd an Acquaintance with Mr. Granville Sharp [1735–1813], and we shall act in Concert in the Affair of Slavery. The Accounts you send me relating to Surinam are indeed terrible."[73] Franklin's letter indicated his growing awareness of the problems of slave trafficking and his clear decision to "act in Concert" regarding the reduction and eventual eradication of slavery. Given the mention of Young's writings in Franklin's letter and Franklin's intention to create a mechanism wherein to reduce slavery's ill effects, it is possible that Wedderburn was making a sly gesture to a knowing audience regarding Franklin presumed plotting against Britain. Was the jibe related to Young's Zanga a telltale jest to insiders who knew the contents of Franklin's letters, even as they all pretended Franklin had acted in a scurrilous and uncivil manner by sending to Massachusetts, as a third party, letters that were someone else's?

Franklin stood for a very long time. He remained silent. Given the circumstances, it is hard to know what other kind of performance than coolness Franklin could have offered to the audience at the Cockpit. The situation forced him to play the subaltern's part: his presence as representative was necessary for this stage, as was his silence. Franklin would later, for an American reading audience, call the situation a bullbaiting, but he evidently kept his face impassive during the lengthy, tiring session. Edward Bancroft, who had been standing near Franklin, later remarked that Franklin's "face was directed towards me, and I had a full uninterrupted view of it and his person, during the whole time in which Mr. Wedderburn spoke." Bancroft noted that "the Doctor . . . stood *conspicuously erect,* without the smallest movement of any part of his body. The muscles of his face had been previously composed, so as to afford a placid tranquill expression of countenance, and he did not suffer the slightest alteration of it to appear during the continuance of the speech in which he was so harshly and improperly treated."[74] Franklin chose not to give the audience any satisfaction by displaying an emotional response to the tirade presented. Yet it was not that Franklin was devoid of feeling, as his friend Priestley could attest. Priestley reported to their friends that as Franklin left the chamber, he "took me by the hand, in a manner that indicated some feeling."[75]

Franklin's hearing was reported in the colonies. A letter dated February 19, 1774, printed April 20 in the *Pennsylvania Gazette* as "Extract of a Letter from London," reported that the solicitor general,

> leaving the Business that was before their Lordships, in a virulent Invective of an Hour, filled with Scurrility, abused him personally, to the great Entertainment of Thirty-five Lords of the Privy-Council, who had been purposely invited as to a Bull-baiting, and not one of them had the Sense to reflect on the Impropriety and Indecency of treating, in so ignominious a Manner, a Public Messenger, whose Character in all Nations, savage as well as civilized, used to be deemed sacred, and his Person under public Protection, even when coming from an Enemy; nor did one of them check the Orator's Extravagance, and recal him to the Point under Consideration, but generally appeared much delighted, chuckling, laughing, and sometimes loudly applauding.[76]

The editors of Franklin's papers indicate Franklin wrote this statement. Franklin considered it important to let colonial Americans see how he was being treated in England, not just so that they would understand imperial intransigence but so that they would see that even someone of his stature in Europe was calculatedly mistreated in England. In his lengthy monologue, Wedderburn had taken up few of the imperial issues that Franklin had been working on for years. Franklin's status as a colonial agent was called into question, because his reliability had been publicly ridiculed. And Franklin had already received quiet communications that he was about to lose the postmaster generalship. There was no legitimate need for the event at the Cockpit on January 29, 1774. The Massachusetts petitioners were seeking the removal of their Crown-appointed governors, and under the existing system of administration, they had no legal or other right to make the request. Franklin had, according to policy in Britain, no legal right to represent Massachusetts, either—a point Wedderburn used in his diatribe—because Franklin had not been appointed by the Crown but selected by Britons in North America.

The Cockpit event was the final attempt by Whitehall to put power on display, a move necessary both internally and externally. Thinking of this situation using a postcolonialist perspective, it is evident that Britain was experiencing the inherent stresses that occur when any political entity is in the process of shifting from colonialism (the settlement by individual communities for commercial purposes) to imperialism (the establishment of a central bureaucracy for ideological and financial reasons).[77] In colony-building, competing interests and competing individuals at court interrupted the possibility of any centralization of administration. In the interim commercial era of midcentury, Britain was moving directly into India with the prospects and intention of establishing in India an imperial center. As the issue of centralized administration for the overseas empire came to the fore, the internal power shifted according to the interests being played out at court in any given moment. In this situation, a person in Franklin's position would (as Franklin did), in effect, run from office to office, courtier to courtier and be told differing stories from all sides. His presence was required to put power on display, but his silence was expected, as a subaltern subject to the administration's control. At the moment when the American colonies were attempting to negotiate, through Benjamin Franklin, a version of a constitutional empire, Great Britain was attempting to consolidate its power in Ireland and make major inroads into India, by massacring and otherwise subduing Indian tribal peoples.

Driven by a mentality that associated colonial peoples with inferiority, the ministry used the Cockpit to display what was, in effect, a good subject (Wedderburn, an assimilated Scot) compared to a bad one (a superficially imperially assimilated but nonetheless upstart colonist from North America). Franklin, in this context, could be treated with the contumely appropriate to his insubordinate position, under express assumptions that he was unassimilable. (He had proven intractable about Ireland and Irish lords just five years earlier.) Scotland had proven itself worthy of Whitehall's regard, for the Scottish elite had been successfully brought into line, having accepted their roles as inferiors and taken on the tasks of becoming "better." Scots peoples who were poor or who could find no place in Scotland or England sailed for North America. The plan of 1707 for Scotland had brought prosperity and economic stability to Scotland, and it created willing subjects, as witnessed in Wedderburn's easy affiliation of himself with the Crown in the use of the imperial "We" during his speeches in the Cockpit.

In the larger context of postcolonialism, it is not surprising that Franklin would be symbolically affiliated with Lucifer or with an enslaved African. That Franklin and Zanga did not obsequiously lick the chains that bound them to their masters revealed the uncultivated and uncultivatable savagery that was ascribed to them as a mark of character, indeed a mark of birth. Here we witness, in this Cockpit display, another version of the ethnizing function of nation-formation discourse, the discursively ideologized effects of power's consolidation over willing and unwilling subjects. We witnessed this earlier in Franklin's manuscript version of his "Observations concerning the Increase of Mankind" (1751), when he spoke as if Germans were darker complected and thus outsiders to the more privileged British people. The ethnizing function of nation-state language creates the situation where ethnized others are, perforce, turned lighter (as Wedderburn) or darker (as Franklin) according to the ease with which they will or will not become part of the system.

However much Franklin might have been—or perhaps precisely because he was—celebrated on the Continent, Franklin's part in this drama of British Empire was to bear the burden of well-documented, much-discussed public censure. Britain would discipline and debase the one whom France celebrated. For Franklin, however, the play did not see its last act when the witnesses of the Cockpit event cleared the hall. This play had a final act for Franklin: he would wear his suit of Manchester velvet to the French-American treaty, a treaty of amity and assistance in the war for independence against Great Britain, in 1778.

Love of Country

While Franklin's imperial theories were in general conversation with those of the leading British and French theorists, it is clear that his ideas were based upon different contingencies, contingencies that arose from his status as a British North American laborer, scientist, and statesman and his understanding of the lived experiences of peoples in the mainland American colonies. The men whose writings he knew well had little experience among laborers, especially laborers in the colonies. Franklin articulated an imperial theory involving a sympathetic concern for the lives of the laborers who would be the source of production of imperial wealth. It was precisely Franklin's condition as a Briton from North America that afforded him an opportunity to consider the failings of any structural policy that emanated outward from an English or European metropolitan center but did not account for the lives of the peoples who were living in colonial circumstances.

Franklin had worked tirelessly, if we take into account the sheer volume of letters he wrote about affairs of state, whether to Britons in England, Scotland, Ireland, or North America; the numbers of meetings he attended both public and private on state matters; the amount of travel he put in to speak with different people, many of whom put him off; the voluminous prose he crafted as letters to the press in an effort to persuade the British people about the affection and interests of British North Americans; and the amount of time it took then (compared to the present) just to take care of the day-to-day matters of living. These time- and labor-intensive efforts had brought him no satisfaction except in knowing that he had attempted to do his part. Franklin had attempted to secure a peaceful solution to the problems between Britain and North America. He had tried to explain that the greatest value to any nation was in its laws enacted by the consent of the governed and in its people, their affections for their leaders, their laws, their land, and their labor. He had tried, and he failed.

According to his friend Joseph Priestley, Franklin and he spent many hours talking about the likelihood of civil war in North America and then its outbreak and progress. Priestley wrote about these times, "I was seldom many days without seeing him, and being members of the same club, we constantly returned together." As the American difficulties deepened, he said, Franklin "urged so much the doctrine of forbearance, that for some time he was unpopular with the Americans on that account, as too much a friend to Great Britain. His advice to them was to bear every thing for the present, as they were sure in time to out-grow all their grievances; as it could not be in the power of the mother country to oppress them long."[78] Franklin understood that some considered him duplicitous, and it was troubling to him. According to Priestley, Franklin "dreaded the war, and often said that, if the difference should come to an open rupture, it would be a war of *ten years*, and he should not live to see the end of it." Priestley also reported that he and Franklin had spent Franklin's last night in London alone. They read the newspapers brought to their rooms. "The last day he spent in England," Priestley said, "we passed together, without any other company; and much of the time was employed in reading American newspapers, especially accounts of the reception which the 'Boston Port Bill,' met with in America." Franklin read about the supportive addresses sent to Boston from the surrounding towns. Priestley said that "as he read the addresses to the inhabitants of Boston, from the places in the neighbourhood, the tears trickled down his cheeks."[79] Priestley painted a picture of Franklin's profound sadness, a longing that events might have gone differently. His account suggests that Franklin took very personally the outcome in war that his long negotiations had yielded. But it also shows Franklin's overwhelming gratitude that the Americans were consolidating their political power and coming together to assist each other. It must have been with a feeling of defeat but also strong commitment to the future that Franklin packed up his trunks and on March 20, 1775, left London for Portsmouth, to set sail to America. He had tried but failed to change events. He left with a better sense of where his allegiance would find harbor—with Britons in America, whose interests and peoples he had long served, for love of country.

Eight

REBELLION TO TYRANTS, OBEDIENCE TO GOD

Almost as soon as he landed in Philadelphia on May 5, 1775, Franklin worked tirelessly to secure the revolution. Some historians have suggested that personal animus, especially after the treatment he received in Britain's Cockpit, drove him to seek Britain's defeat. The situation was much more complicated than mere personal politics. What gnawed at Franklin was the desecration of the early modern ideals he believed Great Britain to have scuttled in the face of the imperial politicking dominating the ministry and Parliament. In Franklin's view, Britain had betrayed its people by ignoring their natural rights, founded in their personal liberty, the foundation of any good government. Whether writing propaganda or political or legal briefs, Franklin consistently voiced positions related to the ideals of freedom (both collective and personal), equity, and justice that, from his youth, he considered ought to be the cornerstone of Britain's great imperial edifice. Franklin's idealism had driven him to continue imagining a possible future for North America in alliance with Great Britain. The memory of England's civil wars that haunted his family's stories was so strong that Franklin sought, in optimism, to believe a workable solution might be found to the political impasses he was witnessing. When political reality presented war as the Americans' only option to secure the rights they believed inalienable, Franklin wanted to be on the side that won that war.

Relative to others in the revolutionary generation, Franklin was advanced in age. He experienced uncertain health. Yet he became a key strategist consulted on many of the decisions made by Congress. Franklin's activities in the midst of the changes he witnessed and adapted to form the basis of his life's final chapters. Highlights of Franklin's activities during his last fifteen years include his propaganda writing; his work in Congress, especially serving the committee that drafted the Declaration of Independence; his crucial role in diplomatic relations between France and British North America during and after the American Revolution; his work to secure the Peace of Paris of 1783; and his final work, with other antislavery advocates, to emancipate Africans and African Americans from slavery. This chapter discusses Franklin's activities from the revolutionary era until the Peace of Paris of 1783. The next treats Franklin's last return across the Atlantic and the major efforts of his last years, including his work toward the abolition of slavery.

Declaring Independence

Upon Franklin's arrival in Philadelphia, the Pennsylvania Assembly chose him a delegate to the Second Continental Congress. Times were tense and the work exhausting, but Franklin was active all during the summer of 1775 on numerous committees established by Congress and the Pennsylvania Assembly. Congress tapped Franklin for a variety of committees: to establish a postal service (May 29, 1775; its report was adopted July 26, and Franklin was named postmaster general); to petition the king (June 3; Congress signed the Olive Branch petition July 8); to introduce saltpeter manufacture (June 10); to draft Washington's statement declaring the reasons for taking up arms (June 23; Congress approved its declaration July 6); to issue paper currency (June 23; Franklin drew up designs and emblems); to protect the American trade (July 12; its resolutions were adopted July 15); to supervise Indian affairs in the middle region of North America (July 13); to consider Lord North's conciliatory resolution (July 22; its rejection was adopted July 31); and to work on the domestic manufacture of lead (July 31). The Pennsylvania Assembly created a committee of safety on June 30 and appointed Franklin to serve on it; he was chosen its president on July 3. In August, Franklin was elected to the Philadelphia committee of inspection and observation. His committee assignments indicate the extent of Franklin's knowledge and influence, and they are reminiscent of Franklin's earliest efforts to secure Pennsylvania's fiscal and border positions and his more recent efforts to produce a workable plan for the confederation of North America.

Understanding from his experience in Britain that the united colonies' political status depended on the legal ramifications of their claims to political sovereignty, Franklin concerned himself with formulating a position on American sovereignty. For much of his life and especially as a Pennsylvania representative, he had worked on various strategies that defined sovereignty as embodied by representative government (e.g., Parliament) or Crown itself. He had been attempting to work out a strategy to enable Britain to have a dominion that was globally dispersed. As we have seen, in more recent years and given Britain's territorial expansion and takeover of lands and peoples in India in addition to its oppression over the native Irish, Franklin created a different line about sovereignty based on a legal justification arising from territorial transfers. As we have seen, Franklin had spent part of 1773 considering the political theory behind sovereignty. Such theory would be brought to bear as the confederation took shape. As he had written to William then, Franklin considered sovereignty in more fluid terms than typical in imperial courts. To Franklin, sovereignty could emerge from a legal, agreed-upon transfer of lands. He reasoned that if a people "purchase Territory in another Country," their sovereignty over the land would be open to be established anew. They might choose to submit "to the Sovereignty and Laws before established therein," or they might choose "Freedom from that Sovereignty" as this "may be purchas'd with the Land." He reasoned that "This latter [was] the Case[?] with respect[?] to Lands purchas'd of the Indian Nations in America." He concluded, "If a Freedom from the Sovereignty is purchased with the Land, the Purchasers may either introduce there the Sovereignty of their former Prince, if they chuse it as needing his Protection; or they may erect a new one of their own, if they are sufficient to their own Defence."[1]

Franklin brought this reasoning—considered radical at the time—to the tables of Congress in 1775. In drafting the Articles of Confederation for Congress in July, he asserted that Americans held political sovereignty over their lands. Because they had purchased Indian lands from the Native people, original sovereignty transferred to and thus resided in the American people, who had set up their own governments over their acquired lands. Franklin's drafts of the Articles (which he read aloud and left on the table for amendment) sought to empower the united colonies to decide upon and amend their own individual constitutions, to create new colonies and settle existing disputes, to make alliances and declare war and peace, and to send and receive ambassadors. Franklin's plan also included provisions for proportional representation in government and for preventing injustices to Native peoples. The plan, in other words, declared independence by its very high degree of American autonomy. If Britain surrendered to the Americans, then the united colonies "would return to their former Connection," but if Britain did not surrender, then all parts of British North America that entered into the Articles would remain permanently beyond the authority of Parliament or Crown. Franklin's draft of his Articles were not entered into congressional records. Indeed, several of Franklin's ideas—especially those related to sovereignty and autonomy, Indian affairs, and proportional representation—were tabled as too radical. Congress was unwilling to embrace such a bold approach. As the editors of Franklin's papers have explained, "Franklin was far ahead of most of the delegates in his readiness to separate from Britain."[2] Yet the plan that ultimately emerged from the committee in June 1776 included many of Franklin's provisions.[3]

Also noteworthy among Franklin's proposals during the summer of 1775 were his working blueprints for a free trade policy, formulated while he was a member of the committee to create resolutions on trade. Unrestrained trade had been his goal from his first days of entering political life and formulating political and economic theory, back in 1729 when he published his paper currency tract. The idea finally gained some traction in Britain and Europe when Franklin's friend, Adam Smith (1723–1790), published his *Wealth of Nations* (1776). Britain's Restraining Acts of March and April had been particularly galling to Franklin and Congress. In an effort to protect the colonies' trade, Franklin joined the committee on trade and wrote up proposals arguing for freedom of trade from all governmental constraints for at least two years. He proposed that trade take place without duties. Franklin essentially called for commercial independence, but he was unsuccessful in convincing the other delegates, who had grown accustomed to the compromises required by Britain's Navigation Acts. Franklin's ideas were shelved for a time, then acted upon nearly nine months later. Even then, his resolution was adopted on April 6, 1776, with a provision that individual colonies could impose their own import duties.[4]

Most of Franklin's work from the fall of 1775 through the spring 1776 led to an obvious conclusion in his appointment to the committee to draft the Declaration of Independence. On August 23, 1775, the king declared the colonies to be in rebellion. When Congress reconvened in September, Franklin was appointed on September 19 to a standing secret committee to supervise the importation of arms and ammunition and to another committee designed to evaluate the state of trade in North America. Franklin then was sent to Cambridge to confer with George Washington. He returned in early November to several committee reappointments, among these a standing committee of secret correspondence to handle foreign affairs. The assault on Quebec and the death on December 31 of General Richard Montgomery (1738–1775), an Irish-born soldier trained for the British army but singularly successful in the Canadian campaign of the Continental Army, proved a tragic loss for the Americans.

The need for assistance prompted informal meetings with representatives from France in the fall of 1775. As a member of the committee of secret correspondence, Franklin took part in December in meetings with the Chevalier de Bonvouloir (1749–1783), a secret agent of the French court who was connected to Charles Gravier (1717–1787), comte de Vergennes, the French minister for foreign affairs. Cloaked in darkness, three secret meetings with Bonvouloir took place in Carpenter's Hall. Vergennes had instructed Bonvouloir to assure the Americans that the French were interested in assisting them and to indicate clearly that the French had no designs on Canada. These secret meetings and assurances of assistance fueled the Americans' desire for independence. Franklin continued as often as possible to explore diplomatic channels open to him through older and newer British friends, among them David Hartley (1732–1813), Edmund Burke (1729–1797), and William Pitt (1708–1778), Lord Chatham, but he conceived that the British would continue to stall any progress toward peace. Indeed, the more he heard about how the American situation was being vetted in Britain, the more he grew convinced that reconciliation was as undesirable as it was politically impossible.

The winter months running from late 1775 to early 1776 found Franklin engaged in a number of different missions, among them a major propaganda effort. He wrote several essays and songs supporting the war. Much of the British Americans' propaganda about their revolution against the British Empire attested that the rebellion was part of their God's plan, as if by adhering to the logic of the rights of nature and of nations, Americans were merely seeking to fulfill a biblical prophecy that required redressing Britain's (in the figure of the king, his ministers, and Parliament) usurpation of those rights. Franklin contributed a good deal of the writing and cartoons to the wartime propaganda campaign, especially during 1775 and 1776.

Perhaps the most famous of Franklin's expressions, one later taken as a personal motto by Thomas Jefferson, was "Rebellion to Tyrants is Obedience to God." The assertion first appeared in Franklin's mock epitaph for John Bradshaw (1602–1659), president of the High Court that had tried Charles I and framed the sentence of his death. [See Figure 8.1.] The epitaph, published in the *Pennsylvania Evening Post*, December 14, 1775, underscored the presumed high-mindedness of the Americans' intentions, and it clearly affiliated the rebellion of Britons in North America with the patriotic liberalism—that is, the necessity of self-governance—of the English Civil War, conceived in propaganda at the time as a classic battle in behalf of the people's rights against the Crown's tyranny.

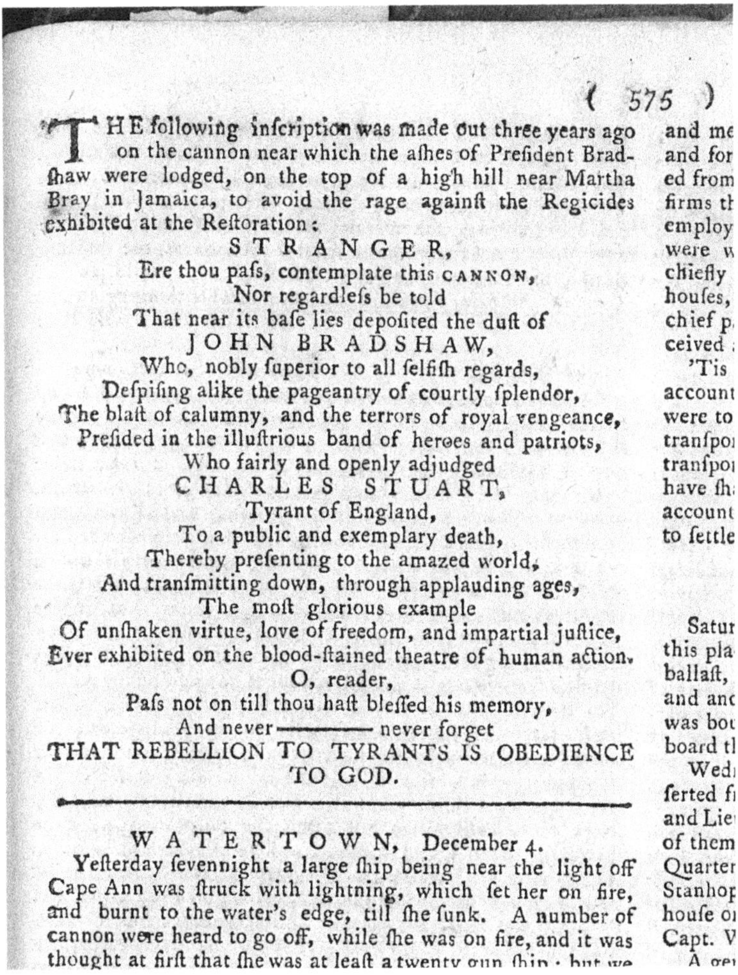

(575)

THE following inscription was made out three years ago on the cannon near which the ashes of President Bradshaw were lodged, on the top of a high hill near Martha Bray in Jamaica, to avoid the rage against the Regicides exhibited at the Restoration:

STRANGER,
Ere thou pass, contemplate this CANNON,
Nor regardless be told
That near its base lies deposited the dust of
JOHN BRADSHAW,
Who, nobly superior to all selfish regards,
Despising alike the pageantry of courtly splendor,
The blast of calumny, and the terrors of royal vengeance,
Presided in the illustrious band of heroes and patriots,
Who fairly and openly adjudged
CHARLES STUART,
Tyrant of England,
To a public and exemplary death,
Thereby presenting to the amazed world,
And transmitting down, through applauding ages,
The most glorious example
Of unshaken virtue, love of freedom, and impartial justice,
Ever exhibited on the blood-stained theatre of human action.
O, reader,
Pass not on till thou hast blessed his memory,
And never ———— never forget
THAT REBELLION TO TYRANTS IS OBEDIENCE TO GOD.

WATERTOWN, December 4.
Yesterday sevennight a large ship being near the light off Cape Ann was struck with lightning, which set her on fire, and burnt to the water's edge, till she sunk. A number of cannon were heard to go off, while she was on fire, and it was thought at first that she was at least a twenty gun ship; but we

Figure 8.1 The Bradshaw Epitaph. During his propaganda campaign for the American Revolution, Franklin devised an epitaph for Judge John Bradshaw, the judge presiding over the trial of Charles I. The epitaph was published in the *Pennsylvania Evening Post*, December 14, 1775. Courtesy, Library Company of Philadelphia.

By recalling Bradshaw's unprecedented efforts, propagandized as courageous and dangerous, Franklin was attaching the bravery of the Americans
to that of the commonwealthmen, especially President Judge Bradshaw,
who took on a post that several others had rejected because they did not
wish to preside over the trial of the king, which would likely result in a
death sentence. In Franklin's hands, Bradshaw was "nobly superior to all
selfish regards," "Despising alike the pagentry of courtly splendor, / The
blast of calumny, and the terrors of royal vengeance." Franklin's Bradshaw
"Presided in the illustrious band of heroes and patriots," who "fairly
and openly adjudged" the king, Charles Stuart (1600–1649), "Tyrant of
England," and sentenced him to "a public and exemplary death." Such
action "present[ed]," Franklin wrote, "to the amazed world" a "most glorious example" of bravery, "Of unshaken virtue, love of freedom, and
impartial justice, / Ever exhibited on the blood-stained theatre of human
action." At the conclusion of his mock epitaph, Franklin implored the
reader to remember the antecedents of their present action. "O reader,"
he wrote:

> Pass not on till thou hast blessed his memory
> And never—never forget
> THAT REBELLION TO TYRANTS IS OBEDIENCE TO
> GOD.[5]

By invoking the memory of the English Civil War, Franklin idealized the
new revolution, affiliating it with the earlier one fostered under the ban-
ners of justice, equity, and natural right. In effect, such an appeal called
into being for the current generation a heroic British past, one descending
from the Magna Carta, made visible during the English Civil War, and
brought forward to the present as evidence of freedom's descent, as a kind
of *translatio libertatis*, across time and space.

Franklin would use the expression about rebellion being obedience
to God again when he proposed (as a member of the committee) the
text and image for the Great Seal of the United States, sometime before
August 1776. For that, Franklin proposed the figure of "Moses standing
on the Shore, and extending his Hand over the Sea, thereby causing the
same to overwhelm Pharoah who is sitting in an open Chariot, a Crown
on his Head and a Sword in his hand." His original plan had suggested
that Moses be "in the Dress of a High Priest," but the committee canceled
his descriptive words.[6] He conceived that the image might be enhanced
by "Rays from a Pillar of Fire in the Clouds reaching to Moses, to express

that he acts by Command of the Deity," with the "Motto" being *Rebellion to Tyrants Is Obedience to God*.[7] Such images of fire coming from the sky were common in emblem books of the early modern era. The Great Seal committee did consult several emblem books, among them a book owned and used at the time by Franklin, *Joachimi Camerarii Symbolorun ac Emblematum Ethico-Politicorum Centuriae Quator*.[8] A similar image of Oliver Cromwell was used during the English Civil War, where Cromwell drew fire from a cloud in the heavens. This image had appeared in Clement Walker's *Anarchia Anglicana: or the History of Independency*, another title Franklin probably consulted.[9] Bradshaw's name is invoked in the description of that emblem, as well. In addition to calling up a heroic memory of John Bradshaw, Franklin used many other metaphors that were commonly being used for revolutionary purposes.

Franklin's propaganda underscores the extent to which he devoted himself to his congressional duties in 1776. He resigned from his Pennsylvania appointments and worked with redoubled effort to shore up the fiscal well-being of the revolutionary government. When Congress ordered new designs for fractional currency (dollars), Franklin created a device of thirteen intertwined circles and the "Fugio" design used on wartime paper currency and then later used on the first US coin, the Fugio cent. [See Figure 8.2.] Appointed in March a commissioner to Canada, Franklin made the arduous late winter journey, traveling to New York, Fort Constitution, Albany, Saratoga, and St. Johns. He left in late March, despite suffering from swelling in his legs, large boils, and dizziness. In early May, the Americans began their retreat from Quebec, and Franklin began the long return to Philadelphia. The trip from Canada, through ice, snow, and poor road conditions sometimes forced him to sleep on waterborne flatboats with little covering but a canvas awning. The seventy-year-old Franklin was ill and tired from travels that challenged much younger men.

Franklin faced emotional struggles that he did not talk much about. When Congress resolved to take William Franklin's governorship away from him and the New Jersey militia took action to implement the decision, Franklin did not intercede for his son. Franklin threw himself into his work. In June 1776, the same month when William Franklin was sent to prison in Connecticut, Benjamin Franklin was appointed by Congress to a committee to draft the Declaration of Independence. In recent years, scholars have been critical of Franklin for abandoning his son at this time. Franklin had indeed relied on William during his years in London, and the two had shared plans to develop their own land grants in the

Figure 8.2 Franklin's Fugio and Interlocked Circles on Continental Currency. Franklin's design of the sun shining down on a sundial (Fugio, meaning "I flee" or "I fly"—indicating that time flies), with the motto, "MIND YOUR BUSINESS," was used first on continental paper currency in a series of issues during 1776. The Fugio design appeared on one side of the currency, with Franklin's thirteen interlocking circles on the other side. The Fugio cent was later authorized by Congress in 1787 as the first official copper penny of the new government. Private collection.

Illinois territory. They had chosen different political paths, given their different upbringings. William, trained in the Inns of Court, had distinct Tory leanings. His youth had not been spent listening to stories of England's civil wars. Too, family relations then, as now, are complicated. The Franklin family's relationships were complicated by Franklin's long absences from home, first representing Pennsylvania and then representing the united colonies.[10] Franklin did fulfill more family obligations than some often credit. It was Benjamin Franklin—not William—who oversaw the boyhood of William Temple Franklin (William's illegitimate son). He brought him over from London with him when he returned to Philadelphia in May 1775. William Temple Franklin would meet his father William for the first time that June as a growing young man whose life events had been overseen by his grandfather, not by his own father. The Franklin family's relations were further complicated by a difference of political opinion as to the best course of action in the face of aggressive and punitive government measures imposed on an unwilling (and nonconsenting) populace. To attempt to measure the relationship in such a way that faults Benjamin Franklin seems to favor Americans' contemporary standards of family values, values different from those governing eighteenth-century life.

The subjects of political independence, internal confederation, trade and monetary policy, munitions, and foreign alliances preoccupied Congress and Franklin's committee work after his return from Canada. Richard Henry Lee (1732–1794), the Virginia representative, offered the second Congress a set of resolutions in behalf of independence. Franklin was there for the vote on July 2 in favor of the motion by Lee, and he was elected on June 11 to the five-member committee to draft the Declaration. But Franklin was struggling to recover from poor health resulting from his difficult return from Canada. His gout made walking painful and hazardous. Sally Franklin's family was overflowing in his home in Philadelphia, so he took up residence in Benfield, in the stone farmhouse of his good friend (who would become his executor), clockmaker Edward Duffield (1720–1802). Franklin received Jefferson's draft of the Declaration sometime after its completion on June 18 and read it sometime between June 21 and 28. His suggestions were few, with the most interesting change the introduction of the phrase "under absolute Despotism" to supply the place of "to arbitrary power" in describing the treatment the Americans had received. After making a number of now-famous excisions from the Declaration, Congress adopted it on July 4.[11]

The rest of the summer's events pressed Franklin into action. He continued to be called upon by Pennsylvania for various posts, having been elected a delegate to the Pennsylvania State Convention on July 8, then chosen its president on July 16. He became Pennsylvania's congressional delegate on July 20. The work of the Assembly had often gone on without Franklin's presence, because he was busy fulfilling obligations in Congress or else remained at home, too uncomfortable to get out. Factionalism in the Assembly proved difficult for him, because some of his oldest friends and political allies—Joseph Galloway (1731–1803), particularly—favored conciliation and loyalty to Britain. By the fall, when the Assembly would normally have reconvened, it was dissolved in behalf of a provisional revolutionary government.

Franklin spent his summer working on congressional matters. He had learned from David Barclay (1729–1809), an English Quaker merchant friend, that Lord Richard Howe (1726–1799), viscount and commissioner representing the British Crown, was setting out from London and aimed to meet with him. Howe was, Barclay reported, well disposed toward the Americans. In fact, upon his arrival, Howe sent circular letters to all colonial governors promising pardons if they would declare allegiance to Britain. While sitting in Congress, Franklin received a personal message from Howe. Franklin opened the letter there in Congress, read it, and asked for it to be read aloud. He then sought congressional permission to answer Howe's letter. Franklin's famous reply, July 20, 1776, contains one of his most affective and poignant metaphors—the British Empire as a "China Vase"—employed in his last years.

Franklin's exchange with Howe in July 1776 suggests the complexities of his political life at this juncture. In England, Franklin had attempted, across the decades of the 1750s, 1760s, and the early 1770s, to bring the British Crown, ministry, Parliament, and people to acknowledge the constrained situation of Britons in North America regarding trade, manufacture, representation, settlement, and culture. One of Franklin's last London efforts, a private meeting where he again offered his plan for a workable solution to the imperial crisis, had been with Howe, under the now-famous ruse of a game of chess with Howe's sister. Recollecting that meeting two years later, in his public letter to Howe, Franklin wrote, "Long did I endeavour with unfeigned and unwearied Zeal, to preserve from breaking, that fine and noble China Vase the British Empire: for I knew that being once broken, the separate Parts could not retain even their Share of the Strength or Value that existed in the Whole, and that a perfect Re-Union of those Parts could scarce even be hoped for."[12] The expression equating the empire with a China vase was well chosen and richly evocative. At its most basic level, the image emphasized both the beauty and fragility of any imperial system, especially one that would not give credence to the situation of Britons living apart from England in British colonial holdings. But also, by employing an image of the British Empire as a vase from China,[13] Franklin metaphorically revealed his long-standing interest in finding a structural system to further the British Empire around the globe. The China vase image symbolized a recognition that the British Empire and thus its trade possibilities faced both East (toward Asia) and West (toward North and South America and the so-called West Indies). If a useful system benefiting the colonies as well as the homeland were in place, Britons around the globe might gain fruitful sustenance and prosper. Taken in this way, the image implicated the functional relationship between trade and British global expansion. If the British Empire were to be sustained by trade, the vase needed to be kept intact, for the several parts could not be self-sustaining. The strength of the system resided, as Franklin was articulating, in its fragile and as yet unfractured whole.

Because Franklin had long supported developing a working interconnected trading relationship between British North America and Britain, some of the American colonists involved in independence movements doubted his allegiances and whether he truly wished to secure independence from Britain. His letter to Howe, written while his son was incarcerated in Connecticut, importantly marked, especially for colonial leaders, Franklin's clear allegiance to the cause of Britons in North America rather than to the Crown and the British Empire. The letter unambiguously performed Franklin's disentanglement from Britain. His letter became a very public performance before Congress: Howe's original overture to Franklin had been read to Congress, and Franklin's response, this letter, was authorized by Congress and, when written, read before Congress, prior to being conveyed to Howe. If anyone in Congress doubted Franklin's allegiances, the performance may have assisted in alleviating those doubts. Franklin later conceived it appropriate to draft a private letter to Howe, reiterating his sense that "To propose now to the Colonies a Submission to the Crown of Great Britain, would be fruitless. The Time is past."[14] He received criticism for this letter in late August and so wrote once more to Howe, September 8, remarking that he "found that my Corresponding with your Lordship was dislik'd by some Members of Congress."[15]

In the late summer, Congress debated concerns over state political formation and individual rights. Franklin took part in these debates, arguing consistently for a more open and radical agenda than most in Congress could accept. For instance, he argued—unsuccessfully—for proportional rather than equal representation in Congress during the debates over the Articles of Confederation.[16] Sometime prior to August 15, Franklin drafted a revision of Pennsylvania's Declaration of Rights that included a provision that states could discourage large concentrations of property, because "an enormous Proportion of Property vested in a few Individuals is dangerous to the Rights, and destructive of the Common Happiness, of Mankind." The Declaration also called for freedom of religious worship and the accountability of government to the people. Here Franklin argued that "all Power being originally inherent in, and consequently derived from, the People, therefore all Officers of Government, whether Legislative or Executive, are their Trustees and Servants, and at all Times accountable to them."[17] Franklin was attempting to draw up articles related to positions he had been arguing at least since he created the Albany Plan of Union. These positions essentially laid the groundwork for the failure of any conciliatory measures between Great Britain and the united colonies, for they insisted upon goals of representation and independence of governance that the Crown would reject.

An official rejection came, in fact, in September, when Franklin formed part of a congressional commission to meet with Howe to discuss the situation. With John Adams (1735–1826) and Edward Rutledge (1749–1800), Franklin met with Howe on Staten Island on September 11. To Howe's question, "Is there no way of treading back this Step of Independency, and opening the door to full discussion?" Franklin replied that "America could not return again to the Domination of Great Britain." Attentive to the legal ramifications of their meeting, John Adams confirmed Franklin's statement by insisting that he appeared at the meeting as an individual and member of an American commission but not "in any Character . . . of a British Subject." Adams reminded Howe that "the Resolution of the Congress to declare Independency was not taken up upon their own Authority" but by "*all* the Colonies." He insisted, as did Rutledge, that he would "not depart from the Idea of Independency." When Howe balked at continuing the meeting, because he had not been authorized "to treat with the Colonies as States independent of the Crown of Great Britain,"

Franklin cut the meeting off, saying that "unconditional Submission" would not be accepted by their constituents."[18] When Franklin offered to return to Congress so that the committee could gain farther instruction and then submit some papers to Howe, for presentation to the Crown, Howe indicated that he would submit the congressional papers but thought little would come of such an effort. This meeting—the only meeting that would take place between official representatives of Congress and of the British Crown prior to the final peace negotiations of 1783—had reached a stalemate. The sticking points—the sovereign authority of the colonies for self-determination and independence—would remain with Franklin through the duration of his diplomatic stay in France and especially through the difficult treaty meetings from 1781 to 1783.

The Mission to France

When he was selected by Congress for the mission to France, Franklin was ready with ideas about what war and peace should entail. During the fall of 1776, he had drafted his "Sketch of Propositions for a Peace," which would require that Britain cede Canada to the United States. As his mission became better known to him, Franklin's plans for conducting war and securing peace involved three key issues: the original sovereignty of the British North Americans, reparations for Americans who suffered from the British takeover of their lands and estates, and the freeing of prisoners of war, particularly those taken at sea. Franklin left Philadelphia for France, sailing out on October 27, 1776, taking with him his grandsons William Temple Franklin and Benjamin Franklin Bache (the eldest of Sarah's children) with him. He landed at Auray December 3 and proceeded immediately to Paris. On December 28, he met secretly with Vergennes, with whom he would form a valuable friendship. Vergennes held a long-standing animosity for Britain as a result of Britain's dominance during the war for empire in North America. Franklin learned this and used it to the advantage of the Americans. On January 5, 1777, the American commissioners formally requested French aid in its war against Britain. In a matter of days, Louis XVI approved a favorable response to the commissioners, and on January 13, they received verbal promise of two million livres.

Because of the difficulty of conducting a diplomatic mission in the city of Paris, where people gawked at him and printers might not retain confidentiality with state papers, Franklin decided to establish quarters in a suburb. He moved to Passy and settled in at l'Hôtel de Valentinois, the lovely estate along the Seine and in sight of Paris owned by a well-to-do merchant, Jacques-Donatien Le Ray de Chaumont (1726–1803).[19] The setting evidently had great charm for Franklin, who was housed in a pavilion of the house that had garden walkways along a high bluff. The terraced gardens linked the pavilion to the Seine, and along the wooded paths were breaks in the trees, where visitors could see Paris in the distance. Franklin arrived with his group sometime between February 26 and February 28, 1777. By March 2, according to the editors of Franklin's papers, the master of the household "began to lay in large supplies of food: meat, vegetables, fruit, wine, bread 'pour les maitres' and 'pour les gens.' A great deal of equipment was also required, not only such obvious items as candles and shoebrushes and wax, but also a coffee mill, a 'Diable' for roasting the coffee, a sugargrater, [and] a feather duster for Franklin's desk."[20] Franklin was arranging his household for a long stay.

Franklin set about finding type for a press, which he set up to print congressional documents and other papers both public and private. During the summer of 1777, he approached the famous typefounding family, the Fourniers, about getting type for his small printing press.[21] On August 25, 1777, Franklin ordered fifty pounds of type. The quantity of type originally ordered indicates he was planning to print only small notes, forms, and documents. Special type began arriving as early as September. But with additional purchases of type in 1778 and 1779, Franklin's operation turned into a much larger endeavor. He occasionally employed printers and assistants from 1779 through 1783 to work on larger documents, pamphlets, and books. (He probably printed small pieces, e.g., his bagatelles, by himself.) By the time his diplomatic mission concluded Franklin had a very well-appointed press, with standard English and French fonts, and with special fonts the Fourniers had made explicitly for his Passy press.[22]

"Eripuit coelo fulmen sceptrumque tyrannis": Franklin Chic

Franklin's reputation preceded—by decades—his arrival in France to negotiate financial assistance for the newly independent colonies. His first visit to France with Sir John Pringle (1707–1782) in 1767 had brought him in touch with many of the scientists and economists who admired his electrical experiments, his economic theories regarding land and labor, and his impe-rial writings. During that visit, he was presented to King Louis XV. His sec-ond visit, a trip two years later also taken with Pringle, shored up some of his existing friendships and extended them to additional circles. His friendships with several renowned Frenchmen, among them the writers and economists Pierre Samuel du Pont de Nemours (1739–1817) and Anne-Robert-Jacques Turgot (1727–1781), brought him fame among the Physiocrats, the leading philosophers of economic liberalism in France, and others of the intelligent-sia hovering around court circles. Turgot's famous Latin phrase describing Franklin, "Eripuit coelo fulmen sceptrumque tyrannis" ("He snatched the lightning from the skies, the scepter from tyrants") was referenced in a letter to du Pont de Nemours on June 5, 1776, well before Franklin even appeared in France on his mission. "On the subject of America," Turgot wrote to du Pont, "here are some Latin and French inscriptions for the portrait of Franklin." Turgot adapted lines earlier used in France to describe Franklin's electri-cal experiments (in 1752). The lines struck a chord for French artists and intellectuals. It appeared on a terra cotta medallion of Franklin created in 1777 by Jean-Baptiste Nini (1717–1786). Jean-Antoine Houdon (1741–1828) used it with his famous bust of Franklin in 1778. The epigram became so famous that it was frequently used for various French portraits and other media representations of Franklin through the end of his life.[23] Franklin was celebrated by the intelligentsia, not the aristocracy associated with the French court. And of course he was sought after by the French people. He was accepted at court and indeed admired there, but it is worth noting that eventually King Louis XVI grew so tired of Franklin's popularity that he ordered a line of Sèvres porcelain chamber pots made with an embossed cameo of Franklin's bust on the inside of the pot.

Once he set up at Passy, Franklin was barraged with attention from all quarters—men and women seeking an audience with him merely so they could say they had met him; members of academies and societies seeking his advice on matters of science, politics, and philosophy; and members of the aristocracy who wanted to get to know him for their own pur-poses at court. Franklin was so busy with the attentions of French people high and low that John Adams would eventually complain that around Franklin's mission there was always "a Scene of continual discipation," with "Phylosophers, Accademicians and Economists" pressing Franklin for conversation and with more "humble friends in the Litterary way" hanging around him so that they could translate his writings into French. Perhaps what bothered Adams most were the "Women and children" who showed up, pestering for an audience with the "great" man.[24]

Franklin admired the language and the social play of the French people, and he was especially fond of the philosophes and other liberals to whom he was introduced by Vergennes. Vergenne's connections in France were not among the highest aristocracy but were of the intelligentsia, philosophers such as Claude-Adrien Helvétius (1715–1771), François-Marie Arouet (1694–1778), known as Voltaire, and others. Franklin thus came to know the liberal French aristocracy, not the court circles surrounding Louis XVI. Franklin understood well the importance of wit in French culture, and as a verbal master, he used witticisms and bon mots to gain a hearing on American affairs, whether he were in social company or working with the commissioners and Vergennes to win French aid. He was aware of the war-mongering efforts of the British ambassador to France, David Murray (1727–1796), second Earl of Mansfield, named Viscount Stormont in 1748. Stormont annoyed Franklin by talking in France about British victories and sending news of North America back to Britain. Stormont taunted the American commissioners with British military successes. Aware that reports of the Americans' losses could impact their diplomatic mission to France, Franklin combated Stormont's reports by making fun of his propaganda. One tale that circulated at the time was about a witticism Franklin created, using Stormont's name. When asked in August, 1777, if it were true that six battalions in Washington's army had surrendered to the British, Franklin reportedly answered, "Non, Monsieur, ce n'est pas vérité; est seulement un Stormont" ("No, sir, it is not a truth; it's only a Stormont"). The expression made Stormont's name proverbial for a lie or liar among the Paris wits.[25] Similarly, Franklin found a way to downplay the significance of the taking of Philadelphia by Sir William Howe (1729–1814) by commenting, "It was not he who had taken Philadelphia, but instead, Philadelphia had taken him."[26]

Franklin's years in France have prompted many books about his social activities and his diplomacy, so many that it is unnecessary to rehearse all the events of this momentous time.[27] Rather than tracing Franklin's lively social life—the dinners with intellectuals (women and men) and men of influence, the verbal flirtations with women, intimate chess games and tea parties, musical entertainments, and so forth—we will consider what Franklin conceived to be the central political concerns of his mission: to achieve recognition of American sovereignty, to secure reparations for Americans who had suffered at the hands of the British military and its Indian allies, and to create a reasonable logic to the transfer of Americans taken prisoner at sea by the British navy. As we will see, other issues preoccupied Franklin as well, but these are the dominant concerns.

Minister Plenipotentiary

When news of the British defeat at Saratoga in October arrived in France on December 4, 1777, the commissioners worked assiduously to formalize a French alliance. By importuning the court and court circles, the commissioners gained the attention of decision-makers in France. They were being spied on by both Britain and France. Franklin considered it best to overlook the spying and play the situation to the Americans' advantage. The French, aware that Franklin was also talking with British spies behind closed doors, became eager for a treaty. The commissioners were happy to oblige. They reported to the American Congress in a letter dated January 28, 1778, that a grant of six million livres had been made to America for the year. Petitioning for a formal authorization of the assistance, the commissioners were able to sign treaties of alliance for mutual defense and of amity and commerce on February 6. Marking his own sense of personal triumph, Franklin wore to the signing ceremony the same suit of figured brown Manchester velvet that he had worn during Wedderburn's denunciation of him in the Cockpit of the Privy Council just over four years earlier.[28] The sense of triumph felt by commissioners Franklin and Silas Deane (1737–1789) is evident in their letter to Congress of February 8. Their Treaty of Alliance, they wrote, had as its "great Aim" these goals: to "establish the Liberty, Sovereignty, and Independency absolute and unlimited of the United States as well in Matters of Government as Commerce." The first of Franklin's aims—to find a way to underscore American sovereignty—was acknowledged by France. Writing home to the American representatives, the commissioners remarked that the king and court of France behaved with generosity and understood the conception of mutual sovereignty (i.e., "the most perfect Equality and Reciprocity") in the making of these treaties. The commissioners wrote "with Pleasure" that they "found throughout this Business the greatest Cordiality in this Court." Clarifying that throughout the proceedings they were treated as equals, not subordinates, the commissioners reported that "no Advantage has been taken or attempted to be taken of our present Difficulties, to obtain hard Terms from us." In fact, as a mark of "the King's Magnanimity and Goodness," they said, he proposed no terms but those "we might . . . readily have agreed to in a State of full Prosperity and established Power." They importantly added, "The Principle laid down as the Basis of the Treaty" was "declared in the Preamble [as] 'the most perfect Equality and Reciprocity'" between the nations. Further, they said, "the Privileges in Trade &c. are mutual[,] and none are given to France, but what we are at Liberty to grant to any other Nation."[29] The American commissioners were formally presented to Louis XVI, March 20, 1778.

In late April, Franklin was joined by John Adams, who had been appointed a fellow commissioner to France to replace Silas Deane. John Adams's legal training and his knowledge of the events leading to the American Revolution were both factors that influenced his appointment as commissioner. Yet to the French people and those working with the American commissioners, John Adams and even John Jay (1745–1829) seemed prickly and insistent, telling the French what was wrong with their lax conduct and insisting upon certain formalities with which American representatives should be treated. Jay and Adams did not understand French culture. For instance, they wanted to tell French leaders, as if to persuade France to act, that its commerce would benefit from France's association with America. By contrast, Franklin knew not to mention commercial dealings with members of the aristocracy. Adams was quite vocal in his pique at the French. Eventually, because of the various difficulties Adams was presenting to the mission, Congress elected Franklin to be sole minister plenipotentiary to France in September.[30] At the time of his election to plenipotentiary powers, Franklin was already witnessing the success of his efforts: the well-timed treaties brought additional force from France, which declared war on Britain in June 1778. When Spain also declared war on Britain (June 21, 1779), Franklin was able to obtain an additional three million livres from France for assistance in North America.

Still, the American commissioners were having difficulty with the invoices presented to them, and Franklin was immensely upset about the absence of funding for crucial negotiations. In 1780, he expressed mortification at the idea that the Americans were forced to move from European court to European court seeking financial assistance to support the war and the diplomatic mission. To John Jay, then having little success in Madrid, he remarked on October 2 that "the Storm of Bills which I found coming upon us both, has terrified and vexed me to such a Degree that I have been deprived of Sleep, and so much indisposed by continual Anxiety as to be render'd almost incapable of Writing."[31] He wrote to John Adams (who had been sent to the Netherlands), "I have long been humiliated with the Idea of our running about from Court to Court begging for Money and Friendship, which are the more withheld the more eagerly they are solicited, and would perhaps have been offer'd if they had not been asked. The supposed Necessity is our only Excuse." He felt acutely the position he was placed in regarding the French mission, and he was concerned about having to continue to go to Vergennes for additional aid. Even so, as the letter to Adams revealed, he attempted to keep his wit and good humor in the matter, adapting a homespun story used in both *Poor Richard* and "Father Abraham's Speech": "The Proverb says *God helps them that helps themselves*, and the World too in this Sense is very Godly."[32]

To John Jay, Franklin wrote that he hoped that the Spanish "Court will be wiser than to take Advantage of our Distress and insist on our making Sacrifices by an Agreement." One of the sacrifices to which Franklin would never acquiesce—a clear indication of his belief in North America's bounty—was American rights to the Mississippi River: "I would rather agree with them to buy at a great Price the whole of their Right on the Missisipi than sell a Drop of its Waters.—A Neighbour might as well ask me to sell my Street Door," he wrote.[33] The Spanish mission was in trouble, though, and America was in great debt. Early in 1781, Franklin found himself again appealing to Vergennes for French aid. In February, he wrote to Vergennes that America could "rely on France alone." Again, June 4 and 10, Franklin was forced to ask Vergennes for money to pay congressional bills as well as those of John Adams (still in the Netherlands) and John Jay (in Spain). When General Charles Cornwallis (1738–1805) finally surrendered to Washington at Yorktown, Virginia, October 19, 1781, the need for funding of the American enterprise was still there, but using that money to continue the war was less an issue than determining the cost of peace.

Negotiating the Treaty of Paris

Initial peace negotiations began shortly after the defeat of Cornwallis at Yorktown. At the time the peace commission was being discussed in Congress, Vergennes requested of Congress that the Americans coordinate diplomacy with France and its allies at the same time America negotiated with Britain. This would allow France to become an ally in the bargaining with Britain and thus enable France to gain ascendancy above British requests. It was a fair request, given the amount of aid the French gave to the Americans. The commissioners were instructed by Congress to work with France and not make a separate peace with Britain. Yet, perhaps at Franklin's instigation, the commissioners ended up delaying with Vergennes and negotiating a treaty with Britain first.

The British situation was complicated for Franklin, who had particular points to negotiate with Britain. He did not wish to have demands by the French interfere with his own bargaining. In Britain, the Rockingham

government had two ministers who tended to contest each other's authority: Foreign Secretary Charles James Fox (1749–1806) and Colonial
Secretary William Petty (1737–1805), first Marquess of Lansdowne and
the second Earl of Shelburne, known as Lord Shelburne. Both the foreign
secretary and the colonial secretary sent envoys to Paris. While pretending to entertain both envoys, Franklin privately sought a commission
for Shelburne's envoy, Richard Oswald (1705–1784), a London merchant
and former slave trader for Henry Laurens (1724–1792). Franklin liked
Shelburne and his envoy better, and he would establish articles of peace
with Oswald alone.

Franklin held informal peace negotiations with the British emissar-
ies from March through June 1782. Working with Oswald, he indicated
on April 18, 1782, that Britain should cede Canada to the United States.
On July 10, he established for Oswald the "necessary" terms for peace
with the Americans—this without previously communicating his points
to Vergennes as instructed and required by Congress. Franklin concurred with Jay's view, which was an established legal opinion much like
Franklin's theoretical one from 1773, that the Americans had sovereignty
and that Britain must express, prior to formal negotiations, a recognition
of American sovereignty and independence. Such recognition would, they
insisted, be the precondition for proceeding with formal negotiation. By
September 21, Oswald had a new commission from Britain that effectively
recognized the independence of the United States. The stage was set for
formal negotiations. Adams arrived in Paris on October 26, and joined
the commissioners' negotiations. Oswald and the American commissioners signed preliminary articles of a peace agreement with Britain on
November 30, 1782. Franklin went to talk with Vergennes only after the
treaty articles with Britain were in letter packets already aboard ships sailing to North America and Congress. Vergennes was dumbfounded when
Franklin told him the preliminary treaty agreement with Britain had been
established. Franklin admitted the impropriety, expressed his gratitude
to France, and asked for another loan. He must have been very persuasive: Vergennes assured him of six million livres.

Franklin's Savage Eloquence

During the complicated negotiation process of 1782, Franklin turned his
hand to satire. He wrote a hoax newssheet that he circulated to newspapers in the Netherlands, Spain, and England. The satire reveals Franklin's

preoccupation with questions of sovereignty, reparations for Americans whose lives and properties had suffered at the hands of the British military and its Native allies, and fair treatment for American prisoners of war taken at sea. Although he was over seventy-five years old, Franklin's wit was intact, as we will see from his artful means of rendering for a wide and public audience—even as the negotiations were going forward in the spring of 1782—the Americans' contentions aired behind closed doors. Sometime between April 19 and 22, Franklin printed at his press at Passy a purported supplement to the *Boston Independent Chronicle*. Franklin's enduring fascination with print technology is evident in the supplement. Numbering his paper "No. 705," Franklin created a broadsheet of "news" mimicking in both size and approach the content of Boston's actual *Independent Chronicle and Universal Advertiser*. He used the number (i.e., 705) of the *Independent Chronicle*'s issue for March, as if this were an actual addendum to that printing, which had probably just reached Europe.[34] [See Figure 8.3.]

The supplement's two articles reflect Franklin's recognition of the complicated wartime situation for Americans both at home and at sea. The treatment that Britons in North America were receiving at the hands of Native peoples, particularly the Iroquois, whose skirmishes against the colonists had been backed by Great Britain, formed the target of the satire on the front of the fake newssheet. The brutal jailing of Americans taken (as acts of piracy) prisoners at sea was the target of satire on the fake newssheet's back side. That Franklin hurriedly prepared the supplement in the days immediately following a series of conversations with Richard Oswald, just after Oswald began a return journey to England to report on Franklin's most recent negotiation points,[35] suggests Franklin wanted to speak to the British people directly regarding the Americans' losses and what it would take for a lasting peace to emerge.

Franklin was deeply troubled by Britain's conduct of the war on North America. Britain was sending Germans over to the colonies to fight what he considered the king's battles.[36] Americans feared that Britain was also attempting to incite local Germans and enslaved Africans to overthrow the local colonial governments.[37] Franklin was also deeply troubled by Britain's alliances with, arming, and training of Iroquoian peoples explicitly to attack colonial settlers and American militia indiscriminately. The arming of Native peoples was a strategy Britain had used with success during the Seven Years War against the French in the 1740s to 1750s. Britain's alliance with the Iroquois in this present war against the Americans irritated Franklin immensely. He used the scalping letter in the supplement to

Numb. 705.

SUPPLEMENT

TO THE BOSTON

INDEPENDENT CHRONICLE.

BOSTON, March 12.

Extract of a Letter from Capt. Gerrish, of the New-England Militia, dated Albany, March 7.

THE Peltry taken in the Expedition [*See the Account of the Expedition to Oswegatchie on the River St. Laurence, in our Paper of the 1st Instant.*] will as you see amount to a good deal of Money. The Possession of this Booty at first gave us Pleasure; but we were struck with Horror to find among the Packages, 8 large ones containing SCALPS of our unhappy Country-folks, taken in the three last Years by the Senneka Indians from the Inhabitants of the Frontiers of New-York, New-Jersey, Pennsylvania, and Virginia, and sent by them as a Present to Col. Haldimand, Governor of Canada, in order to be by him transmitted to England. They were accompanied by the following curious Letter to that Gentleman.

May it please your Excellency, Teoga, Jan. 3d, 1782.

" At the Request of the Senneka Chiefs I send herewith to your Excellency, under the Care of James Boyd, eight Packs of Scalps, cured, dried, hooped and painted, with all the Indian triumphal Marks, of which the following is Invoice and Explanation.

No. 1. Containing 43 Scalps of Congress Soldiers killed in different Skirmishes; these are stretched on black Hoops, 4 Inches diameter; the inside of the Skin painted red, with a small black Spot to note their being killed with Bullets. Also 62 of Farmers, killed in their Houses; the Hoops red; the Skin painted brown, and marked with a Hoe; a black Circle all round, to denote their being surprised in the Night; and a black Hatchet in the Middle, signifying their being killed with that Weapon.

No. 2. Containing 98 of Farmers killed in their Houses; Hoops red; Figure of a Hoe, to mark their Profession; a great white Circle and Sun, to shew they were surprised in the Day-time; a little red Foot, to shew they stood upon their Defence, and died fighting for their Lives and Families.

No. 3. Containing 97 of Farmers; Hoops green, to shew they were killed in their Fields; a large white Circle with a little round Mark on it for the Sun, to shew that it was in the Day-time; black Bullet-mark on some, Hatchet on others.

No. 4. Containing 102 of Farmers, mixed of the several Marks above; only 18 marked with a little yellow Flame, to denote their being of Prisoners burnt alive, after being scalped, their Nails pulled out by the Roots, and other Torments; one of these latter supposed to be of a rebel Clergyman, his Band being fixed to the Hoop of his Scalp. Most of the Farmers appear by the Hair to have been young or middle-aged Men; there being but 67 very grey Heads among them all; which makes the Service more essential.

No. 5. Containing 88 Scalps of Women; Hair long, braided in the Indian Fashion, to shew they were Mothers; Hoops blue; Skin yellow Ground, with little red Tadpoles to represent, by way of Triumph, the Tears of Grief occasioned to their Relations; a black scalping Knife or Hatchet at the Bottom, to mark their being killed with those Instruments. 17 others, Hair very grey; black Hoops; plain brown Colour; no Mark but the short Club or Casseteto, to shew they were knocked down dead, or had their Brains beat out.

No. 6. Containing 193 Boys' Scalps, of various Ages; small green Hoops; whitish Ground on the Skin, with red Tears in the Middle, and black Bullet-marks, Knife, Hatchet, or Club, as their Deaths happened.

No. 7. 211 Girls' Scalps, big and little; small yellow Hoops; white Ground; Tears; Hatchet, Club, scalping Knife, &c.

No. 8. This Package is a Mixture of all the Varieties above-mention'd, to the Number of 122; with a Box of Birch Bark, containing 29 little Infants' Scalps of various Sizes; small white Hoops; white Ground; no Tears; and only a little black Knife in the Middle, to shew they were ript out of their Mothers' Bellies.

With these Packs, the Chiefs send to your Excellency the following Speech, delivered by Conejogatchie in Council, interpreted by the elder Moore, the Trader, and taken down by me in Writing.

Father,

We send you herewith many Scalps, that you may see we are not idle Friends. *A blue Belt.*

Father,

We wish you to send these Scalps over the Water to the great King, that he may regard them and be refreshed; and that he may see our faithfulness in destroying his Enemies, and be convinced that his Presents have not been made to ungrateful People.

A blue and white Belt with red Tassels.

Father,

Attend to what I am now going to say: it is a Matter of much Weight. The great King's Enemies are many, and they grow fast in Number. They were formerly like young Panthers: they could nei-

ther bite nor scratch: we could play with them safely; we feared nothing they could do to us. But now their Bodies are become big as the Elk, and strong as the Buffalo: they have also got great and sharp Claws. They have driven us out of our Country for taking Part in your Quarrel. We expect the great King will give us another Country, that our Children may live after us, and be his Friends and Children, as we are. Say this for us to the great King. To enforce it we give this Belt.

A great white Belt with blue Tassels.

Father,

We have only to say farther that your Traders exact more than ever for their Goods; and our Hunting is lessened by the War, so that we have fewer Skins to give for them. This ruins us. Think of some Remedy. We are poor: and you have Plenty of every Thing. We know you will send us Powder and Guns, and Knives and Hatchets: but we also want Shirts and Blankets.

A little white Belt.

I do not doubt but that your Excellency will think it proper to give some farther Encouragement to those honest People. The high Prices they complain of, are the necessary Effect of the War. Whatever Presents may be sent for them through my Hands, shall be distributed with Prudence and Fidelity. I have the Honour of being

Your Excellency's most obedient
And most humble Servant,
JAMES CRAUFURD."

It was at first proposed to bury these Scalps: but Lieutenant Fitzgerald, who you know has got Leave of Absence to go for Ireland on his private Affairs, said he thought it better they should proceed to their Destination: and if they were given to him, he would undertake to carry them to England, and hang them all up in some dark Night on the Trees in St. James's Park, where they could be seen from the King and Queen's Palaces in the Morning: for that the Sight of them might perhaps strike Muley Ishmael (as he called him) with some Compunction of Conscience. They were accordingly delivered to Fitz, and he has brought them safe hither. To-morrow they go with his Baggage in a Waggon for Boston, and will probably be there in a few Days after this Letter.

I am, &c.
SAMUEL GERRISH.

BOSTON, March 20.

Monday last arrived here Lieutenant Fitzgerald abovementioned, and Yesterday the Waggon with the Scalps. Thousands of People are flocking to see them this Morning, and all Mouths are full of execrations. Fixing them to the Trees is not approved. It is now proposed to make them upon decent little Packets, seal and direct them; one to the King, containing a Sample of every Sort for his Museum; one to the Queen, with little red Tadpoles to represent, by way of the Rest to be distributed among both Houses of Parliament; a double Quantity to the Bishops.

TO BE SOLD,

A convenient Tan-Yard, lying in Medfield, on the Post Road, Half a Mile from the Meeting-House, with a good Dwelling-House and Barn, and about 20 Acres of Land, consisting of Mowing, Plowing, and Pasturing, and an excellent Orchard. For further Particulars enquire of Adam Peters, on the Premises.

TO BE SOLD,

A large Tract of LAND, lying partly in Oxford, and partly in Charlton, in the County of Worcester. It is situated on a great Country Road, about Half a Mile from Charlton Meeting-House, and is capable of making a Number of fine Settlements. For further Particulars enquire of Joseph Blaney, of Salem, or Doctor Samuel Danforth, of Boston.

All Persons indebted to, or that have any Demands on, the Estate of Richard Greenleaf, late of Newbury-Port, Esq; deceased, are requested to bring in their Accounts to Moses Frazier and Mary Greenleaf, Executors to the last Will and Testament of the deceased, for an immediate Settlement.

TO BE SOLD,

A small new Brick HOUSE, two Rooms on a Floor, at the South Part of the Town.—Enquire of the Printer.

Strayed or stolen from the Subscriber, living in Salem, a Bay Horse, about seven Years old, a Rocky well set Horse, marked I. C. on his off Thigh, trots all. Whoever shall take up said Horse and return him to the Owner, shall be handsomely rewarded, HENRY WHITE.

Figure 8.3 Supplement to the Boston *Independent Chronicle*, No. 705, April 1782. Franklin's hoax newssheet, which he printed himself on his press at Passy, mimicked the actual *Independent Chronicle* of Boston. Only a very discerning reader would have recognized that the type Franklin employed was more diverse than most printers could afford. More of the font was French-made than English. Indeed, only a very interested printer would have been able to discover the unique italic script that Simon-Pierre Fournier, the younger, had devised exclusively for Franklin's use at his Passy press and used in this fake newspaper. Courtesy, American Philosophical Society.

are engaged in it, more juſtly deſerve the name of pirates, which you beſtow on me. It is, indeed, a war that coincides with the general ſpirit of your nation. Your common people in their ale-houſes ſing the twenty-four ſongs of Robin Hood, and applaud his deer-ſtealing and his robberies on the highway: thoſe who have juſt learning enough to read, are delighted with your hiſtories of the pirates and of the buccaniers: and often your ſcholars, in the univerſities, ſtudy Quintus Curtius; and are taught to admire Alexander, for what they call his conqueſts in the Indies. Severe laws and the hangmen keep down the effects of this ſpirit, ſomewhat among yourſelves, (though in your little iſland you have, nevertheleſs, more highway robberies than there is in all the reſt of Europe put together): but a foreign war gives it full ſcope. It is then that, with infinite pleaſure, it lets itſelf looſe to ſtrip of their property honeſt merchants, employed in the innocent and uſeful occupation of ſupplying the mutual wants of mankind. Hence, having lately no war with your ancient enemies, rather than be without a war, you choſe to make one upon your friends. In this your piratical war with America, the mariners of your fleets, and the owners of your privateers were animated againſt us by the act of your parliament, which repealed the law of God—" Thou ſhalt not ſteal,"—by declaring it lawful for them to rob us of all our property that they could meet with on the Ocean. This act too had a retroſpect, and, going beyond bulls of pardon, declared that all the robberies you had committed, previous to the act, ſhould be deemed juſt and lawful. Your ſoldiers too were promiſed the plunder of our cities: and your officers were flattered with the diviſion of our lands. You had even the baſeneſs to corrupt our ſervants, the ſailors employed by us, and encourage them to rob their maſters, and bring to you the ſhips and goods they were entruſted with. Is there any ſociety of pirates on the ſea or land; who, in declaring wrong to be right, and right wrong, have leſs authority than your parliament? Do any of them more juſtly than your parliament deſerve the title you beſtow on me?

You will tell me that we forfeited all our eſtates by our refuſal to pay the taxes your nation would have impoſed on us, without the conſent of our colony parliaments. Have you then forgot the inconteſtible principle, which was the foundation of Hambden's glorious lawſuit with Charles the firſt, that "what an Engliſh king has no right to demand, an Engliſh ſubject has a right to refuſe?" But you cannot ſo ſoon have forgotten the inſtructions of your late honourable father, who, being himſelf a ſound Whig, taught you certainly the principles of the Revolution, and that, "if ſubjects might in ſome caſes forfeit their property, kings alſo might forfeit their title, and all claim to the allegiance of their ſubjects." I muſt then ſuppoſe you well acquainted with thoſe Whig principles, on which permit me, Sir, to ask a few queſtions.

Is not protection as juſtly due from a king to his people, as obedience from the people to their king?

If then a king declares his people to be out of his protection:

If he violates and deprives them of their conſtitutional rights;

If he wages war againſt them:

If he plunders their merchants, ravages their coaſts, burns their towns, and deſtroys their lives:

If he hires foreign mercenaries to help him in their deſtruction:

If he engages ſavages to murder their defenceleſs farmers, women, and children:

If he cruelly forces ſuch of his ſubjects as fall into his hands, to bear arms againſt their country, and become executioners of their friends and brethren:

If he ſells others of them into bondage, in Africa and the Eaſt Indies:

If he excites domeſtic inſurrections among their ſervants, and encourages ſervants to murder their maſters:——

Does not ſo atrocious a conduct towards his ſubjects, diſſolve their allegiance?

If not,—pleaſe to ſay how or by what means it can poſſibly be diſſolved?

All this horrible wickedneſs and barbarity has been and daily is practiſed by the king your maſter (as you call him in your memorial) upon the Americans, whom he is ſtill pleaſed to claim as his ſubjects.

During theſe ſix years paſt, he has deſtroyed not leſs than forty thouſand of thoſe ſubjects, by battles on land or ſea, or by ſtarving them, or poiſoning them to death, in the unwholeſome air, with the unwholeſome food of his priſons. And he has waſted the lives of at leaſt an equal number of his own ſoldiers and ſailors; many of whom have been forced into this odious ſervice, and dragged from their families and friends, by the outrageous violence of his illegal preſs-gangs. You are a gentleman of letters, and have read hiſtory: do you recollect any inſtance of any tyrant, ſince the beginning of the world, who, in the courſe of ſo few years, had done ſo much miſchief, by murdering ſo many of his own people? Let us view one of the worſt and blackeſt of them, Nero. He put to death a few of his courtiers, placemen, and penſioners; and among the reſt his tutor. Had George the third done the ſame, and no more, his crime, though deteſtable, as an act of lawleſs power, might have been as uſeful to his nation, as that of Nero was hurtful to Rome; conſidering the different characters and merits of the ſufferers. Nero indeed wiſhed that the people of Rome had but one neck, that he might behead them all by one ſtroke: but this was a ſimple wiſh. George is carrying on with as faſt as he can into execution; and, by continuing in his preſent courſe a few years longer, will have deſtroyed more of the Britiſh people than Nero could have found inhabitants in Rome. Hence, the expreſſion of Milton, in ſpeaking of Charles the firſt, that he was " merum Neronior," is ſtill more applicable to George the third. Like Nero and all other tyrants, while they lived, he indeed has his flatterers, his addreſſers, his applauders. Penſions, places, and hopes of preferment, can bribe even biſhops to approve his conduct: but, when thoſe fulſome, purchaſed addreſſes and panegyrics are ſunk and loſt in oblivion or contempt, impartial hiſtory will ſtep forth, ſpeak honeſt truth, and rank him among public calamities. The only difference will be, that plagues, peſtilences, and famines are of this world, and ariſe from the nature of things: but voluntary malice, miſchief, and murder are from Hell: and this king will, therefore, ſtand foremoſt in the liſt of diabolical, bloody, and execrable tyrants. His baſe-bought parliaments too, who ſell him their ſouls, and extort from the people the money with which they aid his deſtructive purpoſes, as they ſhare his guilt, will ſhare his infamy,——parliaments, who to pleaſe him, have repeatedly, by different votes year after year, dipped their hands in human blood, inſomuch that methinks I ſee it dried and caked ſo thick upon them, that if they could waſh it off in the Thames which flows under their windows, the whole river would run red to the Ocean.

One is provoked by enormous wickedneſs: but one is aſhamed and humiliated at the view of human baſeneſs. It afflicts me, therefore, to ſee a gentleman of Sir Joſeph York's education and talents, for the ſake of a red riband and a paltry ſtipend, mean enough to ſtile ſuch a monſter his maſter, wear his livery, and hold himſelf ready at his command even to cut the throats of fellow-ſubjects. This makes it impoſſible for me to end my letter with the civility of a compliment, and obliges me to ſubſcribe myſelf ſimply,

JOHN PAUL JONES,

whom you are pleaſed to ſtile a *Pirate*.

Figure 8.3 Continued

bring home a sense of the cruelty of the bloodshed of war, along with the dastardliness of a British policy to incite groups of the Iroquois—in this case, and accurately, the Senecas—to kill colonists in undefended areas. Franklin's ultimate goal was to secure reparations for American Britons who suffered losses of person and property as a result of British-sponsored invasions and attacks.

The policy of Europeans using Indian allies to fight their battles was employed in the earliest colonial times by all European cultures.[38] On the one hand, it would seem that Franklin, having lived in British North America and having negotiated at one time with Iroquoian peoples, should readily have accepted the British policy of arming different Iroquoians and offering bounties on scalps as a policy of any European nation at war. During the Seven Years War in North America, bounties for scalps were offered on all sides, including the Pennsylvanians involved in negotiations and activities in the western part of the colony.[39] Such a practice played into mourning war rituals of Iroquoian peoples, and it secured loyalties and changed significantly the social economy within Iroquoia from a polity-based culture to a capital- or commodity-based culture.[40] On the other hand, however, as evidenced by his many letters in English newspapers, Franklin well understood even middling-level Britons' self-regard as "civilized" people: his unmistakable assumption was that middling-level people, the ultimately preferred target readers for the supplement, would find the idea of the British-sponsored Indian scalping of Britons in North America shocking beyond belief.

The "scalping" hoax is a purported letter from a Captain Samuel Gerrish, of the New England militia, to his commander, reporting on the booty taken in a recent capture of British military goods. Gerrish was horrified that one James Crauford, in the British service, was attempting to transmit to England, "at the Request of the Senneka Chiefs," a large package including "eight Packs of [colonists'] Scalps, cured, dried, hooped and painted, with all the Indian triumphal Marks." Crauford's supposed letter detailed how and where the scalps were taken, how they were marked in the package, and the relative age of the people thus taken. The grisly torments are elucidated in the supposed Senecas orator's speech recorded by Crauford. For instance, packet "No. 1" included

> 43 Scalps of Congress Soldiers killed in different Skirmishes; these are stretched on black Hoops, 4 Inches diameter; the inside of the Skin pointed red, with a small black Spot to note their being killed with Bullets. Also 62 of Farmers, killed in their Houses; the Hoops

red; the Skin painted brown, and marked with a Hoe; a black Circle all round, to denote their being surprised in the Night; and a black Hatchet in the Middle, signifying their being killed with that Weapon.

The idea that "Congress Soldiers" and "Farmers"—that is, militia members, civilians, who should have been excluded from deadly attack under "normal" wartime expectations—were "surprised in the Night" evokes the Indians' famous "skulking ways" in war, something Franklin's "civilized" British readers might have difficulty accepting. Yet what is identified in the first packet is rather mild compared to what is reported to have been included in packet number 4. Packet "No. 4" is said to include, in gory clarity, "102 [scalps] of Farmers," with "18 marked with a little yellow Flame, to denote their being Prisoners burnt alive, after being scalped, their Nails pulled out by the Roots and other Torments." Among these scalps was one "supposed to be of a rebel Clergyman, his Band being fixed to the Hoop of his Scalp." Of the others, "Most of the Farmers appear by the Hair to have been young or middle-aged Men; there being but 67 very grey Heads among them all; which makes the Service more essential." The selection brings home the seediness and brutality of British war efforts: Britain rewarded, with liberal presents of arms, Indian hatchet-men who otherwise were abhorred, and Britain supported attacks against noncombatant American civilians of British descent.

Franklin concluded this selection with one of his standard points—made as early as the 1750s—about vaunted British liberalities. The Seneca orator observed, "*Father*, We have only to say farther that your Traders exact more than ever for their Goods"—a point of Franklin's earlier hoax captivity of William Henry. The warrior continued, "Our Hunting is lessened by the War, so that we have fewer Skins to give" in trade. "This ruins us," he said, adding, "Think of some Remedy. We are poor: and you have Plenty of every Thing. We know you will send us Powder and Guns, and Knives and Hatchets: but we also want Shirts and Blankets." The supplication for raiment elucidates the real situation that might have brought the Seneca peoples to such a pass that they would supply scalps for money rather than for their own culture's traditional reasons, in behalf of a blood feud or as a part of a mourning war ritual. Franklin's prodding hook has a double barb: the British are pushing the Iroquois to fight against colonial Britons, and the British ministry could care less, in reality, about those Indians who are purportedly on their side. To a careful reader, Franklin's critique relayed that the Iroquois had reached a place where they had had to choose a side, and Britain was doing to the Indian peoples what it was seeking to do to the colonists: it sought to make them impoverished, dependent, abject, and thus quiescent.

If we read the "scalping" letter in the context of Franklin's peace negotiations and his other writings on the problems with the British ministry, the hoax is not really about the Iroquois so much as it is about British atrocities against their own countrypeople. The Iroquois, like the American Britons, were being manipulated by an uncaring ministry implementing an atrocious imperial policy. In negotiating with Oswald in April, Franklin realized it was time to recuperate his plan for reparations for Americans. If the request for reparations were to take hold, the British people themselves would have to agree that such redress were morally and fiscally required, given the sufferings of the Britons in America. This is what leads me to conclude that Franklin was targeting general readers of the British press especially, hoping to incite them against the ministry's prosecution of a war that they could neither morally nor physically (with their own British troops) support.

One other interesting allusion in Franklin's satire is worthy of remark here, especially in the context of the second part of the supplement. Regarding the final disposition of the discovered scalps, the colonial militiaman, Samuel Gerrish, suggests in the conclusion of his letter that an Irishman, Lieutenant Fitzgerald, has offered to take them over to England. Fitzgerald "said he thought it better" that the scalps "should proceed to their Destination," so he offered "to carry them to England, and hang them all up in some dark Night on the Trees in St. James's Park, where they could be seen from the King and Queen's Palaces in the Morning." He conceived that "the Sight of them might perhaps strike Muley Ishmael (as he has called him) with some Compunction of Conscience." Franklin was targeting anyone who could not have "compunction of conscience" in the face of such "evidence" as he was providing in this purported letter. How fitting that an Irishman proved willing to hang the scalps on display in the park.

The allusion to "Muley Ishmael" is quite interesting. Known in Britain and Europe as "Muley Ismail," Mawlây Ismâ'îl (1646–1727), sultan of Morocco from 1672 to 1727, was infamous among Christians in Britain and Europe, for his reputed ill treatment of Christians held captive in Morocco. Pointing out that the sultan was "held by his compatriots to have been a great ruler, a title which is due to one who reigned over a turbulent, largely medieval, empire for fifty-five years," historian Nevill Barbour has remarked that "it is due to the experiences of some hundreds of Christian prisoners among the thousands of forced labourers employed" on the great monuments and buildings marking his empire "that the ruler acquired the reputation for cruelty by which he is known in Europe."[41] The name Muley Ishmael seems to have been proverbial among British people, Europeans, and Americans. In *Candide* (1759), Voltaire made reference to "Muley-Ismaël" and his reputation for destruction in the narrative (chapter 11) of the "Princesse de Palestrine." In *Candide*, the "princess," who had been carried off into slavery in Morocco while at sea and heading, for respite, to Gaeta (Italy), reported that she and her mother had been very strong in enduring the things they endured while held captive in Morocco. Morocco, she reported to Candide, "nageait dans le sang quand nous arrivames. Cinquante fils de l'Empereur Muley-Ismaël avaient chacun leur parti: ce qui produisant en effet cinquante querres civiles, de noirs contre noirs, de noirs contre bazanés, de mulâtres contre mulâtres. C'était un carnage continuel dans toute l'étendue de l'Empire."[42] In the middle of the eighteenth century, then, this Moroccan ruler was notorious for his conquests and eventually the dissolution of his own empire. The name continued to resonate through the end of the century. Horace Walpole, for instance, mentioned in a 1792 letter to a friend that this sultan "used for a morning's exercise to dispatch a dozen or two of his subjects."[43]

As for Franklin, when he transmitted the supplement to John Adams in 1782, he commented, "I believe the Number of People actually scalp'd in this murdering War by the Indians to exceed what is mention'd in the Invoice, and that Muley Istmael (a happy Name for a Prince as obstinate as a Mule) is full as black a Tyrant as he is represented in Paul Jones's pretended Letter."[44] Franklin was drawing a comparison between King George III and a Moroccan leader despised in England and Europe. The comparison made between George III and the Moroccan ruler underscores, from Franklin's vantage point, destruction caused by the reign of Britain's king, a destruction forcing his subjects to wage bloody war against each other. The serious barbs behind Franklin's critique of inhumane tyranny, where "savagery" obtains just as easily in the presumed "civilized" society as in the presumed non-"civilized" world, formed a theme Franklin would take up within the next year, while still at Passy, in his "Remarks Concerning the Savages of North America." Of course, the criticism also reinforces Franklin's overall contention in these years that British people owed reparations to Britons in North America.

The second item of Franklin's supplement addresses Franklin's disgust, as a humanitarian and diplomat, with the way that Americans taken at sea were being held as prisoners of war. The background for the second hoax were events that had occurred in the late 1770s. Almost from the moment he set foot in France, Franklin worked in behalf of the release of prisoners taken captive at sea.[45] His goals were twofold: to promote and implement a general exchange of prisoners, as soon as possible, and, in the interim, to provide relief of a humanitarian and financial sort to those held captive. In neither goal was he reasonably successful, largely because even the best assistance was unreliable, and negotiations with Britain continued to break down over disparities of interpretation of the laws and customs of prisoner exchange. As the years wore on, however, Franklin seems to have become more and more aware that while it was necessary that he deal with Stormont, and while Stormont's official agreement was essential to the success of this aspect of Franklin's diplomatic mission (i.e., the prisoner exchange), one of the very real sources of Franklin's problems resided in the failure of diplomacy of the opinionated and sometimes irascible Sir Joseph Yorke (1724–1792), Britain's influential ambassador to the Netherlands.[46]

Franklin faced repeated difficulties while trying to arrange to get hundreds of prisoners out of disgusting circumstances in three prisons in England and smaller "holding" prisons or detention centers in Ireland and Scotland. According to historian Catherine Prelinger, there were two main prisons, the Forton and the Old Mill prisons and another, smaller prison in Deal, England. Detention centers were also used in Scotland and Ireland, where one, Kinsale prison, held over three hundred Americans.[47] Britain considered itself free to commandeer ships and remove Americans as rebels (rather than simply as prisoners of war, who would not suffer hanging but eventual release). Britain could house the men, in whatever quarters selected, indefinitely. Franklin and the commissioners, on the other hand, were not in a position to harbor prisoners for long, because until 1778, no open alliance existed with France, and the Netherlands remained neutral territory. The commissioners in effect had no holding area for British seaman who had been captured. Britain took advantage of this situation. At the time when an opportunity for a first prisoner exchange occurred, there were no English prisoners to exchange for the Americans. This is not to say that Americans held no war prisoners. Britain would not accept prisoners of the land war in the colonies as an even exchange. Stormont required that all prisoners in exchange be taken at sea. The Americans had taken captive several British seamen, but lacking a place to house them, they had to let their prisoners go. Franklin forced sea prisoners being released to sign paroles, but Stormont would not accept in exchange prisoners who had been thus paroled.

The mounting difficulties prompted Franklin to look into other means by which to pester Britain into an exchange, including teaming up with individuals within and outside formal political channels. Several individuals and groups came to his assistance, perhaps none more incensed against Britain than John Paul Jones (1747–1792). An American naval captain, Jones was as single-minded about prisoner exchange as Franklin. What troubled Jones the most about the situation was that American *soldiers* were, in effect, given political status as belligerents (and thus were eligible for exchange), whereas American *seamen* were, according to Britain's naval code, held as traitors and could call upon no legal status for easy exchange.[48] Jones offered his services readily, perhaps less for the benefit of obtaining prizes than for the satisfaction of relieving seamen unjustly held captive by Britain.

Jones had several plans he wanted to implement, perhaps the most famous being his attempt to capture and abduct Dunbar Douglas (1722–1799), fourth Earl of Selkirk, from his Irish estate at St. Mary's Isle in April 1778. The situation was notorious because, when he did not find Selkirk at home, Jones permitted his men to steal a significant amount of jewelry and other goods from the estate, and then, suffering remorse, he flamboyantly, using his own money, bought back the goods thus stolen and in a grand gesture returned them to Selkirk. Jones had numerous suggestions for retaliation: engaging in raids on the Irish Sea; making attacks on the coastlines of England, Ireland, and Scotland; taking merchant shippers as prizes; and destroying fishery off Greenland.[49] Interrupting the sea traffic off the coasts of England was an idea that pleased Jones significantly, given the interruptions, piracies, and impressments suffered by Americans at sea.

Franklin embraced Jones's enthusiasm if not his flamboyant style. Yet Franklin was exuberant when Jones's *Bonhomme Richard* was, despite its sinking, victorious over the British ship *Serapis* in a heated battle off Flamborough Head in the first days of October 1779. Jones took over the *Serapis* and triumphantly sailed into the Texel, neutral island territory of the Netherlands, with 504 British seamen as prisoners. Here, Jones made an agreement with Yorke that he would release all but one prisoner, the commander of the *Serapis*.[50] Jones also insisted on keeping the key British ships he had seized. Yorke later refused to honor the agreement and wrote two memorials or testimonies stating his view of the matter. He called upon Britain to seize the two ships anchored in the Texel. Yorke's October 8 memorial to the States General, quoted in the October 15 (No. 83) *Gazette de Leyde*, called Jones both a rebel and a pirate. Yorke's memorial was repeated in the *London Chronicle*, October 19–21, 1779. Jones's behavior, Yorke protested, "falls," "according to treaties and laws of war," into "the class of rebels and pirates," and should be treated accordingly.[51] When the States General refused his request that the ships be seized in the name of Britain, Yorke wrote a second memorial, referring excoriatingly to "the pirate Paul Jones of Scotland, who is a rebel subject, and a criminal of the State."[52] All of this, Jones's success in taking at sea over five hundred British prisoners, his loss of those prisoners at the hands of somewhat unclear agreements among British, French, and Dutch authorities, and his denunciation by Yorke for doing exactly what British seamen had been doing for years, must have been as fresh for Franklin in the spring of 1782 as if nearly two and a half years had not intervened.

Franklin used the supplement to mock Yorke's two memorials thoroughly. The hoax letter, supposedly written by John Paul Jones to Sir Joseph Yorke, reveals Franklin's mastery at rhetorical inversion or transvaluation, wherein the object originally targeted for ridicule (in this case, Jones, as the target of Yorke) turns the tables on his abuser, making the original abuser the object of satire. Franklin must have seen the testimonies of Yorke, and he had to have enjoyed this little game of making a response. In effect, the Jones of Franklin's long letter ends up calling Yorke and men like him "pirates" because—and this is a typical Franklin catalog of complaints against the king and Parliament—they do not give people due process of their constitutional rights; they wage war against them, plundering them of their goods and well-being; they send "foreign mercenaries" and "savages" to "murder defenceless farmers, women, and children"; they excite (this with regard to enslaved Africans in North America) "domestic insurrections among their servants." All of these things, "Jones" says, form part of the whole "horrible wickedness and barbarity" that is "daily . . . practiced by the king your master (as you call him . . .)." The catalog of abuses is a summary catalog of the central points on which Franklin had been writing for many years and attempting to negotiate legal recognition and reparations for in more recent years.

The Jones of Franklin's letter gives Yorke a schoolbook lesson in vocabulary: "A pirate makes war for the sake of rapine. This is not the kind of war I am engaged in against England," he remarks. Here the rhetorical inversion is completed: "Our's is a war in defence of liberty," thus making it "the most just of all wars," and a defense "of our properties, which your nation would have taken from us, without our consent, in violation of our rights, and by an armed force." Franklin's Jones concludes, "Your's, therefore, is a war of rapine; of course, a piratical war: and those who approve of it, and are engaged in it, more justly deserve the name of pirates, which you bestow on me." This part of the letter successfully relies upon a method Franklin often used. He transvalued referents—in this case, the word *pirate*—so that the object of reference (Jones) becomes itself the one making the claim. Such rhetorical inversion is common in Franklin's satires and jeux d'esprits, and they reveal his remarkable linguistic and metaphoric agility. This part of the letter also points, as did the "scalping" letter, to the loss of persons and property, so that Franklin's requests for reparations would have clear justification.

But Franklin's Jones goes beyond a war of words into a commentary on Yorke's stubborn miscalculation, based on old Whig political attitudes, regarding Britain's lines of alliance in Europe and the rights of kings and subjects. Yorke adhered to what some historians have called the "Old System," the traditional belief that the old alliance between London, the Hague, and Vienna "should," as historian Hamish M. Scott has phrased it, "be the foundation of British security." Such traditional values and self-styled Whiggish principles blinded Yorke to the slow decline of the Dutch Republic in Europe, the growing powers of Prussia and Russia, the declining powers of France, and the galloping preoccupation in Britain with its colonial holdings (thus diminishing its standing as a European threat).[53] By appealing to Britain and to the States General to seize Jones's prizes, Yorke had betrayed a misunderstanding of the Dutch Republic's current situation, one of relative decline, and Austria's newer alliance with France.

Calling upon some of the same Whig principles with which Yorke himself would have been raised, Franklin bespoke his own early modern liberal values. Franklin's Jones instructed (and thus chastised) Yorke with an evocative reference to the famous stand by John Hampden (c. 1595–1643) against King Charles I's imposition of forced loans and ship money, helping to spark the English Civil War. Franklin's Jones queried Yorke, "Have you then forgot the incontestable principle, which was the foundation of Hambden's glorious lawsuit with Charles the first, that 'what an English king has no right to demand, an English subject has a right to refuse?'" Surely, Franklin taunted, "you cannot so soon have forgotten the instructions of your late honourable father, . . . who, being himself a sound Whig, taught you certainly the principles of the Revolution." The central lesson of his father that Yorke had not understood was this: "if subjects might in some cases forfeit their property, kings also might forfeit their title, and all claim to the allegiance of their subjects." The reference was to Yorke's father, Philip Yorke (1690–1764), Lord Chancellor and first Earl of

Hardwicke, under whose services to the administration the Jacobite uprising of 1745 had been suppressed.

Franklin's Jones made a mockery of Yorke's vaunted liberal Whig values by engaging in a series of rhetorical questions on issues that were at
the center of the American peace commissioners' negotiations, all problems associated with the legal conception of the king in council. The list
includes most of the key issues troubling Franklin about Britain's prosecution of the war in North America: the legal and constitutional rights of
Britons in North America; sea piracy; the hiring of "foreign mercenaries"
to prosecute the war; the use of Indians to massacre the colonists; the plundering and murder of colonial merchants, farmers, women, and children,
numbering to 40,000; the incitement of insurrections among domestic servants (slaves); the selling of wartime captives into bondage in Africa and
Asia (East India). "Does not so atrocious a conduct towards his subjects,
dissolve their allegiance" to their king? Franklin/Jones asks. "All of this
horrible wickedness and barbarity has been and daily is practiced by the
king your master (as you call him in your memorial) upon the Americans,
whom he is still pleased to claim as his subjects," Jones taunts.

The critique of the political and social havoc Britain had wrought in the
colonists' lives is thus personalized and merged with the critique of Yorke's
presumed Whig values. Franklin's Jones challenges Yorke in very direct
and personal ways. Picking up on his own theme of the absolute necessity
of reparations because the king has overseen the murder of his own people
and the losses of their properties, Franklin has Jones taunt: "You are a gentleman of letters, and have read history: do you recollect any instance of any
tyrant, since the beginning of the world, who, in the course of so few years,
had done so much mischief, by murdering so many of his own people?"
As a follow-up to the question, Franklin/Jones makes a running commentary on Nero, concluding that George III has, as Charles I did before him,
out-Nero'd Nero. "Hence the expression of Milton, in speaking of Charles
the first, that he was 'Nerone Neronior,' is still more applicable to George
the third," who has provoked his Parliament (in prosecuting the war on the
colonies) in such a way that all have "dipped their hands in human blood,
insomuch that methinks I see it dried and caked so thick upon them, that
if they could wash it off in the Thames which flows under their windows,
the whole river would run red to the Ocean." Franklin was evoking the
popular author, John Milton (1608–1674). The phrase "Nerone Neronior,"
which seems to have been equally admired by John Adams, is from the
first chapter of Milton's *Defensio Pro Populo Anglicano Prima* (1651), where
Milton asserted that the English clergy were engaged in preaching to their

congregations that their struggle was not against just any king but against a tyrant greater than any Saul or Ahab, a tyrant more like Nero himself.[54] In strong language and with tellingly bloody metaphors, Franklin used the Jones letter to comment upon social and political matters while drawing attention to Yorke's duplicity in preventing the American commissioners from recovering American prisoners in a just exchange. The echoes of Milton and Hampden in the Jones letter are telling reminders of the failure of the king and Parliament to live up to the principles that had served as the foundations of the English civil wars and the cornerstone of the so-called Glorious Revolution with the peaceful emergence of William and Mary of Orange as leaders in the 1680s. Franklin was thus returning to themes common in his earlier writings, themes he associated with articulations about the freedoms he always associated with early modern liberalism.

Both hoaxes take up issues important to Franklin, then, and both reveal propaganda strategies he commonly employed in these years of protracted diplomatic activity. For Franklin, now that it seemed that serious peace negotiations were possible, it was time to make a last stand against British atrocities, in an effort to convince Britons of the nefarious blows dealt against Britons in North America and the essential importance of reparations. The supplement was public propaganda. Franklin distributed it to key locales where American diplomacy was occurring: London, Amsterdam, and Madrid. In the context of the events taking place, his transmittal letters suggest that it would be useful to have the supplement circulated or printed in England. Of his correspondents, James Hutton seems to have taken the supplement quite seriously. After Franklin sent him the supplement, he returned a letter regarding the Moravian Indians but including some commentary on the supplement's "scalping" letter. "That article in the Boston Paper must be a Romance," he wrote. "All of it invention, cruel forgery I hope & believe." He made some further comments on the supplement, changed the subject, then returned to it at the end of his letter, as if still troubled by the supplement's contents, to say, "The Scalp Bales are so very abominable that I can not prevail upon my self to believe it, as I know the Dispositions here [toward the colonists]."[55]

Franklin knew his supplement would reach the British press. It arrived at London's *Public Advertiser* offices in September and was printed September 27, 1782. It is possible that the supplement made it into other newspapers as well. The supplement did have some effect, as evidenced in a letter Horace Walpole (1717–1797) wrote to the Countess of Ossory, October 1, 1782, commenting on the letter supposedly from John Paul Jones to Sir Joseph Yorke. "Dr[.] Franklin himself I should think was the author," remarked Walpole. "It is certainly written by a first-rate pen, and not by a common man-of-war. The Royal George is out of luck!" Walpole quipped.[56]

If Great Britain were seeking a real reconciliation with the colonists, reparations to the colonists for their losses were necessary to make the reconciliation durable beyond mere words on paper.[57] "Reconciliation," Franklin wrote in his notes in preparation for one of his many meetings with Oswald at this time, "is a sweet Word. It means much more than a mere Peace, & is heartily to be wish'd for." He continued, "Nations may make Peace whenever they are both weary of making War. But if one of them has made War upon the other unjustly, and has wantonly and unnecessarily done it great Injuries, and refuses Reparation; tho' there may for the present be Peace, the Resentment of those Injuries will remain, and . . . the Peace will never be secure; nor can any Cordiality subsist between them."[58] Reparations to those who suffered losses, protection from incursions by the British and their Iroquoian allies during the war, and the complete release of Americans taken captive during the war—these issues were central, in Franklin's view of the situation, to regaining colonial Americans' trust and cooperation with Britain.

Franklin had hoped as well to influence public opinion in the Americans' favor in the Netherlands and Spain. He sent it to John Adams, then negotiating in the Netherlands. Without identifying his own authorship but hinting nonetheless the provenance of the supplement, Franklin wrote that if it "were re-publish'd in England it might make them a little asham'd of themselves."[59] Perhaps to be assured that French agents for North America knew of his efforts to bring attention to his concerns, Franklin also sent the supplement to Charles-Guillaume-Frédéric Dumas (1721–1796), agent in the Netherlands, with a request that Dumas circulate the supplement without indicating how he got it: "Make any use of them [the supplement's stories] you may think proper to shame your Anglomanes but do not let it be Known thro' what hands they come."[60]

John Jay was facing many difficulties in Madrid. Franklin sent the supplement to Jay with additional notes about the prisoner situation. He continued his affectation of disputing the provenance of the supplement, but his investment in the prisoner problem betrayed his authorship. To Jay, Franklin wrote, "In consequence of a Proposition I sent over, the Parliament of Britain have just passed an Act for exchanging American Prisoners." He let Jay know that "they have near 1100 in the Goals [sic] of England & Ireland, all committed as charged with high Treason. The Act is to impower the King, notwithstanding such Commitments to consider them as Prisoners of War according to the Law of Nations, and exchange them as such." Franklin took this as a good sign: "This seems to be giving up their Pretensions of considering us as rebellious Subjects, and is a kind of Acknowledgment of our Independence." He explained further that "Transports are now taking up to carry back to their Country the poor brave Fellows who have borne for Years their cruel Captivity, rather than serve our Enemies; and an equal Number of English are to be deliver'd in Return. I have upon Desire furnish'd Passports for the Vessels."[61] Franklin himself printed the passports on the Passy press, using the very special italic font, "Le Franklin," that the Fourniers had created at his request.[62]

Franklin's targeted circulation of his supplement paid off. As noted earlier, the supplement, or part of it, appeared in at least one newspaper, London's *Public Advertiser*, on September 27, 1782, where the publisher hinted it might have been penned by Jones himself, and if not, then by someone who had "contemptuous insolence," because then it would be "the Production of some audacious Rebel." The very tone of the publisher's commentary seems to implicate Franklin. It is unclear which avenue among Franklin's correspondents brought the supplement to the eyes of the British people. Yet Franklin had hit his mark, if the commentary by Walpole is any indication.

Celebrating the Peace of Paris

The 1783 Peace of Paris, as it was frequently called, was one of a series of treaties signed in France that year establishing peace between Great Britain and the allied nations of France, Spain, and the Netherlands. Based on preliminary treaty articles Franklin and the commissioners had negotiated in 1782, the agreement recognized the independence of the United States and granted significant western territory to the nation. As we have seen, Franklin brought to bear on his negotiations his significant skill at managing complicated political entanglements. In working with the French ministry and with British representatives, Franklin had managed a public stance of transparency while observing a private policy of working with those most likely to further his diplomatic agenda. Yet he wanted to develop an agreement with Britain prior to letting France know. This was a risky decision, and it seems to have been Franklin's decision. He secured other treaties as well. On January 20, 1783, he attended (with

Adams) at Versailles the signing of the Anglo-French and Anglo-Spanish preliminary articles of treaty, and the commissioners were able to declare an armistice. He had also skillfully maintained a favorable relationship with Vergennes. Five days after witnessing the signing of preliminary treaty articles at Versailles, he requested—and received—another six million livres of support from France. This brought the total borrowed from France to twenty million livres.[63] On April 3, he signed a treaty of amity and commerce with Sweden.

The year 1783 proved a tiring but heady time for Franklin. He was crowned with laurel and myrtle on March 6 at the Musée de Paris, celebrating the successful conclusion of the war. He was consulted on how the United States of America would form a government and on many aspects of international relations. So frequently was he consulted on American affairs—from the organization of the states to location of key ports to relations with the Indians to policies related to internal commercial activity—that Franklin sought and received Vergennes's permission to print French translations of many of the most important American state materials. Franklin asked his friend, Louis-Alexandre (1743–1792), duc de La Roche-Guyon et de La Rochefoucauld, to translate the material. The *Constitutions des trieze Etats-Unis de l'Amérique*—the translated compilation of the different state constitutions published by Congress in 1781 and the several founding documents of the country, with recent treaties—was published in July. Franklin sent two volumes to each member in the European diplomatic corps, one for the monarch and one for the relevant diplomat. King Louis XVI received a copy printed on vellum and bound in gold-tooled Moroccan leather.[64]

Franklin considered that the initial public display and reception of the United States would influence future national success. Transmitting from Passy a copy of the volume to Robert R. Livingston (1746–1813), the US secretary for foreign affairs (1781–1783), Franklin wrote about a number of diplomatic matters, including the final release of all prisoners of war held in Britain, and commented on the newly published collection of legal documents, which he enclosed. He indicated that the documents were "much admired by the Politicians here, and it is thought will induce considerable Emigrations of substantial People from different Parts of Europe to America." He expressed the significant admiration of the American leaders that he had been witnessing: "It is particularly a Matter of Wonder, that in the Midst of a cruel War raging in the Bowels of our Country, our Sages should have the firmness of Mind to sit down calmly and form such compleat Plans of Government. They add considerably to the Reputation of the United States."[65]

Diplomacy was on his mind in the years 1783 and 1784, along with concerns about the numerous Europeans who were pestering him, as he wrote to Charles Thomson (1729–1824) in March 1784, about ways of life in North America. Many who consulted Franklin expected that if they moved to America, their lives would be easy, because of the "land of milk and honey" rumors floating about Europe. "I am pestered continually with Numbers of Letters from People in different Parts of Europe, who would go to settle in America," Franklin complained to Thomson, observing that many of the people petitioning him for passports to America "manifest very extravagant Expectations, such as I can by no means encourage; and who appear otherwise to be very improper Persons." He was frustrated with having to give audience to and receive letters from such people. "To save myself Trouble I have just printed some Copies of the enclosed little Piece, which I purpose to send hereafter in Answer to such Letters."[66] Franklin was referring to his pamphlet *Information to Those Who Would Remove to America*, which he wrote around 1782 and published on his press at Passy in 1783.[67] In response to the extravagant publicity about North America's fecundity and potential, Franklin had to emphasize that in America people worked for their living and took joy in the labor: "There are few great Proprietors of the Soil, and few Tenants," he wrote. Seeking to convey the situation in detail, he added, "most People cultivate their own Lands, or follow some Handicraft or Merchandise." Franklin drew a clear contrast between life in America and life in Britain or Europe. "Very few," he said, are "rich enough to live idly upon their Rents or Incomes; or to pay the high Prices given in Europe, for Paintings, Statues, Architecture and the other Works of Art that are more curious than useful." The contrast explained why in America so many with "natural Geniuses" in the arts "have uniformly quitted that Country for Europe, where they can be more suitably rewarded."[68] In response to the effete cultural expectations of the Europeans with whom he was living, he invoked "country" ideology, emphasizing the importance of labor for leading a pure life, the importance of education in practical matters, and the belief that a man ought to be judged not by his name and heritage but by his ability in the agricultural and mechanic trades.

During this period, Franklin also found time to write some jeux d'esprits for his friends, but even in some of these pieces, he used his position as a wise diplomatic sage to elucidate for his private reading audience many of the differences between the living circumstances in North America and in Paris. Almost as if he were seeking to balance the portrayals of Indian atrocities he had formulated for his supplement to the *Independent*

Chronicle, he wrote a very different piece that he published himself on his press at Passy in both English and French translation. In its French title, Franklin's *Remarques sur la politesse des sauvages de l'Amérique septentrio-nale* emphasizes the ideas of the politeness and purity of "natural men" then circulating in Europe. Its English version, *Remarks concerning the Savages of North America,* did not come close to indicating how the piece would play on tropes of city/country and savagism/civility in order to reveal the complications of European culture, which appropriated to itself superior cultural value simply because its systems were not based in nature but in the artifices of high society in Europe. Franklin's pamphlet also provided an oblique treatment of the presumed civilizing tendencies of enlightened commercial activity, as represented by free trade, which he was fond of mentioning to all who inquired about America's commercial possibilities. The *Remarks* in effect critiqued, from the colonial vantage point, any state policy that did not align itself with enlightened civility, a civility best attained by people living close to the natural world and laboring with their own hands. It thus served as an able evaluation of most systems of state in Europe in the latter half of the eighteenth century.

Franklin opened his piece with the statement, "Savages we call them, because their manners differ from ours, which we think the Perfection of Civility; they think the same of theirs."[69] The opening would have reminded his learned French readers of the well-known essay "Of Cannibals" by Michel de Montaigne (1533–1592). In Montaigne's essay, the effect was to show a story of civility about supposed "savage" peoples. For Franklin, the goal was to create an urbane and funny critique of the ethnocentrism of Europeans who would assume theirs was a more civilized culture, despite the warlike nature of Europeans, their clear affection for disputation, and their desire to acquire land only to privatize and thus squander its general usefulness for the community.[70]

European pretensions were not the sole butt of Franklin's satire during this period. In a letter to his daughter Sally, Franklin mocked the aristocratic pretensions of members of the newly organized Society of the Cincinnati, an organization meant to privilege veterans of the American Revolution. The Society was formed so that special privileges would descend to succeeding generations. "I only wonder," he wrote to Sally, "that when the united Wisdom of our Nation had, in the Articles of Confederation, manifested their Dislike of establishing Ranks of Nobility, by Authority either of the Congress or of any particular State, a Number of private Persons should think proper to distinguish themselves and their Posterity from their Fellow Citizens, and form an Order of hereditary

Knights, in direct Opposition to the solemnly declared Sense of their Country."[71] Franklin continued with a comparative cultural history lesson, situating the Americans amid their European and ancient Chinese counterparts and finding the Chinese model best suited to happiness. He used the Chinese to exemplify his own values:

> Thus among the Chinese, the most antient, and, from long Experience, the wisest of Nations, Honour does not *descend* but *ascends*. If a Man from his Learning, his Wisdom or his Valour, is promoted by the Emperor to the Rank of Mandarin, his Parents are immediately intitled to all the same Ceremonies of Respect from the People, that are establish'd as due to the Mandarin himself; on this Supposition, that it must have been owing to the Education, Instruction, and good Example afforded him by his Parents that he was rendered capable of Serving the Publick. This *ascending Honour* is therefore useful to the State as it encourages Parents to give their Children a good and virtuous Education. But the *descending Honour*, to Posterity who could have had no Share in obtaining it, is not only groundless and absurd, but often hurtful to that Posterity, since it is apt to make them proud, disdaining to be employed in useful Arts, and thence falling into Poverty and all the Meannesses, Servility and Wretchedness attending it; which is the present case with much of what is called the *Noblesse* in Europe.

Here again Franklin was giving evidence of his consistent position favoring hard work; good education, including education on matters of virtue; and public service for the betterment of the community. These were themes common in his writings throughout his life, but they emerged especially strongly as the peace was announced and the work of forming a new American social and political order was at hand.

Concluding the Mission

The definitive treaty of peace between Great Britain and the United States was signed September 3, 1783, by David Hartley for the British and by Adams, Franklin, and Jay for the United States. In July, Franklin had been approached by the papal nuncio in Paris seeking to organize a Roman Catholic Church in North America. Ecumenical in his personal orientation and interested in establishing freedom of religious practice as a tenet of American political life, Franklin suggested that John Carroll (1735–1815) be appointed the church's head in North America. Other activities followed, as he entertained the idea that he was finally concluding his diplomatic mission. He embraced the opportunity to return to some of his scientific interests. For instance, Franklin journeyed out to see the first two manned flights of balloons, the first on November 21 and the second on December 1, 1783. In March 1784, Franklin was asked by King Louis XVI to examine and test the theories of animal magnetism promoted by Franz Anton Mesmer (1734–1815). After conducting several public tests, Franklin concluded in a *Rapport* (August 11) and *Exposé* (read to the Academy of Sciences on September 4) that Mesmer's theories were unfounded. He was elected as an honorary fellow of the Royal Society of Edinburgh. Such activities occupied Franklin's time as he waited for the formal mission to conclude.

The formal ratification of the peace treaty with Great Britain took place on May 12, 1784. The day after the ratification, Franklin sat down to write his petition that Congress relieve him of his post, so that he could return home. As he awaited news on his request, Franklin drafted the second part of his autobiography. Then news arrived that Congress had named Adams, Franklin, and Jefferson joint commissioners to negotiate treaties with all the European nations and the Barbary States. Franklin acquiesced to his appointment, and the commissioners began their work on August 30, 1784. On May 2, 1785, Franklin finally received the long-awaited word that Congress would permit him to leave his role as minister plenipotentiary, so that he could return home. (Thomas Jefferson was his successor.) Before setting sail for North America, Franklin (July 9) signed a treaty with Prussia that confirmed Franklin's idealistic political positions on neutrality, privateering, and the exemption of private property from capture at sea. He left Passy on July 12, supplied with one of Queen Marie Antoinette's litters, so that the pain from his bladder stones might be alleviated. He sailed from Havre on July 24, landing at Southampton, England, where he was visited by his son, William, with whom he had reconciled the year before, along with Jonathan Shipley (1714–1788), bishop of St. Asaph, and others of his closest friends. On July 28, Franklin set sail for Philadelphia.

He was finally going home for his last journey. Franklin had attempted to articulate, for much of his life, a position about ideology—or, more accurately, the fractures of ideology—that would arise within any presumed commonwealth that allowed for an empire of *haves* who willingly worked to undermine possibilities for the majority, the *have-nots*. His preoccupation with these concerns lasted even through the period of peacemaking.

To his close friend Jonathan Shipley in England, he wrote from Passy, March 17, 1783, "Let us now forgive and forget." He explained, "Let each Country seek its Advancement in its own internal Advantages of Arts & Agriculture, not in retarding or preventing the Prosperity of the other." Ever the idealist, Franklin wrote that "America will, with God's Blessing, become a great & happy Country; and England, if she has at length gain'd Wisdom, will have gain'd something more valuable, & more essential to her Prosperity, than all she has lost; and will still be a great and respectable Nation."[72] Although he continued in his letter to excoriate the avarice and ambitions of those seeking office in Britain, Franklin nonetheless favored the idea that "much Public Spirit and Virtue" could still work to abolish fundamental greed, if Britain would, in effect, learn from its experience in North America. In reply, Shipley expressed concern that Franklin had idealized Britain's potential. Complaining about the "Band" of men surrounding Lord North seeking places and emolument, Shipley remarked, "How different is all this from the liberal Spirit with which your thirteen States have formd their Constitutions! availing themselves of the Lights & Experience of all former Times and Countries with the courage to hazard any great Trial that inventive Philosophy may suggest."[73] Franklin's idealism, matched as it was by many of his generation, would face yet another great challenge when he returned to North America. His life's last endeavor in behalf of freedom for all people—the abolition of slavery—awaited him on the other side of the Atlantic.

${\mathcal{N}ine}$

"I INTENDED WELL, AND I HOPE ALL WILL END WELL"

Franklin's Last Years

On landing at Philadelphia September 14, 1785, Benjamin Franklin heard pealing bells, cannon salutes, and cheering crowds. The trip had been tiring but beneficial for his health, and he met the crowds with becoming dignity. In addition to the crowds at the wharf, Franklin was greeted by newspaper encomia and celebratory proclamations from all the local social organizations. Members of the Constitutional Society, for instance, greeted him with an address underscoring Franklin's deft negotiations to conclude a "long and bloody war." We are, they said, "deeply indebted to your wisdom and vigilance for the frequent support we have received from the friendly powers in Europe, and especially from our great and good allies." Recognizing Franklin's role in developing and seeing the peace accord through to the signing, they thanked Franklin for "bringing that war to a happy conclusion, by the late honourable peace." Such work, they said, "has also entitled you to the gratitude of every American; and we doubt not those important services will be remembered and acknowledged as long as time shall endure."[1] News of the accolades offered to Franklin quickly spread to Britain and Europe via the newspapers and letters trafficking across the Atlantic.

The voyage must truly have refreshed him. He reported on October 1 to Thomas Jefferson (who remained in France), "I find myself the better for my Voyage."[2] Franklin was happy to be home. Others might readily have retired from public life, but not Franklin. Writing to his friend Jonathan Shipley (1714–1788), Franklin acknowledged that his "Reception here, was . . . very honourable indeed." It was so honorable, Franklin wrote, that "I was betray'd by it and by some Remains of Ambition, from which I had imagin'd myself free, to accept of the Chair of Government for the State of Pennsylvania, when the proper thing for me was Repose and a private Life."[3] His private life offered him much happiness. Describing his household to Polly Stevenson Hewson (1734–1795), Franklin offered an intimate family picture. "I have found my Family here in Health, good Circumstances and well respected by their Fellow Citizens," he happily wrote. Remarking that his youthful "Companions . . . are indeed almost all departed," he nonetheless found "an agreable Society among their Children and Grandchildren." Franklin offered a picture of his daily activities: "I have public Business enough to preserve me from *Ennuy*, and private Amusement besides in Conversation, Books, my Garden, and *Cribbidge*." Additional amusements included "Cards," which the family "sometimes play[ed] here in long Winter Evenings, but it is as they play at Chess, not for Money but for Honour or the Pleasure of Beating one another."[4] Franklin was enjoying family life for the first time in decades. He was also happy to see a flourishing marketplace in Philadelphia and to create a garden with walkways and trees around his house. Like others who had accumulated wealth in the middle of the century, Franklin had shifted the grounds surrounding his home from an emphasis on utility to that of ornament. "Considering our well-furnish'd plentiful Market as the best of Gardens," he said to Polly, "I am turning mine, in the midst of which my House stands, into Grass Plots and Gravel Walks, with Trees and Flowering Shrubs." The family no longer needed a kitchen garden, because the marketplace was close. Making a treed walkway and flower garden marked Franklin's status as someone who no longer labored for his living. Franklin had hoped that Polly Hewson, now a widow, and her children would come over to live in Philadelphia, as she had promised to do while he was working on the Peace of Paris. In the meantime, though, Franklin wrote to her that "we jog on in Life as pleasantly as you do in England." Yet Franklin was much busier than he acknowledged to Polly, certainly much busier than simply working to keep himself from boredom.

From the moment he arrived, Franklin took up affairs of local and national importance, thus continuing his lifelong pattern of service to local and national communities. He was elected (October 11, 1785) for a three-year term to the Supreme Executive Council of Pennsylvania and elected to be its president October 18. He was unanimously re-elected to the Council presidency in the two ensuing years; he donated his salary to charity. To be assured that the study of the science of government would be as well tended to as that of nature (studied by the American Philosophical Society, which often met at his home), Franklin devised and helped initiate the Society for Political Enquiries, which he presided over. His young friend Thomas Paine (1737–1809) became a member. He was named president of the reorganized Pennsylvania Society for Promoting the Abolition of Slavery on April 23, 1787. And he served from May 28 to September 17, 1787, as a Pennsylvania delegate to Federal Constitutional Convention. Franklin's public efforts at this stage of his life conformed with those from his earliest years in political life. He believed in and worked toward the political materialization of several related principles: the necessity for keeping peace, especially in contested areas; the importance of creating a government where the will of the governed fundamentally influenced laws and government decision-making; and the rights of all citizens—of whatever background—to work for themselves and their own families. This chapter will discuss Franklin's last years in light of these concerns.

"We are daily more and more enlightened": Propagandizing "American Realities"

Franklin pursued a propaganda campaign about America's potential prosperity. To Franklin, keeping Americans at peace was essential to furthering the laboring and commercial activities of the people. Indeed, as he and other leaders saw it, the commercial viability of the new confederation was on the line. Leaders, merchants, shippers, and laborers in Europe needed to know, he thought, about America's social and political stability, despite the recent war, and its commercial potential. If America could not remain stable, its citizens' productivity would be shattered, because they would be spending time arming against each other rather than working for a common good, the agricultural and commercial success of the new nation. If produce for export were unavailable, Americans would have to rely on an import trade, which always occurred at greater risk and expense than if citizens were to buy internally supplied produce and manufactured goods.

Franklin's letters back to Europe convey an aching utopian energy that the country succeed beyond all possible expectation. He wrote to Thomas Jefferson, for instance, in the first batch of letters he sat down to write. Jefferson, the new minister plenipotentiary in France, would need to make positive reports from Franklin about affairs in America. Franklin insisted in his brief letter, October 1, 1785, that "in general the Affairs of our Country seem to be in good Train: the last Harvest good, our own Produce high, foreign Supplies both European and West Indian low." He admitted that there were "some Party Wranglings" but quickly added that "no free Country was ever without them; and I do not think they are likely to produce any considerable bad Consequences."[5]

The commercial potential of America was high, making the reliance on imports small. Any disturbances should be expected, because this was a free country, and people were permitted to air their views, he reported. To David Hartley (c. 1730–1813), his scientist friend and British statesman who assisted with the Paris treaty, Franklin's comments were similar, but more extensive. He wrote Hartley on October 27, "Your newspapers are filled with accounts of distresses and miseries that these states are plunged into since their separation from Britain. You may believe me when I tell you that there is no truth in those accounts." He offered Hartley extended and inflated remarks about the stability of property holders and property values, the fecundity of the earth and the high marketability of its produce, the reduced need for imports, the happiness of the laborers, and the happiness and contentment of the American people with their government. "I find all property in lands and houses augmented vastly in value . . . that of houses and towns at least four-fold." He continued, "The crops have been plentiful, and yet the produce sells high, to the great profit of the farmer." Americans had little need for imports, but even so, "All imported goods sell at low rates, some cheaper than the first cost." Further, he claimed, "Working people have plenty of employ and high pay for their labour. These appear to me as certain signs of public prosperity." Franklin's goal was to dispel rumors about the instability of the new country resulting from absence of specie and thus an inability for states to pay back their war debt and to pay returning soldiers. He also presented a view that commercial and other debts held in Britain against Americans resulted from merchants and others who had ventured capital based on their expectation that Britain would win the war and open American markets abroad. Even though the Americans had won the war, the shores of America were filled with "too many traders who have crowded hither from all parts of Europe with more goods than the natural demand of the country requires." He argued that "what in Europe is called the debt of America is chiefly the debt of these adventurers and supercargoes to their principals, with which the settled inhabitants of America, who never paid better, for what they want and buy, have nothing to do." People were quite happy, he said, as free citizens: "As to the contentment of the inhabitants with the change of government, methinks a stronger proof cannot be desired, than what they have given in my reception. You know the part I had in that change, and you see in the papers the addresses from all ranks with which your friend was welcomed home, and the sentiments they contain confirmed yesterday in the choice of him for President by the council and new assembly, which was unanimous, a single voice in seventy seven excepted."[6] Franklin thus attempted to construct a vision of peace and prosperity, knowing that if such news spread in Europe, it would stabilize the Atlantic market exchange. Franklin was on a propaganda campaign. He repeatedly spoke about Americans' industry, the stability of their state and federal governments, the marketability of their products, and the readiness of merchants to trade with all partners. He staked his reputation on the success of the United States.

His efforts did not diminish as time wore on. Instead, they increased. Early in 1786, he grew preoccupied by the negative propaganda about America, especially the presumed instability of the American markets, which were taken to be the cause of American debts. To his old friend Jonathan Shipley he wrote February 24, 1786, defending Americans against the calumnies presented in the public press in England: "Your Newspapers are fill'd with ficticious Accounts of Anarchy, Confusion, Distresses and Miseries we are suppos'd to be involv'd in, as Consequences of the Revolution." The negative publicity came from the loyalists' exaggerated accounts, Franklin thought. He explained that "the few remaining Friends of the old Government among us, take pains to magnify every little Inconvenience a Change in the Course of Commerce may have occasioned."[7] Concerned that the negative accounts of Americans might create doubts among the French about the potential for American prosperity, Franklin wrote to his old French friend Louis-Guillaume Le Veillard (1733–1794) on March 6, "Be assured that all the stories spread in the English papers of our distresses, and confusions, and discontents with our new governments, are as chimerical as the history of my being in chains at Algiers," he insisted. "They exist only in the wishes of our enemies," he said, adding, "America never was in higher prosperity, her produce abundant and bearing a good price, her working people all employed and well paid, and all property in lands and houses of more than treble the value it bore before the war." With "our commerce being no longer the monopoly of British merchants," he pointed out that Americans were "furnished with all the foreign commodities we need, at much more reasonable rates than heretofore." He used this point to insist that American debt would be repaid: "We have no doubt of being able to discharge more speedily the debt incurred by the war than at first was apprehended."[8] The content of this letter was much like that in his letter to Rodolphe-Ferdinand Grand written the previous day: "The English Papers . . . are sending all the United States to Destruction: By their Account you would think we are in the utmost Distress, in Want of every thing, all in Confusion, no Government, and wishing again for that of England." He insisted that his friends should be assured that "these are all Fictions, mere English Wishes, not American Realities." In fact, he insisted, "I never saw greater and more indubitable Marks of public Prosperity in any Country." He spoke to agricultural and manufacturing stability: "The Produce of our Agriculture bears a good Price, and is all paid for in ready hard Money, all the labouring People have high Wages, every body is well cloth'd and well-lodg'd." Knowing of the beginning of turmoil in France, he added that "the Poor [were] provided for or assisted, and all Estates in Town and Country much increas'd in Value. As to wishing for the English Government we should as soon wish for that of Morocco."[9] Franklin believed that if the markets were free of government interference and political intrigue, everyone would have greater confidence in their own ability to thrive, they would labor more readily, and the markets would take off. "Let the merchants on both sides treat with one another," he wrote to his old friend George Whatley (c. 1709–1791), on May 18, 1787, adding, "Laissez les faire."[10]

Some of the negative publicity about America resulted from anxiety about the form that the government would take. Franklin acknowledged that turmoil was evident in some places, but he typically assured his friends, as he had assured Jefferson initially upon his return, that disagreements are to be expected in free and representative governments. His letter to Shipley gives us a good example of his approach to the question of the American government: "We are, I think, in the right Road of Improvement," he said, "for we are making Experiments." Always the conciliator, Franklin said, "I do not oppose all that seems wrong, for the Multitude are more effectually set right by Experience, than kept from going wrong by Reasoning with them." He insisted that "we are daily more and more enlightened: So that I have no doubt of our obtaining in a few Years as much public Felicity as good Government is capable of affording."[11] His utopian optimism, an expressed position about essential eventual success, bespoke his having spent a lifetime trying to achieve the end of good government.

Franklin's propaganda about America resulted from his lifelong consideration of the problems of trade, defense, and taxation. He was determined to cast a positive light on American life. To some of his friends he sent along some of his remarks on the defense of American trade. Two documents dating to 1786 illustrate the point. The first, "The Retort Courteous," probably written early in 1786, took its cue from the calumnies in the British papers. Franklin offered his version of the history of commerce in the colonies to assail the mock pretensions of Britain and draw attention to Britain's unwillingness to give over the frontier posts in the interior, as promised in treaty, because American debt had not been met. Franklin's "retort" against Britain traces a history of commerce and interactions from roughly the 1750s to the end of the war. His goal was to show that oppressive British policies against the Americans were the cause of any debt in the first place. He argued that "the present Inability of many American Merchants to discharge their Debts contracted before the War, is not so much their Fault as the Fault of the crediting Nation who by making an unjust War on them, obstructing their Commerce, plundering and devastating their Country were the Cause of that Inability I have answered the Purpose of writing this Paper." He sent copies of his "Retort" to his French and British friends, "chearfully submit[ing them] to the World's impartial Judgment."[12] He knew his paper would be circulated among his friends in the European republic of letters, and it was.

In addition to viewing American debt as a consequence of Britain's extensive suppressive policies, Franklin wrote another essay about the same time, this one a satire offering to pay back such "debt" with the convicts foisted on British North America back in the 1750s. Here Franklin was recalling his earlier anger about Britain's Navigation Acts and their global impact on commerce, anger that prompted his "Rattlesnakes for Felons" satire of 1751. With his usual biting sarcasm, Franklin (as "A.B.") opened this new essay by recollecting the act for transporting felons to the colonies: "We may all remember the Time when our Mother Country, as a Mark of her parental Tenderness, emptied her Jails into our Habitations, '*for the* BETTER *Peopling,* as she express'd it, *of the Colonies.*'" Adopting the presumably dispassionate tone of a statesman, Franklin continued that he was "certain that no due Returns have yet been made for these valuable Consignments." Calling up his favorite claim about the increase of mankind in North America, Franklin announced that "the felons she [i.e., Britain] planted among us have produc'd such an amazing Increase" that America was "now enabled to make ample Remittance in the same Commodity." He proposed that

> every English Ship arriving in our Ports with Goods for Sale, should be obliged to give Bond, before she is permitted to Trade, engaging that she will carry back to Britain, at least One Felon for every

Fifty Tons of her Burthen. Thus we shall not only discharge sooner our Debts, but furnish our old Friends with the means of "*better Peopling*" and with more Expedition, their promising new Colony at Botany Bay.[13]

Franklin was specifically addressing problems between Britain and the United States, but his writings from these years evince a global vision rather than a provincial one. He was determined to show that Britain had an empire both expansive and oppressive. He was concerned about Britain's imperial expansion into India, Australia, and New Zealand, so he spoke as much to the oppressive policies behind Britain's imperial expansion as to the immediate problem of the negative propaganda flowing freely in British papers about North America.

Securing the Peace

Franklin always believed that most people would seek out and protect their own best interests, which would also be the interests of their community. Yet even Franklin could not have been sanguine about the situation in North America. The Peace of Paris might have secured for American settlement the trans-Appalachian region extending to the Mississippi River, but this did not mean that the territory would remain uncontested by other Europeans or that Native peoples were quiescent and happy to accept the European decisions made about their ancestral homelands. Nor did it make it possible for debts to soldiers to be paid, even in land to the west, or for merchants' debt to be erased from the rolls in Britain and Europe. States still had significant debt to pay, and some states, such as Massachusetts, were determined to pay off the debt sooner rather than later by increasing taxes on lands.

Problems with war debt and taxation were widespread. In Massachusetts, many farmers recently returned home from the war were unable to make payments on their farms and thus forced to sell at a loss in order to repay debts and to pay taxes. The situation caused an uprising from 1786 to 1787 by Daniel Shays (c. 1747–1825), a former Continental soldier from western Massachusetts, who initiated an alarm for all the states facing similar debt crises. Debt had become a national crisis, however much Franklin pretended otherwise in his letters to friends in Britain and Europe. When he first learned of Daniel Shays's October 1786 uprising from newspaper accounts and then from his correspondents, George Washington expressed his dismay to Henry ("Light Horse Harry") Lee III (1756–1818), "I am mortified beyond expression when I view the clouds that have spread over the brightest morn that ever dawned upon any Country." In postwar retirement at Mount Vernon, Washington wrote that he was "lost in amazement when I behold what intrigue, the interested views of desperate characters, ignorance and jealousy of the minor part, are capable of effecting, as a scourge on the major part of our fellow Citizens of the Union." The uprisings brought the realities of life for common people to the attention of those whose lives were secured by wealth or prestige. Worse, the uprisings would confirm what those in Europe and especially in Britain might have hoped for: the immediate demise of Americans once the Peace of Paris had concluded. Washington further remarked, "The picture which you have exhibited, and the accounts which are published of the commotions, and temper of numerous bodies in the Eastern States, are equally to be lamented and deprecated." He ruminated, "They exhibit a melancholy proof of what our trans-Atlantic foe has predicted; and of another thing perhaps, which is still more to be regretted, and is yet more unaccountable, that mankind when left to themselves are unfit for their own Government."[14]

Washington was less optimistic than Franklin about the ability of people to govern themselves. The problems in the northeastern states served an important reminder that men who had already participated in a war in behalf of liberty and especially freedom from tax policies with which they did not concur could just as easily seek their own means of justice against a perceived tyrannical taxation. When internal strife and civil warfare threatened the nation and especially the nation's interests abroad, self-governance was thus put to the test.

Franklin always hoped that people would see to their own success after the war was resolved in favor of North America, so he was especially annoyed by the factionalism and agitation taking place in the states. Such local controversies formed only one set of problems brought to Franklin's attention during these years. Spain still controlled much of the traffic on the lower Mississippi River, including New Orleans, a major port. In 1784, the Spanish government closed the use of the Mississippi to everyone except Spanish traffickers. About that time, Britain decided, via the Privy Council, to close most American commerce to the British West India islands. In addition, though it had agreed to vacate its frontier posts in forts to the west, Britain argued that it could not abandon its Native allies. Britain thus held onto the rich fur trade and its Native allies, negating, in effect, its agreement to vacate. Adding to the complications Americans were facing, their ships were being seized—because they were no longer protected by the British navy—by the "Barbary States" of North Africa, Algiers, Tunis, and Morocco. Americans were being held captive or else sold into North African slavery. This is why Franklin stressed in those letters to Europe (for example, the letter to Rodolphe-Ferdinand Grand of March 5, 1786), that he was not in chains in Morocco! Rumors had been circulating with abandon.

While Franklin was propagandizing his British and European friends about the industry and enlightenment of the American people, he was also addressing important local and national problems that continued to plague the new republic. Throughout his three consecutive terms as president of Pennsylvania's Supreme Executive Council, Franklin had to address serious matters cropping up in Pennsylvania. Most noteworthy in this regard were the repeated problems in northeastern Pennsylvania caused by New Englanders attempting to lay claim to territory there. The history of the uprisings in the Luzerne area (typically called the Valley of the Wyoming) lay in mixed grants during the colonial era, with tracts of the same land in northeastern Pennsylvania being claimed by charter both to Pennsylvania and to Connecticut. Problems had originated in the late 1760s with a series of local wars, known as the Yankee-Pennamite wars, prompted by settlers from Connecticut who were attempting to lay claim to the Wyoming area, based on a charter to John Winthrop (1606–1676), governor of Connecticut, in 1662. In a decree rendered at Trenton, New Jersey, in 1782 by the new federal government, the Wyoming Valley was determined to be part of Pennsylvania. Yet under the leadership of one John Franklin (n.d.), settlers from Connecticut, New York, and Massachusetts charged onto the land in an effort to claim it first for Connecticut and then for an independent state to be called Westmoreland.[15]

Franklin spent many months from 1786 through 1788 hearing petitions, answering letters, and writing to the governors of New York and several New England states. Ethan Allen (1738–1789) and, later, Daniel Shays became involved, hoping to incite a general uprising of farmers against the new state and federal governments. Franklin was forced to handle a range of different petitions about the matter. He finally composed a proclamation about the rights of Pennsylvanians to use the land granted to them originally by charter. As he expressed it to George Clinton (1739–1812), governor of New York, on June 1, 1786, he was troubled by these events, because they were unlawful and kept the people from their proper labors. As he had done with the New England governors, he requested that Clinton do whatever was necessary "to prevent these restless Spirits from exciting Disturbances, that may divert the People's Attention from their Industry, and be attended with mischievous Consequences."[16] These disturbances weighed on Franklin, but he seems to have believed in the power of the confederation to quell disturbances. Unlike Washington, who was willing to use federal intervention and arrest the disgruntled New Englanders, Franklin spent a good deal of time trying to negotiate with John Franklin and others for a peaceful outcome.[17]

In addition to overseeing Pennsylvania's problems, Franklin was elected to serve as a Pennsylvania representative to the federal convention, originally called by Virginians concerned about the inadequacy of the Articles of Confederation to secure internal peace and create policies related to commerce and defense. Americans lacked clear means of defense, including a navy, and America had neither an external nor internal federal commercial policy. From May until September 1787, Franklin represented Pennsylvania at the federal convention being held in New York. His activities there, some of them recorded by James Madison (1751–1836), indicate his continued mental strength, especially his problem-solving capacity and his interest in preserving opportunities for all people. Here he articulated several positions based on his unfailing idealism that common people could be relied on to make good decisions. Among the more famous of Franklin's proposals were those related to representation of the states in federal life and to a general extension of the franchise. On June 11, 1787, Franklin argued that representation to Congress should be proportional to population. Having spent decades in England speaking to matters supporting the rights of common citizens and their abilities for self-rule, it is not surprising that Franklin argued (August 7 and 10) to extend the right to vote as widely as possible. He disliked the idea of having property be the qualification for voting and officeholding. When issues in representation threatened completely to stall the meeting, Franklin came up with what has been called the "great compromise" in representation. He argued on July 3, 1787, that representation might be proportional to population in the House and equal by state in the Senate. His proposal was approved by the Grand Committee and enacted by the whole Convention on July 16, 1787.

Yet Franklin's most famous request for compromise occurred at the conclusion of the convention. He urged—through James Wilson, who read aloud Franklin's closing speech at the convention on September 17, 1787—that every member make an effort to "doubt a little of his own Infallibility," put aside his specific reservations, and vote unanimously for approval of the Constitution. "Much of the Strength and Efficiency of any Government in procuring and securing Happiness to the People," Franklin said, "depends on Opinion, on the general Opinion of the Goodness of that Government as well as of the Wisdom and Integrity of its Governors." Given the importance of public opinion, he expressed hope "that for our own Sakes, as a Part of the People, and for the sake of our Posterity we shall act heartily and unanimously in recommending this Constitution."[18] It seems fitting that Franklin's last speech insisted on the importance of compromise, because, as historian Barbara Oberg once pointed out, "A stand for compromise, even [one] deftly and eloquently expressed," while it is "not the stuff of heroism, virtue, or moral certainty," is "the essence of the democratic process."[19]

Other matters Franklin addressed in the federal convention, matters less frequently discussed by Franklin biographers, related to Native peoples, the Cherokees particularly. Franklin consistently expressed a view that the Native peoples should be secured to the Americans' side. The Spanish controlled traffic on the Mississippi, especially at the useful port of New Orleans. The British retained Canada and a significant standing in forts on the frontier. As we have seen in previous chapters, Franklin understood the importance of Native rights to land, and their rights weighed heavily in his views about land tenure and sovereignty. A cluster of Franklin's papers reveals his work in the convention in this area of concern, particularly with regard to an effort, headed up by John Sevier (1745–1815), to establish a state of Franklin. Among Franklin's papers are several letters to and from a group of Cherokees and Franklin's remonstrances to Sevier and others who were creating disturbances for the state government of North Carolina and the Cherokees.

A group of southerners were seeking, under the proposed governorship of John Sevier, to carve a state called Franklin from territory held by the Cherokees and under contested jurisdiction between North Carolina and what is now Tennessee. Franklin was embroiled in the matter because of the titular significance of the state and his work in the convention. Sevier and his group had shown signs of militancy like that posed by Daniel Shays in New England. When discussions reached an impasse with the government of North Carolina, which denied the political sovereignty of the separatist Franklinite faction, Sevier wrote to North Carolina governor Richard Caswell (1729–1789), "We shall continue to Act as Independent and would rather Suffer death in all its Various and frightful shapes then Conform to any thing that is disgraceful." Sevier and his group were as divisive among the settler peoples as among the Chickamaugas and Overhill Cherokees. The Treaty at Hopewell Plantation between the Confederation Congress and the Cherokees and Chickasaws (1786), and Choctaws (1786)—a treaty between the United States and Native peoples—was meant to open

territory for settlement but also to create a western boundary for settlement, leaving Native lands free beyond the boundary line. Nonetheless,
settlers extended beyond the articulated boundaries, and Native peoples
were justifiably outraged, seeing their homelands taken over by squatters
who had no right to be there. The Cherokees preferred the Hopewell treaty,
because it undermined an earlier, less generous treaty and dispensed with
the Sevier group's Franklin treaty of Dumplin Creek, which had forced
the Cherokees to accept what were, from the state and federal standpoints,
illegal land claims against their territory.[20]

Franklin was incensed against the settlers. He learned firsthand about
the land takeover from a delegation of Cherokees who reported that unin-
vited and aggressive settlers were causing stress in their communities. The
Cherokees' representatives had traveled northward hoping to find the convention in session. They wanted to explain their concerns about the takeover of their territory by settler people. Franklin wrote to Sevier on June
30, 1787, explaining his displeasure with the proceedings. "There are only
two Things that Humanity induces me to wish you may succeed in," he
said. He wanted Sevier and his group to work on "Accommodating your
Misunderstanding with the Government of North Carolina by amicable
Means" and "Avoiding an Indian War by preventing Encroachments on
their Lands." Having seen the turmoil in Pennsylvania when settlers took
over Indian lands without clear title to them, Franklin was angry and ada-
mant that no war occur: "Such Encroachments are the more unjustifiable,
as these People in the fair Way of Purchase usually give very good Bargains."
It was inefficient to go to war for land, especially when good land could, he
argued, be had cheaply. "In one Year's war with them," he pointed out, "you
may suffer a Loss of Property, and be put to an Expense, vastly exceeding in
Value what would have contented them perfectly in fairly buying the Lands
they can spare."

Franklin was most troubled by the fact that the issues had reached such
a head that Cherokee representatives were sent to treat at the federal convention. Having considered fully the political ramifications of sovereignty,
Franklin sided with the Cherokees, whose lands were being taken rather
than tendered to the settlers by purchase under treaty and law. Frustration
emerged in every line of Franklin's letter to Sevier: "Here is one of their
People, who was going to Congress with a Complaint from the Chiefs of
the Cherokees, that the North Carolinians on one Side, and the People
of your State on the other, encroach upon them daily." He concluded by
pointing out that "the strongest Governments are hardly able to restrain
the disorderly People who are generally on the Frontiers, from Excesses of

various kinds." He assured Sevier that if war ensued from such encroachments, the federal government would not assist settlers on any Indian
lands.[21] Franklin was unwilling to have the federal government intervene
in such a war over lands already acknowledged as Indian territory. Based
on his views of sovereignty, he consistently argued that settlers must purchase land in order to lay claim to it.

For their parts, the Cherokees wrote to Franklin indicating their
understanding that they had sovereignty over their own land (especially
Chota, their sacred birthplace and home) and that their young men were
prepared to defend their ancestral lands against any who sought to take
them by force. In September, Franklin received a written down message
from Katteuha, "The Beloved woman of Chota," that their young men had
come home with Franklin's replies to their entreaties against Sevier and
his group. She wrote to say that she was "in hopes my Brothers and the
Beloved men near the water side will heare from me" (i.e., listen to her),
because "This day I filled the pipes that they smoaked in piece [peace], and
I am in hopes the smoake has Reached up to the skies above." Katteuha
underscored that she was speaking as a woman, the mother of all creation,
to ensure that (as she conceived it) the men in Congress would pay attention to her. "I have Taken the privelage to Speak to you as my own Children,
and the same as if you had sucked my Breast," Katteuha said, adding, "I am
in hopes you have a beloved woman amongst you who will help to put her
Children Right if they do wrong, as I shall do the same." In her message, she
acknowledged that "the great men have all promised to Keep the path clear
and straight," thus reiterating, to make a record of it, what the Cherokees
had been promised. She added that "my Children shall Keep the path clear
and white so that the Messengers shall go and come in safety Between us."
Katteuha's aim that her people keep the path "clear and white" records her
promise that the Cherokees will work to maintain peace and happiness as
long as the "great men" of the Congress will do so. She indicated in her
message that it was difficult for the elders to keep the young men from war-
ring on the insulting settlers: "The old people is never done Talking to their
Children—which makes me say so much as I do." Drawing attention to the
fact that she was a woman ("I am a woman giving you this Talk," she said),
Katteuha confirmed that she was "in hopes that you and all the Beloved
men in Congress will pay particular Attention to it, as I am Delivering it to
you from the Bottom of my heart." Her aim was "that they will Lay this on
the white stool in Congress," because she was "wishing them all well and
success in all their undertakings." She concluded by remarking, "I hold fast
the good Talk I Received from you my Brother," thus indicating that what

the Cherokee representatives reported on their return to her would become part of the remembered record of the meeting held with Franklin and other American leaders, a record that served like law among the Cherokees. The Cherokees insisted on their rights to their own lands, and they wanted to be clear to those in government that they were prepared to defend those rights—their young men were especially willing to do so—if the encroachments continued. Franklin understood and respected the message, having been part of Native and settler meetings that took place in Pennsylvania decades earlier.[22]

Franklin believed in the potential efficacy of federal governance. His letters betray his idealistic assumption that the new government would be able to resolve most matters that states were ineffectual in handling. He also believed that an educated citizenry could go a long way toward avoiding future war either with British and European states or with Native peoples. He believed that if people were educated about the costs of war, they would surely choose peace above war. If people could be educated about their best interests, they would understand that war prevented people from laboring for their own betterment, which for Franklin was (as witnessed in his earlier years) the betterment of the nation.

We gain a sense of Franklin's belief in the potential of all common people from the records of James Madison at the federal convention. When Franklin rose to speak against the idea that only wealthy people should be considered for presidential office, he expressed clearly his idealistic trust in the abilities of common people to do what was best for themselves. He also showed an acute awareness of the impact of their deliberations on state policies in Europe. Madison's journal for Friday, August 10, 1787, provides a record of Franklin's speech:

> DOC^{tr} FRANKLIN expressed his dislike of every thing that tended to debase the spirit of the common people. If honesty was often the companion of wealth, and if poverty was exposed to peculiar temptation, it was not less true that the possession of property increased the desire of more property. Some of the greatest rogues he was ever acquainted with, were the richest rogues. We should remember the character which the Scripture requires in Rulers, that they should be men hating covetousness. This Constitution will be much read and attended to in Europe, and if it should betray a great partiality to the rich, will not only hurt us in the esteem of the most liberal and enlightened men there, but discourage the common people from removing into this Country.[23]

Franklin's public expressions consistently evinced a recognition of human frailty—especially selfishness and covetousness—and human possibility. His democratic spirit was, as many have remarked, unusual at the federal convention. In his last remarks to the convention, he was expressing an idealism about the potential government they had framed and a radical understanding of the importance of solidarity. What had happened behind the closed doors of the convention would have global consequences. For that reason, Franklin recommended that everyone in the room should trust his own fallibility, compromise a bit, and stand unified behind the new federal Constitution. It is as if Franklin had listened to all the debates and cut to the essential, foundational meanings behind the many divergent positions: forming the nation would require flexibility, humanity, humility, and a significant acknowledgment of human fallibility.

"The pestilential detestable traffic in the bodies and souls of men"

Franklin late in his life made an effort to come to terms with one specific area of his own fallibility, the area of racial prejudice and the inhumane trafficking in slaves that he had overlooked as a problem in his earlier days. On the issue of abolition and the improvement of life for Africans and African Americans in British North America, Franklin had hedged, for a good part of his life. Yet when he returned from France, he decided to use his tremendous influence to work with others in Philadelphia toward the gradual emancipation of blacks from slavery and toward equality before the law—at both the state and federal levels—for all free blacks.

For Franklin as for many in his generation, the tension between economic self-interest and the ideology of freedom grew during the eighteenth century. In his earliest years, as we have seen, Franklin considered that economic self-interest could be aligned with ancient British liberties. His parents had not owned slaves, though people in Boston—including their friends and associates—did have slaves in their households. When he got to Philadelphia and developed his own newspaper, Franklin published advertisements for slaves in his newspapers. When he discovered that the German domestic workers would not work well with Deborah, Franklin brought slaves into their household.[24] So did many of the well-to-do Quakers in his circle in this early part of the eighteenth century. John Woolman, Anthony Benezet, and some others were beginning an antislavery crusade, but as Gary Nash and Jean Soderlund have acknowledged, "Quaker opponents of slavery had limited influence in the years before 1750."[25]

The economic situation in Pennsylvania was difficult for those in the cities who had jobs to offer. Indentured laborers tended to work off their indentures and buy their own plots of land and work for themselves. These were conditions Franklin had praised in his tracts of the 1750s and 1760s. But these conditions also led affluent Pennsylvanians, Friends and non-Friends alike, to purchase slaves when suitable laborers could not be found. As Nash and Soderlund have pointed out, when free labor was chronically short due to the availability of land, "slaves bound in perpetuity" became preferable to indentured white servants bound for merely four to seven years. In such circumstances, both slaves and indentured laborers "provided labor for craftsmen, merchants, farmers, millers, and mariners who needed more assistance than their families could supply."[26] The labor shortage, ill-timed because of the interior war-stimulated economy in the 1750s, prompted Philadelphians to turn to enslaved Africans to supply their labor needs. Nash and Soderlund have indicated that between 1759 and 1762 well over 850 blacks were brought up the Delaware River to Philadelphia. Both Quakers and non-Quakers participated in the trade and bought slaves for their own use.[27]

Yet by the 1760s, abolitionist efforts had begun to gain traction among many Quakers, with greater attention paid to a rhetoric of freedom as it showed up in Philadelphia's Yearly Meetings, even if not more generally across the colonies.[28] In a society that held some people in bondage—those darker skinned, those speaking a different language, those whose religious views differed, those whose land was sought—while others, even uneducated people and miscreants, could be free, tensions grew inordinately high. Educated Africans, Native peoples, and African Americans were proving to their British, European, and American counterparts that native genius—indeed, humanity—could reside in someone from another race. Humanitarian efforts became mainstream among a new generation of Friends in Philadelphia, yet they could not convince their associates to emancipate their slaves nor even to stop buying slaves. They did gain a hearing for abolition when a platform of gradual emancipation began to emerge, but even then, success occurred not among the lawmakers but among laboring people, who were the first to form abolition societies.

Franklin spent his mature years questioning some of his own racial assumptions. While in London as a colonial representative, Franklin was learning more about Africans from members of the Associates of Dr. Bray, an Anglican group founded by Thomas Bray (1656–1730) to support mission schools in North America. By the middle eighteenth century, the group embraced the idea of educating Africans. Eventually they supported emancipation in Britain and in the American colonies. Under the influence of the Associates during the 1760s, Franklin began to consider Africans in a light different from either the imperial vision of the export trade or that of the Philadelphia tradesman needing workers to assist in domestic work.[29] As he explained in 1763 to John Waring (1716–1794), Anglican clergyman and member of the late Dr. Bray's circle, he found himself surprised at the accomplishments of blacks when he visited the local Negro School upon his return to Philadelphia. He had gone to visit the school taught by William Sturgeon (c. 1722–1770), an Anglican graduate of Yale who had become an assistant at Christ Church and catechized the students. The Negro School, funded by the London Society for the Propagation of the Gospel in Foreign Parts and the Associates of Dr. Bray, had an interested following among Philadelphians. Franklin was in the process of reconsidering the presumed inferiority of blacks. "I was on the whole much pleas'd," he wrote to Waring. He attested that "from what I then saw" he had "conceiv'd a higher Opinion of the natural Capacities of the black Race, than I had ever before entertained." Indeed, he began to doubt of any real difference between Africans and Europeans: "Their Apprehension seems as quick, their Memory as strong, and their Docility in every Respect equal to that of white Children," he concluded.[30] He admitted that he had had "Prejudices," formerly. He also indicated he would not attempt to justify those prejudices.

Like many of his friends in London, Paris, and Philadelphia, Franklin grew more and more ambivalent about slaveholding, especially in light of the rhetoric of liberty then circulating about the American colonies.[31] The liberal wing of politicians in London, like their French aristocratic counterparts, created articulate messages about natural rights that lent themselves to a critique of the slave trade and enslavement more generally. Franklin embraced antislavery rhetoric in several writings from the 1760s through the early 1770s. In his "A Conversation on Slavery" (printed in the *Public Advertiser*, January 30, 1770), Franklin discussed slavery from the perspective of an Englishman, an American, and a Scotsman. Franklin's Englishman chastised the American for the Americans' insistence upon the natural rights of all people to be free despite their own use of slaves: "You Americans make a great Clamour upon every little imaginary Infringement of what you take to be your Liberties; and yet there are no People upon Earth such Enemies to Liberty, such absolute Tyrants, where you have the Opportunity, as you yourselves are." The foundation of the criticism arose, Franklin said, from Sharp's "*A Book upon Slavery*," Franklin's shorthand reference for *A Representation of the Injustice and*

Dangerous Tendency of Tolerating Slavery or of Admitting the Least Claim of Private in the Persons of Men in England (London, 1769) by Granville Sharp (1735–1813), a civil officeholder who became an outspoken abolitionist and social reformer. Franklin had met Sharp on several occasions and later enjoyed a correspondence with him.[32] In the "Conversation," Franklin argued that not all Americans had the same views about slaves. New England had few slaves, the American said, adding that "the same may be said of the next populous Provinces, New-York, New Jersey, and Pensylvania." Where slaves were numerous—"Virginia, Maryland, and the Carolinas"—they were chiefly held by people of old wealth in the region. In fact, he said, "Many Thousands there abhor the Slave Trade as much as Mr. Sharpe can do, conscientiously avoid being concerned with it, and do every Thing in their Power to abolish it."

Franklin was defending a situation that was for many indefensible in terms of morality and humanity. So he used his "Conversation" to argue two key points for Americans, first, that Britain's treatment of its own working poor did not significantly differ from Americans' use of slaves, and second, that Britain's taxation and navigation policies, in effect, caused the slave trade originally and were responsible for its perpetuation in North America. The working poor had no rights in England. And if slavery proved abhorrent, the root of that abhorrent practice was in England, he insisted: "As to the Share England has in these Enormities of America, remember, Sir, that she began the Slave Trade; that her Merchants of London, Bristol, Liverpool and Glasgow, send their Ships to Africa for the Purpose of purchasing Slaves." Franklin then pointed to the Navigation Laws that, he said, forced slavery upon the Americans. "If any unjust Methods are used to procure them; if Wars are fomented to obtain Prisoners; if free People are enticed on board, and then confined and brought away; if petty Princes are bribed to sell their Subjects, who indeed are already a Kind of Slaves, is America to have all the Blame of this Wickedness?" Britain was at fault: "This you have not only done and continue to do, but several Laws heretofore made in our Colonies, to discourage the Importation of Slaves, by laying a heavy Duty, payable by the Importer, have been disapproved and repealed by your Government here, as being prejudicial, forsooth, to the Interest of the African Company." In this interpretation, Britain's navigation policies made it impossible for Americans to avoid the use of slaves. Further, by keeping British laborers on the island and preventing their emigration to North America, Britain created the situation where American manufacturers were forced to employ enslaved labor in order to meet demands of production. The "Conversation on Slavery" spoke to key abolitionist arguments while addressing Franklin's particular political concerns about the oppression of Americans. His views articulated an anti-slavery message couched in his standard economic defense of Americans who, he said, engaged in the slave trade because of an absence of specie, the necessities imposed by the Navigation Acts, and the absence of skilled laborers from England in the wake of the series of laws constraining laborers from moving off the island.

Within two years, his antislavery views became less pragmatic and more dramatically humanitarian. He wrote an unsigned letter to the *London Chronicle*, June 18–20, 1772, where he addressed the recent legal decision being lauded in the newspapers, *Somerset v. Stewart*, wherein William Murray (1705–1793), first Earl of Mansfield, rendered a decision that chattel slavery was not, upon examination, justified in England by English and Welsh law. Slavery could not be supported *in England* by English law, but the ruling did not extend to the Empire's claimed lands elsewhere. The decision was taken to be an abolitionist decision, but in truth, the narrow judgment was simply that a slave could not be forcibly removed from England against his will. Somerset the slave—whom Stewart had attempted to transport out of England and back into slavery—was set free. Franklin used the opportunity to create a bitter argument against Britain couched in moral terms about the inhumanity of enslaving Africans, not just those that happened to be on soil in England. Franklin's brief article, "The Sommersett Case and the Slave Trade," expressed gratitude for the success of the Somerset case, but it offered a bitter castigation of a society that had, in effect, enforced slavery in colonial areas while congratulating itself about its own humanity in setting a single man free at home.

Franklin wrote that he hoped Britain would now create a law "procuring liberty for those that remain in our Colonies, [or] at least to obtain a law for abolishing the African commerce in Slaves, and declaring the children of present Slaves free after they become of age." The article pictured in serious and sentimental terms the plight of Africans: "the yearly importation is about one hundred thousand," Franklin computed, "of which number about one third perish by the gaol distemper on the passage, and in the sickness called the *seasoning* before they are set to labour." Drawing attention to the labor, particularly in the South and the sugar colonies of the Caribbean, Franklin highlighted the "distempers occasioned by excessive labour, bad nourishment, uncomfortable accommodation, and broken spirits" of Africans forced into bondage. He taunted his readers with a series of rhetorical questions: "Can sweetening our tea, &c. with sugar, be a circumstance of such absolute necessity? Can the petty pleasure thence arising to the taste, compensate for so much misery produced among our fellow creatures, and such a constant butchery of the human species by this pestilential detestable traffic in the bodies and souls of men?" Then, pointing to the hypocrisy of British pretention, he expostulated, "*Pharisaical Britain!* to pride thyself in setting free *a single Slave* that happens to land on thy coasts, while thy Merchants in all thy ports are encouraged by thy laws to continue a commerce whereby so many *hundreds of thousands* are dragged into a slavery that can scarce be said to end with their lives, since it is entailed on their posterity!" Franklin's "Sommersett" article drew attention to the debasing economics and the inhumanity of slave trafficking while pointing the finger at British self-satisfaction. He was disgusted by the hypocrisy of British people who were drawing attention to themselves as being extra special because they had freed a slave. The article clarified Franklin's view that slavery was, in effect, imposed on Americans because British people liked the productions from North America and the Caribbean. The British would not consider giving up delicacies they had grown accustomed to using. Franklin here revealed the telltale signs of his personal recognition that his rhetoric of liberty, which he had relied on all along, also applied to Africans.

Franklin had argued for the importance of the individual laborer and the inherent rights of British subjects to engage in their own labor for themselves. So why had Franklin not been an abolitionist all along, given his views about liberty and individual rights? How could he ever have participated in slavery? Perhaps the answer relates to the "Prejudices" he admitted to having back in 1763 (in his letter to Waring) and earlier, as evident in the first draft of his 1750s *Observations concerning the Increase of Mankind*, where he said that all people are partial to their own complexion. Perhaps it had to do with the complications of getting good labor in Philadelphia, when he lived there. The Franklin households (primarily the households run by Deborah and then Sally, during his long absences from home, and the household of his son, William) held five slaves: King, who was William's domestic servant; Peter and Jemima (a couple), who served the Franklin household primarily by assisting Deborah and who probably had a son, also called Peter, who worked for the Franklins; Othello, purchased by Deborah; and George, given to Franklin (really, to Sally Franklin, in her father's absence abroad) in lieu of money owed him by James Parker. With Deborah, Franklin had purchased King, Peter, and Jemima. When William and his father went to London in the 1750s, they took King and young Peter (the son of Peter and Jemima) with them. While in London, King ran off to live with a woman who educated him.[33] Franklin knew where he was, but he let him stay in England. Peter stayed with Franklin, probably because the two liked one another and he was well treated; Peter returned to America with Franklin. Deborah purchased Othello shortly after young Peter's departure with Franklin, so that she would have assistance; Othello was not an aged man, but he died before Franklin returned from his second trip to England.[34] George, who had been given to Franklin by James Parker as partial payment of a debt (George was valued at £100 New York currency), took on Othello's domestic roles in Deborah and Sally Franklin's household. George was passed by Franklin to Sally when he returned from England in 1775. George died in 1782, when Franklin was in Paris and after an illness for which Sally hospitalized him so he would be well cared for.[35] Why did Franklin hold onto slaves and pass them into his children's generation? He had told his mother in 1750 that he and Deborah "do not like Negro Servants,"[36] but they nonetheless held onto King, Peter, and Jemima, and their child long after this, and they added Othello and George into the household.

During the years he spent in Britain and Europe, Franklin seems to have been emotionally distant from the everyday situation of slaveholding—so much so that the idea of slaves in the household, as reported in Deborah's and Sally's letters, might have seemed a distant problem when compared to the political and social negotiations that made up his own everyday experience. Perhaps like many in his generation, Franklin continued to consider slaves as property, movable goods,[37] despite the rhetoric of liberty he propelled in behalf of American economic independence. The idea that Britain was ultimately responsible for the Americans' slaveholding surely helped him rationalize about the issue of trafficking in humans. Even so, such political rhetoric does not satisfy fully the real sense of responsibility for human misery that slaveholding called into being for many slaveholders, including—eventually—sometime abolitionists like Franklin. Perhaps he conceived that in his household, the slaves were treated well, and in the absence of education and improved social attitudes, they would be safer in the Franklin household than manumitted and set free to shift for themselves. The question of why Franklin held slaves in his family is perplexing and troublesome, especially given Franklin's lifelong views about the importance of an individual's owning himself and his own labor.

Franklin finally seems to have been convinced by his friends among the Associates of Dr. Bray, by Granville Sharp and Anthony Benezet, and by some others involved in abolitionism that trafficking in Africans was wrong and slaveholding morally reprehensible. In 1773, he wrote to his Irish friend Richard Woodward (1726–1794), dean of Clogher and chancellor of St. Patrick's in Dublin, enclosing either his "Conversation on Slavery" or more likely his "Somersett Case and the Slave Trade." They must have talked about slavery at the time Franklin met him in Dublin, because Franklin wrote, "I have since [meeting you in Dublin] had the Satisfaction to learn that a Disposition to abolish Slavery prevails in North America, that many of the Pennsylvanians have set their Slaves at liberty, [and] that even the Virginia Assembly have petitioned [the] King for Permission to make a Law for preventing the Importation of more Slaves into that Colony." He was coming around to a full understanding of the severe injustice being done to Africans in North America. To Benjamin Rush, also in 1773, he remarked, "The Friends to Liberty and Humanity will get the better of a Practice that has so long disgrac'd our Nation and Religion."[38] He had finally come around to understanding what many but by no means all Quakers—some of whose antislavery works he had printed back in the late 1720s and 1730s—had been arguing all along.[39]

As soon as he landed in Philadelphia, Franklin involved himself with antislavery activities locally and nationally. When asked to join the newly reorganized abolition society of Pennsylvania—formally called the Pennsylvania Society for Promoting the Abolition of Slavery, and the Relief of Free Negroes, Unlawfully Held in Bondage—Franklin readily assented. Franklin joined a renewed effort of Pennsylvanians, this time one that included men of high status and leading Quakers, not just to assist African Americans on a case-by-case basis but to work toward the eventual eradication of slavery in North America.

Franklin's membership—and presidency—was crucial to the success of the Pennsylvania Abolition Society. During the years from 1786 to 1789, Franklin wrote to many of his old friends in England and France inviting them to develop similar groups on their side of the Atlantic and to coordinate efforts with the Americans to see that slavery would no longer be tolerated. The Society worked locally to create legislation against slavery. It pressed the Pennsylvania legislature to enact laws that would outlaw in Philadelphia the outfitting of ships bound for the slave trade, prevent the separation of enslaved families, impose severe fines on those attempting to enslave free blacks or to sell blacks to the South, and legislate several related measures.[40] It worked to coordinate its efforts not just with the local Quaker societies for relief of Africans but with international associations designed to abolish slavery. Most notably, under Franklin's leadership and his signature, the Society presented an antislavery memorial to Congress on February 3, 1790, to bring national attention to abolition.

Franklin seems to have understood that for slavery to be eradicated, the problem needed to be addressed federally, globally, and locally. By appealing to the federal notion of equal liberty under the law and to ideals of humanity, the Society sought the Constitutional Convention's acknowledgment of the extreme irregularity caused by slavery, because the nation, founded on the ideals of liberty, still permitted slavery. "Mankind are all formed by the same Almighty Being," the memorial opened, indicating that all mankind are "alike objects of [the Almighty Being's] Care, and equally designed for the Enjoyment of Happiness the Christian Religion teaches us to believe" to be mankind's portion. "The Political Creed of America fully coincides with the Position" on equality in the religious and social realms. Thus it was the "duty of Congress" to secure "the blessings of liberty" to all people in the United States, "without distinction of color." Congress was implored to grant liberty to those enslaved:

> From a persuasion that equal liberty was originally the Portion, and is still the Birthright of all Men, and influenced by the strong ties of Humanity and the Principles of their Institution, your Memorialists conceive themselves bound to use all justifiable endeavors to loosen the bands of Slavery and promote a general Enjoyment of the blessings of Freedom. Under these Impressions they earnestly entreat your serious attention to the subject of Slavery; that you will be pleased to countenance the Restoration of liberty to those unhappy Men, who alone in this land of Freedom are degraded into perpetual Bondage, and who amidst the general Joy of Surrounding Free men are groaning in servile Subjection, that you will devise means for removing this Inconsistency from the Character of the American People, that you will promote Mercy and Justice towards the distressed Race, and that you will step to the very verge of the Powers vested in you, for discouraging every Species of Traffick in the Persons of our fellow Men.[41]

Slavery was not simply morally reprehensible but repugnant, because it undermined the ideals for which the war had been fought and around which the "American People" stood united. Notably, the call in the memorial was for stopping the slave trade, not for complete and immediate emancipation. Franklin believed in freedom for all people but understood that if the proposal were to be acceptable in Congress, especially to congressional leaders who themselves owned slaves, freedom would have to come by degrees.

Two months prior to his death, then, Benjamin Franklin was putting into action ideals about humankind that he had been considering for some time but not acting on. While I like to conceive that his goals were humanitarian—I believe they were—I also suspect that he was troubled by the political inconsistency of the national stance on slaveholding. Slaveholding interfered with the ideals of his mature years, specifically the view that people should have freedom to move about for work and to own their own labor while working for themselves. Inequities among the states and certainly among the United States' peoples could only arise if slaveholding remained. Furthermore, federal power and international relations would always suffer if inconsistencies in the American system were allowed to remain in place.

Congress eventually accepted the memorial, but the discussion about it that ensued was deeply troubling to Franklin. James Jackson (1757–1806), an Englishman who ended up serving in the Revolutionary War on the side of the Americans and who entered Congress for Georgia, roundly denounced the petition, arguing that the Bible gave open sanction to slavery and that civil war would be imminent if slavery were abolished. "There never was a Government on the face of the earth," Jackson taunted, "but what permitted slavery. The purest sons of freedom in the Grecian Republics, the citizens of Athens and Lacedaemon, all held slaves," he said.[42] The insolent outburst proved too outrageous for Franklin not to reply.

Franklin wrote a letter signed "Historicus" that commented on a purported letter by one "Sidi Mehemet Ibrahim, a member of the Divan of Algiers, which may be seen in Martin's account of his consulship, anno 1687." In the letter supposedly by Ibrahim, Franklin turned around the signification of slavery and told a story supporting Algerians holding Christian slaves. Under the dateline March 23, when it appeared in the *Federal Gazette* (March 25, 1790), Historicus remarked, "Reading last night in your excellent paper the speech of Mr. Jackson in Congress, against meddling with the affair of slavery, or attempting to mend the condition of slaves," he was put in mind of Sidi Mehemet Ibrahim's comments of 1687. In a devastating satirical thrust, Franklin placed Jackson in the camp of traditionalist Algerians, and he used Jackson's reasons for keeping slaves as if they arose from a reasonable-seeming Muslim who lived in Algiers during the seventeenth century. Franklin adapted key points of Jackson's arguments:

If we cease our cruises against the christians, how shall we be furnished with the commodities their countries produce, and which are so necessary for us? If we forbear to make slaves of their people, who, in this hot climate, are to cultivate our lands? Who are to perform the common labours of our city, and in our families? Must we not then be our own slaves? And is there not more compassion and more favour due to us Mussulmen, than to these christian dogs?

Franklin's comments place economics above Christian humanism, self-concern above compassion. They also target British and the European powers for condoning wage tyranny. Franklin mockingly articulated Jackson's "happy slave" position that would become popular among pro-slavery advocates in ensuing decades. According to Ibrahim, slavery is beneficial to the Christians taken captive. They are better off as slaves, "for here they are brought into a land where the sun of Islamism gives forth its light, and shines in full splendor, and they have an opportunity of making themselves acquainted with the true doctrine, and thereby saving their immortal souls. Those who remain at home have not that happiness." As for what would happen were the Christians emancipated, Ibrahim argued that former slaves could not associate easily in the mix of peoples in Algiers, the same argument made about freed African slaves in North America. The favorite argument of Granville Sharp and others who wanted to establish a separate state for freed slaves back in Africa is alluded to but also criticized:

Sending the slaves home . . . would be sending them out of light into darkness. I repeat the question, what is to be done with them? I have heard it suggested, that they may be planted in the wilderness, where there is plenty of land for them to subsist on, and where they may flourish as a free state; but they are, I doubt, too little disposed to labour without compulsion, as well as too ignorant to establish a good government, and the wild Arabs would soon molest and destroy or again enslave them.[43]

Franklin's parody of Jackson's speech in Congress aptly characterized the pro-slavery rhetoric of his era. Gradual emancipation, the keystone of the abolitionists' social construction, was unthinkable to pro-slavery advocates, as was the idea of enabling former slaves to live side by side with their former slaveowners. The moral equation Franklin drew up—that the slaveholders were no different than Algerian princes of the seventeenth century—scathingly attacked the southern Christian power block interested in creating economic superiority for their region by using a reprehensible method of ensuring work from enslaved labor.

Franklin's lively and provocative satire provides a clear sense of his finally fully developed moral and ethical stance against keeping African Americans in perpetual bondage. So much for the idea of moderation and compromise Franklin had articulated at the closing of the Constitutional Convention! As Claude-Ann Lopez and Eugenia Herbert remarked long ago, the issue of slavery that Franklin ultimately addressed late in life prompted him, at last, to bring to bear on one crucial issue "his faith in the dignity of men, his hatred of arbitrary power, his combativeness tinted with humor."[44] Franklin's satire also reveals his clearly undiminished mental capacities less than a month before his death.

"I only know that I intended well, and I hope all will end well"

During the fall of 1786, Franklin started more frequently to sign the letters to his oldest friends with the expression, "Adieu" rather than using his typical conclusion for his letters such as "my dear friend" or "yours most affectionately."[45] The word *Adieu* has a ring of finality to it, a conclusion much different from other expressions he more typically employed. Franklin's "Adieu" suggests his sense that his death was imminent. But Franklin sometimes talked about his impending death even when a much younger man, as for instance to his good friend, the evangelical preacher George Whitefield (1714–1770), in a letter dated July 2, 1756. To Whitefield, Franklin wrote, "Life, like a dramatic Piece, should not only be conducted with Regularity, but methinks it should finish handsomely." He continued, "Being now in the last Act, I begin to cast about for something fit to end with. Or if mine be more properly compar'd to an Epigram, as some of its few Lines are but barely tolerable, I am very desirous of concluding with a bright Point." The bright point at that time was a utopian idea of settling the Ohio territory with Whitefield as the chaplain, aiming to lead there "a large Strong Body of Religious and Industrious People."[46] To Hugh Roberts on July 7, 1765, Franklin likewise talked about life's conclusions: "We loved and still Love one another, we are Grown Grey together and yet it is too Early to Part." He implored, "Let us Sit till the Evening of Life is spent, the Last Hours were allways the most joyous; when we can Stay no Longer 'tis time enough then to bid each other good Night, separate, and go quietly to bed."[47]

Even though he had talked about his life's conclusion in the middle of the century, Franklin surely had a sense, in the later 1780s, that his time was nearly up. His had been a life of great significance. Working for his country, he had crossed the Atlantic six times (in addition to the two crossings of his youth). He had signed the four most important founding documents of the United States, the Declaration of Independence, the treaty of amity and commerce with France to assist the colonies in their war against Britain, the Peace of Paris (a treaty with Britain and France), and the Constitution. Franklin's last years were preoccupied by bringing the Peace of Paris to bear on American life. He had experienced significant achievement. He had held onto the values of his youth and had spent much of his life attempting to create the best opportunities for the greatest number of people. His old liberal values—that people ought to be able to labor for themselves, own their own land, move about freely, be educated—all of these were values he saw reach fruition in material life. His last effort, to bring these values to bear in the lives of Africans and African Americans in America, was still in progress at the time he died. His old effort, to find ways to treat as equitably as possible with Native peoples, was still unfolding. Yet Franklin had not given up, nor had his energy flagged, at the time when most men his age and in his physical health might have called it a day. Franklin's last years reveal the intensity of his life's work to ensure civil liberty for as many people as possible. He had managed to find a way to bring his ideas about inherent civil liberty to life in American politics, institutions, and daily experience.

To his old friend George Whatley he wrote about the odd circumstance of hearing his one-time friends now called *"old* Mr. such-a-one, to distinguish them from their sons now men grown and in business." He reflected that "by living twelve years beyond David's period, I seem to have intruded myself into the company of posterity, when I ought to have been a-bed and asleep." But he had had too much to do: "Had I gone at seventy it would have cut off twelve of the most active years of my life, employed too in matters of the greatest importance; but whether I have been doing good or mischief is for time to discover. I only know that I intended well, and I hope all will end well."[48]

Conclusion

Benjamin Franklin was America's first Atlantic world intellectual. Inquisitive, energetic, and competitive, he learned about and was proud of his British family and intellectual heritage, British political history, and British culture. From the time of his youth, Franklin embraced a set of values that he attempted, across his long life, to speak about, refine, and implement. Franklin originally conceived of himself a loyal Briton. When he entered political life in Pennsylvania, he determined how the colonies could best assist the British Empire, so that it could retain and enhance its great seaborne imperial agenda. By the 1750s, Franklin recognized that the British colonies of North America could become a separate, powerful, confederated set of states within a network of similar colonial entities, all still part of the British Empire. During his years in London, arguing first on behalf of the Pennsylvania colony and then on behalf of most of the other North American colonies, Franklin witnessed the tendencies of Crown, Privy Council, and Parliament (tendencies embraced by many British people) to view Britons in North America as subjects of Britons in England, not as equal participants in a British commonwealth. The American colonists' deprivations caused by the Navigation Acts and then the Townshend Acts, the constant denial of the validity of the colonial legislatures, the opposition to colonial manufacturing, the prevention of movements of laborers from England to North America—all worked, in Franklin's view, to deprive Britons in North America the dignity of self-determination and the liberal advantages of being part of the British Empire and reaping the benefits of their own defense and labor.

As Franklin took on larger leadership roles in the middle of the eighteenth century, he began explicitly to address in his writings the fractures caused by an imperial system that pitted different parts of the empire and different peoples within the empire against the other parts. To his thinking, such divisions would undermine greater British political and military solidarity, a solidarity that Franklin considered worth establishing. It was precisely during these years that Franklin became fascinated with the natural fecundity of North America, due to its different climates, topography, soils, and animal life. His friendships with Cadwallader Colden, Jared Eliot, James Bowdoin, and John Bartram (1699–1777) flourished, and he was visited by the Swedish naturalist Peter Kalm (1716–1779). His wide knowledge of diverse areas of agriculture brought him election on September 1, 1756, as a corresponding member to the Royal Society of Arts (in London), which sponsored innovative and experimental farming methods and fostered the development and introduction of new crops.

Franklin's knowledge of the environmental circumstances of the colonies enabled him conceive of an empire where the potential of the land could be tapped to benefit all Britons, whether in the Great Britain or North America. The imperialist views Franklin developed were, for the most part, classic ones developed around what has been called a consensual model of political relations.[1] For Franklin, members of the colonial administration and Parliament—essentially, British subjects in Britain—were attempting to interfere with the rights of British subjects in the colonies. They were negatively impacting the British Empire in their selfish attempts to achieve local and personal gain at the expense of the Britons and thus the British nation situated around the globe. Like other economic, social, and political theorists, Franklin imagined a community of people subject to the British Crown all around the globe. His ideas were consonant with some of the earliest writings on British and British American colonialism, and they were spoken in terms assuming that an equal status obtained between the colonists and the king's subjects in Britain. The problem was this: from the standpoint of the colonists, parity could be possible; from the standpoint of those in Britain, parity was unthinkable. In imagining that a group of people could relate together under one flag of commonwealth, colonial theorists were envisioning what Benedict Anderson in *Imagined*

Communities characterized as a sort of "comradeship," where difference would be eased if not erased in the imagined common citizenship.

Under the banner of nationhood, their imagined community would exist as a visionary and potential reality "regardless of the actual inequality and exploitation that [might have] prevail[ed]."[2] Franklin was undoubtedly aware of the actual inequality and exploitation taking place. He was sufficiently realistic to understand that Native peoples would lose their territory, given his understanding of how populations tend to move to live apart from others. But he was idealistic enough to want the territorial acquisition of Indian lands to be both legal and peaceful. Indeed, acquiring land legally was the precondition for the eventual claim of sovereignty, he would eventually argue. Franklin conceived that Britons in North America were the best judges of their own living situation. Indeed, he hoped he might be able to convince leaders in Britain that the path to empire lay—to adapt a metaphor Franklin himself used in 1772—in loosening the imperial reins and letting the more sure-footed horse find its way.[3]

Franklin first articulated his views about the potential happy result that might arise from colonial unity and independence from oppressive measures in his letters, written in the 1750s, to William Shirley, who became a friend and confidante during the years of war for empire in North America. Those letters provide an indication of the radical views Franklin was developing about the American colonies, particularly with regard to self-determination, trade, and defense. Franklin's first ideas about the possibilities for North America—if the colonies were independent of the constraints on trade, defense, and labor—began to emerge in these letters. In reading those letters to Shirley in the context of Franklin's other writings about the British Crown and Parliament, we gain a sense of Franklin's growing distrust of British governance. Yet even as he began seriously to question Britain's unwillingness to listen to his points about the North American colonies and the rights of Britons there, Franklin nonetheless continued to develop and offer strategies whereby the colonies could remain part of a collaborative empire for Britain extending around the globe. Part of Franklin's strategy for devising a collaborative colonial system was to work with leaders and members of the Parliament in England but also in Ireland to develop a cooperative system of trade that might develop into a collaborative political system within the British Empire. He sent his ideas around to correspondents in Europe, Scotland, and Ireland. He wrote for the public press, aiming to inform and influence the general population about conditions of everyday people in North America.

When Franklin read in newspaper reports and in notes about parliamentary proceedings what was happening in India and then when he witnessed firsthand the destitution of the Irish during a visit to Ireland in 1771, where he spent a long, cold day touring the countryside, Franklin recognized that his had been a mistaken mission. Britain would never shift policy to benefit Britons in North America. In Ireland, where Franklin saw firsthand the difference between the lives of wealthy (yet often absent) landlords as opposed to the native laborers in their fields, he grew deeply troubled. The imperial network he had imagined as a global community of equals was impossible. He recognized that Americans would be better off on their own, and he began more strongly to make his views known.

One way to secure American independence, he conceived, would be to clarify the legal issue of sovereignty, so around 1773, he began to theorize about British Americans' sovereignty in their lands, a sovereignty apart from the British Crown, Parliament, and people. His theoretical platform—developed in the context of legal opinions being rendered that year about the militarized takeover of India—held that British Americans alone, because of their personal sacrifice and their purchase of Native Americans' lands, held sovereignty over the territory they had gained peacefully. They owed no allegiance to the British Crown, nor to Britain. They owned their land and they were using it, and thus they were the sovereigns over their territory.

In light of Franklin's developing sense of sovereignty for Americans and his sense—dating as far back as the middle 1750s—that Americans would be in better economic circumstances if on their own, it seems mistaken to say (as many historians still maintain) that Franklin was a pro–British Empire man until he was denounced in Britain's Cockpit by Alexander Wedderburn in the middle 1770s. Franklin was by that time already outside the circle. His thinking had matured into a deliberative and reasoned position regarding American sovereignty, a position he realized, too late, Britons in England would never accept. This is perhaps the strongest reason why he transmitted the purloined letters that he knew would infuriate the Massachusetts representatives. When he was denounced by Alexander Wedderburn in the Cockpit in 1774, that moment made it easier for Franklin to leave England, but it was not a moment of defeat for him nor one marking a change of heart. It was merely the end of any pretense that reconciliation would be possible. When he was called to the Cockpit to face questions, Franklin knew—as he had known for decades—that the independence of the colonies had been inevitable. As he had been arguing from the 1750s onward, if they had to, the colonies could do without the complicated system of British politics and political intrigue, without a system of taxation depriving Americans of their rights of representation, not to mention their productivity and commerce, and without the demeaning and begrudging subjection so frequently thrust their way. If any American could have gained the colonies a fair hearing, Franklin was the man to do so. That he did not succeed in gaining the attention of Britons in England only confirmed what he had known for many years: British Americans could make it without Britain.

Notes

PREFACE

1. Michael Benton, *Literary Biography: An Introduction* (West Sussex, UK: Wiley-Blackwell, 2009), 2.

2. W. A. Wetzel, *Benjamin Franklin as an Economist* (Baltimore, MD: Johns Hopkins Press, 1895).

3. Lewis J. Carey, *Franklin's Economic Views* (Garden City, NY: Doubleday, Doran, 1928).

4. Verner W. Crane, *Benjamin Franklin and a Rising People* (Boston: Little, Brown, 1954) and Crane, ed., *Benjamin Franklin's Letters to the Press, 1758–1775* (Chapel Hill: University of North Carolina Press for the Institute of Early American History and Culture, 1950); Gerald Stourzh, *Benjamin Franklin and American Foreign Policy* (Chicago: University of Chicago Press, 1954); Paul W. Connor, *Poor Richard's Politics: Benjamin Franklin and His New American Order* (New York: Oxford University Press, 1965).

INTRODUCTION

1. BF *Papers* 16:18–19.

2. Franklin to Peter Collinson, May 28, 1754, in BF *Papers* 5:332.

3. While the word *citizen* has particular connotations for those who study nineteenth-century culture after the French Revolution, connotations that do not apply to the eighteenth century, I want to point out that Franklin used the word *citizen* with great frequency when talking about electors and about free people. A search in the Franklin Papers database at http://franklinpapers.org brings up close to four hundred uses of the word in Franklin's papers. Accessed July 15, 2014.

4. See John Brewer, *The Sinews of Power: War, Money and the English State, 1688–1783* (New York: Knopf, 1989), particularly 64–217; quotation at xvii.

5. Reinert argues that the eighteenth century became an era of political emulation, wherein Britain's imperial policies of extensive tariffs, control of trade and navigation, and intrusive market interventions were emulated by European powers such as France, Italy, Germany, and Scandinavia. Sophus A. Reinert, *Translating Empire: Emulation and the Origins of Political Economy* (Cambridge, MA: Harvard University Press, 2011).

6. See, for example, Blair Worden's essays in *Republicanism, Liberty, and Commercial Society, 1649–1776*, ed. David Wootton (Stanford: Stanford University Press, 1994), 45–193, which argue that certain figures serve as a suitable index for

understanding republicanism, despite their significant differences. By contrast, Markku Peltonen has said that a long tradition of civic humanist thought carried on from the sixteenth century through to the civil war era and thus characterizes republicanism. See Peltonen, *Classical Humanism and Republicanism in English Political Thought, 1570–1640* (Cambridge: Cambridge University Press, 1995).

7. My words adapt for use here some of the points made by Annabel Patterson in her book *Early Modern Liberalism* (Cambridge: Cambridge University Press, 1997), 1–26, especially 3–6.

8. Stephen Pincus, "Neither Machiavellian Moment nor Possessive Individualism: Commercial Society and the Defenders of the English Commonwealth," *American Historical Review* 103 (1998): 705–36, quotations at 708.

9. John Brewer points out that the ideology would be adopted by people of different persuasions across the late seventeenth and eighteenth centuries, depending on whatever principle they were arguing for. Scholars have tended to be suspicious of the work of those who espouse the ideology, because it was typically employed by groups from varying sides on the notion of the right of governments to abrogate the people's power whenever they happened to be out of power. I agree that it is not a reliable index of a person's views at any given point, but its frequent use as a touchstone by Franklin suggests its pervasiveness in his intellectual world. For background, see Brewer, *The Sinews of Power*, 115–66. But see also Julian Hoppit, *A Land of Liberty? England, 1689–1727* (Oxford: Oxford University Press, 2002), especially 155–60; H. T. Dickinson, *Liberty and Property: Political Ideology in Eighteenth-Century Britain* (London: Weidenfeld and Nicholson, 1977), and J. R. Jones, *Country and Court: England, 1658–1714* (Cambridge, MA: Harvard University Press, 1978).

10. Samuel Johnson, preface, *Dictionary of the English Language* (London: William Strahan, 1755). The quotations that follow arise from the preface as well.

11. See, for instance, the *Poor Richard Improved* for 1750, where for the month of January Franklin quoted from Johnson's *Vanity of Human Wishes*. BF *Papers* 3:442.

12. *The Genuine Works in Verse and Prose of the Right Honourable George Granville, Baron Lansdowne*, 3 vols. (London: J. and R. Tonson, 1736), 1:113–14. The changes Franklin made in the *Poor Richard* version draw attention to thieving, cheating, and quackery. Franklin added "Thieves" at line 3, emphasizes losses rather than the acquisitions of gold, and speaks to actual costs lost in a cargo. This is the original from Granville:

> Tho' safe thou think'st thy Treasure lies,
> Hidden in Chests from Human Eyes,
> A Fire may come, and it may be
> Bury'd, my Friend, as far from thee.
> Thy Vessel that yon Ocean stems,
> Loaded with golden Dust, and Gems.
> Purchas'd with so much Pains and Cost,
> Yet in a Tempest may be lost
> Pimps, Whores, and Bawds, a thankless Crew,
> Priests, Pick-pockets, and Lawyers too,
> All help by several ways to drain,
> Thanking themselves for what they gain:
> The Liberal are secure alone,
> For what we frankly give, for ever is our own.

13. For background on Franklin's plans, see Carla Mulford, "Benjamin Franklin, Traditions of Liberalism, and Women's Learning in Eighteenth-Century Philadelphia," in *The Good Education of Youth: Worlds of Learning in the Age of Franklin*, ed. John H. Pollack (New Castle, DE: Oak Knoll Press; Philadelphia: University of Pennsylvania Libraries, 2009), 100–121.

14. In his *Proposals Relating to the Education of Youth in Pensilvania* (Philadelphia: [B. Franklin], 1749), Franklin wrote: "The English Language might be taught by Grammar; in which some of our best Writers, as Tillotson, Addison, Pope, Algernon Sidney, Cato's Letters, &c. should be Classicks: The *Stiles* principally to be cultivated, being the *clear* and the *concise*. Reading should also be taught, and pronouncing, properly, distinctly, emphatically; not with an even Tone, which *under-does*, nor a theatrical, which *over-does* Nature": BF *Papers* 3:405–7.

15. The quotation is from *Poor Richard Improved: Being an Almanack and Ephemeris . . . for the Year of our Lord 1750. . . . By Richard Saunders, Philom* (Philadelphia: Printed and Sold by B. Franklin, and D. Hall, 1750). Franklin quotes from "Summer" (1727), part of *The Seasons* (1730) by James Thomson.

16. Thomas Gordon, Cato's Letter No. 15, as quoted by Franklin in the *New-England Courant*, July 9, 1722, and reprinted in BF *Papers* 1:27–28.

CHAPTER 1

1. Tourtellot, 42. Tourtellot's chapter 4 discusses the family's situation. Among recent biographers who have discussed the family's movement across the Atlantic, Walter Isaacson reported, for instance, that Josiah Franklin moved the family primarily for economic reasons: "Josiah's greater concern was for supporting his family," Isaacson commented, concluding, "The story of the Franklin family migration, like the story of Benjamin Franklin, gives a glimpse into the formation of the American character." Isaacson, 8–9. To my knowledge, there is no evidence to suggest that Josiah's primary motive was concern for his family. H. W. Brands spoke to the religious reasons that might have prompted Josiah Franklin to emigrate, but his discussion of what he called the "economics of the move" is much more full, and it does not rely simply on Benjamin Franklin's reportage in the memoir: H. W. Brands, *The First American: The Life and Times of Benjamin Franklin* (New York: Doubleday / Random House, 2000), 13. For background on Josiah Franklin and his family, see Nian-Sheng Huang, *Franklin's Father Josiah: Life of a Colonial Boston Tallow Chandler, 1657–1745* (Philadelphia: American Philosophical Society, 2000).

2. For cost of living information, see Tourtellot, 47–52. A reliable and interesting account of Josiah occurs in Huang; see 6 n. 7.

3. Brian Manning, "Religion and Politics: The Godly People," in *Politics, Religion, and the English Civil War*, ed. Brian Manning (London: Edward Arnold, 1973), 81–123, quotation at 96.

4. Ian Gentles, "The Civil Wars in England," in *The Civil Wars: A Military History of England, Scotland, and Ireland, 1638-1660*, ed. John Kenyon and Jane Ohlmeyer (New York: Oxford University Press, 1998), 103–55, quotation at 104. See Gentles's study of the wars for further information about the range of battles: *The English Revolution and the Wars in the Three Kingdoms, 1638-1752* (Harlow, England: Pearson Longman, 2007).

5. See Roy Sherwood, *The Civil War in the Midlands, 1642–1651* (1974; Phoenix Mill, England: Alan Sutton, 1997), 50.

6. BF Lemay *Writings*, 1311.

7. For Franklin's notes and correspondence about this trip, see BF *Papers* 8:114–21.

8. Uncle Benjamin's nostalgic poem is reprinted in BF *Papers* 8:136. The manuscript commonplace book of Uncle Benjamin (called Benjamin Franklin the Elder) is located at the American Antiquarian Society.

9. She was the daughter of Thomas Franklin, the oldest son born to Josiah's father, Thomas Franklin. For the Franklin genealogy, see BF *Papers* 1:xlix–lxxvii.

10. Documents on the Petition by William Smith are printed in BF *Papers* 8:28–51, quotations at 49, 49, 50.

11. Under Queen Mary, the Crown effectively returned to the Catholic faith, although Mary's half-brother, Edward VI, during his brief reign from 1547 to 1553, had enhanced his father's Protestantism by fostering the first Anglican Book of Common Prayer in 1549 and by requiring, through an Act of Uniformity, that it be used by the English clergy. In general, the reign of Edward VI served to enhance the role of Protestantism in England, but Mary restored the Catholic Mass and liturgy, thus re-establishing the authority of the pope. To enable an increased ritualization in church ceremonies, the administration under Mary created acts requiring that all churches be restored, internally, to the Catholic layout, allowing for the centrality of the priesthood at the church altars, among other changes. Such an effort would have required taxes to be levied in local communities for restoring their churches. In addition, there was a move to restore Catholic Church lands and relics seized by the Crown under Henry VIII's leadership. Most notably, however, uniformity was enforced: Parliament in 1555 confirmed the reinstatement of fourteenth-century heresy laws wherein individuals who did not follow the administration's decrees could be put to death and their properties donated to the Crown. Under Mary's reign, her court had executed, typically by burning, nearly three hundred people of differing ranks and stations.

12. C. William Miller has remarked, basing his information on Paul Leicester Ford's account, that "the *New-England Primer Enlarged* first appeared in Boston in 1690, introduced by its probable compiler, the London writer-printer Benjamin Harris, who had published in London in 1679 an earlier version entitled *The Protestant Tutor*, and who upon returning to London after his Boston sojourn continued to publish revised editions of the book, titled as *The New English Tutor*." Miller, 399 (entry 732). See also Paul Leicester Ford, *The New England Primer* (New York: Dodd, Mead, 1899).

13. Miller, 399 (entry 732).

14. See the preface to *The Speech of Joseph Galloway . . . in Answer to the Speech of John Dickinson* (Philadelphia: W. Dunlap, 1764), in BF *Papers* 11:267–311, mention of Rogers at 303.

15. In the memoir, Franklin attributed the story to his uncle Benjamin, perhaps because Franklin did actually have a number of family notes from his uncle, so when he was working from memory—as he was at Passy in 1771—it is understandable that he would conflate the family stories repeated to him by his uncle and his father. Yet the phrasing that Franklin used in the memoir is very close to that offered him in the letter from his father.

16. BF Lemay *Writings*, 1311–12. Josiah Franklin wrote to Benjamin Franklin about some of the family lore, including this anecdote: "In queen Mary's days, either his [Josiah's great grandfather's] wife, or my grandmother, by father's side, informed my

father that they kept their bible fastened under the top of a joint-stool that they might turn up the book and read in the bible, that when any body came to the dore they turned up the stool for fear of the aparitor, for if it was discovered, they would be in hazard of their lives" (BF *Papers* 2:230–31). The letter, full of additional information about the family, is published from Duane's BF *Works* 1:4–5.

17. The reference to the "English Bible" may be an explicit reference to John Rogers and men like him. This was probably the so-called Great Bible created during the reign of Henry VIII. The Great English Bible was a new translation made by Miles Coverdale, somewhat based on the existing translations by William Tyndale and John Rogers.

18. Uncle Benjamin's "A short account of the Family of Thomas Franklin of Ecton in Northampton Shire. 21 June 1717" is located at the Beinecke Library, Yale University. The account is made available to readers in Huang, 106–13. The quotation here is drawn from 106–7.

19. BF Lemay *Writings*, 1308.

20. Benjamin Franklin's memoir reported, "When I search'd the Register at Ecton, I found an Account of their Births, Marriages and Burials, from the Year 1555 only, there being no Register kept in that Parish at any time preceding. By that Register I perceiv'd that I was the youngest Son of the youngest Son for 5 Generations back." BF Lemay *Writings*, 1309.

21. See Uncle Benjamin's "Short Account" in Huang, 106–13.

22. The spelling of the name varied across the generations and even, sometimes, within the same generation of Franklins. Josiah Franklin gave a lively account of the name in a letter to his son Benjamin Franklin and then concluded: "However our circumstances have been such as that it hath hardly been worth while to concern ourselves much about these things, any farther than to tickle the fancy a little." The letter and useful editorial commentary appear in the BF *Papers* 2:229–32.

23. Uncle Benjamin's "Short Account" in Huang, 106.

24. Uncle Benjamin called Henry Franklin his great-grandfather in his account, but Henry Franklin seems to have been, at least according to the genealogy offered by the editors of Franklin's papers, to have been Uncle Benjamin's great-great-great-grandfather. The last name is variously spelled. Thomas Francklyne (said to have flourished from 1563 to 1573) was this Henry's son, and another Henry (spelled Franklyn, 1573–1631) was Thomas Francklyne's son. The latter Henry was Uncle Benjamin's grandfather, the father of Uncle Benjamin's father Thomas (1598–1682). See Uncle Benjamin's "Short Account" in Huang, 106, and compare with the BF *Papers* 1:l–li. What matters for our purposes here is that the family story that Benjamin Franklin knew was the one his father and Uncle Benjamin would have told.

25. The restrictions mentioned here are derived from William Potts, *A History of Banbury*, 2nd ed., ed. Edward T. Clark (Banbury, England: Gulliver Press, 1978), 133–34.

26. John Palmer (1612–1679) was rector of the Ecton parish and archdeacon of Northampton. Palmer is discussed by John Cole, *The History and Antiquities of Ecton, in the County of Northampton* (Scarborough: John Cole, 1825), 15–17, and John Bridges, *The History and Antiquities of Northamptonshire . . .*, 2 vols. (Oxford: Clarendon Press, 1791), 2:144. See also BF *Papers* 8:137.

27. The children are listed in Uncle Benjamin Franklin's "Short Account" as Thomas, born March 3, 1637; Samuel, born November 5, 1641; John, born February 20, 1643; Joseph, born October 10, 1646; Benjamin, born March 20, 1650; Hannah, born October 29, 1654; and Josiah, born December 25, 1657. Uncle Benjamin remarked,

after providing a list of the children, that his parents "had two sons more, Twins, born befor benjam. but tis tho't they dyed unbaptized because their names are not found in the church Register at Ecton where we were all born & brought up." Huang, 106–7.

28. Ronald Hutton and Wylie Reeves point out that during one particularly long bombardment, "a Parliamentarian in the force beleaguering Banbury Castle in Warwickshire recorded with grim satisfaction how screams were heard from inside every time another grenade exploded." See "Seiges and Fortifications," in *The Civil Wars: A Military History of England, Scotland, and Ireland, 1638–1660,* ed. John Kenyon and Jane Ohlmeyer (New York: Oxford University Press, 1998), 195–233, at 224.

29. Thomas Franklin (1637–1702); Samuel Franklin (1641–1664); John Franklin (1643–1691); Joseph Franklin (1646–1683). See BF *Papers* 1:li.

30. Benjamin Franklin (1650–1727); Hannah Franklin (Morris) (1654–1712); Josiah Franklin (1657–1745).

31. Quoted in Huang, 3. The notebooks are located at the American Antiquarian Society.

32. Quoted from Huang, 107.

33. Information about Wells can be found in in Tourtellot, 31–32.

34. From the short account as in Huang, 110.

35. As in Huang, 112.

36. BF Lemay *Writings,* 1312.

37. BF Lemay *Writings,* 1312.

CHAPTER 2

1. BF Lemay *Writings,* 1317.

2. BF Lemay *Writings,* 1317.

3. Kevin J. Hayes, introduction to Hayes and Edwin Wolf II, *The Library of Benjamin Franklin* (Philadelphia: American Philosophical Society and Library Company of Philadelphia, 2006), 5. For background on these titles and Franklin's reading, see Lemay *Life* 1:44–47, and Tourtellot, 169–87.

4. Joshua Sprigg, *Anglia Rediviva; England's Recovery: being the history of the motions, actions, and successes of the army under the immediate conduct of his excellency Sr. Thomas Fairfax . . . Compiled for the publique good* (London: Printed by R. W. for John Partridge, 1647).

5. Richard Vines, *The Happinesse of Israel. As it was set forth in a sermon preached to both . . . Houses of Parliament . . . upon a solemne day of thanksgiving, March 12th 1644* (London: Printed by G. M. for A. Roper, 1645).

6. Edward Hyde, *The history of the rebellion and Civil Wars in England, begun in the year 1641. With the precedent passages, and actions, that contributed thereunto, and the happy end, and conclusion thereof by the king's blessed restoration, and return upon the 29th of May, in the year 1660,* 3 vols. (Oxford: Printed at the Theater, 1702–4).

7. See Annabel Patterson, *Early Modern Liberalism* (Cambridge: Cambridge University Press, 1997), 13, and Caroline Robbins, *The Eighteenth Century Commonwealthman: Studies in the Transmission, Development, and Circumstance of English Liberal Thought from the Restoration of Charles II until the War with the Thirteen Colonies* (1959; Indianapolis, IN: Liberty Fund, 2004), 3–6.

8. On Defoe's response to Clarendon, see D. N. Deluna, "*Jure Divino*: Defoe's 'Whole Volume in Folio, by Way of Answer to, and Confutation of Clarendon's 'History of the Rebellion,'" *Philological Quarterly* 75 (1996): 43–66.

9. John Oldmixon, *Clarendon and Whitlock Compar'd* (London, 1727), xix, and quoted in Deluna, "*Jure Divino*."

10. BF Lemay *Writings*, 1359.

11. For background on the *Courant* and on James Franklin, see Lemay *Life* 1:84–142.

12. *Freeholder's Journal*, May 18, 1723, and *Weekly Journal, or British Gazetteer*, August 17, 1723. Both are quoted in Jeremy Black, *The English Press in the Eighteenth Century* (Philadelphia: University of Pennsylvania Press, 1987), 13–14.

13. Charles E. Clark, *The Public Prints: The Newspaper in Anglo-American Culture, 1665–1740* (Oxford: Oxford University Press, 1994), 123.

14. J. A. Leo Lemay has said of this printed list, "For Franklin's intellectual development, the inventory is the most significant booklist between his discussion of his early reading in the *Autobiography* and the books ordered annually by the Library Company of Philadelphia (1731–57)": Lemay *Life* 1:163.

15. BF Lemay *Writings*, 1318.

16. See Lemay *Life* 1:52–56.

17. James Franklin's advertisement in the April 25, 1720, *Boston Gazette*, quoted in Lemay *Life* 1:56.

18. James Franklin's imprints can be tracked in a number of ways, but most easily today by searching under James Franklin, publisher, in the *Archive of Americana: America's Historical Newspapers* database supported by Readex's Newsbank system in most research libraries. An exacting examination of James Franklin's printing activities appears in Lemay *Life* 1. Lemay corrects some errors regarding the life of James Franklin, including the story that James trained for the printing trade in London; Lemay shows that James learned the trade in the printing house of Bartholomew Green.

19. Lemay *Life* 1:62.

20. Richard Bernard, *The Isle of Man, Or the Legal Proceedings in Man-Shire against Sin* . . . (Boston: James Franklin, 1719). Bernard was referring in this tract to his earlier book, *A Guide to Grand-Jury Men* (London: Felix Kyngston for Edw. Blackmore, 1627, 1629), which provided instruction as to the treatment of witches and the best manner of authenticating their sorcery.

21. Bernard, *Guide to Grand-Jury Men* (1627), 8–9, 10, 54, 73–74. See Stuart Clark, *Thinking with Demons: The Idea of Witchcraft in Early Modern Europe* (Oxford: Oxford University Press, 1999), 517–18.

22. For additional background on Bernard and witch trials, see Gerald R. Cragg, *Freedom and Authority: A Study of English Thought in the Early Seventeenth Century* (Philadelphia: Westminster Press, 1975), 22 and passim. J. A. Leo Lemay has argued that Benjamin Franklin was highly critical of Samuel Sewall in the Silence Dogood paper No. 9. See Lemay *Life* 1:164–65. Sewall's writings from the time suggest animosity toward the print shop, but not the fear and calumny evident in, for instance, the writings both public and private of Increase and Cotton Mather.

23. Lemay *Life* 1:8–11 provides a useful summary of the situation of religion in Franklin's Boston. But see also Tourtellot.

24. They were called "substantial mechanics" by Rev. Alexander D. D. McKenzie, in "The Religious History of the Provincial Period," in *Memorial History of Boston*, 4 vols., ed. Justin Winsor (Boston: James R. Osgood, 1881), 2:187–248, quotation at 220–21.

25. Those who argued against installing Thacher formed their own church, the New Brick Church, in 1722. See Henry Ware, *Two Discourses Containing the History of the Old North and New Brick Churches United as the Second Church in Boston* (Boston: James W. Burditt, 1821), 25–41, 54–55. The objections are quoted on 54. But see also McKenzie, "Religious History," 2:220–26, and Chandler Robbins, *A History of the Second Church, or Old North in Boston, to Which Is Added a History of the New Brick Church* (Boston: John Wilson and Son, 1852), 170–80.

26. The complete title: *A brief declaration of Mr. Peter Thacher, and Mr. John Webb, Pastors of the New-North-Church in Boston, in behalf of themselves and said church; relating to some of their late ecclesiastical proceedings* (Boston: James Franklin, 1720). The quotations that follow appear on 3, 8, 12.

27. The pamphlet was followed by another one, also published by James Franklin, in which Caleb Lyman defended the New North Church against the several members who defected from it because they questioned Thacher's intentions in shifting his pastorate from Weymouth to Boston.

28. J. A. Leo Lemay speaks about Henry Care and John Wise in *Life* 1:74–75.

29. *English liberties, or The free-born subject's inheritance; containing Magna Charta, Charta de Foresta, the statute De Tallagio non Concedendo, the Habeas Corpus Act, and several other statutes; with comments on each of them . . . with many law-cases throughout the whole. Compiled first by Henry Care, and contiued [sic], with large additions, by W.N. of the Middle-Temple, Esq.* (Boston: Printed by J. Franklin, for N. Buttolph, B. Eliot, and D. Henchman, and sold at their shops, 1721). No date of publication was printed on the original book, but it was published in 1682. See Simon Stern, "Between Local Knowledge and National Politics: Debating Rationales for Jury Nullification after Bushell's Case," *Yale Law Journal* 111 (2002): 1815–59, at nn. 63, 160. The best study of Care is Lois G. Schwoerer, *The Ingenious Mr. Henry Care, Restoration Publicist* (Baltimore, MD: Johns Hopkins University Press, 2001).

30. Schwoerer, *Ingenious Mr. Henry Care*, 44.

31. See William A. Pencak, *War, Politics, and Revolution in Provincial Massachusetts* (Boston: Northeastern University Press, 1981).

32. Care's *English Liberties* was reprinted eight times in England: 1688, 1691, 1692, 1700, 1703, 1719, 1721, and 1766. The volume had originally published laws against Protestants that were eventually removed by Care's friend, Benjamin Harris, who brought out the 1700 edition. Harris substituted for the excisions two new sections, one on justices of the peace and the other on coroners' and constables' obligations to the community. Eventually, the additions were credited to William Nelson (b. 1653), a lawyer of the Middle Temple.

33. See Margaret Ellen Newell, *From Dependency to Independence: Economic Revolution in Colonial New England* (Ithaca, NY: Cornell University Press, 1998).

34. Care, *English Liberties* (Boston: James Franklin, 1721). The prefatory pages are unnumbered. Quotations below derive from 1, 2, and 3, consecutively.

35. I follow Schwoerer's line of reasoning in this regard. For British Americans' admiration of Care and the presence of Care in their libraries, see Schwoerer, *Ingenious Mr. Henry Care*, 232–35.

36. Schwoerer, *Ingenious Mr. Henry Care*, 233. Schwoerer says that pages 2–40 of Care's work appear in Penn's volume.

37. The Library Company also acquired copies of the book in 1764 and 1770. See Schwoerer, *Ingenious Mr. Henry Care*, 234, and Edwin Wolf, *Book Culture of a Colonial American City: Philadelphia Books, Bookmen, and Booksellers* (Oxford: Oxford University Press, 1988), 119–20.

38. Benjamin Colman, *Some Reasons and Arguments Offered to The Good People of Boston And adjacent Places, for The setting up Markets in Boston* (Boston: James Franklin, 1719), 3, 4.

39. Colman, *Some Reasons*, 4.

40. Colman, *Some Reasons*, 6–9.

41. See, for instance, Edward Wigglesworth's *A letter from one in the country to his friend in Boston, containing some remarks upon a late pamphlet, entituled, The distressed state of the town of Boston, &* (Boston: James Franklin, 1720).

42. The complete title: *A discourse, shewing, that the real first cause of the straits and difficulties of this province of Massachusetts Bay, is it's extravagancy, & not paper money: and also what is a safe foundation to raise a bank of credit on, and what not, (with some remarks on Amicus Patriae,) & a projection for emitting of more bills of credit on the province. By way of dialogue, tween a representative in said province, and a certain gentleman concerned for the good of his native country. By Philopatria* (Boston: James Franklin, 1721).

43. Paine, *A Discourse*, 4.

44. Wigglesworth, *Letter*, 4–5.

45. The argument, implied here, occurs on page 11 of the pamphlet.

46. Wigglesworth, *Letter*, 12.

47. Wigglesworth, *Letter*, 18.

48. The pamphlet was printed for booksellers Nicholas Boone, Benjamin Gray, and John Edwards.

49. Colman, *Distressed State*, 1. As Claire Priest has explained it, "Colman believed that the lack of currency was creating unacceptable hardship throughout the colony." See Priest's excellent analysis of the legal ramifications of the currency problems in "Currency Policies and Legal Development in Colonial New England," *Yale Law Journal* 110 (2001): 1303–405, quotation at 1365. Priest details the events occurring around the 1720s currency shortages, 1359–67.

50. See Newell, *From Dependency to Independence*, 108.

51. Wise did not favor the ecclesiastical structure the Mathers supported beginning in 1705, and instead, in a series of pamphlets published in the second decade of the eighteenth century, he argued for the essential right of each congregation to determine both church discipline and pastorate. In *The Churches Quarrel Espoused . . .* (New York: William Bradford, 1713) and *A Vindication of the Government of New England Churches* (Boston: J. Allen for N. Boone, 1717), Wise argued that each person should choose which congregation to belong to, as a matter of fundamental right and natural law. For further background on Wise, see George Allan Cook, *John Wise: American Democrat* (New York: King's Crown Press, 1952); Timothy Breen, *The Character of a Good Ruler: Puritan Political Ideas in New England, 1630–1730* (New York: Norton, 1970); Clinton Rossiter, "John Wise: Colonial Democrat," *New England Quarterly* 22 (1949): 3–32.

52. Wise, *The Freeholder's Address to the Honourable House of Representatives* (Boston: James Franklin, 1721), 4.

53. Wise, *Freeholder's Address*, 4–5.

54. Wise, *Freeholder's Address*, 7.

55. Wise, *Word of Comfort*, 3.

56. Wise, *Word of Comfort*, 3, 4, 5, 7.

57. Wise, *Word of Comfort*, 34.

58. Wise, *Word of Comfort*, 34–35.

59. Newell, *From Dependency to Independence*, 169.

60. Wise, *Word of Comfort*, 21.

61. Defoe (and Silence Dogood) referred to Petty's "Political Arithmetick," thus referring in shorthand to *Another essay in political arithmetick, concerning the growth of the city of London: with the measures, periods, causes, and consequences thereof, 1682* (London: Printed by H.H. for Mark Pardoe, 1683).

62. Defoe, *An essay upon projects* (London: Printed by R.R. for Tho. Cockerill, 1697).

63. Daniel Walker Howe has written about the idea of enlightened self-interest in "Franklin, Edwards, and the Problem of Human Nature," in *Benjamin Franklin, Jonathan Edwards, and the Representation of American Culture*, ed. Barbara B. Oberg and Harry S. Stout (New York: Oxford University Press, 2003), 75–96. On the natural law tradition, see Annie Mitchell, "A *Liberal* Republican 'Cato,'" *American Journal of Political Science* 48 (2004): 588–603. Mitchell's analysis clarifies several confusions in the scholarship on classical republicanism. Her argument is that Trenchard and Gordon were far more complicated in their ideological underpinnings than contemporary scholarship has acknowledged.

64. BF Lemay *Writings*, 1308.

65. Cotton Mather, *The Diary of Cotton Mather*, vol. 2, *1709–1724* (New York: Frederick Ungar, 1957), 663.

66. James Franklin, *New-England Courant*, November 27, 1721. I have written about this interesting controversy in "Pox and 'Hell-Fire': Boston's Smallpox Controversy, the New Science, and Early Modern Liberalism," in *Periodical Literature in Eighteenth-Century America*, ed. Mark L. Kamrath and Sharon M. Harris (Knoxville: University of Tennessee Press, 2005), 7–27.

67. The best discussion to date of the writers surrounding James Franklin appears in Lemay *Life* 1:87–171.

68. Increase Mather published "Advice to the Publick from Dr. Increase Mather," in both the *Boston News-Letter* and the *Boston Gazette*, January 29, 1723. The full statement from the *Gazette* read:

> Whereas a *Wicked Libel* called the *New England Courant*, has represented me as one among the Supporters of it; I do hereby declare, that altho' I had paid the Printer for two or three of them, I then (before that last *Courant* was published) sent him word, that I was *extremely offended* with it! In special, because in one of his *Vile Courants* he insinuates, that if *the Ministers of* GOD *approve of a thing, it is a sign it is of the Devil*, which is a horrid thing to be related. And altho' in one of the *Courants*, it is declared, that the *London Mercury* Sept. 16, 1720. affirms, that *the Great Number of Persons in the Cities and Suburbs are under the Inoculations of the Small Pox*; In his next *Courant*, he asserts, that it was some *Busy Inoculator, that imposed on the Publik in saying so;* whereas I my self saw, and read those words in the *London Mercury*: And he doth frequently abuse the *Ministers* of Religion, and many other worthy Persons in a manner which is intolerable. For these and such like Reasons I signified to the Printer, that I would have no more of their *Wicked Courants*. I that have known what *New England* was from the Beginning, cannot but be troubled to see the Degeneracy of this place. I can well remember when the Civil Government could have taken an effectual Course to suppress such a *Cursed Libel!* which if it be not done I am afraid that some *Awful Judgment* will come upon this Land and that the *Wrath of God will arise, and there will be no Remedy*.

I cannot but pity poor *Franklin*, who tho' but a *Young Man*, it may be *Speedily* he must appear before the Judgement Seat of GOD, and what answer will he give for printing things so vile and abominable? And I cannot help but Advise the Supporters of this *Courant* to consider the consequences of being *Partakers of Other Mens Sin*, and no more to Countenance such a *Wicked Paper*.

69. *Journal of the House of Representatives of Massachusetts*, 51 vols. (Boston: Massachusetts Historical Society, 1919–84), 4:208.

70. *Journal of the House of Representatives*, 4:208–09.

71. Black, *English Press*, 2.

72. Lemay *Life* 1:186.

73. See Lemay *Life* 1:109–206. David Paul Nord called James Franklin's *New-England Courant* "the first overtly heretical newspaper in America," in his essay, "Teleology and News: The Religious Roots of American Journalism, 1630–1730," *Journal of American History* 77 (1990): 9–38; quotation at 35. An additional important assessment of the debates about James Franklin's paper appears in Charles E. Clark, "Boston and the Nurturing of Newspapers: Dimensions of the Cradle, 1690–1741," *New England Quarterly* 64 (1991): 243–71.

74. BF *Papers* 1:27.

75. BF *Papers* 1:31.

76. BF *Papers* 1:33.

77. [Samuel Parker], *Mr. Baxter baptiz'd in bloud, or, A sad history of the unparallel'd cruelty of the Anabaptists in New-England faithfully relating the cruel, barbarous and bloudy murther of Mr. Baxter, an Orthodox minister, who was kill'd by the Anabaptists, and his skin most cruelly flead from his body: with an exact account of all the circumstances and particularities of this barbarous murther/published by his mournfull brother Benjamin Baxter* (London: [n.p.], 1673). The story's fictional basis was uncovered relatively early in its history. See Daniel Neal and Joshua Toulmin, *The History of the Puritans, or, Protestant Nonconformists; from the Reformation in 1517 to the Revolution in 1688 . . . By Daniel Neal. A New Edition in Five Volumes . . .*, 5 vols. (London: n.p. for William Baynes, 1822), 2:383.

78. The opening remarks in his five-page book include the following: "But its a Maxim in Philosophy, Corruptio optimi est pessima, The best things corrupted are the worst; So as the profession of Christianity is a most sacred thing, the doctrine of the Gospel a most holy Rule, the Authour of our Religion an exemplar and pattern of meekness; so when Christians renounce this sacred profession, lay aside this Holy Gospel, and abrenuntiate Christ the pattern of meekness, they soon become the most desperate villains in the world; as may be instanc'd in *Julian* the Apostate, and Sergius the Associate of Mahomet, and compiler of the Alcoran."

79. John Denham, *Poems and Translations with the Sophy* (London: H. Herringman, 1668), 95, 97.

80. The line "the best things corrupted are the worst" appeared also in John Dunton (1659–1733), *A voyage round the world, or, A pocket-library divided into several volumes . . .* (London: [n.p. for Richard Newcome], 1691); Thomas Mace (d. 1709?), *Musick's monument, or, A remembrancer of the best practical musick, both divine and civil, that has ever been known to have been in the world divided into three parts . . .* (London: T. Ratcliffe and N. Thompson for the author, 1676); and a "Person of Quality," *The Devil pursued, or, The Right saddle laid upon the right Mare a satyr upon Madam Celliers standing in the pillory: being convicted for the publishing of a late lying scandalous pamphlet*

called Malice defeated &c. / by a person of quality (London: Printed for T. Davies, 1680), which was reprinted by John Wilmot (1647–1680), Earl of Rochester, as *Rome rhym'd to death being a collection of choice poems, in two parts / written by the E. of R., Dr. Wild, and others of the best modern wits* (London: Printed for John How, 1683).

81. James Franklin, "To the venerable Master JANUS," *New-England Courant*, May 6, 1723.

82. A reference to the debates about whether the "founders" were classical republicans, or neo-Lockeans, or oppositional Whigs. Two useful summary essays are by Alan Gibson, "Ancients, Moderns, and Americans: The Republican-Liberalism Debate Revisited," *History of Political Thought* 21 (2000): 261–307, and Mitchell, "A *Liberal* Republican Cato."

CHAPTER 3

1. BF Lemay *Writings*, 1369.

2. The situation is well described in the BF *Papers* 1:139.

3. BF Lemay *Writings*, 1369.

4. The pamphlet appears in BF *Papers* 1:139–57.

5. The editors of Franklin's papers identify two parts in the argument, whereas there are, to my thinking, five movements within Franklin's presentation. See BF *Papers* 1:140.

6. BF *Papers* 1:142. Underscores (shown here as italics) are in the original text.

7. See chapter 2.

8. See Lars Magnusson, *Mercantilism: The Shaping of an Economic Language* (London: Routledge, 1994), 140.

9. BF *Papers* 1:141, 157.

10. See Magnusson, *Mercantilism*, 4–5, and passim.

11. BF *Papers* 1:147.

12. BF *Papers* 1:147.

13. See Magnusson, *Mercantilism*, 134–35. Tracts of relevance include Josiah Child, *A New Discourse of Trade* (London: John Everingham, 1693); Charles Davenant, *Discourses on the Public Revenues, and on the Trade of England* (London: James Knapton, 1698) and *An Essay upon the Probable Methods of Making People the Gainers in the Balance of Trade* (London: Knapton, 1699); Nicholas Barbon, *A Discourse Concerning the Coining the New Money Lighter* (London: R. Chiswell, 1696) and *A Discourse on Trade* (London: Tho. Milbourne for the Author, 1690); John Pollexfen, *A Discourse of Trade, Coyn, and Paper Credit* (London: Brabazon Aylmer, 1697); and John Cary, *An Essay Toward Regulating the Trade and Employing the Poor of the Kingdom*, 2nd ed. (London: S. Collins for Samuel Mabbat, 1719). Cary, a merchant from Bristol, sought to address the problems of poverty in England less for the sake of the poor than for the sake of the strength of the commonwealth. An interesting argument centered on the influence of John Cary's writings in Britain and Europe is made by Sophus A. Reinert in his book, *Translating Empire: Emulation and the Origins of Political Economy* (Cambridge, MA: Harvard University Press, 2011).

14. See Magnusson, *Mercantilism*, 134–37.

15. BF *Papers* 1:147.

16. Adam Smith, *An Inquiry into the Nature and Causes of the Wealth of Nations*, ed. R. H. Campbell, A. S. Skinner, and W. B. Todd (Oxford: Clarendon Press, 1976), 428.

17. Petty, for instance, concluded his *Political Arithmetick; or A Discourse Concerning the Extent of Lands, People, Buildings . . . as the same relates to . . . the Territories of His Majesty of Great Britain . . .*, 3rd ed. (London: Robert Clavel and Hen. Mortlock, 1690) by remarking that England still had land that could employ many people, so that "inlarging of Stock, both of Mony, and Land" would show that "it is not impossible, nay a very feasible matter, for the King of England's Subjects, to gain the Universal Trade of the whole Commercial World."

18. BF *Papers* 1:148.

19. Magnusson speaks to the idea of the civilizing function of trade among the first generations of mercantilists, *Mercantilism*, 150.

20. Thomas Mun, *England's Treasure by Forraign Trade* (1664) as republished in facsimile (Oxford: Basil Blackwell, 1949), 73, 74.

21. Quotation in Magnusson, *Mercantilism*, 150.

22. Magnusson, *Mercantilism*, 95.

23. Samuel Fortrey, *England's Interest and Improvement* (London: n.p. for Nathaniel Brook, 1673), 16, and [John Houghton], *England's Great Happiness; Or, a Dialogue between Content and Complaint* (London: J.M. for Edward Croft, 1677), 10ff. See Magnusson, from whom I have adapted this point, *Mercantilism*, 101–105.

24. Marian Bowley, *Studies in the History of Economic Thought before 1870* (New York: Macmillan, 1973), 33. See Magnusson, *Mercantilism*, 101, 113.

25. BF *Papers* 1:149.

26. See William Petty, *A Treatise of Taxes and Contributions, shewing the Nature and Measures of Crown Lands . . . . The Same being frequently applied to the present State and affairs of Ireland* (London: X. Brooke, 1662).

27. BF *Papers* 1:150.

28. BF *Papers* 1:150.

29. Magnusson, *Mercantilism*, 121.

30. BF *Papers* 1:151.

31. BF *Papers* 1:151.

32. BF *Papers* 1:152.

33. BF *Papers* 1:153.

34. See Lewis J. Carey, *Franklin's Economic Views* (New York: Doubleday, Doran, 1928). This was a point made by William Petty in his *Treatise of Taxes and Contributions*.

35. BF *Papers* 1:154.

36. By the time the paper money bill passed, after much discussion, the interest level was set at 5 percent, for a period of sixteen years. See BF *Papers* 1:141.

37. Perhaps the first historian of economics to make note of this was William A. Wetzel, in *Benjamin Franklin as an Economist* (Baltimore, MD: Johns Hopkins University Press, 1895), a still useful book. For Wetzel's discussion of Franklin's pamphlet, see 18–22, 30–32.

38. See Magnusson, *Mercantilism*, 9–10, 79.

39. Mun, *England's Treasure*, 58–59.

40. Mun, *England's Treasure*, 59.

41. The point is Magnusson's, *Mercantilism*, 79.

42. BF *Papers* 1:155.

43. BF *Papers* 1:155.

44. BF *Papers* 1:156.

45. BF *Papers* 1:156.

46. Cary, *An Essay, towards Regulating the Trade*. Cary's writings continued to be printed and reprinted during the eighteenth century.

47. BF *Papers* 1:145.

48. Daniel Defoe, *A Plan of the English Commerce. Being a Compleat Prospect of the Trade of this Nation, as Well the Home Trade as the Foreign. In Three Parts* (London: J. Rivington, 1728), 153.

49. North wrote: "Trade is nothing else but a Commutation of Superfluities; for instance: I give of mine, what I can spare, for somewhat of yours, which I want, and you can spare. Thus Trade, whilst it is restrained within the limits of a Town, Country, or Nation, signifieth only the Peoples supplying each other with Conveniences, out of what that Town, Country, or Nation affords. And in this, he who is most diligent, and raiseth most Fruits, or maketh most of Manufactory, will abound most in what others make, or raise; and consequently be free from Want, and enjoy most Conveniences, which is truly to be Rich, altho' there were no such thing as Gold, Silver, or the like amongst them": Dudley North, *Discourses upon Trade, Principally Directed to the Cases of the Interest, Coynage, Clipping, Increase, of Money* (London: Basset, 1691), 2.

50. The point was made by E. A. J. Johnson, in *Predecessors of Adam Smith* (1937; New York: Augustus M. Kelley, 1960), 240.

51. Lewes Roberts, *The Treasure of Traffike, Or A Discourse Of Forraigne Trade* (London: Nicholas Bourne, 1641) [paragraph 180]. Roberts's treatise is available in *A Select Collection of Early English Tracts on Commerce from the Originals of Mun, Roberts, North, and Others, with a Preface and Index*, ed. John Ramsay McCullough (London: Printed for the Political Economy Club, 1856).

52. J. H. Plumb, *England in the Eighteenth Century* (Harmondsworth, England: Penguin, 1950), 179.

53. "The Political Anatomy of Ireland," in *Tracts Chiefly Related to Ireland . . . By the Late Sir William Petty* (Dublin: Boulter Grierson, 1769), 319.

54. See Magnusson, *Mercantilism*, 62.

55. Jonathan Swift, *A Short View of the State of Ireland*, in *The Works of the Rev. Jonathan Swift . . . Arranged by Thomas Sheridan, a New Edition*, 19 vols. (London: J. Johnson, J. Nichols, 1801), 9:199–200.

56. Swift, *Short View*, 9:205.

57. Swift, *Short View*, 9:203.

58. Martyn J. Powell, *Britain and Ireland in the Eighteenth-Century Crisis of Empire* (New York: Palgrave Macmillan, 2003), 6. See Powell for Poynings' Law and the Declaratory Act.

59. See Powell, *Britain and Ireland*, 2.

60. Louis M. Cullen, *The Emergence of Modern Ireland, 1600–1900* (London: Holmes and Meier, 1981), 35.

61. James Kelly, *Prelude to Union: Anglo-Irish Politics in the 1780s* (Cork: Irish Committee of Historical Sciences, 1992), 14.

62. BF *Papers* 1:162.

63. BF *Papers* 1:162n.

64. BF *Papers* 1:260, 263.

65. Benjamin Franklin himself benefited, too, because the Assembly voted that his printing establishment would become the exclusive printer of the paper bills. Franklin devised special identifying marks for his bills, to prevent counterfeiting from occurring.

CHAPTER 4

1. BF Lemay *Writings*, 1334.

2. BF Lemay *Writings*, 1398.

3. Franklin evidently held no quarrels with Keith. Upon reflection, he concluded his character of the man as follows: "He was otherwise an ingenious sensible Man, a pretty good Writer, and a good Governor for the People, tho' not for his Constituents the Proprietaries, whose Instructions he sometimes disregarded. Several of our best Laws were of his Planning, and pass'd during his Administration." BF Lemay *Writings*, 1345.

4. For background on Logan, see the still useful book by Frederick B. Tolles, *James Logan and the Culture of Provincial America* (Boston: Little, Brown, 1957).

5. Background on Richard Peters is available in a number of sources, including Hubertis Cummings, *Richard Peters, Provincial Secretary and Cleric, 1704–1776* (Philadelphia: University of Pennsylvania Press, 1944).

6. BF Lemay *Writings*, 1361.

7. See *"Rules for a Club formerly established in* Philadelphia," published in Benjamin Franklin, *Political, Miscellaneous, and Philosophical Pieces*, ed. Benjamin Vaughan (London: J. Johnson, 1779), 533–36. A draft of the standing queries is archived at the Historical Society of Pennsylvania.

8. For background, see the following: Aaron Spencer Fogelman, *Hopeful Journeys: German Immigration, Settlement, and Political Culture in Colonial America, 1717–1775* (Philadelphia: University of Pennsylvania Press, 1996); Guy Soulliard Klett, *Presbyterians in Colonial Pennsylvania* (Philadelphia: University of Pennsylvania Press, 1937); James T. Lemon, *The Best Poor Man's Country: A Geographical Study of Early Southeastern Pennsylvania* (Baltimore, MD: Johns Hopkins University Press, 1972); A. G. Roeber, *Palatines, Liberty, and Property: German Lutherans in Colonial British America* (Baltimore, MD: Johns Hopkins University Press, 1993); Sally Schwartz, *"A Mixed Multitude": The Struggle for Toleration in Colonial Pennsylvania* (New York: New York University Press, 1987); Marianne Wokeck, *Trade in Strangers: The Beginnings of Mass Migration to North America* (University Park: Pennsylvania State University Press, 1999); Stephanie Grauman Wolf, *Urban Village: Population, Community, and Family Structure in Germantown, Pennsylvania, 1683–1800* (Princeton: Princeton University Press, 1976). For perspectives on immigration, see James H. Merrell, *Into the American Woods: Negotiators on the Pennsylvania Frontier* (New York: W.W. Norton, 1999) and Billy G. Smith, *The "Lower Sort": Philadelphia's Laboring People, 1750–1800* (Ithaca, NY: Cornell University Press, 1990).

9. Mary Maples Dunn, *William Penn: Politics and Conscience* (Princeton: Princeton University Press, 1967), 64. For background on the Penn family see Lorett Treese, *The Storm Gathering: The Penn Family and the American Revolution* (University Park: Pennsylvania State University Press, 1992). A still reliable study of Quakers in Pennsylvania is Gary B. Nash, *Quakers and Politics: Pennsylvania, 1681–1726* (Princeton: Princeton University Press, 1968).

10. See a few of William Penn's tracts: *The Continued Cry of the Oppressed for Justice* (London, 1675; rpt. London: T. Sowle, 1726); *England's Great Interest in the Choice of a New Parliament* (London, [1679], reprinted in 1688 and then by T. Sowle); *England's Present Interest Discovered with Honour to the Prince, and Safety of the People* (London, 1679, reprinted in 1698, 1702, and then by T. Sowle).

11. Joseph E. Illick, review of Nash's *Quakers and Politics*, in *William and Mary Quarterly*, 3rd ser., 26 (1969), 292–95, quotation at 293.

12. See Nash, *Quakers and Politics*, 48–88, esp. 68–69.

13. Dunn, *William Penn*, 152.

14. Dunn, *William Penn*, 153.

15. Nash, *Quakers and Politics*, 189. For background on Randolph, see Michael Garibaldi Hall, *Edward Randolph and the American Colonies, 1676–1703* (Chapel Hill: University of North Carolina Press for the Institute of Early American History and Culture, 1960).

16. See Nash, *Quakers and Politics*, 222–23.

17. See Nash, *Quakers and Politics*, 314–15. See also James A. Henretta, *"Salutary Neglect": Colonial Administration Under the Duke of Newcastle* (Princeton: Princeton University Press, 1972), 57.

18. William S. Hanna, *Benjamin Franklin and Pennsylvania Politics* (Princeton: Princeton University Press, 1964), 15. See also Alan Tully, *William Penn's Legacy* (Baltimore, MD: Johns Hopkins University Press, 1977).

19. See Nash, *Quakers and Politics*, 319–23.

20. James H. Hutson, *Pennsylvania Politics, 1746–1770: The Movement for Royal Government and Its Consequences* (Princeton: Princeton University Press, 1972), 7.

21. Richard Peters to Thomas Penn, June 12, 1752, quoted in Hanna, *Benjamin Franklin and Pennsylvania Politics*, 48.

22. For the standoff between the Assembly and the Proprietary, see James H. Hutson and Benjamin H. Newcomb, *Political Partisanship in the American Middle Colonies, 1700–1776* (Baton Rouge: Louisiana State University Press, 1995).

23. Hanna, *Benjamin Franklin and Pennsylvania Politics*, 78.

24. In Hanna's words, "Before 1751 he had carefully remained outside the political order, letting others have the power and the responsibility of managing political affairs," *Benjamin Franklin and Pennsylvania Politics*, 24.

25. Hanna, *Benjamin Franklin and Pennsylvania Politics*, 25.

26. *The General Magazine, and Historical Chronicle, for all the British Plantations in America* 1 (January 1741): 75.

27. Quoted in BF *Papers* 3:183.

28. Quoted in BF *Papers* 3:183.

29. BF *Papers* 3:219.

30. *Plain Truth*, in BF *Papers* 3:188–204, quotations at 196 and 200.

31. BF *Papers* 3:202.

32. BF *Papers* 3:196.

33. BF *Papers* 3:202.

34. BF *Papers* 3:199.

35. BF *Papers* 3:198.

36. BF *Papers* 3:202.

37. For background see Frederick B. Tolles, *Meeting House and Counting House: The Quaker Merchants of Colonial Philadelphia, 1682–1763* (Chapel Hill: University of North Carolina Press, 1948) and Thomas M. Doerflinger, *A Vigorous Spirit of Enterprise: Merchants and Economic Development in Revolutionary Philadelphia* (Chapel Hill: University of North Carolina Press, 2001).

38. BF *Papers* 3:202–3.

39. James Logan to James Steel, November 18, 1729, and Logan to Thomas Penn, quoted in George W. Franz, *Paxton: A Study of Community Structure and Mobility in the Colonial Pennsylvania Backcountry* (New York: Garland, 1989), 95.

40. BF *Papers* 3:203.

41. See BF *Papers* 3:184. See Barbara A. Gannon, "The Lord Is a Man of War, the God of Love and Peace: The Association Debate, Philadelphia, 1747–1748," *Pennsylvania History* 65 (1998): 46–61.

42. Quoted in BF *Papers* 3:185.

43. BF *Papers* 3:225.

44. BF *Papers* 3:213.

45. BF *Papers* 3:217.

46. BF *Papers* 3:187.

47. BF *Papers* 3:186.

48. For additional background on the situation, see Eric Hinderaker, *Elusive Empires: Constructing Colonialism in the Ohio Valley, 1673–1800* (Cambridge: Cambridge University Press, 1997); R. Douglas Hurt, *The Ohio Frontier: Crucible of the Old Northwest, 1720–1830* (Bloomington: Indiana University Press, 1996); Jane T. Merritt, *At the Crossroads: Indians and Empires on a Mid-Atlantic Frontier, 1700–1763* (Chapel Hill: University of North Carolina Press, 2007); and the several useful essays in *The Sixty Years' War for the Great Lakes, 1754–1814*, ed. David Curtis Skaggs and Larry L. Nelson (East Lansing: Michigan State University Press, 2001).

49. See, for instance, Franklin to James Parker, March 20, 1750/51. The letter was considered by his friends of such singular importance that they asked him to have it compiled with and printed in [Archibald Kennedy], *The Importance of Gaining and Preserving the Friendship of the Indians to the British Interest, Considered* (New York: James Parker, 1751), at 27–32. See also Franklin to Peter Collinson, May 9, 1753, which exists in multiple copies. Both are in BF *Papers* 3:117–21, 477–86.

50. For background on the imperial situation and the battle for empire in the interior, see Fred Anderson, *Crucible of War: The Seven Years' War and the Fate of Empire in British North America, 1754–1766* (New York: Knopf, 2000) and his *The War That Made America: A Short History of the French and Indian War* (New York: Viking, 2005); George Louis Beer, *British Colonial Policy, 1754–1765* (New York: Peter Smith, 1933); Jack M. Sosin, *Whitehall and the Wilderness: The Middle West in British Colonial Policy, 1760–1775* (Lincoln: University of Nebraska Press, 1961); and Skaggs and Nelson, *Sixty Years' War*. For an especially useful resource about the Albany conference, see Timothy J. Shannon, *Indians and Colonists at the Crossroads of Empire: The Albany Congress of 1754* (Ithaca, NY: Cornell University Press and New York State Historical Association, 2000).

51. See the editorial matter in BF *Papers* 3:500–501.

52. See Anderson, *Crucible of War*, 11–32, esp. 18.

53. For background see the editorial matter of the BF *Papers* 5:222 and from Donald H. Kent, *The French Invasion of Western Pennsylvania, 1753* (1954; Harrisburg, PA: Historical and Museum Commission, 1981).

54. Quoted in BF *Papers* 5:222.

55. Anderson has noted, as well, that Dinwiddie had a personal interest in the Ohio area as an investor in the Ohio Company. See Anderson, *Crucible of War*, 37.

56. BF *Papers* 5:270.

57. The proportional count is derived from Beer, *British Colonial Policy*, 17.

58. BF *Papers* 5:270.

59. BF *Papers* 5:274.

60. See Anderson, *Crucible of War*; Francis Jennings, *Empire of Fortune: Crowns, Colonies, and Tribes in the Seven Years War in America* (New York: W.W. Norton, 1988); and Hinderaker, *Elusive Empires*.

61. *Pennsylvania Gazette*, July 18, 1745.

62. These are the remarks as printed by Franklin in November, 1753. BF *Papers* 5:97; subsequent quotations from this speech also appear at 5:97.

63. Published in the *London Chronicle*, June 23–25, and 25–28, 1768.

64. The Assembly received mixed reports about this request, and historical inquiry since then has been contradictory. For background, see BF *Papers* 4:182–84 and notes; Anderson, *Crucible of War*, 24–32; and Nicholas B. Wainwright, *George Croghan: Wilderness Diplomat* (Chapel Hill: University of North Carolina Press, 1959), 35–36, 40–44.

65. See BF *Papers* 5:79–80.

66. BF *Papers* 5:120, 121. Franklin was responding in this letter to the pamphlet by Archibald Kennedy, *The Importance of Gaining and Preserving the Friendship of the Indians to the British Interest, Considered* (New York: James Parker, 1751), to which the letter was appended when published.

67. BF *Papers* 5:111.

68. Quotation from BF *Papers* 5:275. The summary of events surrounding the Albany conference derives from editorial matter in this volume of the Franklin papers and from Anderson, *Crucible of War*. To gain a sense of the contests taking place in Britain and the colonies during the early eighteenth century, see Stanley Nider Katz, *Newcastle's New York: Anglo-American Politics, 1732–1753* (Cambridge, MA: Harvard University Press, 1968).

69. Quoted in BF *Papers* 5:275.

70. This was a particular sticking point for Franklin, because, behind the scenes, different parties (including the Pennsylvania Proprietary) were attempting to negotiate different land deals with the Indians at the conference.

71. Franklin's discussions about empire with William Shirley are taken up in chapter 6.

72. On this point, see Clarke's *Observations on the Late and Present Conduct of the French, with Regard to their Encroachments upon the* British *Colonies in* North America (Boston: S. Kneeland, 1755), 26–31. Franklin took up these relevant points most fully in *The Interest of Great Britain Considered, With Regard to her Colonies, And the Acquisitions of Canada and Guadaloupe* (London: T. Beckett, 1760).

73. On this point, see Clarke, *Observations*, 36–44.

74. Clarke, *Observations*, 33.

75. For background on the interest politics during this era, see Anderson, *Crucible of War*, 66–85, and Henretta, *Salutary Neglect*, 272–318.

76. Franklin to James Parker, March 20, 1751, in BF *Papers* 3:118.

CHAPTER 5

1. For background on the calculating mentality emerging in North America, see Patricia Kline Cohen, *A Calculating People: The Spread of Numeracy in Early America* (Chicago: University of Chicago Press, 1983).

2. BF *Papers* 3:400–401.

3. BF *Papers* 3:417.

4. See BF *Papers* 4:154–91.

5. See BF *Papers* 4:131–32.

6. His essay was reprinted in Hunter's *Virginia Gazette*, May 30, 1751, and the *New York Gazette or Weekly Post-Boy* on June 10.

7. The article appears in BF *Papers* 4:130–33, quotations at 131 and 132. Franklin used this idea of planting objects in London's parks in his hoax newssheet printed in 1782 on his own press at Passy. In the later case, Franklin talked about hanging scalps from the trees in these parks. The hoax is discussed in chapter 8.

8. For background on imperial matters, see, in addition to sources named in previous chapters, Thomas C. Barrow, *Trade and Empire: The British Customs Service in Colonial America, 1660–1775* (Cambridge, MA: Harvard University Press, 1967), 106–86; James A. Henretta, *"Salutary Neglect": Colonial Administration under the Duke of Newcastle* (Princeton: Princeton University Press, 1972), 166–318; Richard Kroebner, *Empire* (Cambridge: Cambridge University Press, 1961), 76–104. Two earlier scholars are always worth re-examining: G. H. Guttridge, *The Colonial Policy of William III* (1922; London: Frank Cass, 1966) and Lawrence Henry Gipson, *The British Empire before the American Revolution*, 15 vols. (Caldwell, ID: Caxton Printers, 1936–70), vols. 1–3.

9. Henretta, *Salutary Neglect*, 317.

10. Henretta, *Salutary Neglect*, 318.

11. See Kroebner, *Empire*, 75–89.

12. Richard H. Grove, *Green Imperialism: Colonial Expansion, Tropical Island Edens and the Origins of Environmentalism, 1600–1860* (Cambridge: Cambridge University Press, 1995), 60.

13. Grove, *Green Imperialism*, 57.

14. Grove, *Green Imperialism*, 58–61, quotation at 60.

15. Grove, *Green Imperialism*, 60.

16. See, for instance, Franklin's 1749–50 exchanges with the governor, written on behalf of the Assembly, regarding issues related to treating with the Indians and to currency matters.

17. For background on the different methods of colonization, see James Axtell, *The Invasion Within: The Contest of Cultures in Colonial North America* (New York: Oxford University Press, 1985), in addition to Grove, *Green Imperialism*.

18. See BF *Papers* 5:464–67.

19. [Charles Davenant], *Discourses on the Public Revenues, and on the Trade of England* (London: James Knapton, 1698), 204.

20. See BF *Papers* 5:464.

21. See Klaus E. Knorr, *British Colonial Theories, 1570–1850* (1944; Toronto: University of Toronto Press, 1968), 71, 73–74.

22. BF *Papers* 4:229.

23. See Knorr, *British Colonial Theories*, 69–70.

24. Knorr, *British Colonial Theories*, 70.

25. BF *Papers* 4:229.

26. See Knorr, *British Colonial Theories*, 67.

27. The issue of Franklin and slavery is taken up in chapter 9. For background, see the chapter on the topic in Claude-Anne Lopez and Eugenia W. Herbert, *The Private Franklin: The Man and His Family* (New York: W.W. Norton, 1975), 291–302. In *Runaway America: Benjamin Franklin, Slavery, and the American Revolution* (New York: Hill and Wang, 2004), David Waldstreicher also discussed Franklin and slavery. See Douglas Anderson's evaluation of Waldstreicher's work in "Benjamin Franklin and His Readers," *Early American Literature* 41 (2006): 535–53.

28. The situation seems to me paradigmatic of what James Clifford in *The Predicament of Culture* called, for the twentieth century, the "loss of traditional orders of difference"

amid the varied emergent inventions of difference that can accrue from such a shift in the cultural matrix. See Clifford, *The Predicament of Culture: Twentieth-Century Ethnography, Literature, and Art* (Cambridge, MA: Harvard University Press, 1988), 230–31.

29. Franklin's essay was added to [William Clarke], *Observations on the late and present Conduct of the French, with Regard to their Encroachments upon the British Colonies in North America. . . . To which is added, wrote by another Hand; Observations concerning the Increase of Mankind, Peopling of Countries, &c.* (Boston: S. Kneeland, 1755). Printed in BF *Papers* 4:225–34.

30. By 1776, the white and black population of the thirteen English colonies reached 2.5 million. The numbers are derived from two sources: Aaron Spencer Fogelman, *Hopeful Journeys: German Immigration, Settlement, and Political Culture* (Philadelphia: University of Pennsylvania Press, 1996), 1–3; and Billy G. Smith, *The "Lower Sort": Philadelphia's Laboring People, 1750–1800* (Ithaca, NY: Cornell University Press, 1990), 40–48.

31. See Ivan Hannaford's very useful survey of racial ideologies in *Race: The History of an Idea in the West* (Baltimore. MD: Johns Hopkins University Press, 1996), especially chapter 7, "The First Stage in the Development of an Idea of Race, 1684–1815." Information provided here is adapted from Hannaford, 202–05; quotations of Linnaeus's character traits are on 204.

32. Bernard Crick, foreword, in Hannaford, *Race*, xv.

33. BF *Papers* 3:202–3.

34. See my essay, "Benjamin Franklin, Pennsylvania Germans, and the Ethnic Origins of Nations," in *Halle Pietism, Colonial North America, and the Young United States*, ed. Hans-Jürgen Grabbe (Stuttgart: Franz Steiner Verlag, 2008), 147–60.

35. A. G. Roeber, "'The Origin of Whatever Is Not English Among Us': The Dutch-Speaking and the German-Speaking Peoples of Colonial British America," in *Strangers within the Realm: Cultural Margins of the First British Empire*, ed. Bernard Bailyn and Philip D. Morgan (Chapel Hill: University of North Carolina Press for the Institute of Early American History and Culture, 1991), 220–83, here, 255. In the middle 1760s, because reports about troubles in Pennsylvania were so sufficiently dissuading, Germans started sailing for Charleston, SC. Useful discussions of the Germans include Roeber's book, *Palatines, Liberty, and Property: German Lutherans in Colonial British America* (1993; Baltimore, MD: Johns Hopkins University Press, 1998), in addition to the following: Fogelman, *Hopeful Journeys*; Walter Allen Knittle, *Early Eighteenth Century Palatine Emigration* (1937; Baltimore: Genealogical Publishing, 1965); and Philip Otterness, *Becoming German: The 1709 Palatine Migration to New York* (Ithaca, NY: Cornell University Press, 2004).

36. For background on these matters, see BF *Papers* 5:19 and 4:65, 77, 206.

37. See Smith, *Lower Sort*, 40–50. In the year 1750, Gottlieb Mittelberger described his passage, as a paying passenger who had a wooden bunk of two by six feet, as particularly difficult, saying "the ship is full of pitiful signs of distress—smells, fumes, horrors, vomiting, various kinds of sea sickness, fever, dysentery, headaches, heat, constipation, boils, scurvy, cancer, mouth-rot, and similar afflictions . . . as well as . . . very bad and filthy water, . . . [These] bring[] about the miserable destruction and death of many." He also commented that, upon arrival, "the sick were the worst off, for the healthy are preferred and are most readily paid for. The miserable people who are ill must often still remain at sea and in sight of the city for another two or

three weeks—which in many cases means death": *Journey to Pennsylvania by Gottlieb Mittelberger*, ed. and trans. Oscar Handlin and John Clive (Cambridge, MA: Belknap Press of Harvard University Press, 1960), 12–13, 44.

38. Smith, *Lower Sort*, 43 n. 7.

39. The letter was published, as we have seen, with Archibald Kennedy's *The Importance of Gaining and Preserving the Friendship of the Indians to the British Interest* (New York: Parker, 1751). See BF *Papers* 4:120–21.

40. Francis Jennings argued that Franklin "had contempt for Germans as persons" and that Franklin considered Germans a "menace" demanding "reduction": Francis Jennings, *Benjamin Franklin, Politician* (New York: W.W. Norton, 1996), 22. This does not account for the different audiences nor occasions for Franklin's different positions on ethnic populations, Germans particularly.

41. Simon Finger, *The Contagious City: The Politics of Public Health in Early Philadelphia* (Ithaca, NY: Cornell University Press, 2012), 4.

42. BF *Papers* 4:234.

43. BF *Papers* 4:232.

44. BF *Papers* 4:230.

45. BF *Papers* 4: 227.

46. BF *Papers* 4:229.

47. BF *Papers* 4:310.

48. BF *Papers* 4:388.

49. See the correspondence in the Franklin papers between Franklin and the men mentioned: BF *Papers* 4:319–30, 333–34, 388.

50. John Perkins to Franklin, October 16, 1752, in BF *Papers* 4:358.

51. BF *Papers* 4:358.

52. The letter requesting the essay was dated November 29, 1753. See BF *Papers* 5:122.

53. This letter is dated February 13, 1754. See BF *Papers* 5:197.

54. For *Poor Richard* for 1753, see BF *Papers* 4:405. For the dialogue, see BF *Papers* 6:299.

55. BF *Papers* 5:443 (December 3, 1754) and 443–44 (December 4, 1754). See also chapter 6.

56. BF *Papers* 5:449.

57. In his autobiography, Franklin famously and brilliantly explained—by showing while telling—his method of argument. BF Lemay *Writings*, 1321–22.

58. References are to the following: John Graunt, *Natural and Political Observations . . . upon the Bills of Mortality* (London: Thomas Roycroft for John Martin, 1662); Thomas Short, *New Observations, Natural, Moral, Civil, Political, and Medical . . . on Bills of Mortality* (London: T. Longman and A. Millar, 1750), and Robert Wallace, *A Dissertation on the Numbers of Mankind in Antient and Modern Times* (Edinburgh: n.p. for G. Hamilton and J. Balfour, 1753). See A. Owen Aldridge, "Franklin as Demographer," *Journal of Economic History* 9 (May 1949): 25–44, but see as well Lewis J. Carey, *Franklin's Economic Views* (New York: Doubleday, Doran, 1928).

59. *Pennsylvania Gazette* (nos. 143–45) for August 5, 12, and 19, 1731, publishing material from *The Political State of Great Britain* 40 (1731): 203–10, 223–30. As A. Owen Aldridge pointed out, Franklin's goal was to create a comparative analysis between Boston, as he was reporting it, to Edmund Halley's Breslau. See Aldridge, "Franklin as Demographer," 27.

60. For general background, see Francis Jennings, *The Ambiguous Iroquois Empire: The Covenant Chain Confederation of Indian Tribes with English Colonies*

(New York: W.W. Norton, 1984) and *Empire of Fortune: Crowns, Colonies, and Tribes in the Seven Years War* (New York: W.W. Norton, 1988), and see the introduction by Susan Kalter to her edition of Franklin's treaties, *Benjamin Franklin, Pennsylvania, and the First Nations: The Treaties of 1736–62* (Urbana: University of Illinois Press, 2006).

61. For background related to the situation of Teedyscung and the Delawares, see Alfred A. Cave, *Prophets of the Great Spirit: Native American Revitalization Movements in Eastern North America* (Lincoln: University of Nebraska Press, 2006), 11–44; Jennings, *The Ambiguous Iroquois Empire*, especially 298ff.; Jennings, *Empire of Fortune*, especially 260–80 and 398ff.; Jane T. Merritt, *At the Crossroads: Indians and Empires on a Mid-Atlantic Frontier, 1700–1763* (Chapel Hill: University of North Carolina Press, 2003), especially 198–231; Anthony F. C. Wallace, *King of the Delawares: Teedyuscung* (Philadelphia: University of Pennsylvania Press, 1949), especially 130ff. See also Boyd Stanley Schlenther, "Training for Resistance: Charles Thomson and Indian Affairs in Pennsylvania," *Pennsylvania History* 50 (1983): 185–217, and James H. Merrill, " 'I desire all that I have said . . . may be taken down aright': Revisiting Teedyuscung's 1756 Treaty Council Speeches," *William and Mary Quarterly*, 3rd ser., 63 (2006): 777–826.

62. See Jennings, *Ambiguous Iroquois Empire*, 314 ff.

63. Merrell, "I desire that all I have said," 783.

64. BF *Papers* 4:228.

65. Daniel Richter, *Ordeal of the Longhouse: The Peoples of the Iroquois League in the Era of European Colonization* (Chapel Hill: University of North Carolina Press), 6.

66. The argument among some Native peoples is that Franklin and others pulled their idea of a colonial union from witnessing the cooperative relations among the Haudenosaunee. See, for instance, the following websites: http://firstpeoplesofcanada.com/fp_groups/fp_groups_conflict.html, accessed September 29, 2014; and http://www.smithsoniansource.org/display/primarysource/viewdetails.aspx?PrimarySourceId=1198, accessed September 29, 2014. And see Bruce E. Johansen, *Forgotten Founders: Benjamin Franklin, the Iroquois, and the Rationale for the American Revolution* (Ipswich, MA: Gambit, 1982).

67. On this point and for additional background to settlers' attitudes, see Peter Silver, *Our Savage Neighbors: How Indian War Transformed Early America* (New York: W. W. Norton, 2008).

68. See Alfred P. James, "Benjamin Franklin's Ohio Valley Lands," *Proceedings of the American Philosophical Society* 98, no. 4 (August 16, 1954): 255–65.

69. Pennsylvania Assembly, Reply to the Governor, in *Votes and Proceedings of the House of Representatives of the province of Pennsylvania, met at Philadelphia, on the Fourteenth of October, Anno Domini 1755, and continued by adjournments* (Philadelphia: B. Franklin, 1756), 19–21. Dated November 11, 1755; reprinted in BF *Papers* 6:238–43.

70. Quoted in BF *Papers* 6:241–42.

71. Cato's Letter No. 11, *London Journal*, January 7, 1721.

72. The Pennsylvania Assembly's Reply to the Governor, August 8, 1755, in BF *Papers* 6:131–38, quotations at 137–38.

73. BF Lemay *Writings*, 1456.

74. Richard Peters to Thomas Penn, January 31, 1757, Peters Letterbook, Historical Society of Pennsylvania.

75. Thomas Penn to Richard Peters, May 14, 1757, Thomas Penn Letterbook, Penn Papers, Historical Society of Pennsylvania. The Peters and Penn letters are quoted in BF *Papers* 7:111.

CHAPTER 6

1. Benjamin H. Newcomb, *Franklin and Galloway: A Political Partnership* (New Haven: Yale University Press, 1971), 40. The background on this legal position is drawn from Newcomb, 39–41.

2. Richard Jackson to Benjamin Franklin, April 24, 1758, in BF *Papers* 8:26–27.

3. See Newcomb, *Franklin and Galloway*, 49–51.

4. After granting the concession on taxation, the Penns wrote to the Pennsylvania Assembly, November 28, 1758, that its representative lacked candor: "We shall always be open to Representation and Conviction, and we see no Matters remaining, but such as may, by the desirable Methods of free Conferences with Persons of Candour, and empowered for the Purpose, be well settled to mutual Satisfaction on both Sides," they wrote. BF *Papers* 8:185–86.

5. BF *Papers* 7:360.

6. Thomas Penn to James Hamilton, May 24, 1760, Thomas Penn Letterbook, Penn Papers, Historical Society of Pennsylvania.

7. See BF *Papers* 9:125–73.

8. See BF *Papers* 9:196–211. See the discussion in Newcomb, *Franklin and Galloway*, 66–67.

9. BF *Papers* 8:309–16, quotation at 310.

10. He would not set sail for Pennsylvania until August 1762.

11. See BF *Papers* 8:449–52.

12. The attribution is made by the editors of BF *Papers* 9:52. The pamphlet was printed in London by A. Millar "in the Strand," 1760. The "two great men" were the Duke of Newcastle and William Pitt.

13. The attribution occurs in BF *Papers* 9:53. The pamphlet was advertised as "this day published" by the *London Chronicle*, January 19–22, 1760.

14. BF *Papers* 9:72.

15. BF *Papers* 9:71.

16. The *London Chronicle*, April 15–17, 1760, announced *The Interest of Great Britain Considered* was "This Day" published.

17. BF *Papers* 9:60.

18. BF *Papers* 9:62.

19. BF *Papers* 9:72.

20. BF *Papers* 9:76.

21. BF *Papers* 9:70.

22. The pamphlet had a wide circulation, indicating its importance. The tract was completed in 1751 and sent during the spring of 1752 to Peter Collinson and Richard Jackson, who admired it and sent Franklin a full critique. Several of his friends thought the pamphlet should be published. It reached publication as a text appended to William Clarke's *Observations*, late in 1754. It was reprinted with attribution to Franklin in the *Gentleman's Magazine* for November 1755 and the *Scots Magazine* for April 1756. In 1760 and 1761, it was printed as an appendix to Franklin's *Interest of Great Britain Considered* in London, Dublin, Boston, and Philadelphia, and it was abbreviated and printed in part in the *London Chronicle*, May 20, 1760. Franklin later included it in the fourth edition of his *Experiments and Observations on Electricity* in 1769.

23. For a study of how the marketplace assisted the revolution against Great Britain, see T. H. Breen, *The Marketplace of Revolution: How Consumer Politics Shaped American Independence* (New York: Oxford University Press, 2004).

24. BF *Papers* 9:90.

25. BF *Papers* 9:90.

26. BF *Papers* 9:74.

27. BF *Papers* 9:78.

28. BF *Papers* 9:78.

29. BF *Papers* 9:95.

30. The smaller of the two quakes occurred on October 30, 1759, in the area of Safed. This quake took nearly two thousand lives. The second earthquake occurred nearly a month later, on November 25. This earthquake was much larger; it destroyed villages in the Beqaa Valley and created major damage in the cities of Nablus, Acre, Tyre, Tripoli, and Hama.

31. The record is scant on the matter. He likely attained information about the region from Alexander Russell (1715?–1758) and then his half-brother Patrick Russell (1726–1805), both of whom were surgeons and naturalists, in addition to being fellows of the Royal Society. They both worked in the region, in Aleppo particularly—Alexander Russell until 1753, when Patrick was sent—and created significant records of their experiences there as physicians and naturalists. Franklin's association with the brothers probably began with Alexander Russell, who was a friend of John Fothergill, one of Franklin's most important sponsors of his scientific work. Their letters to the Society were undoubtedly shared at meetings and among Franklin's circle of acquaintance.

32. Indeed, Franklin was so well aware of the power of the region that he would encourage treaties of amity with Algiers, Tunis, and Tripoli in the 1780s, as North America was organizing its goals for a treaty with Great Britain.

33. BF *Papers* 9:74.

34. BF to David Hume, September 27, 1760. BF *Papers* 9:229.

35. BF to David Hume, September 27, 1760. BF *Papers* 9:229.

36. David Hume, "Of the Jealousy of Trade," in *Essays and Treatises on Several Subjects. A New Edition* (London: Millar, Kincaid and Donaldson, 1758), 187. This essay was printed separately, without being interleaved into the edition, as if a later addition to the compiled book, with directions as to its location in the already published edition. Both essays appeared in this volume. In writing to Hume, Franklin seems to have been working from memory. He commingled the two essays and called them Hume's "excellent Essay on the *Jealousy of Commerce*." BF *Papers* 9:229.

37. BF to David Hume, September 27, 1760. BF *Papers* 9:228–29.

38. An allusion, of course, to Bernard Mandeville's *Fable of the Bees: or, Private Vices Publick Benefits*, 2 vols. (Oxford: Clarendon Press, 1714).

39. Franklin, *The Interest of Great Britain Considered, With Regard to her Colonies, And the Acquisitions of Canada and Guadaloupe* (London: T. Becket, 1760), reprinted in BF *Papers* 9:95.

40. Franklin, *The Interest of Great Britain Considered* as in BF *Papers* 9:95.

41. BF *Papers* 4:227–34.

42. BF *Papers* 9:229.

43. See BF *Papers* 9:53.

44. See my essay, "*Caritas* and Capital: Franklin's *Narrative of the Late Massacres*," in *Reappraising Benjamin Franklin: A Bicentennial Perspective*, ed. J. A. Leo Lemay (Newark: University of Delaware Press, 1993), 347–58.

45. *Narrative of the Late Massacres*, published January 30, 1764, as in BF *Papers* 11:45–69; quotations at 68, 65, 56.

46. Verner S. Crane, ed., *Benjamin Franklin's Letters to the Press, 1758–1775*, 60–62, quotation at 60.

47. *Gazetteer*, February 10, 1766; *London Magazine* 35 (February 1766), 91–95; *Gentleman's Magazine* 36 (February 1766), 85–86.

48. This information has been drawn from Crane, *Benjamin Franklin's Letters to the Press*, 60–61.

49. The complete Commons proceedings appear in *Proceedings and Debates of the British Parliaments Respecting North America, 1754–1783*, 6 vols., ed. R. C. Simmons and P. D. G. Thomas (White Plains, NY: Kraus International, 1982), 2:218–51; the proceedings relevant to the point just made appear at 2:247–49. The proceedings are also available, with commentary, in BF *Papers* 13:124–62. See for commentary, Carl Van Doren, *Benjamin Franklin* (New York: Viking, 1938), 327–67.

50. *Proceedings and Debates*, 2:236.

51. *Proceedings and Debates*, 2:238ff.

52. *Proceedings and Debates*, 2:238.

53. *Proceedings and Debates*, 2:251.

54. See the editorial matter, BF *Papers* 15:xxvii.

55. From this distinction was born Franklin's ideas about internal and external regulation, wherein, he argued, colonists ought to have the right to tax themselves for their own self-rule, so long as the external trade obligations were met.

56. BF to Henry Home, Lord Kames, February 25, 1767, in BF *Papers* 14:62–71; quotation at 65.

57. Franklin to the *London Chronicle*, January 5–7, 1768, BF *Papers* 15:10.

58. Franklin in *The Gentleman's Magazine* 38 (1768): 6–7; printed as "Subjects of Subjects" in BF *Papers* 15:36–37.

59. BF to Cadwalader Evans, BF *Papers* 15:51–53, quotation at 52. Evans had helped with the founding of the Pennsylvania Hospital.

60. BF to Cadwalader Evans, BF *Papers* 15:51–53, quotation at 52.

61. Dickinson's letters first appeared in the *Pennsylvania Chronicle*, December 2, 1767, and they appeared through February 15, 1768. They were reprinted in other colonies and then printed again, in a collected, separate edition, with a preface by Franklin, in June 1768.

62. BF to William Franklin, March 13, 1768, in BF *Papers* 15:74–78.

63. We catch fascinating glimpses of Franklin's reading from the marginalia he was in the habit of creating at this time. Take, for instance, the very "loud" comments he wrote into his copy of the *Protest against the Bill To repeal the American Stamp Act, of Last Session* (the protest being by the House of Lords), and the *Second Protest*, both from 1766. In the first pamphlet, he wrote the remark, "How? Strange Policy! Lay an odious Tax and give Bounties to enable People to pay it," in response to Grenville's plan. The comments are remarkable for the amount of Franklin's sheer *engagement* in the issues he was reading about. See the marginalia in BF *Papers* 13:207–32.

64. Franklin used the newspapers to burlesque newswriters' nonsense during the Stamp Act controversies in 1765. As "The Spectator," Franklin published a fictitious account of the Duke of York's travels in the *Public Advertiser*, May 10, 1765, and he replied to this report as "A Traveller" in the *Public Advertiser*, May 22. The reply included his wonderful hoax, which readers took to be true, about how "Cod, like other Fish, when attacked by their Enemies, fly into any Water where they think they can be safest; that Whales, when they have a mind to eat Cod, pursue them wherever they fly; and that the grand Leap of the Whale in that Chace up the Fall of Niagara is

esteemed by all who have seen it, as one of the finest Spectacles in Nature!" Of course, the article includes an interesting potential metaphor, if we might take the cod to represent British North Americans, who eventually flew into the laps of the French, their supposed enemies, thanks to Franklin's negotiations. There are interesting grains of truth in many of Franklin's most fabulous hoaxes.

65. It is reprinted in BF *Papers* 15:145–57. Authorship questions are discussed by A. O. Aldridge and James Masterson: A. O. Aldridge, "Franklin's Deistical Indians," *Proceedings of the American Philosophical Society* 94, no. 4 (August 1950): 398–410; James R. Masterson, "'A Foolish *Oneida* Tale,'" *American Literature* 10 (1938–39): 53–65.

66. The statement signals Franklin's own latter eighteenth-century version of captivity, in which the *exemplum fidei* offered the reader is one that bespeaks a commercial rather than spiritual redemption supporting the "do unto others" lesson as a result of the spirit of commerce rather than *caritas*. In other words, Benjamin Franklin's 1768 "Extract from an Account of the Captivity of William Henry in 1755" offers, among other things, a satiric parable about commerce in the guise of a captivity narrative.

67. BF *Papers* 15:154.

68. BF *Papers* 15. Quotations at 154, 155–56, 157.

69. See Alfred O. Aldridge, "Jacques Barbeu-Dubourg, a French Disciple of Benjamin Franklin," *Proceedings of the American Philosophical Society* 45 (1951): 331–92. Information in this paragraph is derived from this article and from Aldridge's book *Benjamin Franklin and His French Contemporaries* (Washington Square: New York University Press, 1957), especially 21–38.

70. Franklin's "On the Price of Corn, and Management of the Poor," was originally published in the *London Chronicle*, November 27–29, 1766; the published statement about his examination before Commons was published in the *London Chronicle*, July 4 and July 7, 1767; "Positions to be Examined" was published in the *Chronicle* on June 29, 1769. See Aldridge, *Benjamin Franklin and His French Contemporaries*.

71. "Mithologie et Morale Iroquoises," *Ephémérides du citoyen, ou bibliothèque raisonnée des sciences morales et politiques* 2 (February 1769): 56–78.

72. BF to William Franklin, March 13, 1768, in BF *Papers* 15:74–78, quotation at 78.

73. BF *Papers* 15:220–22, quotations at 222.

74. BF to the *London Chronicle,* October 18–20, 1768, in BF *Papers* 15:233–37, quotations at 233–34. See Verner W. Crane, "Benjamin Franklin and the Stamp Act," *Publications of the Colonial Society of Massachusetts* 32 (1937): 70–77, and *Benjamin Franklin: Englishman and American* (Baltimore, MD: William and Wilkins, for Brown University, 1936), 116–31.

CHAPTER 7

1. See, for instance, the letters discussed in what follows, written to Joshua Babcock and Thomas Cushing, but also those written to between 1768 to 1775 to DuPont du Nemours and Barbeu-Dubourg; Henry Home, Lord Kames; and David Hume. For marginalia, see, for example, Franklin's marginalia in [Anon.], *An Inquiry into the Nature and Causes of the Present Disputes between the British Colonies in America and Their Mother-Country . . .* (London: J. Wilkie, 1769), in BF *Papers* 17:317 ff.

2. The "Aphorisms" were, the editors of Franklin's papers surmise, his "Positions." BF *Papers* 16:4.

3. BF *Papers* 16:47.

4. The article appeared in James Anderson's *The Bee, Or Literary Weekly Intelligencer, Consisting of Original Pieces, and Selections from Performances of Merit, Foreign and Domestic. A Work Calculated to Disseminate Useful Knowledge Among All Ranks of People at a Small Expence*, 12, issue 108 (1792), and in many different editions of Franklin's life and works published posthumously. The article or portions of it had a posthumous run in several periodicals from Scotland to Hawaii.

5. Franklin, "Positions to be Examined," in BF *Papers* 16:107–9; quoted passages are drawn from all three pages, in sequence.

6. Joanna Innes, "Jonathan Clark, Social History, and England's Ancien Regime," *Past and Present* 115 (1987): 178.

7. See Kathleen Wilson, *The Sense of the People: Politics, Culture, and Imperialism in England, 1715–1785* (Cambridge: Cambridge University Press, 1995), and Paul Langford, *A Polite and Commercial People: England, 1727–1783* (New York: Oxford University Press, 1994).

8. Paul Langford, *The Eighteenth Century, 1688–1815* (London: Adam and Charles Black, 1976), 390.

9. Marginalia quoted in BF *Papers* 16:294.

10. The question of Franklin's authorship of all or part of the numbers in this essay series has been a matter of contention. Franklin was first named the author of the complete series by Verner W. Crane, in *Benjamin Franklin's Letters to the Press, 1758–1775*. The editors of Franklin's papers allowed that James Burgh might be a likely coauthor of some of the essays, in whole or in part (see BF *Papers* 17:5). The authorship was contested by Carla H. Hay in two essays, "Benjamin Franklin, James Burgh, and the Authorship of 'The Colonist's Advocate' Letters," *William and Mary Quarterly*, 3rd ser., 32 (1975): 111–24, and "The Making of a Radical: The Case of James Burgh," *Journal of British Studies* 18 (Spring 1979): 90–117, and in her book, *James Burgh, Spokesman for Reform in Hanoverian England* (Washington, DC: University Press of America, 1979). The disparities (across the series) in prose quality and certain arguments suggest that more than two hands were involved in bringing this group of essays to press. I have quoted parts that seem likely to have been Franklin's. Franklin was of such a similar mind with others in the Club of Honest Whigs that the question of *who* authored which essays or portions of essays seems to have been unnecessarily fraught with anxiety in contemporary scholarship. In a study seeking to explore Franklin's intellectual and writerly life, it is just as fruitful to consider his collaborative writings as those individually authored.

11. BF *Papers* 17:28.

12. BF *Papers* 17:54.

13. From "The Colonist's Advocate," No. 3, printed in the *Public Advertiser*, January 11, 1770; BF *Papers* 17:19.

14. BF *Papers* 17:53–54.

15. See, for instance, Sheila L. Skemp, *The Making of a Patriot: Benjamin Franklin at the Cockpit* (New York: Oxford University Press, 2013), 27 and passim; Robert Middlekauff, *Benjamin Franklin and His Enemies* (Berkeley: University of California Press, 1996), 116; Brands, 7, 403; Isaacson, 193–94, 219; Gordon A. Wood, *The Americanization of Benjamin Franklin* (New York: Penguin, 2004), 91, 124, 141; Jerry Weinberger, *Benjamin Franklin Unmasked: The Unity of His Moral, Religious, and Political Thought* (Lawrence: University of Kansas Press, 2005), 220, 288. See J. A. Leo Lemay, *The Life of Benjamin Franklin*, vol. 3, *Soldier, Scientist, and Politician, 1748–1757* (Philadelphia: University of Pennsylvania Press, 2008), appendix 9.

16. See, for example, Sheila Skemp's *The Making of a Patriot* for these arguments.

17. From the preface: "At a Time when England was diffusing the Blessings of Liberty, to a prodigious national Expence, amongst the most remote People of the Continent, it must be matter of just Surprize to the Irish, that far from receiving Assistance from English Legislature, towards repairing the Damages they had sustained, they saw their Independence as a Kingdom, unjustly violated, their Trade wantonly restrained, and Mr. Molineux's modest dispassionate irrefragable Proof of the Rights and Liberties of his native Country, profanely burned by the Hands of the common Hangman." William Molyneux, *The Case of Ireland's being Bound by the Acts of Parliament in England, Stated* (1698; London: J. Almon, 1770), ii. Franklin transmitted the book to Cooper on April 14, 1770. See BF *Papers* 17:124.

18. Oliver W. Ferguson, *Jonathan Swift and Ireland* (Urbana: University of Illinois Press, 1962), 7.

19. For an efficient summary in much greater detail, see Ferguson, *Jonathan Swift and Ireland*, 5–25.

20. See Ferguson, *Jonathan Swift and Ireland*, 13–14. Ferguson also points out that the land was not farmed responsibly; landlords were indifferent to what was going on as long as they got their rents. "Thus the very class of workers who could have effected a real agricultural reform," Ferguson says, "were for the most part never given the chance to do so; and the men who were given the leases deliberately debased agricultural standards," 14.

21. BF *Papers* 17:163n.

22. BF *Papers* 17:163n.

23. See BF *Papers* 18:10–11 and the *Journal of the Commissioners for Trade and Plantations . . . April 1704 to . . . May 1782*, 14 vols. (London: His Majesty's Stationery Office, 1920–38), 1768–75, 10, and *Acts of the Privy Council of England, Colonial Series, 1613–1783*, 6 vols., ed. W. L. Grant and James Munro (Hereford: for HMSO, Anthony Bros., 1908–12), 5:264.

24. The summary of the story was written in Franklin's hand and kept with his papers. The summary appears in BF *Papers* 18:12–16; quotations at 12, 13, 14, and 15.

25. BF *Papers* 18:11.

26. BF *Papers* 18:15–16.

27. BF *Papers* 17:162–63.

28. BF *Papers* 18:28.

29. BF *Papers* 18:126.

30. For background on the situation, see Vincent Morley, *Irish Opinion and the American Revolution, 1760–1783* (Cambridge: Cambridge University Press, 2002). For background on Newenham's relationship with Franklin, see Dixon Wecter, "Benjamin Franklin and an Irish 'Enthusiast,'" *Huntington Library Quarterly* 4 (1941): 205–34. Newenham's life and views are discussed in Eugene A. Coyle, "Eighteenth-Century Dublin Radical," *Dublin Historical Record* 46, no. 1 (1993): 15–30. An entry on Newenham for the online Oxford Dictionary of National Biography appears at http://www.oxforddnb.com/templates/article.jsp?articleid=20006&back=; accessed March 14, 2014.

It is noteworthy that Bushe, then of Kilfane, read a paper on July 10, 1790, to the Royal Irish Academy entitled "An essay towards ascertaining the population of Ireland." He calculated that the population of Ireland was 4,040,000, on basis of hearth-money returns made in 1788. See http://genealogy.links.org/links-cgi/readged?/home/ben/camilla-genealogy/current+c-bushe88933+2-5-0-1-0. Accessed

June 9, 2011. See also J. Bennett Nolan, *Benjamin Franklin in Scotland and Ireland* (Philadelphia: University of Pennsylvania Press, 1938).

31. Franklin to the London *Gazetteer,* January 15, 1766. Franklin's essays appeared in the *Gazetteer* on January 11, 1766 (reprinted in the *Pennsylvania Chronicle,* March 9, 1767) and January 15, 1766 (reprinted in the *Chronicle,* March 23, 1767). As "A Friend to Both Countries," Franklin published an essay in the *Gazetteer and New Daily Advertiser,* January 23, 1766.

32. Franklin (in London) to Joshua Babcock, January 13, 1772, in BF *Papers* 19:7.

33. This discussion is adapted from two sources: Morley, *Irish Opinion,* 42–54; C. A. Bayly, in *Imperial Meridian: The British Empire and the World, 1780–1830* (New York: Longman, 1989), chapter 3, particularly 86–89. But see also Robert E. Burns, "The Catholic Relief Act in Ireland," *Church History* 32 (1963): 181–206, and James Kelly, *Sir Edward Newenham, MP, 1734–1814, Defender of the Protestant Constitution* (Dublin: Four Courts Press, 2004).

34. For background, I have used Charles W. J. Withers, "On Georgics and Geology: James Hutton's 'Elements of Agriculture' and Agricultural Science in Eighteenth-Century Scotland," *Agricultural History Review* 42, no. 1 (1994): 38–48, and Bayly, *Imperial Meridian,* chapter 3, especially 80–88.

35. Kames, *Sketches of the History of Man, In Two Volumes* (Edinburgh: W. Creech and for W. Strahan and T. Cadell, in London), 2:484.

36. Kames, *Sketches,* 2:486.

37. Kames, *The Gentleman Farmer, Being an Attempt to improve Agriculture by subjecting it to the Test of Rational Principles* (Edinburgh: W. Creech, and for T. Cadell, London), "Epistle to Sir John Pringle," iii–vi, quotation at v.

38. Franklin to Babcock, BF *Papers* 19:7, 19:6.

39. Franklin to Thomas Cushing, January 13, 1772. BF *Papers* 19:22–23.

40. The questions appear in BF *Papers* 18:222–23. In August 1772, he sent the questions to a number of different correspondents.

41. Franklin to Cushing, January 13, 1771. BF *Papers* 19:22–23.

42. Franklin gave to the publisher the first volume of the transactions of the American Philosophical Society, just published, and these are described as "no inconsiderable earnest of the great progress the arts and sciences will one day make in this NEW WORLD." *Hibernian Magazine,* October 1771, 491–92, quotation at 492.

43. *Hibernian Magazine,* October 1771, 475–76, quotation at 476.

44. Franklin used the saying "The waves do not rise, but when the winds blow" in the Canada pamphlet in 1760, and he used it again in 1768 as the motto of his "Causes of the American Discontents before 1768."

45. As Franklin reported in a letter to William Franklin, January 30, 1772. BF *Papers* 19:47–48.

46. Franklin to Cushing, January 13, 1772. BF *Papers* 19:21.

47. Franklin to Cushing, January 13, 1772. BF *Papers* 19:21.

48. From Franklin's comments on a proposed act to prevent emigration, designed for the *Public Advertiser,* but never printed. BF *Papers* 20:522–28; quotation at 524.

49. BF to Richard Jackson, February 11, 1764, in BF *Papers* 11:76ff.

50. Gottfried Achenwall's "Some Observations on North America from Oral Information by Dr. Franklin," 1766, in BF *Papers* 13:346ff.

51. BF to the *London Chronicle,* April 11, 1767, in BF *Papers* 14:110–16, quotation at 115.

52. See BF *Papers* 14:115–16n. For information on the East India Company, see Lucy S. Sutherland, *The East India Company in Eighteenth-Century Politics* (Oxford: Oxford University Press, 1951), 136–76.

53. This is probably the information he was referring to in his report on a debate in the House of Lords, extracted in the *Pennsylvania Chronicle*, June 1–8, 1767 (BF *Papers* 14:109).

54. BF *Papers* 15:238–41, quotation at 240.

55. BF to Joseph Galloway, BF *Papers* 19:418–21, quotations at 419, 420.

56. Marginal remarks in [Anon.], *The Constitutional Means* (London: Becket and DeHondt, 1769), as printed in BF *Papers* 16:291-92. The second pamphlet with Franklin's marginalia is Matthew Wheelock's *Reflections Moral and Political on Great Britain and her Colonies* (London: Becket, 1770) in BF *Papers* 17:385.

57. Skemp, *Making of a Patriot*, 152, 153.

58. James Srodes, *Franklin: The Essential Founding Father* (Washington, DC: Regnery Publishing, 2002), 247. The OED defines the Cockpit thus: "The name of the block of buildings on or near the site of the Cockpit erected by Henry VIII opposite Whitehall, London, used from the seventeenth century as government offices; hence put familiarly for 'the Treasury,' and 'the Privy Council chambers.' *Obs.*" *Oxford English Dictionary Online*, http://www.oed.com.ezaccess.libraries.psu.edu/view/Entry/35477?redirectedFrom=Cockpit#eid, accessed August 27, 2014.

59. See the editorial comment in BF *Papers* 21:20n. The information about Wedderburn that follows is derived from the same source.

60. Listeners who reported on the speech said it took over an hour to deliver. As the editors of Franklin's papers point out, it is difficult to ascertain exactly what was said in the Cockpit hearing, but because several different reliable witnesses recorded all or parts of the speech, we can with some degree of certainty know the kinds of remarks Wedderburn made. Thus, while exact wording might be unrecoverable, the import of Wedderburn's long speech becomes quite clear from the different testimonies available to us, testimonies carefully examined by the editors of Franklin's papers. See BF *Papers* 21:37–43.

61. Quoted in BF *Papers* 21:40n, following a citation in *Massachusetts Historical Society Collections*, 6th ser., 9 (1897): 338.

62. BF *Papers* 21:60.

63. BF *Papers* 21:48.

64. BF *Papers* 21:48–49.

65. BF *Papers* 21:60.

66. BF *Papers* 21:44.

67. BF *Papers* 21:46.

68. BF *Papers* 21:46.

69. BF *Papers* 21:56.

70. BF *Papers* 21:58.

71. BF *Papers* 21:60–61.

72. BF *Papers* 21:59.

73. BF *Papers* 20:40–41.

74. BF *Papers* 21:40.

75. Quoted in William Temple Franklin's *Memoirs of the Life and Writings of Benjamin Franklin, LLD, FRS &c*, 3 vols. (London: Henry Colburn, 1817–18), 1:185.

76. Reprinted in BF *Papers* 21:112–13.

77. The distinction is made by Robert Young in *Postcolonialism: An Historical Introduction* (Oxford: Blackwell, 2001): "The term 'empire' has been widely used for many centuries without, however necessarily signifying 'imperialism.' Here a basic

difference emerges between an empire that was bureaucratically controlled by a government from the centre, and which was developed for ideological as well as financial reasons, a structure that can be called imperialism, and an empire that was developed for settlement by individual communities or for commercial purposes by a trading company, a structure that can be called colonial" (16).

78. Joseph Priestley, *The Memoirs of the Rev. Dr. Joseph Priestley to the Year 1795. Written by Himself. With a Continuation to the Time of His Decease, by His Son, Joseph Priestley* (London: Joseph Johnson for the Unitarian Societies in England, 1809), 78–79.

79. Priestley, *Memoirs,* 79.

CHAPTER 8

1. BF to William Franklin, July 14, 1773, in BF *Papers* 20:303–04.

2. BF *Papers* 20:121.

3. BF *Papers* 20:120–25.

4. BF *Papers* 20:126–28.

5. The mock epitaph is reprinted in BF *Papers* 22:303.

6. The original notations by Franklin lie among the papers of Thomas Jefferson. See Richard S. Patterson and Richardson Dougall, *The Eagle and the Shield: A History of the Great Seal of the United States* (Washington, DC: Department of State, 1978), 13–14.

7. See BF *Papers* 22:562.

8. That is, Joachim Camerarius's *Four Centuries of Ethico-Political Symbols and Emblems.* For background on the different editions of Camerarius consulted by the Great Seal committee, see Patterson and Dougall, *The Eagle and the Shield,* 95–102. Franklin's own book was a 1702 Mainz edition.

9. Clement Walker, *Anarchia Anglicana: or the History of Independency* (London: R. Royston, 1660).

10. Franklin's family relations have been studied most notably by Claude-Anne Lopez and Eugenia Herbert in *The Private Franklin: The Man and His Family* (New York: W.W. Norton, 1975) and Sheila L. Skemp, *William Franklin: Son of a Patriot, Servant of a King* (New York: Oxford University Press, 1990).

11. An engaging and still useful resource for studying the drafts of the Declaration is James Munves, *Thomas Jefferson and the Declaration of Independence: The Writing and Editing of the Document that Marked the Birth of the United States of America* (New York: Charles Scribner's Sons, 1976).

12. BF to Richard Howe, July 20, 1776, BF *Papers* 22:520. Howe had arrived at Sandy Hook, New York, after first landing at Halifax, Nova Scotia, in June.

13. In Franklin's day, the word *China* was used to modify nouns in this way, to implicate the thing's having a Chinese origination or a style like that from China. China ware, a porcelain of high-quality, finely wrought semitransparent earthenware, was first manufactured in China and brought to Europe by the Portuguese in the sixteenth century. By the early eighteenth century, it had achieved significant popularity and forms like the porcelain originally called "China ware" were produced in Britain and Europe. See the Oxford English Dictionary, online edition, s.v. "China." Accessed January 19, 2008.

14. The letter is dated August 20, 1776. BF *Papers* 22:575.

15. BF *Papers* 22:593.

16. BF *Papers* 22:571–75.

17. BF *Papers* 22:529–33; quotations above and here at 533 and 530.

18. The record of the meeting appears in BF *Papers* 22:598–605, quotations at 603, 604, 605.

19. For background on Chaumont and events of these years (especially for a correction of charges of duplicity raised against Chaumont by the noted historian of John Paul Jones, Samuel Eliot Morison), see Thomas J. Schaeper, *France and America in the Revolutionary Era: The Life of Jacques-Donatien Leray de Chaumont, 1725–1803* (Providence, RI: Berghahn, 1995).

20. See BF *Papers* 23:112–13, 244–46.

21. See BF *Papers* 24:500–501. The best resource on Franklin's press at Passy is Luther S. Livingston, *Franklin and His Press at Passy: An Account of the Books, Pamphlets, and Leaflets Printed There, Including the Long-Lost Bagatelles* (New York: Grolier Club, 1914). According to Livingston, "the famous typefounding house of Fournier" was "the oldest in its line in France." Established during the early sixteenth century by Claude Garamond, the house was taken up later by Guillaume Le Bé, who passed it on to the elder Fournier, whose son, Pierre-Simon Fournier, author of *Manuel Typographique* (1764–66), became Franklin's supplier in September 1777, although Franklin dealt with several members of the Fournier family at different times. See Livingston, *Franklin and His Press*, 111–12. Livingston acknowledged that the uses of the press were many but that Franklin's original impulse in setting up a press related to his obligations of his office. "It seems probable that Franklin's first idea in putting a press and types in his house at Passy, was to print government documents and legal blanks which he required in the transaction of the affairs of his office," 78.

22. According to Livingston, the English typefoundry that Franklin likely used during his Passy years was the house of Caslon. Franklin bought a significant amount of type from the Caslon family. "William Caslon the elder, from whom Franklin had purchased many hundreds of pounds of type for his printing offices in Philadelphia and other American cities, had died in 1766. He was succeeded in the business by his son William Caslon II, who died in 1778, and was in turn succeeded by his son, William Caslon III": Livingston, *Franklin and His Press*, 121. Franklin arranged that his orders passed through others. In 1780, a very large order, probably to the house of Caslon, was arranged through Charles Dumas, then at The Hague.

23. For background on the lines and their use in France, see Alfred O. Aldridge, *Franklin and His French Contemporaries* (Washington Square: New York University Press, 1957), 124–36.

24. See John Adams's diary for these details: *The Diary and Autobiography of John Adams*, 4 vols., ed. Lyman H. Butterfield (Cambridge, MA: Harvard University Press, 1961), 4:118.

25. See Aldridge, *Franklin and His French Contemporaries*, 196.

26. BF Lemay *Writings*, 1489.

27. Background on these years has been garnered from the following sources: Aldridge, *Franklin and His French Contemporaries*; Ellen R. Cohn, "The Printer at Passy," in *Benjamin Franklin in Search of a Better World*, ed. Page Talbott (New Haven: Yale University Press, 2005), 234–71; Livingston, *Franklin and His Press*; Carla Mulford, "Benjamin Franklin's Savage Eloquence: Hoaxes from the Press at Passy, 1782," *Proceedings of the American Philosophical Society* 152, no. 4 (December 2008): 490–520; Stacy Schiff, *A Great Improvisation: Franklin, France, and the Birth of America* (New York: Henry Holt, 2005); David Schoenbrun, *Triumph*

in Paris: The Exploits of Benjamin Franklin (New York: Harper and Row, 1976); and Gerald Stourzh, *Benjamin Franklin and American Foreign Policy* (Chicago: University of Chicago Press, 1954). An interesting popular account is Willis Steell, *Benjamin Franklin of Paris* (New York: Minton, Balch, 1928). Documentary studies include an important early source, Edward Everett Hale and Edward Everett Hale Jr., *Franklin in France*, 2 vols. (Boston: Roberts Bros., 1887, 1888), and *Letters from France: The Private Diplomatic Correspondence of Benjamin Franklin, 1776–1785*, ed. Brett F. Woods (New York: Algora Publishing, 2006).

28. Some who have written about this event report that the suit was blue, probably thinking it the suit figured in the famous painting featuring Franklin at a desk, looking over papers, completed in 1767 by David Martin (1737–1797). Thus, for instance, Walter Isaacson remarks that the suit was blue in his biography, 277, 347. The coat might have been brown, however, as evidenced by a brief article by Richard Meade Bache, "Franklin's Ceremonial Coat," *Pennsylvania Magazine of History & Biography* 23 (1899): 444–52. Pieces of one of Franklin's coats, perhaps the same coat, are exhibited with the Benjamin Franklin Tercentary exhibition and viewable online: http://www.benfranklin300.org/frankliniana/result.php?id=158&sec=1. Accessed March 12, 2014.

29. BF *Papers* 25:634, 634–35.

30. Adams and Franklin had not been happy together, as we have seen. By 1780, Franklin would report to Congress that Adams, now a commissioner to assist in negotiating peace with Britain, had given distinct offense to the French court by way of repeated insults in letters to Vergennes. On August 9, 1780, Franklin sent copies of the letters to Congress, at the request of Vergennes. This action would prompt Adams to become openly hostile not just to the French but to Franklin. Still, the two had to work on the mission together, but this was made easier when Adams was sent to the Netherlands. Personality differences, differences in diplomacy methods, differences in interpretations of the mission fueled the disputes between Adams and Franklin.

31. BF *Papers* 33:356.

32. BF *Papers* 33:354. The proverb was used by "Poor Richard" in June 1736, along with several bits about being in debt, including a statement similar to the philosophy he was offering in this letter, "He that sells upon trust, loses many friends, and always wants money" (BF *Papers* 2:140). It also became part of "Father Abraham's Speech" in 1758 (BF *Papers* 7:341).

33. BF *Papers* 33:357.

34. The supplement was printed in two editions, a first version with just one selection and a second (the broadside Franklin eventually circulated), with two selections. Franklin worked out the first version, a single-sided broadsheet, in an effort to bring attention to the complicity of the British military and its war tactics. This single-sided first edition offers a "scalping letter," a purported letter from an American militiaman Captain Samuel Gerrish. The sheet is filled out with imitation advertisements for a tanning yard, a tract of land, and a "stocky, well set" stolen or stray bay horse, along with an estate notice. Franklin probably prepared this sheet, ran some copies, and then decided to target one other issue that had rankled him for some time, the treatment that John Paul Jones had received over two years earlier for taking British ships as prizes and not releasing them. In the second version, the John Paul Jones letter draws attention to British captures of American vessels and the execrable treatment of colonial Britons at the hands of those who seized American vessels, even as it makes

an explicit attestation to the grievances of Britons in North America. The second version is completed with some of the advertisements used in the first run of the first sheet Franklin had produced. The Historical Society of Pennsylvania has a copy of the first edition of the supplement but not the second. The American Philosophical Society and the Library of Congress house copies of both editions. The supplement is available in BF *Papers* 37:184–96. There is no evidence that the first version was sent out, according to the editors of Franklin's papers: BF *Papers* 37:185.

35. Franklin dined with Richard Oswald on April 18, and he asked for one more meeting with Oswald the next morning, April 19, so that Franklin would be able, he said, to draft a letter to the Earl of Shelburne. Franklin used the opportunity of that letter to speak directly in behalf of their creating a "General Peace" and of a speedy prisoner exchange, a related subject of the hoax John Paul Jones letter in the supplement.

36. Evidence of Franklin's disgust with Britain's sending Germans to fight the American war appear in several places in his correspondence and in a newspaper essay from 1777 long attributed to him, often called "The Sale of the Hessians" and printed in BF *Papers* 23:480–84.

37. It is clear that Britain used Germans in part to keep the English mainland population from creating a general outcry against the war in the colonies. Historian Eliga Gould has made an interesting point about the political maneuverings of the various ministries prosecuting the war in the colonies: "Although the inconclusive contest required the British people to make enormous sacrifices, Lord North's defenders succeeded in casting the war in the colonies as a patriotic struggle for the integrity of Britain's blue water empire. Moreover, despite the costs generated by so many distant campaigns, the government managed to avoid making the sorts of military and fiscal demands that might have triggered a more sustained popular backlash." See Eliga Gould, *The Persistence of Empire: British Political Culture in the Age of the American Revolution* (Chapel Hill: University of North Carolina Press, 2000), 150.

38. A point under contention has been whether Native peoples engaged in scalping practices before the invasions of the Americas by Europeans. Scalping seems to have been a traditional practice among many peoples, whether those in the Americas or those from Europe. For background on the question, see James Axtell and William C. Sturtevant, "The Unkindest Cut, or Who Invented Scalping," *William and Mary Quarterly*, 3rd ser., 37 (1980): 451–72. See also, however, Daniel Richter, "Whose Indian History?" *William and Mary Quarterly* 3rd ser., 50 (1993): 379–93.

39. Francis Jennings, *Empire of Fortune: Crowns, Colonies, and Tribes in the Seven Years War in America* (New York: W.W. Norton, 1988), 267ff. Jennings has explained, "On 10 April 1756, while Franklin was away in Virginia, the remaining four commissioners proposed formally to [Deputy Governor Robert Hunter] Morris 'that it is necessary for this Province immediately to declare War against the Delawares and all other Enemy Indians' and promised to supply funds for scalp bounties. They appended a neat schedule of prices, including one of 50 dollars 'for the Scalp of every Indian Woman' and 130 dollars for 'every Male Indian above Ten Years old.'" Jennings, 268. Historian Fred Anderson has remarked, as well, that "scalpings were common in the New England–raised ranger companies" at this time. Fred Anderson, *Crucible of War: The Seven Years' War and the Fate of Empire in British North America, 1754–1766* (New York: Knopf, 2000), 788–89 n. 1.

40. See Axtell, "Scalping: The Ethnohistory of a Moral Question," in *The European and the Indian: Essays in the Ethnohistory of Colonial North America* (New York: Oxford University Press, 1981), 207–41, esp. 218ff. For background

on mourning wars in Iroquoian tradition, see Daniel Richter, *The Ordeal of the Longhouse: The Peoples of the Iroquois League in the Era of European Colonization* (Chapel Hill: University of North Carolina Press, 1992). A discussion of scalping and the "whiteness" question occurs in Gregory T. Knouff, "Whiteness and Warfare on a Revolutionary Frontier," in *Friends and Enemies in Penn's Woods: Indians, Colonists, and the Racial Construction of Pennsylvania*, ed. William A. Pencak and Daniel K. Richter (University Park: Pennsylvania State University Press, 2004), 238–57.

41. Nevill Barbour, "North West Africa from the Fifteenth to Nineteenth Centuries," in *The Last Great Muslim Empires: History of the Muslim World*, ed. H. J. Kissling et al. (1969; Princeton: Marcus Wiener, 1996), 107–8.

42. Voltaire (François Marie Arouet), *Candide*, as published in *Candide, ou L'Optimisme: Edition Critique*, ed. André Morize (Paris: Librarie E. Droz, 1931), 62. My own loose translation of this passage is "Morocco was swimming in blood when we arrived. Fifty sons of the Emperor Muley-Ismaël had each his own party (faction), which produced, in effect, fifty civil wars, of blacks against blacks, blacks against brown people (people of mixed race), brown peoples against brown peoples, of mulattos against mulattos. This was continual carnage, throughout the extent of the empire."

43. Walpole to Lady Ossory, September 10, 1792, and to Governor Pownall, October 27, 1783, as quoted in *The Yale Edition of Horace Walpole's Correspondence*, 48 vols., ed. W. S. Lewis (New Haven: Yale University Press, 1944), 2:207 n. 18.

44. Franklin to Adams, April 22, 1782, in BF *Papers* 37:197.

45. According to Catherine Prelinger, "Franklin turned his attention to the prisoners soon after his arrival. The ship that carried him to France, the *Reprisal*, commanded by Lambert Wickes, set sail almost immediately after disembarking its passengers to cruise for prizes and prisoners in the English Channel": Prelinger, "Benjamin Franklin and the American Prisoners of War in England during the American Revolution," *William and Mary Quarterly*, 3rd ser., 32 (1975): 261–94, quotation at 262. Information about Franklin's activities in this era are derived from the Franklin papers volumes covering the years 1777 to 1782 and Prelinger's essay.

46. The importance of Yorke to the prosecution of various aspects of the suppression of the American Britons is discussed in H. M. Scott, "Sir Joseph Yorke, Dutch Politics, and the Origins of the Fourth Anglo-Dutch War," *Historical Journal* 31 (1988): 571–89.

47. Prelinger, "Franklin and American Prisoners of War," 267 n. 19.

48. See Prelinger, "Franklin and American Prisoners of War," 272, and Samuel Eliot Morison, *John Paul Jones: A Sailor's Biography* (Boston: Little, Brown, 1959), 135. See also Thomas J. Schaeper, *John Paul Jones and the Battle Off Flamborough Head, a Reconsideration* (New York: Peter Lang, 1989).

49. See BF *Papers* 30:30 n. 6.

50. See Jones's letter to Franklin, BF *Papers* 30:520–21.

51. Quoted in BF *Papers* 37:191.

52. Quoted in BF *Papers* 37:191 n2.

53. Scott, "Sir Joseph Yorke," 577.

54. See Michele Valerie Ronnick, "The Phrase 'Nerone Neronior' in Walter of Châtillon, John Milton, and John Adams," *Notes and Queries* 239 (1994): 169–70.

55. BF *Papers* 37:667.

56. Horace Walpole to Lady Ossory, October 1, 1782, in *Horace Walpole's Correspondence*, 33:355–58.

57. See BF *Papers* 37:184, and his notes for his conversation with Oswald. The conversation took place on or before April 19, 1782. See BF *Papers* 37:169–72.

58. From Franklin's notes on his conversation with Richard Oswald, written on or before April 19, 1782. See BF *Papers* 37:170.

59. BF *Papers* 37:197.

60. BF to Charles Dumas, May 3, 1782, BF *Papers* 37:268.

61. BF *Papers* 37:206. About the supplement, Franklin wrote: "I inclose what I suspect to be a pretended American Paper, which, however, tho' it should be found fictitious as to the Form, is undoubtedly true as to the Substance. For the English cannot deny such a Number of Murders having been really committed by their Instigation."

62. See BF *Papers* 37: xxvii, lviii, 283. See also Luther S. Livingston, *The Passports Printed by Benjamin Franklin at his Passy Press* (Ann Arbor, MI: William L. Clements Library, 1925).

63. Lemay *Writings*, 1491–92.

64. See BF *Papers* 40:lvii.

65. BF to Robert R. Livingston, July 22[–26], 1783, in BF *Papers* 40:355–70, quotation at 368.

66. BF to Charles Thomson, March 9, 1784. Currently unpublished but available in the online Franklin Papers project, associated with the Yale edition of Franklin's papers. http://franklinpapers.org/franklin//framedVolumes.jsp: accessed January 9, 2014.

67. See Aldridge, *Franklin and His French Contemporaries*, 30.

68. Online edition associated with the Franklin Papers project. http://franklinpapers.org/franklin//framedVolumes.jsp: accessed January 9, 2014.

69. "Remarks Concerning the Savages of North America" is printed in BF Lemay *Writings*, 969–74; the quotation is on 969. Franklin intended neither the *Information* nor the *Remarks* for publication, but he learned of their appearance in London in 1784. He asked his friend, Benjamin Vaughan, about the circumstances of their publication, and Vaughan responded, November 21, "I know not *who* published your pieces on the Indians & Imigrations, nor have I yet seen them. The latter piece the Abbé Morellet sent to Lord Shelburne, from whom I had it; The Bishop of St. Asaph's family afterwards had my whole packet of your pieces for many weeks." Quoted in Aldridge, *Franklin and His French Contemporaries*, 36.

70. For further discussion of the *Remarks*, see my two essays, "Benjamin Franklin, Native Americans, and the Commerce of Civility," in *Revolutionary Histories: Transatlantic Cultural Nationalism, 1775–1815*, ed. W. M. Verhoeven (New York: Palgrave Press of St. Martin's Press, 2002), 48–61, and "Benjamin Franklin, Native Americans, and European Cultures of Civility," *Prospects* 24 (1999): 49–66.

71. BF to Sally Franklin Bache, January 26, 1784; unpublished but in the Franklin papers online edition, http://franklinpapers.org/franklin//framedVolumes.jsp. Accessed January 9, 2014.

72. BF to Jonathan Shipley, BF *Papers* 39:349.

73. Jonathan Shipley to BF, April 24, 1783; BF *Papers* 39:501–2.

CHAPTER 9

1. The address was printed in *The Pennsylvania Packet*, September 19, 1785, 3. For background on the Philadelphia to which Franklin returned, see Ronald Schultz, *The Republic of Labor: Philadelphia Artisans and the Politics of Class, 1720–1830* (New York: Oxford University Press, 1993). For general background on

the era, see Richard Beeman, *Plain, Honest Men: The Making of the Constitution* (New York: Random House, 2009); Richard Buel Jr., *Securing the Revolution: Ideology in American Politics, 1789–1815* (Ithaca, NY: Cornell University Press, 1972); Alan Gibson, *Interpreting the Founding: Guide to the Enduring Debates over the Origins and Foundations of the American Republic* (Lawrence: University Press of Kansas, 2006); P. J. Marshall, *Remaking the British Atlantic: The United States and the British Empire after American Independence* (New York: Oxford University Press, 2012); and *Founding Choices: American Economic Policy in the 1790s*, ed. Douglas A. Irwin and Richard Sylla (Chicago: University of Chicago Press, 2011).

2. BF to Thomas Jefferson, October 1, 1785; letter at franklinpapers.org, accessed February 8, 2014.

3. BF to Jonathan Shipley, February 24, 1786; letter at franklinpapers.org, accessed February 8, 2014. Also in BF Lemay *Writings*, 1161–63, quotation at 1161, and BF Smyth *Writings* 9:488–91; quotation at 488.

4. BF to Mary Stevenson Hewson, May 6, 1786; letter at franklinpapers.org, accessed February 8, 2014. Also in BF Smyth *Writings* 9:510–13, quotation at 511, 512.

5. BF to Thomas Jefferson, October 1, 1785; letter at franklinpapers.org, accessed February 8, 2014.

6. BF to David Hartley, October 27, 1785; letter at franklinpapers.org, accessed February 8, 2014. Also in BF Smyth *Writings* 9:472–73.

7. BF to Jonathan Shipley, February 24, 1786; letter at franklinpapers.org, accessed February 8, 2014. Also in BF Lemay *Writings*, 1161–63, quotation at 1161–62, and in BF Smyth *Writings* 9:488–92, quotation at 489.

8. BF to Louis-Guillaume Le Veillard, March 6, 1786; letter at franklinpapers.org, accessed February 8, 2014. Also in BF Smyth *Writings* 9:495–97, quotation at 495–96. Smith dates the letter March 16, 1786.

9. BF to Rodolphe-Ferdinand Grand, March 5, 1786; letter at franklinpapers.org, accessed February 8, 2014. Also in BF Smyth *Writings* 9:492–94, quotation at 493.

10. BF to George Whatley, May 18, 1787; at franklinpapers.org, accessed February 8, 2014. Also in BF Smyth *Writings* 9:587–89, quotation at 587.

11. BF to Jonathan Shipley, February 24, 1786; letter at franklinpapers.org, accessed February 8, 2014. Also in BF Lemay *Writings*, 1161–63, and in BF Smyth *Writings* 9:488–91.

12. "The Retort Courteous," BF Lemay *Writings*, 1122–30, quotation at 1130; BF Smyth *Writings* 10:105–16, quotation at 115–16. Franklin prepared an additional manuscript that was not published at the time, now called "A.B. to ——" and probably intended for submission to a newspaper. See "A.B. to ——" at franklinpapers.org (c. 1786), accessed February 8, 2014.

13. BF as "A.B." to the *Pennsylvania Gazette* (probably not published), c. 1786, at franklinpapers.org, accessed February 8, 2014. Also in BF Smyth *Writings* 9:628–30.

14. George Washington to Henry Lee, October 31, 1786, in The George Washington Papers at the Library of Congress, available online at http://teachingamericanhistory.org/library/document/letter-to-henry-lee-3/, accessed February 10, 2014.

15. For background on these events, see Edward Hake Phillips, "A Frontier Interlude: Timothy Pickering and the Wyoming Valley," *Rice Institute Pamphlet* 37, no. 1 (1950): 48–74.

16. BF, as President of the Supreme Executive Council, to George Clinton, June 1, 1786; the letter mentions Ethan Allen. See also his later letter to Clinton, mentioning Daniel Shays, September 20, 1787. Letter at franklinpapers.org, accessed February 8, 2014.

17. See a series of Franklin's letters about these events, all available at franklinpapers.org, accessed February 10, 2014: BF to William Shaw, May 27, 1786; BF to William Montgomery, May 27, 1786; BF to George Clinton, June 1, 1786; BF to John Franklin, William Hooker Smith, and John Jenkins, June 11, 1786, in BF Smyth *Writings* 9:515-16; BF to Charles Pettit, October 10, 1786, in BF Smyth *Writings* 9:543-45; BF to James Bowdoin, March 6, 1787; the Proclamation of 1787; BF to Thomas Jefferson, April 19, 1787, BF Smyth *Writings* 9:573-75; BF to George Clinton, September 20, 1787; BF to John Craig, September 26, 1787; the Lieutenant of Luzerne to BF, October 6, 1787; BF to Nathan Dennisen: October 10, 1787; and BF Address to the Pennsylvania General Assembly, September 6, 1788. See the letters at franklinpapers.org, accessed February 8, 2014.

18. Franklin's closing speech, as read by James Wilson, September 17, 1787, available at franklinpapers.org, accessed February 10, 2014. Also available in BF Lemay *Writings*, 1139-41, quotation at 1141, and BF Smyth *Writings* 9:607-9, quotation at 609, 608-9. Other issues Franklin proposed in the convention that were found unacceptable included his opposition to having salaries for highest executive positions. The view might strike us as undemocratic today, because it seemed to suggest a favoring of wealthy people. Franklin conceived that if salaries of significance were offered, individuals might seek office in order to secure the financial reward rather than to serve the people. Another proposal found unacceptable was his motion on June 28, 1787, as the convention faced significant impasse, that sessions of the Convention be opened with prayer. The motion, proving controversial, was dropped.

19. See Barbara B. Oberg, "'Plain, insinuating, persuasive': Benjamin Franklin's Final Speech to the Constitutional Convention of 1787," in *Reappraising Benjamin Franklin: A Bicentennial Perspective*, ed. J. A. Leo Lemay (Newark: University of Delaware Press, 1993), 175-92, quotation at 189.

20. Information is derived from Kevin T. Barksdale, *The Lost State of Franklin: America's First Secession* (Lexington: University Press of Kentucky, 2009), 99-117, 121-27. Sevier's letter to Governor Caswell is quoted at 123.

21. BF to John Sevier, June 30, 1787, in franklinpapers.org, accessed February 10, 2014. For background on the secession movement in the Tennessee Valley and the proposed state of Franklin, see Barksdale, *Lost State of Franklin*; Noel B. Gerson, *Franklin: America's Lost State* (New York: Crowell-Collier Press, 1968); and Samuel Cole Williams, *History of the Lost State of Franklin*, rev. ed. (New York: Press of the Pioneers, 1933). There are a series of letters related to this subject in Franklin's papers. See, for instance, the following: BF to John Jay, July 6, 1786, in BF Smyth *Writings* 9:525-26; Certificate for Chief Scotash, July 7, 1786; BF to William Cocke, August 12, 1786, BF Smyth *Writings* 9:534-35; BF to the "Cherokee Indian Queen," June 30, 1787; BF to John Sevier, June 30, 1787; Talk to the Old Chiefs, June 30, 1787; Talk to Cornstalk, June 30, 1787; and the letter from Cherokee Indian Women, September 8, 1787.

22. Katteuha's message is available at franklinpapers.org, accessed February 21, 2014. It is discussed in a number of works related to the Cherokees, particularly Cherokee women. See Virginia Moore Carney, *Eastern Band Cherokee Women: Cultural Persistence in Their Letters and Speeches* (Knoxville: University of Tennessee Press, 2014) and Karen Kilcup, *Fallen Forests: Emotion, Embodiment, and Ethics in American Women's Environmental Writing, 1782-1924* (Athens: University of Georgia Press, 2013).

23. Madison's journals are widely available. The quotation is available online at http://www.constitution.org/dfc/dfc_0810.htm, accessed February 12, 2014.

24. On Franklin's slaveholding see the still useful study by Claude-Anne Lopez and Eugenia W. Herbert, *The Private Franklin: The Man and His Family* (New York: W.W. Norton, 1975), 291–302. See also Kevin J. Hayes, "New Light on Peter and King, the Two Slaves Benjamin Franklin Brought to England," *Notes and Queries* 60, no. 2 (June 2013): 205–9. Useful contextual information for Philadelphia is available in Gary B. Nash and Jean R. Soderlund, *Freedom by Degrees: Emancipation in Pennsylvania and its Aftermath* (New York: Oxford University Press, 1991). David Waldstreicher has taken a different view of Franklin and slavery in *Runaway America: Franklin, Slavery, and the American Revolution* (New York: Hill and Wang, 2004).

25. Nash and Soderlund, *Freedom by Degrees*, 48.

26. Nash and Soderlund, *Freedom by Degrees*, 48.

27. Nash and Soderlund, *Freedom by Degrees*, 55.

28. See Nash and Soderlund, *Freedom by Degrees*, 54–57.

29. For background on the Associates of Dr. Bray, see John Van Horne, ed., *Religious Philanthropy and Colonial Slavery: The American Correspondence of the Associates of Dr. Bray, 1717–1777* (Urbana: University of Illinois Press, 1985). See also Richard I. Shelling, "Benjamin Franklin and the Dr. Bray Associates," *Pennsylvania Magazine of History and Biography* 63 (1939): 282–93.

30. BF to John Waring, BF *Papers* 10:395–96, quotation at 396. For additional Franklin materials related to the Associates of Dr. Bray and their educational activities, see BF *Papers* 7:98–99, 100–101, 252–53, 256, 377–79; 8:425; 9:12–13, 20–21, 174; 10:298–300.

31. Information has been derived from Nash and Soderlund, *Freedom by Degrees*.

32. Granville Sharp, *A Representation of the Injustice and Dangerous Tendency of Tolerating Slavery or of Admitting the Least Claim of Private in the Persons of Men in England, in Four Parts* (London: Benjamin White, 1769).

33. For interesting new background on King, see Hayes, "New Light on Peter and King."

34. As Franklin had pointed out in his *Observations concerning the Increase of Mankind*, in the northern colonies, slave deaths always outnumbered slave births, making a continual supply from Africa necessary to maintain a labor force.

35. For background on the slaves in the Franklin family, see Nash and Soderlund, *Freedom by Degrees*, ix–xiv; Lopez and Herbert, *The Private Franklin*, 291–302; and Hayes, "New Light on Peter and King."

36. BF to Abiah Franklin, April 12, 1750; BF *Papers* 3:474.

37. For background on the attitudes of Pennsylvanians during Franklin's time, see Nash and Soderlund, *Freedom by Degrees*, 99–134.

38. BF to Richard Woodward, April 10, 1773, in BF *Papers* 20:155–56; BF to Benjamin Rush, July 14, 1773, in BF *Papers* 20:314.

39. Franklin had published the antislavery tracts of both Benjamin Lay and Ralph Sandiford.

40. See Nash and Soderlund, *Freedom by Degrees*, 127.

41. The memorial has been reprinted in several places and is available at franklin-papers.org, accessed February 16, 2014.

42. *Annals of Congress* known as *Debates and Proceedings in the Congress of the United States. . . .* 42 vols., ed Joseph Gales et al. (Washington, DC: Gales and Seaton, 1834–1856), House of Representatives, 1st Congress, 2nd Session (February 12, 1790), 1241. Available online at http://memory.loc.gov/cgi-bin/ampage, accessed February 23, 2014.

For background on such views, see Elizabeth Fox-Genovese and Eugene D. Genovese, *The Mind of the Master Class: History and Faith in the Southern Slaveholders' Worldview* (Cambridge: Cambridge University Press, 2005).

43. Benjamin Franklin as Historicus to *The Federal Gazette*, March 23, 1780.

44. Lopez and Herbert, *The Private Franklin*, 289–90.

45. See, for example, the following letters: BF to Jan Ingenhousz, September 2, 1786; BF to Alexander Small, February 19, 1787, in BF Smyth *Writings* 9:555–57; BF to George Whatley, May 18, 1787, in BF Smyth *Writings* 9:587–89; and BF to Jane Mecom, September 20, 1787, in BF Smyth *Writings* 9:612–14. At franklinpapers.org, accessed February 23, 2014.

46. BF to George Whitefield, July 2, 1756, in BF *Papers* 6:468–69.

47. BF to Hugh Roberts: BF *Papers* 12:201–02.

48. BF to George Whatley, May 18, 1787, in BF Smyth *Writings* 9:587–89, quotation at 588–89, and at franklinpapers.org, accessed February 23, 2014.

CONCLUSION

1. According to Verner Crane, "By 1774, Franklin's formula for empire had become the American formula of John Adams, James Wilson, and Thomas Jefferson. It was the formula implied in the Declaration of Independence": Verner W. Crane, *Benjamin Franklin and a Rising People* (Boston: Little, Brown, 1954), 128.

2. Benedict Anderson, *Imagined Communities: Reflections on the Origin and Spread of Nationalism*, rev. ed. (1983; New York: Verso, 1991), 7.

3. BF to Thomas Cushing, January 13, 1772. BF *Papers* 19:21.

Abbreviations

In the notes to the chapters, several abbreviations have been used for frequently cited materials related to Franklin.

BF *Papers* volume: page	Franklin, Benjamin. *The Papers of Benjamin Franklin*. 40 vols. [through 2011]. Ed. Leonard W. Labaree et al. New Haven: Yale University Press, 1959—.
BF Lemay *Writings*	Franklin, Benjamin. *Benjamin Franklin: Writings*. Ed. J. A. Leo Lemay. New York: Library of America, 1987.
BF Smyth *Writings* volume: page	Franklin, Benjamin. *The Writings of Benjamin Franklin*. 10 vols. Ed. Albert Henry Smyth. New York: Macmillan, 1907.
BF *Works* volume: page	Franklin, Benjamin. *The Works of Dr. Benjamin Franklin*. 6 vols. Ed. William Duane. Philadelphia: William Duane, 1808–18.
Huang	Huang, Nian-Sheng. *Franklin's Father Josiah: Life of a Colonial Boston Tallow Chandler, 1657–1745*. Transactions of the American Philosophical Society, v. 90, pt. 3. Philadelphia: American Philosophical Society, 2000.
Isaacson	Isaacson, Walter. *Benjamin Franklin, An American Life*. New York: Simon and Schuster, 2003.

Lemay *Life* 1: page   Lemay, J. A. Leo. *The Life of Benjamin Franklin: Vol. 1, Journalist, 1706–1730.* Philadelphia: University of Pennsylvania Press, 2006.

Miller   Miller, C. William *Benjamin Franklin's Philadelphia Printing, 1728–1766: A Descriptive Bibliography.* Philadelphia: American Philosophical Society, 1974.

Tourtellot   Tourtellot, Arthur Bernon. *Benjamin Franklin: The Shaping of Genius, the Boston Years.* Garden City, NY: Doubleday, 1977.

Bibliography of Printed Sources

PRIMARY SOURCES

Franklin's Writings (exclusive of individual publications, which are indexed)

Benjamin Franklin's Letters to the Press, 1758–1775. Ed. Verner Crane. Chapel Hill: University of North Carolina Press, 1950.

Franklin: Writings. Ed. J. A. Leo Lemay. New York: Library of America, 1987.

Letters from France: The Private Diplomatic Correspondence of Benjamin Franklin, 1776–1785. Ed. Brett F. Woods. New York: Algora Publishing, 2006.

Memoirs of the Life and Writings of Benjamin Franklin, LLD, FRS &c. 3 vols. Ed. William Temple Franklin. London: Henry Colburn, 1817–18.

Political, Miscellaneous, and Philosophical Pieces, Now First Collected, with Explanatory Plates, Notes, and Index to the Whole. Ed. Benjamin Vaughan. London: J. Johnson, 1779.

The Works of Dr. Benjamin Franklin. 6 vols. Ed. William Duane. Philadelphia: William Duane, 1808–18.

The Papers of Benjamin Franklin. 40 vols. (to 2011). Ed. Leonard W. Labaree et al. New Haven: Yale University Press, 1959—.

The Writings of Benjamin Franklin. 10 vols. Ed. Albert Henry Smyth. New York: Macmillan, 1905–7.

Collections

Acts of the Privy Council of England, Colonial Series, 1613–1783. 6 vols. Ed. W. L. Grant and James Munro. Hereford: For HMSO, Anthony Bros., 1908–12.

Debates and Proceedings in the Congress of the United States . . . . 42 vols. Ed. Joseph Gales et al. Washington, DC: Gales and Seaton, 1834–56.

Journal of the Commissioners for Trade and Plantations . . . April 1704 to . . . May 1782. 14 vols. Ed. K. H. Ledward. London: His Majesty's Stationery Office, 1920–38.

Journals of the House of Representatives of Massachusetts. 50 vols. Ed. Max R. Hall et al. Boston: Massachusetts Historical Society, 1919–90.

Proceedings and Debates of the British Parliaments Respecting North America, 1754–1783. 6 vols. Ed. R. C. Simmons and P. D. G. Thomas. White Plains, NY: Kraus International, 1982.

A Select Collection of Early English Tracts on Commerce from the Originals of Mun, Roberts, North, and Others, with a Preface and Index. Ed. John Ramsay McCullough. London: Printed for the Political Economy Club, 1856.

Periodicals, Newspapers, and Magazines

Athenian Oracle
Boston Gazette
Boston News-Letter
Ephémérides du Citoyen
Freeholder's Journal (London)
Gentleman's Magazine
Guardian
Hibernian Magazine, or Compendium of Entertaining Knowledge
London Gazette
London Gazetteer
London Journal
London Magazine
New-England Courant
New York Weekly Journal
New York Weekly Post Boy
Pennsylvania Chronicle
Pennsylvania Gazette
Political State of Great Britain
Providence Gazette
Scots Magazine
Spectator
Vermont Gazette, or Freeman's Repository
Virginia Gazette
Weekly Journal; Or, British Gazetteer

Contemporaneous Writings

Anon. ["A Person of Quality"]. *The Devil pursued, or, The Right saddle laid upon the right Mare: a satyr upon Madam Celliers standing in the pillory, being convicted for the publishing of a late lying scandalous pamphlet called Malice defeated &c.* London: T. Davies, 1680.

Anon. *An Inquiry into the Nature and Causes of the Present Disputes between the British Colonies in America and Their Mother-Country. . . .* London: J. Wilkie, 1769.

Anon. *Protest Against the Bill to Repeal the American Stamp Act, The Last Session.* Paris: Chez J.W., 1766.

Anon. *Second Protest, with a List of Voters against the Bill to Repeal the American Stamp Act, of Last Session.* Paris: Chez J.W., 1766.

Anon. *The True Constitutional Means for Putting an End to the Disputes between Great Britain and the American Colonies.* London: T. Becket and P.A. DeHondt, 1769.

Adams, John. *The Diary and Autobiography of John Adams.* 4 vols. Ed. Lyman H. Butterfield. Cambridge: Harvard University Press, 1961.

Anderson, James. *The Bee, Or Literary Weekly Intelligencer, Consisting of Original Pieces, and Selections from Performances of Merit, Foreign and Domestic. A Work Calculated to Disseminate Useful Knowledge Among All Ranks of People at Small Expence.* 16 vols. Edinburgh: Mundell, 1791–92.

Barbon, Nicholas. *A Discourse Concerning the Coining the New Money Lighter. in Answer to Mr. Lock's Considerations about Raising the Value of Money.* London: R. Chiswell, 1696.

———. *A Discourse on Trade*. London: Tho. Milbourne for the Author, 1690.

Bernard, Richard. *A Guide to Grand-Jury Men, Divided into Two Books. . . .* London: Felix Kyngston for Edw. Blackmore, 1627, 1629.

———. *The Isle of Man, Or the Legal Proceedings in Man-Shire against Sin. . . .* Boston: James Franklin, 1719.

Bolt, William. *Considerations on India Affairs, Particularly Respecting the Present State of Bengal and Its Dependencies . . . .* London: J. Almon, 1772.

Bridges, John. *The History and Antiquities of Northamptonshire. Compiled from the Manuscript Collections of the Late Learned Antiquary John Bridges, Esq.* 2 vols. Comp. Peter Whalley. Oxford: Clarendon Press, 1791.

Bunyan, John. *The Pilgrim's Progress from This World to That which is to come.* London: Nath. Ponder, 1678.

Burgh, James. *The Dignity of Human Nature; or, a Brief Account of the . . . Means for Attaining the True End of our Existence.* London: W.B. for J. and P. Knapton, 1754.

———. *Political Disquisitions; Or, An Enquiry into Public Errors, Defects, and Abuses.* 2 vols. London: n.p. for E. and C. Dilly, 1774.

Burke, William. *Remarks on the Letter Address'd to Two Great Men. In a Letter to the Author of That Piece.* London: n.p., 1760.

Burton, R. [Nathaniel Crouch]. *Historical Collections.* 120 vols. London: [Nathaniel Crouch], 1681–1736.

Bushe, Gervase Parker. *The Case of Great Britain and America.* 2nd ed. London: n.p. for T. Becket and P.A. DeHondt, 1769.

Camerarius, Joachim. *Symbolorum ac Emblematum Ethico-Politicorum Centuriae Quatuor.* Mainz: Bourgeat, 1702.

Care, Henry. *English Liberties, or The Free-born Subject's Inheritance; Containing Magna Charta, Charta De Foresta, the Statute De Tallagio Non Concedendo, the Habeas Corpus Act, and Several Other Statutes; with Comments on Each of Them . . . with Many Law-cases throughout the Whole. Compiled First by Henry Care, and Contiued [sic], with Large Additions, by W.N. of the Middle-Temple, Esq.* Boston: James Franklin for N. Buttolph, B. Eliot, and D. Henchman, 1721.

Cary, John. *An Essay Toward Regulating the Trade and Employing the Poor of the Kingdom. The second edition. Whereunto is added, an essay towards paying off the publick debts.* London: S. Collins for Samuel Mabbat, 1719.

Child, Josiah. *A New Discourse of Trade wherein is Recommended Several Weighty Points Relating to Companies of Merchants; the Act of Navigation, Naturalization of Strangers, and Our Woollen Manufactures, the Balance of Trade, and the Nature of Plantations, and Their Consequences . . . to the Kingdom.* London: John Everingham, 1693.

Clarke, William. *Observations on the Late and Present Conduct of the French, with Regard to Their Encroachments upon the British Colonies in North America. . . . To which is added, wrote by another Hand; Observations concerning the Increase of Mankind, Peopling of Countries, &c.* Boston: S. Kneeland, 1755.

Colman, Benjamin. *Some Reasons and Arguments Offered to The Good People of Boston And Adjacent Places, for The Setting up Markets in Boston.* Boston: James Franklin, 1719.

Colman, John. *The Distressed State of the Town of Boston, &c. Considered. In a Letter from a Gentleman in the Town, to His Friend in the Countrey.* Boston: James Franklin, 1720.

Davenant, Charles. *Discourses on the Public Revenues, and on the Trade of England.* London: James Knapton, 1698.

———. *An Essay upon the Probable Methods of Making People the Gainers in the Balance of Trade*. London: Knapton, 1699.

De Re Rustica; Or, Repository for Select Papers on Agriculture, Arts, and Manufactures. 2 vols. London: R. Davis, and L. Davis, 1769.

Defoe, Daniel. *An Essay upon Projects.* London: R.R. for Tho. Cockerill, 1697.

———. *Jure Divino: A Satyr. In Twelve Books.* London: n.p., 1706.

———. *A Plan of the English Commerce. Being a Compleat Prospect of the Trade of This Nation, as Well the Home Trade as the Foreign. In Three Parts.* London: J. Rivington, 1728.

Denham John. *Poems and Translations; with the Sophy, a Tragedy.* London: H. Herringman, 1668.

Douglas, John. *A Letter Addressed to Two Great Men, on the Prospect of Peace; and on the Terms Necessary to Be Insisted upon in the Negotiation.* London: A. Millar, 1760.

Dunton, John. *A Voyage round the World, Or, A Pocket-library Divided into Several Volumes. . . .* London: N.p. for Richard Newcome, 1691.

Eliot, Jared. *Essays upon Field Husbandry in New England, As it Is or May Be Ordered.* Boston: Edes and Gill, 1761.

Fortrey, Samuel. *England's Interest and Improvement. Consisting in the Increase of the Store, and Trade of this Kingdom.* London: n.p. for Nathaniel Brook, 1673.

Fournier, Pierre-Simon. *Manuel Typographique.* 2 vols. Paris: Fournier, 1764–65.

Galloway, Joseph. *The Speech of Joseph Galloway . . . in Answer to the Speech of John Dickinson.* Philadelphia: W. Dunlap, 1764.

Gervaise, Isaac. *The System or Theory of the Trade of the World.* London: H. Woodfall, 1720.

Granville, George. *The Genuine Works in Verse and Prose of the Right Honourable George Granville, Baron Lansdowne.* London: J. and R. Tonson, 1736.

Graunt, John. *Natural and Political Observations . . . upon the Bills of Mortality.* London: Thomas Roycroft for John Martin, 1662.

[Harris, Benjamin.] *The New England Primer.* Boston: Benjamin Harris, 1690.

[Harris, Benjamin.] *The New English Tutor Enlarged, for the More Easy Attaining the True Reading of English. To which is Added, Milk for Babes.* Boston: Benjamin Harris, 1710.

[Harris, Benjamin.] *The Protestant Tutor.* London: Benjamin Harris, 1679.

Hobbes, Thomas. *Leviathan, Or, The Matter, Forme, and Power of a Common Wealth, Ecclesiasticall and Civil.* London: Printed for Andrew Crooke, 1651.

Hodder, James. *Hodder's arithmetick: or, That necessary art made most easy. Being explained in a way familiar to the capacity of any that desire to learn it in a little time.* Boston: Printed by J. Franklin, for S. Phillips, N. Buttolph, B. Elliot, D. Henchman, G. Phillips, J. Elliot, and E. Negus, 1719.

Houghton, John. *England's Great Happiness; Or, a Dialogue between Content and Complaint. . . .* London: J.M. for Edward Croft, 1677.

Hume, David. *Essays and Treatises on Several Subjects. A New Edition.* London: Millar, Kincaid and Donaldson, 1758.

Hyde, Edward. *The History of the Rebellion and Civil Wars in England, Begun in the Year 1641. With the Precedent Passages, and Actions, That Contributed Thereunto, and the Happy End, and Conclusion Thereof by the King's Blessed Restoration, and Return upon the 29th of May, in the Year 1660.* 3 vols. Oxford: Printed at the Theater, 1702–4.

Johnson, Samuel. *Preface. In Dictionary of the English Language.* London: William Strahan, 1755.

Kames, Henry Home, Lord. *The Gentleman Farmer, Being an Attempt to Improve Agriculture by Subjecting It to the Test of Rational Principles.* Edinburgh: W. Creech, and for T. Cadell, London.

———. *Sketches of the History of Man, In Two Volumes.* Edinburgh: W. Creech and for W. Strahan and T. Cadell, in London, 1774.

Kennedy, Archibald. *The Importance of Gaining and Preserving the Friendship of the Indians to the British Interest, Considered.* New York: James Parker, 1751.

Linnaeus, Carl. *Systema Naturae.* Leyden: Theodorum Haak, 1735.

Locke, John. *Two Treatises of Government.* London: n.p. for Awnsham and John Churchill, 1690.

Logan, James. *To Robert Jordan, and others of the Friends of the Yearly Meeting for Business, now conven'd in Philadelphia.* Philadelphia: Benjamin Franklin, 1741.

Mace, Thomas. *Musick's Monument, Or, A Remembrancer of the Best Practical Musick, Both Divine and Civil, That Has Ever Been Known to Have Been in the World Divided into Three Parts. . . .* London: T. Ratcliffe and N. Thompson for the Author, 1676.

Mandeville, Bernard. *Fable of the Bees: or, Private Vices Publick Benefits.* 2 vols. Oxford: Clarendon Press, 1714.

Mather, Cotton. *Bonifacious, An Essay upon the Good.* Boston: B. Green for Samuel Gerrish, 1710.

———. *The Diary of Cotton Mather.* 2 vols. Ed. Worthington Chauncy Ford. 1911–12; rpt. New York: Frederick Ungar, 1957.

Misselden, Edward. *The Circle of Commerce or the Ballance of Trade, in Defense of Free Trade. . . .* London: John Dawson for Nicholas Bourne, 1623.

———. *Free Trade or the Meanes to Make Trade Flourish.* London: John Legatt for Simon Waterson, 1622.

Mittelberger, Gottlieb. *Journey to Pennsylvania by Gottlieb Mittelberger.* Ed. Oscar Handlin and John Clive. Cambridge, MA: Belknap Press of Harvard University Press, 1960.

Molyneux, William. *The Case of Ireland's Being Bound by the Acts of Parliament in England, Stated.* 1698; rpt. London: J. Almon, 1770.

Mun, Thomas. *England's Treasure by Forraign Trade: Or, the Ballance of our Forraign Trade is the Rule of our Treasure.* London: F. G. for Thomas Clark, 1662.

Nollet, Jean-Antoine. *Lettres sur l'électricité Dans lesquelles on examine les dernières Découvertes qui ont été faites sur cette Matière, & les conséquences que l'on en peut tirer.* Paris: Hippolyte-Louis Guérin, & Louis-François Delatour, 1753.

North, Dudley. *Discourses upon Trade, Principally Directed to the Cases of the Interest, Coynage, Clipping, Increase, of Money.* London: Basset, 1691.

Oldmixon, John. *Clarendon and Whitlock Compar'd. To which is . . . Added a Comparison Between the History of the Rebellion and Other Histories of the Civil War, Proving . . . that the Editors of the Lord Clarendon's History, Have Hardly Left One Fact, Or One Character on the Parliament Side Fairly Represented; that the Characters are All Satire, Or Panegyrick.* London: J. Pemberton, 1727.

Paine, Thomas. *A Discourse, Shewing, That the Real First Cause of the Straits and Difficulties of This Province of Massachusetts Bay, Is It's Extravagancy, & Not Paper Money: And Also What Is a Safe Foundation to Raise a Bank of Credit On, and What Not (with Some Remarks on Amicus Patriae,) & a Projection for Emitting of More Bills of Credit on the Province. By Way of Dialogue, Tween a Representative in Said Province, and a Certain Gentleman Concerned for the Good of His Native Country. By Philopatria.* Boston: James Franklin, 1721.

[Parker, Samuel]. *Mr. Baxter Baptiz'd in Bloud, Or, A Sad History of the Unparallel'd Cruelty of the Anabaptists in New-England Faithfully Relating the Cruel, Barbarous and Bloudy Murther of Mr. Baxter, an Orthodox Minister, Who Was Kill'd by the Anabaptists, and His Skin Most Cruelly Flead from His Body: With an Exact Account of All the Circumstances and Particularities of This Barbarous Murther / Published by His Mournfull Brother Benjamin Baxter*. London: [Laurance Savill], 1673.

Penn, William. *The Continued Cry of the Oppressed for Justice*. London, 1675; rpt. London: T. Sowle, 1726.

———. *England's Great Interest in the Choice of New Parliament*. London, 1679; rpt. London: T. Sowle, 1726.

———. *England's Present Interest Discovered with Honour to the Prince, and Safety of the People*. London, 1679; rpt. London: T. Sowle, 1726.

———. *The Excellent Priviledge of Liberty and Property Being the Birth-right of the Free-born Subjects of England*. Philadelphia: William Bradford, 1687.

Petty, William. *Another Essay in Political Arithmetick, concerning the Growth of the City of London: With the Measures, Periods, Causes, and Consequences Thereof, 1682*. London: H.H. for Mark Pardoe, 1683.

———. *The Political Anatomy of Ireland . . . To which is added . . . an Account of the Wealth and Expenses of England, and the Method of Raising Taxes in the Most Equal Manner*. [1672]. Dublin: D. Brown, W. Rogers, 1691.

———. *Tracts Chiefly Related to Ireland . . . By the Late Sir William Petty*. Dublin: Boulter Grierson, 1769.

———. *A Treatise of Taxes and Contributions, Shewing the Nature and Measures of Crown Lands . . . The Same Being Frequently Applied to the Present State and Affairs of Ireland*. London: X. Brooke, 1662.

Pownall, Thomas. *The Administration of the British Colonies. The Fifth Edition. Wherein Their Rights and Constitution are Discussed and Stated*. 2 vols. London: n.p. for J. Walter, 1774.

Priestley, Joseph. *The History and Present State of Electricity, with Original Experiments*. London: Dodsley, Johnson, and Cadell, 1767.

———. *The Memoirs of the Rev. Dr. Joseph Priestley to the Year 1795. Written by Himself. With a Continuation to the Time of His Decease, by His Son, Joseph Priestley*. London: Joseph Johnson for the Unitarian Societies in England, 1809.

Pollexfen, John. *A Discourse of Trade, Coyn, and Paper Credit*. London: Brabazon Aylmer, 1697.

[Ramsey, Allan.] *Thoughts on the Origin and Nature of Government, Occasioned by the Late Disputes between Great Britain and Her American Colonies: Written in the Year 1766*. London: T. Becket and P.A. De Hondt, 1769.

Roberts, Lewes. *The Treasure of Traffike, Or A Discourse Of Forraigne Trade*. London, Nicholas Bourne, 1641.

Robie, Thomas. *A Letter to a Certain Gentleman*. Boston: Printed by J. Franklin, for Daniel Henchman, 1719.

Robinson, Henry. *Certain Proposals in Order to the People's Freedom and Accommodation in some Particulars, with the Advancement of Trade and Navigation of this Commonwealth in General*. London: M. Simmons, 1652.

Short, Thomas. *Natural, Moral, Civil, Political, and Medical . . . on Bills of Morality*. London: T. Longman and A. Millar, 1750.

Smith, Adam. *An Inquiry into the Nature and Causes of the Wealth of Nations.* Ed. R. H. Campbell, A. S. Skinner, and W. B. Todd. Oxford: Clarendon Press, 1976.

Sprigg, Joshua. *Anglia Rediviva; England's Recovery: Being the History of the Motions, Actions, and Successes of the Army under the Immediate Conduct of His Excellency Sr. Thomas Fairfax . . . Compiled for the Publique Good.* London: R.W. for John Partridge, 1647.

Swift, Jonathan. *A Short View of the State of Ireland.* In *The Works of the Rev. Jonathan Swift . . . Arranged by Thomas Sheridan, a New Edition.* Ed. John Nichols. 19 vols. London: J. Johnson, J. Nichols, 1801.

Thacher, Peter. *A Brief Declaration of Mr. Peter Thacher, and Mr. John Webb, Pastors of the New-North-Church in Boston, in Behalf of Themselves and Said Church; Relating to Some of Their Late Ecclesiastical Proceedings.* Boston: James Franklin, 1720.

Vanderlint, Jacob. *Money Answers to All Things, Or, An Essay to Make Money Sufficiently Plentiful.* London: T. Cox, 1734.

Vines, Richard. *The Happinesse of Israel. As It Was Set Forth in a Sermon Preached to Both . . . Houses of Parliament . . . upon a Solemne Day of Thanksgiving, March 12th 1644.* London: G. M. for A. Roper, 1645.

Voltaire [Arouet, Francois Marie]. *Candide* (1759). In *Candide, ou L'Optimisme: Edition Critique,* ed. André Morize. Paris: Librarie E. Droz, 1931.

Walker, Clement. *Anarchia Anglicana: or the History of Independency.* 2 vols. London: n.p., 1648–49.

Wallace, Robert. *A Dissertation on the Numbers of Mankind in Antient and Modern Times.* Edinburgh: n.p. for G. Hamilton and J. Balfour, 1753.

Walpole, Horace. *The Yale Edition of Horace Walpole's Correspondence.* 48 vols. Ed. W. S. Lewis. New Haven: Yale University Press, 1937–83.

Ware, Henry. *Two Discourses Containing the History of the Old North and New Brick Churches United as the Second Church in Boston.* Boston: James W. Burditt, 1821.

Wigglesworth, Edward. *A Letter from One in the Country to His Friend in Boston, Containing Some Remarks upon a late Pamphlet, entituled, The Distressed State of the Town of Boston, &c.* Boston: James Franklin, 1720.

Wilmot, John. *Rome Rhym'd to Death, Being a Collection of Choice Poems, in Two Parts. Written by the E. of R., Dr. Wild, and Others of the Best Modern Wits.* London: n.p. for John How, 1683.

Wise, John. *The Churches Quarrel Espoused. . . .* New York: William Bradford, 1713.

———. *The Freeholder's Address to the Honourable House of Representatives.* Boston: James Franklin, 1721.

———. *A Friendly Check, from a Kind Relation.* Boston: James Franklin, 1721.

———. *A Vindication of the Government of New England Churches.* Boston: J. Allen, 1717.

———. *A Word of Comfort to a Melancholy Country. Or The bank of credit erected in the Massachusetts-Bay, fairly defended by a discovery of the great benefit, accruing by it to the whole province with a remedy for recovering a civil state when sinking under desperation by defeat on their bank of credit.* Boston: James Franklin, 1721.

Young, Edward. *The Complaint, Or, Night Thoughts on Life, Death, and Immorality.* 9 parts. London: n.p. for R. Dodsley, 1743–45.

———. *The Revenge, A Tragedy: As It Is Acted at the Theatre-Royal in Drury-Lane.* London: n.p. for W. Chetwood and S. Chapman, 1721.

SECONDARY SOURCES

Monographs and Collections of Essays: Benjamin Franklin and His Family

Aldridge, Alfred O. *Franklin and His French Contemporaries.* Washington Square: New York University Press, 1957.

Brands, H. W. *The First American: The Life and Times of Benjamin Franklin.* New York: Doubleday / Random House, 2000.

Carey, Lewis J. *Franklin's Economic Views.* New York: Doubleday, Doran, 1928.

Crane, Verner W. *Benjamin Franklin and a Rising People.* Boston: Little, Brown, 1954.

———. *Benjamin Franklin: Englishman and American.* Baltimore, MD: William and Wilkins, 1936.

Cole, John. *The History and Antiquities of Ecton, in the County of Northampton.* Scarborough: John Cole, 1825.

Conner, Paul W. *Poor Richard's Politicks: Benjamin Franklin and His New American Order.* New York: Oxford University Press, 1965.

Currey, Cecil B. *Road to Revolution: Benjamin Franklin in England, 1765–1775.* New York: Peter Smith, 1968.

Hale, Edward Everett, and Edward Everett Hale Jr. *Franklin in France, from Original Documents, most of which are now published for the first time.* 2 vols. Boston: Roberts Bros., 1887.

Hanna, William S. *Benjamin Franklin and Pennsylvania Politics.* Princeton: Princeton University Press, 1964.

Hayes, Kevin J., and Edwin Wolf II. *The Library of Benjamin Franklin.* Philadelphia: American Philosophical Society and Library Company of Philadelphia, 2006.

Huang, Nian-Sheng. *Franklin's Father Josiah: Life of a Colonial Boston Tallow Chandler, 1657–1745.* Philadelphia: American Philosophical Society, 2000.

Isaacson, Walter. *Benjamin Franklin: An American Life.* New York: Simon and Schuster, 2003.

Jennings, Francis. *Benjamin Franklin, Politician.* New York: W. W. Norton, 1996.

Lemay, J. A. Leo. *The Life of Benjamin Franklin.* Vol. 1, *Journalist, 1706–1730.* Philadelphia: University of Pennsylvania Press, 2005.

———. *The Life of Benjamin Franklin.* Vol. 2, *Printer and Publisher, 1730–1747.* Philadelphia: University of Pennsylvania Press, 2005.

———. *The Life of Benjamin Franklin.* Vol. 3, *Soldier, Scientist, and Politician, 1748–1757.* Philadelphia: University of Pennsylvania Press, 2008.

———, ed. *The Oldest Revolutionary: Essays on Benjamin Franklin.* Philadelphia: University of Pennsylvania Press, 1976.

———, ed. *Reappraising Benjamin Franklin: A Bicentennial Perspective.* Newark: University of Delaware Press, 1993.

Livingston, Luther S. *Franklin and His Press at Passy: An Account of the Books, Pamphlets, and Leaflets Printed There, Including the Long-Lost Bagatelles.* New York: Grolier Club, 1914.

———. *The Passports Printed by Benjamin Franklin at His Passy Press.* Ann Arbor, MI: William L. Clements Library, 1925.

Lopez, Claude-Anne. *Mon Cher Papa, Franklin and the Ladies of Paris.* New Haven: Yale University Press, 1966.

Lopez, Claude-Anne, and Eugenia W. Herbert. *The Private Franklin: The Man and His Family.* New York: W. W. Norton, 1975.

Middlekauff, Robert. *Benjamin Franklin and His Enemies*. Berkeley: University of California Press, 1996.

Miller, C. William. *Benjamin Franklin's Philadelphia Printing, 1728–1766: A Descriptive Bibliography*. Philadelphia: American Philosophical Society, 1974.

Morgan, David T. *The Devious Dr. Franklin, Colonial Agent: Benjamin Franklin's Years in London*. Macon, GA: Mercer University Press, 1996.

Morgan, Edmund S. *Benjamin Franklin*. New Haven: Yale University Press, 2002.

Newcomb, Benjamin H. *Franklin and Galloway, a Political Partnership*. New Haven: Yale University Press, 1962.

Nolan, J. Bennett. *Benjamin Franklin in Scotland and Ireland*. Philadelphia: University of Pennsylvania Press, 1938.

Pangle, Lorraine Smith. *The Political Philosophy of Benjamin Franklin*. Baltimore, MD: Johns Hopkins University Press, 2007.

Randall, Willard Sterne. *A Little Revenge: Benjamin Franklin and His Son*. Boston: Little, Brown, 1984.

Schiff, Stacy. *A Great Improvisation: Franklin, France, and the Birth of America*. New York: Henry Holt, 2005.

Schoenbrun, David. *Triumph in Paris: The Exploits of Benjamin Franklin*. New York: Harper and Row, 1976.

Seavey, Ormond. *Becoming Benjamin Franklin: The Autobiography and the Life*. Philadelphia: University of Pennsylvania Press, 1988.

Skemp, Sheila L. *The Making of a Patriot: Benjamin Franklin at the Cockpit*. New York: Oxford University Press, 2013.

———. *William Franklin: Son of a Patriot, Servant of a King*. New York: Oxford University Press, 1990.

Srodes, James. *Franklin: The Essential Founding Father*. Washington, DC: Regnery Publishing, 2002.

Steell, Willis. *Benjamin Franklin of Paris, 1776–1785*. New York: Minton, Balch, 1928.

Stourzh, Gerald. *Benjamin Franklin and American Foreign Policy*. Chicago: University of Chicago Press, 1954.

Tise, Larry E. *Benjamin Franklin and Women*. University Park: Pennsylvania State University Press, 2000.

Tourtellot, Arthur Bernon. *Benjamin Franklin: The Shaping of Genius, the Boston Years*. Garden City, NY: Doubleday, 1977.

Treese, Lorette. *The Storm Gathering: The Penn Family and the American Revolution*. University Park: Pennsylvania State University Press, 1992.

Van Doren, Carl. *Benjamin Franklin*. New York: Viking, 1938.

———, ed. *Indian Treaties Printed by Benjamin Franklin*. Philadelphia: Historical Society of Pennsylvania, 1938.

Waldstreicher, David. *Runaway America: Franklin, Slavery, and the American Revolution*. New York: Hill and Wang, 2004.

Weinberger, Jerry. *Benjamin Franklin Unmasked: The Unity of His Moral, Religious, and Political Thought*. Lawrence: University of Kansas Press, 2005.

Wetzel, William A. *Benjamin Franklin as an Economist*. Baltimore, MD: Johns Hopkins University Press, 1895.

Wood, Gordon A. *The Americanization of Benjamin Franklin*. New York: Penguin, 2004.

Wright, Esmond. *Franklin of Philadelphia*. Cambridge, MA: Harvard University Press, 1986.

Journal Articles and Book Chapters: Franklin and His Family

Aldridge, Alfred O. "Franklin as Demographer." *Journal of Economic History* 9 (May 1949): 25–44.

——. "Franklin's Deistical Indians." *Proceedings of the American Philosophical Society* 94, no. 4 (August 1950): 398–410.

——. "Jacques Barbeu-Dubourg, a French Disciple of Benjamin Franklin." *Proceedings of the American Philosophical Society* 45 (1951): 331–92.

Anderson, Douglas. "Benjamin Franklin and His Readers." *Early American Literature* 41 (2006): 535–53.

Bache, Richard Meade. "Franklin's Ceremonial Coat." *Pennsylvania Magazine of History and Biography*, 1899, 444–52.

Cohn, Ellen R. "The Printer at Passy." In *Benjamin Franklin in Search of a Better World*, ed. Page Talbott, 234–71. New Haven: Yale University Press, 2005.

Crane, Verner W. "Benjamin Franklin and the Stamp Act." *Publications of the Colonial Society of Massachusetts* 32 (1937): 70–77.

Gleason, J. Philip. "A Scurrilous Colonial Election and Franklin's Reputation." *William and Mary Quarterly*, 3rd ser., 18 (1961): 68–84.

Greene, Jack P. "The Alienation of Benjamin Franklin, British American." *Journal of the Royal Society for the Arts* (now *RSA Journal*) 124 (1976): 52–73. Rpt. Greene, *Understanding the American Revolution* (Charlottesville: University Press of Virginia, 1995), 247–84.

Hay, Carla H. "Benjamin Franklin, James Burgh, and the Authorship of 'The Colonist's Advocate' Letters." *William and Mary Quarterly*, 3rd ser., 32 (1975): 111–24.

Hayes, Kevin J. "New Light on Peter and King, the Two Slaves Benjamin Franklin Brought to England." *Notes and Queries* 60, no. 1 (June 2013): 205–9.

Howe, Daniel Walker. "Franklin, Edwards, and the Problem of Human Nature." In *Benjamin Franklin, Jonathan Edwards, and the Representation of American Culture*, ed. Barbara B. Oberg and Harry S. Stout, 75–96. New York: Oxford University Press, 2003.

James, Alfred P. "Benjamin Franklin's Ohio Valley Lands." *Proceedings of the American Philosophical Society* 98, no. 4. (August 16, 1954): 255–65.

Marshall, Peter. "Lord Hillsborough, Samuel Wharton and the Ohio Grant, 1769–1775." *English Historical Review* 80, no. 317 (1965): 717–39.

Masterson, James R. "'A Foolish Oneida Tale.'" *American Literature* 10 (1938–39): 53–65.

Mulford, Carla. "Benjamin Franklin, Native Americans, and the Commerce of Civility." In *Revolutionary Histories: Transatlantic Cultural Nationalism, 1775–1815*, ed. W. M. Verhoeven, 48–61. Houndsmills, England: Palgrave Press of St. Martin's Press, 2002.

——. "Benjamin Franklin, Native Americans, and European Cultures of Civility." *Prospects* 24 (1999): 49–66.

——. "Benjamin Franklin, Pennsylvania Germans, and the Ethnic Origins of Nations." In *Halle Pietism, Colonial North America, and the Young United States*, ed. Hans-Jürgen Grabbe, 147–60. Stuttgart: Franz Steiner Verlag, 2008.

——. "Benjamin Franklin, Traditions of Liberalism, and Women's Learning in Eighteenth-Century Philadelphia." In *The Good Education of Youth: Worlds of Learning in the Age of Franklin*, ed. John H. Pollack, 100–121. New Castle: Oak Knoll Press and University of Pennsylvania Libraries, 2009.

———. "Benjamin Franklin's Savage Eloquence: Hoaxes from the Press at Passy, 1782." *Proceedings of the American Philosophical Society* 152, no. 4 (December 2008): 490–520.

———. "*Caritas* and Capital: Franklin's Narrative of the Late Massacres." In *Reappraising Benjamin Franklin: A Bicentennial Perspective*, by J. A. Leo Lemay, 347–58. Newark: University of Delaware Press, 1993.

Oberg, Barbara B. "'Plain, Insinuating, Persuasive': Benjamin Franklin's Final Speech to the Constitutional Convention of 1787." In *Reappraising Benjamin Franklin: A Bicentennial Perspective*, ed. J. A. Leo Lemay, 175–92. Newark: University of Delaware Press, 1993.

Prelinger, Catherine. "Benjamin Franklin and the American Prisoners of War in England during the American Revolution." *William and Mary Quarterly*, 3rd ser., 32 (1975): 261–94.

Shelling, Richard I. "Benjamin Franklin and the Dr. Bray Associates." *Pennsylvania Magazine of History and Biography* 63 (1939): 282–93.

Wecter, Dixon. "Benjamin Franklin and an Irish 'Enthusiast.'" *Huntington Library Quarterly* 4 (1941): 205–34.

Monographs and Collections of Essays: Historical Studies

Alvord, Clarence Walworth. *The Mississippi Valley in British Politics; a Study of the Trade, Land Speculation and Experiments in Imperialism Culminating in the American Revolution*. New York: Russell & Russell, 1959.

Anderson, Benedict. *Imagined Communities: Reflections on the Origin and Spread of Nationalism*. Rev. ed. London: Verso, 1991.

Anderson, Fred. *Crucible of War: The Seven Years' War and the Fate of Empire in British North America, 1754–1766*. New York: Alfred A. Knopf, 2000.

———. *The War That Made America: A Short History of the French and Indian War*. New York: Viking, 2005.

Axtell, James. *The European and the Indian: Essays in the Ethnohistory of Colonial North America*. New York: Oxford University Press, 1981.

———. *The Invasion Within: The Contest of Cultures in Colonial North America*. New York: Oxford University Press, 1985.

Barksdale, Kevin T. *The Lost State of Franklin: America's First Secession*. Lexington: University Press of Kentucky, 2009.

Barrow, Thomas C. *Trade and Empire: The British Customs Service in Colonial America, 1660–1775*. Cambridge, MA: Harvard University Press, 1967.

Bayly, C. A. *Imperial Meridian: The British Empire and the World, 1780–1830*. London: Longman, 1989.

Beeman, Richard. *Plain, Honest Men: The Making of the Constitution*. New York: Random House, 2009.

Beer, George Louis. *British Colonial Policy, 1754–1765*. New York: Peter Smith, 1933.

Benton, Michael. *Literary Biography: An Introduction*. West Sussex, UK: Wiley-Blackwell, 2009.

Black, Jeremy. *The English Press in the Eighteenth Century*. Philadelphia: University of Pennsylvania Press, 1987.

Bowley, Marian. *Studies in the History of Economic Thought before 1870*. London: Macmillan, 1973.

Breen, Timothy H. *The Character of a Good Ruler: Puritan Political Ideas in New England, 1630–1730*. New York: Norton, 1970.

———. *The Marketplace of Revolution: How Consumer Politics Shaped American Independence*. New York: Oxford University Press, 2004.

Brewer, John. *The Sinews of Power: War, Money, and the English State, 1688–1783*. New York: Knopf, 1989.

Bridges, John. *The History and Antiquities of Northamptonshire, Compiled from the Manuscript Collections of . . . John Bridges, Esq. by the Rev. Peter Whalley*. 2 vols. Ed. Peter Whalley. Oxford: Clarendon Press, 1791.

Brunhouse, Robert L. *The Counter-revolution in Pennsylvania, 1776–1790*. 1942; Harrisburg: Pennsylvania Historical and Museum Commission, 1971.

Buel, Richard, Jr. *Securing the Revolution: Ideology in American Politics, 1789–1815*. Ithaca, NY: Cornell University Press, 1972.

Calloway, Colin G. *The Scratch of a Pen: 1763 and the Transformation of North America*. Oxford: Oxford University Press, 2006.

Carney, Virginia Moore. *Eastern Band Cherokee Women: Cultural Persistence in Their Letters and Speeches*. Knoxville: University of Tennessee Press, 2014.

Cave, Alfred A. *Prophets of the Great Spirit: Native American Revitalization Movements in Eastern North America*. Lincoln: University of Nebraska Press, 2006.

Clark, Charles E. *The Public Prints: The Newspaper in Anglo-American Culture, 1665–1740*. New York: Oxford University Press, 1994.

Clark, Stuart. *Thinking with Demons: The Idea of Witchcraft in Early Modern Europe*. Oxford: Oxford University Press, 1999.

Clifford, James. *The Predicament of Culture: Twentieth-Century Ethnography, Literature, and Art*. Cambridge, MA: Harvard University Press, 1988.

Cohen, Patricia Kline. *A Calculating People: The Spread of Numeracy in Early America*. Chicago: University of Chicago Press, 1983.

Cole, John. *The History and Antiquities of Ecton, in the County of Northampton*. Scarborough: John Cole, 1825.

Colley, Linda. *Britons: Forging the Nation, 1707–1837*. New Haven: Yale University Press, 1992.

Cook, George Allan. *John Wise: American Democrat*. New York: King's Crown Press, 1952.

Cragg, Gerald R. *Freedom and Authority: A Study of English Thought in the Early Seventeenth Century*. Philadelphia: Westminster Press, 1975.

Cullen, Louis M. *The Emergence of Modern Ireland, 1600–1900*. London: Holmes and Meier, 1981.

Cummings, Hubertis. *Richard Peters, Provincial Secretary and Cleric, 1704–1776*. Philadelphia: University of Pennsylvania Press, 1944.

Dickinson, H. T. *Liberty and Property: Political Ideology in Eighteenth-Century Britain*. London: Weidenfeld and Nicholson, 1977.

Doerflinger, Thomas M. *A Vigorous Spirit of Enterprise: Merchants and Economic Development in Revolutionary Philadelphia*. Chapel Hill: University of North Carolina Press, 2001.

Dunn, Mary Maples. *William Penn: Politics and Conscience*. Princeton: Princeton University Press, 1967.

Ferguson, Oliver. *Jonathan Swift and Ireland*. Urbana: University of Illinois Press, 1962.

Finger, Simon. *The Contagious City: The Politics of Public Health in Early Philadelphia*. Ithaca, NY: Cornell University Press, 2012.

Fogelman, Aaron Spencer. *Hopeful Journeys: German Immigration, Settlement, and Political Culture in Colonial America, 1717–1775*. Philadelphia: University of Pennsylvania Press, 1996.

Ford, Paul Leicester. *The New England Primer.* New York: Dodd, Mead, 1899.

Fox-Genovese, Elizabeth, and Eugene D. Genovese. *The Mind of the Master Class: History and Faith in the Southern Slaveholders' Worldview.* Cambridge: Cambridge University Press, 2005.

Franz, George W. *Paxton: A Study of Community Structure and Mobility in the Colonial Pennsylvania Backcountry.* New York: Garland, 1989.

Gentles, Ian. *The English Revolution and the Wars in the Three Kingdoms, 1638–1752.* Harlow, England: Pearson Longman, 2007.

Gerson, Noel B. *Franklin: America's Lost State.* New York: Crowell-Collier Press, 1968.

Gibson, Alan. *Interpreting the Founding: Guide to the Enduring Debates over the Origins and Foundations of the American Republic.* Lawrence: University Press of Kansas, 2006.

Gipson, Lawrence Henry. *The British Isles and the American Colonies.* Vol. 1, *Great Britain and Ireland, 1748–1754.* Caldwell, ID: Caxton, 1936.

Gould, Eliga. *The Persistence of Empire: British Political Culture in the Age of the American Revolution.* Chapel Hill: University of North Carolina Press, 2000.

Greene, Jack P. *Understanding the American Revolution: Issues and Actors.* Charlottesville: University Press of Virginia, 1995.

Grove, Richard H. *Green Imperialism: Colonial Expansion, Tropical Island Edens and the Origins of Environmentalism, 1600–1860.* Cambridge: Cambridge University Press, 1995.

Guttridge, G. H. *The Colonial Policy of William III.* London: Frank Cass, 1966.

Hall, Michael Garibaldi. *Edward Randolph and the American Colonies, 1676–1703.* Chapel Hill: University of North Carolina Press for the Institute of Early American History and Culture, 1960.

Hannaford, Ivan. *Race: The History of an Idea in the West.* Baltimore, MD: Johns Hopkins University Press, 1996.

Hay, Carla H. *James Burgh, Spokesman for Reform in Hanoverian England.* Washington, DC: University Press of America, 1979.

Henretta, James A. *Salutary Neglect: Colonial Administration under the Duke of Newcastle.* Princeton: Princeton University Press, 1972.

Hinderaker, Eric. *Elusive Empires: Constructing Colonialism in the Ohio Valley, 1673–1800.* Cambridge: Cambridge University Press, 1997.

Hoppit, Julian. *A Land of Liberty? England, 1689–1727.* Oxford: Oxford University Press, 2002.

Hurt, R. Douglas. *The Ohio Frontier: Crucible of the Old Northwest, 1720–1830.* Bloomington: Indiana University Press, 1996.

Hutson, James H. *Pennsylvania Politics, 1746–1770: The Movement for Royal Government and Its Consequences.* Princeton: Princeton University Press, 1972.

Irwin, Douglas A., and Richard Sylla, eds. *Founding Choices: American Economic Policy in the 1790s.* Chicago: University of Chicago Press, 2011.

Jennings, Francis. *The Ambiguous Iroquois Empire: The Covenant Chain Confederation of Indian Tribes with English Colonies.* New York: W. W. Norton, 1984.

———. *Empire of Fortune: Crowns, Colonies, and Tribes in the Seven Years War in America.* New York: W. W. Norton, 1988.

Johansen, Bruce E. *Forgotten Founders: Benjamin Franklin, the Iroquois, and the Rationale for the American Revolution.* Ipswich, MA: Gambit, 1982.

Johnson, E. A. J. *Predecessors of Adam Smith.* New York: Augustus M. Kelly, 1960.

Jones, J. R. *Country and Court: England, 1658–1714.* Cambridge, MA: Harvard University Press, 1978.

Kammen, Michael J. *A Rope of Sand: The Colonial Agents, British Politics and the American Revolution*. Ithaca, NY: Cornell University Press, 1968.

Katz, Stanley Nider. *Newcastle's New York: Anglo-American Politics, 1732–1753*. Cambridge, MA: Harvard University Press, 1968.

Kelly, James. *Prelude to Union: Anglo-Irish Politics in the 1780s*. Cork: Irish Committee of Historical Sciences, 1992.

———. *Sir Edward Newenham, MP, 1734–1814, Defender of the Protestant Constitution*. Dublin: Four Courts Press, 2004.

Kent, Donald H. *The French Invasion of Western Pennsylvania, 1753*. Harrisburg, PA: Historical and Museum Commission, 1981.

Kilcup, Karen. *Fallen Forests: Emotion, Embodiment, and Ethics in American Women's Environmental Writing, 1782–1924*. Athens: University of Georgia Press, 2013.

Klett, Guy Soulliard. *Presbyterians in Colonial Pennsylvania*. Philadelphia: University of Pennsylvania Press, 1937.

Knittle, Walter Allen. *Early Eighteenth Century Palatine Emigration*. Baltimore, MD: Genealogical Publishing, 1965.

Knorr, Klaus E. *British Colonial Theories, 1570–1850*. Toronto: University of Toronto Press, 1968.

Kroebner, Richard. *Empire*. Cambridge: Cambridge University Press, 1961.

Langford, Paul. *The Eighteenth Century, 1688–1815*. London: Adam and Charles Black, 1976.

———. *The First Rockingham Administration: 1765–1766 / by P. Langford*. Oxford: Oxford University Press, 1973.

———. *A Polite and Commercial People: England, 1727–1783*. New York: Oxford University Press, 1994.

Lemay, J. A. Leo. *Ebenezer Kinnersley, Franklin's Friend*. Philadelphia: University of Pennsylvania Press, 1964.

Lemon, James T. *The Best Poor Man's Country: A Geographical Study of Early Southeastern Pennsylvania*. Baltimore, MD: Johns Hopkins University Press, 1972.

Magnusson, Lars. *Mercantilism: The Shaping of an Economic Language*. London: Routledge, 1994.

Marshall, Peter J. *Remaking the British Atlantic: The United States and the British Empire after American Independence*. New York: Oxford University Press, 2012.

Marshall, Peter J., and Glyndwr Williams. *The British Atlantic Empire before the American Revolution*. London: Cass, 1980.

Merrell, James H. *Into the American Woods: Negotiators on the Pennsylvania Frontier*. New York: W. W. Norton, 1999.

Merritt, Jane T. *At the Crossroads: Indians and Empires on a Mid-Atlantic Frontier, 1700–1763*. Chapel Hill: University of North Carolina Press, 2007.

Morison, Samuel Eliot. *John Paul Jones: A Sailor's Biography*. Boston: Little, Brown, 1959.

Morley, Vincent. *Irish Opinion and the American Revolution, 1760–1783*. Cambridge: Cambridge University Press, 2002.

Munves, James. *Thomas Jefferson and the Declaration of Independence: The Writing and Editing of the Document That Marked the Birth of the United States of America*. New York: Charles Scribner's Sons, 1976.

Nash, Gary B. *Quakers and Politics: Pennsylvania, 1681–1726*. Princeton: Princeton University Press, 1968.

Nash, Gary B., and Jean R. Soderlund. *Freedom by Degrees: Emancipation in Pennsylvania and Its Aftermath*. New York: Oxford University Press, 1991.

Neal, Daniel, and Joshua Toulmin. *The History of the Puritans, or, Protestant Nonconformists; from the Reformation in 1517 to the Revolution in 1688 ... By Daniel Neal. A New Edition in Five Volumes. . . .* London: n.p. for William Baynes, 1822.

Newcomb, Benjamin H. *Political Partisanship in the American Middle Colonies, 1700-1776*. Baton Rouge: Louisiana State University Press, 1995.

Newell, Margaret Ellen. *From Dependency to Independence: Economic Revolution in Colonial New England*. Ithaca, NY: Cornell University Press, 1998.

Olson, Alison Gilbert. *Anglo-American Politics*. Oxford: Clarendon Press, 1973.

Otterness, Philip. *Becoming German: The 1709 Palatine Migration to New York*. Ithaca, NY: Cornell University Press, 2004.

Patterson, Annabel. *Early Modern Liberalism*. Cambridge: Cambridge University Press, 1997.

Patterson, Richard S., and Richardson Dougall. *The Eagle and the Shield: A History of the Great Seal of the United States*. Washington, DC: Department of State, 1978.

Peltonen, Markku. *Classical Humanism and Republicanism in English Political Thought, 1570-1640*. Cambridge: Cambridge University Press, 1995.

Pencak, William A. *War, Politics, and Revolution in Provincial Massachusetts*. Boston: Northeastern University Press, 1981.

Plumb, J. H. *England in the Eighteenth Century*. Harmondsworth, England: Penguin, 1950.

Potts, William. *A History of Banbury*. 2nd ed. Ed. Edward T. Clark. Banbury, England: Gulliver Press, 1978.

Powell, Martyn J. *Britain and Ireland in the Eighteenth-Century Crisis of Empire*. Houndsmills, England: Palgrave Macmillan, 2003.

Reinert, Sophus A. *Translating Empire: Emulation and the Origins of Political Economy* Cambridge, MA: Harvard University Press, 2011.

Richter, Daniel. *Ordeal of the Longhouse: The Peoples of the Iroquois League in the Era of European Colonization*. Chapel Hill: University of North Carolina Press, 1992.

Robbins, Caroline. *The Eighteenth Century Commonwealthman: Studies in the Transmission, Development, and Circumstance of English Liberal Thought from the Restoration of Charles II until the War with the Thirteen Colonies*. Cambridge, MA: Harvard University Press, 1959.

Robbins, Chandler. *A History of the Second Church, or Old North in Boston, to Which Is Added a History of the New Brick Church*. Boston: John Wilson and Son, 1852.

Roeber, A. G. *Palatines, Liberty, and Property: German Lutherans in Colonial British America*. Baltimore, MD: Johns Hopkins University Press, 1993.

Schaeper, Thomas J. *France and America in the Revolutionary Era: The Life of Jacques-Donatien Leray De Chaumont, 1725-1803*. Providence, RI: Berghahn, 1995.

———. *John Paul Jones and the Battle Off Flamborough Head: A Reconsideration*. New York: Peter Lang, 1989.

Schultz, Ronald. *The Republic of Labor: Philadelphia Artisans and the Politics of Class, 1720-1830*. New York: Oxford University Press, 1993.

Schwartz, Sally. *"A Mixed Multitude": The Struggle for Toleration in Colonial Pennsylvania*. New York: New York University Press, 1987.

Schwoerer, Lois G. *The Ingenious Mr. Henry Care, Restoration Publicist*. Baltimore, MD: Johns Hopkins University Press, 2001.

Shannon, Timothy J. *Indians and Colonists at the Crossroads of Empire: The Albany Congress of 1754*. Ithaca, NY: Cornell University Press and New York State Historical Association, 2000.

Sherwood, Roy. *The Civil War in the Midlands, 1642–1651*. 1974; Phoenix Mill, England: Alan Sutton, 1997.

Silver, Peter. *Our Savage Neighbors: How Indian War Transformed Early America*. New York: W.W. Norton, 2009.

Skaggs, David Curtis, and Larry L. Nelson, eds. *The Sixty Years' War for the Great Lakes, 1754–1814*. East Lansing: Michigan State University Press, 2001.

Smith, Billy G. *The "Lower Sort": Philadelphia's Laboring People, 1750–1800*. Ithaca, NY: Cornell University Press, 1990.

Sosin, Jack M. *Whitehall and the Wilderness: The Middle West in British Colonial Policy, 1760–1775*. Lincoln: University of Nebraska Press, 1961.

Sutherland, Lucy S. *The East India Company in Eighteenth-Century Politics*. Oxford: Oxford University Press, 1951.

Thomas, Peter D. G. *The Townshend Duties Crisis: The Second Phase of the American Revolution, 1767–1773*. Oxford: Oxford University Press, 1987.

Tolles, Frederick B. *James Logan and the Culture of Provincial America*. Boston: Little Brown, 1957.

———. *Meeting House and Counting House: The Quaker Merchants of Colonial Philadelphia, 1682–1763*. Chapel Hill: University of North Carolina Press, 1948.

Treese, Lorett. *The Storm Gathering: The Penn Family and the American Revolution*. University Park: Pennsylvania State University Press, 1992.

Tucker, Robert W., and David C. Hendrickson. *The Fall of the First British Empire: Origins of the War of American Independence*. Baltimore, MD: Johns Hopkins University Press, 1982.

Tully, Alan. *William Penn's Legacy*. Baltimore, MD: Johns Hopkins University Press, 1977.

Van Horne, John, ed. *Religious Philanthropy and Colonial Slavery: The American Correspondence of the Associates of Dr. Bray, 1717–1777*. Urbana: University of Illinois Press, 1985.

Wainwright, Nicholas B. *George Croghan: Wilderness Diplomat*. Chapel Hill: University of North Carolina Press, 1959.

Wallace, Anthony F. C. *King of the Delawares: Teedyuscung*. Philadelphia: University of Pennsylvania Press, 1949.

Ware, Henry. *Two Discourses Containing the History of the Old North and New Brick Churches United as the Second Church in Boston*. Boston: James W. Burditt, 1821.

Williams, Samuel Cole. *History of the Lost State of Franklin*. New York: Press of the Pioneers, 1933.

Wilson, Kathleen. *The Sense of the People: Politics, Culture, and Imperialism in England, 1715–1785*. Cambridge: Cambridge University Press, 1995.

Wokeck, Marianne. *Trade in Strangers: The Beginnings of Mass Migration to North America*. University Park: Pennsylvania State University Press, 1999.

Wolf, Edwin. *Book Culture of a Colonial American City: Philadelphia Books, Bookmen, and Booksellers*. Oxford: Oxford University Press, 1988.

Wolf, Stephanie Grauman. *Urban Village: Population, Community, and Family Structure in Germantown, Pennsylvania, 1683–1800*. Princeton: Princeton University Press, 1976.

Young, Robert. *Postcolonialism: An Historical Introduction*. Oxford: Blackwell, 2001.

Journal Articles and Book Chapters: Historical Studies

Axtell, James, and William C. Sturtevant. "The Unkindest Cut, or Who Invented Scalping." *William and Mary Quarterly*, 3rd ser., 37 (1980): 451–72.

Barbour, Nevill. "North West Africa from the Fifteenth to Nineteenth Centuries." In *The Last Great Muslim Empires: History of the Muslim World*, ed. H. J. Kissling, 107–8. Princeton: Marcus Wiener, 1996.

Burns, Robert E. "The Catholic Relief Act in Ireland." *Church History* 32 (1963): 181–206.

Clark, Charles E. "Boston and the Nurturing of Newspapers: Dimensions of the Cradle, 1690–1741." *New England Quarterly* 64 (1991): 243–71.

Coyle, Eugene A. "Eighteenth-Century Dublin Radical." *Dublin Historical Record* 46, no. 1 (1993): 15–30.

Deluna, D. N. "*Jure Divino*: Defoe's 'Whole Volume in Folio, by Way of Answer To, and Confutation of Clarendon's 'History of the Rebellion'" *Philological Quarterly* 75 (1996): 43–66.

Gannon, Barbara A. "The Lord Is a Man of War, the God of Love and Peace: The Association Debate, Philadelphia, 1747–1748." *Pennsylvania History* 65 (1998): 46–61.

Gentles, Ian. "The Civil Wars in England." In *The Civil Wars: A Military History of England, Scotland, and Ireland, 1638–1660*, ed. John Kenyon and Jane Ohlmeyer, 103–55. Oxford: Oxford University Press, 1998.

Gibson, Alan. "Ancients, Moderns, and Americans: The Republican-Liberalism Debate Revisited." *History of Political Thought* 21 (2000): 261–307.

Hay, Carla H. "The Making of a Radical: The Case of James Burgh." *Journal of British Studies* 18 (Spring 1979): 90–117.

Hutton, Ronald, and Wylie Reeves. "Seiges and Fortifications." In *The Civil Wars: A Military History of England, Scotland, and Ireland, 1638–1660*, ed. John Kenyon and Jane Ohlmeyer, 195–233. Oxford: Oxford University Press, 1998.

Illick, Joseph E. Review of Gary B. Nash's *Quakers and Politics*. *William and Mary Quarterly*, 3rd ser., 26 (1969): 292–95.

Innes, Joanna. "Jonathan Clark, Social History, and England's Ancien Regime." *Past and Present* 115 (1987): 165–200.

Knouff, Gregory T. "Whiteness and Warfare on a Revolutionary Frontier." In *Friends and Enemies in Penn's Woods: Indians, Colonists, and the Racial Construction of Pennsylvania*, ed. William A. Pencak and Daniel K. Richter, 238–57. University Park: Pennsylvania State University Press, 2004.

Manning, Brian. "Religion and Politics: The Godly People." In *Politics, Religion, and the English Civil War*, ed. Brian Manning, 81–123. London: Edward Arnold, 1973.

McKenzie, Alexander D. D. "The Religious History of the Provincial Period." In *Memorial History of Boston*, ed. Justin Winsor, 2:187–248. Boston: James R. Osgood, 1881.

Merrill, James H. "'I Desire All That I Have Said . . . May Be Taken down Aright': Revisiting Teedyuscung's 1756 Treaty Council Speeches." *William and Mary Quarterly*, 3rd ser., 63 (2006): 777–826.

Mitchell, Annie. "A Liberal Republican 'Cato.'" *American Journal of Political Science* 48 (2004): 588–603.

Mulford, Carla. "Pox and 'Hell-Fire': Boston's Smallpox Controversy, the New Science, and Early Modern Liberalism." In *Periodical Literature in Eighteenth-Century America*, ed. Mark L. Kamrath and Sharon M. Harris, 7–27. Knoxville: University of Tennessee Press, 2005.

Nord, David Paul. "Teleology and News: The Religious Roots of American Journalism, 1630–1730." *Journal of American History* 77 (1990): 9–38.

Phillips, Edward Hake. "A Frontier Interlude: Timothy Pickering and the Wyoming Valley." *Rice Institute Pamphlet* 37, no. 1 (1950): 48–74.

Pincus, Steven C. A. "Neither Machiavellian Moment nor Possessive Individualism: Commercial Society and the Defenders of the English Commonwealth." *American Historical Review* 103 (1998): 705–36.

Priest, Claire. "Currency Policies and Legal Development in Colonial New England." *Yale Law Journal* 110 (2001): 1303–405.

Richter, Daniel. "Whose Indian History?" *William and Mary Quarterly*, 3rd ser., 50 (1993): 379–93.

Roeber, A. G. "'The Origin of Whatever Is Not English Among Us': The Dutch-Speaking and the German-Speaking Peoples of Colonial British America." In *Strangers within the Realm: Cultural Margins of the First British Empire*, ed. Bernard Bailyn and Philip D. Morgan, 220–83. Chapel Hill: University of North Carolina Press for the Institute of Early American History and Culture, 1991.

Ronnick, Michele Valerie. "The Phrase 'Nerone Neronior' in Walter of Châtillon, John Milton, and John Adams." *Notes and Queries* 239 (1994): 169–70.

Rossiter, Clinton. "John Wise: Colonial Democrat." *New England Quarterly* 22 (1949): 3–32.

Schlenther, Boyd Stanley. "Training for Resistance: Charles Thomson and Indian Affairs in Pennsylvania." *Pennsylvania History* 50 (1983): 185–217.

Scott, H. M. "Sir Joseph Yorke, Dutch Politics, and the Origins of the Fourth Anglo-Dutch War." *The Historical Journal* 31 (1988): 571–89.

Stern, Simon. "Between Local Knowledge and National Politics: Debating Rationales for Jury Nullification after Bushell's Case." *Yale Law Journal* 111 (2002): 1815–59.

Withers, Charles W. J. "On Georgics and Geology: James Hutton's 'Elements of Agriculture' and Agricultural Science in Eighteenth-Century Scotland." *Agricultural History Review* 42, no. 1 (1994): 38–48.

Worden, Blair. "Harrington's 'Oceana': Origins and Aftermath, 1651–1660." In *Republicanism, Liberty, and Commercial Society, 1649–1776*, ed. David Wootton, 111–38. Stanford: Stanford University Press, 1994.

———. "James Harrington and 'The Commonwealth of Oceana,' 1656." In *Republicanism, Liberty, and Commercial Society, 1649–1776*, ed. David Wootton, 82–110. Stanford: Stanford University Press, 1994.

———. "Marchamont Nedham and the Beginnings of English Republicanism, 1649–1656." In *Republicanism, Liberty, and Commercial Society, 1649–1776*, ed. David Wootton, 45–81. Stanford: Stanford University Press, 1994.

———. "Republicanism and the Restoration, 1660–1683." In *Republicanism, Liberty, and Commercial Society, 1649–1776*, ed. David Wootton, 139–96. Stanford: Stanford University Press, 1994.

Index

systems of exchange and, 76, 77, 83,
100, 362
time as, 56
usury and, 63, 78, 80–81, 89–92
value of, intrinsically and extrinsi-
cally, 88–89, 95
Monongahela, Battle of the, 140
Monongahela River, 130
Montagu-Dunk, George, 159
Montaigne, Michel, 312
Montgomery, Richard, 278
Morellet, Abbé, 384
Morris, Robert Hunter, 177, 179, 180, 382
Mun, Thomas, 78, 84, 90–91, 361, 362
Murray, David, 290
as Stormont, 290, 302
Murray, William, 190, 335

Nablus (city), 372
Nash, Gary, 111, 112, 331, 332, 363,
364, 387
Nelson, William, 356
Nero, 306–7
Netherlands, 3, 183, 292, 293, 294, 302,
308, 381, 383
Adams sent to, 292, 293, 308
decline of Dutch Republic, 305
Jones sent ship *Serapis* to, 303
Mun's jealousy of success of, 84
Peace of Paris and, 309
people of, as "Dutch," 84, 110, 368
States General, oversight of
Texel, 303–5
Neville, Henry, 42
New England Primer, 25
The New English Tutor and, 25
imprint of, by Franklin and Hall, 26
New North Church, 49–50, 51, 356
Newcastle. *See* Pelham-Holles, Thomas
Newcomb, Benjamin, 188, 364, 371
Newell, Margaret Ellen, 53, 60, 63,
356, 357
Newenham, Edward, 246, 247, 250,
376, 377
Nini, Jean-Baptiste, 289
Nollet, Abbé, 181
Norris, Isaac, 136
North, Dudley, 95, 362
North, Frederick, 264, 275, 315, 382

North Carolina, 327, 328
North Church. *See* Second Church
Northampton (town in England), 29
Northamptonshire, 22, 28, 31

Oberg, Barbara, 327, 386
Ohio, 128–34
Delaware Indians and, 172
Gnadenhutten, 180
Indians in, 119, 133
lands in, sought by Franklin, 236, 342
Pontiac's activities in, 206
settlements in, sought by Virginia and
Pennsylvania, 128, 129, 159, 180,
212, 342, 365
territory, French in, 128, 129, 130, 133, 212
treaty in, 134
Valley, 128, 176, 365, 370
Ohio River, 127
Oldmixon, John, 42, 45, 355
Olive Branch Petition, 275
Oliver, Andrew, 261
Oneidas, 133. *See also* Iroquois
fictional account of, 222, 374
Oswald, Richard, 294, 295, 300, 308,
382, 384
Othello (slave), 336, 337
Overhill Cherokees, 327
Oxford (town in England), 19, 31, 33
Oxfordshire, 22, 28, 31

Paine, Thomas (of Boston), 57–59, 63, 357
Paine, Thomas (political writer), 318
Palatine Germans. *See* Germans
Palmer, Anthony, 120
Palmer, John, 30, 353
Paoli, Pasquale, 1
paper, as money or medium of trade,
57–63, 77–78, 81–89, 92–94, 104,
114–15, 116, 147, 152, 166, 209,
275, 277, 281, 357, 360, 361, 362.
See also economics; money
Paris, Peace of, 186, 275, 293, 309, 317,
323, 324, 343
Parker, James, 137, 141, 160, 161, 365, 366
as printer of Franklin's woodcut of
Louisbourg, 132
as supplier of slave named George to
Franklin family, 336, 337